The Interpretation of Dreams

The Interpretation of Dreams

Sigmund Freud's

MAPLE PRESS

THE INTERPRETATION OF DREAMS

Reprint : 2015

Author : Sigmund Freud's

Copyright © Publisher

No part of this book may be reproduced in a retrieval system or transmitted in any form or by any means electronics, mechanical, photocopying, recording and or without permission of the publisher.

Published by : Maple Press Pvt. Ltd.
A-63, Sector-58
Noida, (U.P.) – 201 301
☏ (0120) - , 4553583
Email : info@maplepress.co.in

Printed at
B.B. Press, A-37, Sec-67, NOIDA-201301

CONTENTS

    Introductory Note   7
1. The Scientific Literature of Dream-Problems (Up to 1900)   9
2. The Method of Dream Interpretation   102
3. The Dream as Wish-Fulfilment   128
4. Distortion in Dreams   139
5. The Material and Sources   166
6. The Dream-Work   273
7. The Psychology of the Dream Processes   473

INTRODUCTORY NOTE
(to the first edition)

In this volume I have attempted to expound the methods and results of dream-interpretation; and in so doing I do not think I have overstepped the boundary of neuro-pathological science. For the dream proves on psychological investigation to be the first of a series of abnormal psychic formations, a series whose succeeding members - the hysterical phobias, the obsessions, the delusions - must, for practical reasons, claim the attention of the physician. The dream, as we shall see, has no title to such practical importance, but for that very reason its theoretical value as a typical formation is all the greater, and the physician who cannot explain the origin of dream-images will strive in vain to understand the phobias and the obsessive and delusional ideas, or to influence them by therapeutic methods. But the very context to which our subject owes its importance must be held responsible for the deficiencies of the following chapters. The abundant lacunae in this exposition represent so many points of contact at which the problem of dream-formation is linked up with the more comprehensive problems of psycho-pathology; problems which cannot be treated in these pages, but which, if time and powers suffice and if further material presents itself, may be elaborated elsewhere. The peculiar nature of the material employed to exemplify the interpretation of dreams has made the writing even of this treatise a difficult task. Consideration of the methods of dream-interpretation will show why the dreams recorded in the literature on the subject, or those collected by persons unknown to me, were useless for my purpose; I had only the choice between my own dreams and those of the patients whom I was treating by psychoanalytic methods. But this later material was inadmissible, since the dream-processes were undesirably complicated by the intervention of neurotic characters. And if I relate my own dreams I must inevitably reveal to the gaze of strangers more of the intimacies of my psychic life than is agreeable to me, and more than seems fitting in a writer who is not a poet but a scientific investigator. To do so is painful, but unavoidable; I have submitted to the necessity, for otherwise I could not have demonstrated my psychological conclusions. Sometimes, of course, I could not resist the temptation to mitigate my indiscretions by omissions and substitutions; but wherever I have done so the value of the example cited has been very definitely diminished. I can only express the hope that my readers will understand my difficult position, and will be indulgent; and further, that all those persons who are in any way concerned in the dreams recorded will not seek to forbid our dream-life at all events to exercise freedom of thought!

Chapter 1

The Scientific Literature Of Dream-problems (Up To 1900)

In the following pages I shall demonstrate that there is a psychological technique which makes it possible to interpret dreams, and that on the application of this technique every dream will reveal itself as a psychological structure, full of significance, and one which may be assigned to a specific place in the psychic activities of the waking state. Further, I shall endeavour to elucidate the processes which underlie the strangeness and obscurity of dreams, and to deduce from these processes the nature of the psychic forces whose conflict or cooperation is responsible for our dreams. This done, my investigation will terminate, as it will have reached the point where the problem of the dream merges into more comprehensive problems, and to solve these we must have recourse to material of a different kind. I shall begin by giving a short account of the views of earlier writers on this subject, and of the status of the dream-problem in contemporary science; since in the course of this treatise I shall not often have occasion to refer to either. In spite of thousands of years of endeavour, little progress has been made in the scientific understanding of dreams. This fact has been so universally acknowledged by previous writers on the subject that it seems hardly necessary to quote individual opinions. The reader will find, in the works listed at the end of this work, many stimulating observations, and plenty of interesting material relating to our subject, but little or nothing that concerns the true nature of the dream, or that solves definitely any of its enigmas. The educated layman, of course, knows even less of the matter.

The conception of the dream that was held in prehistoric ages by primitive peoples, and the influence which it may have exerted on the formation of their conceptions of the universe, and of the soul, is a theme of such great interest that it is only with reluctance that I refrain from dealing with it in these pages. I will refer the reader to the well-known works of Sir John Lubbock (Lord Avebury), Herbert Spencer, E. B. Tylor, and other writers; I will only add that we shall not realize the importance of these problems and speculations until we have completed the task of dreaminterpretation that lies before us.

A reminiscence of the concept of the dream that was held in primitive times seems to underlie the evaluation of the dream which was current among the peoples of classical antiquity.[1] They took it for granted that dreams were related to the world of the supernatural beings in whom they believed, and that they brought inspirations from the gods and demons. Moreover, it appeared to them that dreams must serve a special purpose in respect of the dreamer; that, as a rule, they predicted the future. The extraordinary variations in the content of dreams, and in the impressions which they produced on the dreamer, made it, of course, very difficult to formulate a coherent conception of them, and necessitated manifold differentiations and group-formations, according to their value and reliability. The valuation of dreams by the individual philosophers of antiquity naturally depended on the importance which they were prepared to attribute to manticism in general. In the two works of Aristotle in which there is mention of dreams, they are already regarded as constituting a problem of psychology. We are told that the dream is not god-sent, that it is not of divine but of demonic origin. For nature is really demonic, not divine; that is to say, the dream is not a supernatural revelation, but is subject to the laws of the human spirit, which has, of course, a kinship with the divine. The dream is defined as the psychic activity of the sleeper, inasmuch as he is asleep. Aristotle was acquainted with some of

---

[1] The following remarks are based on Buchsenschutz's careful essay, Traum und Traumdeutung im Altertum (Berlin 1868).

the characteristics of the dream-life; for example, he knew that a dream converts the slight sensations perceived in sleep into intense sensations ("one imagines that one is walking through fire, and feels hot, if this or that part of the body becomes only quite slightly warm"), which led him to conclude that dreams might easily betray to the physician the first indications of an incipient physical change which escaped observation during the day.[2]

As has been said, those writers of antiquity who preceded Aristotle did not regard the dream as a product of the dreaming psyche, but as an inspiration of divine origin, and in ancient times the two opposing tendencies which we shall find throughout the ages in respect of the evaluation of the dream-life were already perceptible. The ancients distinguished between the true and valuable dreams which were sent to the dreamer as warnings, or to foretell future events, and the vain, fraudulent, and empty dreams whose object was to misguide him or lead him to destruction. Gruppe[3] speaks of such a classification of dreams, citing Macrobius and Artemidorus:

"Dreams were divided into two classes; the first class was believed to be influenced only by the present (or the past), and was unimportant in respect of the future; it included the enuknia (insomnia), which directly reproduce a given idea or its opposite; e.g., hunger or its satiation; and the phantasmata, which elaborate the given idea phantastically, as e.g. the nightmare, ephialtes. The second class of dreams, on the other hand, was determinative of the future. To this belonged: 1. Direct prophecies received in the dream (chrematismos, oraculum); 2. the foretelling of a future event (orama, visio); 3. the symbolic dream, which requires interpretation (oneiros, somnium.) This theory survived for many centuries."

Connected with these varying estimations of the dream was the problem of "dream-interpretation." Dreams in general were expected to yield important solutions, but not every dream was immediately understood, and it was impossible to be sure that a

---
[2] The relationship between dreams and disease is discussed by Hippocrates in a chapter of his famous work.
[3] Griechische Mythologie und Religionsgeschichte.

certain incomprehensible dream did not really foretell something of importance, so that an effort was made to replace the incomprehensible content of the dream by something that should be at once comprehensible and significant. In later antiquity Artemidorus of Daldis was regarded as the greatest authority on dreaminterpretation. His comprehensive works must serve to compensate us for the lost works of a similar nature[4] The pre-scientific conception of the dream which obtained among the ancients was, of course, in perfect keeping with their general conception of the universe, which was accustomed to project as an external reality that which possessed reality only in the life of the psyche. Further, it accounted for the main impression made upon the waking life by the morning memory of the dream; for in this memory the dream, as compared with the rest of the psychic content, seems to be something alien, coming, as it were, from another world. It would be an error to suppose that theory of the supernatural origin of dreams lacks followers even in our own times; for quite apart from pietistic and mystical writers - who cling, as they are perfectly justified in doing, to the remnants of the once predominant realm of the supernatural until these remnants have been swept away by scientific explanation - we not infrequently find that quite intelligent persons, who in other respects are averse from anything of a romantic nature, go so far as to base their religious belief in the existence and co-operation of superhuman spiritual powers on the inexplicable nature of the phenomena of dreams (Haffner).

The validity ascribed to the dream-life by certain schools of philosophy - for example, by the school of Schelling - is a distinct reminiscence of the undisputed belief in the divinity of dreams which prevailed in antiquity; and for some thinkers the mantic

---

[4] For the later history of dream-interpretation in the Middle Ages consult Diepgen, and the special investigations of M. Forster, Gotthard, and others. The interpretation of dreams among the Jews has been studied by Amoli, Amram, and Lowinger, and recently, with reference to the psycho-analytic standpoint, by Lauer. Details of the Arabic methods of dream-interpretation are furnished by Drexl, F. Schwarz, and the missionary Tfinkdji. The interpretation of dreams among the Japanese has been investigated by Miura and Iwaya, among the Chinese by Secker, and among the Indians by Negelein.

or prophetic power of dreams is still a subject of debate. This is due to the fact that the explanations attempted by psychology are too inadequate to cope with the accumulated material, however strongly the scientific thinker may feel that such superstitious doctrines should be repudiated. To write strongly the history of our scientific knowledge of the dream-problem is extremely difficult, because, valuable though this knowledge may be in certain respects, no real progress in a definite direction is as yet discernible. No real foundation of verified results has hitherto been established on which future investigators might continue to build. Every new author approaches the same problems afresh, and from the very beginning.

If I were to enumerate such authors in chronological order, giving a survey of the opinions which each has held concerning the problems of the dream, I should be quite unable to draw a clear and complete picture of the present state of our knowledge on the subject. I have therefore preferred to base my method of treatment on themes rather than on authors, and in attempting the solution of each problem of the dream I shall cite the material found in the literature of the subject.

But as I have not succeeded in mastering the whole of this literature - for it is widely dispersed, and interwoven with the literature of other subjects - I must ask my readers to rest content with my survey as it stands, provided that no fundamental fact or important point of view has been overlooked. Until recently most authors have been inclined to deal with the subjects of sleep and dreams in conjunction, and together with these they have commonly dealt with analogous conditions of a psycho-pathological nature, and other dream-like phenomena, such as hallucinations, visions, etc. In recent works, on the other hand, there has been a tendency to keep more closely to the theme, and to consider, as a special subject, the separate problems of the dream-life. In this change I should like to perceive an expression of the growing conviction that enlightenment and agreement in such obscure matters may be attained only by a series of detailed investigations. Such a detailed investigation, and one of a special psychological nature, is expounded in these pages. I have had little occasion to concern myself with the problem of sleep, as this is essentially a physiological problem, although the changes in the functional determination of the psychic apparatus should be included in a description of the sleeping state. The literature of sleep will therefore not be considered here. A scientific interest in the phenomena of dreams as such leads us to propound the following problems, which to a certain extent, interdependent, merge into one another.

A. The Relation of the Dream to the Waking State

The naive judgment of the dreamer on waking assumes that the dream - even if it does not come from another world - has at all events transported the dreamer into another world. The old physiologist, Burdach, to whom we are indebted for a careful and discriminating description of the phenomena of dreams, expressed this conviction in a frequently quoted passage:

"The waking life, with its trials and joys, its pleasures and pains, is never repeated; on the contrary, the dream aims at relieving us of these. Even when our whole mind is filled with one subject, when our hearts are rent by bitter grief, or when some task has been taxing our mental capacity to the utmost, the dream either gives us something entirely alien, or it selects for its combinations only a few elements of reality; or it merely enters into the key of our mood, and symbolizes reality."

J. H. Fichte speaks in precisely the same sense of supplementary dreams, calling them one of the secret, self-healing benefits of the psyche. L. Strumpell expresses himself to the same effect in his Natur und Entstehung der Traume, a study which is deservedly held in high esteem.

"He who dreams turns his back upon the world of waking consciousness"; "In the dream the memory of the orderly content of waking consciousness and its normal behaviour is almost entirely lost"; "The almost complete and unencumbered isolation of the psyche in the dream from the regular normal content and course of the waking state...".

Yet the overwhelming majority of writers on the subject have adopted the contrary view of the relation of the dream to waking life. Thus Haffner: "To begin with, the dream continues the waking life. Our dreams always connect themselves with such ideas as have shortly before been present in our consciousness. Careful examination will nearly always detect a thread by which the dream has linked itself to the experiences of the previous day."

Weygandt flatly contradicts the statement of Burdach. "For it may often be observed, apparently indeed in the great majority of dreams, that they lead us directly back into everyday life, instead of releasing us from it."

Maury expresses the same idea in a concise formula: "Nous revons de ce que nous avons vu, dit, desire, ou fait."[5] Jessen, in his Psychologie, published in 1855, is rather more explicit: "The content of dreams is always more or less determined by the personality, the age, sex, station in life, education and habits, and by the events and experiences of the whole past life of the individual."

The philosopher, I. G. E. Maas, adopts the most unequivocal attitude in respect of this question (Uber die Leidenschaften, 1805): "Experience corroborates our assertion that we dream most frequently of those things toward which our warmest passions are directed. This shows us that our passions must influence the generation of our dreams. The ambitious man dreams of the laurels which he has won (perhaps only in imagination), or has still to win, while the lover occupies himself, in his dreams, with the object of his dearest hopes.... All the sensual desires and loathings which slumber in the heart, if they are stimulated by any cause, may combine with other ideas and give rise to a dream; or these ideas may mingle in an already existing dream."[6]

The ancients entertained the same idea concerning the dependence of the dream-content on life. I will quote Radestock: "When Xerxes, before his expedition against Greece, was dissuaded

---

[5] We dream of what we have seen, said, desired, or done.
[6] Communicated by Winterstein to the Zentralblatt fur Psychoanalyse.

from his resolution by good counsel, but was again and again incited by dreams to undertake it, one of the old, rational dream-interpreters of the Persians, Artabanus, told him, and very appropriately, that dream-images for the most part contain that of which one has been thinking in the waking state."

In the didactic poem of Lucretius, On the Nature of Things, there occurs this passage:

"Et quo quisque fere studio devinctus adhaeret, aut quibus in rebus multum sumus ante morati atque in ea ratione fuit contenta magis mens, in somnis eadem plerumque videmur obire; causidici causas agere et componere leges, induperatores pugnare ac proelia obire,"... etc., etc.[7] Cicero (De Divinatione, II. LXVII) says, in a similar strain, as does also Maury many centuries later: "Maximeque 'reliquiae' rerum earum moventur in animis et agitantur, de quibus vigilantes aut cogitavimus aut egimus."[8]

The contradiction between these two views concerning the relation between dream life and waking life seems indeed irresolvable. Here we may usefully cite the opinion of F. W. Hildebrandt (1875), who held that on the whole the peculiarities of the dream can only be described as "a series of contrasts which apparently amount to contradictions". "The first of these contrasts is formed by the strict isolation or seclusion of the dream from true and actual life on the one hand, and on the other hand by the continuous encroachment of the one upon the other, and the constant dependence of the one upon the other. The dream is something absolutely divorced from the reality experienced during the waking state; one may call it an existence hermetically sealed up and insulated from real life by an unbridgeable chasm. It frees us from reality, blots out the normal recollection of reality, and sets us in another world and a totally different life, which fundamentally has nothing in common with real life...."

[7] And whatever be the pursuit to which one clings with devotion, whatever the things on which we have been occupied much in the past, the mind being thus more intent upon that pursuit, it is generally the same things that we seem to encounter in dreams; pleaders to plead their cause and collate laws, generals to contend and engage battle.
[8] And especially the "remnant" of our waking thoughts and deeds move and stir within the soul.

Hildebrandt then asserts that in falling asleep our whole being, with its forms of existence, disappears "as through an invisible trapdoor."

In one's dream one is perhaps making a voyage to St. Helena in order to offer the imprisoned Napoleon an exquisite vintage of Moselle. One is most affably received by the ex-emperor, and one feels almost sorry when, on waking, the interesting illusion is destroyed. But let us now compare the situation existing in the dream with the actual reality. The dreamer has never been a wine-merchant, and has no desire to become one. He has never made a sea-voyage, and St. Helena is the last place in the world that he would choose as the destination of such a voyage. The dreamer feels no sympathy for Napoleon, but on the contrary a strong patriotic aversion. And lastly, the dreamer was not yet among the living when Napoleon died on the island of St. Helena; so that it was beyond the realms of possibility that he should have had any personal relations with Napoleon. The dream-experience thus appears as something entirely foreign, interpolated between two mutually related and successive periods of time.

"Nevertheless," continues Hildebrandt, "the apparent contrary is just as true and correct. I believe that side by side with this seclusion and insulation there may still exist the most intimate interrelation. We may therefore justly say: Whatever the dream may offer us, it derives its material from reality, and from the psychic life centered upon this reality. However extraordinary the dream may seem, it can never detach itself from the real world, and its most sublime as well as its most ridiculous constructions must always borrow their elementary material either from that which our eyes have beheld in the outer world, or from that which has already found a place somewhere in our waking thoughts; in other words, it must be taken from that which we have already experienced, either objectively or subjectively."

B. The Material of Dreams - Memory in Dreams

That all the material composing the content of a dream is somehow derived from experience, that it is reproduced or remembered in the dream – this at least may be accepted as an incontestable fact. Yet it would be wrong to assume that such a connection between the dream-content and reality will be easily obvious from a comparison between the two. On the contrary, the connection must be carefully sought, and in quite a number of cases it may for a long while elude discovery. The reason for this is to be found in a number of peculiarities evinced by the faculty of memory in dreams; which peculiarities, though generally observed, have hitherto defied explanation. It will be worth our while to examine these characteristics exhaustively.

To begin with, it happens that certain material appears in the dream-content which cannot be subsequently recognized, in the waking state, as being part of one's knowledge and experience. One remembers clearly enough having dreamed of the thing in question, but one cannot recall the actual experience or the time of its occurrence. The dreamer is therefore in the dark as to the source which the dream has tapped, and is even tempted to believe in an independent productive activity on the part of the dream, until, often long afterwards, a fresh episode restores the memory of that former experience, which had been given up for lost, and so reveals the source of the dream. One is therefore forced to admit that in the dream something was known and remembered that cannot be remembered in the waking state.[9]

Delboeuf relates from his own experience an especially impressive example of this kind. He saw in his dream the courtyard of his house covered with snow, and found there two little lizards, half-frozen and buried in the snow. Being a lover of animals he picked them up, warmed them, and put them back into the hole in the wall which was reserved especially for them. He also gave them a few fronds of a little fern which was growing on the wall, and of which he knew they were very fond. In the dream he knew the name of the plant; Asplenium ruta muralis. The dream continued returning after a digression to the lizards,

---

[9] Vaschide even maintains that it has often been observed that in one's dreams one speaks foreign languages more fluently and with greater purity than in the waking state.

and to his astonishment Delboeuf saw two other little lizards falling upon what was left of the ferns. On turning his eyes to the open fields he saw a fifth and a sixth lizard making for the hole in the wall, and finally the whole road was covered by a procession of lizards, all wandering in the same direction.

In his waking state Delboeuf knew only a few Latin names of plants, and nothing of any Asplenium. To his great surprise he discovered that a fern of this name did actually exist, and that the correct name was Asplenium ruta muraria, which the dream had slightly distorted. An accidental coincidence was of course inconceivable; yet where he got his knowledge of the name Asplenium in the dream remained a mystery to him. The dream occurred in 1862. Sixteen years later, while at the house of one of his friends, the philosopher noticed a small album containing dried plants, such as are sold as souvenirs to visitors in many parts of Switzerland. A sudden recollection came to him: he opened the herbarium, discovered therein the Asplenium of his dream, and recognized his own handwriting in the accompanying Latin name. The connection could now be traced. In 1860, two years before the date of the lizard dream, one of his friend's sisters, while on her wedding-journey, had paid a visit to Delboeuf. She had with her at the time this very album, which was intended for her brother, and Delboeuf had taken the trouble to write, at the dictation of a botanist, the Latin name under each of the dried plants.

The same good fortune which gave this example its unusual value enabled Delboeuf to trace yet another portion of this dream to its forgotten source. One day in 1877 he came upon an old volume of an illustrated periodical, in which he found the whole procession of lizards pictured, just as he had dreamt of it in 1862. The volume bore the date 1861, and Delboeuf remembered that he had subscribed to the journal since its first appearance.

That dreams have at their disposal recollections which are inaccessible to the waking state is such a remarkable and theoretically important fact that I should like to draw attention to the point by recording yet other hypermnesic dreams. Maury relates that for some time the word Mussidan used to occur to him during the day. He knew it to be the name of a French city, but that was all. One night he dreamed of a conversation with a certain person, who told him that she came from Mussidan, and, in answer to his question as to where the city was, she replied: "Mussidan is the principal town of a district in the department of Dordogne." On waking, Maury gave no credence to the information received in his dream; but the gazetteer showed it to be perfectly correct. In this case the superior knowledge of the dreamer was confirmed, but it was not possible to trace the forgotten source of this knowledge.

Jessen refers to a very similar incident, the period of which is more remote. "Among others we may here mention the dream of the elder Scaliger, who wrote a poem in praise of the famous men of Verona, and to whom a man named Brugnolus appeared in a dream, complaining that he had been neglected. Though Scaliger could not remember that he had heard of the man, he wrote some verses in his honour, and his son learned subsequently that a certain Brugnolus had at one time been famed in Verona as a critic."

A hypermnesic dream, especially remarkable for the fact that a memory not at first recalled was afterwards recognized in a dream which followed the first, is narrated by the Marquis d'Hervey de St. Denis:[10] "I once dreamed of a young woman with fair golden hair, whom I saw chatting with my sister as she showed her a piece of embroidery. In my dream she seemed familiar to me; I thought, indeed, that I had seen her repeatedly. After waking, her face was still quite vividly before me, but I was absolutely unable to recognize it. I fell asleep again; the dream-picture repeated itself. In this new dream I addressed the golden-haired lady and asked her whether I had not had the pleasure of meeting her somewhere. 'Of course,' she replied; 'don't you remember the bathing-place at Pornic?' Thereupon I awoke, and I was then able to recall with certainty

---
[10] See Vaschide.

and in detail the incidents with which this charming dream-face was connected."

The same author[11] recorded that a musician of his acquaintance once heard in a dream a melody which was absolutely new to him. Not until many years later did he find it in an old collection of musical compositions, though still he could not remember ever having seen it before. I believe that Myers has published a whole collection of such hypermnesic dreams in the Proceedings of the Society for Psychical Research, but these, unfortunately, are inaccessible to me. I think everyone who occupies himself with dreams will recognize, as a very common phenomenon, the fact that a dream will give proof of the knowledge and recollection of matters of which the dreamer, in his waking state, did not imagine himself to be cognizant. In my analytic investigations of nervous patients, of which I shall speak later, I find that it happens many times every week that I am able to convince them, from their dreams, that they are perfectly well acquainted with quotations, obscene expressions, etc., and make use of them in their dreams, although they have forgotten them in their waking state. I shall here cite an innocent example of dreamhypermnesia, because it was easy to trace the source of the knowledge which was accessible only in the dream. A patient dreamed amongst other things (in a rather long dream) that he ordered a kontuszowka in a cafe, and after telling me this he asked me what it could be, as he had never heard the name before. I was able to tell him that kontuszowka was a Polish liqueur, which he could not have invented in his dream, as the name had long been familiar to me from the advertisements. At first the patient would not believe me, but some days later, after he had allowed his dream of the cafe to become a reality, he noticed the name on a signboard at a street corner which for some months he had been passing at least twice a day.

I have learned from my own dreams how largely the discovery of the origin of individual dream-elements may be dependent on

---

[11] Vaschide.

chance. Thus, for some years before I had thought of writing this book, I was haunted by the picture of a church tower of fairly simple construction, which I could not remember ever having seen. I then suddenly recognized it, with absolute certainty, at a small station between Salzburg and Reichenhall. This was in the late nineties, and the first time I had travelled over this route was in 1886. In later years, when I was already busily engaged in the study of dreams, I was quite annoyed by the frequent recurrence of the dream-image of a certain peculiar locality. I saw, in definite orientation to my own person - on my left - a dark space in which a number of grotesque sandstone figures stood out. A glimmering recollection, which I did not quite believe, told me that it was the entrance to a beer-cellar; but I could explain neither the meaning nor the origin of this dream-picture. In 1907 I happened to go to Padua, which, to my regret, I had been unable to visit since 1895. My first visit to this beautiful university city had been unsatisfactory. I had been unable to see Giotto's frescoes in the church of the Madonna dell' Arena: I set out for the church, but turned back on being informed that it was closed for the day. On my second visit, twelve years later, I thought I would compensate myself for this disappointment, and before doing anything else I set out for Madonna dell' Arena. In the street leading to it, on my left, probably at the spot where I had turned back in 1895, I discovered the place, with its sandstone figures, which I had so often seen in my dream. It was, in fact, the entrance to a restaurant garden.

One of the sources from which dreams draw material for reproduction - material of which some part is not recalled or utilized in our waking thoughts - is to be found in childhood. Here I will cite only a few of the authors who have observed and emphasized this fact: Hildebrandt: "It has already been expressly admitted that a dream sometimes brings back to the mind, with a wonderful power of reproduction, remote and even forgotten experiences from the earliest periods of one's life."

Strumpell: "The subject becomes more interesting still when

we remember how the dream sometimes drags out, as it were, from the deepest and densest psychic deposits which later years have piled upon the earliest experiences of childhood, the pictures of certain persons, places and things, quite intact, and in all their original freshness. This is confined not merely to such impressions as were vividly perceived at the time of their occurrence, or were associated with intense psychological values, to recur later in the dream as actual reminiscences which give pleasure to the waking mind. On the contrary, the depths of the dream-memory rather contain such images of persons, places, things and early experiences as either possessed but little consciousness and no psychic value whatsoever, or have long since lost both, and therefore appear totally strange and unknown, both in the dream and in the waking state, until their early origin is revealed."

Volkelt: "It is especially to be remarked how readily infantile and youthful reminiscences enter into our dreams. What we have long ceased to think about, what has long since lost all importance for us, is constantly recalled by the dream."

The control which the dream exercises over material from our childhood, most of which, as is well known, falls into the lacunae of our conscious memory, is responsible for the production of interesting hypermnesic dreams, of which I shall cite a few more examples. Maury relates that as a child he often went from his native city, Meaux, to the neighbouring Trilport, where his father was superintending the construction of a bridge. One night a dream transported him to Trilport and he was once more playing in the streets there. A man approached him, wearing a sort of uniform. Maury asked him his name, and he introduced himself, saying that his name was C, and that he was a bridgeguard.

On waking, Maury, who still doubted the actuality of the reminiscence, asked his old servant, who had been with him in his childhood, whether she remembered a man of this name. "Of course," was the reply; "he used to be watchman on the bridge which your father was building then."

Maury records another example, which demonstrates no less

clearly the reliability of the reminiscences of childhood that emerge in our dreams. M. F., who as a child had lived in Montbrison, decided, after an absence of twenty-five years, to visit his home and the old friends of his family.

The night before his departure he dreamt that he had reached his destination, and that near Montbrison he met a man whom he did not know by sight, and who told him that he was M. F., a friend of his father's. The dreamer remembered that as a child he had known a gentleman of this name, but on waking he could no longer recall his features. Several days later, having actually arrived at Montbrison, he found once more the locality of his dream, which he had thought was unknown to him, and there he met a man whom he at once recognized as the M. F. of his dream, with only this difference, that the real person was very much older than his dream-image.

Here I might relate one of my own dreams, in which the recalled impression takes the form of an association. In my dream I saw a man whom I recognized, while dreaming, as the doctor of my native town. His face was not distinct, but his features were blended with those of one of my schoolmasters, whom I still meet from time to time. What association there was between the two persons I could not discover on waking, but upon questioning my mother concerning the doctor I learned that he was a one-eyed man. The schoolmaster, whose image in my dream obscured that of the physician, had also only one eye. I had not seen the doctor for thirty-eight years, and as far as I know I had never thought of him in my waking state, although a scar on my chin might have reminded me of his professional attentions.

As though to counterbalance the excessive part which is played in our dreams by the impressions of childhood, many authors assert that the majority of dreams reveal elements drawn from our most recent experiences. Robert even declares that the normal dream generally occupies itself only with the impressions of the last few days. We shall find, indeed, that the theory of the dream advanced by Robert absolutely requires that our oldest impressions should be thrust into the background, and our most recent ones brought to the fore. However, the fact here stated by Robert is correct; this I can confirm from my own investigations. Nelson, an American author, holds that the impressions received in a dream most frequently date from the second day before the dream, or from the third day before it, as though the impressions of the day immediately preceding the dream were not sufficiently weakened and remote.

Many authors who are unwilling to question the intimate connection between the dream-content and the waking state have been struck by the fact that the impressions which have intensely occupied the waking mind appear in dreams only after they have been to some extent removed from the mental activities of the day. Thus, as a rule, we do not dream of a beloved person who is dead while we are still overwhelmed with sorrow (Delage).

Yet Miss Hallam, one of the most recent observers, has collected examples which reveal the very opposite behaviour in this respect, and upholds the claims of psychological individuality in this matter. The third, most remarkable, and at the same time most incomprehensible, peculiarity of memory in dreams is shown in the selection of the material reproduced; for here it is not, as in the waking state, only the most significant things that are held to be worth remembering, but also the most indifferent and insignificant details. In this connection I will quote those authors who have expressed their surprise in the most emphatic language.

Hildebrandt: "For it is a remarkable fact that dreams do not, as a rule, take their elements from important and far-reaching events, or from the intense and urgent interests of the preceding day, but from unimportant incidents, from the worthless odds and ends of recent experience or of the remoter past. The most shocking death in our family, the impressions of which keep us awake long into the night, is obliterated from our memories until the first moment of waking brings it back to us with distressing force. On the other hand, the wart on the forehead of a passing stranger, to whom we did not give a moment's thought once he was out of sight, finds a place in our dreams."

Strumpell speaks of "cases in which the analysis of a dream brings to light elements which, although derived from the experiences of yesterday or the day before yesterday, were yet so unimportant and worthless for the waking state that they were forgotten soon after they were experienced. Some experiences may be the chance-heard remarks of other persons, or their superficially observed actions, or, fleeting perceptions of things or persons, or isolated phrases that we have read, etc."

Havelock Ellis: "The profound emotions of waking life, the questions and problems on which we spend our chief voluntary mental energy, are not those which usually present themselves at once to dream-consciousness. It is, so far as the immediate past is concerned, mostly the trifling, the incidental, the 'forgotten' impressions of daily life which reappear in our dreams. The psychic activities that are awake most intensely are those that sleep most profoundly."

It is precisely in connection with these characteristics of memory in dreams that Binz finds occasion to express dissatisfaction with the explanations of dreams which he himself had favoured: "And the normal dream raises similar questions. Why do we not always dream of mental impressions of the day before, instead of going back, without any perceptible reason, to the almost forgotten past, now lying far behind us? Why, in a dream, does consciousness so often revive the impression of indifferent memory-pictures, while the cerebral cells that bear the most sensitive records of experience remain for the most part inert and numb, unless an acute revival during the waking state has quite recently excited them?"

We can readily understand how the strange preference shown by the dream-memory for the indifferent and therefore disregarded details of daily experience must commonly lead us altogether to overlook the dependence of dreams on the waking state, or must at least make it difficult for us to prove this dependence in any individual case. Thus it happened that in the statistical treatment of her own and her friend's dream, Miss Whiton Calkins found that 11 per cent of the entire number showed no relation to the waking state. Hildebrandt was certainly correct in his assertion that all our dream-images could be genetically explained if we devoted enough time and material to the tracing of their origin. To be sure, he calls this "a most tedious and thankless job. For most often it would lead us to ferret out all sorts of psychically worthless things from the remotest corners of our storehouse of memories, and to bring to light all sorts of quite indifferent events of long ago from the oblivion which may have overtaken them an hour after their occurrence." I must, however, express my regret that this discerning author refrained from following the path which at first sight seemed so unpromising, for it would have led him directly to the central point of the explanation of dreams.

The behaviour of memory in dreams is surely most significant for any theory of memory whatsoever. It teaches us that "nothing which we have once psychically possessed is ever entirely lost"; or as Delboeuf puts it, "que toute impression, meme la plus insignificante, laisse une trace inalterable, indifiniment susceptible de reparaitre au jour";[12] a conclusion to which we are urged by so many other pathological manifestations of mental life. Let us bear in mind this extraordinary capacity of the memory in dreams, in order the more keenly to realize the contradiction which has to be put forward in certain dream-theories to be mentioned later, which seek to explain the absurdities and incoherences of dreams by a partial forgetting of what we have known during the day.

It might even occur to one to reduce the phenomenon of dreaming to that of remembering, and to regard the dream as the manifestation of a reproductive activity, unresting even at night, which is an end in itself. This would seem to be in agreement with statements such as those made by Pilcz, according to which definite relations between the time of dreaming and the contents

---

[12] That every impression, even the most insignificant, leaves an ineradicable mark, indefinitely capable of reappearing by day.

of a dream may be demonstrated, inasmuch as the impressions reproduced by the dream in deep sleep belong to the remote past, while those reproduced towards morning are of recent origin. But such a conception is rendered improbable from the outset by the manner in which the dream deals with the material to be remembered. Strumpell rightly calls our attention to the fact that repetitions of experiences do not occur in dreams. It is true that a dream will make a beginning in that direction, but the next link is wanting; it appears in a different form, or is replaced by something entirely novel. The dream gives us only fragmentary reproductions; this is so far the rule that it permits of a theoretical generalization. Still, there are exceptions in which an episode is repeated in a dream as completely as it can be reproduced by our waking memory. Delboeuf relates of one of his university colleagues that a dream of his repeated, in all its details, a perilous drive in which he escaped accident as if by miracle. Miss Calkins mentions two dreams the contents of which exactly reproduced an experience of the previous day, and in a later chapter I shall have occasion to give an example that came to my knowledge of a childish experience which recurred unchanged in a dream.[13]

C. Dream-Stimuli and Sources

What is meant by dream-stimuli and dream-sources may be explained by a reference to the popular saying: "Dreams come from the stomach."

This notion covers a theory which conceives the dream as resulting from a disturbance of sleep. We should not have dreamed if some disturbing element had not come into play during our sleep, and the dream is the reaction against this disturbance.

The discussion of the exciting causes of dreams occupies a great deal of space in the literature of dreams. It is obvious that this problem could have made its appearance only after dreams

---

[13] From subsequent experience I am able to state that it is not at all rare to find in dreams reproductions of simple and unimportant occupations of everyday life, such as packing trunks, preparing food in the kitchen, etc., but in such dreams the dreamer himself emphasizes not the character of the recollection but its "reality" - "I really did this during the day."

had become an object of biological investigation. The ancients, who conceived of dreams as divine inspirations, had no need to look for stimuli; for them a dream was due to the will of divine or demonic powers, and its content was the product of their special knowledge and intention. Science, however, immediately raised the question whether the stimuli of dreams were single or multiple, and this in turn led to the consideration whether the causal explanation of dreams belonged to the region of psychology or to that of physiology. Most authors appear to assume that disturbance of sleep, and hence dreams, may arise from various causes, and that physical as well as mental stimuli may play the part of dream-excitants. Opinions differ widely in preferring this or the other factor as the cause of dreams, and in classifying them in the order of importance.

Whenever the sources of dreams are completely enumerated they fall into the following four categories, which have also been employed in the classification of dreams: (1) external (objective) sensory stimuli; (2) internal (subjective) sensory stimuli; (3) internal (organic) physical stimuli; (4) Purely psychical sources of excitation.

1. External sensory stimuli

The younger Strumpell, the son of the philosopher, whose work on dreams has already more than once served us as a guide in considering the problems of dreams, has, as is well known, recorded his observations of a patient afflicted with general anaesthesia of the skin and with paralysis of several of the higher sensory organs. This man would laps into sleep whenever the few remaining sensory paths between himself and the outer world were closed. When we wish to fall asleep we are accustomed to strive for a condition similar to that obtaining in Strumpell's experiment.

We close the most important sensory portals, the eyes, and we endeavour to protect the other senses from all stimuli or from any change of the stimuli already acting upon them. We then fall asleep, although our preparations are never wholly successful. For we can never completely insulate the sensory organs, nor can we entirely abolish the excitability of the sensory organs themselves. That we may at any time be awakened by intenser stimuli should prove to us "that the mind has remained in constant communication with the external world even during sleep." The sensory stimuli that reach us during sleep may easily become the source of dreams.

There are a great many stimuli of this nature, ranging from those unavoidable stimuli which are proper to the state of sleep or occasionally admitted by it, to those fortuitous stimuli which are calculated to wake the sleeper. Thus a strong light may fall upon the eyes, a noise may be heard, or an odour may irritate the mucous membranes of the nose. In our unintentional movements during sleep we may lay bare parts of the body, and thus expose them to a sensation of cold, or by a change of position we may excite sensations of pressure and touch. A mosquito may bite us, or a slight nocturnal mischance may simultaneously attack more than one sense-organ. Observers have called attention to a whole series of dreams in which the stimulus ascertained on waking and some part of the dream-content corresponded to such a degree that the stimulus could be recognized as the source of the dream. I shall here cite a number of such dreams, collected by Jessen, which are traceable to more or less accidental objective sensory stimuli.

Every noise indistinctly perceived gives rise to corresponding dream-representations; the rolling of thunder takes us into the thick of battle, the crowing of a cock may be transformed into human shrieks of terror, and the creaking of a door may conjure up dreams of burglars breaking into the house. When one of our blankets slips off us at night we may dream that we are walking about naked, or falling into water. If we lie diagonally across the bed with our feet extending beyond the edge, we may dream of standing on the brink of a terrifying precipice, or of falling from a great height. Should our head accidentally get under the pillow we may imagine a huge rock overhanging us and about to crush us under its weight. An accumulation of semen produces voluptuous dreams, and local pains give rise to ideas of suffering ill-treatment, of hostile attacks, or of accidental bodily injuries....

"Meier (Versuch einer Erklarung des Nachtwandelns, Halle, 1758) once dreamed of being attacked by several men who threw him flat on the ground and drove a stake into the earth between his first and second toes. While imagining this in his dream he suddenly awoke and felt a piece of straw sticking between his toes. The same author, according to Hemmings (Von den Traumen und Nachtwandlern, Weimar, 1784), "dreamed on another occasion, when his nightshirt was rather too tight round his neck, that he was being hanged. In his youth Hoffbauer dreamed of having fallen from a high wall, and found, on waking, that the bedstead had come apart, and that he had actually fallen on to the floor.... Gregory relates that he once applied a hot-water bottle to his feet, and dreamed of taking a trip to the summit of Mount Etna, where he found the heat of the soil almost unbearable. After having a blister applied to his head, another man dreamed of being scalped by Indians; still another, whose shirt was damp, dreamed that he was dragged through a stream. An attack of gout caused a patient to believe that he was in the hands of the Inquisition, and suffering the pains of torture (Macnish)."

The argument that there is a resemblance between the dream-stimulus and the dream-content would be confirmed if, by a systematic induction of stimuli, we should succeed in producing dreams corresponding to these stimuli. According to Macnish such experiments had already been made by Giron de Buzareingues. "He left his knee exposed and dreamed of travelling on a mail-coach by night. He remarked, in this connection, that travellers were well aware how cold the knees become in a coach at night. On another occasion he left the back of his head uncovered, and dreamed that he was taking part in a religious ceremony in the open air. In the country where he lived it was customary to keep the head always covered except on occasions of this kind."

Maury reports fresh observation on self-induced dreams of his own. (A number of other experiments were unsuccessful.)

1. He was tickled with a feather on his lips and on the tip of his nose. He dreamed of an awful torture, viz., that a mask of pitch was stuck to his face and then forcibly torn off, bringing the skin with it.

2. Scissors were whetted against a pair of tweezers. He heard bells ringing, then sounds of tumult which took him back to the days of the Revolution of 1848.

3. Eau de Cologne was held to his nostrils. He found himself in Cairo, in the shop of Johann Maria Farina. This was followed by fantastic adventures which he was not able to recall.

4. His neck was lightly pinched. He dreamed that a blister was being applied, and thought of a doctor who had treated him in childhood.

5. A hot iron was brought near his face. He dreamed that chauffeurs[14] had broken into the house, and were forcing the occupants to give up their money by thrusting their feet into braziers. The Duchesse d'Abrantes, whose secretary he imagined himself to be then entered the room.

6. A drop of water was allowed to fall on to his forehead. He imagined himself in Italy, perspiring heavily, and drinking the white wine of Orvieto.

7. When the light of a candle screened with red paper was allowed to fall on his face, he dreamed of thunder, of heat, and of a storm at sea which he once witnessed in the English Channel.

Hervey, Weygandt, and others have made attempts to produce dreams experimentally.

Many have observed the striking skill of the dream in interweaving into its structure sudden impressions from the outer world, in such a manner as to represent a gradually approaching catastrophe (Hildebrandt). "In former years," this author relates,

---

[14] Chauffeurs were bands of robbers in the Vendee who resorted to this form of torture.

"I occasionally made use of an alarmclock in order to wake punctually at a certain hour in the morning. It probably happened hundreds of times that the sound of this instrument fitted into an apparently very long and connected dream, as though the entire dream had been especially designed for it, as though it found in this sound its appropriate and logically indispensable climax, its inevitable denouement."

I shall presently have occasion to cite three of these alarm-clock dreams in a different connection. Volkelt relates: "A composer once dreamed that he was teaching a class, and was just explaining something to his pupils. When he had finished he turned to one of the boys with the question: 'Did you understand me?' The boy cried out like one possessed 'Oh, ja!' Annoyed by this, he reprimanded his pupil for shouting. But now the entire class was screaming 'Orja,' then 'Eurjo,' and finally 'Feuerjo.' He was then aroused by the actual fire alarm in the street."

Garnier (Traite des facultes de l'ame, 1865), on the authority of Radestock, relates that Napoleon I, while sleeping in a carriage, was awakened from a dream by an explosion which took him back to the crossing of the Tagliamento and the bombardment of the Austrians, so that he started up, crying, "We have been undermined."

The following dream of Maury's has become celebrated: He was ill in bed; his mother was sitting beside him. He dreamed of the Reign of Terror during the Revolution. He witnessed some terrible scenes of murder, and finally he himself was summoned before the Tribunal. There he saw Robespierre, Marat, Fouquier-Tinville, and all the sorry heroes of those terrible days; he had to give an account of himself, and after all manner of incidents which did not fix themselves in his memory, he was sentenced to death. Accompanied by an enormous crowd, he was led to the place of execution. He mounted the scaffold; the executioner tied him to the plank, it tipped over, and the knife of the guillotine fell. He felt his head severed from his trunk, and awakened in terrible anxiety, only to find that the head-board of the bed had fallen, and had actually struck the cervical vertebrae just where the knife of the guillotine would have fallen.

This dream gave rise to an interesting discussion, initiated by Le Lorrain and Egger in the Revue Philosophique, as to whether, and how, it was possible for the dreamer to crowd together an amount of dream-content apparently so large in the short space of time elapsing between the perception of the waking stimulus and the moment of actual waking. Examples of this nature show that objective stimuli occurring in sleep are among the most firmly-established of all the sources of dreams; they are, indeed, the only stimuli of which the layman knows anything whatever. If we ask an educated person who is not familiar with the literature of dreams how dreams originate, he is certain to reply by a reference to a case known to him in which a dream has been explained after waking by a recognized objective stimulus. Science, however, cannot stop here, but is incited to further investigation by the observation that the stimulus influencing the senses during sleep does not appear in the dream at all in its true form, but is replaced by some other representation, which is in some way related to it. But the relation existing between the stimulus and the resulting dream is, according to Maury, "une affinite quelconque mais qui n'est pas unique et exclusive"[15]. If we read, for example, three of Hildebrandt's "alarm-clock dreams," we shall be compelled to ask why the same casual stimulus evoked so many different results, and why just these results and no others. "I am taking a walk on a beautiful spring morning. I stroll through the green meadows to a neighbouring village, where I see numbers of the inhabitants going to church, wearing their best clothes and carrying their hymn-books under their arms. I remember that it is Sunday, and that the morning service will soon begin. I decide to attend it, but as I am rather overheated I think I will wait in the churchyard until I am cooler.

While reading the various epitaphs, I hear the sexton climbing the church-tower, and I see above me the small bell which is about to ring for the beginning of service. For a little while it

---

[15] A sort of relation which is, however, neither unique nor exclusive.

hangs motionless; then it begins to swing, and suddenly its notes resound so clearly and penetratingly that my sleep comes to an end. But the notes of the bell come from the alarm-clock."

"A second combination. It is a bright winter day; the streets are deep in snow. I have promised to go on a sleigh-ride, but I have to wait some time before I am told that the sleigh is at the door. Now I am preparing to get into the sleigh. I put on my furs, the foot-warmer is put in, and at last I have taken my seat. But still my departure is delayed. At last the reins are twitched, the horses start, and the sleigh bells, now violently shaken, strike up their familiar music with a force that instantly tears the gossamer of my dream. Again it is only the shrill note of my alarm-clock."

"Yet a third example. I see the kitchen-maid walking along the passage to the dining-room, with a pile of several dozen plates. The porcelain column in her arms seems to me to be in danger of losing its equilibrium. 'Take care,' I exclaim, 'you will drop the whole pile!' The usual retort is naturally made - that she is used to such things, etc. Meanwhile I continue to follow her with my anxious gaze, and behold, at the threshold the fragile plates fall and crash and roll across the floor in hundreds of pieces. But I soon perceive that the endless din is not really a rattling but a true ringing, and with this ringing the dreamer now becomes aware that the alarm-clock has done its duty."

The question why the dreaming mind misjudges the nature of the objective sensory stimulus has been answered by Strumpell, and in an almost identical fashion by Wundt; their explanation is that the reaction of the mind to the stimulus attacking sleep is complicated and confused by the formation of illusions. A sensory impression is recognized by us and correctly interpreted - that is, it is classed with the memory-group to which it belongs according to all previous experience if the impression is strong, clear, and sufficiently prolonged, and if we have sufficient time to submit it to those mental processes. But if these conditions are not fulfilled we mistake the object which gives rise to the impression, and on the basis of this impression we construct an illusion. "If one takes a walk in an open field and perceives indistinctly a distant object, it may happen that one will at first take it for a horse."

On closer inspection the image of a cow, resting, may obtrude itself, and the picture may finally resolve itself with certainty into a group of people sitting on the ground. The impressions which the mind receives during sleep from external stimuli are of a similarly indistinct nature; they give rise to illusions because the impression evokes a greater or lesser number of memory-images, through which it acquires its psychic value. As for the question, in which of the many possible spheres of memory the corresponding images are aroused, and which of the possible associative connections are brought into play, that - to quote Strumpell again - is indeterminable, and is left, as it were, to the caprices of the mind.

Here we may take our choice. We may admit that the laws of dream-formation cannot really be traced any further, and so refrain from asking whether or not the interpretation of the illusion evoked by the sensory impression depends upon still other conditions; or we may assume that the objective sensory stimulus encroaching upon sleep plays only a modest role as a dream-source, and that other factors determine the choice of the memory-image to be evoked. Indeed, on carefully examining Maury's experimentally produced dreams, which I have purposely cited in detail, one is inclined to object that his investigations trace the origin of only one element of the dreams, and that the rest of the dream-content seems too independent and too full of detail to be explained by a single requirement, namely, that it must correspond with the element experimentally introduced. Indeed, one even begins to doubt the illusion theory, and the power of objective impressions to shape the dream, when one realizes that such impressions are sometimes subjected to the most peculiar and far-fetched interpretations in our dreams. Thus M. Simon tells of a dream in which he saw persons of gigantic stature[16] seated at a table, and heard distinctly the horrible clattering produced by the impact of their jaws as they chewed their food. On waking he heard the clatter of a horse's hooves as it galloped past his window. If in this case the sound of the horse's hooves had revived ideas from the memory-sphere of Gulliver's Travels, the sojourn with the giants of Brobdingnag, and the virtuous horse-like creatures - as I should perhaps interpret the dream without any assistance on the author's part - ought not the choice of a memorysphere so alien to the stimulus to be further elucidated by other motives?

2. Internal (subjective) sensory stimuli

All objections to the contrary notwithstanding, we must admit that the role of the objective sensory stimuli as producers of dreams has been indisputably established, and if, having regard to their nature and their frequency, these stimuli seem perhaps insufficient to explain all dreampictures, this indicates that we should look for other dream-sources which act in a similar fashion. I do not know where the idea first arose that together with the external sensory stimuli the internal (subjective) stimuli should also be considered, but as a matter of fact this has been done more or less explicitly in all the more recent descriptions of the aetiology of dreams. "I believe," says Wundt, "that an important part is played in dream-illusions by those subjective sensations of sight and hearing which are familiar to us in the waking state as a luminous chaos in the dark field of the vision, and a ringing, buzzing, etc., of the ears, and in especial, subjective irritations of the retina.

This explains the remarkable tendency of dreams to delude the eyes with numbers of similar or identical objects. Thus we see outspread before our eyes innumerable birds, butterflies, fishes, coloured beads, flowers, etc. Here the luminous dust in the dark field of vision has assumed fantastic forms, and the many luminous points of which it consists are embodied in our dreams

---

[16] Gigantic persons in a dream justify the assumption that the dream is dealing with a scene from the dreamer's childhood. This interpretation of the dream as a reminiscence of Gulliver's Travels is, by the way, a good example of how an interpretation should not be made. The dreaminterpreter should not permit his own intelligence to operate in disregard of the dreamer's impressions.

in as many single images, which, owing to the mobility of the luminous chaos, are seen as moving objects. This is perhaps the reason of the dream's decided preference for the most varied animal forms, for owing to the multiplicity of such forms they can readily adapt themselves to the subjective luminous images."

The subjective sensory stimuli as a source of dreams have the obvious advantage that, unlike objective stimuli, they are independent of external accidents. They are, so to speak, at the disposal of the interpretation whenever they are required. But they are inferior to the objective sensory stimuli by the fact that their claim to the role of dream-inciters - which observation and experiment have established in the case of objective stimuli - can in their case be verified with difficulty or not at all. The main proof of the dream-inciting power of subjective sensory stimuli is afforded by the so-called hypnogogic hallucinations, which have been described by Johann Muller as "phantastic visual manifestations."

They are those very vivid and changeable pictures which with many people occur constantly during the period of falling asleep, and which may linger for a while even after the eyes have been opened. Maury, who was very subject to these pictures, made a thorough study of them, and maintained that they were related to or rather identical with dream-images. This had already been asserted by Johann Muller. Maury maintains that a certain psychic passivity is necessary for their origin; that it requires a relaxation of the intensity of attention. But one may perceive a hypnogogic hallucination in any frame of mind if one falls into such a lethargy for a moment, after which one may perhaps wake up, until this oft-repeated process terminates in sleep.

According to Maury, if one wakes up shortly after such an experience, it is often possible to trace in the dream the images which one has perceived before falling asleep as hypnogogic hallucinations. Thus Maury on one occasion saw a series of images of grotesque figures with distorted features and curiously dressed hair, which obtruded themselves upon him with incredible importunity during the period of falling asleep, and which, upon waking, he recalled having seen in his dream. On another occasion, while suffering from hunger, because he was subjecting himself to a rather strict diet, he saw in one of his hypnogogic states a plate, and a hand armed with a fork taking some food from the plate. In his dream he found himself at a table abundantly supplied with food, and heard the clatter of the diner's forks. On yet another occasion, after falling asleep with strained and painful eyes, he had a hypnogogic hallucination of microscopically small characters, which he was able to decipher, one by one, only with a great effort; and on waking from sleep an hour later he recalled a dream in which there was an open book with very small letters, which he was obliged to read through with laborious effort.

Not only pictures, but auditory hallucinations of words, names, etc., may also occur hypnogogically, and then repeat themselves in the dream, like an overture announcing the principal motif of the opera which is to follow.

A more recent observer of hypnogogic hallucinations, G. Trumbull Ladd, follows the same lines as Johann Muller and Maury. By dint of practice he succeeded in acquiring the faculty of suddenly arousing himself, without opening his eyes, two to five minutes after gradually falling asleep. This enabled him to compare the disappearing retinal sensations with the dream-images remaining in his memory. He assures us that an intimate relation between the two can always be recognized, inasmuch as the luminous dots and lines of light spontaneously perceived by the retina produce, so to speak, the outline or scheme of the psychically perceived dream-images. For example, a dream in which he saw before him clearly printed lines, which he read and studied, corresponded with a number of luminous spots arranged in parallel lines; or, to express it in his own words: The clearly printed page resolved itself into an object which appeared to his waking perception like part of an actual printed page seen through a small hole in a sheet of paper, but at a distance too great to permit of its being read. Without in any way underestimating the central element of the phenomenon, Ladd believes that hardly any visual dream occurs in our minds that is not based on material furnished by this internal condition of retinal irritability. This is particularly true of dreams which occur shortly after falling asleep in a dark room, while dreams occurring in the morning, near the period of waking, receive their stimulus from the objective light penetrating the eye in a brightly-lit room.

The shifting and infinitely variable character of the spontaneous luminous excitations of the retina exactly corresponds with the fitful succession of images presented to us in our dreams. If we attach any importance to Ladd's observations, we cannot underrate the productiveness of this subjective source of stimuli; for visual images, as we know, are the principal constituents of our dreams. The share contributed by the other senses, excepting, perhaps, the sense of hearing, is relatively insignificant and inconstant.

3. Internal (organic) physical stimuli

If we are disposed to look for the sources of dreams not outside but inside the organism, we must remember that almost all our internal organs, which in a state of health hardly remind us of their existence, may, in states of excitation - as we call them - or in disease, become a source of the most painful sensations, and must therefore be put on a par with the external excitants of pain and sensation. Strumpell, for example, gives expression to a long-familiar experience when he declares that "during sleep the psyche becomes far more deeply and broadly conscious of its coporality than in the waking state, and it is compelled to receive and to be influenced by certain stimulating impressions originating in parts of the body, and in alterations of the body, of which it is unconscious in the waking state."

Even Aristotle declares it to be quite possible that a dream may draw our attention to incipient morbid conditions which we have not noticed in the waking state (owing to the exaggerated intensity of the impressions experienced in the dream; and some medical authors, who certainly did not believe in the prophetic nature of dreams, have admitted the significance of dreams, at least in so far as the predicting of disease is concerned. [Cf. M. Simon and many earlier writers.][17]

Among the Greeks there were dream oracles, which were vouchsafed to patients in quest of recovery. The patient betook himself to the temple of Apollo or Aesculapius; there he was subjected to various ceremonies, bathed, rubbed and perfumed. A state of exaltation having been thus induced, he was made to lie down in the temple on the skin of a sacrificial ram. He fell asleep and dreamed of remedies, which he saw in their natural form, or in symbolic images which the priests afterwards interpreted.

For further references concerning the remedial dreams of the Greeks, cf. Lehmann, i, 74; Bouche-Leclerq; Hermann, Gottesd. Altert. d. Gr., SS 41; Privataltert. SS 38, 16; Bottinger in Sprengel's Beitr. z. Gesch. d. Med., ii, et seq.; W. Lloyd, Magnetism and Mesmerism in Antiquity, London, 1877; Dollinger, Heidentum und Judentum. Even in our days there seems to be no lack of authenticated examples of such diagnostic achievements on the part of dreams. Thus Tissie cites from Artigues (Essai sur la valeur semeiologique des Reves) the history of a woman of forty-three, who, during several years of apparently perfect health, was troubled with anxiety-dreams, and in whom a medical examination subsequently revealed an incipient affection of the heart, to which she presently succumbed.

Serious derangements of the internal organs clearly excite dreams in quite a number of persons. The frequency of anxiety-dreams in diseases of the heart and lungs has been generally realized; indeed, this function of the dream-life is emphasized by so many writers that I shall here content myself with a reference to the literature of the subject (Radestock, Spitta, Maury, M. Simon, Tissie). Tissie even believes that the diseased organs impress upon the dream-content its characteristic features. The dreams of persons suffering from diseases of the heart are generally very

---

[17] In addition to the diagnostic valuation of dreams (e.g., by Hippocrates) mention must also be made of their therapeutic significance in antiquity.

brief, and end in a terrified awakening; death under terrible circumstances almost always find a place in their content. Those suffering from diseases of the lungs dream of suffocation, of being crushed, and of flight, and a great many of them are subject to the familiar nightmare - which, by the way, Borner has succeeded in inducing experimentally by lying on the face and covering the mouth and nostrils. In digestive disturbances the dream contains ideas from the sphere of gustatory enjoyment and disgust. Finally, the influence of sexual excitement on the dream-content is obvious enough in everyone's experience, and provides the strongest confirmation of the whole theory of dream-instigation by organic sensation.

Moreover, if we study the literature of dreams it becomes quite evident that some writers (Maury, Weygandt) have been led to the study of dreamproblems by the influence their own pathological state has had on the content of their dreams. The enlargement of the number of dream-sources by such undeniably established facts is, however, not so important as one might be led to suppose; for dreams are, after all, phenomena which occur in healthy persons - perhaps in all persons, and every night - and a pathological state of the organs is evidently not one of the indispensable conditions. For us, however, the question is not whence particular dreams originate, but rather: what is the exciting cause of ordinary dreams in normal people?

But we have only to go a step farther to find a source of dreams which is more prolific than any of those mentioned above, and which promises indeed to be inexhaustible. If it is established that the bodily organs become, in sickness, an exciting source of dreams, and if we admit that the mind, when diverted during sleep from the outer world, can devote more of its attention to the interior of the body, we may readily assume that the organs need not necessarily become diseased in order to permit stimuli, which in one way or another grow into dream-images, to reach the sleeping mind. What in the waking state we vaguely perceive as a general sensation, perceptible by its quality alone - a sensation to which, in the opinion of physicians, all the organic systems contribute their share - this general sensation would at night attain a greater potency, and, acting through its individual components, would constitute the most prolific as well as the most usual source of dream-representations. We should then have to discover the laws by which organic stimuli are translated into dream-representations.

This theory of the origin of dreams is the one most favoured by all medical writers. The obscurity which conceals the essence of our being - the "moi splanchnique" as Tissie terms it - from our knowledge, and the obscurity of the origin of dreams, correspond so closely that it was inevitable that they should be brought into relation with one another. The theory according to which the organic sensations are responsible for dreams has, moreover, another attraction for the physician, inasmuch as it favours the aetiological union of the dream with mental derangement, both of which reveal so many points of agreement in their manifestations, since changes in the general organic massive sensation and in the stimuli emanating from the internal organs are also considered to have a far-reaching significance as regards the origin of the psychoses. It is therefore not surprising that the organic stimulus theory can be traced to several writers who have propounded this theory independently.

A number of writers have followed the train of thought developed by Schopenhauer in 1851. Our conception of the universe has its origin in the recasting by the intellect of the impressions which reach it from without in the moulds of time, space and causality. During the day the stimuli proceeding from the interior of the organism, from the sympathetic nervous system, exert at most an unconscious influence on our mood. At night, however, when the overwhelming effect of the impressions of the day is no longer operative, the impressions that surge upward from within are able to force themselves on our attention - just as in the night we hear the rippling of the brook that was drowned in the clamour of the day. But how else can the intellect react to these stimuli than by transforming them in accordance with its own function into things which occupy space and time and follow the lines of causality? - and so a dream originates. Thus Scherner, and after him Volkelt, endeavoured to discover the more intimate relations between physical sensations and dream-pictures; but we shall reserve the discussion of this point for our chapter on the theory of dreams.

As a result of a singularly logical analysis, the psychiatrist Krauss referred the origin of dreams, and also of deliria and delusions, to the same element, namely, to organically determined sensations. According to him, there is hardly any part of the organism which might not become the starting-point of a dream or a delusion. Organically determined sensations, he says, "may be divided into two classes: (1) general sensations - those affecting the whole system; (2) specific sensations - those that are immanent in the principal systems of the vegetative organism, and which may in turn be subdivided into five groups: (a) the muscular, (b) the pneumatic, (c) the gastric, (d) the sexual, (e) the peripheral sensations."

The origin of the dream-image from physical sensations is conceived by Krauss as follows: The awakened sensation, in accordance with some law of association, evokes an idea or image bearing some relation to it, and combines with this idea or image, forming an organic structure, towards which, however, the consciousness does not maintain its normal attitude. For it does not bestow any attention on the sensation, but concerns itself entirely with the accompanying ideas; and this explains why the facts of the case have been so long misunderstood.

Krauss even gives this process the special name of "transubstantiation of the sensations into dream-images". The influence of organic physical stimuli on the formation of dreams is today almost universally admitted, but the question as to the nature of the law underlying this relation is answered in various ways, and often obscurely. On the basis of the theory of physical excitation the special task of dream-interpretation is to trace back the content of a dream to the causative organic stimulus, and if we do not accept the rules of interpretation advanced by Scherner, we shall often find ourselves confronted by the awkward fact that the organic source of excitation reveals itself only in the content of the dream.

A certain agreement, however, appears in the interpretation of the various forms of dreams which have been designated as "typical," because they recur in so many persons with almost the same content. Among these are the well-known dreams of falling from a height, of the dropping out of teeth, of flying, and of embarrassment because one is naked or scantily clad. This last type of dream is said to be caused simply by the dreamer's perception, felt in his sleep, that he has thrown off the bedclothes and is uncovered. The dream that one's teeth are dropping out is explained by "dental irritation," which does not, however, of necessity imply a morbid condition of irritability in the teeth. According to Strumpell, the flying dream is the adequate image employed by the mind to interpret the quantum of stimulus emanating from the rising and sinking of the pulmonary lobes when the cutaneous sensation of the thorax has lapsed into insensibility. This latter condition causes the sensation which gives rise to images of hovering in the air. The dream of falling from a height is said to be due to the fact that an arm falls away from the body, or a flexed knee is suddenly extended, after unconsciousness of the sensation of cutaneous pressure has supervened, whereupon this sensation returns to consciousness, and the transition from unconsciousness to consciousness embodies itself psychically as a dream of falling. The weakness of these fairly plausible attempts at explanation clearly lies in the fact that without any further elucidation they allow this or that group of organic sensations to disappear from psychic perception, or to obtrude themselves upon it, until the constellation favourable for the explanation has been established. Later on, however, I shall have occasion to return to the subject of typical dreams and their origin.

From a comparison of a series of similar dreams, M. Simon

endeavoured to formulate certain rules governing the influence of organic sensations on the nature of the resulting dream. He says: "If during sleep any organic apparatus, which normally participates in the expression of an affect, for any reason enters into the state of excitation to which it is usually aroused by the affect, the dream thus produced will contain representations which harmonize with that affect."

Another rule reads as follows: "If, during sleep, an organic apparatus is in a state of activity, stimulation, or disturbance, the dream will present ideas which correspond with the nature of the organic function performed by that apparatus." Mourly Vold has undertaken to prove the supposed influence of bodily sensation on the production of dreams by experimenting on a single physiological territory. He changed the positions of a sleeper's limbs, and compared the resulting dreams with these changes. He recorded the following results:

1. The position of a limb in a dream corresponds approximately to that of reality, i.e., we dream of a static condition of the limb which corresponds with the actual condition.

2. When one dreams of a moving limb it always happens that one of the positions occurring in the execution of this movement corresponds with the actual position.

3. The position of one's own limb may in the dream be attributed to another person.

4. One may also dream that the movement in question is impeded.

5. The limb in any particular position may appear in the dream as an animal or monster, in which case a certain analogy between the two is established.

6. The behaviour of a limb may in the dream incite ideas which bear some relation or other to this limb. Thus, for example, if we are using our fingers we dream of numerals.

Results such as these would lead me to conclude that even the theory of organic stimulation cannot entirely abolish the apparent freedom of the determination of the dream-picture which will be evoked.[18]

4. Psychic sources of excitation

When considering the relation of dreams to waking life, and the provenance of the material of dreams, we learned that the earliest as well as the most recent investigators are agreed that men dream of what they do during the day, and of the things that interest them in the waking state. This interest, continued from waking life into sleep, is not only a psychic bond, joining the dream to life, but it is also a source of dreams whose importance must not be underestimated, and which, taken together with those stimuli which become active and of interest during sleep, suffices to explain the origin of all dream-images. Yet we have also heard the very contrary of this asserted; namely, that dreams bear the sleeper away from the interests of the day, and that in most cases we do not dream of things which have occupied our attention during the day until after they have lost, for our waking life, the stimulating force of belonging to the present. Hence in the analysis of dream-life we are reminded at every step that it is inadmissible to frame general rules without making provision for qualifications by introducing such terms as "frequently," "as a rule," "in most cases," and without being prepared to admit the validity of exceptions.

If interest during the waking state together with the internal and external stimuli that occur during sleep, sufficed to cover the whole aetiology of dreams, we should be in a position to give a satisfactory account of the origin of all the elements of a dream; the problem of the dream-sources would then be solved, leaving us only the task of discriminating between the part played by the psychic and that played by the somatic dreamstimuli in individual dreams. But as a matter of fact no such complete solution of a dream has ever been achieved in any case, and everyone who has attempted such a solution has found that components of the dream - and usually a great many of them - are left whose source

---

[18] See below for a further discussion of the two volumes of records of dreams since published by this writer.

he is unable to trace. The interests of the day as a psychic source of dreams are obviously not so influential as to justify the confident assertion that every dreamer continues the activities of his waking life in his dreams.

Other dream-sources of a psychic nature are not known. Hence, with the exception perhaps of the explanation of dreams given by Scherner, to which reference will be made later on, all the explanations found in the literature of the subject show a considerable hiatus whenever there is a question of tracing the images and ideas which are the most characteristic material of dreams. In this dilemma the majority of authors have developed a tendency to belittle as far as possible the share of the psychic factor, which is so difficult to determine, in the evocation of dreams. To be sure, they distinguish as major divisions the nerve-stimulus dream and the association-dream, and assert that the latter has its source exclusively in reproduction, but they cannot dismiss the doubt as to "whether they appear without any impulsion from organic stimuli". And even the characteristic quality of the pure association-dream disappears. To quote Volkelt: "In the association-dream proper, there is no longer any question of such a stable nucleus. Here the loose grouping penetrates even to the very centre of the dream. The imaginative life, already released from the control of reason and intellect, is here no longer held together by the more important psychical and physical stimuli, but is left to its own uncontrolled and confused divagations." Wundt, too, attempts to belittle the psychic factor in the evocation of dreams by asserting that "the phantasms of the dream are perhaps unjustly regarded as pure hallucinations. Probably most dream representations are really illusions, inasmuch as they emanate from the slight sensory impressions which are never extinguished during sleep". Weygandt has adopted this view, and generalizes upon it. He asserts that "the most immediate causes of all dream-representations are sensory stimuli to which reproductive associations then attach themselves". Tissie goes still further in suppressing the psychic sources of excitation: "Les reves d'origine absolument psychique n'existent pas";[19] and elsewhere, "Les pensees de nos reves nous viennent de dehors...."[20]

Those writers who, like the eminent philosopher Wundt, adopt a middle course, do not hesitate to assert that in most dreams there is a cooperation of the somatic stimuli and psychic stimuli which are either unknown or are identified with the interests of the day. We shall learn later that the problem of dream-formation may be solved by the disclosure of an entirely unsuspected psychic source of excitation.

In the meanwhile we shall not be surprised at the overestimation of the influence of those stimuli which do not originate in the psychic life. It is not merely because they alone may easily be found, and even confirmed by experiment, but because the somatic conception of the origin of dreams entirely corresponds with the mode of thought prevalent in modern psychiatry. Here, it is true, the mastery of the brain over the organism is most emphatically stressed; but everything that might show that the psychic life is independent of demonstrable organic changes, or spontaneous in its manifestations, is alarming to the contemporary psychiatrist, as though such an admission must mean a return to the old-world natural philosophy and the metaphysical conception of the nature of the soul.

The distrust of the psychiatrist has placed the psyche under tutelage, so to speak; it requires that none of the impulses of the psyche shall reveal an autonomous power. Yet this attitude merely betrays a lack of confidence in the stability of the causal concatenation between the physical and the psychic. Even where on investigation the psychic may be recognized as the primary cause of a phenomenon, a more profound comprehension of the subject will one day succeed in following up the path that leads to the organic basis of the psychic. But where the psychic must, in the present state of our knowledge, be accepted as the terminus, it need not on that account be disavowed.

---
[19] Dreams do not exist whose origin is totally psychic.
[20] The thoughts of our dreams come from outside.

D. Why Dreams Are Forgotten After Waking

That a dream fades away in the morning is proverbial. It is, indeed, possible to recall it. For we know the dream, of course, only by recalling it after waking; but we very often believe that we remember it incompletely, that during the night there was more of it than we remember. We may observe how the memory of a dream which in the morning was still vivid fades in the course of the day, leaving only a few trifling remnants. We are often aware that we have been dreaming, but we do not know of what we have dreamed; and we are so well used to this fact - that the dream is liable to be forgotten - that we do not reject as absurd the possibility that we may have been dreaming even when, in the morning, we know nothing either of the content of the dream or of the fact that we have dreamed. On the other hand, it often happens that dreams manifest an extraordinary power of maintaining themselves in the memory. I have had occasion to analyse, with my patients, dreams which occurred to them twenty-five years or more previously, and I can remember a dream of my own which is divided from the present day by at least thirty-seven years, and yet has lost nothing of its freshness in my memory. All this is very remarkable, and for the present incomprehensible. The forgetting of dreams is treated in the most detailed manner by Strumpell. This forgetting is evidently a complex phenomenon; for Strumpell attributes it not to a single cause, but to quite a number of causes. In the first place, all those factors which induce forgetfulness in the waking state determine also the forgetting of dreams. In the waking state we commonly very soon forget a great many sensations and perceptions because they are too slight to remember, and because they are charged with only a slight amount of emotional feeling. This is true also of many dream-images; they are forgotten because they are too weak, while the stronger images in their neighbourhood are remembered. However, the factor of intensity is in itself not the only determinant of the preservation of dream-images; Strumpell, as well as other authors (Calkins), admits that dream-images are often rapidly forgotten although they are known to have been vivid, whereas, among those that are retained in the memory, there are many that are very shadowy and unmeaning. Besides, in the waking state one is wont to forget rather easily things that have happened only once, and to remember more readily things which occur repeatedly. But most dream-images are unique experiences,[21] and this peculiarity would contribute towards the forgetting of all dreams equally.

Of much greater significance is a third cause of forgetting. In order that feelings, representations, ideas and the like should attain a certain degree of memorability, it is important that they should not remain isolated, but that they should enter into connections and associations of an appropriate nature. If the words of a verse of poetry are taken and mixed together, it will be very difficult to remember them. "Properly placed, in a significant sequence, one word helps another, and the whole, making sense, remains and is easily and lastingly fixed in the memory. Contradictions, as a rule, are retained with just as much difficulty and just as rarely as things that are confused and disorderly." Now dreams, in most cases, lack sense and order. Dream-compositions, by their very nature, are insusceptible of being remembered, and they are forgotten because as a rule they fall to pieces the very next moment. To be sure, these conclusions are not entirely consistent with Radestock's observation, that we most readily retain just those dreams which are most peculiar.

According to Strumpell, other factors, deriving from the relation of the dream to the waking state, are even more effective in causing us to forget our dreams. The forgetfulness of dreams manifested by the waking consciousness is evidently merely the counterpart of the fact already mentioned, namely, that the dream hardly ever takes over an orderly series of memories from the waking state, but only certain details of these memories, which it removes from the habitual psychic connections in which they are remembered in the waking state. The dream-composition, therefore, has no place in the community of the psychic series

---

[21] Periodically recurrent dreams have been observed repeatedly. Compare the collection made by Chabaneix.

which fill the mind. It lacks all mnemonic aids. "In this manner the dream-structure rises, as it were, from the soil of our psychic life, and floats in psychic space like a cloud in the sky, quickly dispelled by the first breath of reawakening life". This situation is accentuated by the fact that on waking the attention is immediately besieged by the inrushing world of sensation, so that very few dream-images are capable of withstanding its force. They fade away before the impressions of the new day like the stars before the light of the sun.

Finally, we should remember that the fact that most people take but little interest in their dreams is conducive to the forgetting of dreams. Anyone who for some time applies himself to the investigation of dreams, and takes a special interest in them, usually dreams more during that period than at any other; he remembers his dreams more easily and more frequently.

Two other reasons for the forgetting of dreams, which Bonatelli (cited by Benini) adds to those adduced by Strumpell, have already been included in those enumerated above; namely, (1) that the difference of the general sensation in the sleeping and the waking state is unfavourable to mutual reproduction, and (2) that the different arrangement of the material in the dream makes the dream untranslatable, so to speak, for the waking consciousness.

It is therefore all the more remarkable, as Strumpell himself observes, that, in spite of all these reasons for forgetting the dream, so many dreams are retained in the memory. The continual efforts of those who have written on the subject to formulate laws for the remembering of dreams amount to an admission that here, too, there is something puzzling and unexplained. Certain peculiarities relating to the remembering of dreams have attracted particular attention of late; for example, the fact that the dream which is believed to be forgotten in the morning may be recalled in the course of the day on the occasion of some perception which accidentally touches the forgotten content of the dream (Radestock,

Tissie). But the whole recollection of dreams is open to an objection which is calculated greatly to depreciate its value in critical eyes. One may doubt whether our memory, which omits so much from the dream, does not falsify what it retains. This doubt as to the exactness of the reproduction of dreams is expressed by Strumpell when he says: "It may therefore easily happen that the waking consciousness involuntarily interpolates a great many things in the recollection of the dream; one imagines that one has dreamt all sorts of things which the actual dream did not contain."

Jessen expresses himself in very decided terms:

"Moreover, we must not lose sight of the fact, hitherto little heeded, that in the investigation and interpretation of coherent and logical dreams we almost always take liberties with the truth when we recall a dream to memory. Unconsciously and unintentionally we fill up the gaps and supplement the dream-images. Rarely, and perhaps never, has a connected dream been as connected as it appears to us in memory. Even the most truth-loving person can hardly relate a dream without exaggerating and embellishing it in some degree. The human mind so greatly tends to perceive everything in a connected form that it intentionally supplies the missing links in any dream which is in some degree incoherent."

The observations of V. Eggers, though of course independently conceived, read almost like a translation of Jessen's words:

"...L'observation des reves a ses difficultes speciales et le seul moyen d'eviter toute erreur en pareille matiere est de confier au papier sans le moindre retard ce que l'on vient d'eprouver et de remarquer; sinon, l'oubli vient vite ou total ou partiel; l'oubli total est sans gravite; mais l'oubli partiel est perfide: car si l'on se met ensuite a raconter ce que l'on n'a pas oublie, on est expose a completer par imagination les fragments incoherents et disjoints fourni par la memoire... on devient artiste a son insu, et le recit, periodiquement repete s'impose a la creance de son auteur, qui, de bonne foi, le presente comme un fait authentique, dument etabli selon les bonnes methodes...."[22]

Similarly Spitta, who seems to think that it is only in the attempt to reproduce the dream that we bring order and arrangement into loosely associated dream-elements--"turning juxtaposition into concatenation; that is, adding the process of logical connection which is absent in the dream."

Since we can test the reliability of our memory only by objective means, and since such a test is impossible in the case of dreams, which are our own personal experience, and for which we know no other source than our memory, what value do our recollections of our dreams possess?

E. The Psychological Peculiarities of Dreams In our scientific investigation of dreams we start with the assumption that dreams are a phenomenon of our own psychic activity; yet the completed dream appears to us as something alien, whose authorship we are so little inclined to recognize that we should be just as willing to say "A dream came to me," as "I dreamed."

Whence this "psychic strangeness" of dreams? According to our exposition of the sources of dreams, we must assume that it is not determined by the material which finds its way into the dream-content, since this is for the most part common both to dream-life and waking life.

We might ask ourselves whether this impression is not evoked by modifications of the psychic processes in dreams, and we might even attempt to suggest that the existence of such changes is the psychological characteristic of dreams.

---

[22] ...The observation of dreams has its special difficulties, and the only way to avoid all error in such matter is to put on paper without the least delay what has just been experienced and noticed; otherwise, totally or partially the dream is quickly forgotten; total forgetting is without seriousness; but partial forgetting is treacherous: for, if one then starts to recount what has not been forgotten, one is likely to supplement from the imagination the incoherent and disjointed fragments provided by the memory.... unconsciously one becomes an artist, and the story, repeated from time to time, imposes itself on the belief of its author, who, in good faith, tells it as authentic fact, regularly established according to proper methods....

No one has more strongly emphasized the essential difference between dream-life and waking life and drawn more far reaching conclusions from this difference than G. Th. Fechner in certain observations contained in his Elemente der Psychophysik.

He believes that "neither the simple depression of conscious psychic life under the main threshold," nor the distraction of the attention from the influences of the outer world, suffices to explain the peculiarities of dream-life as compared with waking life. He believes, rather, that the arena of dreams is other than the arena of the waking life of the mind.

"If the arena of psychophysical activity were the same during the sleeping and the waking state, the dream, in my opinion, could only be a continuation of the waking ideational life at a lower degree of intensity, so that it would have to partake of the form and material of the latter. But this is by no means the case."

What Fechner really meant by such a transposition of the psychic activity has never been made clear, nor has anybody else, to my knowledge, followed the path which he indicates in this remark. An anatomical interpretation in the sense of physiological localization in the brain, or even a histological stratification of the cerebral cortex, must of course be excluded. The idea might, however, prove ingenious and fruitful if it could refer to a psychical apparatus built up of a number of successive and connected systems.

Other authors have been content to give prominence to this or that palpable psychological peculiarity of the dream-life, and even to take this as a starting-point for more comprehensive attempts at explanation. It has been justly remarked that one of the chief peculiarities of dream-life makes its appearance even in the state of falling asleep, and may be defined as the sleep-heralding phenomenon. According to Schleiermacher, the distinguishing characteristic of the waking state is the fact that its psychic activity occurs in the form of ideas rather than in that of images. But the dream thinks mainly in visual images, and it may be noted that with the approach of sleep the voluntary activities become impeded in proportion as involuntary representations make their appearance, the latter belonging entirely to the category of images.

The incapacity for such ideational activities as we feel to be deliberately willed, and the emergence of visual images, which is regularly connected with this distraction - these are two constant characteristics of dreams, and on psychological analysis we are compelled to recognize them as essential characteristics of dream-life. As for the images themselves the hypnogogic hallucinations - we have learned that even in their content they are identical with dream-images.[23]

Dreams, then, think preponderantly, but not exclusively, in visual images. They make use also of auditory images, and, to a lesser extent, of the other sensory impressions. Moreover, in dreams, as in the waking state, many things are simply thought or imagined (probably with the help of remnants of verbal conceptions).

Characteristic of dreams, however, are only those elements of their contents which behave like images, that is, which more closely resemble perceptions than mnemonic representations. Without entering upon a discussion of the nature of hallucinations - a discussion familiar to every psychiatrist - we may say, with every well-informed authority, that the dream hallucinates- that is, that it replaces thoughts by hallucinations. In this respect visual and acoustic impressions behave in the same way. It has been observed that the recollection of a succession of notes heard as we are falling asleep becomes transformed, when we have fallen asleep, into a hallucination of the same melody, to give place, each time we wake, to the fainter and qualitatively different representations of the memory, and resuming, each time we doze off again, its hallucinatory character.

---

[23] Silberer has shown by excellent examples how in the state of falling asleep even abstract thoughts may be changed into visible plastic images, which, of course, express them. (Jahrbuch, Bleuler-Freud, vol. i, 1900.) I shall return to the discussion of his findings later on.

The transformation of an idea into a hallucination is not the only departure of the dream from the more or less corresponding waking thought.

From these images the dream creates a situation; it represents something as actually present; it dramatizes an idea, as Spitta puts it. But the peculiar character of this aspect of the dream-life is completely intelligible only if we admit that in dreaming we do not as a rule (the exceptions call for special examination) suppose ourselves to be thinking, but actually experiencing; that is, we accept the hallucination in perfectly good faith.

The criticism that one has experienced nothing, but that one has merely been thinking in a peculiar manner - dreaming - occurs to us only on waking. It is this characteristic which distinguishes the genuine dream from the day-dream, which is never confused with reality.

The characteristics of the dream-life thus far considered have been summed up by Burdach as follows: "As characteristic features of the dream we may state (a) that the subjective activity of our psyche appears as objective, inasmuch as our perceptive faculties apprehend the products of phantasy as though they were sensory activities... (b) that sleep abrogates our voluntary action; hence falling asleep involves a certain degree of passivity... The images of sleep are conditioned by the relaxation of our powers of will."

It now remains to account for the credulity of the mind in respect to the dream-hallucinations which are able to make their appearance only after the suspension of certain voluntary powers. Strumpell asserts that in this respect the psyche behaves correctly and in conformity with its mechanism. The dream-elements are by no means mere representations, but true and actual experiences of the psyche, similar to those which come to the waking state by way of the senses. Whereas in the waking state the mind thinks and imagines by means of verbal images and language, in dreams it thinks and imagines in actual perceptual images. Dreams, moreover, reveal a spatial consciousness, inasmuch as in dreams, just as in the waking state, sensations and images are transposed into outer space. It must therefore be admitted that in dreams the mind preserves the same attitude in respect of images and perceptions as in the waking state. And if it forms erroneous conclusions in respect of these images and perceptions, this is due to the fact that in sleep it is deprived of that criterion which alone can distinguish between sensory perceptions emanating from within and those coming from without. It is unable to subject its images to those tests which alone can prove their objective reality.

Further, it neglects to differentiate between those images which can be exchanged at will and those in respect of which there is no free choice. It errs because it cannot apply the law of causality to the content of its dreams. In brief, its alienation from the outer world is the very reason for its belief in its subjective dream-world.

Delboeuf arrives at the same conclusion through a somewhat different line of argument. We believe in the reality of dream-pictures because in sleep we have no other impressions with which to compare them; because we are cut off from the outer world. But it is not because we are unable, when asleep, to test our hallucinations that we believe in their reality. Dreams can make us believe that we are applying such tests - that we are touching, say, the rose that we see in our dream; and yet we are dreaming. According to Delboeuf there is no valid criterion that can show whether something is a dream or a waking reality, except - and that only pragmatically - the fact of waking. "I conclude that all that has been experienced between falling asleep and waking is a delusion, if I find on waking that I am lying undressed in bed". "I considered the images of my dream real while I was asleep on account of the unsleeping mental habit of assuming an outer world with which I can contrast my ego."[24]

---

[24] Haffner, like Delboeuf, has attempted to explain the act of dreaming by the alteration which an abnormally introduced condition must have upon the otherwise correct functioning of the intact psychic apparatus; but he describes this condition in somewhat different terms. He states that the first distinguishing mark of dreams is the abolition of time and space, i.e., the emancipation of the representation from the individual's position in the spatial and temporal order. Associated with this is the second fundamental character of dreams, the mistaking of the hallucinations, imaginations, and phantasy-combinations for objective perceptions. "The sum-total of the higher psychic functions, particularly the formation of concepts, judgments, and conclusions on the one hand, and free self-determination on the

If the turning-away from the outer world is accepted as the decisive cause of the most conspicuous characteristics of our dreams, it will be worth our while to consider certain subtle observations of Burdach's, which will throw some light on the relation of the sleeping psyche to the outer world, and at the same time serve to prevent our over-estimating the importance of the above deductions. "Sleep," says Burdach, "results only under the condition that the mind is not excited by sensory stimuli... yet it is not so much a lack of sensory stimuli that conditions sleep as a lack of interest in them;[25] some sensory impressions are even necessary in so far as they serve to calm the mind; thus the miller can fall asleep only when he hears the clatter of his mill, and he who finds it necessary, as a matter of precaution, to burn a light at night, cannot fall asleep in the dark".

"During sleep the psyche isolates itself from the outer world, and withdraws from the periphery.... Nevertheless, the connection is not entirely broken; if one did not hear and feel during sleep, but only after waking, one would assuredly never be awakened at all. The continuance of sensation is even more plainly shown by the fact that we are not always awakened by the mere force of the sensory impression, but by its relation to the psyche. An indifferent word does not arouse the sleeper, but if called by name he wakes... so that even in sleep the psyche discriminates between sensations.... Hence one may even be awakened by the obliteration

---

other hand, combine with the sensory phantasy-images, and at all times have these as a substratum. These activities too, therefore, participate in the erratic nature of the dream-representations. We say they participate, for our faculties of judgment and will are in themselves unaltered during sleep. As far as their activity is concerned, we are just as shrewd and just as free as in the waking state. A man cannot violate the laws of thought; that is, even in a dream he cannot judge things to be identical which present themselves to him as opposites. He can desire in a dream only that which he regards as a good (sub ratione boni). But in this application of the laws of thought and will the human intellect is led astray in dreams by confusing one notion with another. Thus it happens that in dreams we formulate and commit the greatest of contradictions, while, on the other hand, we display the shrewdest judgment and arrive at the most logical conclusions, and are able to make the most virtuous and sacred resolutions. The lack of orientation is the whole secret of our flights of phantasy in dreams, and the lack of critical reflection and agreement with other minds is the main source of the reckless extravagances of our judgments, hopes and wishes in dreams".

[25] Compare with this the element of "Desinteret," in which Claparede (1905) finds the mechanism of falling asleep.

of a sensory stimulus, if this is related to anything of imagined importance. Thus one man wakes when the nightlight is extinguished, and the miller when his mill comes to a standstill; that is, waking is due to the cessation of a sensory activity, and this presupposes that the activity has been perceived, but has not disturbed the mind, its effect being indifferent, or actually reassuring".

Even if we are willing to disregard these by no means trifling objections, we must yet admit that the qualities of dream-life hitherto considered, which are attributed to withdrawal from the outer world, cannot fully account for the strangeness of dreams. For otherwise it would be possible to reconvert the hallucinations of the dream into mental images, and the situations of the dream into thoughts, and thus to achieve the task of dreaminterpretation.

Now this is precisely what we do when we reproduce a dream from memory after waking, and no matter whether we are fully or only partially successful in this retranslation, the dream still remains as mysterious as before. Furthermore, all writers unhesitatingly assume that still other and profounder changes take place in the plastic material of waking life. Strumpell seeks to isolate one of these changes as follows: "With the cessation of active sensory perception and of normal consciousness, the psyche is deprived of the soil in which its feelings, desires, interests, and activities are rooted. Those psychic states, feelings, interests, and valuations, which in the waking state adhere to memory-images, succumb to an obscuring pressure, in consequence of which their connection with these images is severed; the perceptual images of things, persons, localities, events and actions of the waking state are, individually, abundantly reproduced, but none of these brings with it its psychic value. Deprived of this, they hover in the mind dependent on their own resources..."

This annihilation of psychic values, which is in turn referred to a turning away from the outer world, is, according to Strumpell, very largely responsible for the impression of strangeness with which the dream is coloured in our memory. We have seen that the very fact of falling asleep involves a renunciation of one of the psychic activities - namely, the voluntary guidance of the flow of ideas. Thus the supposition obtrudes itself (though it is in any case a natural one) that the state of sleep may extend even to the psychic functions. One or another of these functions is perhaps entirely suspended; we have now to consider whether the rest continue to operate undisturbed, whether they are able to perform their normal work under the circumstances. The idea occurs to us that the peculiarities of the dream may be explained by the restricted activity of the psyche during sleep, and the impression made by the dream upon our waking judgment tends to confirm this view.

The dream is incoherent; it reconciles, without hesitation, the worst contradictions; it admits impossibilities; it disregards the authoritative knowledge of the waking state, and it shows us as ethically and morally obtuse. He who should behave in the waking state as his dreams represent him as behaving would be considered insane. He who in the waking state should speak as he does in his dreams, or relate such things as occur in his dreams, would impress us as a feeble-minded or muddle-headed person. It seems to us, then, that we are merely speaking in accordance with the facts of the case when we rate psychic activity in dreams very low, and especially when we assert that in dreams the higher intellectual activities are suspended or at least greatly impaired.

With unusual unanimity (the exceptions will be dealt with elsewhere) the writers on the subject have pronounced such judgments as lead immediately to a definite theory or explanation of dream-life. It is now time to supplement the resume which I have just given by a series of quotations from a number of authors - philosophers and physicians - bearing upon the psychological characteristics of the dream.

According to Lemoine, the incoherence of the dream-images is the sole essential characteristic of the dream. Maury agrees with him (Le Sommeil): "Il n'y a pas des reves absolument raisonnables et qui ne contiennent quelque incoherence, quelque absurdite."[26]

According to Hegel, quoted by Spitta, the dream lacks any intelligible objective coherence. Dugas says: "Les reve, c'est l'anarchie psychique, affective et mentale, c'est le jeu des fonctions livrees a elles-memes et s'exercant sans controle et sans but; dans le reve l'esprit est un automate spirituel."[27]

"The relaxation, dissolution, and promiscuous confusion of the world of ideas and images held together in waking life by the logical power of the central ego" is conceded even by Volkelt, according to whose theory the psychic activity during sleep appears to be by no means aimless.

The absurdity of the associations of ideas which occur in dreams can hardly be more strongly stigmatized than it was by Cicero (De Divinatione, II. lxxi): "Nihil tam praepostere, tam incondite, tam monstruose cogitari potest, quod non possimus somniare."[28]

Fechner says: "It is as though the psychological activity of the brain of a reasonable person were to migrate into that of a fool."

Radestock: "It seems indeed impossible to recognize any stable laws in this preposterous behaviour. Withdrawing itself from the strict policing of the rational will that guides our waking ideas, and from the processes of attention, the dream, in crazy sport, whirls all things about in kaleidoscopic confusion."

Hildebrandt: "What wonderful jumps the dreamer permits himself, for instance, in his chain of reasoning! With what unconcern he sees the most familiar laws of experience turned upside down!

---

[26] There are no dreams which are absolutely reasonable which do not contain some incoherence, some absurdity.

[27] The dream is psychic anarchy, emotional and intellectual, the playing of functions, freed of themselves and performing without control and without end; in the dream, the mind is a spiritual automaton.

[28] There is no imaginable thing too absurd, too involved, or too abnormal for us to dream about.

What ridiculous contradictions he is able to tolerate in the order of nature and of society, before things go too far, and the very excess of nonsense leads to an awakening! Sometimes we quite innocently calculate that three times three make twenty; and we are not in the least surprised if a dog recites poetry to us, if a dead person walks to his grave, or if a rock floats on the water.

We solemnly go to visit the duchy of Bernburg or the principality of Liechtenstein in order to inspect its navy; or we allow ourselves to be recruited as a volunteer by Charles XII just before the battle of Poltava."

Binz, referring to the theory of dreams resulting from these impressions, says: "Of ten dreams nine at least have an absurd content. We unite in them persons or things which do not bear the slightest relation to one another. In the next moment, as in a kaleidoscope, the grouping changes to one, if possible, even more nonsensical and irrational than before; and so the shifting play of the drowsy brain continues, until we wake, put a hand to our forehead, and ask ourselves whether we still really possess the faculty of rational imagination and thought."

Maury, Le Sommeil makes, in respect of the relation of the dream-image to the waking thoughts, a comparison which a physician will find especially impressive:

"La production de ces images que chez l'homme eveille fait le plus souvent naitre la volonte, correspond, pour l'intelligence, a ce que sont pour la motilite certains mouvements que nous offrent la choree et les affections paralytiques...."[29] For the rest, he considers the dream "toute une serie de degradations de la faculte pensante et raisonnante"[30].

It is hardly necessary to cite the utterances of those authors who repeat Maury's assertion in respect of the higher individual

---

[29] The production of those images which, in the waking man, most often excite the will, correspond, for the mind, to those which are, for the motility, certain movements that offer St. Vitus' dance and paralytic affections...

[30] A whole series of degradations of the faculty of thinking and reasoning.

psychic activities. According to Strumpell, in dreams - and even, of course, where the nonsensical nature of the dream is not obvious - all the logical operations of the mind, based on relations and associations, recede into the background. According to Spitta ideas in dreams are entirely withdrawn from the laws of causality; while Radestock and others emphasize the feebleness of judgment and logical inference peculiar to dreams.

According to Jodl, there is no criticism in dreams, no correcting of a series of perceptions by the content of consciousness as a whole. The same author states that "All the activities of consciousness occur in dreams, but they are imperfect, inhibited, and mutually isolated." The contradictions of our conscious knowledge which occur in dreams are explained by Stricker and many others on the ground that facts are forgotten in dreams, or that the logical relations between ideas are lost, etc., etc.

Those authors who, in general, judge so unfavourably of the psychic activities of the dreamer nevertheless agree that dreams do retain a certain remnant of psychic activity. Wundt, whose teaching has influenced so many other investigators of dream-problems, expressly admits this. We may ask, what are the nature and composition of the remnants of normal psychic life which manifest themselves in dreams? It is pretty generally acknowledged that the reproductive faculty, the memory, seems to be the least affected in dreams; it may, indeed, show a certain superiority over the same function in waking life, even though some of the absurdities of dreams are to be explained by the forgetfulness of dream-life. According to Spitta, it is the sentimental life of the psyche which is not affected by sleep, and which thus directs our dreams. By sentiment (Gemut) he means "the constant sum of the emotions as the inmost subjective essence of the man".

Scholz sees in dreams a psychic activity which manifests itself in the "allegorizing interpretation" to which the dream-material is subjected. Siebeck likewise perceives in dreams a "supplementary interpretative activity" of the psyche, which applies itself to all that is observed and perceived. Any judgment of the part played in dreams by what is presumed to be the highest psychical function, i.e., consciousness, presents a peculiar difficulty. Since it is only through consciousness that we can know anything of dreams, there can be no doubt as to its being retained. Spitta, however, believes that only consciousness is retained in the dream, but not self-consciousness. Delboeuf confesses that he is unable to comprehend this distinction.

The laws of association which connect our mental images hold good also for what is represented in dreams; indeed, in dreams the dominance of these laws is more obvious and complete than in the waking state. Strumpell says: "Dreams would appear to proceed either exclusively in accordance with the laws of pure representation, or in accordance with the laws of organic stimuli accompanied by such representations; that is, without being influenced by reflection, reason, aesthetic taste, or moral judgment."

The authors whose opinions I here reproduce conceive the formation of the dream somewhat as follows: The sum of sensory stimuli of varying origin (discussed elsewhere) that are operative in sleep at first awaken in the psyche a number of images which present themselves as hallucinations (according to Wundt, it is more correct to say "as illusions," because of their origin in external and internal stimuli). These combine with one another in accordance with the known laws of association, and, in accordance with the same laws, they in turn evoke a new series of representations (images).

The whole of this material is then elaborated as far as possible by the still active remnant of the thinking and organizing faculties of the psyche (cf. Wundt and Weygandt). Thus far, however, no one has been successful in discerning the motive which would decide what particular law of association is to be obeyed by those images which do not originate in external stimuli.

But it has been repeatedly observed that the associations which connect the dream-images with one another are of a particular kind, differing from those found in the activities of the waking mind. Thus Volkelt:

"In dreams the ideas chase and seize upon one another on the strength of accidental similarities and barely perceptible connections. All dreams are pervaded by casual and unconstrained associations of this kind." Maury attaches great value to this characteristic of the connection of ideas, for it allows him to draw a closer analogy between the dream-life and certain mental derangements. He recognizes two main characteristics of "deliria": "(1) une action spontanee et comme automatique de l'esprit; (2) une association vicieuse et irreguliere des idees"[31]. Maury gives us two excellent examples from his own dreams, in which the mere similarity of sound decides the connection between the dream-representations. Once he dreamed that he was on a pilgrimage (pelerinage) to Jerusalem, or to Mecca. After many adventures he found himself in the company of the chemist Pelletier; the latter, after some conversation, gave him a galvanized shovel (pelle) which became his great broadsword in the next portion of the dream. In another dream he was walking along a highway where he read the distances on the kilometre-stones; presently he found himself at a grocer's who had a large pair of scales; a man put kilogramme weights into the scales, in order to weigh Maury; the grocer then said to him: "You are not in Paris, but on the island Gilolo." This was followed by a number of pictures, in which he saw the flower lobelia, and then General Lopez, of whose death he had read a little while previously. Finally he awoke as he was playing a game of lotto.[32]

We are, indeed, quite well aware that this low estimate of the psychic activities of the dream has not been allowed to pass without contradiction from various quarters. Yet here contradiction would seem rather difficult. It is not a matter of much significance that one of the depreciators of dream-life, Spitta, should assure us that the same psychological laws which govern the waking state rule the dream also, or that another (Dugas) should state: "Le reve n'est pas deraison ni meme irraison pure,"[33] so long as neither

---

[31] An action of the mind spontaneous and as though automatic; (2) a defective and irregular association of ideas.

[32] Later on we shall be able to understand the meaning of dreams like these which are full of words with similar sounds or the same initial letters.

[33] The dream is neither pure derangement nor pure irrationality.

of them has attempted to bring this opinion into harmony with the psychic anarchy and dissolution of all mental functions in the dream which they themselves have described. However, the possibility seems to have dawned upon others that the madness of the dream is perhaps not without its method- that it is perhaps only a disguise, a dramatic pretence, like that of Hamlet, to whose madness this perspicacious judgment refers. These authors must either have refrained from judging by appearances, or the appearances were, in their case, altogether different.

Without lingering over its superficial absurdity, Havelock Ellis considers the dream as "an archaic world of vast emotions and imperfect thoughts," the study of which may acquaint us with the primitive stages of the development of mental life. J. Sully presents the same conception of the dream in a still more comprehensive and penetrating fashion. His statements deserve all the more consideration when it is added that he, perhaps more than any other psychologist, was convinced of the veiled significance of the dream. "Now our dreams are a means of conserving these successive personalities. When asleep we go back to the old ways of looking at things and of feeling about them, to impulses and activities which long ago dominated us." A thinker like Delboeuf asserts - without, indeed, adducing proof in the face of contradictory data, and hence without real justification - "Dans le sommeil, hormis la perception, toutes les facultes de l'esprit, intelligence, imagination, memoire, volonte, moralite, restent intactes dans leur essence; seulement, elles s'appliquent a des objets imaginaires et mobiles. Le songeur est un acteur qui joue a volonte les fous et les sages, les bourreaux et les victimes, les nains et les geants, les demons et les anges"[34]. The Marquis Hervey,[35] who is flatly contradicted by Maury, and whose essay I have been unable to obtain despite all my efforts, appears emphatically to protest against the under-estimation of the psychic capacity in the dream. Maury speaks of him as follows: "M. le Marquis

---

[34] In sleep, excepting perception, all the faculties of the mind intellect, imagination, memory, will, morality - remain intact in their essence; only, they are applied to imaginary and variable objects. The dreamer is an actor who plays at will the mad and the wise, executioner and victim, dwarf and giant, devil and angel.

[35] Hervey de St. Denys.

Hervey prete a l'intelligence durant le sommeil toute sa liberte d'action et d'attention, et il ne semble faire consister le sommeil que dans l'occlusion des sens, dans leur fermeture au monde exterieur; en sorte que l'homme qui dort ne se distingue guere, selon sa maniere de voir, de l'homme qui laisse vaguer sa pensee en se bouchant les sens; toute la difference qui separe alors la pensee ordinaire du celle du dormeur c'est que, chez celui-ci, l'idee prend une forme visible, objective, et ressemble, a s'y meprendre, a la sensation determinee par les objets exterieurs; le souvenir revet l'apparence du fait present."[36]

Maury adds, however, "qu'il y a une difference de plus et capitale a savoir que les facultes intellectuelles de l'homme endormi n'offrent pas l'equilibre qu'elles gardent chez l'homme eveille."[37] In Vaschide, who gives us fully information as to Hervey's book, we find that this author expresses himself as follows, in respect to the apparent incoherence of dreams: "L'image du reve est la copie de l'idee. Le principal est l'idee; la vision n'est pas qu'accessoire. Ceci etabli, il faut savoir suivre la marche des idees, il faut savoir analyser le tissu des reves; l'incoherence devient alors comprehensible, les conceptions les plus fantasques deviennent des faits simples et parfaitement logiques"[38]. And: "Les reves les plus bizarres trouvent meme une explication des plus logiques quand on sait les analyser."[39]

J. Starke has drawn attention to the fact that a similar solution of the incoherence of dreams was put forward in 1799 by an old writer, Wolf Davidson, who was unknown to me: "The peculiar leaps of our

---

[36] The Marquis Hervey attributes to the intelligence during sleep all its freedom of action and attention, and he seems to make sleep consist only of the shutting of the senses, of their closing to the outside world; except for his manner of seeing, the man asleep is hardly distinguishable from the man who allows his mind to wander while he obstructs his senses; the whole difference, then, between ordinary thought and that of the sleeper, is that with the latter the idea takes an objective and visible shape, which resembles, to all appearances, sensation determined by exterior objects; memory takes on the appearance of present fact.

[37] That there is a further and important difference in that the mental faculties of the sleeping man do not offer the equilibrium which they keep in the waking state.

[38] The image in a dream is a copy of an idea. The main thing is the idea; the vision is only accessory. This established, it is necessary to know how to follow the progression of ideas, how to analyse the texture of the dreams; incoherence then is understandable, the most fantastic concepts become simple and perfectly logical facts.

[39] Even the most bizarre dreams find a most logical explanation when one knows how to analyse them.

imaginings in the dream-state all have their cause in the laws of association, but this connection often occurs very obscurely in the soul, so that we frequently seem to observe a leap of the imagination where none really exists."

The evaluation of the dream as a psychic product in the literature of the subject varies over a very wide scale; it extends from the extreme of under-estimation, as we have already seen, through premonitions that it may have a value as yet unrevealed, to an exaggerated over-estimation, which sets the dream-life far above the capacities of waking life. In his psychological characterization of dream-life, Hildebrandt, as we know, groups it into three antinomies, and he combines in the third of these antinomies the two extreme points of this scale of values: "It is the contrast between, on the one hand, an enhancement, an increase of potentiality, which often amounts to virtuosity, and on the other hand a decided diminution and enfeeblement of the psychic life, often to a sub-human level."

"As regards the first, who is there that cannot confirm from his own experience the fact that in the workings and weavings of the genius of dreams, there are sometimes exhibited a profundity and sincerity of emotion, a tenderness of feeling, a clearness of view, a subtlety of observation and a readiness of wit, such as we should have modestly to deny that we always possessed in our waking life? Dreams have a wonderful poetry, an apposite allegory, an incomparable sense of humour, a delightful irony. They see the world in the light of a peculiar idealization, and often intensify the effect of their phenomena by the most ingenious understanding of the reality underlying them. They show us earthly beauty in a truly heavenly radiance, the sublime in its supremest majesty, and that which we know to be terrible in its most frightful form, while the ridiculous becomes indescribably and drastically comical. And on waking we are sometimes still so full of one of these impressions that it will occur to us that such things have never yet been offered to us by the real world."

One might here ask oneself: do these depreciatory remarks and these enthusiastic praises really refer to the self-same phenomenon? Have somewriters overlooked the foolish and others the profound and sensitive dreams? And if both kinds of dreams do occur - that is, dreams that merit both these judgments - does it not seem idle to seek a psychological characterization of the dream? Would it not suffice to state that everything is possible in the dream, from the lowest degradation of the psychic life to its flight to heights unknown in the waking state? Convenient as such a solution might be, it has this against it: that behind the efforts of all the investigators of dreams there seems to lurk the assumption that there is in dreams some characteristic which is universally valid in its essential features, and which must eliminate all these contradictions.

It is unquestionably true that the mental capacities of dreams found readier and warmer recognition in the intellectual period now lying behind us, when philosophy rather than exact natural science ruled the more intelligent minds. Statements like that of Schubert, to the effect that the dream frees the mind from the power of external nature, that it liberates the soul from the chains of sensory life, together with similar opinions expressed by the younger Fichte[40] and others, who represent dreams as a soaring of the mind to a higher plane - all these seem hardly conceivable to us today; they are repeated at present only by mystics and devotees.[41] With the advance of a scientific mode of thought a reaction took place in the estimation of dreams. It is the medical writers who are most inclined to underrate the psychic activity in dreams, as being insignificant and valueless; while philosophers and unprofessional observers - amateur psychologists - whose contributions to the subject in especial must not be overlooked, have for the most part, in agreement with popular belief, laid emphasis on the psychological value of dreams. Those who are inclined to underrate the psychic activity of dreams naturally show a preference for the somatic sources of excitation in the aetiology

---

[40] Cf. Haffner and Spitta.
[41] That brilliant mystic, Du Prel, one of the few writers for the omission of whose name in earlier editions of this book I should like to apologize, has said that, so far as the human mind is concerned, it is not the waking state but dreams which are the gateway to metaphysics (Philosophie der Mystik).

of the dream; those who admit that the dreaming mind may retain the greater part of its waking faculties naturally have no motive for denying the existence of autonomous stimulations Among the superior accomplishments which one may be tempted, even on a sober comparison, to ascribe to the dream-life, that of memory is the most impressive. We have fully discussed the by no means rare experiences which prove this superiority. Another privilege of the dream-life, often extolled by the older writers - namely, the fact that it can overstep the limitations of time and space - is easily recognized as an illusion. This privilege, as Hildebrandt remarks, is merely illusory; dreams disregard time and space only as does waking thought, and only because dreaming is itself a form of thinking. Dreams are supposed to enjoy a further advantage in respect of time - to be independent of the passage of time in yet another sense. Dreams like Maury's dream of his execution seem to show that the perceptual content which the dream can compress into a very short space of time far exceeds that which can be mastered by our psychic activity in its waking thoughts. These conclusions have, however, been disputed. The essays of Le Lorrain and Egger on The Apparent Duration of Dreams gave rise to a long and interesting discussion, which in all probability has not yet found the final explanation of this profound and delicate problem.[42]

That dreams are able to continue the intellectual activities of the day and to carry them to a point which could not be arrived at during the day, that they may resolve doubts and problems, and that they may be the source of fresh inspiration in poets and composers, seems, in the light of numerous records, and of the collection of instances compiled by Chabaneix, to be proved beyond question. But even though the facts may be beyond dispute, their interpretation is subject to many doubts on wider grounds.[43]

Finally, the alleged divinatory power of the dream has become

---

[42] For the further literature of the subject, and a critical discussion of these problems, the reader is referred to Tobowolska's dissertation (Paris, 1900).

[43] Compare Havelock Ellis's criticism in The World of Dreams.

a subject of contention in which almost insuperable objections are confronted by obstinate and reiterated assertions. It is, of course, right that we should refrain from denying that this view has any basis whatever in fact, since it is quite possible that a number of such cases may before long be explained on purely natural psychological grounds.

F. The Ethical Sense in Dreams

For reasons which will be intelligible only after a consideration of my own investigations of dreams, I have isolated from the psychology of the dream the subsidiary problem as to whether and to what extent the moral dispositions and feelings of waking life extend into dream-life. The same contradictions which we were surprised to observe in the descriptions by various authors of all the other psychic activities will surprise us again here. Some writers flatly assert that dreams know nothing of moral obligations; others as decidedly declare that the moral nature of man persists even in his dream-life.

Our ordinary experience of dreams seems to confirm beyond all doubt the correctness of the first assertion. Jessen says: "Nor does one become better or more virtuous during sleep; on the contrary, it seems that conscience is silent in our dreams, inasmuch as one feels no compassion and can commit the worst crimes, such as theft, murder, and homicide, with perfect indifference and without subsequent remorse."

Radestock says: "It is to be noted that in dreams associations are effected and ideas combined without being in any way influenced by reflection, reason, aesthetic taste, and moral judgment; the judgment is extremely weak, and ethical indifference reigns supreme." Volkelt expresses himself as follows: "As every one knows, dreams are especially unbridled in sexual matters. Just as the dreamer himself is shameless in the extreme, and wholly lacking in moral feeling and judgment, so likewise does he see others, even the most respected persons, doing things which, even in his thoughts, he would blush to associate with them in his waking state."

Utterances like those of Schopenhauer, that in dreams every man acts and talks in complete accordance with his character, are in sharpest contradiction to those mentioned above. R. Ph. Fischer[44] maintains that the subjective feelings and desires, or affects and passions, manifest themselves in the wilfulness of the dream-life, and that the moral characteristics of a man are mirrored in his dreams.

Haffner says: "With rare exceptions... a virtuous man will be virtuous also in his dreams; he will resist temptation, and show no sympathy for hatred, envy, anger, and all other vices; whereas the sinful man will, as a rule, encounter in his dreams the images which he has before him in the waking state."

Scholz: "In dreams there is truth; despite all camouflage of nobility or degradation, we recognize our own true selves.... The honest man does not commit a dishonouring crime even in his dreams, or, if he does, he is appalled by it as by something foreign to his nature. The Roman emperor who ordered one of his subjects to be executed because he dreamed that he had cut off the emperor's head was not far wrong in justifying his action on the ground that he who has such dreams must have similar thoughts while awake. Significantly enough, we say of things that find no place even in our intimate thoughts: 'I would never even dream of such a thing.'"

Plato, on the other hand, considers that they are the best men who only dream the things which other men do. Plaff,[45] varying a familiar proverb, says: "Tell me your dreams for a time and I will tell you what you are within."

The little essay of Hildebrandt's from which I have already taken so many quotations (the best-expressed and most suggestive contribution to the literature of the dream-problem which I have hitherto discovered), takes for its central theme the problem of morality in dreams. For Hildebrandt, too, it is an established rule that the purer the life, the purer the dream; the impurer the life, the impurer the dream.

[44] Grundzuge des Systems der Anthropologie. Erlangen, 1850 (quoted by Spitta).

The moral nature of man persists even in dreams. "But while we are not offended or made suspicious by an arithmetical error, no matter how obvious, by a reversal of scientific fact, no matter how romantic, or by an anachronism, no matter how ridiculous, we nevertheless do not lose sight of the difference between good and evil, right and wrong, virtue and vice. No matter how much of that which accompanies us during the day may vanish in our hours of sleep, Kant's categorical imperative dogs our steps as an inseparable companion, of whom we cannot rid ourselves even in our slumber.... This can be explained only by the fact that the fundamental element of human nature, the moral essence, is too firmly fixed to be subjected to the kaleidoscopic shaking-up to which phantasy, reason, memory, and other faculties of the same order succumb in our dreams".

In the further discussion of the subject we find in both these groups of authors remarkable evasions and inconsequences. Strictly speaking, all interest in immoral dreams should be at an end for those who assert that the moral personality of the individual falls to pieces in his dreams. They could as coolly reject all attempts to hold the dreamer responsible for his dreams, or to infer from the immorality of his dreams that there is an immoral strain in his nature, as they have rejected the apparently analogous attempt to prove from the absurdity of his dreams the worthlessness of his intellectual life in the waking state. The others, according to whom the categorical imperative extends even into the dream, ought to accept in toto the notion of full responsibility for immoral dreams; and we can only hope that their own reprehensible dreams do not lead them to abandon their otherwise firm belief in their own moral worth.

As a matter of fact, however, it would seem that although no one is positively certain just how good or how bad he is, he can hardly deny that he can recollect immoral dreams of his own. That there are such dreams no one denies; the only question is: how do they originate? So that, in spite of their conflicting

---

[45] Das Traumleben und seine Deutung, 1868 (cited by Spitta, p. 192).

judgments of dream-morality, both groups of authors are at pains to explain the genesis of the immoral dream; and here a new conflict arises, as to whether its origin is to be sought in the normal functions of the psychic life, or in the somatically conditioned encroachments upon this life. The nature of the facts compels both those who argue for and those who argue against moral responsibility in dream-life to agree in recognizing a special psychic source for the immorality of dreams.

Those who maintain that morality continues to function in our dream-life nevertheless refrain from assuming full responsibility for their dreams. Haffner says: "We are not responsible for our dreams, because that basis which alone gives our life truth and reality is withdrawn from our thoughts and our will. Hence the wishes and actions of our dreams cannot be virtuous or sinful." Yet the dreamer is responsible for the sinful dream in so far as indirectly he brings it about. Thus, as in waking life, it is his duty, just before going to sleep, morally to cleanse his mind.

The analysis of this admixture of denial and recognition of responsibility for the moral content of dreams is carried much further by Hildebrandt.

After arguing that the dramatic method of representation characteristic of dreams, the condensation of the most complicated processes of reflection into the briefest periods of time, and the debasement and confusion of the imaginative elements of dreams, which even he admits must be allowed for in respect of the immoral appearance of dreams, he nevertheless confesses that there are the most serious objections to flatly denying all responsibility for the lapses and offenses of which we are guilty in our dreams.

"If we wish to repudiate very decisively any sort of unjust accusation, and especially one which has reference to our intentions and convictions, we use the expression: 'We should never have dreamt of such a thing.' By this, it is true, we mean on the one hand that we consider the region of dreams the last and remotest place in which we could be held responsible for our thoughts, because there these thoughts are so loosely and incoherently connected with our real being that we can, after all, hardly regard them as our own; but inasmuch as we feel impelled expressly to deny the existence of such thoughts even in this region, we are at the same time indirectly admitting that our justification would not be complete unless it extended even thus far. And I believe that here, although unconsciously, we are speaking the language of truth."

"No dream-action can be imagined whose first beginnings have not in some shape already passed through the mind during our waking hours, in the form of wish, desire, or impulse." Concerning this original impulse we must say: The dream has not discovered it - it has only imitated and extended it; it has only elaborated into dramatic form a scrap of historical material which it found already existing within us; it brings to our mind the words of the Apostle that he who hates his brother is a murderer. And though, after we wake, being conscious of our moral strength, we may smile at the whole widely elaborated structure of the depraved dream, yet the original material out of which we formed it cannot be laughed away. One feels responsible for the transgressions of one's dreaming self; not for the whole sum of them, but yet for a certain percentage. "In short, if in this sense, which can hardly be impugned, we understand the words of Christ, that out of the heart come evil thoughts, then we can hardly help being convinced that every sin committed in our dreams brings with it at least a vague minimum of guilt."

Thus Hildebrandt finds the source of the immorality of dreams in the germs and hints of evil impulses which pass through our minds during the day as mental temptations, and he does not hesitate to include these immoral elements in the ethical evaluation of the personality. These same thoughts, and the same evaluation of these thoughts, have, as we know, caused devout and holy men of all ages to lament that they were wicked sinners.[46]

---

[46] It is not uninteresting to consider the attitude of the Inquisition to this problem. In the Tractatus de Officio sanctissimae Inquisitionis of Thomas Carena (Lyons edit., 1659) one finds the following passage: "Should anyone utter heresies in his dreams, the inquisitors shall consider this a reason for investigating his conduct in life, for that is wont to return in sleep which occupies a man during the day" (Dr. Ehniger, St. Urban, Switzerland).

The general occurrence of these contrasting thoughts in the majority of men, and even in other regions than the ethical, is of course established beyond a doubt. They have sometimes been judged in a less serious spirit. Spitta quotes a relevant passage from A. Zeller (Article "Irre," in the Allgemeine Encyklopadie der Wissenschaften, Ersch and Gruber): "An intellect is rarely so happily organized as to be in full command of itself at all times and seasons, and never to be disturbed in the lucid and constant processes of thought by ideas not merely unessential, but absolutely grotesque and nonsensical; indeed, the greatest thinkers have had cause to complain of this dream-like, tormenting and distressing rabble of ideas, which disturbs their profoundest contemplations and their most pious and earnest meditations."

A clearer light is thrown on the psychological meaning of these contrasting thoughts by a further observation of Hildebrandt's, to the effect that dreams permit us an occasional glimpse of the deepest and innermost recesses of our being, which are generally closed to us in our waking state. A recognition of this fact is betrayed by Kant in his Anthropology, when he states that our dreams may perhaps be intended to reveal to us not what we are but what we might have been if we had had another upbringing; and by Radestock, who suggests that dreams disclose to us what we do not wish to admit to ourselves, and that we therefore unjustly condemn them as lying and deceptive. J. E. Erdmann asserts: "A dream has never told me what I ought to think of a person, but, to my great surprise, a dream has more than once taught me what I do really think of him and feel about him." And J. H. Fichte expresses himself in a like manner: "The character of our dreams gives a far truer reflection of our general disposition than anything that we can learn by self-observation in the waking state." Such remarks as this of Benini's call our attention to the fact that the emergence of impulses which are foreign to our ethical consciousness is merely analogous to the manner, already familiar to us, in which the dream disposes of other representative material: "Certe nostre inclinazioni che si credevano soffocate e spente da un pezzo, si ridestano; passioni vecchie e sepolte revivono; cose e persone a cui non pensiamo mai, ci vengono dinanzi". Volkelt expresses himself in a similar fashion: "Even ideas which have entered into our consciousness almost unnoticed, and which, perhaps, it has never before called out of oblivion, often announce their presence in the mind through a dream". Finally, we may remember that according to Schleiermacher the state of falling asleep is accompanied by the appearance of undesired imaginings.

We may include in such "undesired imaginings" the whole of that imaginative material the occurrence of which surprises us in immoral as well as in absurd dreams. The only important difference consists in the fact that the undesired imaginings in the moral sphere are in opposition to our usual feelings, whereas the others merely appear strange to us. So far nothing has been done to enable us to reconcile this difference by a profounder understanding. But what is the significance of the emergence of undesired representations in dreams? What conclusions can the psychology of the waking and dreaming mind draw from these nocturnal manifestations of contrasting ethical impulses? Here we find a fresh diversity of opinion, and also a different grouping of the authors who have treated of the subject. The line of thought followed by Hildebrandt, and by others who share his fundamental opinion, cannot be continued otherwise than by ascribing to the immoral impulses, even in the waking state, a latent vitality, which is indeed inhibited from proceeding to action, and by asserting that during sleep something falls away from us which, having the effect of an inhibition, has kept us from becoming aware of the existence of such impulses. Dreams therefore, reveal the true, if not the whole, nature of the dreamer, and are one means of making the hidden life of the psyche accessible to our understanding. It is only on such hypotheses that Hildebrandt can attribute to the dream the role of a monitor who calls our attention to the secret mischief in the soul, just as, according to the physicians, it may announce a hitherto unobserved physical disorder. Spitta, too, must be influenced by this conception when he refers, for example, to the stream of excitations which flow in upon the psyche during puberty, and consoles the dreamer by assuring him that he has done all that is in his power to do if he has led a strictly virtuous life during his waking state, if he has made an effort to suppress the sinful thoughts as often as they arise, and has kept them from maturing and turning into action. According to this conception, we might designate as "undesired imaginings" those that are suppressed during the day, and we must recognize in their emergence a genuine psychic phenomenon.

According to certain other authors, we have no right to draw this last inference. For Jessen the undesired ideas and images, in the dream as in the waking state, and also in the delirium of fever, etc., possess "the character of a voluntary activity laid to rest, and of a procession, to some extent mechanical, of images and ideas evoked by inner impulses." An immoral dream proves nothing in respect of the psychic life of the dreamer except that he has somehow become cognizant of the imaginative content in question; it is certainly no proof of a psychic impulse of his own mind. Another writer, Maury, makes us wonder whether he, too, does not ascribe to the dream-state the power of dividing the psychic activity into its components, instead of aimlessly destroying it. He speaks as follows of dreams in which one oversteps the bounds of morality: "Ce sont nos penchants qui parlent et qui nous font agir, sans que la conscience nous retienne, bien que parfois elle nous avertisse. J'ai mes defauts et mes penchants vicieux; a l'etat de veille, je tache de lutter contre eux, et il m'arrive assez souvent de n'y pas succomber. Mais dans mes songes j'y succombe toujours, ou pour mieux dire j'agis par leur impulsion, sans crainte et sans remords.... Evidemment les visions qui se deroulent devant ma pensee, et qui constituent le reve, me sont suggerees par les incitations que je ressens et que ma volonte absente ne cherche pas a refouler."[47] Le Sommeil.

---

[47] Our tendencies speak and make us act, without being restrained by our conscience, although it sometimes warns us. I have my faults and vicious tendencies; awake I try to fight against them, and often enough I do not succumb to them. But in my dreams I always succumb, or, rather, I act at their direction, without fear or remorse.... Evidently, the visions which unfold in my thoughts, and which constitute the dream, are suggested by the stimuli which I feel and which my absent will does not try to repel.

If one believed in the power of the dream to reveal an actually existing, but suppressed or concealed, immoral disposition of the dreamer, one could not express one's opinion more emphatically than in the words of Maury: "En reve l'homme se revele donc tout entier a soi-meme dans sa nudite et sa misere natives. Des qu'il suspend l'exercise de sa volonte, il devient le jouet de toutes les passions contre lesquelles, a l'etat de veille, la conscience, le sentiment d'honneur, la crainte nous defendent."[48] In another place makes the striking assertion: "Dans le reve, c'est surtout l'homme instinctif que se revele.... L'homme revient pour ainsi dire l'etat de nature quand il reve; mais moins les idees acquises ont penetre dans son esprit, plus 'les penchants en desaccord' avec elles conservent encore sur lui d'influence dans le rive."[49] He then mentions, as an example, that his own dreams often reveal him as a victim of just those superstitions which he has most vigorously attacked in his writings. The value of all these acute observations is, however, impaired in Maury's case, because he refuses to recognize in the phenomena which he has so accurately observed anything more than a proof of the automatisme psychologique which in his own opinion dominates the dream-life. He conceives this automatism as the complete opposite of psychic activity.

A passage in Stricker's Studien uber das Bewusstsein reads: "Dreams do not consist purely and simply of delusions; for example, if one is afraid of robbers in a dream, the robbers indeed are imaginary, but the fear is real." Our attention is here called to the fact that the affective development of a dream does not admit of the judgment which one bestows upon the rest of the dream-content, and the problem then arises: What part of the psychic processes in a dream may be real? That is to say, what part of

---

[48] In a dream, a man is totally revealed to himself in his naked and wretched state. As he suspends the exercise of his will, he becomes the toy of all the passions from which, when awake, our conscience, horror, and fear defend us.

[49] In a dream, it is above all the instinctive man who is revealed.... Man returns, so to speak, to the natural state when he dreams; but the less acquired ideas have penetrated into his mind, the more his "tendencies to disagreement" with them keep their hold on him in his dreams.

them may claim to be enrolled among the psychic processes of the waking state?

G. Dream-Theories and the Function of the Dream

A statement concerning the dream which seeks to explain as many as possible of its observed characteristics from a single point of view, and which at the same time defines the relation of the dream to a more comprehensive sphere of phenomena, may be described as a theory of the dream. The individual theories of the dream will be distinguished from one another by their designating as essential this or that characteristic of dreams, and relating thereto their data and their explanations. It is not absolutely necessary that we should deduce from the theory of the dream a function, i.e., a use or any such similar role, but expectation, being as a matter of habit teleologically inclined, will nevertheless welcome those theories which afford us some insight into a function of dreams.

We have already become acquainted with many conceptions of the dream, which in this sense are more or less deserving of the name of dreamtheories. The belief of the ancients that dreams were sent by the gods in order to guide the actions of man was a complete theory of the dream, which told them all that was worth knowing about dreams. Since dreams have become an object of biological research we have a greater number of theories, some of which, however, are very incomplete.

Provided we make no claim to completeness, we might venture on the following rough grouping of dream-theories, based on their fundamental conception of the degree and mode of the psychic activity in dreams:

1. Theories, like those of Delboeuf, which allow the full psychic activity of the waking state to continue in our dreams. Here the psyche does not sleep; its apparatus remains intact; but under the conditions of the sleeping state, which differ from those of the waking state, it must in its normal functioning give results which differ from those of the waking state. As regards these theories, it may be questioned whether their authors are in a position to derive the distinction between dreaming and waking

thought entirely from the conditions of the sleeping state. Moreover, they lack one possible access to a function of dreams; one does not understand to what purpose one dreams - why the complicated mechanism of the psychic apparatus should continue to operate even when it is placed under conditions to which it does not appear to be adapted. There are only two purposeful reactions in the place of the reaction of dreaming: to sleep dreamlessly, or to wake when affected by disturbing stimuli. 2. Theories which, on the contrary, assume for the dream a diminution of the psychic activity, a loosening of connections, and an impoverishment of the available material. In accordance with these theories, one must assume for sleep a psychological character entirely different from that given by Delboeuf. Sleep encroaches widely upon the psyche; it does not consist in the mere shutting it off from the outer world; on the contrary, it enters into its mechanism, and makes it for the time being unserviceable. If I may draw a comparison from psychiatry, I would say that the first group of theories construes the dream like a paranoia, while the second represents it as a type of mental deficiency or amentia. The theory that only a fragment of the psychic activity paralysed by sleep finds expression in dreams is that by far the most favoured by medical writers, and by scientists in general. In so far as one may presuppose a general interest in dream-interpretation, one may indeed describe it as the most popular theory of dreams. It is remarkable how nimbly this particular theory avoids the greatest danger that threatens every dreaminterpretation; that is, shipwreck on one of the contrasts incorporated in dreams. Since this theory regards dreams as the result of a partial waking (or, as Herbart puts it in his Psychologie uber den Traum, "a gradual, partial, and at the same time very anomalous waking"), it is able to cover the whole series, from the inferior activities of dreams, which betray themselves by their absurdity, to fully concentrated intellectual activity, by a series of states of progressive awakening, ending in complete wakefulness.

Those who find the physiological mode of expression indispensable, or who deem it more scientific, will find this theory of dreams summarized in Binz's description :

"This state (of torpor), however, gradually comes to an end in the hours of early morning. The accumulated products of fatigue in the albumen of the brain gradually diminish. They are slowly decomposed, or carried away by the constantly flowing blood-stream. Here and there individual groups of cells can be distinguished as being awake, while around them all is still in a state of torpidity. The isolated work of the individual groups now appears before our clouded consciousness, which is still powerless to control other parts of the brain, which govern the associations. Hence the pictures created, which for the most part correspond to the objective impressions of the immediate past, combine with one another in a wild and uncontrolled fashion. As the number of brain-cells set free constantly increases, the irrationality of the dream becomes constantly less."

The conception of the dream as an incomplete, partial waking state, or traces of the influence of this conception, will of course be found in the works of all the modern physiologists and philosophers. It is most completely represented by Maury. It often seems as though this author conceives the state of being awake or asleep as susceptible of shifting from one anatomical region to another; each anatomical region seeming to him to be connected with a definite psychic function. Here I will merely suggest that even if the theory of partial waking were confirmed, its finer superstructure would still call for exhaustive consideration.

No function of dreams, of course, can emerge from this conception of the dream-life. On the contrary, Binz, one of the chief proponents of this theory, consistently enough denies that dreams have any status or importance. He says: "All the facts, as we see them, urge us to characterize the dream as a physical process, in all cases useless, and in many cases definitely morbid."

The expression physical in reference to dreams (the word is emphasized by the author) points, of course, in more than one direction. In the first place, it refers to the aetiology of dreams, which was of special interest to Binz, as he was studying the experimental production of dreams by the administration of drugs.

It is certainly in keeping with this kind of dream-theory to ascribe the incitement to dreaming, whenever possible, exclusively to somatic origins. Presented in the most extreme form the theory is as follows: After we have put ourselves to sleep by the banishment of stimuli, there would be no need to dream, and no reason for dreaming until the morning, when the gradual awakening through the fresh invasion of stimuli might be reflected in the phenomenon of dreaming. But, as a matter of fact, it is not possible to protect our sleep from stimuli; like the germs of life of which Mephistopheles complained, stimuli come to the sleeper from all directions - from without, from within, and even from all those bodily regions which never trouble us during the waking state. Thus our sleep is disturbed; now this, now that little corner of the psyche is jogged into the waking state, and the psyche functions for a while with the awakened fraction, yet is thankful to fall asleep again. The dream is the reaction to the disturbance of sleep caused by the stimulus, but it is, when all is said, a purely superfluous reaction.

The description of the dream - which, after all, remains an activity of the psychic organ - as a physical process has yet another connotation. So to describe it is to deny that the dream has the dignity of a psychic process. The old simile of "the ten fingers of a person ignorant of music running over the keyboard of an instrument" perhaps best illustrates in what esteem the dream is commonly held by the representatives of exact science. Thus conceived, it becomes something wholly insusceptible of interpretation. How could the ten fingers of a player ignorant of music perform a musical composition?

The theory of partial wakefulness did not escape criticism even by the earlier writers. Thus Burdach wrote in 1830: "If we say that dreaming is a partial waking, then, in the first place, neither the waking nor the sleeping state is explained thereby; secondly, this amounts only to saying that certain powers of the mind are active in dreams while others are at rest. But such irregularities occur throughout life...".

The prevailing dream-theory which conceives the dream as a "physical" process finds a certain support in a very interesting conception of the dream which was first propounded by Robert in 1866, and which is seductive because it assigns to the dream a function or a useful result. As the basis of his theory Robert takes two objectively observable facts which we have already discussed in our consideration of dream-material (chapter I., B). These facts are: (1) that one very often dreams about the most insignificant impressions of the day; and (2) that one rarely carries over into the dream the absorbing interests of the day. Robert asserts as an indisputable fact that those matters which have been fully settled and solved never evoke dreams, but only such as lie incompleted in the mind, or touch it merely in passing. "For this reason we cannot usually explain our dreams, since their causes are to be found in sensory impressions of the preceding day which have not attained sufficient recognition on the part of the dreamer." The condition permitting an impression to reach the dream is, therefore, that this impression has been disturbed in its elaboration, or that it was too insignificant to lay claim to such elaboration. Robert therefore conceives the dream "as a physical process of elimination which in its psychic reaction reaches the consciousness." Dreams are eliminations of thoughts nipped in the bud. "A man deprived of the capacity for dreaming would in time become mentally unbalanced, because an immense number of unfinished and unsolved thoughts and superficial impressions would accumulate in his brain, under the pressure of which all that should be incorporated in the memory as a completed whole would be stifled." The dream acts as a safety-valve for the overburdened brain. Dreams possess a healing and unburdening power.

We should misunderstand Robert if we were to ask him how representation in the dream could bring about an unburdening of the mind. The writer apparently concluded from these two peculiarities of the dream-material that during sleep such an elimination of worthless impressions is effected somehow as a somatic process; and that dreaming is not a special psychic process, but only the information which we receive of such elimination.

Moreover, elimination is not the only thing that takes place in the mind during sleep. Robert himself adds that the stimuli of the day are likewise elaborated, and "what cannot be eliminated from the undigested thought-material lying in the mind is bound up into a completed whole by mental clues borrowed from the imagination, and is thus enrolled in the memory as a harmless phantasy-picture".

But it is in his criticism of the sources of dreams that Robert is most flatly opposed to the prevailing theory. Whereas according to this theory there would be no dream if the external and internal sensory stimuli did not repeatedly wake the mind, according to Robert the impulse to dream lies in the mind itself. It lies in the overloading of the mind, which demands discharge, and Robert considers, quite consistently, that those causes conditioning the dream which depend on the physical condition assume a subordinate rank, and could not incite dreams in a mind which contained no material for dream-formation derived from the waking consciousness. It is admitted, however, that the phantasy-images originating in the depths of the mind may be influenced by nervous stimuli. Thus, according to Robert, dreams are not, after all, wholly dependent on the somatic element. Dreaming is, of course, not a psychic process, and it has no place among the psychic processes of the waking state; it is a nocturnal somatic process in the apparatus of mental activity, and has a function to perform, viz., to guard this apparatus against excessive strain, or, if we may be allowed to change the comparison, to cleanse the mind.

Another author, Yves Delage, bases his theory on the same characteristics of the dream-characteristics which are perceptible in the selection of the dream-material, and it is instructive to observe how a trifling twist in the conception of the same things gives a final result entirely different in its bearings. Delage, having lost through death a person very dear to him, found that we either do not dream at all of what occupies us intently during the day, or that we begin to dream of it only after it is overshadowed by the other interests of the day. His investigations in respect of other persons corroborated the universality of this state of affairs. Concerning the dreams of newly-married people, he makes a comment which is admirable if it should prove to be generally true: "S'ils ont ete fortement epris, presque jamais ils n'ont reve l'un de l'autre avant le mariage ou pendant la lune de miel; et s'ils ont reve d'amour c'est pour etre infideles avec quelque personne indifferente ou odieuse.[50]" But of what does one dream? Delage recognizes that the material of our dreams consists of fragments and remnants of impressions, both from the last few days and from earlier periods. All that appears in our dreams, all that we may at first be inclined to consider the creation of the dream-life, proves on closer investigation to be unrecognized reproduction, "souvenir inconscient." But this representative material reveals one common characteristic; it originates from impressions which have probably affected our senses more forcibly than our mind, or from which the attention has been deflected soon after their occurrence. The less conscious, and at the same time the stronger an impression, the greater the prospect of its playing a part in our next dream.

These two categories of impressions - the insignificant and the undisposed-of - are essentially the same as those which were emphasized by Robert, but Delage gives them another significance, inasmuch as he believes that these impressions are capable of exciting dreams not because they are indifferent, but because they are not disposed of. The insignificant impressions also are, in a sense, not fully disposed of; they, too, owing to their character of new impressions, are "autant de ressorts tendus,"[51] which will be relaxed during sleep. Still more entitled to a role in the dream than a weak and almost unnoticed impression is a vivid impression which has been accidentally retarded in its elaboration, or intentionally repressed. The psychic energy accumulated during

---

[50] If they are very much in love, they have almost never dreamed of each other before the marriage or during the honeymoon; and if they have dreamed of love, it was to be unfaithful with someone unimportant or distasteful.

[51] So many taut lines.

the day by inhibition or suppression becomes the mainspring of the dream at night. In dreams psychically suppressed material achieves expression.[52]

Unfortunately Delage does not pursue this line of thought any farther; he is able to ascribe only the most insignificant role in our dreams to an independent psychic activity, and thus, in his theory of dreams, he reverts to the prevailing doctrine of a partial slumber of the brain: "En somme le reve est le produit de la pensee errante, sans but et sans direction, se fixant successivement sur les souvenirs, qui ont garde assez d'intensite pour se placer sur sa route et l'arreter au passage, etablissant entre eux un lien tantot faible et indecis, tantot plus fort et plus serre, selon que l'activite actuelle du cerveau est plus ou moins abolie par le sommeil."[53]

3. In a third group we may include those dream-theories which ascribe to the dreaming mind the capacity for and propensity to special psychic activities, which in the waking state it is able to exert either not at all or imperfectly. In most cases the manifestation of these activities is held to result in a useful function of dreams. The evaluations of dreams by the earlier psychologists fall chiefly within this category. I shall content myself, however, with quoting in their stead the assertion of Burdach, to the effect that dreaming "is the natural activity of the mind, which is not limited by the power of the individuality, nor disturbed by self-consciousness, nor directed by self-determination, but is the vitality of the sensible focus indulging in free play".

Burdach and others evidently consider this revelling in the free use of its own powers as a state in which the mind refreshes itself and gathers fresh strength for the day's work; something, indeed,

---

[52] A novelist, Anatole France, expresses himself to a similar effect (Le Lys Rouge): "Ce que nous voyons la nuit ce sont les restes malheureux que nous avons negligé dans la veille. Le reve est souvent la revanche des choses qu'on meprise ou le reproche des etres abandonnes." [What we see at night are the unhappy relics that we neglected while awake. The dream is often the revenge of things scorned or the reproach of beings deserted.]

[53] In short, the dream is the product of wandering thought, without end or direction, successively fixing on memories which have retained sufficient intensity to put themselves in the way and block the passage, establishing between themselves a connection sometimes weak and loose, sometimes stronger and closer, according to whether the actual work of the brain is more or less suppressed by sleep.

after the fashion of a vacation. Burdach therefore cites with approval the admirable words in which the poet Novalis lauds the power of the dream: "The dream is a bulwark against the regularity and commonplace character of life, a free recreation of the fettered phantasy, in which it intermingles all the images of life and interrupts the constant seriousness of the adult by the joyful play of the child. Without the dream we should surely grow old earlier, so that the dream may be considered, if not precisely as a gift from above, yet as a delightful exercise, a friendly companion on our pilgrimage to the grave."

The refreshing and healing activity of dreams is even more impressively described by Purkinje. "The productive dreams in particular would perform these functions. These are the unconstrained play of the imagination, and have no connection with the events of the day. The mind is loth to continue the tension of the waking life, but wishes to relax it and recuperate from it. It creates, in the first place conditions opposed to those of the waking state. It cures sadness by joy, worry by hope and cheerfully distracting images, hatred by love and friendliness, and fear by courage and confidence; it appeases doubt by conviction and firm belief, and vain expectation by realization. Sleep heals many sore spots in the mind, which the day keeps continually open, by covering them and guarding them against fresh irritation. On this depends in some degree the consoling action of time." We all feel that sleep is beneficial to the psychic life, and the vague surmise of the popular consciousness is apparently loth to surrender the notion that dreaming is one of the ways in which sleep bestows its benefits. The most original and most comprehensive attempt to explain dreaming as a special activity of the mind, which can freely unfold itself only in the sleeping state, is that made by Scherner in 1861. Scherner's book is written in a heavy and bombastic style and is inspired by an almost intoxicated enthusiasm for the subject, which is bound to repel us unless it can carry us away with it. It places so many difficulties in the way of an analysis that we gladly resort to the clearer and conciser presentation of Scherner's theories made by the philosopher Volkelt: "From these mystical conglomerations, from all these outbursts of splendour and radiance, there indeed flashes and shines an ominous semblance of meaning; but the path of the philosopher is not illumined thereby." Such is the criticism of Scherner's exposition by one of his own followers.

Scherner is not one of those writers for whom the mind carries its undiminished faculties into the dream-life. He even explains how, in our dreams, the centrality and spontaneous energy of the ego become enervated; how cognition, feeling, will, and imagination are transformed by this decentralization; how the remnant of these psychic forces has not a truly intellectual character, but is rather of the nature of a mechanism. But, on the other hand, that activity of the psyche which may be described as phantasy, freed from all rational governance, and hence no longer strictly controlled, rises to absolute supremacy in our dreams. To be sure, it borrows all its building-material from the memory of the waking state, but with this material it builds up structures which differ from those of the waking state as day differs from night. In our dreams it reveals itself as not only reproductive but also productive. Its peculiarities give the dream-life its singular character. It shows a preference for the unlimited, the exaggerated, the prodigious; but by its liberation from the inhibiting categories of thought, it gains a greater flexibility and agility, and indulges in pleasurable turns. It is excessively sensitive to the delicate emotional stimuli of the mind, to its stirring and disturbing affects, and it rapidly recasts the inner life into an external, plastic visibility. The dream-phantasy lacks the language of concepts. What it wishes to say it must express in visible form; and since in this case the concept does not exert an inhibitory control, it depicts it in all the fulness, power, and breadth of visible form. But hereby its language, plain though it is, becomes cumbersome, awkward, and prolix. Plain speaking is rendered especially difficult by the fact that it dislikes expressing an object by its actual image, but prefers to select an alien image, if only the latter is able to express that particular aspect of the object which it is anxious to represent. Such is the symbolizing activity of the phantasy.... It is, moreover, very significant that the dream-phantasy reproduces objects not in detail, but only in outline, and in the freest possible manner. Its paintings, therefore, are like light and brilliant sketches. The dream-phantasy, however, does not stop at the mere representation of the object, but feels an internal urge to implicate the dream-ego to some extent with the object, and thus to give rise to action. The visual dream, for example, depicts gold coins lying in the street; the dreamer picks them up, rejoices, and carries them away.

According to Scherner, the material upon which the dream-phantasy exerts its artistic activity consists preponderantly of the organic sensory stimuli which are so obscure during the day (cf. p. 151 above); hence it is that the over-fantastic theory of Scherner, and perhaps too matter-offact theories of Wundt and other physiologists, though otherwise diametrically opposed to each other, are in perfect agreement in their assumptions with regard to dream-sources and dream-stimuli. But whereas, according to the physiological theory, the psychic reaction to the inner physical stimuli becomes exhausted with the arousing of any of the ideas appropriate to these stimuli (as these ideas then, by way of association, call to their aid other ideas, so that on reaching this stage the chain of psychic processes appears to terminate), according to Scherner, on the other hand, the physical stimuli merely supply the psyche with material which it may utilize in fulfilling its phantastic intentions. For Scherner dream-formation begins where, according to the views of other writers, it comes to an end.

What the dream-phantasy does with the physical stimuli cannot, of course, be regarded as purposeful. The phantasy plays a tantalizing game with them, and represents the organic source of the stimuli of the dream in question by any sort of plastic symbolism. Indeed, Scherner holds - though here Volkelt and others differ from him - that the dream-phantasy has a certain favourite symbol for the organism as a whole: namely, the house.

Fortunately, however, for its representations, it does not seem to limit itself to this material; it may also employ a whole series of houses to designate a single organ; for example, very long streets of houses for the intestinal stimulus. In other dreams particular parts of the house may actually represent particular regions of the body, as in the headache-dream, when the ceiling of the room (which the dream sees covered with disgusting toad-like spiders) represents the head.

Quite apart from the symbol of the house, any other suitable object may be employed to represent those parts of the body which excite the dream.

"Thus the breathing lungs find their symbol in the flaming stove with its windy roaring, the heart in hollow chests and baskets, the bladder in round, ball-shaped, or simply hollow objects. The man's dreams, when due to the sexual stimulus, make the dreamer find in the street the upper portion of a clarinet, or the mouthpiece of a tobacco-pipe, or, again, a piece of fur. The clarinet and tobacco-pipe represent the approximate form of the male sexual organ, while the fur represents the pubic hair. In the sexual dreams of the female, the tightness of the closed thighs may be symbolized by a narrow courtyard surrounded by houses, and the vagina by a very narrow, slippery and soft footpath, leading through the courtyard, upon which the dreamer is obliged to walk, in order perhaps to carry a letter to a man". It is particularly noteworthy that at the end of such a physically stimulated dream the phantasy, as it were, unmasks itself by representing the exciting organ or its function unconcealed. Thus the "tooth-excited dream" usually ends with the dreamer taking a tooth out of his mouth.

The dream-phantasy may, however, direct its attention not merely to the form of the exciting organ, but may even make the substance contained therein the object of symbolization. Thus, for example, the dream excited by the intestinal stimuli may lead us through muddy streets, the dream due to stimuli from the bladder to foaming water. Or the stimulus as such, the nature of its excitation, and the object which it covets, are represented symbolically. Or, again, the dream-ego enters into a concrete association with the symbolization of its own state; as, for example, when in the case of painful stimuli we struggle desperately with vicious dogs or raging bulls, or when in a sexual dream the dreamer sees herself pursued by a naked man. Disregarding all the possible prolixity of elaboration, a phantastic symbolizing activity remains as the central force of every dream. Volkelt, in his fine and enthusiastic essay, attempted to penetrate still further into the character of this phantasy, and to assign to the psychic activity thus recognized its position in a system of philosophical ideas, which, however, remains altogether too difficult of comprehension for anyone who is not prepared by previous training for the intuitive comprehension of philosophical modes of thought.

Scherner attributes no useful function to the activity of the symbolizing phantasy in dreams. In dreams the psyche plays with the stimuli which are offered to it. One might conjecture that it plays in a mischievous fashion. And we might be asked whether our detailed consideration of Scherner's dream-theory, the arbitrariness of which, and its deviation from the rules of all forms of research are only too obvious, can lead to any useful results. We might fitly reply that to reject Scherner's theory without previous examination would be imposing too arrogant a veto. This theory is based on the impressions produced by his dreams on a man who paid close attention to them, and who would appear to be personally very well equipped for tracing obscure psychic phenomena. Furthermore, it treats of a subject which (though rich in its contents and relations) has for thousands of years appeared mysterious to humanity, and to the elucidation of which science, strictly so called, has, as it confesses, contributed nothing beyond attempting - in uncompromising opposition to popular sentiment - to deny its content and significance. Finally, let us frankly admit that it seems as though we cannot very well avoid the phantastical in our attempts to explain dreams. We must remember also that there is such a thing as a phantasy of ganglion cells; the passage cited from a sober and exact investigator like Binz, which describes how the dawn of awakening floods the dormant cell-masses of the cerebral cortex, is not a whit less fanciful and improbable than Scherner's attempts at interpretation. I hope to be able to demonstrate that there is something real underlying these attempts, though the phenomena which he describes have been only vaguely recognized, and do not possess the character of universality that should entitle them to be the basis of a theory of dreams. For the present, Scherner's theory of dreams, in contrast to the medical theory, may perhaps lead us to realize between what extremes the explanation of dream-life is still unsteadily vacillating.

H. The Relation between Dreams and Mental Diseases

When we speak of the relation of dreams to mental derangement, we may mean three different things: (1) aetiological and clinical relations, as when a dream represents or initiates a psychotic condition, or occurs subsequently to such a condition; (2) changes which the dream-life undergoes in cases of mental disease; (3) inner relations between dreams and psychoses, analogies which point to an intimate relationship. These manifold relations between the two series of phenomena were in the early days of medical science - and are once more at the present time - a favourite theme of medical writers, as we may learn from the literature on the subject collated by Spitta, Radestock, Maury, and Tissie. Recently Sante de Sanctis has directed his attention to this relationship.[54] For the purposes of our discussion it will suffice merely to glance at this important subject.

As to the clinical and aetiological relations between dreams and the psychoses, I will report the following observations as examples: Hohnbaum asserts (see Krauss) that the first attack of insanity is frequently connected with a terrifying anxiety-dream, and that the predominating idea is related to this dream. Sante de Sanctis adduces similar observations in respect of paranoiacs, and declares the dream to be, in some of them, "la vraie cause determinante de la folie."[55] The psychosis may come to life quite suddenly, simultaneously with the dream that contains its

---

[54] Among the more recent authors who have occupied themselves with these relations are: Fere, Ideler, Lasegue, Pichon, Regis Vespa, Giessler, Kazodowsky, Pachantoni, and others.

[55] The real determining cause of the madness.

effective and delusive explanation, or it may develop slowly through subsequent dreams that have still to struggle against doubt. In one of de Sanctis's cases an intensively moving dream was accompanied by slight hysterical attacks, which, in their turn, were followed by an anxious melancholic state. Fere (cited by Tissie) refers to a dream which was followed by hysterical paralysis. Here the dream is presented as the aetiology of mental derangement, although we should be making a statement equally consistent with the facts were we to say that the first manifestation of the mental derangement occurred in the dream-life, that the disorder first broke through in the dream. In other instances, the morbid symptoms are included in the dream-life, or the psychosis remains confined to the dream-life. Thus Thomayer calls our attention to anxiety-dreams which must be conceived as the equivalent of epileptic attacks. Allison has described cases of nocturnal insanity (see Radestock), in which the subjects are apparently perfectly well in the day-time, while hallucinations, fits of frenzy, and the like regularly make their appearance at night. De Sanctis and Tissie record similar observations (the equivalent of a paranoic dream in an alcoholic, voices accusing a wife of infidelity). Tissie records many observations of recent date in which behaviour of a pathological character (based on delusory hypotheses, obsessive impulses) had their origin in dreams. Guislain describes a case in which sleep was replaced by an intermittent insanity.

We cannot doubt that one day the physician will concern himself not only with the psychology, but also with the psychopathology of dreams.

In cases of convalescence from insanity, it is often especially obvious that while the functions may be healthy by day the dream-life may still partake of the psychosis. Gregory is said to have been the first to call attention to such cases (see Krauss). Macario (cited by Tissie) gives an account of a maniac who, a week after his complete recovery, once more experienced in dreams the flux of ideas and the unbridled impulses of his disease.

Concerning the changes which the dream-life undergoes in chronic psychotics, little research has been undertaken as yet. On the other hand, early attention was given to the inner relationship between dreams and mental disturbances, a relationship which is demonstrated by the complete agreement of the manifestations occurring in each. According to Maury, Cabanis, in his Rapports du Physique et du Moral, was the first to call attention to this relationship; he was followed by Lelut, J. Moreau, and more particularly the philosopher Maine de Biran. The comparison between the two is of course older still. Radestock begins the chapter in which he deals with the subject by citing a number of opinions which insist on the analogy between insanity and dreaming. Kant says somewhere: "The lunatic is a dreamer in the waking state." According to Krauss, "Insanity is a dream in which the senses are awake." Schopenhauer terms the dream a brief insanity, and insanity a long dream. Hagen describes delirium as a dream-life which is inducted not by sleep but by disease. Wundt, in his Physiologische Psychologie, declares: "As a matter of fact we ourselves may in dreams experience almost all the manifestations which we observe in the asylums for the insane."

The specific points of agreement in consequence of which such a comparison commends itself to our judgment are enumerated by Spitta, who groups them (very much as Maury has done) as follows: "(1) Suspension, or at least retardation of self-consciousness, and consequently ignorance of the condition as such, the impossibility of astonishment, and a lack of moral consciousness. (2) Modified perception of the sensory organs; that is, perception is as a rule diminished in dreams, and greatly enhanced in insanity. (3) Mutual combination of ideas exclusively in accordance with the laws of association and reproduction, hence automatic series-formations: hence again a lack of proportion in the relations between ideas (exaggerations, phantasms); and the results of all this: (4) Changes in - for example, inversions of - the personality, and sometimes of the idiosyncrasies of the character (perversities)."

Radestock adds a few additional data concerning the analogous nature of the material of dreams and of mental derangement: "The greatest number of hallucinations and illusions are found in the sphere of the senses of sight and hearing and general sensation. As in dreams, the fewest elements are supplied by the senses of smell and taste. The fever-patient, like the dreamer, is assailed by reminiscences from the remote past; what the waking and healthy man seems to have forgotten is recollected in sleep and in disease." The analogy between dreams and the psychoses receives its full value only when, like a family resemblance, it is extended to the subtler points of mimicry, and even the individual peculiarities of facial expression.

"To him who is tortured by physical and mental sufferings the dream accords what has been denied him by reality, to wit, physical well-being, and happiness; so, too, the insane see radiant images of happiness, eminence, and wealth. The supposed possession of estates and the imaginary fulfilment of wishes, the denial or destruction of which have actually been a psychic cause of the insanity, often form the main content of the delirium. The woman who has lost a dearly beloved child experiences in her delirium the joys of maternity; the man who has suffered reverses of fortune deems himself immensely wealthy; and the jilted girl sees herself tenderly beloved."

(This passage from Radestock is an abstract of a brilliant exposition of Griesinger's, which reveals, with the greatest clarity, wishfulfilment as a characteristic of the imagination common to dreams and to the psychoses. My own investigations have taught me that here is to be found the key to a psychological theory of dreams and of the psychoses.) "Absurd combinations of ideas and weakness of judgment are the main characteristics of the dream and of insanity." The over-estimation of one's own mental capacity, which appears absurd to sober judgment, is found alike in both, and the rapid flux of imaginings in the dream corresponds to the flux of ideas in the psychoses. Both are devoid of any measure of time. The splitting of the personality in dreams, which, for instance, distributes one's own knowledge between two persons, one of whom, the strange person, corrects one's own ego in the dream, entirely corresponds with the well-known splitting of the personality in hallucinatory paranoia; the dreamer, too, hears his own thoughts expressed by strange voices. Even the constant delusive ideas find their analogy in the stereotyped and recurring pathological dream (reve obsedant). After recovering from delirium, patients not infrequently declare that the whole period of their illness appeared to them like an uncomfortable dream; indeed, they inform us that sometimes during their illness they have suspected that they were only dreaming, just as often happens in the sleepdream. In view of all this, it is not surprising that Radestock should summarize his own opinion, and that of many others, in the following words: "Insanity, an abnormal morbid phenomenon, is to be regarded as an enhancement of the periodically recurring normal dream-state".

Krauss attempted to base the relationship between the dream and insanity upon their aetiology (or rather upon the sources of excitation), thus, perhaps, making the relationship even more intimate than was possible on the basis of the analogous nature of the phenomena manifested. According to him, the fundamental element common to both is, as we have already learned, the organically conditioned sensation, the sensation of physical stimuli, the general sensation arising out of contributions from all the organs.

The undeniable agreement between dreams and mental derangement, extending even to characteristic details, constitutes one of the strongest confirmations of the medical theory of dream-life, according to which the dream is represented as a useless and disturbing process, and as the expression of a diminished psychic activity. One cannot expect, for the present, to derive the final explanation of the dream from the psychic derangements, since, as is well known, our understanding of the origin of the latter is still highly unsatisfactory. It is very probable, however, that a modified conception of the dream must also influence our views regarding the inner mechanism of mental disorders, and hence we may say that we are working towards the explanation of the psychoses when we endeavour to elucidate the mystery of dreams.

ADDENDUM 1909

I shall have to justify myself for not extending my summary of the literature of dream-problems to cover the period between the first appearance of this book and the publication of the second edition. This justification may not seem very satisfactory to the reader; none the less, to me it was decisive. The motives which induced me to summarize the treatment of dreams in the literature of the subject have been exhausted by the foregoing introduction; to have continued this would have cost me a great deal of effort and would not have been particularly useful or instructive. For the interval in question - a period of nine years - has yielded nothing new or valuable as regards the conception of dreams, either in actual material or in novel points of view. In most of the literature which has appeared since the publication of my own work the latter has not been mentioned or discussed; it has, of course, received the least attention from the so-called "research-workers on dreams," who have thus afforded a brilliant example of the aversion to learning anything new so characteristic of the scientist. "Les savants ne sont pas curieux,"[56] said the scoffer Anatole France. If there were such a thing in science as the right of revenge, I in my turn should be justified in ignoring the literature which has appeared since the publication of this book. The few reviews which have appeared in the scientific journals are so full of misconceptions and lack of comprehension that my only possible answer to my critics would be a request that they should read this book over again - or perhaps merely that they should read it!

In the works of those physicians who make use of the psycho-analytic method of treatment a great many dreams have been recorded and interpreted in accordance with my directions. In so far as these works go beyond the confirmation of my own

---

[56] The learned are not inquisitive.

assertions, I have noted their results in the context of my exposition. A supplementary bibliography at the end of this volume comprises the most important of these new publications.

The comprehensive work on the dream by Sante de Sanctis, of which a German translation appeared soon after its publication, was produced simultaneously with my own, so that I could not review his results, nor could he comment upon mine. I am sorry to have to express the opinion that this laborious work is exceedingly poor in ideas, so poor that one could never divine from it the possibility of the problems which I have treated in these pages.

I can think of only two publications which touch on my own treatment of the dream-problems. A young philosopher, H. Swoboda, who has ventured to extend W. Fliess's discovery of biological periodicity (in series of twenty-three and twenty-eight days) to the psychic field, has produced an imaginative essay,[57] in which, among other things, he has used this key to solve the riddle of dreams. Such a solution, however, would be an inadequate estimate of the significance of dreams. The material content of dreams would be explained by the coincidence of all those memories which, on the night of the dream, complete one of these biological periods for the first or the nth time. A personal communication of the author's led me to assume that he himself no longer took this theory very seriously. But it seems that I was mistaken in this conclusion: I shall record in another place some observations made with reference to Swoboda's thesis, which did not, however, yield convincing results. It gave me far greater pleasure to find by chance, in an unexpected quarter, a conception of the dream which is in complete agreement with the essence of my own. The relevant dates preclude the possibility that this conception was influenced by reading my book: I must therefore hail this as the only demonstrable concurrence with the essentials of my theory of dreams to be found in the literature of the subject. The book which contains the passage that I have in mind was published (in its second edition) in 1910, by Lynkeus, under the title Phantasien eines Realisten.

---

[57] H. Swoboda, Die Perioden des Menschlichen Organismus, 1904.

ADDENDUM 1914

The above apologia was written in 1909. Since then, the state of affairs has certainly undergone a change; my contribution to the "interpretation of dreams" is no longer ignored in the literature of the subject. But the new situation makes it even more impossible to continue the foregoing summary. The Interpretation of Dreams has evoked a whole series of new contentions and problems, which have been expounded by the authors in the most varied fashions. But I cannot discuss these works until I have developed the theories to which their authors have referred. Whatever has appeared to me as valuable in this recent literature I have accordingly reviewed in the course of the following exposition.

Chapter 2

The Method Of Dream Interpretation

The Analysis of a Specimen Dream

The epigraph on the title-page of this volume indicates the tradition to which I prefer to ally myself in my conception of the dream. I am proposing to show that dreams are capable of interpretation; and any contributions to the solution of the problems which have already been discussed will emerge only as possible by-products in the accomplishment of my special task. On the hypothesis that dreams are susceptible of interpretation, I at once find myself in disagreement with the prevailing doctrine of dreams - in fact, with all the theories of dreams, excepting only that of Scherner, for to interpret a dream is to specify its meaning, to replace it by something which takes its position in the concatenation of our psychic activities as a link of definite importance and value. But, as we have seen, the scientific theories of the dream leave no room for a problem of dream-interpretation; since, in the first place, according to these theories, dreaming is not a psychic activity at all, but a somatic process which makes itself known to the psychic apparatus by means of symbols. Lay opinion has always been opposed to these theories. It asserts its privilege of proceeding illogically, and although it admits that dreams are incomprehensible and absurd, it cannot summon up the courage to deny that dreams have any significance. Led by a dim intuition, it seems rather to assume that dreams have a meaning, albeit a hidden one; that they are intended as a substitute for some other thought-process, and that we have only to disclose this substitute correctly in order to discover the hidden meaning of the dream.

The unscientific world, therefore, has always endeavoured

to interpret dreams, and by applying one or the other of two essentially different methods. The first of these methods envisages the dream-content as a whole, and seeks to replace it by another content, which is intelligible and in certain respects analogous. This is symbolic dream-interpretation; and of course it goes to pieces at the very outset in the case of those dreams which are not only unintelligible but confused. The construction which the biblical Joseph placed upon the dream of Pharaoh furnishes an example of this method. The seven fat kine, after which came seven lean ones that devoured the former, were a symbolic substitute for seven years of famine in the land of Egypt, which according to the prediction were to consume all the surplus that seven fruitful years had produced.

Most of the artificial dreams contrived by the poets[1] are intended for some such symbolic interpretation, for they reproduce the thought conceived by the poet in a guise not unlike the disguise which we are wont to find in our dreams.

The idea that the dream concerns itself chiefly with the future, whose form it surmises in advance - a relic of the prophetic significance with which dreams were once invested - now becomes the motive for translating into the future the meaning of the dream which has been found by means of symbolic interpretation.

A demonstration of the manner in which one arrives at such a symbolic interpretation cannot, of course, be given. Success remains a matter of ingenious conjecture, of direct intuition, and for this reason dream-interpretation has naturally been elevated into an art which seems to depend upon extraordinary gifts.[2]

---

[1] In a novel Gradiva, by the poet W. Jensen, I chanced to discover several fictitious dreams, which were perfectly correct in their construction, and could be interpreted as though they had not been invented, but had been dreamt by actual persons. The poet declared, upon my inquiry, that he was unacquainted with my theory of dreams. I have made use of this agreement between my investigations and the creations of the poet as a proof of the correctness of my method of dream-analysis (Der Wahn und die Traume in W. Jenson's Gradiva, vol. i of the Schriften zur angewandten Seelenkunde, 1906, edited by myself, Ges. Schriften, vol. ix).

The second of the two popular methods of dream-interpretation entirely abandons such claims. It might be described as the cipher method, since it treats the dream as a kind of secret code in which every sign is translated into another sign of known meaning, according to an established key. For example, I have dreamt of a letter, and also of a funeral or the like; I consult a "dream-book," and I find that "letter" is to be translated by "vexation" and "funeral" by "engagement." It now remains to establish a connection, which I am again to assume as pertaining to the future, by means of the rigmarole which I have deciphered. An interesting variant of this cipher procedure, a variant in which its character of purely mechanical transference is to a certain extent corrected, is presented in the work on dream-interpretation by Artemidoros of Daldis.[3] Here not only the dream-content, but also the personality and social position of the dreamer are taken into consideration, so that the same dream-content has a

[2] Aristotle expressed himself in this connection by saying that the best interpreter of dreams is he who can best grasp similarities. For dreampictures, like pictures in water, are disfigured by the motion (of the water), so that he hits the target best who is able to recognize the true picture in the distorted one (Buchsenschutz, p. 65).

[3] Artemidoros of Daldis, born probably in the beginning of the second century of our calendar, has furnished us with the most complete and careful elaboration of dream-interpretation as it existed in the Graeco-Roman world. As Gompertz has emphasized, he ascribed great importance to the consideration that dreams ought to be interpreted on the basis of observation and experience, and he drew a definite line between his own art and other methods, which he considered fraudulent. The principle of his art of interpretation is, according to Gompertz, identical with that of magic: i.e., the principle of association. The thing dreamed meant what it recalled to the memory - to the memory, of course, of the dreaminterpreter! This fact - that the dream may remind the interpreter of various things, and every interpreter of different things - leads, of course, to uncontrollable arbitrariness and uncertainty. The technique which I am about to describe differs from that of the ancients in one essential point, namely, in that it imposes upon the dreamer himself the work of interpretation. Instead of taking into account whatever may occur to the dreaminterpreter, it considers only what occurs to the dreamer in connection with the dream-element concerned. According to the recent records of the missionary, Tfinkdjit (Anthropos, 1913), it would seem that the modern dream-interpreters of the Orient likewise attribute much importance to the co-operation of the dreamer. Of the dream-interpreters among the Mesopotamian Arabs this writer relates as follows: "Pour interpreter exactement un songe les oniromanciens les plus habiles s'informent de ceux qui les consultent de toutes les circonstances qu'ils regardent necessaires pour la bonne explication.... En un mot, nos oniromanciens ne laissent aucune circonstance leur echapper et ne donnent l'interpretation desiree avant d'avoir parfaitement saisi et recu toutes les interrogations desirables." [To interpret a dream exactly, the most practised interpreters of dreams learn from those who consult them all circumstances which they regard as necessary for a good explanation.... In a word, our interpreters allow no circumstance to be overlooked and do not give the desired interpretation before perfectly taking and apprehending all desirable questions.] Among these questions one always finds demands for precise information in respect to near relatives (parents, wife, children) as well as the following formula: habistine in hoc nocte copulam conjugalem ante vel post somnium [Did you this night have conjugal copulation before or after the dream?] "L'idee dominante dans l'interpretation des songes consiste a expliquer le reve par son oppose." [The dominant idea in the interpretation of dreams consists in explaining the dream by its opposite.]

significance for the rich man, the married man, or the orator, which is different from that which applies to the poor man, the bachelor, or, let us say, the merchant. The essential point, then, in this procedure is that the work of interpretation is not applied to the entirety of the dream, but to each portion of the dream-content severally, as though the dream were a conglomerate in which each fragment calls for special treatment. Incoherent and confused dreams are certainly those that have been responsible for the invention of the cipher method.[4]

The worthlessness of both these popular methods of interpretation does not admit of discussion. As regards the scientific treatment of the subject, the symbolic method is limited in its application, and is not susceptible of a general exposition. In the cipher method everything depends upon whether the key, the dream-book, is reliable, and for that all guarantees are lacking. So that one might be tempted to grant the contention of the philosophers and psychiatrists, and to dismiss the problem of dream-interpretation as altogether fanciful.[5]

I have, however, come to think differently. I have been forced to perceive that here, once more, we have one of those not

[4] Dr. Alfred Robitsek calls my attention to the fact that Oriental dream-books, of which ours are pitiful plagiarisms, commonly undertake the interpretation of dream-elements in accordance with the assonance and similarity of words. Since these relationships must be lost by translation into our language, the incomprehensibility of the equivalents in our popular "dream-books" is hereby explained. Information as to the extraordinary significance of puns and the play upon words in the old Oriental cultures may be found in the writings of Hugo Winckler. The finest example of a dream-interpretation which has come down to us from antiquity is based on a play upon words. Artemidoros relates the following (p. 225): "But it seems to me that Aristandros gave a most happy interpretation to Alexander of Macedon. When the latter held Tyros encompassed and in a state of siege, and was angry and depressed over the great waste of time, he dreamed that he saw a Satyr dancing on his shield. It happened that Aristandros was in the neighbourhood of Tyros, and in the escort of the king, who was waging war on the Syrians. By dividing the word Satyros into sa and turos, he induced the king to become more aggressive in the siege. And thus Alexander became master of the city." (Sa Turos = Thine is Tyros.) The dream, indeed, is so intimately connected with verbal expression that Ferenczi justly remarks that every tongue has its own dream-language. A dream is, as a rule, not to be translated into other languages.

[5] After the completion of my manuscript, a paper by Stumpf came to my notice which agrees with my work in attempting to prove that the dream is full of meaning and capable of interpretation. But the interpretation is undertaken by means of an allegorizing symbolism, and there is no guarantee that the procedure is generally applicable.

infrequent cases where an ancient and stubbornly retained popular belief seems to have come nearer to the truth of the matter than the opinion of modern science. I must insist that the dream actually does possess a meaning, and that a scientific method of dream-interpretation is possible. I arrived at my knowledge of this method in the following manner:

For years I have been occupied with the resolution of certain psycho-pathological structures - hysterical phobias, obsessional ideas, and the like - with therapeutic intentions. I have been so occupied, in fact, ever since I heard the significant statement of Joseph Breuer, to the effect that in these structures, regarded as morbid symptoms, solution and treatment go hand in hand.[6] Where it has been possible to trace a pathological idea back to those elements in the psychic life of the patient to which it owed its origin, this idea has crumbled away, and the patient has been relieved of it. In view of the failure of our other therapeutic efforts, and in the face of the mysterious character of these pathological conditions, it seemed to me tempting, in spite of all the difficulties, to follow the method initiated by Breuer until a complete elucidation of the subject had been achieved. I shall have occasion elsewhere to give a detailed account of the form which the technique of this procedure has finally assumed, and of the results of my efforts. In the course of these psycho-analytic studies, I happened upon the question of dream-interpretation. My patients, after I had pledged them to inform me of all the ideas and thoughts which occurred to them in connection with a given theme, related their dreams, and thus taught me that a dream may be interpolated in the psychic concatenation, which may be followed backwards from a pathological idea into the patient's memory. The next step was to treat the dream itself as a symptom, and to apply to it the method of interpretation which had been worked out for such symptoms.

---

[6] Studien uber Hysterie, 1895. [Compare page 26 above.]

For this a certain psychic preparation on the part of the patient is necessary. A twofold effort is made, to stimulate his attentiveness in respect of his psychic perceptions, and to eliminate the critical spirit in which he is ordinarily in the habit of viewing such thoughts as come to the surface.

For the purpose of self-observation with concentrated attention it is advantageous that the patient should take up a restful position and close his eyes; he must be explicitly instructed to renounce all criticism of the thought-formations which he may perceive. He must also be told that the success of the psycho-analysis depends upon his noting and communicating everything that passes through his mind, and that he must not allow himself to suppress one idea because it seems to him unimportant or irrelevant to the subject, or another because it seems nonsensical. He must preserve an absolute impartiality in respect to his ideas; for if he is unsuccessful in finding the desired solution of the dream, the obsessional idea, or the like, it will be because he permits himself to be critical of them.

I have noticed in the course of my psycho-analytical work that the psychological state of a man in an attitude of reflection is entirely different from that of a man who is observing his psychic processes. In reflection there is a greater play of psychic activity than in the most attentive selfobservation; this is shown even by the tense attitude and the wrinkled brow of the man in a state of reflection, as opposed to the mimic tranquillity of the man observing himself. In both cases there must be concentrated attention, but the reflective man makes use of his critical faculties, with the result that he rejects some of the thoughts which rise into consciousness after he has become aware of them, and abruptly interrupts others, so that he does not follow the lines of thought which they would otherwise open up for him; while in respect of yet other thoughts he is able to behave in such a manner that they do not become conscious at all - that is to say, they are suppressed before they are perceived. In selfobservation, on the other hand, he has but one task - that of suppressing criticism; if he succeeds in doing this, an unlimited number of thoughts enter his consciousness which would otherwise have eluded his grasp. With the aid of the material thus obtained - material which is new to the self-observer - it is possible to achieve the interpretation of pathological ideas, and also that of dream-formations. As will be seen, the point is to induce a psychic state which is in some degree analogous, as regards the distribution of psychic energy (mobile attention), to the state of the mind before falling asleep - and also, of course, to the hypnotic state. On falling asleep the undesired ideas emerge, owing to the slackening of a certain arbitrary (and, of course, also critical) action, which is allowed to influence the trend of our ideas; we are accustomed to speak of fatigue as the reason of this slackening; the emerging undesired ideas are changed into visual and auditory images. In the condition which it utilized for the analysis of dreams and pathological ideas, this activity is purposely and deliberately renounced, and the psychic energy thus saved (or some part of it) is employed in attentively tracking the undesired thoughts which now come to the surface - thoughts which retain their identity as ideas (in which the condition differs from the state of falling asleep). Undesired ideas are thus changed into desired ones.

There are many people who do not seem to find it easy to adopt the required attitude toward the apparently "freely rising" ideas, and to renounce the criticism which is otherwise applied to them. The "undesired ideas" habitually evoke the most violent resistance, which seeks to prevent them from coming to the surface. But if we may credit our great poet-philosopher Friedrich Schiller, the essential condition of poetical creation includes a very similar attitude. In a certain passage in his correspondence with Korner (for the tracing of which we are indebted to Otto Rank), Schiller replies in the following words to a friend who complains of his lack of creative power: "The reason for your complaint lies, it seems to me, in the constraint which your intellect imposes upon your imagination. Here I will make an observation, and illustrate it by an allegory.

Apparently it is not good - and indeed it hinders the creative work of the mind - if the intellect examines too closely the ideas already pouring in, as it were, at the gates. Regarded in isolation, an idea may be quite insignificant, and venturesome in the extreme, but it may acquire importance from an idea which follows it; perhaps, in a certain collocation with other ideas, which may seem equally absurd, it may be capable of furnishing a very serviceable link. The intellect cannot judge all these ideas unless it can retain them until it has considered them in connection with these other ideas. In the case of a creative mind, it seems to me, the intellect has withdrawn its watchers from the gates, and the ideas rush in pell-mell, and only then does it review and inspect the multitude. You worthy critics, or whatever you may call yourselves, are ashamed or afraid of the momentary and passing madness which is found in all real creators, the longer or shorter duration of which distinguishes the thinking artist from the dreamer. Hence your complaints of unfruitfulness, for you reject too soon and discriminate too severely" (letter of December 1, 1788).

And yet, such a withdrawal of the watchers from the gates of the intellect, as Schiller puts it, such a translation into the condition of uncritical selfobservation, is by no means difficult.

Most of my patients accomplish it after my first instructions. I myself can do so very completely, if I assist the process by writing down the ideas that flash through my mind. The quantum of psychic energy by which the critical activity is thus reduced, and by which the intensity of selfobservation may be increased, varies considerably according to the subject-matter upon which the attention is to be fixed.

The first step in the application of this procedure teaches us that one cannot make the dream as a whole the object of one's attention, but only the individual components of its content. If I ask a patient who is as yet unpractised: "What occurs to you in connection with this dream?" he is unable, as a rule, to fix upon anything in his psychic field of vision. I must first dissect the dream for him; then, in connection with each fragment, he gives me a number of ideas which may be described as the thoughts behind this part of the dream. In this first and important condition, then, the method of dream-interpretation which I employ diverges from the popular, historical and legendary method of interpretation by symbolism and approaches more nearly to the second or cipher method. Like this, it is an interpretation in detail, not en masse; like this, it conceives the dream, from the outset, as something built up, as a conglomerate of psychic formations.

In the course of my psycho-analysis of neurotics I have already subjected perhaps more than a thousand dreams to interpretation, but I do not wish to use this material now as an introduction to the theory and technique of dream-interpretation. For quite apart from the fact that I should lay myself open to the objection that these are the dreams of neuropaths, so that the conclusions drawn from them would not apply to the dreams of healthy persons, there is another reason that impels me to reject them. The theme to which these dreams point is, of course, always the history of the malady that is responsible for the neurosis. Hence every dream would require a very long introduction, and an investigation of the nature and aetiological conditions of the psychoneuroses, matters which are in themselves novel and exceedingly strange, and which would therefore distract attention from the dream-problem proper. My purpose is rather to prepare the way, by the solution of the dream-problem, for the solution of the more difficult problems of the psychology of the neuroses. But if I eliminate the dreams of neurotics, which constitute my principal material, I cannot be too fastidious in my treatment of the rest. Only those dreams are left which have been incidentally related to me by healthy persons of my acquaintance, or which I find given as examples in the literature of dream-life. Unfortunately, in all these dreams I am deprived of the analysis without which I cannot find the meaning of the dream. My mode of procedure is, of course, less easy than that of the popular cipher method, which translates the given dream-content by reference to an established key; I, on the contrary, hold that the same dream-content may conceal a different meaning in the case of different persons, or in different connections. I must, therefore, resort to my own dreams as a source of abundant and convenient material, furnished by a person who is more or less normal, and containing references to many incidents of everyday life. I shall certainly be confronted with doubts as to the trustworthiness of these self-analyses and it will be said that arbitrariness is by no means excluded in such analyses. In my own judgment, conditions are more likely to be favourable in self-observation than in the observation of others; in any case, it is permissible to investigate how much can be accomplished in the matter of dream-interpretation by means of self-analysis. There are other difficulties which must be overcome in my own inner self. One has a comprehensible aversion to exposing so many intimate details of one's own psychic life, and one does not feel secure against the misinterpretations of strangers. But one must be able to transcend such considerations. "Tout psychologiste," writes Delboeuf, "est oblige de faire l'aveu meme de ses faiblesses s'il croit par la jeter du jour sur quelque probleme obscur."[7]

And I may assume for the reader that his initial interest in the indiscretions which I must commit will very soon give way to an exclusive engrossment in the psychological problems elucidated by them.'[8]

I shall therefore select one of my own dreams for the purpose of elucidating my method of interpretation. Every such dream necessitates a preliminary statement; so that I must now beg the reader to make my interests his own for a time, and to become absorbed, with me, in the most trifling details of my life; for an interest in the hidden significance of dreams imperatively demands just such a transference.

Preliminary Statement

---

[7] Every psychologist is obliged to admit even his own weaknesses, if he thinks by that he may throw light on a difficult problem.

[8] However, I will not omit to mention, in qualification of the above statement, that I have practically never reported a complete interpretation of a dream of my own. And I was probably right not to trust too far to the reader's discretion.

In the summer of 1895 I had treated psycho-analytically a young lady who was an intimate friend of mine and of my family. It will be understood that such complicated relations may excite manifold feelings in the physician, and especially the psychotherapist. The personal interest of the physician is greater, but his authority less. If he fails, his friendship with the patient's relatives is in danger of being undermined. In this case, however, the treatment ended in partial success; the patient was cured of her hysterical anxiety, but not of all her somatic symptoms. At that time I was not yet quite sure of the criteria which denote the final cure of an hysterical case, and I expected her to accept a solution which did not seem acceptable to her. In the midst of this disagreement, we discontinued the treatment for the summer holidays. One day a younger colleague, one of my most intimate friends, who had visited the patient - Irma - and her family in their country residence, called upon me. I asked him how Irma was, and received the reply: "She is better, but not quite well." I realize that these words of my friend Otto's, or the tone of voice in which they were spoken, annoyed me. I thought I heard a reproach in the words, perhaps to the effect that I had promised the patient too much, and - rightly or wrongly - I attributed Otto's apparent taking sides against me to the influence of the patient's relatives, who, I assumed, had never approved of my treatment. This disagreeable impression, however, did not become clear to me, nor did I speak of it. That same evening I wrote the clinical history of Irma's case, in order to give it, as though to justify myself, to Dr. M, a mutual friend, who was at that time the leading personality in our circle. During the night (or rather in the early morning) I had the following dream, which I recorded immediately after waking.[9]

Dream of July 23-24, 1895

A great hall - a number of guests, whom we are receiving - among them Irma, whom I immediately take aside, as though to answer her letter, and to reproach her for not yet accepting the

---

[9] This is the first dream which I subjected to an exhaustive interpretation.

"solution." I say to her: "If you still have pains, it is really only your own fault." - She answers: "If you only knew what pains I have now in the throat, stomach, and abdomen - I am choked by them." I am startled, and look at her. She looks pale and puffy. I think that after all I must be overlooking some organic affection. I take her to the window and look into her throat. She offers some resistance to this, like a woman who has a set of false teeth. I think, surely, she doesn't need them. - The mouth then opens wide, and I find a large white spot on the right, and elsewhere I see extensive grayish-white scabs adhering to curiously curled formations, which are evidently shaped like the turbinal bones of the nose. - I quickly call Dr. M, who repeats the examination and confirms it.... Dr. M looks quite unlike his usual self; he is very pale, he limps, and his chin is clean-shaven.... Now my friend Otto, too, is standing beside her, and my friend Leopold percusses her covered chest, and says "She has a dullness below, on the left," and also calls attention to an infiltrated portion of skin on the left shoulder (which I can feel, in spite of the dress).... M says: "There's no doubt that it's an infection, but it doesn't matter; dysentery will follow and the poison will be eliminated." ... We know, too, precisely how the infection originated. My friend Otto, not long ago, gave her, when she was feeling unwell, an injection of a preparation of propyl... propyls... propionic acid... trimethylamin (the formula of which I see before me, printed in heavy type)....

One doesn't give such injections so rashly.... Probably, too, the syringe was not clean.

This dream has an advantage over many others. It is at once obvious to what events of the preceding day it is related, and of what subject it treats.

The preliminary statement explains these matters. The news of Irma's health which I had received from Otto, and the clinical history, which I was writing late into the night, had occupied my psychic activities even during sleep. Nevertheless, no one who had read the preliminary report, and had knowledge of the content of the dream, could guess what the dream signified. Nor do I myself know. I am puzzled by the morbid symptoms of which Irma complains in the dream, for they are not the symptoms for which I treated her. I smile at the nonsensical idea of an injection of propionic acid, and at Dr. M's attempt at consolation. Towards the end the dream seems more obscure and quicker in tempo than at the beginning. In order to learn the significance of all these details I resolve to undertake an exhaustive analysis. Analysis The hall - a number of guests, whom we are receiving. We were living that summer at Bellevue, an isolated house on one of the hills adjoining the Kahlenberg. This house was originally built as a place of entertainment, and therefore has unusually lofty, hall-like rooms. The dream was dreamed in Bellevue, a few days before my wife's birthday. During the day my wife had mentioned that she expected several friends, and among them Irma, to come to us as guests for her birthday. My dream, then, anticipates this situation: It is my wife's birthday, and we are receiving a number of people, among them Irma, as guests in the large hall of Bellevue.

I reproach Irma for not having accepted the "solution." I say, "If you still have pains, it is really your own fault." I might even have said this while awake; I may have actually said it. At that time I was of the opinion (recognized later to be incorrect) that my task was limited to informing patients of the hidden meaning of their symptoms. Whether they then accepted or did not accept the solution upon which success depended - for that I was not responsible. I am grateful to this error, which, fortunately, has now been overcome, since it made life easier for me at a time when, with all my unavoidable ignorance, I was expected to effect successful cures. But I note that, in the speech which I make to Irma in the dream, I am above all anxious that I shall not be blamed for the pains which she still suffers. If it is Irma's own fault, it cannot be mine. Should the purpose of the dream be looked for in this quarter?

Irma's complaints - pains in the neck, abdomen, and stomach; she is choked by them. Pains in the stomach belonged to the symptom - complex of my patient, but they were not very prominent; she complained rather of qualms and a feeling of nausea. Pains in the neck and abdomen and constriction of the throat played hardly any part in her case. I wonder why I have decided upon this choice of symptoms in the dream; for the moment I cannot discover the reason.

She looks pale and puffy. My patient had always a rosy complexion. I suspect that here another person is being substituted for her.

I am startled at the idea that I may have overlooked some organic affection. This, as the reader will readily believe, is a constant fear with the specialist who sees neurotics almost exclusively, and who is accustomed to ascribe to hysteria so many manifestations which other physicians treat as organic. On the other hand, I am haunted by a faint doubt - I do not know whence it comes - whether my alarm is altogether honest. If Irma's pains are indeed of organic origin, it is not my duty to cure them. My treatment, of course, removes only hysterical pains. It seems to me, in fact, that I wish to find an error in the diagnosis; for then I could not be reproached with failure to effect a cure.

I take her to the window in order to look into her throat. She resists a little, like a woman who has false teeth. I think to myself, she does not need them. I had never had occasion to inspect Irma's oral cavity. The incident in the dream reminds me of an examination, made some time before, of a governess who at first produced an impression of youthful beauty, but who, upon opening her mouth, took certain measures to conceal her denture. Other memories of medical examinations, and of petty secrets revealed by them, to the embarrassment of both physician and patient, associate themselves with this case. - "She surely does not need them," is perhaps in the first place a compliment to Irma; but I suspect yet another meaning. In a careful analysis one is able to feel whether or not the arriere-pensees which are to be expected have all been exhausted. The way in which Irma stands at the window suddenly reminds me of another experience. Irma has an intimate woman friend of whom I think very highly. One evening, on paying her a visit, I found her at the window in the position reproduced in the dream, and her physician, the same Dr. M, declared that she had a diphtheritic membrane. The person of Dr. M and the membrane return, indeed, in the course of the dream. Now it occurs to me that during the past few months I have had every reason to suppose that this lady too is hysterical. Yes, Irma herself betrayed the fact to me. But what do I know of her condition? Only the one thing, that like Irma in the dream she suffers from hysterical choking. Thus, in the dream I have replaced my patient by her friend. Now I remember that I have often played with the supposition that this lady, too, might ask me to relieve her of her symptoms. But even at the time I thought it improbable, since she is extremely reserved. She resists, as the dream shows. Another explanation might be that she does not need it; in fact, until now she has shown herself strong enough to master her condition without outside help. Now only a few features remain, which I can assign neither to Irma nor to her friend; pale, puffy, false teeth. The false teeth led me to the governess; I now feel inclined to be satisfied with bad teeth. Here another person, to whom these features may allude, occurs to me. She is not my patient, and I do not wish her to be my patient, for I have noticed that she is not at her ease with me, and I do not consider her a docile patient.

She is generally pale, and once, when she had not felt particularly well, she was puffy.[10] I have thus compared my patient Irma with two others, who would likewise resist treatment. What is the meaning of the fact that I have exchanged her for her friend in the dream? Perhaps that I wish to exchange her; either her friend arouses in me stronger sympathies, or I have a higher regard for her intelligence. For I consider Irma foolish

---

[10] The complaint of pains in the abdomen, as yet unexplained, may also be referred to this third person. It is my own wife, of course, who is in question; the abdominal pains remind me of one of the occasions on which her shyness became evident to me. I must admit that I do not treat Irma and my wife very gallantly in this dream, but let it be said, in my defence, that I am measuring both of them against the ideal of the courageous and docile female patient.

because she does not accept my solution. The other woman would be more sensible, and would thus be more likely to yield. The mouth then opens readily; she would tell more than Irma.[11]

What I see in the throat: a white spot and scabby turbinal bones. The white spot recalls diphtheria, and thus Irma's friend, but it also recalls the grave illness of my eldest daughter two years earlier, and all the anxiety of that unhappy time. The scab on the turbinal bones reminds me of my anxiety concerning my own health. At that time I frequently used cocaine in order to suppress distressing swellings in the nose, and I had heard a few days previously that a lady patient who did likewise had contracted an extensive necrosis of the nasal mucous membrane. In 1885 it was I who had recommended the use of cocaine, and I had been gravely reproached in consequence. A dear friend, who had died before the date of this dream, had hastened his end by the misuse of this remedy.

I quickly call Dr. M, who repeats the examination. This would simply correspond to the position which M occupied among us. But the word quickly is striking enough to demand a special examination. It reminds me of a sad medical experience. By continually prescribing a drug (sulphonal), which at that time was still considered harmless, I was once responsible for a condition of acute poisoning in the case of a woman patient, and hastily turned for assistance to my older and more experienced colleague. The fact that I really had this case in mind is confirmed by a subsidiary circumstance. The patient, who succumbed to the toxic effects of the drug, bore the same name as my eldest daughter. I had never thought of this until now; but now it seems to me almost like a retribution of fate - as though the substitution of persons had to be continued in another sense: this Matilda for that Matilda; an eye for an eye, a tooth for a tooth. It is as though I were seeking every opportunity to reproach myself for a lack of medical conscientiousness.

---

[11] I suspect that the interpretation of this portion has not been carried far enough to follow every hidden meaning. If I were to continue the comparison of the three women, I should go far afield. Every dream has at least one point at which it is unfathomable: a central point, as it were, connecting it with the unknown.

Dr. M is pale; his chin is shaven, and he limps. Of this so much is correct, that his unhealthy appearance often arouses the concern of his friends.

The other two characteristics must belong to another person. An elder brother living abroad occurs to me, for he, too, shaves his chin, and if I remember him rightly, the M of the dream bears on the whole a certain resemblance to him. And some days previously the news arrived that he was limping on account of an arthritic affection of the hip. There must be some reason why I fuse the two persons into one in my dream. I remember that, in fact, I was on bad terms with both of them for similar reasons. Both had rejected a certain proposal which I had recently made them.

My friend Otto is now standing next to the patient, and my friend Leopold examines her and calls attention to a dulness low down on the left side.

My friend Leopold also is a physician, and a relative of Otto's. Since the two practice the same specialty, fate has made them competitors, so that they are constantly being compared with one another. Both of them assisted me for years, while I was still directing a public clinic for neurotic children. There, scenes like that reproduced in my dream had often taken place. While I would be discussing the diagnosis of a case with Otto, Leopold would examine the child anew and make an unexpected contribution towards our decision. There was a difference of character between the two men like that between Inspector Brasig and his friend Karl. Otto was remarkably prompt and alert; Leopold was slow and thoughtful, but thorough. If I contrast Otto and the cautious Leopold in the dream I do so, apparently, in order to extol Leopold. The comparison is like that made above between the disobedient patient Irma and her friend, who was believed to be more sensible. I now become aware of one of the tracks along which the association of ideas in the dream proceeds: from the sick child to the children's clinic. Concerning the dulness low on the left side, I have the impression that it corresponds with a certain case of which all the details were similar, a case in which Leopold impressed me by his thoroughness. I thought vaguely, too, of something like a metastatic affection, but it might also be a reference to the patient whom I should have liked to have in Irma's place. For this lady, as far as I can gather, exhibited symptoms which imitated tuberculosis.

An infiltrated portion of skin on the left shoulder. I know at once that this is my own rheumatism of the shoulder, which I always feel if I lie awake long at night. The very phrasing of the dream sounds ambiguous: Something which I can feel, as he does, in spite of the dress. "Feel on my own body" is intended. Further, it occurs to me how unusual the phrase infiltrated portion of skin sounds. We are accustomed to the phrase: "an infiltration of the upper posterior left"; this would refer to the lungs, and thus, once more, to tuberculosis.

In spite of the dress. This, to be sure, is only an interpolation. At the clinic the children were, of course, examined undressed; here we have some contrast to the manner in which adult female patients have to be examined. The story used to be told of an eminent physician that he always examined his patients through their clothes. The rest is obscure to me; I have, frankly, no inclination to follow the matter further.

Dr. M says: "It's an infection, but it doesn't matter; dysentery will follow, and the poison will be eliminated." This, at first, seems to me ridiculous; nevertheless, like everything else, it must be carefully analysed; more closely observed it seems after all to have a sort of meaning.

What I had found in the patient was a local diphtheritis. I remember the discussion about diphtheritis and diphtheria at the time of my daughter's illness. Diphtheria is the general infection which proceeds from local diphtheritis. Leopold demonstrates the existence of such a general infection by the dulness, which also suggests a metastatic focus. I believe, however, that just this kind of metastasis does not occur in the case of diphtheria.

It reminds me rather of pyaemia.

It doesn't matter is a consolation. I believe it fits in as follows: The last part of the dream has yielded a content to the effect that the patient's sufferings are the result of a serious organic affection. I begin to suspect that by this I am only trying to shift the blame from myself. Psychic treatment cannot be held responsible for the continued presence of a diphtheritic affection. Now, indeed, I am distressed by the thought of having invented such a serious illness for Irma, for the sole purpose of exculpating myself. It seems so cruel. Accordingly, I need the assurance that the outcome will be benign, and it seems to me that I made a good choice when I put the words that consoled me into the mouth of Dr. M. But here I am placing myself in a position of superiority to the dream; a fact which needs explanation.

But why is this consolation so nonsensical?

Dysentery. Some sort of far-fetched theoretical notion that the toxins of disease might be eliminated through the intestines. Am I thereby trying to make fun of Dr. M's remarkable store of far-fetched explanations, his habit of conceiving curious pathological relations? Dysentery suggests something else. A few months ago I had in my care a young man who was suffering from remarkable intestinal troubles; a case which had been treated by other colleagues as one of "anaemia with malnutrition." I realized that it was a case of hysteria; I was unwilling to use my psychotherapy on him, and sent him off on a sea-voyage. Now a few days previously I had received a despairing letter from him; he wrote from Egypt, saying that he had had a fresh attack, which the doctor had declared to be dysentery. I suspect that the diagnosis is merely an error on the part of an ignorant colleague, who is allowing himself to be fooled by the hysteria; yet I cannot help reproaching myself for putting the invalid in a position where he might contract some organic affection of the bowels in addition to his hysteria. Furthermore, dysentery sounds not unlike diphtheria, a word which does not occur in the dream.

Yes, it must be the case that with the consoling prognosis,

Dysentery will develop, etc., I am making fun of Dr. M, for I recollect that years ago he once jestingly told a very similar story of a colleague. He had been called in to consult with him in the case of a woman who was very seriously ill, and he felt obliged to confront his colleague, who seemed very hopeful, with the fact that he found albumen in the patient's urine. His colleague, however, did not allow this to worry him, but answered calmly: "That does not matter, my dear sir; the albumen will soon be excreted!" Thus I can no longer doubt that this part of the dream expresses derision for those of my colleagues who are ignorant of hysteria. And, as though in confirmation, the thought enters my mind: "Does Dr. M know that the appearances in Irma's friend, his patient, which gave him reason to fear tuberculosis, are likewise due to hysteria? Has he recognized this hysteria, or has he allowed himself to be fooled?"

But what can be my motive in treating this friend so badly? That is simple enough: Dr. M agrees with my solution as little as does Irma herself. Thus, in this dream I have already revenged myself on two persons: on Irma in the words, If you still have pains, it is your own fault, and on Dr. M in the wording of the nonsensical consolation which has been put into his mouth.

We know precisely how the infection originated. This precise knowledge in the dream is remarkable. Only a moment before this we did not yet know of the infection, since it was first demonstrated by Leopold.

My friend Otto gave her an injection not long ago, when she was feeling unwell. Otto had actually related during his short visit to Irma's family that he had been called in to a neighbouring hotel in order to give an injection to someone who had been suddenly taken ill. Injections remind me once more of the unfortunate friend who poisoned himself with cocaine. I had recommended the remedy for internal use only during the withdrawal of morphia; but he immediately gave himself injections of cocaine.

With a preparation of propyl... propyls... propionic acid. How on earth did this occur to me? On the evening of the day after I had written the clinical history and dreamed about the case, my wife opened a bottle of liqueur labelled "Ananas,"[12] which was a present from our friend Otto.

He had, as a matter of fact, a habit of making presents on every possible occasion; I hope he will some day be cured of this by a wife.[13] This liqueur smelt so strongly of fusel oil that I refused to drink it. My wife suggested: "We will give the bottle to the servants," and I, more prudent, objected, with the philanthropic remark: "They shan't be poisoned either." The smell of fusel oil (amyl...) has now apparently awakened my memory of the whole series: propyl, methyl, etc., which furnished the preparation of propyl mentioned in the dream. Here, indeed, I have effected a substitution: I dreamt of propyl after smelling amyl; but substitutions of this kind are perhaps permissible, especially in organic chemistry. - Trimethylamin. In the dream I see the chemical formula of this substance - which at all events is evidence of a great effort on the part of my memory - and the formula is even printed in heavy type, as though to distinguish it from the context as something of particular importance. And where does trimethylamin, thus forced on my attention, lead me? To a conversation with another friend, who for years has been familiar with all my germinating ideas, and I with his. At that time he had just informed me of certain ideas concerning a sexual chemistry, and had mentioned, among others, that he thought he had found in trimethylamin one of the products of sexual metabolism. This substance thus leads me to sexuality, the factor to which I attribute the greatest significance in respect of the origin of these nervous affections which I am trying to cure. My patient Irma is a young widow; if I am required to excuse my failure to cure her, I shall perhaps do best to refer to this condition, which her admirers would be glad to terminate. But

---

[12] "Ananas," moreover, has a remarkable assonance with the family name of my patient Irma.

[13] In this the dream did not turn out to be prophetic. But in another sense it proved correct, for the "unsolved" stomach pains, for which I did not want to be blamed, were the forerunners of a serious illness, due to gall-stones.

in what a singular fashion such a dream is fitted together! The friend who in my dream becomes my patient in Irma's place is likewise a young widow.

I surmise why it is that the formula of trimethylamin is so insistent in the dream. So many important things are centered about this one word: trimethylamin is an allusion, not merely to the all-important factor of sexuality, but also to a friend whose sympathy I remember with satisfaction whenever I feel isolated in my opinions. And this friend, who plays such a large part in my life: will he not appear yet again in the concatenation of ideas peculiar to this dream? Of course; he has a special knowledge of the results of affections of the nose and the sinuses, and has revealed to science several highly remarkable relations between the turbinal bones and the female sexual organs. (The three curly formations in Irma's throat.) I got him to examine Irma, in order to determine whether her gastric pains were of nasal origin. But he himself suffers from suppurative rhinitis, which gives me concern, and to this perhaps there is an allusion in pyaemia, which hovers before me in the metastasis of the dream.

One doesn't give such injections so rashly. Here the reproach of rashness is hurled directly at my friend Otto. I believe I had some such thought in the afternoon, when he seemed to indicate, by word and look, that he had taken sides against me. It was, perhaps: "How easily he is influenced; how irresponsibly he pronounces judgment." Further, the above sentence points once more to my deceased friend, who so irresponsibly resorted to cocaine injections. As I have said, I had not intended that injections of the drug should be taken. I note that in reproaching Otto I once more touch upon the story of the unfortunate Matilda, which was the pretext for the same reproach against me. Here, obviously, I am collecting examples of my conscientiousness, and also of the reverse.

Probably too the syringe was not clean. Another reproach directed at Otto, but originating elsewhere. On the previous day I happened to meet the son of an old lady of eighty-two, to whom I am obliged to give two injections of morphia daily. At present she is in the country, and I have heard that she is suffering from phlebitis. I immediately thought that this might be a case of infiltration caused by a dirty syringe. It is my pride that in two years I have not given her a single infiltration; I am always careful, of course, to see that the syringe is perfectly clean. For I am conscientious. From the phlebitis I return to my wife, who once suffered from thrombosis during a period of pregnancy, and now three related situations come to the surface in my memory, involving my wife, Irma, and the dead Matilda, whose identity has apparently justified my putting these three persons in one another's places.

I have now completed the interpretation of the dream.[14] In the course of this interpretation I have taken great pains to avoid all those notions which must have been suggested by a comparison of the dream-content with the dream-thoughts hidden behind this content. Meanwhile the meaning of the dream has dawned upon me. I have noted an intention which is realized through the dream, and which must have been my motive in dreaming. The dream fulfills several wishes, which were awakened within me by the events of the previous evening (Otto's news, and the writing of the clinical history). For the result of the dream is that it is not I who am to blame for the pain which Irma is still suffering, but that Otto is to blame for it. Now Otto has annoyed me by his remark about Irma's imperfect cure; the dream avenges me upon him, in that it turns the reproach upon himself. The dream acquits me of responsibility for Irma's condition, as it refers this condition to other causes (which do, indeed, furnish quite a number of explanations). The dream represents a certain state of affairs, such as I might wish to exist; the content of the dream is thus the fulfilment of a wish; its motive is a wish.

This much is apparent at first sight. But many other details of the dream become intelligible when regarded from the standpoint of wishfulfilment. I take my revenge on Otto, not merely for too readily taking sides against me. in that I accuse him of careless

---

[14] Even if I have not, as might be expected, accounted for everything that occurred to me in connection with the work of interpretation.

medical treatment (the injection), but I revenge myself also for the bad liqueur which smells of fusel oil, and I find an expression in the dream which unites both these reproaches: the injection of a preparation of propyl. Still I am not satisfied, but continue to avenge myself by comparing him with his more reliable colleague. Thereby I seem to say: "I like him better than you." But Otto is not the only person who must be made to feel the weight of my anger. I take my revenge on the disobedient patient, by exchanging her for a more sensible and more docile one. Nor do I pass over Dr. M's contradiction; for I express, in an obvious allusion, my opinion of him: namely, that his attitude in this case is that of an ignoramus (Dysentery will develop, etc.). Indeed, it seems as though I were appealing from him to someone better informed (my friend, who told me about trimethylamin), just as I have turned from Irma to her friend, and from Otto to Leopold. It is as though I were to say: Rid me of these three persons, replace them by three others of my own choice, and I shall be rid of the reproaches which I am not willing to admit that I deserve! In my dream the unreasonableness of these reproaches is demonstrated for me in the most elaborate manner. Irma's pains are not attributable to me, since she herself is to blame for them, in that she refuses to accept my solution. They do not concern me, for being as they are of an organic nature, they cannot possibly be cured by psychic treatment. Irma's sufferings are satisfactorily explained by her widowhood (trimethylamin!); a state which I cannot alter. Irma's illness has been caused by an incautious injection administered by Otto, an injection of an unsuitable drug, such as I should never have administered. Irma's complaint is the result of an injection made with an unclean syringe, like the phlebitis of my old lady patient, whereas my injections have never caused any ill effects. I am aware that these explanations of Irma's illness, which unite in acquitting me, do not agree with one another; that they even exclude one another. The whole plea - for this dream is nothing else - recalls vividly the defence offered by a man who was accused by his neighbour of having returned a kettle in a damaged condition. In the first place, he had returned the kettle undamaged; in the second place it already had holes in it when he borrowed it; and in the third place, he had never borrowed it at all. A complicated defence, but so much the better; if only one of these three lines of defence is recognized as valid, the man must be acquitted.

Still other themes play a part in the dream, and their relation to my non-responsibility for Irma's illness is not so apparent: my daughter's illness, and that of a patient with the same name; the harmfulness of cocaine; the affection of my patient, who was traveling in Egypt; concern about the health of my wife; my brother, and Dr. M; my own physical troubles, and anxiety concerning my absent friend, who is suffering from suppurative rhinitis. But if I keep all these things in view, they combine into a single train of thought, which might be labelled: Concern for the health of myself and others; professional conscientiousness. I recall a vaguely disagreeable feeling when Otto gave me the news of Irma's condition. Lastly, I am inclined, after the event, to find an expression of this fleeting sensation in the train of thoughts which forms part of the dream. It is as though Otto had said to me: "You do not take your medical duties seriously enough; you are not conscientious; you do not perform what you promise."

Thereupon this train of thought placed itself at my service, in order that I might give proof of my extreme conscientiousness, of my intimate concern about the health of my relatives, friends and patients. Curiously enough, there are also some painful memories in this material, which confirm the blame attached to Otto rather than my own exculpation. The material is apparently impartial, but the connection between this broader material, on which the dream is based, and the more limited theme from which emerges the wish to be innocent of Irma's illness, is, nevertheless, unmistakable.

I do not wish to assert that I have entirely revealed the meaning of the dream, or that my interpretation is flawless. I could still spend much time upon it; I could draw further explanations from it, and discuss further problems which it seems to propound. I can even perceive the points from which further mental associations might be traced; but such considerations as are always involved in every dream of one's own prevent me from interpreting it farther. Those who are overready to condemn such reserve should make the experiment of trying to be more straightforward. For the present I am content with the one fresh discovery which has just been made: If the method of dream interpretation here indicated is followed, it will be found that dreams do really possess a meaning, and are by no means the expression of a disintegrated cerebral activity, as the writers on the subject would have us believe. When the work of interpretation has been completed the dream can be recognized as a wish fulfilment.

Chapter 3

The Dream As Wish-fulfilment

When, after passing through a narrow defile, one suddenly reaches a height beyond which the ways part and a rich prospect lies outspread in different directions, it is well to stop for a moment and consider whither one shall turn next. We are in somewhat the same position after we have mastered this first interpretation of a dream. We find ourselves standing in the light of a sudden discovery. The dream is not comparable to the irregular sounds of a musical instrument, which, instead of being played by the hand of a musician, is struck by some external force; the dream is not meaningless, not absurd, does not presuppose that one part of our store of ideas is dormant while another part begins to awake. It is a perfectly valid psychic phenomenon, actually a wish-fulfilment; it may be enrolled in the continuity of the intelligible psychic activities of the waking state; it is built up by a highly complicated intellectual activity. But at the very moment when we are about to rejoice in this discovery a host of problems besets us. If the dream, as this theory defines it, represents a fulfilled wish, what is the cause of the striking and unfamiliar manner in which this fulfilment is expressed? What transformation has occurred in our dream-thoughts before the manifest dream, as we remember it on waking, shapes itself out of them? How has this transformation taken place? Whence comes the material that is worked up into the dream? What causes many of the peculiarities which are to be observed in our dream-thoughts; for example, how is it that they are able to contradict one another? Is the dream capable of teaching us something new concerning our internal psychic processes and can its content correct opinions which we have held during the day? I suggest that for the present all these problems be laid aside, and that a single path be pursued. We have found that the dream represents a wish as fulfilled. Our next purpose should be to ascertain whether this is a general characteristic of dreams, or whether it is only the accidental content of the particular dream (the dream about Irma's injection) with which we have begun our analysis; for even if we conclude that every dream has a meaning and psychic value, we must nevertheless allow for the possibility that this meaning may not be the same in every dream. The first dream which we have considered was the fulfilment of a wish; another may turn out to be the realization of an apprehension; a third may have a reflection as its content; a fourth may simply reproduce a reminiscence. Are there, then dreams other than wishdreams; or are there none but wish-dreams? -

It is easy to show that the wish-fulfilment in dreams is often undisguised and easy to recognize, so that one may wonder why the language of dreams has not long since been understood. There is, for example, a dream which I can evoke as often as I please, experimentally, as it were. If, in the evening, I eat anchovies, olives, or other strongly salted foods, I am thirsty at night, and therefore I wake. The waking, however, is preceded by a dream, which has always the same content, namely, that I am drinking. I am drinking long draughts of water; it tastes as delicious as only a cool drink can taste when one's throat is parched; and then I wake, and find that I have an actual desire to drink. The cause of this dream is thirst, which I perceive when I wake. From this sensation arises the wish to drink, and the dream shows me this wish as fulfilled. It thereby serves a function, the nature of which I soon surmise. I sleep well, and am not accustomed to being waked by a bodily need. If I succeed in appeasing my thirst by means of the dream that I am drinking, I need not wake up in order to satisfy that thirst. It is thus a dream of convenience. The dream takes the place of action, as elsewhere in life. Unfortunately, the need of water to quench the thirst cannot be satisfied by a dream, as can my thirst for revenge upon Otto and Dr. M, but the intention is the same. Not long ago I had the same dream in a somewhat modified form. On this occasion I felt thirsty before going to bed, and emptied the glass of water which stood on the little chest beside my bed. Some hours later, during the night, my thirst returned, with the consequent discomfort. In order to obtain water, I should have had to get up and fetch the glass which stood on my wife's bed-table. I thus quite appropriately dreamt that my wife was giving me a drink from a vase; this vase was an Etruscan cinerary urn, which I had brought home from Italy and had since given away. But the water in it tasted so salt (apparently on account of the ashes) that I was forced to wake. It may be observed how conveniently the dream is capable of arranging matters. Since the fulfilment of a wish is its only purpose, it may be perfectly egoistic. Love of comfort is really not compatible with consideration for others. The introduction of the cinerary urn is probably once again the fulfilment of a wish; I regret that I no longer possess this vase; it, like the glass of water at my wife's side, is inaccessible to me. The cinerary urn is appropriate also in connection with the sensation of an increasingly salty taste, which I know will compel me to wake.[1] - Such convenience-dreams came very frequently to me in my youth. Accustomed as I had always been to working until late at night, early waking was always a matter of difficulty. I used then to dream that I was out of bed and standing at the wash-stand. After a while I could no longer shut out the knowledge that I was not yet up; but in the meantime I had continued to sleep. The same sort of lethargy-dream was

---

[1] The facts relating to dreams of thirst were known also to Weygandt, who speaks of them as follows: "It is just this sensation of thirst which is registered most accurately of all; it always causes a representation of quenching the thirst. The manner in which the dream represents the act of quenching the thirst is manifold, and is specified in accordance with some recent recollection. A universal phenomenon noticeable here is the fact that the representation of quenching the thirst is immediately followed by disappointment in the inefficacy of the imagined refreshment." But he overlooks the universal character of the reaction of the dream to the stimulus. If other persons who are troubled by thirst at night awake without dreaming beforehand, this does not constitute an objection to my experiment, but characterizes them as persons who sleep less soundly. Cf. Isaiah, 29. 8.

dreamed by a young colleague of mine, who appears to share my propensity for sleep. With him it assumed a particularly amusing form. The landlady with whom he was lodging in the neighbourhood of the hospital had strict orders to wake him every morning at a given hour, but she found it by no means easy to carry out his orders. One morning sleep was especially sweet to him. The woman called into his room: "Herr Pepi, get up; you've got to go to the hospital." Whereupon the sleeper dreamt of a room in the hospital, of a bed in which he was lying, and of a chart pinned over his head, which read as follows: "Pepi M, medical student, 22 years of age." He told himself in the dream: "If I am already at the hospital, I don't have to go there," turned over, and slept on. He had thus frankly admitted to himself his motive for dreaming.

Here is yet another dream of which the stimulus was active during sleep: One of my women patients, who had been obliged to undergo an unsuccessful operation on the jaw, was instructed by her physicians to wear by day and night a cooling apparatus on the affected cheek; but she was in the habit of throwing it off as soon as she had fallen asleep. One day I was asked to reprove her for doing so; she had again thrown the apparatus on the floor. The patient defended herself as follows: "This time I really couldn't help it; it was the result of a dream which I had during the night. In the dream I was in a box at the opera, and was taking a lively interest in the performance. But Herr Karl Meyer was lying in the sanatorium and complaining pitifully on account of pains in his jaw. I said to myself, 'Since I haven't the pains, I don't need the apparatus either'; that's why I threw it away." The dream of this poor sufferer reminds me of an expression which comes to our lips when we are in a disagreeable situation: "Well, I can imagine more amusing things!" The dream presents these "more amusing things!" Herr Karl Meyer, to whom the dreamer attributed her pains, was the most casual acquaintance of whom she could think. It is quite as simple a matter to discover the wish-fulfilment in several other dreams which I have collected from healthy persons. A friend who was acquainted with my theory of dreams, and had explained it to his wife, said to me one day: "My wife asked me to tell you that she dreamt yesterday that she was having her menses. You will know what that means." Of course I know: if the young wife dreams that she is having her menses, the menses have stopped. I can well imagine that she would have liked to enjoy her freedom a little longer, before the discomforts of maternity began. It was a clever way of giving notice of her first pregnancy. Another friend writes that his wife had dreamt not long ago that she noticed milk-stains on the front of her blouse. This also is an indication of pregnancy, but not of the first one; the young mother hoped she would have more nourishment for the second child than she had for the first.

A young woman who for weeks had been cut off from all society because she was nursing a child who was suffering from an infectious disease dreamt, after the child had recovered, of a company of people in which Alphonse Daudet, Paul Bourget, Marcel Prevost and others were present; they were all very pleasant to her and amused her enormously. In her dream these different authors had the features which their portraits give them. M. Prevost, with whose portrait she is not familiar, looked like the man who had disinfected the sickroom the day before, the first outsider to enter it for a long time. Obviously the dream is to be translated thus: "It is about time now for something more entertaining than this eternal nursing."

Perhaps this collection will suffice to prove that frequently, and under the most complex conditions, dreams may be noted which can be understood only as wish-fulfilments, and which present their content without concealment. In most cases these are short and simple dreams, and they stand in pleasant contrast to the confused and overloaded dream-compositions which have almost exclusively attracted the attention of the writers on the subject. But it will repay us if we give some time to the examination of these simple dreams. The simplest dreams of all are, I suppose, to be expected in the case of children whose psychic activities are certainly less complicated than those of adults. Child psychology, in my opinion, is destined to render the same services to the psychology of adults as a study of the structure or development of the lower animals renders to the investigation of the structure of the higher orders of animals. Hitherto but few deliberate efforts have been made to make use of the psychology of the child for such a purpose.

The dreams of little children are often simple fulfilments of wishes, and for this reason are, as compared with the dreams of adults, by no means interesting. They present no problem to be solved, but they are invaluable as affording proof that the dream, in its inmost essence, is the fulfilment of a wish. I have been able to collect several examples of such dreams from the material furnished by my own children.

For two dreams, one that of a daughter of mine, at that time eight and a half years of age, and the other that of a boy of five and a quarter, I am indebted to an excursion to Hallstatt, in the summer of 1806. I must first explain that we were living that summer on a hill near Aussee, from which, when the weather was fine, we enjoyed a splendid view of the Dachstein. With a telescope we could easily distinguish the Simony hut.

The children often tried to see it through the telescope - I do not know with what success. Before the excursion I had told the children that Hallstatt lay at the foot of the Dachstein. They looked forward to the outing with the greatest delight. From Hallstatt we entered the valley of Eschern, which enchanted the children with its constantly changing scenery. One of them, however, the boy of five, gradually became discontented. As often as a mountain came into view, he would ask: "Is that the Dachstein?" whereupon I had to reply: "No, only a foot-hill."

After this question had been repeated several times he fell quite silent, and did not wish to accompany us up the steps leading to the waterfall. I thought he was tired. But the next morning he came to me, perfectly happy, and said: "Last night I dreamt that we went to the Simony hut." I understood him now; he had expected, when I spoke of the Dachstein, that on our excursion to Hallstatt he would climb the mountain, and would see at close quarters the hut which had been so often mentioned when the telescope was used. When he learned that he was expected to content himself with foot-hills and a waterfall he was disappointed, and became discontented. But the dream compensated him for all this. I tried to learn some details of the dream; they were scanty. "You go up steps for six hours," as he had been told.

On this excursion the girl of eight and a half had likewise cherished wishes which had to be satisfied by a dream. We had taken with us to Hallstatt our neighbour's twelve-year-old boy; quite a polished little gentleman, who, it seemed to me, had already won the little woman's sympathies. Next morning she related the following dream: "Just think, I dreamt that Emil was one of the family, that he said 'papa' and 'mamma' to you, and slept at our house, in the big room, like one of the boys. Then mamma came into the room and threw a handful of big bars of chocolate, wrapped in blue and green paper, under our beds." The girl's brothers, who evidently had not inherited an understanding of dreaminterpretation, declared, just as the writers we have quoted would have done: "That dream is nonsense." The girl defended at least one part of the dream, and from the standpoint of the theory of the neuroses it is interesting to learn which part it was that she defended: "That Emil was one of the family was nonsense, but that about the bars of chocolate wasn't." It was just this latter part that was obscure to me, until my wife furnished the explanation. On the way home from the railway-station the children had stopped in front of a slot-machine, and had wanted exactly such bars of chocolate, wrapped in paper with a metallic lustre, such as the machine, in their experience, provided. But the mother thought, and rightly so, that the day had brought them enough wish-fulfilments, and therefore left this wish to be satisfied in the dream. This little scene had escaped me.

That portion of the dream which had been condemned by my daughter I understood without any difficulty. I myself had heard the well-behaved little guest enjoining the children, as they were walking ahead of us, to wait until "papa" or "mamma" had come up. For the little girl the dream turned this temporary relationship into a permanent adoption. Her affection could not as yet conceive of any other way of enjoying her friend's company permanently than the adoption pictured in her dream, which was suggested by her brothers. Why the bars of chocolate were thrown under the bed could not, of course, be explained without questioning the child.

From a friend I have learned of a dream very much like that of my little boy. It was dreamed by a little girl of eight. Her father, accompanied by several children, had started on a walk to Dornbach, with the intention of visiting the Rohrer hut, but had turned back, as it was growing late, promising the children to take them some other time. On the way back they passed a signpost which pointed to the Hameau. The children now asked him to take them to the Hameau, but once more, and for the same reason, they had to be content with the promise that they should go there some other day. Next morning the little girl went to her father and told him, with a satisfied air: "Papa, I dreamed last night that you were with us at the Rohrer hut, and on the Hameau." Thus, in the dream her impatience had anticipated the fulfilment of the promise made by her father.

Another dream, with which the picturesque beauty of the Aussee inspired my daughter, at that time three and a quarter years of age, is equally straightforward. The little girl had crossed the lake for the first time, and the trip had passed too quickly for her. She did not want to leave the boat at the landing, and cried bitterly. The next morning she told us: "Last night I was sailing on the lake." Let us hope that the duration of this dreamvoyage was more satisfactory to her.

My eldest boy, at that time eight years of age, was already dreaming of the realization of his fancies. He had ridden in a chariot with Achilles, with Diomedes as charioteer. On the previous day he had shown a lively interest in a book on the myths of Greece which had been given to his elder sister.

If it can be admitted that the talking of children in their sleep belongs to the sphere of dreams, I can relate the following as one of the earliest dreams in my collection: My youngest daughter, at that time nineteen months old, vomited one morning, and was therefore kept without food all day. During the night she was heard to call excitedly in her sleep: "Anna F(r)eud, St'awbewy, wild st'awbewy, om'lette, pap!" She used her name in this way in order to express the act of appropriation; the menu presumably included everything that would seem to her a desirable meal; the fact that two varieties of strawberry appeared in it was demonstration against the sanitary regulations of the household, and was based on the circumstance, which she had by no means overlooked, that the nurse had ascribed her indisposition to an over-plentiful consumption of strawberries; so in her dream she avenged herself for this opinion which met with her disapproval.[2]

When we call childhood happy because it does not yet know sexual desire, we must not forget what a fruitful source of disappointment and renunciation, and therefore of dream-stimulation, the other great vital impulse may be for the child.[3] Here is a second example. My nephew, twenty-two months of age, had been instructed to congratulate me on my birthday, and to give me a present of a small basket of cherries, which at that time of the year were scarce, being hardly in season. He seemed to find the task a difficult one, for he repeated again and again: "Cherries in it," and could not be induced to let the little basket

---

[2] The dream afterwards accomplished the same purpose in the case of the child's grandmother, who is older than the child by about seventy years. After she had been forced to go hungry for a day on account of the restlessness of her floating kidney, she dreamed, being apparently translated into the happy years of her girlhood, that she had been asked out, invited to lunch and dinner, and had at each meal been served with the most delicious titbits.

[3] A more searching investigation into the psychic life of the child teaches us, of course, that sexual motives, in infantile forms, play a very considerable part, which has been too long overlooked, in the psychic activity of the child. This permits us to doubt to some extent the happiness of the child, as imagined later by adults. Cf. Three Contributions to the Theory of Sex.

go out of his hands. But he knew how to indemnify himself. He had, until then, been in the habit of telling his mother every morning that he had dreamt of the "white soldier," an officer of the guard in a white cloak, whom he had once admired in the street. On the day after the sacrifice on my birthday he woke up joyfully with the announcement, which could have referred only to a dream: "He [r] man eaten all the cherries!"[4]

What animals dream of I do not know. A proverb, for which I am indebted to one of my pupils, professes to tell us, for it asks the question: "What does the goose dream of?" and answers: "Of maize."[5] The whole theory that the dream is the fulfilment of a wish is contained in these two sentences.[6]

We now perceive that we should have reached our theory of the hidden meaning of dreams by the shortest route had we merely consulted the vernacular. Proverbial wisdom, it is true, often speaks contemptuously enough of dreams - it apparently seeks to justify the scientists when it says that "dreams are bubbles"; but in colloquial language the dream is predominantly the gracious fulfiller of wishes. "I should never have imagined that in my wildest dreams," we exclaim in delight if we find that the reality surpasses our expectations.

---

[4] It should be mentioned that young children often have more complex and obscure dreams, while, on the other hand, adults, in certain circumstances, often have dreams of a simple and infantile character. How rich in unsuspected content the dreams of children no more than four or five years of age may be is shown by the examples in my "Analysis of a Phobia in a five-year old Boy," Collected Papers, III, and Jung's "Experiences Concerning the Psychic Life of the Child," translated by Brill, American Journal of Psychology. April, 1910. For analytically interpreted dreams of children, see also von Hug-Hellmuth, Putnam, Raalte, Spielrein, and Tausk; others by Banchieri, Busemann, Doglia, and especially Wigam, who emphasizes the wish-fulfilling tendency of such dreams. On the other hand, it seems that dreams of an infantile type reappear with especial frequency in adults who are transferred into the midst of unfamiliar conditions. Thus Otto Nordenskjold, in his book, Antarctic (1904, vol. i, p. 336), writes as follows of the crew who spent the winter with him: "Very characteristic of the trend of our inmost thoughts were our dreams, which were never more vivid and more numerous. Even those of our comrades with whom dreaming was formerly exceptional had long stories to tell in the morning, when we exchanged our experiences in the world of phantasy. They all had reference to that outside world which was now so far removed from us, but they often fitted into our immediate circumstances. An especially characteristic dream was that in which one of our comrades believed himself back at school, where the task was assigned to him of skinning miniature seals, which were manufactured especially for purposes of instruction. Eating and drinking constituted

the pivot around which most of our dreams revolved. One of us, who was especially fond of going to big dinner-parties, was delighted if he could report in the morning 'that he had had a three-course dinner.' Another dreamed of tobacco, whole mountains of tobacco; yet another dreamed of a ship approaching on the open sea under full sail. Still another dream deserves to be mentioned: The postman brought the post and gave a long explanation of why it was so long delayed; he had delivered it at the wrong address, and only with great trouble was he able to get it back. To be sure, we were often occupied in our sleep with still more impossible things, but the lack of phantasy in almost all the dreams which I myself dreamed, or heard others relate, was quite striking. It would certainly have been of great psychological interest if all these dreams could have been recorded. But one can readily understand how we longed for sleep. That alone could afford us everything that we all most ardently desired." I will continue by a quotation from Du Prel (p. 231): "Mungo Park, nearly dying of thirst on one of his African expeditions, dreamed constantly of the well-watered valleys and meadows of his home. Similarly Trenck, tortured by hunger in the fortress of Magdeburg, saw himself surrounded by copious meals. And George Back, a member of Franklin's first expedition, when he was on the point of death by starvation, dreamed continually and invariably of plenteous meals."

[5] A Hungarian proverb cited by Ferenczi states more explicitly that "the pig dreams of acorns, the goose of maize." A Jewish proverb asks: "Of what does the hen dream?" - "Of millet" (Sammlung jud. Sprichw. u. Redensarten., edit. by Bernstein, 2nd ed., p. 116).

[6] I am far from wishing to assert that no previous writer has ever thought of tracing a dream to a wish. (Cf. the first passages of the next chapter.) Those interested in the subject will find that even in antiquity the physician Herophilos, who lived under the First Ptolemy, distinguished between three kinds of dreams: dreams sent by the gods; natural dreams - those which come about whenever the soul creates for itself an image of that which is beneficial to it, and will come to pass; and mixed dreams - those which originate spontaneously from the juxtaposition of images, when we see that which we desire. From the examples collected by Scherner, J. Starcke cites a dream which was described by the author himself as a wish-fulfilment (p. 239). Scherner says: "The phantasy immediately fulfills the dreamer's wish, simply because this existed vividly in the mind." This dream belongs to the "emotional dreams." Akin to it are dreams due to "masculine and feminine erotic longing," and to "irritable moods." As will readily be seen, Scherner does not ascribe to the wish any further significance for the dream than to any other psychic condition of the waking state; least of all does he insist on the connection between the wish and the essential nature of the dream.

Chapter 4
Distortion In Dreams

If I now declare that wish-fulfilment is the meaning of every dream, so that there cannot be any dreams other than wish-dreams, I know beforehand that I shall meet with the most emphatic contradiction. My critics will object: "The fact that there are dreams which are to be understood as fulfilments of wishes is not new, but has long since been recognized by such writers as Radestock, Volkelt, Purkinje, Griesinger and others.[1] That there can be no other dreams than those of wish-fulfilments is yet one more unjustified generalization, which, fortunately, can be easily refuted. Dreams which present the most painful content, and not the least trace of wish-fulfilment, occur frequently enough. The pessimistic philosopher, Eduard von Hartmann, is perhaps most completely opposed to the theory of wish-fulfilment. In his Philosophy of the Unconscious, Part II (Stereotyped German edition), he says: 'As regards the dream, with it all the troubles of waking life pass over into the sleeping state; all save the one thing which may in some degree reconcile the cultured person with life - scientific and artistic enjoyment....' But even less pessimistic observers have emphasized the fact that in our dreams pain and disgust are more frequent than pleasure. Two ladies, Sarah Weed and Florence Hallam, have even worked out, on the basis of their dreams, a numerical value for the preponderance of distress and discomfort in dreams. They find that 58 per cent of dreams are disagreeable, and only 28.6

---

[1] Already Plotinus, the neo-Platonist, said: "When desire bestirs itself, then comes phantasy, and presents to us, as it were, the object of desire".

positively pleasant. Besides those dreams that convey into our sleep the many painful emotions of life, there are also anxiety-dreams, in which this most terrible of all the painful emotions torments us until we wake. Now it is precisely by these anxiety dreams that children are so often haunted (cf. Debacker on Pavor nocturnus); and yet it was in children that you found the wish-fulfilment dream in its most obvious form."

The anxiety-dream does really seem to preclude a generalization of the thesis deduced from the examples given in the last chapter, that dreams are wish-fulfilments, and even to condemn it as an absurdity.

Nevertheless, it is not difficult to parry these apparently invincible objections. It is merely necessary to observe that our doctrine is not based upon the estimates of the obvious dream-content, but relates to the thought-content, which, in the course of interpretation, is found to lie behind the dream. Let us compare and contrast the manifest and the latent dream-content. It is true that there are dreams the manifest content of which is of the most painful nature. But has anyone ever tried to interpret these dreams - to discover their latent thought-content? If not, the two objections to our doctrine are no longer valid; for there is always the possibility that even our painful and terrifying dreams may, upon interpretation, prove to be wish fulfilments.[2]

In scientific research it is often advantageous, if the solution of one problem presents difficulties, to add to it a second problem;

---

[2] It is quite incredible with what obstinacy readers and critics have excluded this consideration and disregarded the fundamental differentiation between the manifest and the latent dream-content. Nothing in the literature of the subject approaches so closely to my own conception of dreams as a passage in J. Sully's essay, Dreams as a Revelation (and it is not because I do not think it valuable that I allude to it here for the first time): "It would seem then, after all, that dreams are not the utter nonsense they have been said to be by such authorities as Chaucer, Shakespeare, and Milton. The chaotic aggregations of our night-fancy have a significance, and communicate new knowledge. Like some letter in cipher, the dreaminscription when scrutinized closely loses its first look of balderdash and takes on the aspect of a serious, intelligible message. Or, to vary the figure slightly, we may say that, like some palimpsest, the dream discloses beneath its worthless surface-characters traces of an old and precious communication.

just as it is easier to crack two nuts together instead of separately. Thus, we are confronted not only with the problem: How can painful and terrifying dreams be the fulfilments of wishes? but we may add to this a second problem which arises from the foregoing discussion of the general problem of the dream: Why do not the dreams that show an indifferent content, and yet turn out to be wish-fulfilments, reveal their meaning without disguise? Take the exhaustively treated dream of Irma's injection: it is by no means of a painful character, and it may be recognized, upon interpretation, as a striking wish-fulfilment. But why is an interpretation necessary at all? Why does not the dream say directly what it means? As a matter of fact, the dream of Irma's injection does not at first produce the impression that it represents a wish of the dreamer's as fulfilled. The reader will not have received this impression, and even I myself was not aware of the fact until I had undertaken the analysis. If we call this peculiarity of dreams - namely, that they need elucidation - the phenomenon of distortion in dreams, a second question then arises: What is the origin of this distortion in dreams? If one's first thoughts on this subject were consulted, several possible solutions might suggest themselves: for example, that during sleep one is incapable of finding an adequate expression for one's dream-thoughts. The analysis of certain dreams, however, compels us to offer another explanation. I shall demonstrate this by means of a second dream of my own, which again involves numerous indiscretions, but which compensates for this personal sacrifice by affording a thorough elucidation of the problem.

Preliminary Statement

In the spring of 1897 I learnt that two professors of our university had proposed me for the title of Professor Extraordinarius (assistant professor).

The news came as a surprise to me, and pleased me considerably as an expression of appreciation on the part of two eminent men which could not be explained by personal interest. But I told myself immediately that I must not expect anything to come of their proposal. For some years past the Ministry had disregarded such proposals, and several colleagues of mine, who were my seniors and at least my equals in desert, had been waiting in vain all this time for the appointment. I had no reason to suppose that I should fare any better. I resolved, therefore, to resign myself to disappointment. I am not, so far as I know, ambitious, and I was following my profession with gratifying success even without the recommendation of a professorial title. Whether I considered the grapes to be sweet or sour did not matter, since they undoubtedly hung too high for me.

One evening a friend of mine called to see me; one of those colleagues whose fate I had regarded as a warning. As he had long been a candidate for promotion to the professorate (which in our society makes the doctor a demigod to his patients), and as he was less resigned than I, he was accustomed from time to time to remind the authorities of his claims in the hope of advancing his interests. It was after one of these visits that he called on me. He said that this time he had driven the exalted gentleman into a corner, and had asked him frankly whether considerations of religious denomination were not really responsible for the postponement of his appointment. The answer was: His Excellency had to admit that in the present state of public opinion he was not in a position, etc. "Now at least I know where I stand," my friend concluded his narrative, which told me nothing new, but which was calculated to confirm me in my resignation. For the same denominational considerations would apply to my own case.

On the morning after my friend's visit I had the following dream, which was notable also on account of its form. It consisted of two thoughts and two images, so that a thought and an image emerged alternately. But here I shall record only the first half of the dream, since the second half has no relation to the purpose for which I cite the dream.

I. My friend R is my uncle - I have a great affection for him.

II. I see before me his face, somewhat altered. It seems to be elongated; a yellow beard, which surrounds it, is seen with peculiar distinctness.

Then follow the other two portions of the dream, again a thought and an image, which I omit.

The interpretation of this dream was arrived at in the following manner: When I recollected the dream in the course of the morning, I laughed outright and said, "The dream is nonsense." But I could not get it out of my mind, and I was pursued by it all day, until at last, in the evening, I reproached myself in these words: "If in the course of a dream-interpretation one of your patients could find nothing better to say than 'That is nonsense,' you would reprove him, and you would suspect that behind the dream there was hidden some disagreeable affair, the exposure of which he wanted to spare himself. Apply the same thing to your own case; your opinion that the dream is nonsense probably signifies merely an inner resistance to its interpretation. Don't let yourself be put off." I then proceeded with the interpretation.

R is my uncle. What can that mean? I had only one uncle, my uncle Joseph.[3] His story, to be sure, was a sad one. Once, more than thirty years ago, hoping to make money, he allowed himself to be involved in transactions of a kind which the law punishes severely, and paid the penalty.

My father, whose hair turned grey with grief within a few days, used always to say that uncle Joseph had never been a bad man, but, after all, he was a simpleton. If, then, my friend R is my uncle Joseph, that is equivalent to saying: "R is a simpleton." Hardly credible, and very disagreeable! But there is the face that I saw in the dream, with its elongated features and its yellow beard. My uncle actually had such a face - long, and framed in a handsome yellow beard. My friend R was extremely swarthy,

---

[3] It is astonishing to see how my memory here restricts itself - in the aking state! - for the purposes of analysis. I have known five of my uncles and I loved and honoured one of them. But at the moment when I overcame my resistance to the interpretation of the dream, I said to myself: "I have only one uncle, the one who is intended in the dream."

but when black-haired people begin to grow grey they pay for the glory of their youth. Their black beards undergo an unpleasant change of colour, hair by hair; first they turn a reddish brown, then a yellowish brown, and then definitely grey. My friend R's beard is now in this stage; so, for that matter, is my own, a fact which I note with regret. The face that I see in my dream is at once that of my friend R and that of my uncle. It is like one of those composite photographs of Galton's; in order to emphasize family resemblances Galton had several faces photographed on the same plate. No doubt is now possible; it is really my opinion that my friend R is a simpleton - like my uncle Joseph.

I have still no idea for what purpose I have worked out this relationship. It is certainly one to which I must unreservedly object. Yet it is not very profound, for my uncle was a criminal, and my friend R is not, except in so far as he was once fined for knocking down an apprentice with his bicycle. Can I be thinking of this offence? That would make the comparison ridiculous. Here I recollect another conversation, which I had some days ago with another colleague, N; as a matter of fact, on the same subject. I met N in the street; he, too, has been nominated for a professorship, and having heard that I had been similarly honoured he congratulated me. I refused his congratulations, saying: "You are the last man to jest about the matter, for you know from your own experience what the nomination is worth." Thereupon he said, though probably not in earnest; "You can't be sure of that. There is a special objection in my case. Don't you know that a woman once brought a criminal accusation against me? I need hardly assure you that the matter was put right. It was a mean attempt at blackmail, and it was all I could do to save the plaintiff from punishment. But it may be that the affair is remembered against me at the Ministry. You, on the other hand, are above reproach." Here, then, I have the criminal, and at the same time the interpretation and tendency of my dream. My uncle Joseph represents both of my colleagues who have not been appointed to the professorship - the one as a simpleton, the other as a criminal. Now, too, I know for what purpose I need this representation. If denominational considerations are a determining factor in the postponement of my two friends' appointment, then my own appointment is likewise in jeopardy. But if I can refer the rejection of my two friends to other causes, which do not apply to my own case, my hopes are unaffected. This is the procedure followed by my dream: it makes the one friend R, a simpleton, and the other, N, a criminal. But since I am neither one nor the other, there is nothing in common between us. I have a right to enjoy my appointment to the title of professor, and have avoided the distressing application to my own case of the information which the official gave to my friend R.

I must pursue the interpretation of this dream still farther; for I have a feeling that it is not yet satisfactorily elucidated. I still feel disquieted by the ease with which I have degraded two respected colleagues in order to clear my own way to the professorship. My dissatisfaction with this procedure has, of course, been mitigated since I have learned to estimate the testimony of dreams at its true value. I should contradict anyone who suggested that I really considered R a simpleton, or that I did not believe N's account of the blackmailing incident. And of course I do not believe that Irma has been made seriously ill by an injection of a preparation of propyl administered by Otto. Here, as before, what the dream expresses is only my wish that things might be so. The statement in which my wish is realized sounds less absurd in the second dream than in the first; it is here made with a skilful use of actual points of support in establishing something like a plausible slander, one of which one could say that "there is something in it." For at that time my friend R had to contend with the adverse vote of a university professor of his own department, and my friend N had himself, all unsuspectingly, provided me with material for the calumny. Nevertheless, I repeat, it still seems to me that the dream requires further elucidation.

I remember now that the dream contained yet another portion which has hitherto been ignored by the interpretation. After it occurred to me that my friend R was my uncle, I felt in the dream a great affection for him. To whom is this feeling directed? For my uncle Joseph, of course, I have never had any feelings of affection. R has for many years been a dearly loved friend, but if I were to go to him and express my affection for him in terms approaching the degree of affection which I felt in the dream, he would undoubtedly be surprised. My affection, if it was for him, seems false and exaggerated, as does my judgment of his intellectual qualities, which I expressed by merging his personality in that of my uncle; but exaggerated in the opposite direction. Now, however, a new state of affairs dawns upon me. The affection in the dream does not belong to the latent content, to the thoughts behind the dream; it stands in opposition to this content; it is calculated to conceal the knowledge conveyed by the interpretation. Probably this is precisely its function. I remember with what reluctance I undertook the interpretation, how long I tried to postpone it, and how I declared the dream to be sheer nonsense. I know from my psycho-analytic practice how such a condemnation is to be interpreted. It has no informative value, but merely expresses an affect. If my little daughter does not like an apple which is offered her, she asserts that the apple is bitter, without even tasting it. If my patients behave thus, I know that we are dealing with an idea which they are trying to repress. The same thing applies to my dream. I do not want to interpret it because there is something in the interpretation to which I object. After the interpretation of the dream is completed, I discover what it was to which I objected; it was the assertion that R is a simpleton. I can refer the affection which I feel for R not to the latent dream-thoughts, but rather to this unwillingness of mine. If my dream, as compared with its latent content, is disguised at this point, and actually misrepresents things by producing their opposites, then the manifest affection in the dream serves the purpose of the misrepresentation: in other words, the distortion is here shown to be intentional - it is a means of disguise. My dream-thoughts of R are derogatory, and so that I may not become aware of this the very opposite of defamation - a tender affection for him - enters into the dream.

This discovery may prove to be generally valid. As the examples in Chapter III have demonstrated, there are, of course, dreams which are undisguised wish-fulfilments. Wherever a wish-fulfilment is unrecognizable and disguised there must be present a tendency to defend oneself against this wish, and in consequence of this defence the wish is unable to express itself save in a distorted form. I will try to find a parallel in social life to this occurrence in the inner psychic life. Where in social life can a similar misrepresentation be found? Only where two persons are concerned, one of whom possesses a certain power while the other has to act with a certain consideration on account of this power. The second person will then distort his psychic actions: or, as we say, he will mask himself. The politeness which I practise every day is largely a disguise of this kind; if I interpret my dreams for the benefit of my readers, I am forced to make misrepresentations of this kind. The poet even complains of the necessity of such misrepresentation: Das Beste, was du wissen kannst, darfst du den Buben doch nicht sagen: "The best that thou canst know thou mayst not tell to boys."

The political writer who has unpleasant truths to tell to those in power finds himself in a like position. If he tells everything without reserve, the Government will suppress them - retrospectively in the case of a verbal expression of opinion, preventively if they are to be published in the Press. The writer stands in fear of the censorship; he therefore moderates and disguises the expression of his opinions. He finds himself compelled, in accordance with the sensibilities of the censor, either to refrain altogether from certain forms of attack or to express himself in allusions instead of by direct assertions; or he must conceal his objectionable statement in an apparently innocent disguise. He may, for instance, tell of a contretemps between two Chinese mandarins, while he really has in mind the officials of his own country. The stricter the domination of the censorship, the more thorough becomes the disguise, and, often enough, the more ingenious the means employed to put the reader on the track of the actual meaning.

The detailed correspondence between the phenomena of censorship and the phenomena of dream-distortion justifies us in presupposing similar conditions for both. We should then assume that in every human being there exist, as the primary cause of dream-formation, two psychic forces (tendencies or systems), one of which forms the wish expressed by the dream, while the other exercises a censorship over this dream-wish, thereby enforcing on it a distortion. The question is: What is the nature of the authority of this second agency by virtue of which it is able to exercise its censorship? If we remember that the latent dream-thoughts are not conscious before analysis, but that the manifest dream-content emerging from them is consciously remembered, it is not a far-fetched assumption that admittance to the consciousness is the prerogative of the second agency. Nothing can reach the consciousness from the first system which has not previously passed the second instance; and the second instance lets nothing pass without exercising its rights, and forcing such modifications as are pleasing to itself upon the candidates for admission to consciousness. Here we arrive at a very definite conception of the essence of consciousness; for us the state of becoming conscious is a special psychic act, different from and independent of the process of becoming fixed or represented, and consciousness appears to us as a sensory organ which perceives a content proceeding from another source. It may be shown that psycho-pathology simply cannot dispense with these fundamental assumptions. But we shall reserve for another time a more exhaustive examination of the subject.

If I bear in mind the notion of the two psychic instances and their relation to the consciousness, I find in the sphere of politics a perfectly appropriate analogy to the extraordinary affection which I feel for my friend R, who is so disparaged in the dream-interpretation. I refer to the political life of a State in which the ruler, jealous of his rights, and an active public opinion are in mutual conflict. The people, protesting against the actions of an unpopular official, demand his dismissal. The autocrat, on the other hand, in order to show his contempt for the popular will, may then deliberately confer upon the official some exceptional distinction which otherwise would not have been conferred. Similarly, my second instance, controlling the access to my consciousness, distinguishes my friend R with a rush of extraordinary affection, because the wishtendencies of the first system, in view of a particular interest on which they are just then intent, would like to disparage him as a simpleton.[4] We may now perhaps begin to suspect that dream-interpretation is capable of yielding information concerning the structure of our psychic apparatus which we have hitherto vainly expected from philosophy. We shall not, however, follow up this trail, but shall return to our original problem as soon as we have elucidated the problem of dream-distortion. The question arose, how dreams with a disagreeable content can be analysed as wish-fulfillments. We see now that this is possible where a dream-distortion has occurred, when the disagreeable content serves only to disguise the thing wished for. With regard to our assumptions respecting the two psychic instances, we can now also say that disagreeable dreams contain, as a matter of fact, something which is disagreeable to the second instance, but which at the same time fulfills a wish of the first instance. They are wish-dreams in so far as every dream emanates from the first instance, while the second instance behaves towards the dream only in a defensive, not in a constructive manner.[5] Were we to limit ourselves to a consideration of what the second instance contributes to the dream we should never understand the dream, and all the problems which the writers on the subject have discovered in the dream would have to remain unsolved.

---

[4] Such hypocritical dreams are not rare, either with me or with others. While I have been working at a certain scientific problem, I have been visited for several nights, at quite short intervals, by a somewhat confusing dream which has as its content a reconciliation with a friend dropped long ago. After three or four attempts I finally succeeded in grasping the meaning of this dream. It was in the nature of an encouragment to give up the remnant of consideration still surviving for the person in question, to make myself quite free from him, but it hypocritically disguised itself in its antithesis. I have recorded a "hypocritical Oedipus dream" in which the hostile feelings and death-wishes of the dream-thoughts were replaced by manifest tenderness ("Typisches Beispiel eines verkappten Oedipustraumes." Zentralblatt fur Psychoanalyse, Vol. I, No. I-II [1910]). Another class of hypocritical dreams will be recorded in another place (see Chap vi, "The Dream-Work").

[5] Later on we shall become acquainted with cases in which, on the contrary, the dream expresses a wish of this second instance. -

That the dream actually has a secret meaning, which proves to be a wish-fulfillment, must be proved afresh in every case by analysis. I will therefore select a few dreams which have painful contents, and endeavour to analyse them. Some of them are dreams of hysterical subjects, which therefore call for a long preliminary statement, and in some passages an examination of the psychic processes occurring in hysteria. This, though it will complicate the presentation, is unavoidable.

When I treat a psychoneurotic patient analytically, his dreams regularly, as I have said, become a theme of our conversations. I must therefore give him all the psychological explanations with whose aid I myself have succeeded in understanding his symptoms. And here I encounter unsparing criticism, which is perhaps no less shrewd than that which I have to expect from my colleagues. With perfect uniformity, my patients contradict the doctrine that dreams are the fulfillments of wishes. Here are several examples of the sort of dream-material which is adduced in refutation of my theory.

"You are always saying that a dream is a wish fulfilled," begins an intelligent lady patient. "Now I shall tell you a dream in which the content is quite the opposite, in which a wish of mine is not fulfilled. How do you reconcile that with your theory? The dream was as follows: I want to give a supper, but I have nothing available except some smoked salmon. I think I will go shopping, but I remember that it is Sunday afternoon, when all the shops are closed. I then try to ring up a few caterers, but the telephone is out of order. Accordingly I have to renounce my desire to give a supper."

I reply, of course, that only the analysis can decide the meaning of this dream, although I admit that at first sight it seems sensible and coherent and looks like the opposite of a wish-fulfilment. "But what occurrence gave rise to this dream?" I ask. "You know that the stimulus of a dream always lies among the experiences of the preceding day."

Analysis

The patient's husband, an honest and capable meat salesman, had told her the day before that he was growing too fat, and that he meant to undergo treatment for obesity. He would rise early, take physical exercise, keep to a strict diet, and above all accept no more invitations to supper.

She proceeds jestingly to relate how her husband, at a table d'hote, had made the acquaintance of an artist, who insisted upon painting his portrait, because he, the painter, had never seen such an expressive head. But her husband had answered in his downright fashion, that while he was much obliged, he would rather not be painted; and he was quite convinced that a bit of a pretty girl's posterior would please the artist better than his whole face.[6] She is very much in love with her husband, and teases him a good deal. She has asked him not to give her any caviar. What can that mean?

Goethe: And if he has no backside, How can the nobleman sit? As a matter of fact, she had wanted for a long time to eat a caviar sandwich every morning, but had grudged the expense. Of course she could get the caviar from her husband at once if she asked for it. But she has, on the contrary, begged him not to give her any caviar, so that she might tease him about it a little longer.

(To me this explanation seems thin. Unconfessed motives are wont to conceal themselves behind just such unsatisfying explanations. We are reminded of the subjects hypnotized by Bernheim, who carried out a post-hypnotic order, and who, on being questioned as to their motives, instead of answering: "I do not know why I did that." had to invent a reason that was obviously inadequate. There is probably something similar to this in the case of my patient's caviar. I see that in waking life she is compelled to invent an unfulfilled wish. Her dream also shows her the nonfulfillment of her wish. But why does she need an unfulfilled wish?) The ideas elicited so far are insufficient for the interpretation of the dream. I press for more. After a short pause, which corresponds to the overcoming of a resistance, she reports

---

[6] To sit for the painter.

that the day before she had paid a visit to a friend of whom she is really jealous because her husband is always praising this lady so highly. Fortunately this friend is very thin and lanky, and her husband likes full figures. Now of what did this thin friend speak? Of course, of her wish to become rather plumper. She also asked my patient: "When are you going to invite us again? You always have such good food."

Now the meaning of the dream is clear. I am able to tell the patient: "It is just as though you had thought at the moment of her asking you that: 'Of course, I'm to invite you so that you can eat at my house and get fat and become still more pleasing to my husband! I would rather give no more suppers!' The dream then tells you that you cannot give a supper, thereby fulfilling your wish not to contribute anything to the rounding out of your friend's figure. Your husband's resolution to accept no more invitations to supper in order that he may grow thin teaches you that one grows fat on food eaten at other people's tables." Nothing is lacking now but some sort of coincidence which will confirm the solution. The smoked salmon in the dream has not yet been traced. - "How did you come to think of salmon in your dream?" - "Smoked salmon is my friend's favourite dish," she replied. It happens that I know the lady, and am able to affirm that she grudges herself salmon just as my patient grudges herself caviar.

This dream admits of yet another and more exact interpretation - one which is actually necessitated only by a subsidiary circumstance. The two interpretations do not contradict one another, but rather dovetail into one another, and furnish an excellent example of the usual ambiguity of dreams, as of all other psycho-pathological formations. We have heard that at the time of her dream of a denied wish the patient was impelled to deny herself a real wish (the wish to eat caviar sandwiches). Her friend, too, had expressed a wish, namely, to get fatter, and it would not surprise us if our patient had dreamt that this wish of her friend's - the wish to increase in weight - was not to be fulfilled. Instead of this, however, she dreamt that one of her own wishes was not fulfilled. The dream becomes capable of a new interpretation if in the dream she does not mean herself, but her friend, if she has put herself in the place of her friend, or, as we may say, has identified herself with her friend.

I think she has actually done this, and as a sign of this identification she has created for herself in real life an unfulfilled wish. But what is the meaning of this hysterical identification? To elucidate this a more exhaustive exposition is necessary. Identification is a highly important motive in the mechanism of hysterical symptoms; by this means patients are enabled to express in their symptoms not merely their own experiences, but the experiences of quite a number of other persons; they can suffer, as it were, for a whole mass of people, and fill all the parts of a drama with their own personalities. It will here be objected that this is the well-known hysterical imitation, the ability of hysterical subjects to imitate all the symptoms which impress them when they occur in others, as though pity were aroused to the point of reproduction. This, however, only indicates the path which the psychic process follows in hysterical imitation. But the path itself and the psychic act which follows this path are two different matters. The act itself is slightly more complicated than we are prone to believe the imitation of the hysterical to be; it corresponds to an unconscious end-process, as an example will show. The physician who has, in the same ward with other patients, a female patient suffering from a particular kind of twitching, is not surprised if one morning he learns that this peculiar hysterical affection has found imitators. He merely tells himself: The others have seen her, and have imitated her; this is psychic infection. Yes, but psychic infection occurs somewhat in the following manner: As a rule, patients know more about one another than the physician knows about any one of them, and they are concerned about one another when the doctor's visit is over. One of them has an attack to-day: at once it is known to the rest that a letter from home, a recrudescence of lovesickness, or the like, is the cause. Their sympathy is aroused, and although it does not emerge into consciousness they form the following conclusion:

"If it is possible to suffer such an attack from such a cause, I too may suffer this sort of an attack, for I have the same occasion for it."

If this were a conclusion capable of becoming conscious, it would perhaps express itself in dread of suffering a like attack; but it is formed in another psychic region, and consequently ends in the realization of the dreaded symptoms. Thus identification is not mere imitation, but an assimilation based upon the same aetiological claim; it expresses a just like, and refers to some common condition which has remained in the unconscious.

In hysteria, identification is most frequently employed to express a sexual community. The hysterical woman identifies herself by her symptoms most readily - though not exclusively - with persons with whom she has had sexual relations, or who have had sexual intercourse with the same persons as herself. Language takes cognizance of this tendency: two lovers are said to be "one." In hysterical phantasy, as well as in dreams, identification may ensue if one simply thinks of sexual relations; they need not necessarily become actual. The patient is merely following the rules of the hysterical processes of thought when she expresses her jealousy of her friend (which, for that matter, she herself admits to be unjustified) by putting herself in her friend's place in her dream, and identifying herself with her by fabricating a symptom (the denied wish). One might further elucidate the process by saying: In the dream she puts herself in the place of her friend, because her friend has taken her own place in relation to her husband, and because she would like to take her friend's place in her husband's esteem.[7] - The contradiction of my theory of dreams on the part of another female patient, the most intelligent of all my dreamers, was solved in a simpler fashion, though still in accordance with the principle that the non-fulfilment of one wish signified the fulfilment of

---

[7] I myself regret the inclusion of such passages from the psycho-pathology of hysteria, which, because of their fragmentary presentation, and because they are torn out of their context, cannot prove to be very illuminating. If these passages are capable of throwing any light upon the intimate relations between dream and the psycho-neurosis, they have served the intention with which I have included them.

another. I had one day explained to her that a dream is a wish-fulfilment. On the following day she related a dream to the effect that she was travelling with her mother-in- law to the place in which they were both to spend the summer. Now I knew that she had violently protested against spending the summer in the neighbourhood of her mother-in-law. I also knew that she had fortunately been able to avoid doing so, since she had recently succeeded in renting a house in a place quite remote from that to which her mother-in-law was going. And now the dream reversed this desired solution. Was not this a flat contradiction of my theory of wish-fulfilment? One had only to draw the inferences from this dream in order to arrive at its interpretation. According to this dream, I was wrong; but it was her wish that I should be wrong, and this wish the dream showed her as fulfilled. But the wish that I should be wrong, which was fulfilled in the theme of the country house, referred in reality to another and more serious matter. At that time I had inferred, from the material furnished by her analysis, that something of significance in respect to her illness must have occurred at a certain time in her life. She had denied this, because it was not present in her memory. We soon came to see that I was right. Thus her wish that I should prove to be wrong, which was transformed into the dream that she was going into the country with her mother-in-law, corresponded with the justifiable wish that those things which were then only suspected had never occurred. Without an analysis, and merely by means of an assumption, I took the liberty of interpreting a little incident in the life of a friend, who had been my companion through eight classes at school. He once heard a lecture of mine, delivered to a small audience, on the novel idea that dreams are wish-fulfilments. He went home, dreamt that he had lost all his lawsuits - he was a lawyer - and then complained to me about it. I took refuge in the evasion: "One can't win all one's cases"; but I thought to myself: "If, for eight years, I sat as primus on the first bench, while he moved up and down somewhere in the middle of the class, may he not naturally have had the wish, ever since his boyhood, that I too might for once make a fool of myself?" Yet another dream of a more gloomy character was offered me by a female patient in contradiction of my theory of the wish-dream. This patient, a young girl, began as follows: "You remember that my sister has now only one boy, Charles. She lost the elder one, Otto, while I was still living with her. Otto was my favourite; it was I who really brought him up. I like the other little fellow, too, but, of course, not nearly as much as his dead brother. Now I dreamt last night that I saw Charles lying dead before me. He was lying in his little coffin, his hands folded; there were candles all about; and, in short, it was just as it was at the time of little Otto's death, which gave me such a shock. Now tell me, what does this mean? You know me - am I really so bad as to wish that my sister should lose the only child she has left? Or does the dream mean that I wish that Charles had died rather than Otto, whom I liked so much better?"

I assured her that this latter interpretation was impossible. After some reflection, I was able to give her the interpretation of the dream, which she subsequently confirmed. I was able to do so because the whole previous history of the dreamer was known to me.

Having become an orphan at an early age, the girl had been brought up in the home of a much older sister, and had met, among the friends and visitors who frequented the house, a man who made a lasting impression upon her affections. It looked for a time as though these barely explicit relations would end in marriage, but this happy culmination was frustrated by the sister, whose motives were never completely explained. After the rupture the man whom my patient loved avoided the house; she herself attained her independence some time after the death of little Otto, to whom, meanwhile, her affections had turned. But she did not succeed in freeing herself from the dependence due to her affection for her sister's friend. Her pride bade her avoid him, but she found it impossible to transfer her love to the other suitors who successively presented themselves. Whenever the man she loved, who was a member of the literary profession, announced a lecture anywhere, she was certain to be found among the audience; and she seized every other opportunity of seeing him unobserved. I remembered that on the previous day she had told me that the Professor was going to a certain concert, and that she too was going, in order to enjoy the sight of him. This was on the day before the dream; and the concert was to be given on the day on which she told me the dream. I could now easily see the correct interpretation, and I asked her whether she could think of any particular event which had occurred after Otto's death. She replied immediately: "Of course; the Professor returned then, after a long absence, and I saw him once more beside little Otto's coffin." It was just as I had expected. I interpreted the dream as follows: "If now the other boy were to die, the same thing would happen again. You would spend the day with your sister; the Professor would certainly come to offer his condolences, and you would see him once more under the same circumstances as before. The dream signifies nothing more than this wish of yours to see him again - a wish against which you are fighting inwardly. I know that you have the ticket for today's concert in your bag. Your dream is a dream of impatience; it has anticipated by several hours the meeting which is to take place to-day."

In order to disguise her wish she had obviously selected a situation in which wishes of the sort are commonly suppressed - a situation so sorrowful that love is not even thought of. And yet it is entirely possible that even in the actual situation beside the coffin of the elder, more dearly loved boy, she had not been able to suppress her tender affection for the visitor whom she had missed for so long.

A different explanation was found in the case of a similar dream of another patient, who in earlier life had been distinguished for her quick wit and her cheerful disposition, and who still displayed these qualities, at all events in the free associations which occurred to her during treatment.

In the course of a longer dream, it seemed to this lady that she saw her fifteen-year-old daughter lying dead before her in a box. She was strongly inclined to use this dream-image as an objection to the theory of wish-fulfilment, although she herself suspected that the detail of the box must lead to a different conception of the dream.[8] For in the course of the analysis it occurred to her that on the previous evening the conversation of the people in whose company she found herself had turned on the English word box, and upon the numerous translations of it into German such as Schachtel (box), Loge (box at the theatre), Kasten (chest), Ohrfeige (box on the ear), etc. From other components of the same dream it was now possible to add the fact that the lady had guessed at the relationship between the English word "box" and the German Buchse, and had then been haunted by the recollection that Buchse is used in vulgar parlance to denote the female genitals. It was therefore possible, treating her knowledge of topographical anatomy with a certain indulgence, to assume that the child in the box signified a child in the mother's womb. At this stage of the explanation she no longer denied that the picture in the dream actually corresponded with a wish of hers. Like so many other young women, she was by no means happy on finding that she was pregnant, and she had confessed to me more than once the wish that her child might die before its birth; in a fit of anger, following a violent scene with her husband, she had even struck her abdomen with her fists, in order to injure the child within. The dead child was therefore, really the fulfilment of a wish, but a wish which had been put aside for fifteen years, and it is not surprising that the fulfilment of the wish was no longer recognized after so long an interval. For there had been many changes in the meantime.

The group of dreams (having as content the death of beloved relatives) to which belong the last two mentioned will be considered again under the head of "Typical Dreams." I shall then be able to show by new examples that in spite of their undesirable content all these dreams must be interpreted as wish - fulfilments. For the following dream, which again was told me in order to deter me from a hasty generalization of my theory, I am indebted,

---

[8] As in the dream of the deferred supper and the smoked salmon. -

not to a patient, but to an intelligent jurist of my acquaintance. "I dream," my informant tells me, "that I am walking in front of my house with a lady on my arm. Here a closed carriage is waiting; a man steps up to me, shows me his authorization as a police officer, and requests me to follow him. I ask only for time in which to arrange my affairs." The jurist then asks me: "Can you possibly suppose that it is my wish to be arrested?" - "Of course not," I have to admit. "Do you happen to know upon what charge you were arrested?" - "Yes; I believe for infanticide." -

"Infanticide? But you know that only a mother can commit this crime upon her new-born child?" - "That is true."[9] "And under what circumstances did you dream this? What happened on the evening before?" - "I would rather not tell you - it is a delicate matter." - "But I need it, otherwise we must forgo the interpretation of the dream." - "Well, then, I will tell you. I spent the night, not at home, but in the house of a lady who means a great deal to me. When we awoke in the morning, something again passed between us. Then I went to sleep again, and dreamt what I have told you." - "The woman is married?" - "Yes." - "And you do not wish her to conceive?" - "No; that might betray us." - "Then you do not practice normal coitus?" - "I take the precaution to withdraw before ejaculation." - "Am I to assume that you took this precaution several times during the night, and that in the morning you were not quite sure whether you had succeeded?" - "That might be so." - "Then your dream is the fulfilment of a wish. By the dream you are assured that you have not begotten a child, or, what amounts to the same thing, that you have killed the child. I can easily demonstrate the connecting-links. Do you remember, a few days ago we were talking about the troubles of matrimony, and about the inconsistency of permitting coitus so long as no impregnation takes place, while at the same time any preventive act committed after the ovum

---

[9] It often happens that a dream is told incompletely, and that a recollection of the omitted portions appears only in the course of the analysis. These portions, when subsequently fitted in, invariably furnish the key to the interpretation. Cf. Chapter VII, on forgetting of dreams.

and the semen meet and a foetus is formed is punished as a crime? In this connection we recalled the medieval controversy about the moment of time at which the soul actually enters into the foetus, since the concept of murder becomes admissible only from that point onwards. Of course, too, you know the gruesome poem by Lenau, which puts infanticide and birth-control on the same plane." - "Strangely enough, I happened, as though by chance, to think of Lenau this morning." - "Another echo of your dream. And now I shall show you yet another incidental wish-fulfilment in your dream. You walk up to your house with the lady on your arm. So you take her home, instead of spending the night at her house, as you did in reality. The fact that the wish-fulfilment, which is the essence of the dream, disguises itself in such an unpleasant form, has perhaps more than one explanation. From my essay on the aetiology of anxiety neurosis, you will see that I note coitus interruptus as one of the factors responsible for the development of neurotic fear. It would be consistent with this if, after repeated coitus of this kind, you were left in an uncomfortable frame of mind, which now becomes an element of the composition of your dream. You even make use of this uncomfortable state of mind to conceal the wish-fulfilment. At the same time, the mention of infanticide has not yet been explained. Why does this crime, which is peculiar to females, occur to you?" - "I will confess to you that I was involved in such an affair years ago. I was responsible for the fact that a girl tried to protect herself from the consequences of a liaison with me by procuring an abortion. I had nothing to do with the carrying out of her plan, but for a long time I was naturally worried in case the affair might be discovered." - "I understand. This recollection furnished a second reason why the supposition that you had performed coitus interruptus clumsily must have been painful to you."

A young physician, who heard this dream related in my lecture-room, must have felt that it fitted him, for he hastened to imitate it by a dream of his own, applying its mode of thinking to another theme. On the previous day he had furnished a statement of his income; a quite straightforward statement, because he had little to state. He dreamt that an acquaintance of his came from a meeting of the tax commission and informed him that all the other statements had passed unquestioned, but that his own had aroused general suspicion, with the result that he would be punished with a heavy fine. This dream is a poorly disguised fulfilment of the wish to be known as a physician with a large income. It also calls to mind the story of the young girl who was advised against accepting her suitor because he was a man of quick temper, who would assuredly beat her after their marriage. Her answer was: "I wish he would strike me!" Her wish to be married was so intense that she had taken into consideration the discomforts predicted for this marriage; she had even raised them to the plane of a wish. If I group together the very frequent dreams of this sort, which seem flatly to contradict my theory, in that they embody the denial of a wish or some occurrence obviously undesired, under the head of counter-wish-dreams, I find that they may all be referred to two principles, one of which has not yet been mentioned, though it plays a large part in waking as well as dream-life. One of the motives inspiring these dreams is the wish that I should appear in the wrong. These dreams occur regularly in the course of treatment whenever the patient is in a state of resistance; indeed, I can with a great degree of certainty count on evoking such a dream once I have explained to the patient my theory that the dream is a wishfulfilment.[10] Indeed, I have reason to expect that many of my readers will have such dreams, merely to fulfil the wish that I may prove to be wrong. The last dream which I shall recount from among those occurring in the course of treatment once more demonstrates this very thing. A young girl who had struggled hard to continue my treatment, against the will of her relatives and the authorities whom they had consulted, dreamt the following dream: At home she is forbidden to come to me any more. She then reminds me of the

---

[10] Similar counter-wish-dreams have been repeatedly reported to me within the last few years, by those who attend my lectures, as their reaction to their first encounter with the wish-theory of dreams.

promise I made her to treat her for nothing if necessary, and I tell her: "I can show no consideration in money matters."

It is not at all easy in this case to demonstrate the fulfilment of a wish, but in all cases of this kind there is a second problem, the solution of which helps also to solve the first. Where does she get the words which she puts into my mouth? Of course, I have never told her anything of the kind; but one of her brothers, the one who has the greatest influence over her, has been kind enough to make this remark about me. It is then the purpose of the dream to show that her brother is right; and she does not try to justify this brother merely in the dream; it is her purpose in life and the motive of her illness.

A dream which at first sight presents peculiar difficulties for the theory of wish-fulfilment was dreamed by a physician (Aug. Starcke) and interpreted by him: "I have and see on the last phalange of my left forefinger a primary syphilitic affection."

One may perhaps be inclined to refrain from analysing this dream, since it seems clear and coherent, except for its unwished-for content.

However, if one takes the trouble to make an analysis, one learns that primary affection reduces itself to prima affectio (first love), and that the repulsive sore, in the words of Starcke, proves to be "the representative of wish-fulfilments charged with intense emotion."[11]

The other motive for counter-wish-dreams is so clear that there is a danger of overlooking it, as happened in my own case for a long time. In the sexual constitution of many persons there is a masochistic component, which has arisen through the conversion of the aggressive, sadistic component into its opposite. Such people are called ideal masochists if they seek pleasure not in the bodily pain which may be inflicted upon them, but in humiliation and psychic chastisement. It is obvious that such persons may have counter-wish-dreams and disagreeable dreams, yet these are

---

[11] Zentralblatt fur Psychoanalyse, Jahrg. II, 1911-12.

for them nothing more than wish-fulfilments, which satisfy their masochistic inclinations. Here is such a dream: A young man, who in earlier youth greatly tormented his elder brother, toward whom he was homosexually inclined, but who has since undergone a complete change of character, has the following dream, which consists of three parts: (1) He is "teased" by his brother. (2) Two adults are caressing each other with homosexual intentions. (3) His brother has sold the business the management of which the young man had reserved for his own future. From this last dream he awakens with the most unpleasant feelings; and yet it is a masochistic wish-dream, which might be translated: It would serve me right if my brother were to make that sale against my interests. It would be my punishment for all the torments he has suffered at my hands. I hope that the examples given above will suffice - until some further objection appears - to make it seem credible that even dreams with a painful content are to be analysed as wish-fulfilments.[12] Nor should it be considered a mere matter of chance that, in the course of interpretation, one always happens upon subjects about which one does not like to speak or think. The disagreeable sensation which such dreams arouse is of course precisely identical with the antipathy which would, and usually does, restrain us from treating or discussing such subjects - an antipathy which must be overcome by all of us if we find ourselves obliged to attack the problem of such dreams. But this disagreeable feeling which recurs in our dreams does not preclude the existence of a wish; everyone has wishes which he would not like to confess to others, which he does not care to admit even to himself. On the other hand, we feel justified in connecting the unpleasant character of all these dreams with the fact of dreamdistortion, and in concluding that these dreams are distorted, and that their wish-fulfilment is disguised beyond recognition, precisely because there is a strong revulsion against - a will to repress - the subject-matter of the dream, or the wish created by it. Dream-distortion, then, proves

---

[12] I will here observe that we have not yet disposed of this theme; we shall discuss it again later.

in reality to be an act of censorship. We shall have included everything which the analysis of disagreeable dreams has brought to light if we reword our formula thus: The dream is the (disguised) fulfilment of a (suppressed, repressed) wish.[13]

I will here anticipate by citing the amplification and modification of this fundamental formula propounded by Otto Rank: "On the basis of and with the aid of repressed infantile-sexual material, dreams regularly represent as fulfilled current, and as a rule also erotic, wishes in a disguised and symbolic form" (Ein Traum, der sich selbst deutet).

Nowhere have I said that I have accepted this formula of Rank's. The shorter version contained in the text seems to me sufficient. But the fact that I merely mentioned Rank's modification was enough to expose psycho-analysis to the oft-repeated reproach that it asserts that all dreams have a sexual content. If one understands this sentence as it is intended to be understood, it only proves how little conscientiousness our critics are wont to display, and how ready our opponents are to overlook statements if they do not accord with their aggressive inclinations. Only a few pages back I mentioned the manifold wish-fulfilments of children's dreams (to make an excursion on land and or water, to make up for an omitted meal, etc.). Elsewhere I have mentioned dreams excited by thirst and the desire to evacuate, and mere comfort - or convenience-dreams. Even Rank does not make an absolute assertion. He says "as a rule also erotic wishes," and this can be completely confirmed in the case of most dreams of adults.

The matter has, however, a different aspect if we employ the word sexual in the sense of Eros, as the word is understood by psycho-analysts. But the interesting problem of whether all dreams are not produced by libidinal motives (in opposition to destructive ones) has hardly been considered by our opponents.

Now there still remain to be considered, as a particular sub-

---

[13] A great contemporary poet, who, I am told, will hear nothing of psycho-analysis and dream-interpretation, has nevertheless derived from his own experience an almost identical formula for the nature of the dream: "Unauthorized emergence of suppressed yearnings under false features and names" (C. Spitteler, "Meine fruhesten Erlebnisse," in Suddeutsche Monatshefte, October, 1913).

order of dreams with painful content, the anxiety-dreams, the inclusion of which among the wish-dreams will be still less acceptable to the uninitiated. But I can here deal very cursorily with the problem of anxiety-dreams; what they have to reveal is not a new aspect of the dream-problem; here the problem is that of understanding neurotic anxiety in general. The anxiety which we experience in dreams is only apparently explained by the dream-content. If we subject that content to analysis, we become aware that the dream-anxiety is no more justified by the dream-content than the anxiety in a phobia is justified by the idea to which the phobia is attached. For example, it is true that it is possible to fall out of a window, and that a certain care should be exercised when one is at a window, but it is not obvious why the anxiety in the corresponding phobia is so great, and why it torments its victims more than its cause would warrant. The same explanation which applies to the phobia applies also to the anxiety-dream. In either case, the anxiety is only fastened on to the idea which accompanies it, and is derived from another source.

On account of this intimate relation of dream-anxiety to neurotic anxiety, the discussion of the former obliges me to refer to the latter. In a little essay on Anxiety Neurosis,[14] written in 1895, I maintain that neurotic anxiety has its origin in the sexual life, and corresponds to a libido which has been deflected from its object and has found no employment. The accuracy of this formula has since then been demonstrated with everincreasing certainty. From it we may deduce the doctrine that anxiety-dreams are dreams of sexual content, and that the libido appertaining to this content has been transformed into anxiety. Later on I shall have an opportunity of confirming this assertion by the analysis of several dreams of neurotics. In my further attempts to arrive at a theory of dreams I shall again have occasion to revert to the conditions of anxiety-dreams and their compatibility with the theory of wish-fulfilment.

Chapter 5

The Material And Sources Of Dreams

Having realized, as a result of analysing the dream of Irma's injection, that the dream was the fulfilment of a wish, we were immediately interested to ascertain whether we had thereby discovered a general characteristic of dreams, and for the time being we put aside every other scientific problem which may have suggested itself in the course of the interpretation. Now that we have reached the goal on this one path, we may turn back and select a new point of departure for exploring dream-problems, even though we may for a time lose sight of the theme of wishfulfilment, which has still to be further considered.

Now that we are able, by applying our process of interpretation, to detect a latent dream-content whose significance far surpasses that of the manifest dream-content, we are naturally impelled to return to the individual dream-problems, in order to see whether the riddles and contradictions which seemed to elude us when we had only the manifest content to work upon may not now be satisfactorily solved.

The opinions of previous writers on the relation of dreams to waking life, and the origin of the material of dreams, have not been given here. We may recall however three peculiarities of the memory in dreams, which have been often noted, but never explained:

1. That the dream clearly prefers the impressions of the last few days (Robert, Strumpell, Hildebrandt; also Weed-Hallam);

2. That it makes a selection in accordance with principles other than those governing our waking memory, in that it recalls not essential and important, but subordinate and disregarded things;

3. That it has at its disposal the earliest impressions of our childhood, and brings to light details from this period of life, which, again, seem trivial to us, and which in waking life were believed to have been long since forgotten.[1]

These peculiarities in the dream's choice of material have, of course, been observed by previous writers in the manifest dream-content.

A. Recent and Indifferent Impressions in the Dream

If I now consult my own experience with regard to the origin of the elements appearing in the dream-content, I must in the first place express the opinion that in every dream we may find some reference to the experiences of the preceding day. Whatever dream I turn to, whether my own or someone else's, this experience is always confirmed. Knowing this, I may perhaps begin the work of interpretation by looking for the experience of the preceding day which has stimulated the dream; in many cases this is indeed the quickest way. With the two dreams which I subjected to a close analysis in the last chapter (the dreams of Irma's injection, and of the uncle with the yellow beard) the reference to the preceding day is so evident that it needs no further elucidation. But in order to show how constantly this reference may be demonstrated, I shall examine a portion of my own dream-chronicle, I shall relate only so much of the dreams as is necessary for the detection of the dream-source in question.

1. I pay a call at a house to which I gain admittance only with difficulty, etc., and meanwhile I am keeping a woman waiting for me.

---

[1] It is evident that Robert's idea- that the dream is intended to rid our memory of the useless impressions which it has received during the day- is no longer tenable if indifferent memories of our childhood appear in our dreams with some degree of frequency. We should be obliged to conclude that our dreams generally perform their prescribed task very inadequately.

Source: A conversation during the evening with a female relative to the effect that she would have to wait for a remittance for which she had asked, until... etc.

2. I have written a monograph on a species (uncertain) of plant.

Source: In the morning I had seen in a bookseller's window a monograph on the genus Cyclamen.

3. I see two women in the street, mother and daughter, the latter being a patient.

Source: A female patient who is under treatment had told me in the evening what difficulties her mother puts in the way of her continuing the treatment.

4. At S and R's bookshop I subscribe to a periodical which costs 20 florins annually.

Source: During the day my wife has reminded me that I still owe her 20 florins of her weekly allowance.

5. I receive a communication from the Social Democratic Committee, in which I am addressed as a member.

Source: I have received simultaneous communications from the Liberal Committee on Elections and from the president of the Humanitarian Society, of which latter I am actually a member.

6. A man on a steep rock rising from the sea, in the manner of Bocklin.

Source: Dreyfus on Devil's Island; also news from my relatives in England, etc.

The question might be raised, whether a dream invariably refers to the events of the preceding day only, or whether the reference may be extended to include impressions from a longer period of time in the immediate past. This question is probably not of the first importance, but I am inclined to decide in favour of the exclusive priority of the day before the dream (the dream-day). Whenever I thought I had found a case where an impression two or three days old was the source of the dream, I was able to convince myself after careful investigation that this impression had been remembered the day before; that is, that a demonstrable reproduction on the day before had been interpolated between the day of the event and the time of the dream; and further, I was able to point to the recent occasion which might have given rise to the recollection of the older impression. On the other hand, I was unable to convince myself that a regular interval of biological significance (H. Swoboda gives the first interval of this kind as eighteen hours) elapses between the dream-exciting daytime impression and its recurrence in the dream.

I believe, therefore, that for every dream a dream-stimulus may be found among these experiences "on which one has not yet slept."

Havelock Ellis, who has likewise given attention to this problem, states that he has not been able to find any such periodicity of reproduction in his dreams, although he has looked for it. He relates a dream in which he found himself in Spain; he wanted to travel to a place called Daraus, Varaus, or Zaraus. On awaking he was unable to recall any such place-names, and thought no more of the matter. A few months later he actually found the name Zaraus; it was that of a railway-station between San Sebastian and Bilbao, through which he had passed in the train eight months (250 days) before the date of the dream.

Thus the impressions of the immediate past (with the exception of the day before the night of the dream) stand in the same relation to the dreamcontent as those of periods indefinitely remote. The dream may select its material from any period of life, provided only that a chain of thought leads back from the experiences of the day of the dream (the recent impressions) of that earlier period.

But why this preference for recent impressions? We shall arrive at some conjectures on this point if we subject one of the dreams already mentioned to a more precise analysis. I select the

Dream of the Botanical Monograph

I have written a monograph on a certain plant. The book lies before me; I am just turning over a folded coloured plate. A dried specimen of the plant, as though from a herbarium, is bound up with every copy.

Analysis

In the morning I saw in a bookseller's window a volume entitled The Genus Cyclamen, apparently a monograph on this plant.

The cyclamen is my wife's favorite flower. I reproach myself for remembering so seldom to bring her flowers, as she would like me to do. In connection with the theme of giving her flowers, I am reminded of a story which I recently told some friends of mine in proof of my assertion that we often forget in obedience to a purpose of the unconscious, and that forgetfulness always enables us to form a deduction about the secret disposition of the forgetful person. A young woman who has been accustomed to receive a bouquet of flowers from her husband on her birthday misses this token of affection on one of her birthdays, and bursts into tears. The husband comes in, and cannot understand why she is crying until she tells him: "Today is my birthday." He claps his hand to his forehead, and exclaims: "Oh, forgive me, I had completely forgotten it!" and proposes to go out immediately in order to get her flowers. But she refuses to be consoled, for she sees in her husband's forgetfulness a proof that she no longer plays the same part in his thoughts as she formerly did. This Frau L met my wife two days ago, told her that she was feeling well, and asked after me. Some years ago she was a patient of mine.

Supplementary facts: I did once actually write something like a monograph on a plant, namely, an essay on the coca plant, which attracted the attention of K. Koller to the anaesthetic properties of cocaine. I had hinted that the alkaloid might be employed as an anaesthetic, but I was not thorough enough to pursue the matter farther. It occurs to me, too, that on the morning of the day following the dream (for the interpretation of which I did not find time until the evening) I had thought of cocaine in a kind of day-dream. If I were ever afflicted with glaucoma, I would go to Berlin, and there undergo an operation, incognito, in the house of my Berlin friend, at the hands of a surgeon whom he would recommend. The surgeon, who would not know the name of his patient, would boast, as usual, how easy these operations had become since the introduction of cocaine; and I should not betray the fact that I myself had a share in this discovery. With this phantasy were connected thoughts of how awkward it really is for a physician to claim the professional services of a colleague. I should be able to pay the Berlin eye specialist, who did not know me, like anyone else. Only after recalling this day-dream do I realize that there is concealed behind it the memory of a definite event. Shortly after Koller's discovery, my father contracted glaucoma; he was operated on by my friend Dr. Koenigstein, the eye specialist. Dr. Koller was in charge of the cocaine anaesthetization, and he made the remark that on this occasion all the three persons who had been responsible for the introduction of cocaine had been brought together.

My thoughts now pass on to the time when I was last reminded of the history of cocaine. This was a few days earlier, when I received a Festschrift, a publication in which grateful pupils had commemorated the jubilee of their teacher and laboratory director. Among the titles to fame of persons connected with the laboratory I found a note to the effect that the discovery of the anaesthetic properties of cocaine had been due to K.

Koller. Now I suddenly become aware that the dream is connected with an experience of the previous evening. I had just accompanied Dr. Koenigstein to his home, and had entered into a discussion of a subject which excites me greatly whenever it is mentioned. While I was talking with him in the entrance-hall Professor Gartner and his young wife came up. I could not refrain from congratulating them both upon their blooming appearance. Now Professor Gartner is one of the authors of the Festschrift of which I have just spoken, and he may well have reminded me of it. And Frau L, of whose birthday disappointment I spoke a little way back, had been mentioned, though of course in another connection, in my conversation with Dr. Koenigstein.

I shall now try to elucidate the other determinants of the dream-content. A dried specimen of the plant accompanies the monograph, as though it were a herbarium. And herbarium reminds me of the Gymnasium. The director of our Gymnasium once called the pupils of the upper classes together, in order that they might examine and clean the Gymnasium herbarium. Small insects had been found- book-worms. The director seemed to have little confidence in my ability to assist, for he entrusted me with only a few of the pages. I know to this day that there were crucifers on them. My interest in botany was never very great. At my preliminary examination in botany I was required to identify a crucifer, and failed to recognize it; had not my theoretical knowledge come to my aid, I should have fared badly indeed. Crucifers suggest composites. The artichoke is really a composite, and in actual fact one which I might call my favourite flower. My wife, more thoughtful than I, often brings this favourite flower of mine home from the market.

I see the monograph which I have written lying before me. Here again there is an association. My friend wrote to me yesterday from Berlin: "I am thinking a great deal about your dream-book. I see it lying before me, completed, and I turn the pages." How I envied him this power of vision! If only I could see it lying before me, already completed!

The folded coloured plate. When I was a medical student I suffered a sort of craze for studying monographs exclusively. In spite of my limited means, I subscribed to a number of the medical periodicals, whose coloured plates afforded me much delight. I was rather proud of this inclination to thoroughness. When I subsequently began to publish books myself, I had to draw the plates for my own treatises, and I remember one of them turned out so badly that a well-meaning colleague ridiculed me for it. With this is associated, I do not exactly know how, a very early memory of my childhood. My father, by the way of a jest, once gave my elder sister and myself a book containing coloured plates (the book was a narrative of a journey through Persia) in order that we might destroy it. From an educational point of view this was hardly to be commended. I was at the time five years old, and my sister less than three, and the picture of us two children blissfully tearing the book to pieces (I should add, like an artichoke, leaf by leaf), is almost the only one from this period of my life which has remained vivid in my memory. When I afterwards became a student, I developed a conspicuous fondness for collecting and possessing books (an analogy to the inclination for studying from monographs, a hobby alluded to in my dream-thoughts, in connection with cyclamen and artichoke). I became a book-worm (cf. herbarium). Ever since I have been engaged in introspection I have always traced this earliest passion of my life to this impression of my childhood: or rather, I have recognized in this childish scene a screen or concealing memory for my subsequent bibliophilia.[2] And of course I learned at an early age that our passions often become our misfortunes. When I was seventeen, I ran up a very considerable account at the bookseller's, with no means with which to settle it, and my father would hardly accept it as an excuse that my passion was at least a respectable one. But the mention of this experience of my youth brings me back to my conversation with my friend Dr. Koenigstein on the evening preceding the dream; for one of the themes of this conversation was the same old reproach- that I am much too absorbed in my hobbies.

For reasons which are not relevant here I shall not continue the interpretation of this dream, but will merely indicate the path which leads to it. In the course of the interpretation I was reminded of my conversation with Dr. Koenigstein, and, indeed, of more than one portion of it. When I consider the subjects touched upon in this conversation, the meaning of the dream immediately becomes clear to me. All the trains of thought which have been started- my own inclinations, and those of my wife, the cocaine, the awkwardness of securing medical treatment from one's own colleagues, my preference for monographical studies,

---

[2] Cf. The Psycho-pathology of Everyday Life.

and my neglect of certain subjects, such as botany- all these are continued in and lead up to one branch or another of this widely-ramified conversation. The dream once more assumes the character of a justification, of a plea for my rights (like the dream of Irma's injection, the first to be analysed); it even continues the theme which that dream introduced, and discusses it in association with the new subject-matter which has been added in the interval between the two dreams. Even the dream's apparently indifferent form of expression at once acquires a meaning. Now it means: "I am indeed the man who has written that valuable and successful treatise (on cocaine)," just as previously I declared in self-justification: "I am after all a thorough and industrious student"; and in both instances I find the meaning: "I can allow myself this." But I may dispense with the further interpretation of the dream, because my only purpose in recording it was to examine the relation of the dream-content to the experience of the previous day which arouses it. As long as I know only the manifest content of this dream, only one relation to any impression of the day is obvious; but after I have completed the interpretation, a second source of the dream becomes apparent in another experience of the same day. The first of these impressions to which the dream refers is an indifferent one, a subordinate circumstance. I see a book in a shop window whose title holds me for a moment, but whose contents would hardly interest me. The second experience was of great psychic value; I talked earnestly with my friend, the eye specialist, for about an hour; I made allusions in this conversation which must have ruffled the feelings of both of us, and which in me awakened memories in connection with which I was aware of a great variety of inner stimuli. Further, this conversation was broken off unfinished, because some acquaintances joined us. What, now, is the relation of these two impressions of the day to one another, and to the dream which followed during the night?

In the manifest dream-content I find merely an allusion to the indifferent impression, and I am thus able to reaffirm that the dream prefers to take up into its content experiences of a non-essential character. In the dream-interpretation, on the contrary, everything converges upon the important and justifiably disturbing event. If I judge the sense of the dream in the only correct way, according to the latent content which is brought to light in the analysis, I find that I have unwittingly lighted upon a new and important discovery. I see that the puzzling theory that the dream deals only with the worthless odds and ends of the day's experiences has no justification; I am also compelled to contradict the assertion that the psychic life of the waking state is not continued in the dream, and that hence, the dream wastes our psychic energy on trivial material. The very opposite is true; what has claimed our attention during the day dominates our dream-thoughts also, and we take pains to dream only in connection with such matters as have given us food for thought during the day.

Perhaps the most immediate explanation of the fact that I dream of the indifferent impression of the day, while the impression which has with good reason excited me causes me to dream, is that here again we are dealing with the phenomenon of dream- distortion, which we have referred to as a psychic force playing the part of a censorship. The recollection of the monograph on the genus cyclamen is utilized as though it were an allusion to the conversation with my friend, just as the mention of my patient's friend in the dream of the deferred supper is represented by the allusion smoked salmon. The only question is: by what intermediate links can the impression of the monograph come to assume the relation of allusion to the conversation with the eye specialist, since such a relation is not at first perceptible? In the example of the deferred supper, the relation is evident at the outset; smoked salmon, as the favourite dish of the patient's friend, belongs to the circle of ideas which the friend's personality would naturally evoke in the mind of the dreamer. In our new example we are dealing with two entirely separate impressions, which at first glance seem to have nothing in common, except indeed that they occur on the same day. The monograph attracts my attention in the morning: in the evening

I take part in the conversation. The answer furnished by the analysis is as follows: Such relations between the two impressions as do not exist from the first are established subsequently between the idea-content of the one impression and the idea-content of the other. I have already picked out the intermediate links emphasized in the course of writing the analysis. Only under some outside influence, perhaps the recollection of the flowers missed by Frau L, would the idea of the monograph on the cyclamen have attached itself to the idea that the cyclamen is my wife's favourite flower. I do not believe that these inconspicuous thoughts would have sufficed to evoke a dream.

There needs no ghost, my lord, come from the grave To tell us this, as we read in Hamlet. But behold! in the analysis I am reminded that the name of the man who interrupted our conversation was Gartner (gardener), and that I thought his wife looked blooming; indeed, now I even remember that one of my female patients, who bears the pretty name of Flora, was for a time the main subject of our conversation. It must have happened that by means of these intermediate links from the sphere of botanical ideas the association was effected between the two events of the day, the indifferent one and the stimulating one. Other relations were then established, that of cocaine for example, which can with perfect appropriateness form a link between the person of Dr. Koenigstein and the botanical monograph which I have written, and thus secure the fusion of the two circles of ideas, so that now a portion of the first experience may be used as an allusion to the second.

I am prepared to find this explanation attacked as either arbitrary or artificial. What would have happened if Professor Gartner and his blooming wife had not appeared, and if the patient who was under discussion had been called, not Flora, but Anna? And yet the answer is not hard to find. If these thought-relations had not been available, others would probably have been selected. It is easy to establish relations of this sort, as the jocular questions and conundrums with which we amuse ourselves suffice to show. The range of wit is unlimited. To go a step farther: if no sufficiently fertile associations between the two impressions of the day could have been established, the dream would simply have followed a different course; another of the indifferent impressions of the day, such as come to us in multitudes and are forgotten, would have taken the place of the monograph in the dream, would have formed an association with the content of the conversation, and would have represented this in the dream. Since it was the impression of the monograph and no other that was fated to perform this function, this impression was probably that most suitable for the purpose. One need not, like Lessing's Hanschen Schlau, be astonished that "only the rich people of the world possess the most money."

Still the psychological process by which, according to our exposition, the indifferent experience substitutes itself for the psychologically important one seems to us odd and open to question. In a later chapter we shall undertake the task of making the peculiarities of this seemingly incorrect operation more intelligible. Here we are concerned only with the result of this process, which we were compelled to accept by constantly recurring experiences in the analysis of dreams. In this process it is as though, in the course of the intermediate steps, a displacement occurs- let us say, of the psychic accent- until ideas of feeble potential, by taking over the charge from ideas which have a stronger initial potential, reach a degree of intensity which enables them to force their way into consciousness. Such displacements do not in the least surprise us when it is a question of the transference of affective magnitudes or of motor activities. That the lonely spinster transfers her affection to animals, that the bachelor becomes a passionate collector, that the soldier defends a scrap of coloured cloth- his flag- with his life-blood, that in a loveaffair a clasp of the hands a moment longer than usual evokes a sensation of bliss, or that in Othello a lost handkerchief causes an outburst of rageall these are examples of psychic displacements which to us seem incontestable. But if, by the same means, and in accordance with the same fundamental principles, a decision is made as to what is to reach our consciousness and what is to be withheld from it- that is to say, what we are to think- this gives us the impression of morbidity, and if it occurs in waking life we call it an error of thought. We may here anticipate the result of a discussion which will be undertaken later, namely, that the psychic process which we have recognized in dream-displacement proves to be not a morbidly deranged process, but one merely differing from the normal, one of a more primary nature.

Thus we interpret the fact that the dream-content takes up remnants of trivial experiences as a manifestation of dream-distortion (by displacement), and we thereupon remember that we have recognized this dream-distortion as the work of a censorship operating between the two psychic instances. We may therefore expect that dream-analysis will constantly show us the real and psychically significant source of the dream in the events of the day, the memory of which has transferred its accentuation to some indifferent memory. This conception is in complete opposition to Robert's theory, which consequently has no further value for us. The fact which Robert was trying to explain simply does not exist; its assumption is based on a misunderstanding, on a failure to substitute the real meaning of the dream for its apparent meaning. A further objection to Robert's doctrine is as follows: If the task of the dream were really to rid our memory, by means of a special psychic activity, of the slag of the day's recollections, our sleep would perforce be more troubled, engaged in more strenuous work, than we can suppose it to be, judging by our waking thoughts. For the number of the indifferent impressions of the day against which we should have to protect our memory is obviously immeasurably large; the whole night would not be long enough to dispose of them all. It is far more probable that the forgetting of the indifferent impressions takes place without any active interference on the part of our psychic powers.

Still, something cautions us against taking leave of Robert's theory without further consideration. We have left unexplained the fact that one of the indifferent impressions of the day- indeed, even of the previous day- constantly makes a contribution to the dream-content. The relations between this impression and the real source of the dream in the unconscious do not always exist from the outset; as we have seen, they are established subsequently, while the dream is actually at work, as though to serve the purpose of the intended displacement. Something, therefore, must necessitate the opening up of connections in the direction of the recent but indifferent impression; this impression must possess some quality that gives it a special fitness. Otherwise it would be just as easy for the dream- thoughts to shift their accentuation to some inessential component of their own sphere of ideas.

Experiences such as the following show us the way to an explanation: If the day has brought us two or more experiences which are worthy to evoke a dream, the dream will blend the allusion of both into a single whole: it obeys a compulsion to make them into a single whole. For example: One summer afternoon I entered a railway carriage in which I found two acquaintances of mine who were unknown to one another. One of them was an influential colleague, the other a member of a distinguished family which I had been attending in my professional capacity. I introduced the two gentlemen to each other; but during the long journey they conversed with each other through me, so that I had to discuss this or that topic now with one, now with the other. I asked my colleague to recommend a mutual acquaintance who had just begun to practise as a physician. He replied that he was convinced of the young man's ability, but that his undistinguished appearance would make it difficult for him to obtain patients in the upper ranks of society. To this I rejoined: "That is precisely why he needs recommendation." A little later, turning to my other fellow-traveller, I inquired after the health of his aunt- the mother of one of my patients- who was at this time prostrated by a serious illness. On the night following this journey I dreamt that the young friend whom I had asked one of my companions to recommend was in a fashionable drawing-room, and with all the bearing of a man of the world was making- before a distinguished company, in which I recognized all the rich and aristocratic persons of my acquaintance- a funeral oration over the old lady (who in my dream had already died) who was the aunt of my second fellow-traveller. (I confess frankly that I had not been on good terms with this lady.) Thus my dream had once more found the connection between the two impressions of the day, and by means of the two had constructed a unified situation. In view of many similar experiences, I am persuaded to advance the proposition that a dream works under a kind of compulsion which forces it to combine into a unified whole all the sources of dream-stimulation which are offered to it.[3] In a subsequent chapter (on the function of dreams) we shall consider this impulse of combination as part of the process of condensation, another primary psychic process.

I shall now consider the question whether the dream-exciting source to which our analysis leads us must always be a recent (and significant) event, or whether a subjective experience- that is to say, the recollection of a psychologically significant event, a train of thought- may assume the role of a dream- stimulus. The very definite answer, derived from numerous analyses, is as follows: The stimulus of the dream may be a subjective transaction, which has been made recent, as it were, by the mental activity of the day.

And this is perhaps the best time to summarize in schematic form the different conditions under which the dream-sources are operative.

The source of a dream may be:

(a) A recent and psychologically significant event which is directly represented in the dream.[4]

(b) Several recent and significant events, which are combined by the dream in a single whole.[5]

---

[3] The tendency of the dream at work to blend everything present of interest into a single transaction has already been noticed by several authors, for instance, by Delage and Delboeuf.
[4] The dream of Irma's injection; the dream of the friend who is my uncle.
[5] The dream of the funeral oration delivered by the young physician.

(c) One or more recent and significant events, which are represented in the dream-content by allusion to a contemporary but indifferent event.[6]

(d) A subjectively significant experience (recollection, train of thought), which is constantly represented in the dream by allusion to a recent but indifferent impression.[7]

As may be seen, in dream-interpretation the condition is always fulfilled that one component of the dream-content repeats a recent impression of the day of the dream. The component which is destined to be represented in the dream may either belong to the same circle of ideas as the dreamstimulus itself (as an essential or even an inessential element of the same); or it may originate in the neighbourhood of an indifferent impression, which has been brought by more or less abundant associations into relation with the sphere of the dream-stimulus. The apparent multiplicity of these conditions results merely from the alternative, that a displacement has or has not occurred, and it may here be noted that this alternative enables us to explain the contrasts of the dream quite as readily as the medical theory of the dream explains the series of states from the partial to the complete waking of the brain cells.

In considering this series of sources we note further that the psychologically significant but not recent element (a train of thought, a recollection) may be replaced for the purposes of dream-formation by a recent but psychologically indifferent element, provided the two following conditions are fulfilled: (1) the dream-content preserves a connection with things recently experienced; (2) the dream-stimulus is still a psychologically significant event. In one single case (a) both these conditions are fulfilled by the same impression. If we now consider that these same indifferent impressions, which are utilized for the dream as long as they are recent, lose this qualification as soon as they are a day (or at most several days) older, we are obliged to assume that

---

[6] The dream of the botanical monograph.
[7] The dreams of my patients during analysis are mostly of this kind.

the very freshness of an impression gives it a certain psychological value for dream-formation, somewhat equivalent to the value of emotionally accentuated memories or trains of thought. Later on, in the light of certain Psychological considerations, we shall be able to divine the explanation of this importance of recent impressions in dream formation.[8]

Incidentally our attention is here called to the fact that at night, and unnoticed by our consciousness, important changes may occur in the material comprised by our ideas and memories. The injunction that before making a final decision in any matter one should sleep on it for a night is obviously fully justified. But at this point we find that we have passed from the psychology of dreaming to the psychology of sleep, a step which there will often be occasion to take.

At this point there arises an objection which threatens to invalidate the conclusions at which we have just arrived. If indifferent impressions can find their way into the dream only so long as they are of recent origin, how does it happen that in the dream-content we find elements also from earlier periods of our lives, which, at the time when they were still recent, possessed, as Strumpell puts it, no psychic value, and which, therefore, ought to have been forgotten long ago; elements, that is, which are neither fresh nor psychologically significant?

This objection can be disposed of completely if we have recourse to the results of the psychoanalysis of neurotics. The solution is as follows: The process of shifting and rearrangement which replaces material of psychic significance by material which is indifferent (whether one is dreaming or thinking) has already taken place in these earlier periods of life, and has since become fixed in the memory. Those elements which were originally indifferent are in fact no longer so, since they have acquired the value of psychologically significant material. That which has actually remained indifferent can never be reproduced in the dream.

---

[8] Cf. Chap. VII on "transference."

From the foregoing exposition the reader may rightly conclude that I assert that there are no indifferent dream-stimuli, and therefore no guileless dreams. This I absolutely and unconditionally believe to be the case, apart from the dreams of children, and perhaps the brief dream-reactions to nocturnal sensations. Apart from these exceptions, whatever one dreams is either plainly recognizable as being psychically significant, or it is distorted and can be judged correctly only after complete interpretation, when it proves, after all, to be of psychic significance. The dream never concerns itself with trifles; we do not allow sleep to be disturbed by trivialities.[9] Dreams which are apparently guileless turn out to be the reverse of innocent, if one takes the trouble to interpret them; if I may be permitted the expression, they ail show "the mark of the beast." Since this is another point on which I may expect contradiction, and since I am glad of an opportunity to show dream-distortion at work, I shall here subject to analysis a number of guileless dreams from my collection.

I

An intelligent and refined young woman, who in real life is distinctly reserved, one of those people of whom one says that "still waters run deep," relates the following dream: "I dreamt that I arrived at the market too late, and could get nothing from either the butcher or the greengrocer woman." Surely a guileless dream, but as it has not the appearance of a real dream I induce her to relate it in detail. Her report then runs as follows: She goes to the market with her cook, who carries the basket. The butcher tells her, after she has asked him for something: "That is no longer to be obtained," and waits to give her something else, with the remark: "That is good, too." She refuses, and goes to the greengrocer woman. The latter tries to sell her a peculiar vegetable, which is bound up in bundles, and is black in colour. She says: "I don't know that, I won't take it."

---

[9] Havelock Ellis, a kindly critic of The Interpretation of Dreams, writes in The World of Dreams (p. 169): "From this point on, not many of us will be able to follow F." But Mr. Ellis has not undertaken any analyses of dreams, and will not believe how unjustifiable it is to judge them by the manifest dream-content. -

The connection of the dream with the preceding day is simple enough. She had really gone to the market too late, and had been unable to buy anything. The meatshop was already closed, comes into one's mind as a description of the experience. But wait, is not that a very vulgar phrase which- or rather, the opposite of which- denotes a certain neglect with regard to man's clothing? The dreamer has not used these words; she has perhaps avoided them: but let us look for the interpretation of the details contained in the dream.

When in a dream something has the character of a spoken utterance- that is, when it is said or heard, not merely thought, and the distinction can usually be made with certainty- then it originates in the utterances of waking life, which have, of course, been treated as raw material, dismembered, and slightly altered, and above all removed from their context.[10] In the work of interpretation we may take such utterances as our starting- point. Where, then, does the butcher's statement, That is no longer to be obtained, come from? From myself; I had explained to her some days previously "that the oldest experiences of childhood are no longer to be obtained as such, but will be replaced in the analysis by transferences and dreams." Thus, I am the butcher, and she refuses to accept these transferences to the present of old ways of thinking and feeling.

Where does her dream utterance, I don't know that, I won't take it, come from? For the purposes of the analysis this has to be dissected. I don't know that she herself had said to her cook, with whom she had a dispute on the previous day, but she had then added: Behave yourself decently.

Here a displacement is palpable; of the two sentences which she spoke to her cook, she included the insignificant one in her dream; but the suppressed sentence, Behave yourself decently! alone fits in with the rest of the dream-content. One might use the words to a man who was making indecent overtures, and had

---

[10] Cf. what is said of speech in dreams in the chapter on "The Dream-Work." Only one of the writers on the subject- Delboeuf- seems to have recognized the origin of the speeches heard in dreams; he compares them with cliches.

neglected "to close his meat-shop." That we have really hit upon the trail of the interpretation is proved by its agreement with the allusions made by the incident with the greengrocer woman. A vegetable which is sold tied up in bundles (a longish vegetable, as she subsequently adds), and is also black: what can this be but a dream-combination of asparagus and black radish? I need not interpret asparagus to the initiated; and the other vegetable, too (think of the exclamation: "Blacky, save yourself!"), seems to me to point to the sexual theme at which we guessed in the beginning, when we wanted to replace the story of the dream by "the meat-shop is closed." We are not here concerned with the full meaning of the dream; so much is certain, that it is full of meaning and by no means guileless.[11]

II

Another guileless dream of the same patient, which in some respects is a pendant to the above. Her husband asks her: "Oughtn't we to have the piano tuned?" She replies: "It's not worth while, the hammers would have to be rebuffed as well." Again we have the reproduction of an actual event of the preceding day. Her husband had asked her such a question, and she had answered it in such words. But what is the meaning of her dreaming it? She says of the piano that it is a disgusting old box which has a bad tone; it belonged to her husband before they were married,[12] etc., but the key to the true solution lies in the phrase: It isn't worth while. This has its origin in a call paid yesterday to a woman friend. She was asked to take off her coat, but declined, saying: "Thanks, it isn't worth while, I must go in

---

[11] For the curious, I may remark that behind the dream there is hidden a phantasy of indecent, sexually provoking conduct on my part, and of repulsion on the part of the lady. If this interpretation should seem preposterous, I would remind the reader of the numerous cases in which physicians have been made the object of such charges by hysterical women, with whom the same phantasy has not appeared in a distorted form as a dream, but has become undisguisedly conscious and delusional. With this dream the patient began her psycho-analytical treatment. It was only later that I learned that with this dream she repeated the initial trauma in which her neurosis originated, and since then I have noticed the same behaviour in other persons who in their childhood were victims of sexual attacks, and now, as it were, wish in their dreams for them to be repeated.

[12] A substitution by the opposite, as will be clear after analysis.

a moment." At this point I recall that yesterday, during the analysis, she suddenly took hold of her coat, of which a button had come undone. It was as though she meant to say: "Please don't look in, it isn't worth while." Thus box becomes chest, and the interpretation of the dream leads to the years when she was growing out of her childhood, when she began to be dissatisfied with her figure. It leads us back, indeed, to earlier periods, if we take into consideration the disgusting and the bad tone, and remember how often in allusions and in dreams the two small hemispheres of the female body take the place- as a substitute and an antithesis- of the large ones.

III

I will interrupt the analysis of this dreamer in order to insert a short, innocent dream which was dreamed by a young man. He dreamt that he was putting on his winter overcoat again; this was terrible. The occasion for this dream is apparently the sudden advent of cold weather. On more careful examination we note that the two brief fragments of the dream do not fit together very well, for what could be terrible about wearing a thick or heavy coat in cold weather? Unfortunately for the innocency of this dream, the first association, under analysis, yields the recollection that yesterday a lady had confidentially confessed to him that her last child owed its existence to the splitting of a condom. He now reconstructs his thoughts in accordance with this suggestion: A thin condom is dangerous, a thick one is bad. The condom is a "pullover" (Ueberzieher = literally pullover), for it is pulled over something: and Uebersieher is the German term for a light overcoat. An experience like that related by the lady would indeed be terrible for an unmarried man.

We will now return to our other innocent dreamer.

IV

She puts a candle into a candlestick; but the candle is broken, so that it does not stand up. The girls at school say she is clumsy; but she replies that it is not her fault.

Here, too, there is an actual occasion for the dream; the day before she had actually put a candle into a candlestick; but this one was not broken.

An obvious symbolism has here been employed. The candle is an object which excites the female genitals; its being broken, so that it does not stand upright, signifies impotence on the man's part (it is not her fault). But does this young woman, carefully brought up, and a stranger to all obscenity, know of such an application of the candle? By chance she is able to tell how she came by this information. While paddling a canoe on the Rhine, a boat passed her which contained some students, who were singing rapturously, or rather yelling: "When the Queen of Sweden, behind closed shutters, with the candles of Apollo..."

She does not hear or else understand the last word. Her husband was asked to give her the required explanation. These verses are then replaced in the dream-content by the innocent recollection of a task which she once performed clumsily at her boarding-school, because of the closed shutters. The connection between the theme of masturbation and that of impotence is clear enough. Apollo in the latent dream-content connects this dream with an earlier one in which the virgin Pallas figured. All this is obviously not innocent.

V

Lest it may seem too easy a matter to draw conclusions from dreams concerning the dreamer's real circumstances, I add another dream originating with the same person, which once more appears innocent. "I dreamt of doing something," she relates, "which I actually did during the day, that is to say, I filled a little trunk so full of books that I had difficulty in closing it. My dream was just like the actual occurrence." Here the dreamer herself emphasizes the correspondence between the dream and the reality. All such criticisms of the dream, and comments on the dream, although they have found a place in the waking thoughts, properly belong to the latent dream-content, as further examples will confirm. We are told, then, that what the dream relates has actually occurred during the day. It would take us too far afield to show how we arrive at the idea of making use of the English language to help us in the interpretation of this dream. Suffice it to say that it is again a question of a little box (cf. chap. IV, the dream of the dead child in the box) which has been filled so full that nothing can go into it. In all these "innocent" dreams the sexual factor as the motive of the censorship is very prominent. But this is a subject of primary significance, which we must consider later.

B. Infantile Experiences as the Source of Dreams

As the third of the peculiarities of the dream-content, we have adduced the fact, in agreement with all other writers on the subject (excepting Robert), that impressions from our childhood may appear in dreams, which do not seem to be at the disposal of the waking memory. It is, of course, difficult to decide how seldom or how frequently this occurs, because after waking the origin of the respective elements of the dream is not recognized. The proof that we are dealing with impressions of our childhood must thus be adduced objectively, and only in rare instances do the conditions favour such proof. The story is told by A. Maury, as being particularly conclusive, of a man who decides to visit his birthplace after an absence of twenty years. On the night before his departure he dreams that he is in a totally unfamiliar locality, and that he there meets a strange man with whom he holds a conversation. Subsequently, upon his return home, he is able to convince himself that this strange locality really exists in the vicinity of his home, and the strange man in the dream turns out to be a friend of his dead father's, who is living in the town. This is, of course, a conclusive proof that in his childhood he had seen both the man and the locality. The dream, moreover, is to be interpreted as a dream of impatience, like the dream of the girl who carries in her pocket the ticket for a concert, the dream of the child whose father had promised him an excursion to the Hameau (ch. III), and so forth. The motives which reproduce just these impressions of childhood for the dreamer cannot, of course, be discovered without analysis.

One of my colleagues, who attended my lectures, and who boasted that his dreams were very rarely subject to distortion, told me that he had sometime previously seen, in a dream, his former tutor in bed with his nurse, who had remained in the household until his eleventh year. The actual location of this scene was realized even in the dream. As he was greatly interested, he related the dream to his elder brother, who laughingly confirmed its reality. The brother said that he remembered the affair very distinctly, for he was six years old at the time. The lovers were in the habit of making him, the elder boy, drunk with beer whenever circumstances were favourable to their nocturnal intercourse. The younger child, our dreamer, at that time three years of age, slept in the same room as the nurse, but was not regarded as an obstacle.

In yet another case it may be definitely established, without the aid of dream-interpretation, that the dream contains elements from childhoodnamely, if the dream is a so-called perennial dream, one which, being first dreamt in childhood, recurs again and again in adult years. I may add a few examples of this sort to those already known, although I have no personal knowledge of perennial dreams. A physician, in his thirties, tells me that a yellow lion, concerning which he is able to give the precisest information, has often appeared in his dream-life, from his earliest childhood up to the present day. This lion, known to him from his dreams, was one day discovered in natura, as a longforgotten china animal. The young man then learned from his mother that the lion had been his favourite toy in early childhood, a fact which he himself could no longer remember.

If we now turn from the manifest dream-content to the dreamthoughts which are revealed only on analysis, the experiences of childhood may be found to recur even in dreams whose content would not have led us to suspect anything of the sort. I owe a particularly delightful and instructive example of such a dream to my esteemed colleague of the "yellow lion." After reading Nansen's account of his polar expedition, he dreamt that he was giving the intrepid explorer electrical treatment on an ice-floe for the sciatica of which the latter complained! During the analysis of this dream he remembered an incident of his childhood, without which the dream would be wholly unintelligible. When he was three or four years of age he was one day listening attentively to the conversation of his elders; they were talking of exploration, and he presently asked his father whether exploration was a bad illness. He had apparently confounded Reisen (journey, trips) with Reissen (gripes, tearing pains), and the derision of his brothers and sisters prevented his ever forgetting the humiliating experience.

We have a precisely similar case when, in the analysis of the dream of the monograph on the genus cyclamen, I stumble upon a memory, retained from childhood, to the effect that when I was five years old my father allowed me to destroy a book embellished with coloured plates. It will perhaps be doubted whether this recollection really entered into the composition of the dream content, and it may be suggested that the connection was established subsequently by the analysis. But the abundance and intricacy of the associative connections vouch for the truth of my explanation: cyclamen- favourite flower- favourite dish- artichoke; to pick to pieces like an artichoke, leaf by leaf (a phrase which at that time one heard daily, a propos of the dividing up of the Chinese empire); herbarium- bookworm, whose favourite food is books. I can further assure the reader that the ultimate meaning of the dream, which I have not given here, is most intimately connected with the content of the scene of childish destruction.

In another series of dreams we learn from analysis that the very wish which has given rise to the dream, and whose fulfilment the dream proves to

be, has itself originated in childhood, so that one is astonished to find that the child with all his impulses survives in the dream.

I shall now continue the interpretation of a dream which has already proved instructive: I refer to the dream in which my friend R is my uncle. We have carried its interpretation far enough for the wish-motive- the wish to be appointed professor- to assert itself palpably; and we have explained the affection felt for my friend R in the dream as the outcome of opposition to, and defiance of, the two colleagues who appear in the dreamthoughts. Thee dream was my own; I may, therefore, continue the analysis by stating that I did not feel quite satisfied with the solution arrived at. I knew that my opinion of these colleagues. who were so badly treated in my dream-thoughts, would have been expressed in very different language in my waking life; the intensity of the wish that I might not share their fate as regards the appointment seemed to me too slight fully to account for the discrepancy between my dream- opinion and my waking opinion. If the desire to be addressed by another title were really so intense, it would be proof of a morbid ambition, which I do not think I cherish, and which I believe I was far from entertaining. I do not know how others who think they know me would judge me; perhaps I really was ambitious; but if I was, my ambition has long since been transferred to objects other than the rank and title of Professor extraordinarius.

Whence, then, the ambition which the dream has ascribed to me? Here I am reminded of a story which I heard often in my childhood, that at my birth an old peasant woman had prophesied to my happy mother (whose first-born I was) that she had brought a great man into the world. Such prophecies must be made very frequently; there are so many happy and expectant mothers, and so many old peasant women, and other old women who, since their mundane powers have deserted them, turn their eyes toward the future; and the prophetess is not likely to suffer for her prophecies. Is it possible that my thirst for greatness has originated from this source? But here I recollect an impression from the later years of my childhood, which might serve even better as an explanation. One evening, at a restaurant on the Prater, where my parents were accustomed to take me when I was eleven or twelve years of age, we noticed a man who was going from table to table and, for a small sum, improvising verses upon any subject that was given him. I was sent to bring the poet to our table, and he showed his gratitude. Before asking for a subject he threw off a few rhymes about myself, and told us that if he could trust his inspiration I should probably one day become a minister. I can still distinctly remember the impression produced by this second prophecy. It was in the days of the "bourgeois Ministry"; my father had recently brought home the portraits of the bourgeois university graduates, Herbst, Giskra, Unger, Berger and others, and we illuminated the house in their honour. There were even Jews among them; so that every diligent Jewish schoolboy carried a ministerial portfolio in his satchel. The impression of that time must be responsible for the fact that until shortly before I went to the university I wanted to study jurisprudence, and changed my mind only at the last moment. A medical man has no chance of becoming a minister. And now for my dream: It is only now that I begin to see that it translates me from the sombre present to the hopeful days of the bourgeois Ministry, and completely fulfils what was then my youthful ambition. In treating my two estimable and learned colleagues, merely because they are Jews, so badly, one as though he were a simpleton and the other as though he were a criminal, I am acting as though I were the Minister; I have put myself in his place. What a revenge I take upon his Excellency! He refuses to appoint me Professor extraordinarius, and so in my dream I put myself in his place.

In another case I note the fact that although the wish that excites the dream is a contemporary wish it is nevertheless greatly reinforced by memories of childhood. I refer to a series of dreams which are based on the longing to go to Rome. For a long time to come I shall probably have to satisfy this longing by means of dreams, since, at the season of the year when I should be able to travel, Rome is to be avoided for reasons of health.[13] Thus I once dreamt that I saw the Tiber and the bridge of Sant' Angelo from the window of a railway carriage; presently the train started, and I realized that I had never entered the city at all. The view that appeared in the dream was modelled after a well-known

---

[13] I long ago learned that the fulfilment of such wishes only called for a little courage, and I then became a zealous pilgrim to Rome. -

engraving which I had casually noticed the day before in the drawing-room of one of my patients. In another dream someone took me up a hill and showed me Rome half shrouded in mist, and so distant that I was astonished at the distinctness of the view. The content of this dream is too rich to be fully reported here. The motive, "to see the promised land afar," is here easily recognizable. The city which I thus saw in the mist is Lubeck; the original of the hill is the Gleichenberg. In a third dream I am at last in Rome. To my disappointment the scenery is anything but urban: it consists of a little stream of black water, on one side of which are black rocks, while on the other are meadows with large white flowers. I notice a certain Herr Zucker (with whom I am superficially acquainted), and resolve to ask him to show me the way into the city. It is obvious that I am trying in vain to see in my dream a city which I have never seen in my waking life. If I resolve the landscape into its elements, the white flowers point to Ravenna, which is known to me, and which once, for a time, replaced Rome as the capital of Italy. In the marshes around Ravenna we had found the most beautiful water-lilies in the midst of black pools of water; the dream makes them grow in the meadows, like the narcissi of our own Aussee, because we found it so troublesome to cull them from the water. The black rock so close to the water vividly recalls the valley of the Tepl at Karlsbad. Karlsbad now enables me to account for the peculiar circumstance that I ask Herr Zucker to show me the way. In the material of which the dream is woven I am able to recognize two of those amusing Jewish anecdotes which conceal such profound and, at times, such bitter worldly wisdom, and which we are so fond of quoting in our letters and conversation. One is the story of the constitution; it tells how a poor Jew sneaks into the Karlsbad express without a ticket; how he is detected, and is treated more and more harshly by the conductor at each succeeding call for tickets; and how, when a friend whom he meets at one of the stations during his miserable journey asks him where he is going, he answers: "To Karlsbad- if my constitution holds out." Associated in memory with this is another story about a Jew who is ignorant of French, and who has express instructions to ask in Paris for the Rue Richelieu. Paris was for many years the goal of my own longing, and I regarded the satisfaction with which I first set foot on the pavements of Paris as a warrant that I should attain to the fulfilment of other wishes also. Moreover, asking the way is a direct allusion to Rome, for, as we know, "all roads lead to Rome." And further, the name Zucker (sugar) again points to Karlsbad, whither we send persons afflicted with the constitutional disease, diabetes (Zuckerkrankheit, sugardisease.) The occasion for this dream was the proposal of my Berlin friend that we should meet in Prague at Easter. A further association with sugar and diabetes might be found in the matters which I had to discuss with him. -

A fourth dream, occurring shortly after the last-mentioned, brings me back to Rome. I see a street corner before me, and am astonished that so many German placards should be posted there. On the previous day, when writing to my friend, I had told him, with truly prophetic vision, that Prague would probably not be a comfortable place for German travellers. The dream, therefore, expressed simultaneously the wish to meet him in Rome instead of in the Bohemian capital, and the desire, which probably originated during my student days, that the German language might be accorded more tolerance in Prague. As a matter of fact, I must have understood the Czech language in the first years of my childhood, for I was born in a small village in Moravia, amidst a Slav population. A Czech nursery rhyme, which I heard in my seventeenth year, became, without effort on my part, so imprinted upon my memory that I can repeat it to this day, although I have no idea of its meaning. Thus in these dreams also there is no lack of manifold relations to the impressions of my early childhood.

During my last Italian journey, which took me past Lake Trasimenus, I at length discovered, after I had seen the Tiber, and had reluctantly turned back some fifty miles from Rome, what a reinforcement my longing for the Eternal City had received from the impressions of my childhood. I had just conceived a plan of travelling to Naples via Rome the following year when this sentence, which I must have read in one of our German classics, occurred to me:[14] "It is a question which of the two paced to and fro in his room the more impatiently after he had conceived the plan of going to Rome- Assistant Headmaster Winckelmann or the great General Hannibal." I myself had walked in Hannibal's footsteps; like him I was destined never to see Rome, and he too had gone to Campania when all were expecting him in Rome. Hannibal, with whom I had achieved this point of similarity, had been my favourite hero during my years at the Gymnasium; like so many boys of my age, I bestowed my sympathies in the Punic war not on the Romans, but on the Carthaginians. Moreover, when I finally came to realize the consequences of belonging to an alien race, and was forced by the anti-Semitic feeling among my classmates to take a definite stand, the figure of the Semitic commander assumed still greater proportions in my imagination. Hannibal and Rome symbolized, in my youthful eyes, the struggle between the tenacity of the Jews and the organization of the Catholic Church. The significance for our emotional life which the anti-Semitic movement has since assumed helped to fix the thoughts and impressions of those earlier days. Thus the desire to go to Rome has in my dream- life become the mask and symbol for a number of warmly cherished wishes, for whose realization one had to work with the tenacity and single-mindedness of the Punic general, though their fulfilment at times seemed as remote as Hannibal's life-long wish to enter Rome. - And now, for the first time, I happened upon the youthful experience which even to-day still expresses its power in all these emotions and dreams. I might have been ten or twelve years old when my father began to take me with him on his walks, and in his conversation to reveal his views on the things of this world. Thus it was that he once told me the following incident, in order to show me that I had been born into happier times than he: "When I was a young man, I was walking one Saturday along the street in the village where you were born; I was well-

---

[14] The writer in whose works I found this passage was probably Jean Paul Richter.

dressed, with a new fur cap on my head. Up comes a Christian, who knocks my cap into the mud, and shouts, 'Jew, get off the pavement!'"- "And what did you do?"- "I went into the street and picked up the cap," he calmly replied. That did not seem heroic on the part of the big, strong man who was leading me, a little fellow, by the hand. I contrasted this situation, which did not please me, with another, more in harmony with my sentimentsthe scene in which Hannibal's father, Hamilcar Barcas, made his son swear before the household altar to take vengeance on the Romans.[15] Ever since then Hannibal has had a place in my phantasies.

I think I can trace my enthusiasm for the Carthaginian general still further back into my childhood, so that it is probably only an instance of an already established emotional relation being transferred to a new vehicle. One of the first books which fell into my childish hands after I learned to read was Thiers' Consulate and Empire. I remember that I pasted on the flat backs of my wooden soldiers little labels bearing the names of the Imperial marshals, and that at that time Massena (as a Jew, Menasse) was already my avowed favourite.[16] This preference is doubtless also to be explained by the fact of my having been born, a hundred years later, on the same date. Napoleon himself is associated with Hannibal through the crossing of the Alps. And perhaps the development of this martial ideal may be traced yet farther back, to the first three years of my childhood, to wishes which my alternately friendly and hostile relations with a boy a year older than myself must have evoked in the weaker of the two playmates.

The deeper we go into the analysis of dreams, the more often are we put on the track of childish experiences which play the part of dream-sources in the latent dream-content.

We have learned that dreams very rarely reproduce memories in such a manner as to constitute, unchanged and unabridged, the sole manifest dream-content. Nevertheless, a few authentic

---

[15] In the first edition of this book I gave here the name "Hasdrubal," an amazing error, which I explained in my Psycho pathology of Everyday Life.
[16] The Jewish descent of the Marshal is somewhat doubtful.

examples which show such reproduction have been recorded, and I can add a few new ones, which once more refer to scenes of childhood. In the case of one of my patients a dream once gave a barely distorted reproduction of a sexual incident, which was immediately recognized as an accurate recollection. The memory of it had never been completely lost in the waking life, but it had been greatly obscured, and it was revivified by the previous work of analysis. The dreamer had at the age of twelve visited a bedridden schoolmate, who had exposed himself, probably only by a chance movement in bed. At the sight of the boy's genitals he was seized by a kind of compulsion, exposed himself, and took hold of the member of the other boy who, however, looked at him in surprise and indignation, whereupon he became embarrassed and let it go. A dream repeated this scene twenty-three years later, with all the details of the accompanying emotions, changing it, however, in this respect, that the dreamer played the passive instead of the active role, while the person of the schoolmate was replaced by a contemporary.

As a rule, of course, a scene from childhood is represented in the manifest dream-content only by an allusion, and must be disentangled from the dream by interpretation. The citation of examples of this kind cannot be very convincing, because any guarantee that they are really experiences of childhood is lacking; if they belong to an earlier period of life, they are no longer recognized by our memory. The conclusion that such childish experiences recur at all in dreams is justified in psychoanalytic work by a great number of factors, which in their combined results appear to be sufficiently reliable. But when, for the purposes of dream-interpretation, such references to childish experiences are torn out of their context, they may not perhaps seem very impressive, especially where I do not even give all the material upon which the interpretation is based. However, I shall not let this deter me from giving a few examples.

I

With one of my female patients all dreams have the character of hurry; she is hurrying so as to be in time, so as not to miss her train, and so on. In one dream she has to visit a girl friend; her mother had told her to ride and not walk; she runs, however, and keeps on calling. The material that emerged in the analysis allowed one to recognize a memory of childish romping, and, especially for one dream, went back to the popular childish game of rapidly repeating the words of a sentence as though it was all one word. All these harmless jokes with little friends were remembered because they replaced other less harmless ones.[17]

II

The following dream was dreamed by another female patient: *She is in a large room in which there are all sorts of machines; it is rather like what she would imagine an orthopaedic institute to be. She hears that I am pressed for time, and that she must undergo treatment along with five others.*

But she resists, and is unwilling to lie down on the bed- or whatever it is- which is intended for her. She stands in a corner, and waits for me to say "It is not true." The others, meanwhile, laugh at her, saying it is all foolishness on her part. At the same time, it is as though she were called upon to make a number of little squares.

The first part of the content of this dream is an allusion to the treatment and to the transference to myself. The second contains an allusion to a scene of childhood; the two portions are connected by the mention of the bed. The orthopaedic institute is an allusion to one of my talks, in which I compared the treatment, with regard to its duration and its nature. to an orthopaedic treatment. At the beginning of the treatment I had to tell her that for the present I had little time to give her, but that later on I would devote a whole hour to her daily. This aroused in her the old sensitiveness, which is a leading characteristic of children who are destined to become hysterical. Their desire for love is insatiable. My patient was the youngest of six brothers and sisters (hence,

---

[17] In the original this paragraph contains many plays on the word Hetz (hurry, chase, scurry, game, etc.).- TR.

with five others), and as such her father's favourite, but in spite of this she seems to have felt that her beloved father devoted far too little time and attention to her. Her waiting for me to say It is not trite was derived as follows: A little tailor's apprentice had brought her a dress, and she had given him the money for it. Then she asked her husband whether she would have to pay the money again if the boy were to lose it. To tease her, her husband answered "Yes" (the teasing in the dream), and she asked again and again, and waited for him to say "It is not true." The thought of the latent dream-content may now be construed as follows: Will she have to pay me double the amount when I devote twice as much time to her?- a thought which is stingy or filthy (the uncleanliness of childhood is often replaced in dreams by greed for money; the word filthy here supplies the bridge). If all the passage referring to her waiting until I say It is not true is intended in the dream as a circumlocution for the word dirty, the standing-in-the-corner and not lying-down-on-the-bed are in keeping with this word, as component parts of a scene of her childhood in which she had soiled her bed, in punishment for which she was put into the corner, with a warning that papa would not love her any more, whereupon her brothers and sisters laughed at her, etc. The little squares refer to her young niece, who showed her the arithmetical trick of writing figures in nine squares (I think) in such a way that on being added together in any direction they make fifteen.

III

Here is a man's dream: He sees two boys tussling with each other; they are cooper's boys, as he concludes from the tools which are lying about; one of the boys has thrown the other down; the prostrate boy is wearing ear-rings with blue stones. He runs towards the assailant with lifted cane, in order to chastise him. The boy takes refuge behind a woman, as though she were his mother, who is standing against a wooden fence. She is the wife of a day-labourer, and she turns her back to the man who is dreaming. Finally she turns about and stares at him with a horrible look, so that he runs away in terror; the red flesh of the lower lid seems to stand out from her eyes. This dream has made abundant use of trivial occurrences from the previous day, in the course of which he actually saw two boys in the street, one of whom threw the other down. When he walked up to them in order to settle the quarrel, both of them took to their heels. Cooper's boys- this is explained only by a subsequent dream, in the analysis of which he used the proverbial expression: "To knock the bottom out of the barrel." Ear-rings with blue stones, according to his observation, are worn chiefly by prostitutes. This suggests a familiar doggerel rhyme about two boys: "The other boy was called Marie": that is, he was a girl. The woman standing by the fence: after the scene with the two boys he went for a walk along the bank of the Danube and, taking advantage of being alone, urinated against a wooden fence. A little farther on a respectably dressed, elderly lady smiled at him very pleasantly and wanted to hand him her card with her address.

Since, in the dream, the woman stood as he had stood while urinating, there is an allusion to a woman urinating, and this explains the horrible look and the prominence of the red flesh, which can only refer to the genitals gaping in a squatting posture; seen in childhood, they had appeared in later recollection as proud flesh, as a wound. The dream unites two occasions upon which, as a little boy, the dreamer was enabled to see the genitals of little girls, once by throwing the little girl down, and once while the child was urinating; and, as is shown by another association, he had retained in his memory the punishment administered or threatened by his father on account of these manifestations of sexual curiosity.

IV

A great mass of childish memories, which have been hastily combined into a phantasy, may be found behind the following dream of an elderly lady: She goes out in a hurry to do some shopping. On the Graben she sinks to her knees as though she had broken down. A number of people collect around her, especially cabdrivers, but no one helps her to get up. She makes many vain attempts; finally she must have succeeded, for she is put into a cab which is to take her home. A large, heavily laden basket (something like a market- basket) is thrown after her through the window.

This is the woman who is always harassed in her dreams; just as she used to be harassed when a child. The first situation of the dream is apparently taken from the sight of a fallen horse; just as broken down points to horse-racing. In her youth she was a rider; still earlier she was probably also a horse. With the idea of falling down is connected her first childish reminiscence of the seventeen-year-old son of the hall porter, who had an epileptic seizure in the street and was brought home in a cab. Of this, of course, she had only heard, but the idea of epileptic fits, of falling down, acquired a great influence over her phantasies, and later on influenced the form of her own hysterical attacks. When a person of the female sex dreams of falling, this almost always has a sexual significance; she becomes a fallen woman, and, for the purpose of the dream under consideration, this interpretation is probably the least doubtful, for she falls in the Graben, the street in Vienna which is known as the concourse of prostitutes. The market-basket admits of more than one interpretation; in the sense of refusal (German, Korb = basket = snub, refusal) it reminds her of the many snubs which she at first administered to her suitors and which, she thinks, she herself received later. This agrees with the detail: no one will help her up, which she herself interprets as being disdained. Further, the market-basket recalls phantasies which have already appeared in the course of analysis, in which she imagines that she has married far beneath her station and now goes to the market as a marketwoman.

Lastly, the market- basket might be interpreted as the mark of a servant. This suggests further memories of her childhood- of a cook who was discharged because she stole; she, too, sank to her knees and begged for mercy. The dreamer was at that time twelve years of age. Then emerges a recollection of a chamber-maid, who was dismissed because she had an affair with the coachman of the household, who, incidentally, married her afterwards. This recollection, therefore, gives us a clue to the cab-drivers in the dream (who, in opposition to the reality, do not stand by the fallen woman). But there still remains to be explained the throwing of the basket; in particular, why it is thrown through the window? This reminds her of the forwarding of luggage by rail, to the custom of Fensterln[18] in the country, and to trivial impressions of a summer resort, of a gentleman who threw some blue plums into the window of a lady's room, and of her little sister, who was frightened because an idiot who was passing looked in at the window. And now, from behind all this emerges an obscure recollection from her tenth year of a nurse in the country to whom one of the men-servants made love (and whose conduct the child may have noticed), and who was sent packing, thrown out, together with her lover (in the dream we have the expression: thrown into); an incident which we have been approaching by several other paths. The luggage or box of a servant is disparagingly described in Vienna as "seven plums." "Pack up your seven plums and get out!" -

My collection, of course, contains a plethora of such patients' dreams, the analysis of which leads back to impressions of childhood, often dating back to the first three years of life, which are remembered obscurely, or not at all. But it is a questionable proceeding to draw conclusions from these and apply them to dreams in general, for they are mostly dreams of neurotic, and especially hysterical, persons; and the part played in these dreams by childish scenes might be conditioned by the nature of the neurosis, and not by the nature of dreams in general. In the interpretation of my own dreams, however, which is assuredly not undertaken on account of grave symptoms of illness, it happens just as frequently that in the latent dreamcontent I am

---

[18] Fensterln is the custom, now falling into disuse, found in rural districts of the German Schwarzwald, of lovers who woo their sweethearts at their bedroom windows, to which they ascend by means of a ladder, enjoying such intimacy that the relation practically amounts to a trial marriage. The reputation of the young woman never suffers on account of Fensterln, unless she becomes intimate with too many suitors.- TR.

unexpectedly confronted with a scene of my childhood, and that a whole series of my dreams will suddenly converge upon the paths proceeding from a single childish experience. I have already given examples of this, and I shall give yet more in different connections. Perhaps I cannot close this chapter more fittingly than by citing several dreams of my own, in which recent events and longforgotten experiences of my childhood appear together as dream-sources.

I

After I have been travelling, and have gone to bed hungry and tired, the prime necessities of life begin to assert their claims in sleep, and I dream as follows: I go into a kitchen in order to ask for some pudding. There three women are standing, one of whom is the hostess; she is rolling something in her hands, as though she were making dumplings. She replies that I must wait until she has finished (not distinctly as a speech). I become impatient, and go away affronted. I want to put on an overcoat; but the first I try on is too long. I take it off, and am somewhat astonished to find that it is trimmed with fur. A second coat has a long strip of cloth with a Turkish design sewn into it. A stranger with a long face and a short, pointed beard comes up and prevents me from putting it on, declaring that it belongs to him. I now show him that it is covered all over with Turkish embroideries. He asks: "How do the Turkish (drawings, strips of cloth...) concern you?" But we soon become quite friendly.

In the analysis of this dream I remember, quite unexpectedly, the first novel which I ever read, or rather, which I began to read from the end of the first volume, when I was perhaps thirteen years of age. I have never learned the name of the novel, or that of its author, but the end remains vividly in my memory. The hero becomes insane, and continually calls out the names of the three women who have brought the greatest happiness and the greatest misfortune into his life. Pelagie is one of these names. I still do not know what to make of this recollection during the analysis. Together with the three women there now emerge the three Parcae, who spin the fates of men, and I know that one of the three women, the hostess in the dream, is the mother who gives life, and who, moreover, as in my own case, gives the child its first nourishment. Love and hunger meet at the mother's breast. A young man- so runs an anecdote- who became a great admirer of womanly beauty, once observed, when the conversation turned upon the handsome wet-nurse who had suckled him as a child, that he was sorry that he had not taken better advantage of his opportunities. I am in the habit of using the anecdote to elucidate the factor of retrospective tendencies in the mechanism of the psychoneuroses.

One of the Parcae, then, is rubbing the palms of her hands together, as though she were making dumplings. A strange occupation for one of the Fates, and urgently in need of explanation! This explanation is furnished by another and earlier memory of my childhood. When I was six years old, and receiving my first lessons from my mother, I was expected to believe that we are made of dust, and must, therefore, return to dust. But this did not please me, and I questioned the doctrine. Thereupon my mother rubbed the palms of her hands together-just as in making dumplings, except that there was no dough between them- and showed me the blackish scales of epidermis which were thus rubbed off, as a proof that it is of dust that we are made. Great was my astonishment at this demonstration ad oculos, and I acquiesced in the idea which I was later to hear expressed in the words: "Thou owest nature a death."[19] Thus the women to whom I go in the kitchen, as I so often did in my childhood when I was hungry and my mother, sitting by the fire, admonished me to wait until lunch was ready, are really the Parcae. And now for the dumplings! At least one of my teachers at the University- the very one to whom I am indebted for my histological knowledge (epidermis)- would be reminded by the name Knodl (Knodl means dumpling), of a person whom he

---

[19] Both the affects pertaining to these childish scenes- astonishment and resignation to the inevitable- appeared in a dream of slightly earlier date, which first reminded me of this incident of my childhood.

had to prosecute for plagiarizing his writings. Committing a plagiarism, taking anything one can lay hands on, even though it belongs to another, obviously leads to the second part of the dream, in which I am treated like the overcoat thief who for some time plied his trade in the lecture halls. I have written the word plagiarism- without definite intention- because it occurred to me, and now I see that it must belong to the latent dream-content and that it will serve as a bridge between the different parts of the manifest dream-content. The chain of associations- Pelagie- plagiarism- plagiostomi[20] (sharks)- fish-bladder- connects the old novel with the affair of Knodl and the overcoats (German: Uberzieher = pullover, overcoat or condom), which obviously refer to an appliance appertaining to the technique of sex. This, it is true, is a very forced and irrational connection, but it is nevertheless one which I could not have established in waking life if it had not already been established by the dream-work. Indeed, as though nothing were sacred to this impulse to enforce associations, the beloved name, Brucke (bridge of words, see above), now serves to remind me of the very institute in which I spent my happiest hours as a student, wanting for nothing. "So will you at the breasts of Wisdom every day more pleasure find"), in the most complete contrast to the desires which plague me (German: plagen) while I dream. And finally, there emerges the recollection of another dear teacher, whose name once more sounds like something edible (Fleischl- Fleisch = meat- like Knodl = dumplings), and of a pathetic scene in which the scales of epidermis play a part (mother- hostess), and mental derangement (the novel), and a remedy from the Latin pharmacopeia (Kuche = kitchen) which numbs the sensation of hunger, namely, cocaine.

In this manner I could follow the intricate trains of thought still farther, and could fully elucidate that part of the dream which is lacking in the analysis; but I must refrain, because the personal sacrifice which this would involve is too great. I shall take up only one of the threads, which will serve to lead us directly to

---

[20] I do not bring in the plagiostomi arbitrarily; they recall a painful incident of disgrace before the same teacher.

one of the dream-thoughts that lie at the bottom of the medley. The stranger with the long face and pointed beard, who wants to prevent me from putting on the overcoat, has the features of a tradesman of Spalato, of whom my wife bought a great deal of Turkish cloth. His name was Popovic, a suspicious name, which even gave the humorist Stettenheim a pretext for a suggestive remark: "He told me his name, and blushingly shook my hand."[21] For the rest, I find the same misuse of names as above in the case of Pelagie, Knodl, Brucke, Fleischl.

No one will deny that such playing with names is a childish trick; if I indulge in it the practice amounts to an act of retribution, for my own name has often enough been the subject of such feeble attempts at wit. Goethe once remarked how sensitive a man is in respect to his name, which he feels that he fills even as he fills his skin; Herder having written the following lines on his name:

Der du von Gottern abstammst, von Gothen oder vom Kote.

So seid ihr Gotterbilder auch zu Staub. -

[Thou who art born of the gods, of the Goths, or of the mud. Thus are thy godlike images even dust.]

I realize that this digression on the misuse of names was intended merely to justify this complaint. But here let us stop.... The purchase at Spalato reminds me of another purchase at Cattaro, where I was too cautious, and missed the opportunity of making an excellent bargain. (Missing an opportunity at the breast of the wet-nurse; see above.) One of the dream-thoughts occasioned by the sensation of hunger really amounts to this:

We should let nothing escape; we should take what we can get, even if we do a little wrong; we should never let an opportunity go by; life is so short, and death inevitable. Because this is meant even sexually, and because desire is unwilling to check itself before the thought of doing wrong, this philosophy of carpe diem has reason to fear the censorship, and must conceal

---

[21] Popo = "backside," in German nursery language.

itself behind a dream. And so all sorts of counter-thoughts find expression, with recollections of the time when spiritual nourishment alone was sufficient for the dreamer, with hindrances of every kind and even threats of disgusting sexual punishments.

II

A second dream requires a longer preliminary statement:

I had driven to the Western Station in order to start on a holiday trip to the Aussee, but I went on to the platform in time for the Ischl train, which leaves earlier. There I saw Count Thun, who was again going to see the Emperor at Ischl. In spite of the rain he arrived in an open carriage, came straight through the entrance-gate for the local trains, and with a curt gesture and not a word of explanation he waved back the gatekeeper, who did not know him and wanted to take his ticket. After he had left in the Ischl train, I was asked to leave the platform and return to the waitingroom; but after some difficulty I obtained permission to remain. I passed the time noting how many people bribed the officials to secure a compartment; I fully intended to make a complaint- that is, to demand the same privilege. Meanwhile I sang something to myself, which I afterwards recognized as the aria from The Marriage of Figaro: -

If my lord Count would tread a measure, tread a measure, Let him but say his pleasure, And I will play the tune.

(Possibly another person would not have recognized the tune.) The whole evening I was in a high-spirited, pugnacious mood; I chaffed the waiter and the cab-driver, I hope without hurting their feelings; and now all kinds of bold and revolutionary thoughts came into my mind, such as would fit themselves to the words of Figaro, and to memories of Beaumarchais' comedy, of which I had seen a performance at the Comedie Francaise.

The speech about the great men who have taken the trouble to be born; the seigneurial right which Count Almaviva wishes to exercise with regard to Susanne; the jokes which our malicious Opposition journalists make on the name of Count Thun

(German, thun = do), calling him Graf Nichtsthun, Count-Do-Nothing. I really do not envy him; he now has a difficult audience with the Emperor before him, and it is I who am the real Count-Do-Nothing, for I am going off for a holiday. I make all sorts of amusing plans for the vacation. Now a gentleman arrives whom I know as a Government representative at the medical examinations, and who has won the flattering nickname of "the Governmental bed-fellow" (literally, by-sleeper) by his activities in this capacity. By insisting on his official status he secured half a first-class compartment, and I heard one guard say to another: "Where are we going to put the gentleman with the first-class half-compartment?" A pretty sort of favouritism! I am paying for a whole first-class compartment. I did actually get a whole compartment to myself, but not in a through carriage, so there was no lavatory at my disposal during the night. My complaints to the guard were fruitless; I revenged myself by suggesting that at least a hole be made in the floor of this compartment, to serve the possible needs of passengers. At a quarter to three in the morning I wake, with an urgent desire to urinate, from the following dream:

A crowd, a students' meeting.... A certain Count (Thun or Taaffe) is making a speech. Being asked to say something about the Germans, he declares, with a contemptuous gesture, that their favourite flower is coltsfoot, and he then puts into his buttonhole something like a torn leaf, really the crumpled skeleton of a leaf. I jump up, and I jump up,[22] but I am surprised at my implied attitude. Then, more indistinctly: It seems as though this were the vestibule (Aula); the exits are thronged, and one must escape. I make my way through a suite of handsomely appointed rooms, evidently ministerial apartments, with furniture of a colour between brown and violet, and at last I come to a corridor in which a housekeeper, a fat, elderly woman, is seated. I try to avoid speaking to her, but she apparently thinks I have a right to pass this way, because she asks whether she shall accompany me

---

[22] This repetition has crept into the text of the dream, apparently through absent-mindedness, and I have left it because analysis shows that it has a meaning. -

with the lamp. I indicate with a gesture, or tell her, that she is to remain standing on the stairs, and it seems to me that I am very clever, for after all I am evading detection. Now I am downstairs, and I find a narrow, steeply rising path, which I follow.

Again indistinctly: It is as though my second task were to get away from the city, just as my first was to get out of the building. I am riding in a one-horse cab, and I tell the driver to take me to a railway station. "I can't drive with you on the railway line itself," I say, when he reproaches me as though I had tired him out. Here it seems as though I had already made a journey in his cab which is usually made by rail. The stations are crowded; I am wondering whether to go to Krems or to Znaim, but I reflect that the Court will be there, and I decide in favour of Graz or some such place. Now I am seated in the railway carriage, which is rather like a tram, and I have in my buttonhole a peculiar long braided thing, on which are violet-brown violets of stiff material, which makes a great impression on people. Here the scene breaks off.

I am once more in front of the railway station, but I am in the company of an elderly gentleman. I think out a scheme for remaining unrecognized, but I see this plan already being carried out. Thinking and experiencing are here, as it were, the same thing. He pretends to be blind, at least in one eye, and I hold before him a male glass urinal (which we have to buy in the city, or have bought). I am thus a sick-nurse, and have to give him the urinal because he is blind. If the conductor sees us in this position, he must pass us by without drawing attention to us. At the same time the position of the elderly man, and his urinating organ, is plastically perceived. Then I wake with a desire to urinate.

The whole dream seems a sort of phantasy, which takes the dreamer back to the year of revolution, 1848, the memory of which had been revived by the jubilee of 1898, as well as by a little excursion to Wachau, on which I visited Emmersdorf, the refuge of the student leader Fischof,[23] to whom several features

---

[23] This is an error and not a slip, for I learned later that the Emmersdorf in Wachau is not identical with the refuge of the revolutionist Fischof, a place of the same name.

of the manifest dream-content might refer. The association of ideas then leads me to England, to the house of my brother, who used in jest to twit his wife with the title of Tennyson's poem *Fifty Years Ago*, whereupon the children were used to correct him: *Fifteen Years Ago*. This phantasy, however, which attaches itself to the thoughts evoked by the sight of Count Thun, is, like the facade of an Italian church, without organic connection with the structure behind it, but unlike such a facade it is full of gaps, and confused, and in many places portions of the interior break through. The first situation of the dream is made up of a number of scenes, into which I am able to dissect it. The arrogant attitude of the Count in the dream is copied from a scene at my school which occurred in my fifteenth year. We had hatched a conspiracy against an unpopular and ignorant teacher; the leading spirit in this conspiracy was a schoolmate who since that time seems to have taken Henry VIII of England as his model. It fell to me to carry out the coup d'etat, and a discussion of the importance of the Danube (German, Donau) to Austria (Wachau!) was the occasion of an open revolt. One of our fellow-conspirators was our only aristocratic schoolmate- he was called "the giraffe" on account of his conspicuous height- and while he was being reprimanded by the tyrant of the school, the professor of the German language, he stood just as the Count stood in the dream. The explanation of the favourite flower, and the putting into a button-hole of something that must have been a flower (which recalls the orchids which I had given that day to a friend, and also a rose of Jericho) prominently recalls the incident in Shakespeare's historical play which opens the civil wars of the Red and the White Roses; the mention of Henry VIII has paved the way to this reminiscence. Now it is not very far from roses to red and white carnations. (Meanwhile two little rhymes, the one German, the other Spanish, insinuate themselves into the analysis: Rosen, Tulpen, Nelken, alle Blumen welken,[24] and Isabelita, no llores, que se marchitan las flores.[25] The Spanish line occurs in Figaro.)

---

[24] Roses, tulips, and carnations, flowers all will wither.
[25] Do not cry, little Isabella because your flowers have faded.

Here in Vienna white carnations have become the badge of the Anti-Semites, red ones of the Social Democrats. Behind this is the recollection of an anti-Semitic challenge during a railway journey in beautiful Saxony (Anglo Saxon). The third scene contributing to the formation of the first situation in the dream dates from my early student days. There was a debate in a German students' club about the relation of philosophy to the general sciences. Being a green youth, full of materialistic doctrines, I thrust myself forward in order to defend an extremely one-sided position. Thereupon a sagacious older fellow-student, who has since then shown his capacity for leading men and organizing the masses, and who, moreover, bears a name belonging to the animal kingdom, rose and gave us a thorough dressing-down; he too, he said, had herded swine in his youth, and had then returned repentant to his father's house. I jumped up (as in the dream), became piggishly rude, and retorted that since I knew he had herded swine, I was not surprised at the tone of his discourse. (In the dream I am surprised at my German Nationalistic feelings.) There was a great commotion, and an almost general demand that I should retract my words, but I stood my ground. The insulted student was too sensible to take the advice which was offered him, that he should send me a challenge, and let the matter drop.

The remaining elements of this scene of the dream are of more remote origin. What does it mean that the Count should make a scornful reference to coltsfoot? Here I must question my train of associations. Coltsfoot (German: Huflattich), Lattice (lettuce), Salathund (the dog that grudges others what he cannot eat himself). Here plenty of opprobrious epithets may be discerned: Gir-affe (German: Affe = monkey, ape), pig, sow, dog; I might even arrive, by way of the name, at donkey, and thereby pour contempt upon an academic professor. Furthermore, I translate coltsfoot (Huflattich)- I do not know whether I do so correctly- by pisse-en-lit. I get this idea from Zola's Germinal, in which some children are told to bring some dandelion salad with them. The dog- chien- has a name sounding not unlike the verb for the major function (chier, as pisser stands for the minor one). Now we shall soon have the indecent in all its three physical categories, for in the same Germinal, which deals with the future revolution, there is a description of a very peculiar contest, which relates to the production of the gaseous excretions known as flatus.[26] And now I cannot but observe how the way to this flatus has been prepared a long while since, beginning with the flowers, and proceeding to the Spanish rhyme of Isabelita, to Ferdinand and Isabella, and, by way of Henry VIII, to English history at the time of the Armada, after the victorious termination of which the English struck a medal with the inscription: Flavit et dissipati sunt, for the storm had scattered the Spanish fleet.[27] I had thought of using this phrase, half jestingly, as the title of a chapter on "Therapy," if I should ever succeed in giving a detailed account of my conception and treatment of hysteria.

I cannot give so detailed an interpretation of the second scene of the dream, out of sheer regard for the censorship. For at this point I put myself in the place of a certain eminent gentleman of the revolutionary period, who had an adventure with an eagle (German: Adler) and who is said to have suffered from incontinence of the bowels, incontinentia and, etc.; and here I believe that I should not be justified in passing the censorship, even though it was an aulic councillor (aula, consiliarizis aulicus) who told me the greater part of this history. The suite of rooms in the dream is suggested by his Excellency's private saloon carriage, into which I was able to glance; but it means, as it so often does in dreams, a woman.[28]

The personality of the housekeeper is an ungrateful allusion to a witty old lady, which ill repays her for the good times and

---

[26] Not in Germinal, but in La Terre- a mistake of which I became aware only in the analysis. Here I would call attention to the identity of letters in Huflattich and Flatus.
[27] An unsolicited biographer, Dr. F. Wittels, reproaches me for having omitted the name of Jehovah from the above motto. The English medal contains the name of the Deity, in Hebrew letters, on the background of a cloud, and placed in such a manner that one may equally well regard it as part of the picture or as part of the inscription.
[28] Frauenzimmer, German, Zimmer-room, is appended to Frauen-woman, in order to imply a slight contempt.- TR.

the many good stories which I have enjoyed in her house. The incident of the lamp goes back to Grillparzer, who notes a charming experience of a similar nature, of which he afterwards made use in Hero and Leander (the waves of the sea and of love- the Armada and the storm).

I must forego a detailed analysis of the two remaining portions of the dream; I shall single out only those elements which lead me back to the two scenes of my childhood for the sake of which alone I have selected the dream. The reader will rightly assume that it is sexual material which necessitates the suppression; but he may not be content with this explanation. There are many things of which one makes no secret to oneself, but which must be treated as secrets in addressing others, and here we are concerned not with the reasons which induce me to conceal the solution, but with the motive of the inner censorship which conceals the real content of the dream even from myself. Concerning this, I will confess that the analysis reveals these three portions of the dream as impertinent boasting, the exuberance of an absurd megalomania, long ago suppressed in my waking life, which, however, dares to show itself, with individual ramifications, even in the manifest dream-content (it seems to me that I am a cunning fellow), making the high-spirited mood of the evening before the dream perfectly intelligible.

Boasting of every kind, indeed thus, the mention of Graz points to the phrase: "What price Graz?" which one is wont to use when one feels unusually wealthy. Readers who recall Master Rabelais's inimitable description of the life and deeds of Gargantua and his son Pantagruel will be able to enroll even the suggested content of the first portion of the dream among the boasts to which I have alluded. But the following belongs to the two scenes of childhood of which I have spoken: I had bought a new trunk for this journey, the colour of which, a brownish violet, appears in the dream several times (violet-brown violets of a stiff cloth, on an object which is known as a girl-catcher- the furniture in the ministerial chambers). Children, we know, believe that one attracts people's attention with anything new. Now I have been told of the following incident of my childhood; my recollection of the occurrence itself has been replaced by my recollection of the story. I am told that at the age of two I still used occasionally to wet my bed, and that when I was reproved for doing so I consoled my father by promising to buy him a beautiful new red bed in N (the nearest large town). Hence, the interpolation in the dream, that we had bought the urinal in the city or had to buy it; one must keep one's promises. (One should note, moreover, the association of the male urinal and the woman's trunk, box.) All the megalomania of the child is contained in this promise. The significance of dreams of urinary difficulties in the case of children has already been considered in the interpretation of an earlier dream (cf. the dream in chapter V., A.). The psycho-analysis of neurotics has taught us to recognize the intimate connection between wetting the bed and the character trait of ambition.

Then, when I was seven or eight years of age another domestic incident occurred which I remember very well. One evening, before going to bed, I had disregarded the dictates of discretion, and had satisfied my needs in my parents' bedroom, and in their presence. Reprimanding me for this delinquency, my father remarked: "That boy will never amount to anything." This must have been a terrible affront to my ambition, for allusions to this scene recur again and again in my dreams, and are constantly coupled with enumerations of my accomplishments and successes, as though I wanted to say: "You see, I have amounted to something after all." This childish scene furnishes the elements for the last image of the dream, in which the roles are interchanged, of course for the purpose of revenge. The elderly man obviously my father, for the blindness in one eye signifies his one-sided glaucoma,[29] is now urinating before me as I once urinated before him. By means of the glaucoma I remind my father of cocaine, which stood him in good stead during his operation, as though I had thereby fulfilled my promise. Besides, I make sport of him;

---

[29] Another interpretation: He is one-eyed like Odin, the father of the gods- Odin's consolation. The consolation in the childish scene: I will buy him a new bed.

since he is blind, I must hold the glass in front of him, and I delight in allusions to my knowledge of the theory of hysteria, of which I am proud.[30]

If the two childish scenes of urination are, according to my theory, closely associated with the desire for greatness, their resuscitation on the journey to the Aussee was further favoured by the accidental circumstance that my compartment had no lavatory, and that I must be prepared to postpone relief during the journey, as actually happened in the morning when I woke with the sensation of a bodily need. I suppose one might be inclined to credit this sensation with being the actual stimulus of the dream; I should, however, prefer a different explanation, namely, that the dream-thoughts first gave rise to the desire to

---

[30] Here is some more material for interpretation: Holding the urine-glass recalls the story of a peasant (illiterate) at the optician's, who tried on now one pair of spectacles, now another, but was still unable to read.- (Peasant-catcher- girl-catcher in the preceding portion of the dream.)- The peasants' treatment of the feeble-minded father in Zola's La Terre.- The tragic atonement, that in his last days my father soiled his bed like a child; hence, I am his nurse in the dream.- "Thinking and experiencing are here, as it were, identical"; this recalls a highly revolutionary closet drama by Oscar Panizza, in which God, the Father, is ignominiously treated as a palsied greybeard. With Him will and deed are one, and in the book he has to be restrained by His archangel, a sort of Ganymede, from scolding and swearing, because His curses would immediately be fulfilled.- Making plans is a reproach against my father, dating from a later period in the development of the critical faculty, much as the whole rebellious content of the dream, which commits lese majeste and scorns authority, may be traced to a revolt against my father. The sovereign is called the father of his country (Landesvater), and the father is the first and oldest, and for the child the only authority, from whose absolutism the other social authorities have evolved in the course of the history of human civilization (in so far as mother-right does not necessitate a qualification of this doctrine).- The words which occurred to me in the dream, "thinking and experiencing are the same thing," refer to the explanation of hysterical symptoms with which the male urinal (glass) is also associated.- I need not explain the principle of Gschnas to a Viennese; it consists in constructing objects of rare and costly appearance out of trivial, and preferably comical and worthless material- for example, making suits of armour out of kitchen utensils, wisps of straw and Salzstangeln (long rolls), as our artists are fond of doing at their jolly parties. I had learned that hysterical subjects do the same thing; besides what really happens to them, they unconsciously conceive for themselves horrible or extravagantly fantastic incidents, which they build up out of the most harmless and commonplace material of actual experience. The symptoms attach themselves primarily to these phantasies, not to the memory of real events, whether serious or trivial. This explanation had helped me to overcome many difficulties, and afforded me much pleasure. I was able to allude to it by means of the dream-element "male urine-glass," because I had been told that at the last Gschnas evening a poison-chalice of Lucretia Borgia's had been exhibited, the chief constituent of which had consisted of a glass urinal for men, such as is used in hospitals.

urinate. It is quite unusual for me to be disturbed in sleep by any physical need, least of all at the time when I woke on this occasion- a quarter to four in the morning. I would forestall a further objection by remarking that I have hardly ever felt a desire to urinate after waking early on other journeys made under more comfortable circumstances. However, I can leave this point undecided without weakening my argument.

Further, since experience in dream-analysis has drawn my attention to the fact that even from dreams the interpretation of which seems at first sight complete, because the dream-sources and the wish-stimuli are easily demonstrable, important trains of thought proceed which reach back into the earliest years of childhood, I had to ask myself whether this characteristic does not even constitute an essential condition of dreaming. If it were permissible to generalize this notion, I should say that every dream is connected through its manifest content with recent experiences, while through its latent content it is connected with the most remote experiences; and I can actually show in the analysis of hysteria that these remote experiences have in a very real sense remained recent right up to the present. But I still find it very difficult to prove this conjecture; I shall have to return to the probable role in dream-formation of the earliest experiences of our childhood in another connection (chapter VII).

Of the three peculiarities of the dream-memory considered above, one- the preference for the unimportant in the dream-content- has been satisfactorily explained by tracing it back to dream distortion. We have succeeded in establishing the existence of the other two peculiarities- the preferential selection of recent and also of infantile material- but we have found it impossible to derive them from the motives of the dream. Let us keep in mind these two characteristics, which we still have to explain or evaluate; a place will have to be found for them elsewhere, either in the discussion of the psychology of the sleeping state, or in the consideration of the structure of the psychic apparatus- which we shall undertake later after we have seen that by means of dream-interpretation we are able to glance as through an inspection-hole into the interior of this apparatus.

But here and now I will emphasize another result of the last few dream-analyses. The dream often appears to have several meanings; not only may several wish-fulfilments be combined in it, as our examples show, but one meaning or one wish-fulfilment may conceal another. until in the lowest stratum one comes upon the fulfilment of a wish from the earliest period of childhood; and here again it may be questioned whether the word often at the beginning of this sentence may not more correctly be replaced by constantly.[31]

C. The Somatic Sources of Dreams

If we attempt to interest a cultured layman in the problems of dreams, and if, with this end in view, we ask him what he believes to be the source of dreams, we shall generally find that he feels quite sure he knows at least this part of the solution. He thinks immediately of the influence exercised on the formation of dreams by a disturbed or impeded digestion ("Dreams come from the stomach"), an accidental position of the body, a trifling occurrence during sleep. He does not seem to suspect that even after all these factors have been duly considered something still remains to be explained.

In the introductory chapter we examined at length the opinion of scientific writers on the role of somatic stimuli in the formation of dreams, so that here we need only recall the results of this inquiry. We have seen that three kinds of somatic stimuli will be distinguished: the objective sensory stimuli which proceed from external objects, the inner states of excitation of the sensory organs, having only a subjective reality, and the bodily stimuli arising within the body; and we have also noticed that the writers on dreams are inclined to thrust into the background any psychic

---

[31] The stratification of the meanings of dreams is one of the most delicate but also one of the most fruitful problems of dream interpretation. Whoever forgets the possibility of such stratification is likely to go astray and to make untenable assertions concerning the nature of dreams. But hitherto this subject has been only too imperfectly investigated. So far, a fairly orderly stratification of symbols in dreams due to urinary stimulus has been subjected to a thorough evaluation only by Otto Ran...

sources of dreams which may operate simultaneously with the somatic stimuli, or to exclude them altogether. In testing the claims made on behalf of these somatic stimuli we have learned that the significance of the objective excitation of the sensory organs- whether accidental stimuli operating during sleep, or such as cannot be excluded from the dormant relation of these dream-images and ideas to the internal bodily stimuli and confirmed by experiment; that the part played by the subjective sensory stimuli appears to be demonstrated by the recurrence of hypnagogic sensory images in dreams; and that, although the broadly accepted relation of these dream-images and ideas to the internal bodily stimuli cannot be exhaustively demonstrated, it is at all events confirmed by the well-known influence which an excited state of the digestive, urinary and sexual organs exercises upon the content of our dreams.

Nerve stimulus and bodily stimulus would thus be the anatomical sources of dreams; that is, according to many writers, the sole and exclusive sources of dreams.

But we have already considered a number of doubtful points, which seem to question not so much the correctness of the somatic theory as its adequacy.

However confident the representatives of this theory may be of its factual basis- especially in respect of the accidental and external nerve stimuli, which may without difficulty be recognized in the dream-content- nevertheless they have all come near to admitting that the rich content of ideas found in dreams cannot be derived from the external nerve-stimuli alone. In this connection Miss Mary Whiton Calkins tested her own dreams, and those of a second person, for a period of six weeks, and found that the element of external sensory perception was demonstrable in only 13.2 per cent and 6.7 percent of these dreams respectively. Only two dreams in the whole collection could be referred to organic sensations. These statistics confirm what a cursory survey of our own experience would already, have led us to suspect.

A distinction has often been made between nerve-stimulus dreams which have already been thoroughly investigated, and other forms of dreams.

Spitta, for example, divided dreams into nervestimulus dreams and association-dreams. But it was obvious that this solution remained unsatisfactory unless the link between the somatic sources of dreams and their ideational content could be indicated.

In addition to the first objection, that of the insufficient frequency of the external sources of stimulus, a second objection presents itself, namely, the inadequacy of the explanations of dreams afforded by this category of dream-sources. There are two things which the representatives of this theory have failed to explain: firstly, why the true nature of the external stimulus is not recognized in the dream, but is constantly mistaken for something else; and secondly, why the result of the reaction of the perceiving mind to this misconceived stimulus should be so indeterminate and variable. We have seen that Strumpell, in answer to these questions, asserts that the mind, since it turns away from the outer world during sleep, is not in a position to give the correct interpretation of the objective sensory stimulus, but is forced to construct illusions on the basis of the indefinite stimulation arriving from many directions. In his own words (Die Natur und Entstehung der Traume, p. 108).

"When by an external or internal nerve-stimulus during sleep a feeling, or a complex of feelings, or any sort of psychic process arises in the mind, and is perceived by the mind, this process calls up from the mind perceptual images belonging to the sphere of the waking experiences, that is to say, earlier perceptions, either unembellished, or with the psychic values appertaining to them. It collects about itself, as it were, a greater or lesser number of such images, from which the impression resulting from the nerve-stimulus receives its psychic value. In this connection it is commonly said, as in ordinary language we say of the waking procedure, that the mind interprets in sleep the impressions of nervous stimuli. The result of this interpretation is the socalled nerve-stimulus dream- that is, a dream the components of which are conditioned by the fact that a nervestimulus produces its psychical effect in the life of the mind in accordance with the laws of reproduction."

In all essential points identical with this doctrine is Wundt's statement that the concepts of dreams proceed, at all events for the most part, from sensory stimuli, and especially from the stimuli of general sensation, and are therefore mostly phantastic illusions- probably only to a small extent pure memory conceptions raised to the condition of hallucinations. To illustrate the relation between dream-content and dream-stimuli which follows from this theory, Strumpell makes use of an excellent simile. It is "as though ten fingers of a person ignorant of music were to stray over the keyboard of an instrument." The implication is that the dream is not a psychic phenomenon, originating from psychic motives, but the result of a physiological stimulus, which expresses itself in psychic symptomatology because the apparatus affected by the stimulus is not capable of any other mode of expression. Upon a similar assumption is based the explanation of obsessions which Meynert attempted in his famous simile of the dial on which individual figures are most deeply embossed.

Popular though this theory of the somatic dream-stimuli has become, and seductive though it may seem, it is none the less easy to detect its weak point. Every somatic dream-stimulus which provokes the psychic apparatus in sleep to interpretation by the formation of illusions may evoke an incalculable number of such attempts at interpretation. It may consequently be represented in the dream- content by an extraordinary number of different concepts.[32] But the theory of Strumpell and Wundt cannot point to any sort of motive which controls the relation between the external stimulus and the dream-concept chosen to interpret

---

[32] I would advise everyone to read the exact and detailed records (collected in two volumes) of the dreams experimentally produced by Mourly Vold in order to convince himself how little the conditions of the experiments help to explain the content of the individual dream, and how little such experiments help us towards an understanding of the problems of dreams.

it, and therefore it cannot explain the "peculiar choice" which the stimuli "often enough make in the course of their productive activity" (Lipps, Grundtatsachen des Seelen-lebens). Other objections may be raised against the fundamental assumption behind the theory of illusions- the assumption that during sleep the mind is not in a condition to recognize the real nature of the objective sensory stimuli. The old physiologist Burdach shows us that the mind is quite capable even during sleep of a correct interpretation of the sensory impressions which reach it, and of reacting in accordance with this correct interpretation, inasmuch as he demonstrates that certain sensory impressions which seem important to the individual may be excepted from the general neglect of the sleeping mind (as in the example of nurse and child), and that one is more surely awakened by one's own name than by an indifferent auditory impression; all of which presupposes, of course, that the mind discriminates between sensations, even in sleep. Burdach infers from these observations that we must not assume that the mind is incapable of interpreting sensory stimuli in the sleeping state, but rather that it is not sufficiently interested in them. The arguments which Burdach employed in 1830 reappear unchanged in the works of Lipps (in the year 1883), where they are employed for the purpose of attacking the theory of somatic stimuli. According to these arguments the mind seems to be like the sleeper in the anecdote, who, on being asked, "Are you asleep?" answers "No," and on being again addressed with the words: "Then lend me ten florins," takes refuge in the excuse: "I am asleep."

The inadequacy of the theory of somatic dream-stimuli may be further demonstrated in another way. Observation shows that external stimuli do not oblige me to dream, even though these stimuli appear in the dream-content as soon as I begin to dream-supposing that I do dream. In response to a touch or pressure stimulus experienced while I am asleep, a variety of reactions are at my disposal. I may overlook it, and find on waking that my leg has become uncovered, or that I have been lying on an arm; indeed, pathology offers me a host of examples of powerfully exciting sensory and motor stimuli of different kinds which remain ineffective during sleep. I may perceive the sensation during sleep, and through my sleep, as it were, as constantly happens in the case of pain stimuli, but without weaving the pain into the texture of a dream. And thirdly, I may wake up in response to the stimulus, simply in order to avoid it. Still another, fourth, reaction is possible: namely, that the nervestimulus may cause me to dream; but the other possible reactions occur quite as frequently as the reaction of dream-formation. This, however, would not be the case if the incentive to dreaming did not lie outside the somatic dream-sources.

Appreciating the importance of the above-mentioned lacunae in the explanation of dreams by somatic stimuli, other writers- Scherner, for example, and, following him, the philosopher Volkelt- endeavoured to determine more precisely the nature of the psychic activities which cause the many-coloured images of our dreams to proceed from the somatic stimuli, and in so doing they approached the problem of the essential nature of dreams as a problem of psychology, and regarded dreaming as a psychic activity. Scherner not only gave a poetical, vivid and glowing description of the psychic peculiarities which unfold themselves in the course of dream-formation, but he also believed that he had hit upon the principle of the method the mind employs in dealing with the stimuli which are offered to it. The dream, according to Scherner, in the free activity of the phantasy, which has been released from the shackles imposed upon it during the day, strives to represent symbolically the nature of the organ from which the stimulus proceeds. Thus there exists a sort of dream-book, a guide to the interpretation of dreams, by means of which bodily sensations, the conditions of the organs, and states of stimulation, may be inferred from the dream-images. "Thus the image of a cat expressed extreme ill-temper; the image of pale, smooth pastry the nudity of the body. The human body as a whole is pictured by the phantasy of the dream as a house, and the individual organs of the body as parts of the house. In toothache-dreams a vaulted vestibule corresponds to the mouth, and a staircase to the descent from the pharynx to the oesophagus; in the headache-dream a ceiling covered with disgusting toad-like spiders is chosen to denote the upper part of the head." "Many different symbols are employed by our dreams for the same organ: thus the breathing lung finds its symbol in a roaring stove, filled with flames, the heart in empty boxes and baskets, and the bladder in round, bag-shaped or merely hollow objects. It is of particular significance that at the close of the dream the stimulating organ or its function is often represented without disguise and usually on the dreamer's own body. Thus the toothache-dream commonly ends by the dreamer drawing a tooth out of his mouth." It cannot be said that this theory of dream-interpretation has found much favour with other writers. It seems, above all, extravagant; and so Scherner's readers have hesitated to give it even the small amount of credit to which it is, in my opinion, entitled. As will be seen, it tends to a revival of dream-interpretation by means of symbolism, a method employed by the ancients; only the province from which the interpretation is to be derived is restricted to the human body. The lack of a scientifically comprehensible technique of interpretation must seriously limit the applicability of Scherner's theory. Arbitrariness in the interpretation of dreams would appear to be by no means excluded, especially since in this case also a stimulus may be expressed in the dream-content by several representative symbols; thus even Scherner's follower Volkelt was unable to confirm the representation of the body as a house. Another objection is that here again the dream-activity is regarded as a useless and aimless activity of the mind, since, according to this theory, the mind is content with merely forming phantasies around the stimulus with which it is dealing, without even remotely attempting to abolish the stimulus.

Scherner's theory of the symbolization of bodily stimuli by the dream is seriously damaged by yet another objection. These bodily stimuli are present at all times, and it is generally assumed that the mind is more accessible to them during sleep than in the waking state. It is therefore impossible to understand why the mind does not dream continuously all night long, and why it does not dream every night about all the organs. If one attempts to evade this objection by positing the condition that special excitations must proceed from the eye, the ear, the teeth, the bowels, etc., in order to arouse the dream-activity, one is confronted with the difficulty of proving that this increase of stimulation is objective; and proof is possible only in a very few cases. If the dream of flying is a symbolization of the upward and downward motion of the pulmonary lobes, either this dream, as has already been remarked by Strumpell, should be dreamt much oftener, or it should be possible to show that respiration is more active during this dream. Yet a third alternative is possible- and it is the most probable of all- namely, that now and again special motives are operative to direct the attention to the visceral sensations which are constantly present. But this would take us far beyond the scope of Scherner's theory.

The value of Scherner's and Volkelt's disquisitions resides in their calling our attention to a number of characteristics of the dream-content which are in need of explanation, and which seem to promise fresh discoveries. It is quite true that symbolizations of the bodily organs and functions do occur in dreams: for example, that water in a dream often signifies a desire to urinate, that the male genital organ may be represented by an upright staff, or a pillar, etc. With dreams which exhibit a very animated field of vision and brilliant colours, in contrast to the dimness of other dreams, the interpretation that they are "dreams due to visual stimulation" can hardly be dismissed, nor can we dispute the participation of illusionformation in dreams which contain noise and a medley of voices. A dream like that of Scherner's, that two rows of fair handsome boys stood facing one another on a bridge, attacking one another, and then resuming their positions, until finally the dreamer himself sat down on a bridge and drew a long tooth from his jaw; or a similar dream of Volkelt's, in which two rows of drawers played a part, and which again ended in the extraction of a tooth; dream-formations of this kind, of which both writers relate a great number, forbid our dismissing

Scherner's theory as an idle invention without seeking the kernel of truth which may be contained in it. We are therefore confronted with the task of finding a different explanation of the supposed symbolization of the alleged dental stimulus. Throughout our consideration of the theory of the somatic sources of dreams, I have refrained from urging the argument which arises from our analyses of dreams. If, by a procedure which has not been followed by other writers in their investigation of dreams, we can prove that the dream possesses intrinsic value as psychic action, that a wish supplies the motive of its formation, and that the experiences of the previous day furnish the most obvious material of its content, any other theory of dreams which neglects such an important method of investigation- and accordingly makes the dream appear a useless and enigmatical psychic reaction to somatic stimuli- may be dismissed without special criticism. For in this case there would have to be- and this is highly improbable- two entirely different kinds of dreams, of which only one kind has come under our observation, while the other kind alone has been observed by the earlier investigators. It only remains now to find a place in our theory of dreams for the facts on which the current doctrine of somatic dream-stimuli is based.

We have already taken the first step in this direction in advancing the thesis that the dream-work is under a compulsion to elaborate into a unified whole all the dream-stimuli which are simultaneously present (chapter V., A, above). We have seen that when two or more experiences capable of making an impression on the mind have been left over from the previous day, the wishes that result from them are united into one dream; similarly, that the impressions possessing psychic value and the indifferent experiences of the previous day unite in the dream-material, provided that connecting ideas between the two can be established. Thus the dream appears to be a reaction to everything which is simultaneously present as actual in the sleeping mind. As far as we have hitherto analysed the dreammaterial, we have discovered it to be a collection of psychic remnants and memory-traces, which we were obliged to credit (on account of the preference shown for recent and for infantile material) with a character of psychological actuality, though the nature of this actuality was not at the time determinable. We shall now have little difficulty in predicting what will happen when to these actualities of the memory fresh material in the form of sensations is added during sleep. These stimuli, again, are of importance to the dream because they are actual; they are united with the other psychic actualities to provide the material for dreamformation. To express it in other words, the stimuli which occur during sleep are elaborated into a wish-fulfilment, of which the other components are the psychic remnants of daily experience with which we are already familiar. This combination, however, is not inevitable; we have seen that more than one kind of behaviour toward the physical stimuli received during sleep is possible. Where this combination is effected, a conceptual material for the dream-content has been found which will represent both kinds of dream-sources, the somatic as well as the psychic. The nature of the dream is not altered when somatic material is added to the psychic dream-sources; it still remains a wish fulfilment, no matter how its expression is determined by the actual material available.

I should like to find room here for a number of peculiarities which are able to modify the significance of external stimuli for the dream. I imagine that a co-operation of individual, physiological and accidental factors, which depend on the circumstances of the moment, determines how one will behave in individual cases of more intensive objective stimulation during sleep; habitual or accidental profundity of sleep, in conjunction with the intensity of the stimulus, will in one case make it possible so to suppress the stimulus that it will not disturb the sleeper, while in another case it will force the sleeper to wake, or will assist the attempt to subdue the stimulus by weaving it into the texture of the dream. In accordance with the multiplicity of these constellations, external objective stimuli will be expressed more rarely or more frequently in the case of one person than in that of another. In my own case. since I am an excellent sleeper, and obstinately refuse to allow myself to be disturbed during sleep on any pretext whatever, this intrusion of external causes of excitation into my dreams is very rare, whereas psychic motives apparently cause me to dream very easily. Indeed, I have noted only a single dream in which an objective, painful source of stimulation is demonstrable, and it will be highly instructive to see what effect the external stimulus had in this particular dream.

I am riding a gray horse, at first timidly and awkwardly, as though I were merely carried along. Then I meet a colleague, P, also on horseback, and dressed in rough frieze; he is sitting erect in the saddle; he calls my attention to something (probably to the fact that I have a very bad seat). Now I begin to feel more and more at ease on the back of my highly intelligent horse; I sit more comfortably, and I find that I am quite at home up here. My saddle is a sort of pad, which completely fills the space between the neck and the rump of the horse. I ride between two vans, and just manage to clear them. After riding up the street for some distance, I turn round and wish to dismount, at first in front of a little open chapel which is built facing on to the street. Then I do really dismount in front of a chapel which stands near the first one; the hotel is in the same street; I might let the horse go there by itself, but I prefer to lead it thither. It seems as though I should be ashamed to arrive there on horseback. In front of the hotel there stands a page-boy, who shows me a note of mine which has been found, and ridicules me on account of it. On the note is written, doubly underlined, "Eat nothing," and then a second sentence (indistinct): something like "Do not work"; at the same time a hazy idea that I am in a strange city, in which I do not work.

It will not at once be apparent that this dream originated under the influence, or rather under the compulsion, of a painstimulus. The day before, however, I had suffered from boils, which made every movement a torture, and at last a boil had grown to the size of an apple at the root of the scrotum, and had caused me the most intolerable pains at every step; a feverish lassitude, lack of appetite, and the hard work which I had nevertheless done during the day, had conspired with the pain to upset me. I was not altogether in a condition to discharge my duties as a physician, but in view of the nature and the location of the malady, it was possible to imagine something else for which I was most of all unfit, namely riding. Now it is this very activity of riding into which I am plunged by the dream; it is the most energetic denial of the pain which imagination could conceive. As a matter of fact, I cannot ride; I do not dream of doing so; I never sat on a horse but once- and then without a saddle- and I did not like it. But in this dream I ride as though I had no boil on the perineum; or rather, I ride, just because I want to have none. To judge from the description, my saddle is the poultice which has enabled me to fall asleep. Probably, being thus comforted, I did not feel anything of my pain during the first few hours of my sleep. Then the painful sensations made themselves felt, and tried to wake me; whereupon the dream came and said to me, soothingly: "Go on sleeping, you are not going to wake! You have no boil, for you are riding on horseback, and with a boil just there no one could ride!" And the dream was successful; the pain was stifled, and I went on sleeping.

But the dream was not satisfied with "suggesting away" the boil by tenaciously holding fast to an idea incompatible with the malady (thus behaving like the hallucinatory insanity of a mother who has lost her child, or of a merchant who has lost his fortune). In addition, the details of the sensation denied and of the image used to suppress it serve the dream also as a means to connect other material actually present in the mind with the situation in the dream, and to give this material representation. I am riding on a gray horse- the colour of the horse exactly corresponds with the pepper-and-salt suit in which I last saw my colleague P in the country. I have been warned that highly seasoned food is the cause of boils, and in any case it is preferable as an aetiological explanation to sugar, which might be thought of in connection with furunculosis. My friend P likes to ride the high horse with me ever since he took my place in the treatment of a female patient, in whose case I had performed great feats (Kuntstucke:

in the dream I sit the horse at first sideways, like a trick-rider, Kunstreiter), but who really, like the horse in the story of the Sunday equestrian, led me wherever she wished. Thus the horse comes to be a symbolic representation of a lady patient (in the dream it is highly intelligent). *I feel quite at home* refers to the position which I occupied in the patient's household until I was replaced by my colleague P. "I thought you were safe in the saddle up there," one of my few wellwishers among the eminent physicians of the city recently said to me, with reference to the same household. And it was a feat to practise psychotherapy for eight to ten hours a day, while suffering such pain, but I know that I cannot continue my peculiarly strenuous work for any length of time without perfect physical health, and the dream is full of dismal allusions to the situation which would result if my illness continued (the note, such as neurasthenics carry and show to their doctors): Do not work, do not eat. On further interpretation I see that the dream activity has succeeded in finding its way from the wish-situation of riding to some very early childish quarrels which must have occurred between myself and a nephew, who is a year older than I, and is now living in England. It has also taken up elements from my journeys in Italy: the street in the dream is built up out of impressions of Verona and Siena. A still deeper interpretation leads to sexual dream-thoughts, and I recall what the dream allusions to that beautiful country were supposed to mean in the dream of a female patient who had never been to Italy (to Italy, German: gen Italien = Genitalien = genitals); at the same time there are references to the house in which I preceded my friend P as physician, and to the place where the boil is located.

In another dream, I was similarly successful in warding off a threatened disturbance of my sleep; this time the threat came from a sensory stimulus. It was only chance, however, that enabled me to discover the connection between the dream and the accidental dream- stimulus, and in this way to understand the dream. One midsummer morning in a Tyrolese mountain resort I woke with the knowledge that I had dreamed: *The Pope is* dead. I was not able to interpret this short, non-visual dream. I could remember only one possible basis of the dream, namely, that shortly before this the newspapers had reported that His Holiness was slightly indisposed. But in the course of the morning my wife asked me: "Did you hear the dreadful tolling of the church bells this morning?" I had no idea that I had heard it, but now I understood my dream. It was the reaction of my need for sleep to the noise by which the pious Tyroleans were trying to wake me. I avenged myself on them by the conclusion which formed the content of my dream, and continued to sleep, without any further interest in the tolling of the bells.

Among the dreams mentioned in the previous chapters there are several which might serve as examples of the elaboration of so called nervestimuli.

The dream of drinking in long draughts is such an example; here the somatic stimulus seems to be the sole source of the dream, and the wish arising from the sensation- thirst- the only motive for dreaming. We find much the same thing in other simple dreams, where the somatic stimulus is able of itself to generate a wish. The dream of the sick woman who throws the cooling apparatus from her cheek at night is an instance of an unusual manner of reacting to a pain-stimulus with a wish fulfilment; it seems as though the patient had temporarily succeeded in making herself analgesic, and accompanied this by ascribing her pains to a stranger.

My dream of the three Parcae is obviously a hunger-dream, but it has contrived to shift the need for food right back to the child's longing for its mother's breast, and to use a harmless desire as a mask for a more serious one that cannot venture to express itself so openly. In the dream of Count Thun we were able to see by what paths an accidental physical need was brought into relation with the strongest, but also the most rigorously repressed impulses of the psychic life. And when, as in the case reported by Garnier, the First Consul incorporates the sound of an exploding infernal machine into a dream of battle before it causes him to wake, the true purpose for which alone psychic activity concerns itself with sensations during sleep is revealed with unusual clarity. A young lawyer, who is full of his first great bankruptcy case, and falls asleep in the afternoon, behaves just as the great Napoleon did. He dreams of a certain G. Reich in Hussiatyn, whose acquaintance he has made in connection with the bankruptcy case, but Hussiatyn (German: husten, to cough) forces itself upon his attention still further; he is obliged to wake, only to hear his wife- who is suffering from bronchial catarrh- violently coughing.

Let us compare the dream of Napoleon I- who, incidentally, was an excellent sleeper- with that of the sleepy student, who was awakened by his landlady with the reminder that he had to go to the hospital, and who thereupon dreamt himself into a bed in the hospital, and then slept on, the underlying reasoning being as follows: If I am already in the hospital, I needn't get up to go there. This is obviously a convenience-dream; the sleeper frankly admits to himself his motive in dreaming; but he thereby reveals one of the secrets of dreaming in general. In a certain sense, all dreams are convenience-dreams; they serve the purpose of continuing to sleep instead of waking. The dream is the guardian of sleep, not its disturber. In another place we shall have occasion to justify this conception in respect to the psychic factors that make for waking; but we can already demonstrate its applicability to the objective external stimuli. Either the mind does not concern itself at all with the causes of sensations during sleep, if it is able to carry this attitude through as against the intensity of the stimuli, and their significance, of which it is well aware; or it employs the dream to deny these stimuli; or, thirdly, if it is obliged to recognize the stimuli, it seeks that interpretation of them which will represent the actual sensation as a component of a desired situation which is compatible with sleep. The actual sensation is woven into the dream in order to deprive it of its reality. Napoleon is permitted to go on sleeping; it is only a dream-memory of the thunder of the guns at Arcole which is trying to disturb him.[33]

---

[33] The two sources from which I know of this dream do not entirely agree as to its content.

The wish to sleep, to which the conscious ego has adjusted itself, and which (together with the dream-censorship and the "secondary elaboration" to be mentioned later) represents the ego's contribution to the dream, must thus always be taken into account as a motive of dream-formation, and every successful dream is a fulfilment of this wish. The relation of this general, constantly present, and unvarying sleep-wish to the other wishes of which now one and now another is fulfilled by the dreamcontent, will be the subject of later consideration. In the wish to sleep we have discovered a motive capable of supplying the deficiency in the theory of Strumpell and Wundt, and of explaining the perversity and capriciousness of the interpretation of the external stimulus. The correct interpretation, of which the sleeping mind is perfectly capable, would involve active interest, and would require the sleeper to wake; hence, of those interpretations which are possible at all, only such are admitted as are acceptable to the dictatorial censorship of the sleep-wish. The logic of dream situations would run, for example: "It is the nightingale, and not the lark." For if it is the lark, love's night is at an end. From among the interpretations of the stimulus which are thus admissible, that one is selected which can secure the best connection with the wish- impulses that are lying in wait in the mind. Thus everything is definitely determined, and nothing is left to caprice. The misinterpretation is not an illusion, but- if you will- an excuse. Here again, as in substitution by displacement in the service of the dream-censorship, we have an act of deflection of the normal psychic procedure.

If the external nerve-stimuli and the inner bodily stimuli are sufficiently intense to compel psychic attention, they represent- that is, if they result in dreaming at all, and not in waking- a fixed point for dream-formation, a nucleus in the dream-material, for which an appropriate wishfulfilment is sought, just as (see above) mediating ideas between two psychical dream-stimuli are sought. To this extent it is true of a number of dreams that the somatic element dictates the dream-content. In this extreme case even a wish that is not actually present may be aroused for the purpose of dream-formation. But the dream cannot do otherwise than represent a wish in some situation as fulfilled; it is, as it were, confronted with the task of discovering what wish can be represented as fulfilled by the given sensation. Even if this given material is of a painful or disagreeable character, yet it is not unserviceable for the purposes of dream-formation. The psychic life has at its disposal even wishes whose fulfilment evokes displeasure, which seems a contradiction, but becomes perfectly intelligible if we take into account the presence of two sorts of psychic instance and the censorship that subsists between them.

In the psychic life there exist, as we have seen, repressed wishes, which belong to the first system, and to whose fulfilment the second system is opposed. We do not mean this in a historic sense- that such wishes have once existed and have subsequently been destroyed. The doctrine of repression, which we need in the study of psychoneuroses, asserts that such repressed wishes still exist, but simultaneously with an inhibition which weighs them down. Language has hit upon the truth when it speaks of the suppression (sub-pression, or pushing under) of such impulses.

The psychic mechanism which enables such suppressed wishes to force their way to realization is retained in being and in working order. But if it happens that such a suppressed wish is fulfilled, the vanquished inhibition of the second system (which is capable of consciousness) is then expressed as discomfort. And, in order to conclude this argument: If sensations of a disagreeable character which originate from somatic sources are present during sleep, this constellation is utilized by the dreamactivity to procure the fulfilment- with more or less maintenance of the censorship- of an otherwise suppressed wish.

This state of affairs makes possible a certain number of anxiety dreams, while others of these dream-formations which are unfavourable to the wish-theory exhibit a different mechanism. For the anxiety in dreams may of course be of a psychoneurotic character, originating in psychosexual excitation, in which case, the anxiety corresponds to repressed libido. Then this anxiety, like the whole anxiety-dream, has the significance of a neurotic symptom, and we stand at the dividing-line where the wish-fulfilling tendency of dreams is frustrated. But in other anxiety-dreams the feeling of anxiety comes from somatic sources (as in the case of persons suffering from pulmonary or cardiac trouble, with occasional difficulty in breathing), and then it is used to help such strongly suppressed wishes to attain fulfilment in a dream, the dreaming of which from psychic motives would have resulted in the same release of anxiety. It is not difficult to reconcile these two apparently contradictory cases. When two psychic formations, an affective inclination and a conceptual content, are intimately connected, either one being actually present will evoke the other, even in a dream; now the anxiety of somatic origin evokes the suppressed conceptual content, now it is the released conceptual content, accompanied by sexual excitement, which causes the release of anxiety. In the one case, it may be said that a somatically determined affect is psychically interpreted; in the other case, all is of psychic origin, but the content which has been suppressed is easily replaced by a somatic interpretation which fits the anxiety. The difficulties which lie in the way of understanding all this have little to do with dreams; they are due to the fact that in discussing these points we are touching upon the problems of the development of anxiety and of repression.

The general aggregate of bodily sensation must undoubtedly be included among the dominant dream-stimuli of internal bodily origin. Not that it is capable of supplying the dream-content; but it forces the dream-thoughts to make a choice from the material destined to serve the purpose of representation in the dream- content, inasmuch as it brings within easy reach that part of the material which is adapted to its own character, and holds the rest at a distance. Moreover, this general feeling, which survives from the preceding day, is of course connected with the psychic residues that are significant for the dream. Moreover, this feeling itself may be either maintained or overcome in the dream, so that it may, if it is painful, veer round into its opposite.

If the somatic sources of excitation during sleep- that is, the sensations of sleep- are not of unusual intensity, the part which they play in dreamformation is, in my judgment, similar to that of those impressions of the day which are still recent, but of no great significance. I mean that they are utilized for the dream formation if they are of such a kind that they can be united with the conceptual content of the psychic dream-source, but not otherwise. They are treated as a cheap ever-ready material, which can be used whenever it is needed, and not as valuable material which itself prescribes the manner in which it must be utilized. I might suggest the analogy of a connoisseur giving an artist a rare stone, a piece of onyx, for example, in order that it may be fashioned into a work of art. Here the size of the stone, its colour, and its markings help to decide what head or what scene shall be represented; while if he is dealing with a uniform and abundant material such as marble or sandstone, the artist is guided only by the idea which takes shape in his mind. Only in this way, it seems to me, can we explain the fact that the dreamcontent furnished by physical stimuli of somatic origin which are not unusually accentuated does not make its appearance in all dreams and every night.[34]

Perhaps an example which takes us back to the interpretation of dreams will best illustrate my meaning. One day I was trying to understand the significance of the sensation of being inhibited, of not being able to move from the spot, of not being able to get something done, etc., which occurs so frequently in dreams, and is so closely allied to anxiety. That night I had the following dream: I am very incompletely dressed, and I go from a flat on the ground-floor up a flight of stairs to an upper story. In doing this I jump up three stairs at a time, and I am glad to find that I can mount the stairs so quickly. Suddenly I notice that a servant-maid is coming down the stairs- that is, towards me. I am ashamed, and try to hurry away, and now comes this feeling of being inhibited; I am glued to the stairs, and cannot move from the spot.

---

[34] Rank has shown, in a number of studies, that certain awakening dreams provoked by organic stimuli (dreams of urination and ejaculation) are especially calculated to demonstrate the conflict between the need for sleep and the demands of the organic need, as well as the influence of the latter on the dreamcontent.

Analysis: The situation of the dream is taken from an everyday reality. In a house in Vienna I have two apartments, which are connected only by the main staircase. My consultation-rooms and my study are on the raised ground-floor, and my living-rooms are on the first floor. Late at night, when I have finished my work downstairs, I go upstairs to my bedroom. On the evening before the dream I had actually gone this short distance with my garments in disarray- that is, I had taken off my collar, tie and cuffs; but in the dream this had changed into a more advanced, but, as usual, indefinite degree of undress. It is a habit of mine to run up two or three steps at a time; moreover, there was a wish-fulfilment recognized even in the dream, for the ease with which I run upstairs reassures me as to the condition of my heart. Further, the manner in which I run upstairs is an effective contrast to the sensation of being inhibited, which occurs in the second half of the dream. It shows me- what needed no proof- that dreams have no difficulty in representing motor actions fully and completely carried out; think, for example, of flying in dreams! But the stairs up which I go are not those of my own house; at first I do not recognize them; only the person coming towards me informs me of their whereabouts. This woman is the maid of an old lady whom I visit twice daily in order to give her hypodermic injections; the stairs, too, are precisely similar to those which I have to climb twice a day in this old lady's house.

How do these stairs and this woman get into my dream? The shame of not being fully dressed is undoubtedly of a sexual character; the servant of whom I dream is older than I, surly, and by no means attractive. These questions remind me of the following incident: When I pay my morning visit at this house I am usually seized with a desire to clear my throat; the sputum falls on the stairs. There is no spittoon on either of the two floors, and I consider that the stairs should be kept clean not at my expense, but rather by the provision of a spittoon. The housekeeper, another elderly, curmudgeonly person, but, as I willingly admit, a woman of cleanly instincts, takes a different view of the matter. She lies in wait for me, to see whether I shall take the liberty referred to, and, if she sees that I do, I can distinctly hear her growl. For days thereafter, when we meet she refuses to greet me with the customary signs of respect. On the day before the dream the housekeeper's attitude was reinforced by that of the maid. I had just furnished my usual hurried visit to the patient when the servant confronted me in the ante-room, observing: "You might as well have wiped your shoes today, doctor, before you came into the room. The red carpet is all dirty again from your feet." This is the only justification for the appearance of the stairs and the maid in my dream.

Between my leaping upstairs and my spitting on the stairs there is an intimate connection. Pharyngitis and cardiac troubles are both supposed to be punishments for the vice of smoking, on account of which vice my own housekeeper does not credit me with excessive tidiness, so that my reputation suffers in both the houses which my dream fuses into one.

I must postpone the further interpretation of this dream until I can indicate the origin of the typical dream of being incompletely clothed. In the meantime, as a provisional deduction from the dream just related, I note that the dream-sensation of inhibited movement is always aroused at a point where a certain connection requires it. A peculiar condition of my motor system during sleep cannot be responsible for this dream-content, since a moment earlier I found myself, as though in confirmation of this fact, skipping lightly up the stairs.

D. Typical Dreams

Generally speaking, we are not in a position to interpret another person's dream if he is unwilling to furnish us with the unconscious thoughts which lie behind the dream-content, and for this reason the practical applicability of our method of dream-interpretation is often seriously restricted.[35] But there are dreams

---

[35] The statement that our method of dream-interpretation is inapplicable when we have not at our disposal the dreamer's association-material must be qualified. In one case our work of interpretation is independent of these associations: namely, when the dreamer make use of symbolic elements in his dream. We then employ what is, strictly speaking, a second auxiliary method of dream-interpretation. (See below).

which exhibit a complete contrast to the individual's customary liberty to endow his dream-world with a special individuality, thereby making it inaccessible to an alien understanding: there are a number of dreams which almost every one has dreamed in the same manner, and of which we are accustomed to assume that they have the same significance in the case of every dreamer. A peculiar interest attaches to these typical dreams, because, no matter who dreams them, they presumably all derive from the same sources, so that they would seem to be particularly fitted to provide us with information as to the sources of dreams.

With quite special expectations, therefore, we shall proceed to test our technique of dream-interpretation on these typical dreams, and only with extreme reluctance shall we admit that precisely in respect of this material our method is not fully verified. In the interpretation of typical dreams we as a rule fail to obtain those associations from the dreamer which in other cases have led us to comprehension of the dream, or else these associations are confused and inadequate, so that they do not help us to solve our problem.

Why this is the case, and how we can remedy this defect in our technique, are points which will be discussed in a later chapter. The reader will then understand why I can deal with only a few of the group of typical dreams in this chapter, and why I have postponed the discussion of the others.

(a) The Embarrassment-Dream of Nakedness

In a dream in which one is naked or scantily clad in the presence of strangers, it sometimes happens that one is not in the least ashamed of one's condition. But the dream of nakedness demands our attention only when shame and embarrassment are felt in it, when one wishes to escape or to hide, and when one feels the strange inhibition of being unable to stir from the spot, and of being utterly powerless to alter the painful situation. It is only in this connection that the dream is typical; otherwise the nucleus of its content may be involved in all sorts of other connections, or may be replaced by individual amplifications. The essential point is that one has a painful feeling of shame, and is anxious to hide one's nakedness, usually by means of locomotion, but is absolutely unable to do so. I believe that the great majority of my readers will at some time have found themselves in this situation in a dream.

The nature and manner of the exposure is usually rather vague. The dreamer will say, perhaps, "I was in my chemise," but this is rarely a clear image; in most cases the lack of clothing is so indeterminate that it is described in narrating the dream by an alternative: "I was in my chemise or my petticoat." As a rule the deficiency in clothing is not serious enough to justify the feeling of shame attached to it. For a man who has served in the army, nakedness is often replaced by a manner of dressing that is contrary to regulations. "I was in the street without my sabre, and I saw some officers approaching," or "I had no collar," or "I was wearing checked civilian trousers," etc.

The persons before whom one is ashamed are almost always strangers, whose faces remain indeterminate. It never happens, in the typical dream, that one is reproved or even noticed on account of the lack of clothing which causes one such embarrassment. On the contrary, the people in the dream appear to be quite indifferent; or, as I was able to note in one particularly vivid dream, they have stiff and solemn expressions. This gives us food for thought.

The dreamer's embarrassment and the spectator's indifference constitute a contradiction such as often occurs in dreams. It would be more in keeping with the dreamer's feelings if the strangers were to look at him in astonishment, or were to laugh at him, or be outraged. I think, however, that this obnoxious feature has been displaced by wish-fulfilment, while the embarrassment is for some reason retained, so that the two components are not in agreement. We have an interesting proof that the dream which is partially distorted by wish-fulfilment has not been properly understood; for it has been made the basis of a fairy-tale familiar to us all in Andersen's version of The Emperor's New Clothes, and it has more recently received poetical treatment by Fulda in *The Talisman*. In Andersen's fairy-tale we are told of two impostors who weave a costly garment for the Emperor, which shall, however, be visible only to the good and true. The Emperor goes forth clad to this invisible garment, and since the imaginary fabric serves as a sort of touchstone, the people are frightened into behaving as though they did not notice the Emperor's nakedness.

But this is really the situation in our dream. It is not very venturesome to assume that the unintelligible dream-content has provided an incentive to invent a state of undress which gives meaning to the situation present in the memory. This situation is thereby robbed of its original meaning, and made to serve alien ends. But we shall see that such a misunderstanding of the dream-content often occurs through the conscious activity of a second psychic system, and is to be recognized as a factor of the final form of the dream; and further, that in the development of obsessions and phobias similar misunderstandings- still, of course, within the same psychic personality- play a decisive part. It is even possible to specify whence the material for the fresh interpretation of the dream is taken. The impostor is the dream, the Emperor is the dreamer himself, and the moralizing tendency betrays a hazy knowledge of the fact that there is a question, in the latent dream-content, of forbidden wishes, victims of repression. The connection in which such dreams appear during my analysis of neurotics proves beyond a doubt that a memory of the dreamer's earliest childhood lies at the foundation of the dream. Only in our childhood was there a time when we were seen by our relatives, as well as by strange nurses, servants and visitors, in a state of insufficient clothing, and at that time we were not ashamed of our nakedness.[36] In the case of many rather older children it may be observed that being undressed has an exciting effect upon them, instead of making them feel ashamed. They laugh, leap about, slap or thump their own bodies; the

---

[36] The child appears in the fairy-tale also, for there a little child suddenly cries out: "But he hasn't anything on at all!"

mother, or whoever is present, scolds them, saying: "Fie, that is shameful- you mustn't do that!"

Children often show a desire to display themselves; it is hardly possible to pass through a village in country districts without meeting a two-or three-year-old child who lifts up his or her blouse or frock before the traveller, possibly in his honour. One of my patients has retained in his conscious memory a scene from his eighth year, in which, after undressing for bed, he wanted to dance into his little sister's room in his shirt, but was prevented by the servant. In the history of the childhood of neurotics, exposure before children of the opposite sex plays a prominent part; in paranoia, the delusion of being observed while dressing and undressing may be directly traced to these experiences; and among those who have remained perverse, there is a class in whom the childish impulse is accentuated into a symptom: the class of exhibitionists.

This age of childhood, in which the sense of shame is unknown, seems a paradise when we look back upon it later, and paradise itself is nothing but the mass-phantasy of the childhood of the individual. This is why in paradise men are naked and unashamed, until the moment arrives when shame and fear awaken; expulsion follows, and sexual life and cultural development begin. Into this paradise dreams can take us back every night; we have already ventured the conjecture that the impressions of our earliest childhood (from the prehistoric period until about the end of the third year) crave reproduction for their own sake, perhaps without further reference to their content, so that their repetition is a wishfulfilment.

Dreams of nakedness, then, are exhibition-dreams.[37]

The nucleus of an exhibition-dream is furnished by one's own person, which is seen not as that of a child, but as it exists in the present, and by the idea of scanty clothing which emerges

---

[37] Ferenczi has recorded a number of interesting dreams of nakedness in women which were without difficulty traced to the infantile delight in exhibitionism, but which differ in may features from the typical dream of nakedness discussed above.

indistinctly, owing to the superimposition of so many later situations of being partially clothed, or out of consideration for the censorship; to these elements are added the persons in whose presence one is ashamed. I know of no example in which the actual spectators of these infantile exhibitions reappear in a dream; for a dream is hardly ever a simple recollection. Strangely enough, those persons who are the objects of our sexual interest in childhood are omitted from all reproductions, in dreams, in hysteria or in obsessional neurosis; paranoia alone restores the spectators, and is fanatically convinced of their presence, although they remain unseen. The substitute for these persons offered by the dream, the number of strangers who take no notice of the spectacle offered them, is precisely the counter- wish to that single intimately-known person for whom the exposure was intended. "A number of strangers," moreover, often occur in dreams in all sorts of other connections; as a counter-wish they always signify a secret.[38] It will be seen that even that restitution of the old state of affairs that occurs in paranoia complies with this counter-tendency. One is no longer alone; one is quite positively being watched; but the spectators are a number of strange, curiously indeterminate people.

Furthermore, repression finds a place in the exhibition-dream. For the disagreeable sensation of the dream is, of course, the reaction on the part of the second psychic instance to the fact that the exhibitionistic scene which has been condemned by the censorship has nevertheless succeeded in presenting itself. The only way to avoid this sensation would be to refrain from reviving the scene.

In a later chapter we shall deal once again with the feeling of inhibition. In our dreams it represents to perfection a conflict of the will, a denial. According to our unconscious purpose, the exhibition is to proceed; according to the demands of the censorship, it is to come to an end.

---

[38] For obvious reasons the presence of the whole family in the dream has the same significance.

The relation of our typical dreams to fairy-tales and other fiction and poetry is neither sporadic nor accidental. Sometimes the penetrating insight of the poet has analytically recognized the process of transformation of which the poet is otherwise the instrument, and has followed it up in the reverse direction; that is to say, has traced a poem to a dream. A friend has called my attention to the following passage in G. Keller's Der Grune Heinrich: "I do not wish, dear Lee, that you should ever come to realize from experience the exquisite and piquant truth in the situation of Odysseus, when he appears, naked and covered with mud, before Nausicaa and her playmates! Would you like to know what it means? Let us for a moment consider the incident closely. If you are ever parted from your home, and from all that is dear to you, and wander about in a strange country; if you have seen much and experienced much; if you have cares and sorrows, and are, perhaps, utterly wretched and forlorn, you will some night inevitably dream that you are approaching your home; you will see it shining and glittering in the loveliest colours; lovely and gracious figures will come to meet you; and then you will suddenly discover that you are ragged, naked, and covered with dust. An indescribable feeling of shame and fear overcomes you; you try to cover yourself, to hide, and you wake up bathed in sweat. As long as humanity exists, this will be the dream of the care-laden, tempest-tossed man, and thus Homer has drawn this situation from the profoundest depths of the eternal nature of humanity."

What are the profoundest depths of the eternal nature of humanity, which the poet commonly hopes to awaken in his listeners, but these stirrings of the psychic life which are rooted in that age of childhood, which subsequently becomes prehistoric? Childish wishes, now suppressed and forbidden, break into the dream behind the unobjectionable and permissibly conscious wishes of the homeless man, and it is for this reason that the dream which is objectified in the legend of Nausicaa regularly develops into an anxiety-dream.

My own dream of hurrying upstairs, which presently changed into being glued to the stairs, is likewise an exhibition-dream, for it reveals the essential ingredients of such a dream. It must therefore be possible to trace it back to experiences in my childhood, and the knowledge of these should enable us to conclude how far the servant's behaviour to me (i.e., her reproach that I had soiled the carpet) helped her to secure the position which she occupies in the dream. Now I am actually able to furnish the desired explanation. One learns in a psycho-analysis to interpret temporal proximity by material connection; two ideas which are apparently without connection, but which occur in immediate succession, belong to a unity which has to be deciphered; just as an a and a b, when written in succession, must be pronounced as one syllable, ab. It is just the same with the interrelations of dreams. The dream of the stairs has been taken from a series of dreams with whose other members I am familiar, having interpreted them. A dream included in this series must belong to the same context. Now, the other dreams of the series are based on the memory of a nurse to whom I was entrusted for a season, from the time when I was still at the breast to the age of two and a half, and of whom a hazy recollection has remained in my consciousness. According to information which I recently obtained from my mother, she was old and ugly, but very intelligent and thorough; according to the inferences which I am justified in drawing from my dreams, she did not always treat me quite kindly, but spoke harshly to me when I showed insufficient understanding of the necessity for cleanliness. Inasmuch as the maid endeavoured to continue my education in this respect, she is entitled to be treated, in my dream, as an incarnation of the prehistoric old woman. It is to be assumed, of course, that the child was fond of his teacher in spite of her harsh behaviour.[39]

(b) Dreams of the death of beloved persons

Another series of dreams which may be called typical are those whose content is that a beloved relative, a parent, brother, sister,

---

[39] A supplementary interpretation of this dream: To spit (spucken) on the stairs, since spuken (to haunt) is the occupation of spirits (cf. English, "spook"), led me by a free translation to espirit d'escalier. "Stairwit" means unreadiness at repartee, (Schlagfertigkeit = literally: "readiness to hit out") with which I really have to reproach myself. But was the nurse deficient in Schlagfertigkeit?

child, or the like, has died. We must at once distinguish two classes of such dreams: those in which the dreamer remains unmoved, and those in which he feels profoundly grieved by the death of the beloved person, even expressing this grief by shedding tears in his sleep.

We may ignore the dreams of the first group; they have no claim to be reckoned as typical. If they are analysed, it is found that they signify something that is not contained in them, that they are intended to mask another wish of some kind. This is the case in the dream of the aunt who sees the only son of her sister lying on a bier (chapter IV). The dream does not mean that she desires the death of her little nephew; as we have learned, it merely conceals the wish to see a certain beloved person again after a long separation- the same person whom she had seen after as long an interval at the funeral of another nephew. This wish, which is the real content of the dream, gives no cause for sorrow, and for that reason no sorrow is felt in the dream. We see here that the feeling contained in the dream does not belong to the manifest, but to the latent dreamcontent, and that the affective content has remained free from the distortion which has befallen the conceptual content.

It is otherwise with those dreams in which the death of a beloved relative is imagined, and in which a painful affect is felt. These signify, as their content tells us, the wish that the person in question might die; and since I may here expect that the feelings of all my readers and of all who have had such dreams will lead them to reject my explanation, I must endeavour to rest my proof on the broadest possible basis.

We have already cited a dream from which we could see that the wishes represented as fulfilled in dreams are not always current wishes. They may also be bygone, discarded, buried and repressed wishes, which we must nevertheless credit with a sort of continued existence, merely on account of their reappearance in a dream. They are not dead, like persons who have died, in the sense that we know death, but are rather like the shades in the Odyssey which awaken to a certain degree of life so soon as they have drunk blood. The dream of the dead child in the box (chapter IV) contained a wish that had been present fifteen years earlier, and which had at that time been frankly admitted as real. Further- and this, perhaps, is not unimportant from the standpoint of the theory of dreams- a recollection from the dreamer's earliest childhood was at the root of this wish also. When the dreamer was a little child- but exactly when cannot be definitely determined- she heard that her mother, during the pregnancy of which she was the outcome, had fallen into a profound emotional depression, and had passionately wished for the death of the child in her womb. Having herself grown up and become pregnant, she was only following the example of her mother.

If anyone dreams that his father or mother, his brother or sister, has died, and his dream expresses grief, I should never adduce this as proof that he wishes any of them dead now. The theory of dreams does not go as far as to require this; it is satisfied with concluding that the dreamer has wished them dead at some time or other during his childhood. I fear, however, that this limitation will not go far to appease my critics; probably they will just as energetically deny the possibility that they ever had such thoughts, as they protest that they do not harbour them now. I must, therefore, reconstruct a portion of the submerged infantile psychology on the basis of the evidence of the present.[40]

Let us first of all consider the relation of children to their brothers and sisters. I do not know why we presuppose that it must be a loving one, since examples of enmity among adult brothers and sisters are frequent in everyone's experience, and since we are so often able to verify the fact that this estrangement originated during childhood, or has always existed. Moreover, many adults who today are devoted to their brothers and sisters, and support them in adversity, lived with them in almost continuous enmity during their childhood. The elder child ill-

---

[40] Cf. also "Analysis of a Phobia in a Five-year-old Boy," Collected Papers, III; and "On the Sexual Theories of Children," Ibid., II.

treated the younger, slandered him, and robbed him of his toys; the younger was consumed with helpless fury against the elder, envied and feared him, or his earliest impulse toward liberty and his first revolt against injustice were directed against his oppressor. The parents say that the children do not agree, and cannot find the reason for it. It is not difficult to see that the character even of a well-behaved child is not the character we should wish to find in an adult. A child is absolutely egoistical; he feels his wants acutely, and strives remorselessly to satisfy them, especially against his competitors, other children, and first of all against his brothers and sisters. And yet we do not on that account call a child wicked-we call him naughty; he is not responsible for his misdeeds, either in our own judgment or in the eyes of the law. And this is as it should be; for we may expect that within the very period of life which we reckon as childhood, altruistic impulses and morality will awake in the little egoist, and that, in the words of Meynert, a secondary ego will overlay and inhibit the primary ego. Morality, of course, does not develop simultaneously in all its departments, and furthermore, the duration of the amoral period of childhood differs in different individuals. Where this morality fails to develop we are prone to speak of degeneration; but here the case is obviously one of arrested development. Where the primary character is already overlaid by the later development it may be at least partially uncovered again by an attack of hysteria. The correspondence between the so-called hysterical character and that of a naughty child is positively striking. The obsessional neurosis, on the other hand, corresponds to a supermorality, which develops as a strong reinforcement against the primary character that is threatening to revive.

Many persons, then, who now love their brothers and sisters, and who would feel bereaved by their death, harbour in their unconscious hostile wishes, survivals from an earlier period, wishes which are able to realize themselves in dreams. It is, however, quite especially interesting to observe the behaviour of little children up to their third and fourth year towards their younger brothers or sisters. So far the child has been the only one; now he is informed that the stork has brought a new baby. The child inspects the new arrival, and expresses his opinion with decision:

"The stork had better take it back again!"[41]

I seriously declare it as my opinion that a child is able to estimate the disadvantages which he has to expect on account of a newcomer. A connection of mine, who now gets on very well with a sister, who is four years her junior, responded to the news of this sister's arrival with the reservation: "But I shan't give her my red cap, anyhow." If the child should come to realize only at a later stage that its happiness may be prejudiced by a younger brother or sister, its enmity will be aroused at this period. I know of a case where a girl, not three years of age, tried to strangle an infant in its cradle, because she suspected that its continued presence boded her no good. Children at this time of life are capable of a jealousy that is perfectly evident and extremely intense. Again, perhaps the little brother or sister really soon disappears, and the child once more draws to himself the whole affection of the household; then a new child is sent by the stork; is it not natural that the favourite should conceive the wish that the new rival may meet the same fate as the earlier one, in order that he may be as happy as he was before the birth of the first child, and during the interval after his death?[42] Of course, this attitude of the child towards the younger brother or sister is, under normal circumstances, a mere function of the difference of age. After a certain interval the maternal instincts of the older girl will be awakened towards the helpless newborn infant.

Feelings of hostility towards brothers and sisters must occur

---

[41] Hans, whose phobia was the subject of the analysis in the above-mentioned publication, cried out at the age of three and a half, while feverish, shortly after the birth of a sister: "But I don't want to have a little sister." In his neurosis, eighteen months later, he frankly confessed the wish that his mother should drop the child into the bath while bathing it, in order that it might die. With all this, Hans was a good-natured, affectionate child, who soon became fond of his sister, and took her under his special protection.

[42] Such cases of death in the experience of children may soon be forgotten in the family, but psycho-analytical investigation shows that they are very significant for a later neurosis.

far more frequently in children than is observed by their obtuse elders.[43]

In the case of my own children, who followed one another rapidly, I missed the opportunity of making such observations, I am now retrieving it, thanks to my little nephew, whose undisputed domination was disturbed after fifteen months by the arrival of a feminine rival. I hear, it is true, that the young man behaves very chivalrously toward his little sister, that he kisses her hand and strokes her; but in spite of this I have convinced myself that even before the completion of his second year he is using his new command of language to criticize this person, who, to him, after all, seems superfluous. Whenever the conversation turns upon her he chimes in, and cries angrily: "Too (l)ittle, too (l)ittle!" During the last few months, since the child has outgrown this disparagement, owing to her splendid development, he has found another reason for his insistence that she does not deserve so much attention. He reminds us, on every suitable pretext: "She hasn't any teeth."[44] We all of us recollect the case of the eldest daughter of another sister of mine. The child, who was then six years of age, spent a full half-hour in going from one aunt to another with the question: "Lucie can't understand that yet, can she?" Lucie was her rival- two and a half years younger.

I have never failed to come across this dream of the death of brothers or sisters, denoting an intense hostility, e.g., I have met it in all my female patients. I have met with only one exception, which could easily be interpreted into a confirmation of the rule.

---

[43] Since the above was written, a great many observations relating to the originally hostile attitude of children toward their brothers and sisters, and toward one of their parents, have been recorded in the literature of psycho-analysis. One writer, Spitteler, gives the following peculiarly sincere and ingenious description of this typical childish attitude as he experienced it in his earliest childhood: "Moreover, there was now a second Adolf. A little creature whom they declared was my brother, but I could not understand what he could be for, or why they should pretend he was a being like myself. I was sufficient unto myself: what did I want with a brother? And he was not only useless, he was also even troublesome. When I plagued my grandmother, he too wanted to plague her; when I was wheeled about in the baby-carriage he sat opposite me, and took up half the room, so that we could not help kicking one another."

[44] The three-and-a-half-year-old Hans embodied his devastating criticism of his little sister in these identical words (loc. cit.). He assumed that she was unable to speak on account of her lack of teeth.

Once, in the course of a sitting, when I was explaining this state of affairs to a female patient, since it seemed to have some bearing on the symptoms under consideration that day, she answered, to my astonishment, that she had never had such dreams. But another dream occurred to her, which presumably had nothing to do with the case- a dream which she had first dreamed at the age of four, when she was the youngest child, and had since then dreamed repeatedly. "A number of children, all her brothers and sisters with her boy and girl cousins, were romping about in a meadow. Suddenly they all grew wings, flew up, and were gone." She had no idea of the significance of this dream; but we can hardly fail to recognize it as a dream of the death of all the brothers and sisters, in its original form, and but little influenced by the censorship. I will venture to add the following analysis of it: on the death of one out of this large number of children- in this case the children of two brothers were brought up together as brothers and sisters- would not our dreamer, at that time not yet four years of age, have asked some wise, grown-up person: "What becomes of children when they are dead?" The answer would probably have been: "They grow wings and become angels." After this explanation. all the brothers and sisters and cousins in the dream now have wings, like angels and- this is the important point- they fly away. Our little angel-maker is left alone: just think, the only one out of such a crowd! That the children romp about a meadow, from which they fly away, points almost certainly to butterflies it is as though the child had been influenced by the same association of ideas which led the ancients to imagine Psyche, the soul, with the wings of a butterfly.

Perhaps some readers will now object that the inimical impulses of children toward their brothers and sisters may perhaps be admitted, but how does the childish character arrive at such heights of wickedness as to desire the death of a rival or a stronger playmate, as though all misdeeds could be atoned for only by death? Those who speak in this fashion forget that the child's idea of being dead has little but the word in common with our own. The child knows nothing of the horrors of decay, of shivering in the cold grave, of the terror of the infinite Nothing, the thought of which the adult, as all the myths of the hereafter testify, finds so intolerable. The fear of death is alien to the child; and so he plays with the horrid word, and threatens another child: "If you do that again, you will die, just like Francis died"; at which the poor mother shudders, unable perhaps to forget that the greater proportion of mortals do not survive beyond the years of childhood. Even at the age of eight, a child returning from a visit to a natural history museum may say to her mother: "Mamma, I do love you so; if you ever die, I am going to have you stuffed and set you up here in the room, so that I can always, always see you!" So different from our own is the childish conception of being dead.[45]

Being dead means, for the child, who has been spared the sight of the suffering that precedes death, much the same as being gone, and ceasing to annoy the survivors. The child does not distinguish the means by which this absence is brought about, whether by distance, or estrangement, or death.[46] If, during the child's prehistoric years, a nurse has been dismissed, and if his mother dies a little while later, the two experiences, as we discover by analysis, form links of a chain in his memory. The fact that the child does not very intensely miss those who are absent has been realized, to her sorrow, by many a mother, when she has returned home from an absence of several weeks, and has been told, upon inquiry: "The children have not asked for their mother

---

[45] To my astonishment, I was told that a highly intelligent boy of ten, after the sudden death of his father, said: "I understand that father is dead, but I can't see why he does not come home to supper." Further material relating to this subject will be found in the section "Kinderseele," edited by Frau Dr. von HugHellmuth, in Imago Vol. i-v, 1912-18.

[46] The observation of a father trained in psycho-analysis was able to detect the very moment when his very intelligent little daughter, age four, realized the difference between being away and being dead. The child was being troublesome at table, and noted that one of the waitresses in the pension was looking at her with an expression of annoyance. "Josephine ought to be dead," she thereupon remarked to her father. "But why dead?" asked the father, soothingly. "Wouldn't it be enough if she went away?" "No," replied the child, "then she would come back again." To the uncurbed self-love (narcissism) of the child, every inconvenience constitutes the crime of lese majeste, and, as in the Draconian code, the child's feelings prescribe for all such crimes the one invariable punishment.

once." But if she really departs to "that undiscovered country from whose bourne no traveller returns," the children seem at first to have forgotten her, and only subsequently do they begin to remember their dead mother.

While, therefore, the child has its motives for desiring the absence of another child, it is lacking in all those restraints which would prevent it from clothing this wish in the form of a death-wish; and the psychic reaction to dreams of a death-wish proves that, in spite of all the differences of content, the wish in the case of the child is after all identical with the corresponding wish in an adult.

If, then, the death-wish of a child in respect of his brothers and sisters is explained by his childish egoism, which makes him regard his brothers and sisters as rivals, how are we to account for the same wish in respect of his parents, who bestow their love on him, and satisfy his needs, and whose preservation he ought to desire for these very egoistical reasons?

Towards a solution of this difficulty we may be guided by our knowledge that the very great majority of dreams of the death of a parent refer to the parent of the same sex as the dreamer, so that a man generally dreams of the death of his father, and a woman of the death of her mother. I do not claim that this happens constantly; but that it happens in a great majority of cases is so evident that it requires explanation by some factor of general significance.[47] Broadly speaking, it is as though a sexual preference made itself felt at an early age, as though the boy regarded his father, and the girl her mother, as a rival in love- by whose removal he or she could but profit.

Before rejecting this idea as monstrous, let the reader again consider the actual relations between parents and children. We must distinguish between the traditional standard of conduct, the filial piety expected in this relation, and what daily observation shows us to be the fact. More than one occasion for enmity lies

---

[47] The situation is frequently disguised by the intervention of a tendency to punishment, which, in the form of a moral reaction, threatens the loss of the beloved parent.

hidden amidst the relations of parents and children; conditions are present in the greatest abundance under which wishes which cannot pass the censorship are bound to arise. Let us first consider the relation between father and son. In my opinion the sanctity with which we have endorsed the injunctions of the Decalogue dulls our perception of the reality. Perhaps we hardly dare permit ourselves to perceive that the greater part of humanity neglects to obey the fifth commandment. In the lowest as well as in the highest strata of human society, filial piety towards parents is wont to recede before other interests. The obscure legends which have been handed down to us from the primeval ages of human society in mythology and folklore give a deplorable idea of the despotic power of the father, and the ruthlessness with which it was exercised. Kronos devours his children, as the wild boar devours the litter of the sow; Zeus emasculates his father[48] and takes his place as ruler.

The more tyrannically the father ruled in the ancient family, the more surely must the son, as his appointed successor, have assumed the position of an enemy, and the greater must have been his impatience to attain to supremacy through the death of his father. Even in our own middle-class families the father commonly fosters the growth of the germ of hatred which is naturally inherent in the paternal relation, by refusing to allow the son to be a free agent or by denying him the means of becoming so. A physician often has occasion to remark that a son's grief at the loss of his father cannot quench his gratification that he has at last obtained his freedom. Fathers, as a rule, cling desperately to as much of the sadly antiquated potestas patris familias[49] as still survives in our modern society, and the poet who, like Ibsen, puts the immemorial strife between father and son in the foreground of his drama is sure of his effect. The

---

[48] At least in some of the mythological accounts. According to others, emasculation was inflicted only by Kronos on his father Uranos. With regard to the mythological significance of this motive, cf. Otto Rank's Der Mythus von der Geburt des Helden, in No. v of Schriften zur angew. Seelen-kunde (1909), and Das Inzestmotiv in Dichtung und Sage (1912), chap. ix, 2.

[49] Authority of the father.

causes of conflict between mother and daughter arise when the daughter grows up and finds herself watched by her mother when she longs for real sexual freedom, while the mother is reminded by the budding beauty of her daughter that for her the time has come to renounce sexual claims.

All these circumstances are obvious to everyone, but they do not help us to explain dreams of the death of their parents in persons for whom filial piety has long since come to be unquestionable. We are, however, prepared by the foregoing discussion to look for the origin of a death-wish in the earliest years of childhood.

In the case of psychoneurotics, analysis confirms this conjecture beyond all doubt. For analysis tells us that the sexual wishes of the child- in so far as they deserve this designation in their nascent state- awaken at a very early age, and that the earliest affection of the girl-child is lavished on the father, while the earliest infantile desires of the boy are directed upon the mother. For the boy the father, and for the girl the mother, becomes an obnoxious rival, and we have already shown, in the case of brothers and sisters, how readily in children this feeling leads to the death-wish. As a general rule, sexual selection soon makes its appearance in the parents; it is a natural tendency for the father to spoil his little daughters, and for the mother to take the part of the sons, while both, so long as the glamour of sex does not prejudice their judgment, are strict in training the children. The child is perfectly conscious of this partiality, and offers resistance to the parent who opposes it. To find love in an adult is for the child not merely the satisfaction of a special need; it means also that the child's will is indulged in all other respects. Thus the child is obeying its own sexual instinct, and at the same time reinforcing the stimulus proceeding from the parents, when its choice between the parents corresponds with their own.

The signs of these infantile tendencies are for the most part over-looked; and yet some of them may be observed even after the early years of childhood. An eight-year-old girl of my acquaintance, whenever her mother is called away from the table, takes advantage of her absence to proclaim herself her successor. "Now I shall be Mamma; Karl, do you want some more vegetables? Have some more, do," etc. A particularly clever and lively little girl, not yet four years of age, in whom this trait of child psychology is unusually transparent, says frankly: "Now mummy can go away; then daddy must marry me, and I will be his wife." Nor does this wish by any means exclude the possibility that the child may most tenderly love its mother. If the little boy is allowed to sleep at his mother's side whenever his father goes on a journey, and if after his father's return he has to go back to the nursery, to a person whom he likes far less, the wish may readily arise that his father might always be absent, so that he might keep his place beside his dear, beautiful mamma; and the father's death is obviously a means for the attainment of this wish; for the child's experience has taught him that dead folks, like grandpapa, for example, are always absent; they never come back.

While such observations of young children readily accommodate themselves to the interpretation suggested, they do not, it is true, carry the complete conviction which is forced upon a physician by the psycho-analysis of adult neurotics. The dreams of neurotic patients are communicated with preliminaries of such a nature that their interpretation as wish-dreams becomes inevitable. One day I find a lady depressed and weeping. She says: "I do not want to see my relatives any more; they must shudder at me." Thereupon, almost without any transition, she tells me that she has remembered a dream, whose significance, of course, she does not understand. She dreamed it when she was four years old, and it was this: A fox or a lynx is walking about the roof; then something falls down, or she falls down, and after that, her mother is carried out of the house- dead; whereat the dreamer weeps bitterly. I have no sooner informed her that this dream must signify a childish wish to see her mother dead, and that it is because of this dream that she thinks that her relatives must shudder at her, than she furnishes material in explanation of the dream. "Lynx-eye" is an opprobrious epithet which a street boy once bestowed on her when she was a very small child; and when she was three years old a brick or tile fell on her mother's head, so that she bled profusely. I once had occasion to make a thorough study of a young girl who was passing through various psychic states. In the state of frenzied confusion with which her illness began, the patient manifested a quite peculiar aversion for her mother; she struck her and abused her whenever she approached the bed, while at the same period she was affectionate and submissive to a much older sister. Then there followed a lucid but rather apathetic condition, with badly disturbed sleep. It was in this phase that I began to treat her and to analyse her dreams. An enormous number of these dealt, in a more or less veiled fashion, with the death of the girl's mother; now she was present at the funeral of an old woman, now she saw herself and her sister sitting at a table, dressed in mourning; the meaning of the dreams could not be doubted. During her progressive improvement hysterical phobias made their appearance, the most distressing of which was the fear that something had happened to her mother. Wherever she might be at the time, she had then to hurry home in order to convince herself that her mother was still alive. Now this case, considered in conjunction with the rest of my experience. was very instructive; it showed, in polyglot translations, as it were, the different ways in which the psychic apparatus reacts to the same exciting idea.

In the state of confusion, which I regard as an overthrow of the second psychic instance by the first instance, at other times suppressed, the unconscious enmity towards the mother gained the upper hand, and found physical expression; then, when the patient became calmer, the insurrection was suppressed, and the domination of the censorship restored, and this enmity had access only to the realms of dreams, in which it realized the wish that the mother might die; and, after the normal condition had been still further strengthened, it created the excessive concern for the mother as a hysterical counter-reaction and defensive phenomenon. In the light of these considerations, it is no longer inexplicable why hysterical girls are so often extravagantly attached to their mothers.

On another occasion I had an opportunity of obtaining a profound insight into the unconscious psychic life of a young man for whom an obsessional neurosis made life almost unendurable, so that he could not go into the streets, because he was tormented by the fear that he would kill everyone he met. He spent his days in contriving evidence of an alibi in case he should be accused of any murder that might have been committed in the city. It goes without saying that this man was as moral as he was highly cultured. The analysis- which, by the way, led to a curerevealed, as the basis of this distressing obsession, murderous impulses in respect of his rather overstrict father- impulses which, to his astonishment, had consciously expressed themselves when he was seven years old, but which, of course, had originated in a much earlier period of his childhood. After the painful illness and death of his father, when the young man was in his thirty-first year, the obsessive reproach made its appearance, which transferred itself to strangers in the form of this phobia. Anyone capable of wishing to push his own father from a mountaintop into an abyss cannot be trusted to spare the lives of persons less closely related to him; he therefore does well to lock himself into his room.

According to my already extensive experience, parents play a leading part in the infantile psychology of all persons who subsequently become psychoneurotics. Falling in love with one parent and hating the other forms part of the permanent stock of the psychic impulses which arise in early childhood, and are of such importance as the material of the subsequent neurosis. But I do not believe that psychoneurotics are to be sharply distinguished in this respect from other persons who remain normal- that is, I do not believe that they are capable of creating something absolutely new and peculiar to themselves. It is far more probable- and this is confirmed by incidental observations of normal children- that in their amorous or hostile attitude toward their parents, psychoneurotics do no more than reveal to us, by magnification, something that occurs less markedly and intensively in the minds of the majority of children. Antiquity has furnished us with legendary matter which corroborates this belief, and the profound and universal validity of the old legends is explicable only by an equally universal validity of the above-mentioned hypothesis of infantile psychology.

I am referring to the legend of King Oedipus and the Oedipus Rex of Sophocles. Oedipus, the son of Laius, king of Thebes, and Jocasta, is exposed as a suckling, because an oracle had informed the father that his son, who was still unborn, would be his murderer. He is rescued, and grows up as a king's son at a foreign court, until, being uncertain of his origin, he, too, consults the oracle, and is warned to avoid his native place, for he is destined to become the murderer of his father and the husband of his mother. On the road leading away from his supposed home he meets King Laius, and in a sudden quarrel strikes him dead. He comes to Thebes, where he solves the riddle of the Sphinx, who is barring the way to the city, whereupon he is elected king by the grateful Thebans, and is rewarded with the hand of Jocasta. He reigns for many years in peace and honour, and begets two sons and two daughters upon his unknown mother, until at last a plague breaks out- which causes the Thebians to consult the oracle anew. Here Sophocles' tragedy begins. The messengers bring the reply that the plague will stop as soon as the murderer of Laius is driven from the country. But where is he?

Where shall be found, Faint, and hard to be known, the trace of the ancient guilt?

The action of the play consists simply in the disclosure, approached step by step and artistically delayed (and comparable to the work of a psychoanalysis) that Oedipus himself is the murderer of Laius, and that he is the son of the murdered man and Jocasta. Shocked by the abominable crime which he has unwittingly committed, Oedipus blinds himself, and departs from his native city. The prophecy of the oracle has been fulfilled.

The Oedipus Rex is a tragedy of fate; its tragic effect depends on the conflict between the all-powerful will of the gods and the vain efforts of human beings threatened with disaster; resignation to the divine will, and the perception of one's own impotence is the lesson which the deeply moved spectator is supposed to learn from the tragedy. Modern authors have therefore sought to achieve a similar tragic effect by expressing the same conflict in stories of their own invention. But the playgoers have looked on unmoved at the unavailing efforts of guiltless men to avert the fulfilment of curse or oracle; the modern tragedies of destiny have failed of their effect.

If the Oedipus Rex is capable of moving a modern reader or playgoer no less powerfully than it moved the contemporary Greeks, the only possible explanation is that the effect of the Greek tragedy does not depend upon the conflict between fate and human will, but upon the peculiar nature of the material by which this conflict is revealed. There must be a voice within us which is prepared to acknowledge the compelling power of fate in the Oedipus, while we are able to condemn the situations occurring in Die Ahnfrau or other tragedies of fate as arbitrary inventions. And there actually is a motive in the story of King Oedipus which explains the verdict of this inner voice. His fate moves us only because it might have been our own, because the oracle laid upon us before our birth the very curse which rested upon him. It may be that we were all destined to direct our first sexual impulses toward our mothers, and our first impulses of hatred and violence toward our fathers; our dreams convince us that we were. King Oedipus, who slew his father Laius and wedded his mother Jocasta, is nothing more or less than a wish-fulfilment- the fulfilment of the wish of our childhood. But we, more fortunate than he, in so far as we have not become psychoneurotics, have since our childhood succeeded in withdrawing our sexual impulses from our mothers, and in forgetting our jealousy of our fathers. We recoil from the person for whom this primitive wish of our childhood has been fulfilled with all the force of the repression which these wishes have undergone in our minds since childhood. As the poet brings the guilt of Oedipus to light by his investigation, he forces us to become aware of our own inner selves, in which the same impulses are still extant, even though they are suppressed. The antithesis with which the chorus departs:

...Behold, this is Oedipus, Who unravelled the great riddle, and was first in power, Whose fortune all the townsmen praised and envied; See in what dread adversity he sank! -this admonition touches us and our own pride, we who, since the years of our childhood, have grown so wise and so powerful in our own estimation. Like Oedipus, we live in ignorance of the desires that offend morality, the desires that nature has forced upon us and after their unveiling we may well prefer to avert our gaze from the scenes of our childhood.[50]

In the very text of Sophocles' tragedy there is an unmistakable reference to the fact that the Oedipus legend had its source in dream-material of immemorial antiquity, the content of which was the painful disturbance of the child's relations to its parents caused by the first impulses of sexuality. Jocasta comforts Oedipus- who is not yet enlightened, but is troubled by the recollection of the oracle- by an allusion to a dream which is often dreamed, though it cannot, in her opinion, mean anything: -

For many a man hath seen himself in dreams His mother's mate, but he who gives no heed To suchlike matters bears the easier life. -

The dream of having sexual intercourse with one's mother was as common then as it is today with many people, who tell it with indignation and astonishment. As may well be imagined, it

---

[50] None of the discoveries of psycho-analytical research has evoked such embittered contradiction, such furious opposition, and also such entertaining acrobatics of criticism, as this indication of the incestuous impulses of childhood which survive in the unconscious. An attempt has even been made recently, in defiance of all experience, to assign only a symbolic significance to incest. Ferenczi has given an ingenious reinterpretation of the Oedipus myth, based on a passage in one of Schopenhauer's letters, in Imago, i, (1912). The Oedipus complex, which was first alluded to here in The Interpretation of Dreams, has through further study of the subject, acquired an unexpected significance for the understanding of human history and the evolution of religion and morality. See Toten and Taboo.

is the key to the tragedy and the complement to the dream of the death of the father. The Oedipus fable is the reaction of phantasy to these two typical dreams, and just as such a dream, when occurring to an adult, is experienced with feelings of aversion, so the content of the fable must include terror and self-chastisement. The form which it subsequently assumed was the result of an uncomprehending secondary elaboration of the material, which sought to make it serve a theological intention.[51] The attempt to reconcile divine omnipotence with human responsibility must, of course, fail with this material as with any other.

Another of the great poetic tragedies, Shakespeare's Hamlet, is rooted in the same soil as Oedipus Rex. But the whole difference in the psychic life of the two widely separated periods of civilization, and the progress, during the course of time, of repression in the emotional life of humanity, is manifested in the differing treatment of the same material. In Oedipus Rex the basic wish-phantasy of the child is brought to light and realized as it is in dreams; in Hamlet it remains repressed, and we learn of its existence- as we discover the relevant facts in a neurosis- only through the inhibitory effects which proceed from it. In the more modern drama, the curious fact that it is possible to remain in complete uncertainty as to the character of the hero has proved to be quite consistent with the over-powering effect of the tragedy. The play is based upon Hamlet's hesitation in accomplishing the task of revenge assigned to him; the text does not give the cause or the motive of this hesitation, nor have the manifold attempts at interpretation succeeded in doing so. According to the still prevailing conception, a conception for which Goethe was first responsible. Hamlet represents the type of man whose active energy is paralyzed by excessive intellectual activity: "Sicklied o'er with the pale cast of thought." According to another conception. the poet has endeavoured to portray a morbid, irresolute character, on the verge of neurasthenia. The plot of the drama, however, shows us that Hamlet is by no means intended to appear as a character wholly incapable of action.

---

[51] Cf. the dream-material of exhibitionism, earlier in this chapter.

On two separate occasions we see him assert himself: once in a sudden outburst of rage, when he stabs the eavesdropper behind the arras, and on the other occasion when he deliberately, and even craftily, with the complete unscrupulousness of a prince of the Renaissance, sends the two courtiers to the death which was intended for himself. What is it, then, that inhibits him in accomplishing the task which his father's ghost has laid upon him? Here the explanation offers itself that it is the peculiar nature of this task. Hamlet is able to do anything but take vengeance upon the man who did away with his father and has taken his father's place with his mother- the man who shows him in realization the repressed desires of his own childhood. The loathing which should have driven him to revenge is thus replaced by self-reproach, by conscientious scruples, which tell him that he himself is no better than the murderer whom he is required to punish. I have here translated into consciousness what had to remain unconscious in the mind of the hero; if anyone wishes to call Hamlet an hysterical subject I cannot but admit that this is the deduction to be drawn from my interpretation. The sexual aversion which Hamlet expresses in conversation with Ophelia is perfectly consistent with this deduction- the same sexual aversion which during the next few years was increasingly to take possession of the poet's soul, until it found its supreme utterance in Timon of Athens. It can, of course, be only the poet's own psychology with which we are confronted in Hamlet; and in a work on Shakespeare by Georg Brandes (1896) I find the statement that the drama was composed immediately after the death of Shakespeare's father (1601)- that is to say, when he was still mourning his loss, and during a revival, as we may fairly assume, of his own childish feelings in respect of his father. It is known, too, that Shakespeare's son, who died in childhood, bore the name of Hamnet (identical with Hamlet). Just as Hamlet treats of the relation of the son to his parents, so Macbeth, which was written about the same period, is based upon the theme of childlessness. Just as all neurotic symptoms, like dreams themselves, are capable of hyper-interpretation, and even require such hyper-interpretation before they become perfectly intelligible, so every genuine poetical creation must have proceeded from more than one motive, more than one impulse in the mind of the poet, and must admit of more than one interpretation. I have here attempted to interpret only the deepest stratum of impulses in the mind of the creative poet.[52]

With regard to typical dreams of the death of relatives, I must add a few words upon their significance from the point of view of the theory of dreams in general. These dreams show us the occurrence of a very unusual state of things; they show us that the dream-thought created by the repressed wish completely escapes the censorship, and is transferred to the dream without alteration. Special conditions must obtain in order to make this possible. The following two factors favour the production of these dreams: first, this is the last wish that we could credit ourselves with harbouring; we believe such a wish "would never occur to us even in a dream"; the dream-censorship is therefore unprepared for this monstrosity, just as the laws of Solon did not foresee the necessity of establishing a penalty for patricide. Secondly, the repressed and unsuspected wish is, in this special case, frequently met half-way by a residue from the day's experience, in the form of some concern for the life of the beloved person.

This anxiety cannot enter into the dream otherwise than by taking advantage of the corresponding wish; but the wish is able to mask itself behind the concern which has been aroused during the day. If one is inclined to think that all this is really a very much simpler process, and to imagine that one merely continues during the night, and in one's dream, what was begun during the

---

[52] These indications in the direction of an analytical understanding of Hamlet were subsequently developed by Dr. Ernest Jones, who defended the above conception against others which have been put forward in the literature of the subject (The Problem of Hamlet and the Oedipus Complex, [1911]). The relation of the material of Hamlet to the myth of the birth of the hero has been demonstrated by O. Rank. Further attempts at an analysis of Macbeth will be found in my essay on "Some Character Types Met with in Psycho-Analytic Work," Collected Papers, IV., in L. Jeckel's "Shakespeare's Macbeth," in Imago, V. (1918) and in "The Oedipus Complex as an Explanation of Hamlet's Mystery: a Study in Motive" (American Journal of Psycology [1910], vol. xxi).

day, one removes the dreams of the death of those dear to us out of all connection with the general explanation of dreams, and a problem that may very well be solved remains a problem needlessly.

It is instructive to trace the relation of these dreams to anxiety-dreams. In dreams of the death of those dear to us the repressed wish has found a way of avoiding the censorship- and the distortion for which the censorship is responsible. An invariable concomitant phenomenon then, is that painful emotions are felt in the dream. Similarly, an anxiety-dream occurs only when the censorship is entirely or partially overpowered, and on the other hand, the overpowering of the censorship is facilitated when the actual sensation of anxiety is already present from somatic sources. It thus becomes obvious for what purpose the censorship performs its office and practises dream-distortion; it does so in order to prevent the development of anxiety or other forms of painful affect.

I have spoken in the foregoing sections of the egoism of the child's psyche, and I now emphasize this peculiarity in order to suggest a connection, for dreams too have retained this characteristic. All dreams are absolutely egoistical; in every dream the beloved ego appears, even though in a disguised form. The wishes that are realized in dreams are invariably the wishes of this ego; it is only a deceptive appearance if interest in another person is believed to have evoked a dream. I will now analyse a few examples which appear to contradict this assertion. -

I

A boy not yet four years of age relates the following dream: He saw a large garnished dish, on which was a large joint of roast meat; and the joint was suddenly- not carved- but eaten up. He did not see the person who ate it.[53]

---

[53] Even the large, over-abundant, immoderate and exaggerated things occurring in dreams may be a childish characteristic. A child wants nothing more intensely than to grow big, and to eat as much of everything as grown-ups do; a child is hard to satisfy; he knows no such word as enough and insatiably demands the repetition of whatever has pleased him or tasted good to him. He learns to practise moderation, to be modest and resigned, only through training. As we know, the neurotic also is inclined to immoderation and excess.

Who can he be, this strange person, of whose luxurious repast the little fellow dreams? The experience of the day must supply the answer. For some days past the boy, in accordance with the doctor's orders, had been living on a milk diet; but on the evening of the dream-day he had been naughty, and, as a punishment, had been deprived of his supper. He had already undergone one such hunger-cure, and had borne his deprivation bravely. He knew that he would get nothing, but he did not even allude to the fact that he was hungry. Training was beginning to produce its effect; this is demonstrated even by the dream, which reveals the beginnings of dream-distortion. There is no doubt that he himself is the person whose desires are directed toward this abundant meal, and a meal of roast meat at that. But since he knows that this is forbidden him, he does not dare, as hungry children do in dreams (cf. my little Anna's dream about strawberries, chapter III), to sit down to the meal himself. The person remains anonymous.

II

One night I dream that I see on a bookseller's counter a new volume of one of those collectors' series, which I am in the habit of buying (monographs on artistic subjects, history, famous artistic centres, etc.). The new collection is entitled "Famous Orators" (or Orations), and the first number bears the name of Dr. Lecher.

On analysis it seems to me improbable that the fame of Dr. Lecher, the long-winded speaker of the German Opposition, should occupy my thoughts while I am dreaming. The fact is that a few days ago I undertook the psychological treatment of some new patients, and am now forced to talk for ten to twelve hours a day. Thus I myself am a long-winded speaker.

III

On another occasion I dream that a university lecturer of my acquaintance says to me: "My son, the myopic." Then follows a dialogue of brief observations and replies. A third portion of the dream follows, in which I and my sons appear, and so far as the latent dream-content is concerned, the father, the son, and

Professor M, are merely lay figures, representing myself and my eldest son. Later on I shall examine this dream again, on account of another peculiarity.

IV

The following dream gives an example of really base, egoistical feelings, which conceal themselves behind an affectionate concern: *My friend Otto looks ill; his face is brown and his eyes protrude.*

Otto is my family physician, to whom I owe a debt greater than I can ever hope to repay, since he has watched for years over the health of my children, has treated them successfully when they have been ill, and, moreover, has given them presents whenever he could find any excuse for doing so. He paid us a visit on the day of the dream, and my wife noticed that he looked tired and exhausted. At night I dream of him, and my dream attributes to him certain of the symptoms of Basedow's disease. If you were to disregard my rules for dream-interpretation you would understand this dream to mean that I am concerned about the health of my friend, and that this concern is realized in the dream. It would thus constitute a contradiction not only of the assertion that a dream is a wish-fulfilment, but also of the assertion that it is accessible only to egoistical impulses. But will those who thus interpret my dream explain why I should fear that Otto has Basedow's disease, for which diagnosis his appearance does not afford the slightest justification? My analysis, on the other hand, furnishes the following material, deriving from an incident which had occurred six years earlier. We were driving- a small party of us, including Professor R- in the dark through the forest of N, which lies at a distance of some hours from where we were staying in the country. The driver, who was not quite sober, overthrew us and the carriage down a bank, and it was only by good fortune that we all escaped unhurt. But we were forced to spend the night at the nearest inn, where the news of our mishap aroused great sympathy. A certain gentleman, who showed unmistakable symptoms of morbus Basedowii- the brownish colour of the skin of the face and the protruding eyes, but no goitre- placed himself entirely at our disposal, and asked what he could do for us. Professor R answered in his decisive way, "Nothing, except lend me a nightshirt." Whereupon our generous friend replied: "I am sorry, but I cannot do that," and left us.

In continuing the analysis, it occurs to me that Basedow is the name not only of a physician but also of a famous pedagogue. (Now that I am wide awake, I do not feel quite sure of this fact.) My friend Otto is the person whom I have asked to take charge of the physical education of my children- especially during the age of puberty (hence the nightshirt) in case anything should happen to me. By seeing Otto in my dream with the morbid symptoms of our above-mentioned generous helper, I clearly mean to say: "If anything happens to me, he will do just as little for my children as Baron L did for us, in spite of his amiable offers." The egoistical flavour of this dream should now be obvious enough.[54]

In justice to this lady with her national pride it may, however, be remarked that the dogma: "the dream is wholly egoistic" must not be misunderstood. For inasmuch as everything that occurs in preconscious inking may appear in dreams (in the content as well as the latent dreamthoughts) the altruistic feelings may possibly occur. Similarly, affectionate or amorous feelings for another person, if they exist in the unconscious, may occur in dreams. The truth of the assertion is therefore restricted to the fact that among the unconscious stimuli of dreams one very often finds egoistical tendencies which seem to have been overcome in the waking state. But where is the wish-fulfilment to be found in this? Not in the vengeance wreaked on my friend Otto (who seems to be fated to be badly treated in my dreams), but in the following circumstance: Inasmuch as in my dream I represented Otto as Baron L, I likewise identified myself with another person,

---

[54] While Dr. Ernest Jones was delivering a lecture before an American scientific society, and was speaking of egoism in dreams, a learned lady took exception to this unscientific generalization. She thought the lecturer was entitled to pronounce such a verdict only on the dreams of Austrians, but had no right to include the dreams of Americans. As for herself, she was sure that all her dreams were strictly altruistic.

namely, with Professor R; for I have asked something of Otto, just as R asked something of Baron L at the time of the incident I have described. And this is the point. For Professor R has gone his way independently, outside academic circles, just as I myself have done, and has only in his later years received the title which he had earned before. Once more, then, I want to be a professor! The very phrase *in his later years* is a wish-fulfilment, for it means that I shall live long enough to steer my boys through the age of puberty myself.

Of other typical dreams, in which one flies with a feeling of ease or falls in terror, I know nothing from my own experience, and whatever I have to say about them I owe to my psychoanalyses. From the information thus obtained one must conclude that these dreams also reproduce impressions made in childhood- that is, that they refer to the games involving rapid motion which have such an extraordinary attraction for children. Where is the uncle who has never made a child fly by running with it across the room with outstretched arms, or has never played at falling with it by rocking it on his knee and then suddenly straightening his leg, or by lifting it above his head and suddenly pretending to withdraw his supporting hand? At such moments children shout with joy, and insatiably demand a repetition of the performance, especially if a little fright and dizziness are involved in the game; in after years they repeat their sensations in dreams. but in dreams they omit the hands that held them, so that now they are free to float or fall. We know that all small children have a fondness for such games as rocking and see-sawing; and if they see gymnastic performances at the circus their recollection of such games is refreshed.[55] In some boys a hysterical attack will consist simply in the reproduction of such performances, which they accomplish with great dexterity. Not infrequently sexual sensations are excited by these games of

---

[55] Psycho-analytic investigation has enabled us to conclude that in the predilection shown by children for gymnastic performances, and in the repetition of these in hysterical attacks, there is, besides the pleasure felt in the organ, yet another factor at work (often unconscious): namely, a memory-picture of sexual intercourse observed in human beings or animals.

movement, which are quite neutral in themselves.[56] To express the matter in a few words: the exciting games of childhood are repeated in dreams of flying, falling, reeling and the like, but the voluptuous feelings are now transformed into anxiety. But, as every mother knows, the excited play of children often enough culminates in quarrelling and tears.

I have therefore good reason for rejecting the explanation that it is the state of our dermal sensations during sleep, the sensation of the movements of the lungs, etc., that evokes dreams of flying and falling. I see that these very sensations have been reproduced from the memory to which the dream refers- and that they are, therefore, dream-content and not dream-sources.

I do not for a moment deny, however, that I am unable to furnish a full explanation of this series of typical dreams. Precisely here my material leaves me in the lurch. I must adhere to the general opinion that all the dermal and kinetic sensations of these typical dreams are awakened as soon as any psychic motive of whatever kind has need of them, and that they are neglected when there is no such need of them. The relation to infantile experiences seems to be confirmed by the indications which I have obtained from the analyses of psychoneurotics. But I am unable to say what other meanings might, in the course of the dreamer's life, have become attached to the memory of these sensations- different, perhaps, in each individual, despite the typical appearance of these dreams- and I should very much like to be in a position to fill this gap with careful analyses of good examples. To those who wonder why I complain of a lack of material, despite the frequency of these dreams of flying, falling, tooth-drawing, etc., I must explain that I myself have never experienced

---

[56] A young colleague, who is entirely free from nervousness, tells me, in this connection: "I know from my own experience that while swinging, and at the moment at which the downward movement was at its maximum, I used to have a curious feeling in my genitals, which, although it was not really pleasing to me, I must describe as a voluptuous feeling." I have often heard from patients that the first erections with voluptuous sensations which they can remember to have had in boyhood occurred while they were climbing. It is established with complete certainty by psycho-analysis that the first sexual sensations often have their origin in the scufflings and wrestlings of childhood.

any such dreams since I have turned my attention to the subject of dreaminterpretation.

The dreams of neurotics which are at my disposal, however, are not all capable of interpretation, and very often it is impossible to penetrate to the farthest point of their hidden intention; a certain psychic force which participated in the building up of the neurosis, and which again becomes active during its dissolution, opposes interpretation of the final problem.

(c) The Examination-Dream

Everyone who has received his certificate of matriculation after passing his final examination at school complains of the persistence with which he is plagued by anxiety-dreams in which he has failed, or must go through his course again, etc. For the holder of a university degree this typical dream is replaced by another, which represents that he has not taken his doctor's degree, to which he vainly objects, while still asleep, that he has already been practising for years, or is already a university lecturer or the senior partner of a firm of lawyers, and so on. These are the ineradicable memories of the punishments we suffered as children for misdeeds which we had committed - memories which were revived in us on the dies irae, dies illa[57] of the gruelling examination at the two critical junctures in our careers as students. The examination-anxiety of neurotics is likewise intensified by this childish fear. When our student days are over, it is no longer our parents or teachers who see to our punishment; the inexorable chain of cause and effect of later life has taken over our further education. Now we dream of our matriculation, or the examination for the doctor's degree- and who has not been faint-hearted on such occasions?- whenever we fear that we may be punished by some unpleasant result because we have done something carelessly or wrongly, because we have not been as thorough as we might have been- in short, whenever we feel the burden of responsibility.

For a further explanation of examination-dreams I have to

---

[57] Day of wrath.

thank a remark made by a colleague who had studied this subject, who once stated, in the course of a scientific discussion, that in his experience the examination-dream occurred only to persons who had passed the examination, never to those who had flunked. We have had increasing confirmation of the fact that the anxiety-dream of examination occurs when the dreamer is anticipating a responsible task on the following day, with the possibility of disgrace; recourse will then be had to an occasion in the past on which a great anxiety proved to have been without real justification, having, indeed, been refuted by the outcome. Such a dream would be a very striking example of the way in which the dream-content is misunderstood by the waking instance. The exclamation which is regarded as a protest against the dream: "But I am already a doctor," etc., would in reality be the consolation offered by the dream, and should, therefore, be worded as follows: "Do not be afraid of the morrow; think of the anxiety which you felt before your matriculation; yet nothing happened to justify it, for now you are a doctor," etc. But the anxiety which we attribute to the dream really has its origin in the residues of the dream-day.

The tests of this interpretation which I have been able to make in my own case, and in that of others, although by no means exhaustive, were entirely in its favour.[58] For example, I failed in my examination for the doctor's degree in medical jurisprudence; never once has the matter worried me in my dreams, while I have often enough been examined in botany, zoology, and chemistry, and I sat for the examinations in these subjects with well-justified anxiety, but escaped disaster, through the clemency of fate, or of the examiner. In my dreams of school examinations, I am always examined in history, a subject in which I passed brilliantly at the time, but only, I must admit, because my good-natured professormy one-eyed benefactor in another dream- did not overlook the fact that on the examination-paper which I returned to him I had crossed out with my fingernail the second of three questions, as a hint that he should not insist on it. One of my

---

[58] See also chapter VI., A.

patients, who withdrew before the matriculation examination. only to pass it later, but failed in the officer's examination, so that he did not become an officer, tells me that he often dreams of the former examination, but never of the latter.

W. Stekel, who was the first to interpret the matriculation dream, maintains that this dream invariably refers to sexual experiences and sexual maturity. This has frequently been confirmed in my experience.

Chapter 6

The Dream-work

All other previous attempts to solve the problems of dreams have concerned themselves directly with the manifest dream-content as it is retained in the memory. They have sought to obtain an interpretation of the dream from this content, or, if they dispensed with an interpretation, to base their conclusions concerning the dream on the evidence provided by this content. We, however, are confronted by a different set of data; for us a new psychic material interposes itself between the dream-content and the results of our investigations: the latent dream-content, or dreamthoughts, which are obtained only by our method. We develop the solution of the dream from this latent content, and not from the manifest dreamcontent.

We are thus confronted with a new problem, an entirely novel task - that of examining and tracing the relations between the latent dreamthoughts and the manifest dream-content, and the processes by which the latter has grown out of the former.

The dream-thoughts and the dream-content present themselves as two descriptions of the same content in two different languages; or, to put it more clearly, the dream-content appears to us as a translation of the dream-thoughts into another mode of expression, whose symbols and laws of composition we must learn by comparing the origin with the translation. The dream-thoughts we can understand without further trouble the moment we have ascertained them. The dream-content is, as it were, presented in hieroglyphics, whose symbols must be translated, one by one, into the language of the dream-thoughts. It would of course, be incorrect to attempt to read these symbols in accordance with their values as pictures, instead of in accordance with their meaning as symbols. For instance, I have before me a picture - puzzle (rebus) - a house, upon whose roof there is a boat; then a single letter; then a running figure, whose head has been omitted, and so on. As a critic I might be tempted to judge this composition and its elements to be nonsensical. A boat is out of place on the roof of a house, and a headless man cannot run; the man, too, is larger than the house, and if the whole thing is meant to represent a landscape the single letters have no right in it, since they do not occur in nature. A correct judgment of the picture-puzzle is possible only if I make no such objections to the whole and its parts, and if, on the contrary, I take the trouble to replace each image by a syllable or word which it may represent by virtue of some allusion or relation. The words thus put together are no longer meaningless, but might constitute the most beautiful and pregnant aphorism. Now a dream is such a picture-puzzle, and our predecessors in the art of dream-interpretation have made the mistake of judging the rebus as an artistic composition. As such, of course, it appears nonsensical and worthless.

A. Condensation

The first thing that becomes clear to the investigator when he compares the dream-content with the dream-thoughts is that a tremendous work of condensation has been accomplished. The dream is meagre, paltry and laconic in comparison with the range and copiousness of the dreamthoughts. The dream, when written down fills half a page; the analysis, which contains the dream-thoughts, requires six, eight, twelve times as much space. The ratio varies with different dreams; but in my experience it is always of the same order. As a rule, the extent of the compression which has been accomplished is under-estimated, owing to the fact that the dream-thoughts which have been brought to light are believed to be the whole of the material, whereas a continuation of the work of interpretation would reveal still further thoughts hidden in the dream. We have already found it necessary to remark that one can never be really sure that one has interpreted a dream completely; even if the solution seems satisfying and flawless, it is always possible that yet another meaning has been manifested by the same dream. Thus the degree of condensation is - strictly speaking - indeterminable. Exception may be taken - and at first sight the objection seems perfectly plausible - to the assertion that the disproportion between dream-content and dream-thoughts justifies the conclusion that a considerable condensation of psychic material occurs in the formation of dreams. For we often have the feeling that we have been dreaming a great deal all night, and have then forgotten most of what we have dreamed. The dream which we remember on waking would thus appear to be merely a remnant of the dream-work, which would surely equal the dream-thoughts in range if only we could remember it completely. To a certain extent this is undoubtedly true; there is no getting away from the fact that a dream is most accurately reproduced if we try to remember it immediately after waking, and that the recollection of it becomes more and more defective as the day goes on. On the other hand, it has to be recognized that the impression that we have dreamed a good deal more than we are able to reproduce is very often based on an illusion, the origin of which we shall explain later on. Moreover, the assumption of a condensation in the dream-work is not affected by the possibility of forgetting a part of dreams, for it may be demonstrated by the multitude of ideas pertaining to those individual parts of the dream which do remain in the memory. If a large part of the dream has really escaped the memory, we are probably deprived of access to a new series of dream-thoughts. We have no justification for expecting that those portions of the dream which have been lost should likewise have referred only to those thoughts which we know from the analysis of the portions which have been preserved.[1]

In view of the very great number of ideas which analysis elicits for each individual element of the dream-content, the principal

---

[1] References to the condensation in dreams are to be found in the works of many writers on the subject. Du Prel states in his Philosophie der Mystik that he is absolutely certain that a condensation-process of the succession of ideas had occurred. -

doubt in the minds of many readers will be whether it is permissible to count everything that subsequently occurs to the mind during analysis as forming part of the dream-thoughts - in other words, to assume that all these thoughts have been active in the sleeping state, and have taken part in the formation of the dream. Is it not more probable that new combinations of thoughts are developed in the course of analysis, which did not participate in the formation of the dream? To this objection I can give only a conditional reply. It is true, of course, that separate combinations of thoughts make their first appearance during the analysis; but one can convince oneself every time this happens that such new combinations have been established only between thoughts which have already been connected in other ways in the dream-thoughts; the new combinations are, so to speak, corollaries, short-circuits, which are made possible by the existence of other, more fundamental modes of connection. In respect of the great majority of the groups of thoughts revealed by analysis, we are obliged to admit that they have already been active in the formation of the dream, for if we work through a succession of such thoughts, which at first sight seem to have played no part in the formation of the dream, we suddenly come upon a thought which occurs in the dream-content, and is indispensable to its interpretation, but which is nevertheless inaccessible except through this chain of thoughts. The reader may here turn to the dream of the botanical monograph, which is obviously the result of an astonishing degree of condensation, even though I have not given the complete analysis.

But how, then, are we to imagine the psychic condition of the sleeper which precedes dreaming? Do all the dream-thoughts exist side by side, or do they pursue one another, or are there several simultaneous trains of thought, proceeding from different centres, which subsequently meet? I do not think it is necessary at this point to form a plastic conception of the psychic condition at the time of dream-formation. But let us not forget that we are concerned with unconscious thinking, and that the process may easily be different from that which we observe in ourselves in deliberate contemplation accompanied by consciousness. The fact, however, is irrefutable that dream-formation is based on a process of condensation. How, then, is this condensation effected?

Now, if we consider that of the dream-thoughts ascertained only the most restricted number are represented in the dream by means of one of their conceptual elements, we might conclude that the condensation is accomplished by means of omission, inasmuch as the dream is not a faithful translation or projection, point by point, of the dream-thoughts, but a very incomplete and defective reproduction of them. This view, as we shall soon perceive, is a very inadequate one. But for the present let us take it as a point of departure, and ask ourselves: If only a few of the elements of the dream-thoughts make their way into the dream-content, what are the conditions that determine their selection?

In order to solve this problem, let us turn our attention to those elements of the dream-content which must have fulfilled the conditions for which we are looking. The most suitable material for this investigation will be a dream to whose formation a particularly intense condensation has contributed. I select the dream, cited in chapter V., of the botanical monograph.

I

Dream-content: I have written a monograph upon a certain (indeterminate) species of plant. The book lies before me. I am just turning over a folded coloured plate. A dried specimen of the plant is bound up in this copy, as in a herbarium.

The most prominent element of this dream is the botanical monograph. This is derived from the impressions of the dream-day; I had actually seen a monograph on the genus Cyclamen in a bookseller's window. The mention of this genus is lacking in the dream-content; only the monograph and its relation to botany have remained. The botanical monograph immediately reveals its relation to the work on cocaine which I once wrote; from cocaine the train of thought proceeds on the one hand to a Festschrift, and on the other to my friend, the oculist, Dr. Koenigstein, who was partly responsible for the introduction of cocaine as a local anaesthetic. Moreover, Dr. Koenigstein is connected with the recollection of an interrupted conversation I had had with him on the previous evening, and with all sorts of ideas relating to the remuneration of medical and surgical services among colleagues. This conversation, then, is the actual dream-stimulus; the monograph on cyclamen is also a real incident, but one of an indifferent nature; as I now see, the botanical monograph of the dream proves to be a common mean between the two experiences of the day, taken over unchanged from an indifferent impression, and bound with the psychically significant experience by means of the most copious associations.

Not only the combined idea of the botanical monograph, however, but also each of its separate elements, botanical and monograph, penetrates farther and farther, by manifold associations, into the confused tangle of the dream-thoughts. To botanical belong the recollections of the person of Professor Gartner (German: Gartner = gardener), of his blooming wife, of my patient, whose name is Flora, and of a lady concerning whom I told the story of the forgotten flowers. Gartner, again, leads me to the laboratory and the conversation with Koenigstein; and the allusion to the two female patients belongs to the same conversation. From the lady with the flowers a train of thoughts branches off to the favourite flowers of my wife, whose other branch leads to the title of the hastily seen monograph. Further, botanical recalls an episode at the Gymnasium, and a university examination; and a fresh subject - that of my hobbies - which was broached in the above-mentioned conversation, is linked up, by means of what is humorously called my favourite flower, the artichoke, with the train of thoughts proceeding from the forgotten flowers; behind artichoke there lies, on the one hand, a recollection of Italy, and on the other a reminiscence of a scene of my childhood, in which I first formed an acquaintance - which has since then grown so intimate - with books. Botanical, then, is a veritable nucleus, and, for the dream, the meetingpoint of many trains of thought; which, I can testify, had all really been brought into connection by the conversation referred to. Here we find ourselves in a thought-factory, in which, as in The Weaver's Masterpiece:

The little shuttles to and fro
Fly, and the threads unnoted flow;
One throw links up a thousand threads.

Monograph in the dream, again, touches two themes: the one-sided nature of my studies, and the costliness of my hobbies.

The impression derived from this first investigation is that the elements botanical and monograph were taken up into the dream-content because they were able to offer the most numerous points of contact with the greatest number of dream-thoughts, and thus represented nodal points at which a great number of the dream-thoughts met together, and because they were of manifold significance in respect of the meaning of the dream.

The fact upon which this explanation is based may be expressed in another form: Every element of the dream-content proves to be overdetermined - that is, it appears several times over in the dream-thoughts.

We shall learn more if we examine the other components of the dream in respect of their occurrence in the dream-thoughts. The coloured plate refers (cf. the analysis in chapter V.) to a new subject, the criticism passed upon my work by colleagues, and also to a subject already represented in the dream - my hobbies - and, further, to a memory of my childhood, in which I pull to pieces a book with coloured plates; the dried specimen of the plant relates to my experience with the herbarium at the Gymnasium, and gives this memory particular emphasis. Thus I perceive the nature of the relation between the dream-content and dream-thoughts: Not only are the elements of the dream determined several times over by the dream-thoughts, but the individual dream-thoughts are represented in the dream by several elements. Starting from an element of the dream, the path of the association leads to a number of dream-thoughts; and from a single dream-thought to several elements of the dream. In the process of dream-formation, therefore, it is not the case that a single dream-thought, or a group of dream-thoughts, supplies the dream-content with an abbreviation of itself as its representative, and that the next dream-thought supplies another abbreviation as its representative (much as representatives are elected from among the population); but rather that the whole mass of the dream-thoughts is subjected to a certain elaboration, in the course of which those elements that receive the strongest and completest support stand out in relief; so that the process might perhaps be likened to election by the scrutin du liste. Whatever dream I may subject to such a dissection, I always find the same fundamental principle confirmed - that the dream-elements have been formed out of the whole mass of the dream-thoughts, and that every one of them appears, in relation to the dream-thoughts, to have a multiple determination.

It is certainly not superfluous to demonstrate this relation of the dream-content to the dream-thoughts by means of a further example, which is distinguished by a particularly artful intertwining of reciprocal relations. The dream is that of a patient whom I am treating for claustrophobia (fear of enclosed spaces). It will soon become evident why I feel myself called upon to entitle this exceptionally clever piece of dream-activity:

II. "A Beautiful Dream"

The dreamer is driving with a great number of companions in X-street, where there is a modest hostelry (which is not the case). A theatrical performance is being given in one of the rooms of the inn. He is first spectator, then actor. Finally the company is told to change their clothes, in order to return to the city. Some of the company are shown into rooms on the ground floor, others to rooms on the first floor. Then a dispute arises. The people upstairs are annoyed because those downstairs have not yet finished changing, so that they cannot come down. His brother is upstairs; he is downstairs; and he is angry with his brother because they are so hurried. (This part obscure.) Besides, it was already decided, upon their arrival, who was to go upstairs and who down. Then he goes alone up the hill towards the city, and he walks so heavily, and with such difficulty, that he cannot move from the spot. An elderly gentleman joins him and talks angrily of the King of Italy. Finally, towards the top of the hill, he is able to walk much more easily.

The difficulty experienced in climbing the hill was so distinct that for some time after waking he was in doubt whether the experience was a dream or the reality.

Judged by the manifest content, this dream can hardly be eulogized. Contrary to the rules, I shall begin the interpretation with that portion to which the dreamer referred as being the most distinct.

The difficulty dreamed of, and probably experienced during the dream - difficulty in climbing, accompanied by dyspnoea - was one of the symptoms which the patient had actually exhibited some years before, and which, in conjunction with other symptoms, was at the time attributed to tuberculosis (probably hysterically simulated). From our study of exhibition-dreams we are already acquainted with this sensation of being inhibited in motion, peculiar to dreams, and here again we find it utilized as material always available for the purposes of any other kind of representation. The part of the dream-content which represents climbing as difficult at first, and easier at the top of the hill, made me think, while it was being related, of the well-known masterly introduction to Daudet's Sappho. Here a young man carries the woman he loves upstairs; she is at first as light as a feather, but the higher he climbs the more she weighs; and this scene is symbolic of the process of their relation, in describing which Daudet seeks to admonish young men not to lavish an earnest affection upon girls of humble origin and dubious antecedents.[2] Although I knew that my patient had recently had a love-affair with an actress, and had broken it off, I hardly expected to find that the interpretation which had occurred to me was correct. The situation in Sappho is actually the reverse of

---

[2] In estimating the significance of this passage we may recall the meaning of dreams of climbing stairs, as explained in the chapter on Symbolism.

that in the dream; for in the dream climbing was difficult at the first and easy later on; in the novel the symbolism is pertinent only if what was at first easily carried finally proves to be a heavy burden. To my astonishment, the patient remarked that the interpretation fitted in very well with the plot of a play which he had seen the previous evening. The play was called Rund um Wien (Round about Vienna), and treated of the career of a girl who was at first respectable, but who subsequently lapsed into the demimonde, and formed relations with highly-placed lovers, thereby climbing, but finally she went downhill faster and faster. This play reminded him of another, entitled Von Stufe zu Stufe (From Step to Step), the poster advertising which had depicted a flight of stairs.

To continue the interpretation: The actress with whom he had had his most recent and complicated affair had lived in X-street. There is no inn in this street. However, while he was spending part of the summer in Vienna for the sake of this lady, he had lodged (German: abgestiegen = stopped, literally stepped off) at a small hotel in the neighbourhood. When he was leaving the hotel, he said to the cab-driver: "I am glad at all events that I didn't get any vermin here!" (Incidentally, the dread of vermin is one of his phobias.) Whereupon the cab-driver answered: "How could anybody stop there! That isn't a hotel at all, it's really nothing but a pub!"

The pub immediately reminded him of a quotation:

Of a wonderful host
I was lately a guest.

But the host in the poem by Uhland is an apple-tree. Now a second quotation continues the train of thought:

FAUST (dancing with the young witch).
A lovely dream once came to me;
I then beheld an apple-tree,
And there two fairest apples shone:
They lured me so, I climbed thereon.

THE FAIR ONE
Apples have been desired by you,
Since first in Paradise they grew;
And I am moved with joy to know
That such within my garden grow.[3]

There is not the slightest doubt what is meant by the apple-tree and the apples. A beautiful bosom stood high among the charms by which the actress had bewitched our dreamer.

Judging from the context of the analysis, we had every reason to assume that the dream referred to an impression of the dreamer's childhood. If this is correct, it must have referred to the wet-nurse of the dreamer, who is now a man of nearly thirty years of age. The bosom of the nurse is in reality an inn for the child. The nurse, as well as Daudet's Sappho, appears as an allusion to his recently abandoned mistress.

The (elder) brother of the patient also appears in the dream-content; he is upstairs, while the dreamer himself is downstairs. This again is an inversion, for the brother, as I happen to know, has lost his social position, while my patient has retained his. In relating the dream-content, the dreamer avoided saying that his brother was upstairs and that he himself was downstairs. This would have been to obvious an expression, for in Austria we say that a man is on the ground floor when he has lost his fortune and social position, just as we say that he has come down. Now the fact that at this point in the dream something is represented as inverted must have a meaning; and the inversion must apply to some other relation between the dream-thoughts and the dream-content. There is an indication which suggests how this inversion is to be understood. It obviously applies to the end of the dream, where the circumstances of climbing are the reverse of those described in Sappho. Now it is evident what inversion is meant: In Sappho the man carries the woman who stands in a sexual relation to him; in the dream-thoughts, conversely, there is a reference to a woman carrying a man: and, as this could occur

---
[3] Faust I.

only in childhood, the reference is once more to the nurse who carries the heavy child. Thus the final portion of the dream succeeds in representing Sappho and the nurse in the same allusion.

Just as the name Sappho has not been selected by the poet without reference to a Lesbian practise, so the portions of the dream in which people are busy upstairs and downstairs, above and beneath, point to fancies of a sexual content with which the dreamer is occupied, and which, as suppressed cravings, are not unconnected with his neurosis. Dream-interpretation itself does not show that these are fancies and not memories of actual happenings; it only furnishes us with a set of thoughts and leaves it to us to determine their actual value. In this case real and imagined happenings appear at first as of equal value - and not only here, but also in the creation of more important psychic structures than dreams. A large company, as we already know, signifies a secret. The brother is none other than a representative, drawn into the scenes of childhood by fancying backwards, of all of the subsequent for women's favours. Through the medium of an experience indifferent in itself, the episode of the gentleman who talks angrily of the King of Italy refers to the intrusion of people of low rank into aristocratic society. It is as though the warning which Daudet gives to young men were to be supplemented by a similar warning applicable to a suckling child.[4]

In the two dreams here cited I have shown by italics where one of the elements of the dream recurs in the dream-thoughts, in order to make the multiple relations of the former more obvious. Since, however, the analysis of these dreams has not been carried to completion, it will probably be worth while to consider a dream with a full analysis, in order to demonstrate the manifold determination of the dream-content. For this purpose I shall select the dream of Irma's injection (see chapter II). From this example

---

[4] The fantastic nature of the situation relating to the dreamer's wet-nurse is shown by the circumstance, objectively ascertained, that the nurse in this case was his mother. Further, I may call attention to the regret of the young man in the anecdote related to p. 222 above (that he had not taken better advantage of his opportunities with his wet-nurse) as the probable source of his dream.

we shall readily see that the condensation-work in the dreamformation has made use of more means than one.

The chief person in the dream-content is my patient Irma, who is seen with the features which belong to her waking life, and who therefore, in the first instance, represents herself. But her attitude, as I examine her at the window, is taken from a recollection of another person, of the lady for whom I should like to exchange my patient, as is shown by the dream-thoughts. Inasmuch as Irma has a diphtheritic membrane, which recalls my anxiety about my eldest daughter, she comes to represent this child of mine, behind whom, connected with her by the identity of their names, is concealed the person of the patient who died from the effects of poison. In the further course of the dream the Significance of Irma's personality changes (without the alteration of her image as it is seen in the dream): she becomes one of the children whom we examine in the public dispensaries for children's diseases, where my friends display the differences in their mental capacities. The transition was obviously effected by the idea of my little daughter. Owing to her unwillingness to open her mouth, the same Irma constitutes an allusion to another lady who was examined by me, and, also in the same connection, to my wife. Further, in the morbid changes which I discover in her throat I have summarized allusions to quite a number of other persons.

All these people whom I encounter as I follow up the associations suggested by Irma do not appear personally in the dream; they are concealed behind the dream-person Irma, who is thus developed into a collective image, which, as might be expected, has contradictory features. Irma comes to represent these other persons, who are discarded in the work of condensation, inasmuch as I allow anything to happen to her which reminds me of these persons, trait by trait.

For the purposes of dream-condensation I may construct a composite person in yet another fashion, by combining the actual features of two or more persons in a single dream-image. It is in this fashion that the Dr. M of my dream was constructed; he bears the name of Dr. M, and he speaks and acts as Dr. M does, but his bodily characteristics and his malady belong to another person, my eldest brother; a single feature, paleness, is doubly determined, owing to the fact that it is common to both persons. Dr. R, in my dream about my uncle, is a similar composite person. But here the dream-image is constructed in yet another fashion. I have not united features peculiar to the one person with the features of the other, thereby abridging by certain features the memory-picture of each; but I have adopted the method employed by Galton in producing family portraits; namely, I have superimposed the two images, so that the common features stand out in stronger relief, while those which do not coincide neutralize one another and become indistinct. In the dream of my uncle the fair beard stands out in relief, as an emphasized feature, from a physiognomy which belongs to two persons, and which is consequently blurred; further, in its reference to growing grey the beard contains an allusion to my father and to myself.

The construction of collective and composite persons is one of the principal methods of dream-condensation. We shall presently have occasion to deal with this in another connection.

The notion of dysentry in the dream of Irma's injection has likewise a multiple determination; on the one hand, because of its paraphasic assonance with diphtheria. and on the other because of its reference to the patient whom I sent to the East, and whose hysteria had been wrongly diagnosed.

The mention of propyls in the dream proves again to be an interesting case of condensation. Not propyls but amyls were included in the dreamthoughts.

One might think that here a simple displacement had occured in the course of dream-formation. This is in fact the case, but the displacement serves the purposes of the condensation, as is shown from the following supplementary analysis: If I dwell for a moment upon the word propylen (German) its assonance with the word propylaeum suggests itself to me. But a propylaeum is to be found not only in Athens, but also in Munich. In the latter city, a year before my dream, I had visited a friend who was seriously ill, and the reference to him in trimethylamin, which follows closely upon propyls, is unmistakable.

I pass over the striking circumstance that here, as elsewhere in the analysis of dreams, associations of the most widely differing values are employed for making thought-connections as though they were equivalent, and I yield to the temptation to regard the procedure by which amyls in the dream-thoughts are replaced in the dream-content by propyls as a sort of plastic process.

On the one hand, here is the group of ideas relating to my friend Otto, who does not understand me, thinks I am in the wrong, and gives me the liqueur that smells of amyls; on the other hand, there is the group of ideas - connected with the first by contrast - relating to my Berlin friend who does understand me, who would always think that I was right, and to whom I am indebted for so much valuable information concerning the chemistry of sexual processes.

What elements in the Otto group are to attract my particular attention are determined by the recent circumstances which are responsible for the dream; amyls belong to the element so distinguished, which are predestined to find their way into the dream-content. The large group of ideas centering upon William is actually stimulated by the contrast between William and Otto, and those elements in it are emphasized which are in tune with those already stirred up in the Otto group. In the whole of this dream I am continually recoiling from somebody who excites my displeasure towards another person with whom I can at will confront the first; trait by trait I appeal to the friend as against the enemy. Thus amyls in the Otto group awakes recollections in the other group, also belonging to the region of chemistry; trimethylamin, which receives support from several quarters, finds its way into the dream-content. Amyls, too, might have got into the dream-content unchanged, but it yields to the influence of the William group, inasmuch as out of the whole range of recollections covered by this name an element is sought out which is able to furnish a double determination for amyls. Propyls is closely associated with amyls; from the William group comes Munich with its propylaeum. Both groups are united in propyls - propylaeum. As though by a compromise, this intermediate element then makes its way into the dream-content.

Here a common mean which permits of a multiple determination has been created. It thus becomes palpable that a multiple determination must facilitate penetration into the dream-content. For the purpose of this mean-formation a displacement of the attention has been unhesitatingly effected from what is really intended to something adjacent to it in the associations.

The study of the dream of Irma's injection has now enabled us to obtain some insight into the process of condensation which occurs in the formation of dreams. We perceive, as peculiarities of the condensing process, a selection of those elements which occur several times over in the dream-content, the formation of new unities (composite persons, mixed images), and the production of common means. The purpose which is served by condensation, and the means by which it is brought about, will be investigated when we come to study in all their bearings the psychic processes at work in the formation of dreams. Let us for the present be content with establishing the fact of dream-condensation as a relation between the dream-thoughts and the dream-content which deserves attention.

The condensation-work of dreams becomes most palpable when it takes words and means as its objects. Generally speaking, words are often treated in dreams as things, and therefore undergo the same combinations as the ideas of things. The results of such dreams are comical and bizarre word-formations.

1. A colleague sent an essay of his, in which he had, in my opinion, overestimated the value of a recent physiological discovery, and had expressed himself, moreover, in extravagant terms. On the following night I dreamed a sentence which obviously referred to this essay: "That is a truly norekdal style."

The solution of this word-formation at first gave me some difficulty; it was unquestionably formed as a parody of the superlatives colossal, pyramidal; but it was not easy to say where it came from. At last the monster fell apart into the two names Nora and Ekdal, from two well-known plays by Ibsen. I had previously read a newspaper article on Ibsen by the writer whose latest work I was now criticizing in my dream.

2. One of my female patients dreams that a man with a fair beard and a peculiar glittering eye is pointing to a sign-board attached to a tree which reads: uclamparia - wet.[5]

Analysis. - The man was rather authoritative-looking, and his peculiar glittering eye at once recalled the church of San Paolo, near Rome, where she had seen the mosaic portraits of the Popes. One of the early Popes had a golden eye (this is really an optical illusion, to which the guides usually call attention). Further associations showed that the general physiognomy of the man corresponded with her own clergyman (pope), and the shape of the fair beard recalled her doctor (myself), while the stature of the man in the dream recalled her father. All these persons stand in the same relation to her; they are all guiding and directing the course of her life. On further questioning, the golden eye recalled gold - money - the rather expensive psycho-analytic treatment, which gives her a great deal of concern. Gold, moreover, recalls the gold cure for alcoholism - Herr D, whom she would have married, if it had not been for his clinging to the disgusting alcohol habit - she does not object to anyone's taking an occasional drink; she herself sometimes drinks beer and liqueurs. This again brings her back to her visit to San Paolo (fuori la mura) and its surroundings. She remembers that in the neighbouring monastery of the Tre Fontane she drank a liqueur made of eucalyptus by the Trappist monks of the monastery. She then relates how the monks transformed this malarial and swampy region into a dry and wholesome neighbourhood by planting numbers of eucalyptus trees. The word uclamparia then resolves itself into eucalyptus

---

[5] Given by translator, as the author's example could not be translated.

and malaria, and the word wet refers to the former swampy nature of the locality. Wet also suggests dry. Dry is actually the name of the man whom she would have married but for his overindulgence in alcohol. The peculiar name of Dry is of Germanic origin (drei = three) and hence, alludes to the monastery of the Three (drei) Fountains. In talking of Mr. Dry's habit she used the strong expression: "He could drink a fountain." Mr. Dry jocosely refers to his habit by saying: "You know I must drink because I am always dry" (referring to his name). The eucalyptus refers also to her neurosis, which was at first diagnosed as malaria. She went to Italy because her attacks of anxiety, which were accompanied by marked rigors and shivering, were thought to be of malarial origin. She bought some eucalyptus oil from the monks, and she maintains that it has done her much good.

The condensation uclamparia - wet is, therefore, the point of junction for the dream as well as for the neurosis.

3. In a rather long and confused dream of my own, the apparent nucleus of which is a sea-voyage, it occurs to me that the next port is Hearsing, and next after that Fliess. The latter is the name of my friend in B, to which city I have often journeyed. But Hearsing is put together from the names of the places in the neighbourhood of Vienna, which so frequently end in "ing": Hietzing, Liesing, Moedling (the old Medelitz, meae deliciae, my joy; that is, my own name, the German for joy being Freude), and the English hearsay, which points to calumny, and establishes the relation to the indifferent dream-stimulus of the day - a poem in Fliegende Blatter about a slanderous dwarf, Sagter Hatergesagt (Saidhe Hashesaid). By the combination of the final syllable ing with the name Fliess, Vlissingen is obtained, which is a real port through which my brother passes when he comes to visit us from England. But the English for Vlissingen is Flushing, which signifies blushing, and recalls patients suffering from erythrophobia (fear of blushing), whom I sometimes treat,

and also a recent publication of Bechterew's, relating to this neurosis, the reading of which angered me.[6]

4. Upon another occasion I had a dream which consisted of two separate parts. The first was the vividly remembered word Autodidasker: the second was a faithful reproduction in the dream-content of a short and harmless fancy which had been developed a few days earlier, and which was to the effect that I must tell Professor N, when I next saw him: "The patient about whose condition I last consulted you is really suffering from a neurosis, just as you suspected." So not only must the newly-coined Autodidasker satisfy the requirement that it should contain or represent a compressed meaning, but this meaning must have a valid connection with my resolve - repeated from waking life - to give Professor N due credit for his diagnosis.

Now Autodidasker is easily separated into author (German, Autor), autodidact, and Lasker, with whom is associated the name Lasalle. The first of these words leads to the occasion of the dream - which this time is significant. I had brought home to my wife several volumes by a wellknown author who is a friend of my brother's, and who, as I have learned, comes from the same neighbourhood as myself (J. J. David). One evening she told me how profoundly impressed she had been by the pathetic sadness of a story in one of David's novels (a story of wasted talents), and our conversation turned upon the signs of talent which we perceive

---

[6] The same analysis and synthesis of syllables - a veritable chemistry of syllables - serves us for many a jest in waking life. "What is the cheapest method of obtaining silver? You go to a field where silverberries are growing and pick them; then the berries are eliminated and the silver remains in a free state." [Translator's example]. The first person who read and criticized this book made the objection - with which other readers will probably agree - that "the dreamer often appears too witty." That is true, so long as it applies to the dreamer; it involves a condemnation only when its application is extended to the interpreter of the dream. In waking reality I can make very little claim to the predicate witty; if my dreams appear witty, this is not the fault of my individuality, but of the peculiar psychological conditions under which the dream is fabricated, and is intimately connected with the theory of wit and the comical. The dream becomes witty because the shortest and most direct way to the expression of its thoughts is barred for it: the dream is under constraint. My readers may convince themselves that the dreams of my patients give the impression of being quite as witty (at least, in intention), as my own, and even more so. Nevertheless, this reproach impelled me to compare the technique of wit with the dream-work.

in our own children. Under the influence of what she had just read, my wife expressed some concern about our children, and I comforted her with the remark that precisely such dangers as she feared can be averted by training. During the night my thoughts proceeded farther, took up my wife's concern for the children, and interwove with it all sorts of other things. Something which the novelist had said to my brother on the subject of marriage showed my thoughts a by-path which might lead to representation in the dream. This path led to Breslau; a lady who was a very good friend of ours had married and gone to live there. I found in Breslau Lasker and Lasalle, two examples to justify the fear lest our boys should be ruined by women, examples which enabled me to represent simultaneously two ways of influencing a man to his undoing.[7] The Cherchez la femme, by which these thoughts may be summarized, leads me, if taken in another sense, to my brother, who is still married and whose name is Alexander. Now I see that Alex, as we abbreviate the name, sounds almost like an inversion of Lasker, and that this fact must have contributed to send my thoughts on a detour by way of Breslau.

But the playing with names and syllables in which I am here engaged has yet another meaning. It represents the wish that my brother may enjoy a happy family life, and this in the following manner: In the novel of artistic life, L'OEuvre, which, by virtue of its content, must have been in association with my dream-thoughts, the author, as is well-known, has incidentally given a description of his own person and his own domestic happiness, and appears under the name of Sandoz. In the metamorphosis of his name he probably went to work as follows: Zola, when inverted (as children are fond of inverting names) gives Aloz. But this was still too undisguised; he therefore replaced the syllable Al, which stands at the beginning of the name Alexander, by the third syllable of the same name, sand, and thus arrived at Sandoz. My autodidasker originated in a similar fashion.

---

[7] Lasker died of progressive paralysis; that is, of the consequences of an infection caught from a woman (syphilis); Lasalle, also a syphilitic, was killed in a duel which he fought on account of the lady whom he had been courting.

My phantasy - that I am telling Professor N that the patient whom we have both seen is suffering from a neurosis - found its way into the dream in the following manner: Shortly before the close of my working year, I had a patient in whose case my powers of diagnosis failed me. A serious organic trouble - possibly some alterative degeneration of the spinal cord - was to be assumed, but could not be conclusively demonstrated. It would have been tempting to diagnose the trouble as a neurosis, and this would have put an end to all my difficulties, but for the fact that the sexual anamnesis, failing which I am unwilling to admit a neurosis, was so energetically denied by the patient. In my embarrassment I called to my assistance the physician whom I respect most of all men (as others do also), and to whose authority I surrender most completely. He listened to my doubts, told me he thought them justified, and then said: "Keep on observing the man, it is probably a neurosis." Since I know that he does not share my opinions concerning the aetiology of the neuroses, I refrained from contradicting him, but I did not conceal my scepticism. A few days later I informed the patient that I did not know what to do with him, and advised him to go to someone else. Thereupon, to my great astonishment, he began to beg my pardon for having lied to me: he had felt so ashamed; and now he revealed to me just that piece of sexual aetiology which I had expected, and which I found necessary for assuming the existence of a neurosis. This was a relief to me, but at the same time a humiliation; for I had to admit that my consultant, who was not disconcerted by the absence of anamnesis, had judged the case more correctly. I made up my mind to tell him, when next I saw him, that he had been right and I had been wrong.

This is just what I do in the dream. But what sort of a wish is fulfilled if I acknowledge that I am mistaken? This is precisely my wish; I wish to be mistaken as regards my fears - that is to say, I wish that my wife, whose fears I have appropriated in my dream-thoughts, may prove to be mistaken. The subject to which the fact of being right or wrong is related in the dream is not far removed from that which is really of interest to the dream-thoughts. We have the same pair of alternatives, of either organic or functional impairment caused by a woman, or actually by the sexual life - either tabetic paralysis or a neurosis - with which latter the nature of Lasalle's undoing is indirectly connected.

In this well-constructed (and on careful analysis quite transparent) dream, Professor N appears not merely on account of this analogy, and my wish to be proved mistaken, or the associated references to Breslau and to the family of our married friend who lives there, but also on account of the following little dialogue which followed our consultation: After he had acquitted himself of his professional duties by making the abovementioned suggestion, Dr. N proceeded to discuss personal matters. "How many children have you now?" - "Six." - A thoughtful and respectful gesture. - "Girls, boys?" - "Three of each. They are my pride and my riches." - "Well, you must be careful; there is no difficulty about the girls, but the boys are a difficulty later on as regards their upbringing." I replied that until now they had been very tractable; obviously this prognosis of my boys' future pleased me as little as his diagnosis of my patient, whom he believed to be suffering only from a neurosis. These two impressions, then, are connected by their continuity, by their being successively received; and when I incorporate the story of the neurosis into the dream, I substitute it for the conversation on the subject of upbringing, which is even more closely connected with the dream-thoughts, since it touches so closely upon the anxiety subsequently expressed by my wife. Thus, even my fear that N may prove to be right in his remarks on the difficulties to be met with in bringing up boys is admitted into the dream-content, inasmuch as it is concealed behind the representation of my wish that I may be wrong to harbour such apprehensions. The same phantasy serves without alteration to represent both the conflicting alternatives.

Examination-dreams present the same difficulties to interpretation that I have already described as characteristic of most typical dreams. The associative material which the dreamer supplies only rarely suffices for interpretation. A deeper understanding of such dreams has to be accumulated from a considerable number of examples. Not long ago I arrived at a conviction that reassurances like "But you already are a doctor," and so on, not only convey a consolation but imply a reproach as well. This would have run: "You are already so old, so far advanced in life, and yet you still commit such follies, are guilty of such childish behaviour." This mixture of self-criticism and consolation would correspond with the examination-dreams. After this it is no longer surprising that the reproaches in the last analysed examples concerning follies and childish behaviour should relate to repetitions of reprehensible sexual acts.

The verbal transformations in dreams are very similar to those which are known to occur in paranoia, and which are observed also in hysteria and obsessions. The linguistic tricks of children, who at a certain age actually treat words as objects, and even invent new languages and artificial syntaxes, are a common source of such occurrences both in dreams and in the psychoneuroses.

The analysis of nonsensical word-formations in dreams is particularly well suited to demonstrate the degree of condensation effected in the dreamwork.

From the small number of the selected examples here considered it must not be concluded that such material is seldom observed or is at all exceptional. It is, on the contrary, very frequent, but, owing to the dependence of dream interpretation on psychoanalytic treatment, very few examples are noted down and reported, and most of the analyses which are reported are comprehensible only to the specialist in neuropathology.

When a spoken utterance, expressly distinguished as such from a thought, occurs in a dream, it is an invariable rule that the dream-speech has originated from a remembered speech in the dream-material. The wording of the speech has either been preserved in its entirety or has been slightly altered in expression. frequently the dream-speech is pieced together from different recollections of spoken remarks; the wording has remained the same, but the sense has perhaps become ambiguous, or differs from the wording. Not infrequently the dream-speech serves merely as an allusion to an incident in connection with which the remembered speech was made.[8]

B. The Work of Displacement

Another and probably no less significant relation must have already forced itself upon our attention while we were collecting examples of dreamcondensation.

We may have noticed that these elements which obtrude themselves in the dream-content as its essential components do not by any means play this same part in the dream-thoughts. As a corollary to this, the converse of this statement is also true. That which is obviously the essential content of the dream-thoughts need not be represented at all in the dream. The dream is, as it were, centred elsewhere; its content is arranged about elements which do not constitute the central point of the dream-thoughts. Thus, for example, in the dream of the botanical monograph the central point of the dream-content is evidently the element botanical; in the dream-thoughts, we are concerned with the complications and conflicts resulting from services rendered between colleagues which place them under mutual obligations; later on with the reproach that I am in the habit of sacrificing too much time to my hobbies; and the element botanical finds no place in this nucleus of the dreamthoughts, unless it is loosely connected with it by antithesis, for botany was never among my favourite subjects. In the Sappho-dream of my patient, ascending and descending, being upstairs and down, is made the central point; the dream, however, is concerned with the danger of sexual relations with persons of low degree; so that only one of the elements of the dream-thoughts seems to have found its way into the dreamcontent, and this is unduly expanded. Again, in the dream of my uncle, the fair beard, which seems to

---

[8] In the case of a young man who was suffering from obsessions, but whose intellectual functions were intact and highly developed, I recently found the only exception to this rule. The speeches which occurred in his dreams did not originate in speeches which he had heard had made himself, but corresponded to the undistorted verbal expression of his obsessive thoughts, which came to his waking consciousness only in an altered form.

be its central point, appears to have no rational connection with the desire for greatness which we have recognized as the nucleus of the dream-thoughts. Such dreams very naturally give us an impression of a displacement. In complete contrast to these examples, the dream of Irma's injection shows that individual elements may claim the same place in dream-formation as that which they occupy in the dream-thoughts. The recognition of this new and utterly inconstant relation between the dream-thoughts and the dream-content will probably astonish us at first. If we find, in a psychic process of normal life, that one idea has been selected from among a number of others, and has acquired a particular emphasis in our consciousness, we are wont to regard this as proof that a peculiar psychic value (a certain degree of interest) attaches to the victorious idea. We now discover that this value of the individual element in the dream-thoughts is not retained in dream-formation, or is not taken into account. For there is no doubt which of the elements of the dream-thoughts are of the highest value; our judgment informs us immediately. In dream-formation the essential elements, those that are emphasized by intensive interest, may be treated as though they were subordinate, while they are replaced in the dream by other elements, which were certainly subordinate in the dream-thoughts. It seems at first as though the psychic intensity[9] of individual ideas were of no account in their selection for dream-formation, but only their greater or lesser multiplicity of determination. One might be inclined to think that what gets into the dream is not what is important in the dream-thoughts, but what is contained in them several times over; but our understanding of dreamformation is not much advanced by this assumption; to begin with, we cannot believe that the two motives of multiple determination and intrinsic value can influence the selection of the dream otherwise than in the same direction. Those ideas in the dream-thoughts which are most important are probably also those which recur most frequently, since the

---

[9] The psychic intensity or value of an idea - the emphasis due to interest - is of course to be distinguished from perceptual or conceptual intensity.

individual dream-thoughts radiate from them as centres. And yet the dream may reject these intensely emphasized and extensively reinforced elements, and may take up into its content other elements which are only extensively reinforced.

This difficulty may be solved if we follow up yet another impression received during the investigation of the over-determination of the dreamcontent.

Many readers of this investigation may already have decided, in their own minds, that the discovery of the multiple determination of the dream-elements is of no great importance, because it is inevitable. Since in analysis we proceed from the dream-elements, and register all the ideas which associate themselves with these elements, is it any wonder that these elements should recur with peculiar frequency in the thoughtmaterial obtained in this manner? While I cannot admit the validity of this objection, I am now going to say something that sounds rather like it:

Among the thoughts which analysis brings to light are many which are far removed from the nucleus of the dream, and which stand out like artificial interpolations made for a definite purpose. Their purpose may readily be detected; they establish a connection, often a forced and farfetched connection, between the dream-content and the dream-thoughts, and in many cases, if these elements were weeded out of the analysis, the components of the dream-content would not only not be over-determined, but they would not be sufficiently determined. We are thus led to the conclusion that multiple determination, decisive as regards the selection made by the dream, is perhaps not always a primary factor in dreamformation, but is often a secondary product of a psychic force which is as yet unknown to us. Nevertheless, it must be of importance for the entrance of the individual elements into the dream, for we may observe that, in cases where multiple determination does not proceed easily from the dream-material, it is brought about with a certain effort.

It now becomes very probable that a psychic force expresses

itself in the dream-work which, on the one hand, strips the elements of the high psychic value of their intensity and, on the other hand, by means of over-determination, creates new significant values from elements of slight value, which new values then make their way into the dream-content. Now if this is the method of procedure, there has occurred in the process of dream-formation a transference and displacement of the psychic intensities of the individual elements, from which results the textual difference between the dream-content and the thought-content. The process which we here assume to be operative is actually the most essential part of the dream-work; it may fitly be called dream-displacement. Dream-displacement and dream-condensation are the two craftsmen to whom we may chiefly ascribe the structure of the dream.

I think it will be easy to recognize the psychic force which expresses itself in dream-displacement. The result of this displacement is that the dream-content no longer has any likeness to the nucleus of the dream-thoughts, and the dream reproduces only a distorted form of the dream-wish in the unconscious. But we are already acquainted with dream-distortion; we have traced it back to the censorship which one psychic instance in the psychic life exercises over another. Dream-displacement is one of the chief means of achieving this distortion. Is fecit, cui profuit.[10] We must assume that dream-displacement is brought about by the influence of this censorship, the endopsychic defence.[11]

"Concerning a man who possesses the remarkable faculty of never dreaming nonsense...."

"Your marvellous faculty of dreaming as if you were awake is based upon your virtues, upon your goodness, your justice, and your love of truth; it is the moral clarity of your nature which makes everything about you intelligible to me."

---

[10] "The doer gained."
[11] Since I regard the attribution of dream-distortion to the censorship as the central point of my conception of the dream, I will here quote the closing passage of a story, Traumen wie Wachen, from Phantasien eines Realisten, by Lynkeus (Vienna, second edition [1900]), in which I find this chief feature of my doctrine reproduced:

"But if I really give thought to the matter," was the reply, "I almost believe that all men are made as I am, and that no one ever dreams nonsense!

A dream which one remembers so distinctly that one can relate it afterwards, and which, therefore, is no dream of delirium, always has a meaning; why, it cannot be otherwise! For that which is in contradiction to itself can never be combined into a whole. The fact that time and space are often thoroughly shaken up, detracts not at all from the real content of the dream, because both are without any significance whatever for its essential content. We often do the same thing in waking life; think of fairy-tales, of so many bold and pregnant creations of fantasy, of which only a foolish person would say: 'That is nonsense! For it isn't possible.'"

"If only it were always possible to interpret dreams correctly, as you have just done with mine!" said the friend.

"That is certainly not an easy task, but with a little attention it must always be possible to the dreamer. You ask why it is generally impossible? In your case there seems to be something veiled in your dreams, something unchaste in a special and exalted fashion, a certain secrecy in your nature, which it is difficult to fathom; and that is why your dreams so often seem to be without meaning, or even nonsensical. But in the profoundest sense, this is by no means the case; indeed it cannot be, for a man is always the same person, whether he wakes or dreams."

The manner in which the factors of displacement, condensation and over-determination interact with one another in dream-formation - which is the ruling factor and which the subordinate one - all this will be reserved as a subject for later investigation. In the meantime, we may state, is a second condition which the elements that find their way into the dream must satisfy, that they must be withdrawn from the resistance of the censorship. But henceforth, in the interpretation of dreams, we shall reckon with dream-displacement as an unquestionable fact.

C. The Means of Representation in Dreams

Besides the two factors of condensation and displacement in dreams, which we have found to be at work in the transformation of the latent dreammaterial into the manifest dream-content, we shall, in the course of this investigation, come upon two further conditions which exercise an unquestionable influence over the selection of the material that eventually appears in the dream. But first, even at the risk of seeming to interrupt our progress, I shall take a preliminary glance at the processes by which the interpretation of dreams is accomplished. I do not deny that the best way of explaining them, and of convincing the critic of their reliability, would be to take a single dream as an example, to detail its interpretation, as I did (in Chapter II) in the case of the dream of Irma's injection, but then to assemble the dream-thoughts which I had discovered, and from them to reconstruct the formation of the dream - that is to say, to supplement dream-analysis by dream-synthesis. I have done this with several specimens for my own instruction; but I cannot undertake to do it here, as I am prevented by a number of considerations (relating to the psychic material necessary for such a demonstration) such as any right-thinking person would approve. In the analysis of dreams these considerations present less difficulty, for an analysis may be incomplete and still retain its value, even if it leads only a little way into the structure of the dream.

I do not see how a synthesis, to be convincing, could be anything short of complete. I could give a complete synthesis only of the dreams of such persons as are unknown to the reading public. Since, however, neurotic patients are the only persons who furnish me with the means of making such a synthesis, this part of the description of dreams must be postponed until I can carry the psychological explanation of the neuroses far enough to

---

[12] I have since given the complete analysis and synthesis of two dreams in the Bruchstuck einer Hysterieanalyse, (1905) (Ges. Schriften, Vol. VIII). "Fragment of an Analysis of a Case of Hysteria," translated by Strachey, Collected Papers, Vol III, (Hogarth Press, London). O. Rank's analysis, Ein Traum der sich selbst deutet, deserves mention as the most complete interpretation of a comparatively long dream.

demonstrate their relation to our subject.[12] This will be done elsewhere.

From my attempts to construct dreams synthetically from their dream-thoughts, I know that the material which is yielded by interpretation varies in value. Part of it consists of the essential dream-thoughts, which would completely replace the dream and would in themselves be a sufficient substitute for it, were there no dream-censorship. To the other part, one is wont to ascribe slight importance, nor does one set any value on the assertion that all these thoughts have participated in the formation of the dream; on the contrary, they may include notions which are associated with experiences that have occurred subsequently to the dream, between the dream and the interpretation. This part comprises not only all the connecting-paths which have led from the manifest to the latent dream-content, but also the intermediate and approximating associations by means of which one has arrived at a knowledge of these connecting-paths during the work of interpretation.

At this point we are interested exclusively in the essential dream-thoughts. These commonly reveal themselves as a complex of thoughts and memories of the most intricate possible construction, with all the characteristics of the thought-processes known to us in waking life. Not infrequently they are trains of thought which proceed from more than one centre, but which are not without points of contact; and almost invariably we find, along with a train of thought, its contradictory counterpart, connected with it by the association of contrast.

The individual parts of this complicated structure naturally stand in the most manifold logical relations to one another. They constitute foreground and background, digressions, illustrations, conditions, lines of argument and objections. When the whole mass of these dream-thoughts is subjected to the pressure of the dream-work, during which the fragments are turned about, broken up and compacted, somewhat like drifting ice, the question arises: What becomes of the logical ties which had hitherto provided the framework of the structure? What representation do if, because, as though, although, either-or and all the other conjunctions, without which we cannot understand a phrase or a sentence, receive in our dreams?

To begin with, we must answer that the dream has at its disposal no means of representing these logical relations between the dream-thoughts. In most cases it disregards all these conjunctions, and undertakes the elaboration only of the material content of the dream-thoughts. It is left to the interpretation of the dream to restore the coherence which the dream-work has destroyed.

If dreams lack the ability to express these relations, the psychic material of which they are wrought must be responsible for this defect. As a matter of fact, the representative arts - painting and sculpture - are similarly restricted, as compared with poetry, which is able to employ speech; and here again the reason for this limitation lies in the material by the elaboration of which the two plastic arts endeavour to express something.

Before the art of painting arrived at an understanding of the laws of expression by which it is bound, it attempted to make up for this deficiency.

In old paintings little labels hung out of the mouths of the persons represented, giving in writing the speech which the artist despaired of expressing in the picture.

Here, perhaps an objection will be raised, challenging the assertion that our dreams dispense with the representation of logical relations. There are dreams in which the most complicated intellectual operations take place; arguments for and against are adduced, jokes and comparisons are made, just as in our waking thoughts. But here again appearances are deceptive; if the interpretation of such dreams is continued it will be found that all these things are dream-material, not the representation of intellectual activity in the dream. The content of the dream-thoughts is reproduced by the apparent thinking in our dreams, but not the relations of the dream-thoughts to one another, in the determination of which relations thinking consists. I shall give some examples of this. But the fact which is most easily established is that all speeches which occur in dreams, and which are expressly designated as such, are unchanged or only slightly modified replicas of speeches which occur likewise among the memories in the dream-material. Often the speech is only an allusion to an event contained in the dream-thoughts; the meaning of the dream is quite different.

However, I shall not dispute the fact that even critical thought - activity, which does not simply repeat material from the dream - thoughts, plays a part in dream-formation. I shall have to explain the influence of this factor at the close of this discussion. It will then become clear that this thought activity is evoked not by the dream-thoughts, but by the dream itself, after it is, in a certain sense, already completed.

Provisionally, then, it is agreed that the logical relations between the dream-thoughts do not obtain any particular representation in the dream. For instance, where there is a contradiction in the dream, this is either a contradiction directed against the dream itself or a contradiction contained in one of the dream-thoughts; a contradiction in the dream corresponds with a contradiction between the dream-thoughts only in the most indirect and intermediate fashion.

But just as the art of painting finally succeeded in depicting, in the persons represented, at least the intentions behind their words - tenderness, menace, admonition, and the like - by other means than by floating labels, so also the dream has found it possible to render an account of certain of the logical relations between its dream-thoughts by an appropriate modification of the peculiar method of dream-representation. It will be found by experience that different dreams go to different lengths in this respect; while one dream will entirely disregard the logical structure of its material, another attempts to indicate it as completely as possible. In so doing, the dream departs more or less widely from the text which it has to elaborate; and its attitude is equally variable in respect to the temporal articulation of the dream-thoughts, if such has been established in the unconscious (as, for example, in the dream of Irma's injection).

But what are the means by which the dream-work is enabled to indicate those relations in the dream-material which are difficult to represent? I shall attempt to enumerate these, one by one.

In the first place, the dream renders an account of the connection which is undeniably present between all the portions of the dream-thoughts by combining this material into a unity as a situation or a proceeding. It reproduces logical connections in the form of simultaneity; in this case it behaves rather like the painter who groups together all the philosophers or poets in a picture of the School of Athens, or Parnassus. They never were assembled in any hall or on any mountain-top, although to the reflective mind they do constitute a community.

The dream carries out in detail this mode of representation. Whenever it shows two elements close together, it vouches for a particularly intimate connection between their corresponding representatives in the dream-thoughts. It is as in our method of writing: to signifies that the two letters are to be pronounced as one syllable; while t with o following a blank space indicates that t is the last letter of one word and o the first letter of another. Consequently, dream-combinations are not made up of arbitrary, completely incongruous elements of the dream-material, but of elements that are pretty intimately related in the dream-thoughts also.

For representing causal relations our dreams employ two methods, which are essentially reducible to one. The method of representation more frequently employed - in cases, for example, where the dream-thoughts are to the effect: "Because this was thus and thus, this and that must happen" - consists in making the subordinate clause a prefatory dream and joining the principal clause on to it in the form of the main dream. If my interpretation is correct, the sequence may likewise be reversed. The principal clause always corresponds to that part of the dream which is elaborated in the greatest detail.

An excellent example of such a representation of causality was once provided by a female patient, whose dream I shall subsequently give in full.

The dream consisted of a short prologue, and of a very circumstantial and very definitely centred dream-composition. I might entitle it "Flowery language." The preliminary dream is as follows: She goes to the two maids in the kitchen and scolds them for taking so long to prepare "a little bite of food." She also sees a very large number of heavy kitchen utensils in the kitchen turned upside down in order to drain, even heaped up in stacks. The two maids go to fetch water, and have, as it were, to climb into a river, which reaches up to the house or into the courtyard.

Then follows the main dream, which begins as follows: She is climbing down from a height over a curiously shaped trellis, and she is glad that her dress doesn't get caught anywhere, etc. Now the preliminary dream refers to the house of the lady's parents. The words which are spoken in the kitchen are words which she has probably often heard spoken by her mother. The piles of clumsy pots and pans are taken from an unpretentious hardware shop located in the same house. The second part of this dream contains an allusion to the dreamer's father, who was always pestering the maids, and who during a flood - for the house stood close to the bank of the river - contracted a fatal illness. The thought which is concealed behind the preliminary dream is something like this: "Because I was born in this house, in such sordid and unpleasant surroundings..." The main dream takes up the same thought, and presents it in a form that has been altered by a wish-fulfilment: "I am of exalted origin." Properly then: "Because I am of such humble origin, the course of my life has been so and so."

As far as I can see, the division of a dream into two unequal portions does not always signify a causal relation between the thoughts of the two portions. It often seems as though in the two dreams the same material were presented from different points of view; this is certainly the case when a series of dreams, dreamed the same night, end in a seminal emission, the somatic need enforcing a more and more definite expression. Or the two dreams have proceeded from two separate centres in the dream-material, and they overlap one another in the content, so that the subject which in one dream constitutes the centre cooperates in the other as an allusion, and vice versa. But in a certain number of dreams the division into short preliminary dreams and long subsequent dreams actually signifies a causal relation between the two portions. The other method of representing the causal relation is employed with less comprehensive material, and consists in the transformation of an image in the dream into another image, whether it be of a person or a thing. Only where this transformation is actually seen occurring in the dream shall we seriously insist on the causal relation; not where we simply note that one thing has taken the place of another. I said that both methods of representing the causal relation are really reducible to the same method; in both cases causation is represented by succession, sometimes by the succession of dreams, sometimes by the immediate transformation of one image into another. In the great majority of cases, of course, the causal relation is not represented at all, but is effaced amidst the succession of elements that is unavoidable even in the dream-process.

Dreams are quite incapable of expressing the alternative either-or; it is their custom to take both members of this alternative into the same context, as though they had an equal right to be there. A classic example of this is contained in the dream of Irma's injection. Its latent thoughts obviously mean: I am not responsible for the persistence of Irma's pains; the responsibility rests either with her resistance to accepting the solution or with the fact that she is living under unfavourable sexual conditions, which I am unable to change, or her pains are not hysterical at all, but organic.

The dream, however, carries out all these possibilities, which are almost mutually exclusive, and is quite ready to add a fourth solution derived from the dream-wish. After interpreting the dream, I then inserted the either-or in its context in the dream-thoughts.

But when in narrating a dream the narrator is inclined to employ the alternative either-or: "It was either a garden or a living-room," etc., there is not really an alternative in the dream-thoughts, but an and - a simple addition. When we use either-or we are as a rule describing a quality of vagueness in some element of the dream, but a vagueness which may still be cleared up. The rule to be applied in this case is as follows: The individual members of the alternative are to be treated as equal and connected by an and. For instance, after waiting long and vainly for the address of a friend who is travelling in Italy, I dream that I receive a telegram which gives me the address. On the telegraph form I see printed in blue letters: the first word is blurred - perhaps via or villa; the second is distinctly Sezerno, or even (Casa). The second word, which reminds me of Italian names, and of our discussions on etymology, also expresses my annoyance in respect of the fact that my friend has kept his address a secret from me; but each of the possible first three words may be recognized on analysis as an independent and equally justifiable starting-point in the concatenation of ideas.

During the night before the funeral of my father I dreamed of a printed placard, a card or poster rather like the notices in the waiting-rooms of railway stations which announce that smoking is prohibited. The sign reads either:

You are requested to shut the eyes

or

You are requested to shut one eye

an alternative which I am in the habit of representing in the following form:

- the You are requested to shut eye(s).
- one

Each of the two versions has its special meaning, and leads along particular paths in the dream-interpretation. I had made the simplest possible funeral arrangements, for I knew what the deceased thought about such matters. Other members of the family, however, did not approve of such puritanical simplicity;

they thought we should feel ashamed in the presence of the other mourners. Hence one of the wordings of the dream asks for the shutting of one eye, that is to say, it asks that people should show consideration. The significance of the vagueness, which is here represented by an either-or, is plainly to be seen. The dream-work has not succeeded in concocting a coherent and yet ambiguous wording for the dream-thoughts. Thus the two principal trains of thought are separated from each other, even in the dream-content.

In some few cases the division of a dream into two equal parts expresses the alternative which the dream finds it so difficult to present.

The attitude of dreams to the category of antithesis and contradiction is very striking. This category is simply ignored; the word No does not seem to exist for a dream. Dreams are particularly fond of reducing antitheses to uniformity. or representing them as one and the same thing. Dreams likewise take the liberty of representing any element whatever by its desired opposite, so that it is at first impossible to tell, in respect of any element which is capable of having an opposite, whether it is contained in the dream-thoughts in the negative or the positive sense.[13] In one of the recently cited dreams, whose introductory portion we have already interpreted ("because my origin is so and so"), the dreamer climbs down over a trellis, and holds a blossoming bough in her hands. Since this picture suggests to her the angel in paintings of the Annunciation (her own name is Mary) bearing a lily-stem in his hand, and the white-robed girls walking in procession on Corpus Christi Day, when the streets are decorated with green boughs, the blossoming bough in the

---

[13] From a work of K. Abel's, Der Gegensinn der Urworte, (1884), see my review of it in the Bleuler-Freud Jahrbuch, ii (1910) (Ges. Schriften Vol. X). I learned the surprising fact, which is confirmed by other philologists, that the oldest languages behaved just as dreams do in this regard. They had originally only one word for both extremes in a series of qualities or activities (strong - weak, old - young, far - near, bind - separate), and formed separate designations for the two opposites only secondarily, by slight modifications of the common primitive word. Abel demonstrates a very large number of those relationships in ancient Egyptian, and points to distinct remnants of the same development in the Semitic and Indo-Germanic languages.

dream is quite clearly an allusion to sexual innocence. But the bough is thickly studded with red blossoms, each of which resembles a camellia. At the end of her walk (so the dream continues) the blossoms are already beginning to fall; then follow unmistakable allusions to menstruation. But this very bough, which is carried like a lily-stem and as though by an innocent girl, is also an allusion to Camille, who, as we know, usually wore a white camellia, but a red one during menstruation. The same blossoming bough ("the flower of maidenhood" in Goethe's songs of the miller's daughter) represents at once sexual innocence and its opposite. Moreover, the same dream, which expresses the dreamer's joy at having succeeded in passing through life unsullied, hints in several places (as in the falling of the blossom) at the opposite train of thought, namely, that she had been guilty of various sins against sexual purity (that is, in her childhood). In the analysis of the dream we may clearly distinguish the two trains of thought, of which the comforting one seems to be superficial, and the reproachful one more profound. The two are diametrically opposed to each other, and their similar yet contrasting elements have been represented by identical dream-elements.

The mechanism of dream-formation is favourable in the highest degree to only one of the logical relations. This relation is that of similarity, agreement, contiguity, just as; a relation which may be represented in our dreams, as no other can be, by the most varied expedients. The screening which occurs in the dream-material, or the cases of just as are the chief points of support for dream-formation, and a not inconsiderable part of the dream-work consists in creating new screenings of this kind in cases where those that already exist are prevented by the resistance of the censorship from making their way into the dream. The effort towards condensation evinced by the dream-work facilitates the representation of a relation of similarity.

Similarity, agreement, community, are quite generally expressed in dreams by contraction into a unity, which is either already found in the dreammaterial or is newly created. The first case may be referred to as identification, the second as composition. Identification is used where the dream is concerned with persons, composition where things constitute the material to be unified; but compositions are also made of persons. Localities are often treated as persons.

Identification consists in giving representation in the dream-content to only one of two or more persons who are related by some common feature, while the second person or other persons appear to be suppressed as far as the dream is concerned. In the dream this one "screening" person enters into all the relations and situations which derive from the persons whom he screens. In cases of composition, however, when persons are combined, there are already present in the dream-image features which are characteristic of, but not common to, the persons in question, so that a new unity, a composite person, appears as the result of the union of these features. The combination itself may be effected in various ways. Either the dream-person bears the name of one of the persons to whom he refers - and in this case we simply know, in a manner that is quite analogous to knowledge in waking life, that this or that person is intended - while the visual features belong to another person; or the dream-image itself is compounded of visual features which in reality are derived from the two. Also, in place of the visual features, the part played by the second person may be represented by the attitudes and gestures which are usually ascribed to him by the words he speaks, or by the situations in which he is placed. In this latter method of characterization the sharp distinction between the identification and the combination of persons begins to disappear. But it may also happen that the formation of such a composite person is unsuccessful. The situations or actions of the dream are then attributed to one person, and the other - as a rule the more important - is introduced as an inactive spectator. Perhaps the dreamer will say: "My mother was there too" (Stekel). Such an element of the dream-content is then comparable to a determinative in hieroglyphic script which is not meant to be expressed, but is intended only to explain another sign.

The common feature which justifies the union of two persons that is to say, which enables it to be made - may either be represented in the dream or it may be absent. As a rule, identification or composition of persons actually serves to avoid the necessity of representing this common feature.

Instead of repeating: "A is ill-disposed towards me, and so is B," I make, in my dream, a composite person of A and B; or I conceive A as doing something which is alien to his character, but which is characteristic of B. The dream-person obtained in this way appears in the dream in some new connection, and the fact that he signifies both A and B justifies my inserting that which is common to both persons - their hostility towards me - at the proper place in the dream-interpretation. In this manner I often achieve a quite extraordinary degree of condensation of the dreamcontent; I am able to dispense with the direct representation of the very complicated relations belonging to one person, if I can find a second person who has an equal claim to some of these relations. It will be readily understood how far this representation by means of identification may circumvent the censoring resistance which sets up such harsh conditions for the dream-work. The thing that offends the censorship may reside in those very ideas which are connected in the dream-material with the one person; I now find a second person, who likewise stands in some relation to the objectionable material, but only to a part of it. Contact at that one point which offends the censorship now justifies my formation of a composite person, who is characterized by the indifferent features of each. This person, the result of combination or identification, being free of the censorship, is now suitable for incorporation in the dream-content. Thus, by the application of dream-condensation, I have satisfied the demands of the dream-censorship.

When a common feature of two persons is represented in a dream, this is usually a hint to look for another concealed common feature, the representation of which is made impossible by the censorship. Here a displacement of the common feature has occurred, which in some degree facilitates representation. From the circumstance that the composite person is shown to me in the dream with an indifferent common feature, I must infer that another common feature which is by no means indifferent exists in the dream-thoughts.

Accordingly, the identification or combination of persons serves various purposes in our dreams; in the first place, that of representing a feature common to two persons; secondly, that of representing a displaced common feature; and, thirdly, that of expressly a community of features which is merely wished for. As the wish for a community of features in two persons often coincides with the interchanging of these persons, this relation also is expressed in dreams by identification. In the dream of Irma's injection I wish to exchange one patient for another - that is to say, I wish this other person to be my patient, as the former person has been; the dream deals with this wish by showing me a person who is called Irma, but who is examined in a position such as I have had occasion to see only the other person occupy. In the dream about my uncle this substitution is made the centre of the dream; I identify myself with the minister by judging and treating my colleagues as shabbily as lie does.

It has been my experience - and to this I have found no exception - that every dream treats of oneself. Dreams are absolutely egoistic.[14] In cases where not my ego but only a strange person occurs in the dream-content, I may safely assume that by means of identification my ego is concealed behind that person. I am permitted to supplement my ego. On other occasions, when my ego appears in the dream, the situation in which it is placed tells me that another person is concealing himself, by means of identification, behind the ego. In this case I must be prepared to find that in the interpretation I should transfer something which is connected with this person - the hidden common feature - to myself. There are also dreams in which my ego appears together with other persons who, when the identification is resolved, once

---

[14] Cf. here the observations made in chapter V.

more show themselves to be my ego. Through these identifications I shall then have to connect with my ego certain ideas to which the censorship has objected. I may also give my ego multiple representation in my dream, either directly or by means of identification with other people. By means of several such identifications an extraordinary amount of thought material may be condensed.[15] That one's ego should appear in the same dream several times or in different forms is fundamentally no more surprising than that it should appear, in conscious thinking, many times and in different places or in different relations: as, for example, in the sentence: "When I think what a healthy child I was."

Still easier than in the case of persons is the resolution of identifications in the case of localities designated by their own names, as here the disturbing influence of the all-powerful ego is lacking. In one of my dreams of Rome (chapter V., B.) the name of the place in which I find myself is Rome: I am surprised, however, by a large number of German placards at a street corner. This last is a wish-fulfilment, which immediately suggests Prague; the wish itself probably originated at a period of my youth when I was imbued with a German nationalistic spirit which today is quite subdued. At the time of my dream I was looking forward to meeting a friend in Prague; the identification of Rome with Prague is therefore explained by a desired common feature; I would rather meet my friend in Rome than in Prague; for the purpose of this meeting I should like to exchange Prague for Rome.

The possibility of creating composite formations is one of the chief causes of the fantastic character so common in dreams. in that it introduces into the dream-content elements which could never have been objects of perception. The psychic process which occurs in the creation of composite formations is obviously the same as that which we employ in conceiving or figuring a dragon

---

[15] If I do not know behind which of the persons appearing in the dream I am to look for my ego. I observe the following rule: That person in the dream who is subject to an emotion which I am aware of while asleep is the one that conceals my ego.

or a centaur in our waking senses. The only difference is that, in the fantastic creations of waking life, the impression intended is itself the decisive factor, while the composite formation in the dream is determined by a factor - the common feature in the dream-thoughts - which is independent of its form. Composite formations in dreams may be achieved in a great many different ways. In the most artless of these methods, only the properties of the one thing are represented, and this representation is accompanied by a knowledge that they refer to another object also. A more careful technique combines features of the one object with those of the other in a new image, while it makes skillful use of any really existing resemblances between the two objects. The new creation may prove to be wholly absurd, or even successful as a phantasy, according as the material and the wit employed in constructing it may permit. If the objects to be condensed into a unity are too incongruous, the dream-work is content with creating a composite formation with a comparatively distinct nucleus, to which are attached more indefinite modifications. The unification into one image has here been to some extent unsuccessful; the two representations overlap one another, and give rise to something like a contest between the visual images. Similar representations might be obtained in a drawing if one were to attempt to give form to a unified abstraction of disparate perceptual images.

Dreams naturally abound in such composite formations; I have given several examples of these in the dreams already analysed, and will now cite more such examples. In the dream earlier in this chapter which describes the career of my patient in flowery language, the dream-ego carries a spray of blossoms in her hand which, as we have seen, signifies at once sexual innocence and sexual transgression. Moreover, from the manner in which the blossoms are set on, they recall cherry-blossom; the blossoms themselves, considered singly, are camellias, and finally the whole spray gives the dreamer the impression of an exotic plant. The common feature in the elements of this composite formation is revealed by the dreamthoughts.

The blossoming spray is made up of allusions to presents by which she was induced or was to have been induced to behave in a manner agreeable to the giver. So it was with cherries in her childhood, and with a camellia-tree in her later years; the exotic character is an allusion to a much-travelled naturalist, who sought to win her favour by means of a drawing of a flower. Another female patient contrives a composite mean out of bathing machines at a seaside resort, country privies, and the attics of our city dwelling-houses. A reference to human nakedness and exposure is common to the first two elements; and we may infer from their connection with the third element that (in her childhood) the garret was likewise the scene of bodily exposure. A dreamer of the male sex makes a composite locality out of two places in which "treatment" is given - my office and the assembly rooms in which he first became acquainted with his wife. Another, a female patient, after her elder brother has promised to regale her with caviar, dreams that his legs are covered all over with black beads of caviar. The two elements, taint in a moral sense and the recollection of a cutaneous eruption in childhood which made her legs look as though studded over with red instead of black spots, have here combined with the beads of caviar to form a new idea - the idea of what she gets from her brother. In this dream parts of the human body are treated as objects, as is usually the case in dreams. In one of the dreams recorded by Ferenczi there occurs a composite formation made up of the person of a physician and a horse, and this composite being wears a nightshirt. The common feature in these three components was revealed in the analysis, after the nightshirt had been recognized as an allusion to the father of the dreamer in a scene of childhood. In each of the three cases there was some object of her sexual curiosity. As a child she had often been taken by her nurse to the army stud, where she had the amplest opportunity to satisfy her curiosity, at that time still uninhibited.

I have already stated that the dream has no means of expressing the relation of contradiction, contrast, negation. I shall now contradict this assertion for the first time. A certain number of cases of what may be summed up under the word contrast obtain representation, as we have seen, simply by means of identification - that is when an exchange, a substitution, can be bound up with the contrast. Of this we have cited repeated examples. Certain other of the contrasts in the dream-thoughts, which perhaps come under the category of inverted, united into the opposite, are represented in dreams in the following remarkable manner, which may almost be described as witty. The inversion does not itself make its way into the dream-content, but manifests its presence in the material by the fact that a part of the already formed dream-content which is, for other reasons, closely connected in context is - as it were subsequently - inverted. It is easier to illustrate this process than to describe it. In the beautiful "Up and Down" dream (this chapter, A.), the dream-representation of ascending is an inversion of its prototype in the dream-thoughts: that is, of the introductory scene of Daudet's Sappho; in the dream, climbing is difficult at first and easy later on, whereas, in the novel, it is easy at first, and later becomes more and more difficult. Again, above and below, with reference to the dreamer's brother, are reversed in the dream. This points to a relation of inversion or contrast between two parts of the material in the dream-thoughts, which indeed we found in them, for in the childish phantasy of the dreamer he is carried by his nurse, while in the novel, on the contrary, the hero carries his beloved. My dream of Goethe's attack on Herr M (to be cited later) likewise contains an inversion of this sort, which must be set right before the dream can be interpreted. In this dream, Goethe attacks a young man, Herr M; the reality, as contained in the dream-thoughts, is that an eminent man, a friend of mine, has been attacked by an unknown young author. In the dream I reckon time from the date of Goethe's death; in reality the reckoning was made from the year in which the paralytic was born. The thought which influences the dream-material reveals itself as my opposition to the treatment of Goethe as though he were a lunatic. "It is the other way about," says the dream; "if you don't understand the book it is you who are feeble-minded, not the author." All these dreams of inversion, moreover, seem to me to imply an allusion to the contemptuous phrase, "to turn one's back upon a person" (German: einem die Kehrseite zeigen, lit. to show a person one's backside): cf. the inversion in respect of the dreamer's brother in the Sappho dream. It is further worth noting how frequently inversion is employed in precisely those dreams which are inspired by repressed homosexual impulses.

Moreover, inversion, or transformation into the opposite, is one of the most favoured and most versatile methods of representation which the dream-work has at its disposal. It serves, in the first place, to enable the wish-fulfilment to prevail against a definite element of the dreamthoughts.

"If only it were the other way about!" is often the best expression for the reaction of the ego against a disagreeable recollection. But inversion becomes extraordinarily useful in the service of the censorship, for it effects, in the material to be represented, a degree of distortion which at first simply paralyses our understanding of the dream. It is therefore always permissible, if a dream stubbornly refuses to surrender its meaning, to venture on the experimental inversion of definite portions of its manifest content. Then, not infrequently, everything becomes clear.

Besides the inversion of content, the temporal inversion must not be overlooked. A frequent device of dream-distortion consists in presenting the final issue of the event or the conclusion of the train of thought at the beginning of the dream, and appending at the end of the dream the premises of the conclusion, or the causes of the event. Anyone who forgets this technical device of dream-distortion stands helpless before the problem of dream-interpretation.[16]

---

[16] The hysterical attack often employs the same device of temporal inversion in order to conceal its meaning from the observer. The attack of a hysterical girl, for example, consists in enacting a little romance, which she has imagined in the unconscious in connection with an encounter in a tram. A man, attracted by the beauty of her foot, addresses her while she is reading, whereupon she goes with him and a passionate love-scene ensues. Her attack begins with the representation of this scene by writhing movements of the body (accompanied by movements of the lips and folding of the arms to signify kisses and embraces), whereupon she hurries into the next room, sits down on a chair, lifts her skirt in order to show her foot, acts as though she were about to read a book, and speaks to me (answers me). Cf. the observation of Artemidorus: "In interpreting dreamstories, one must consider them the first time from the beginning to the end, and the second time from the end to the beginning."

In many cases, indeed, we discover the meaning of the dream only when we have subjected the dream-content to a multiple inversion, in accordance with the different relations. For example, in the dream of a young patient who is suffering from obsessional neurosis, the memory of the childish death-wish directed against a dreaded father concealed itself behind the following words: His father scolds him because he comes home so late, but the context of the psycho-analytic treatment and the impressions of the dreamer show that the sentence must be read as follows:

He is angry with his father, and further, that his father always came home too early (i.e., too soon). He would have preferred that his father should not come home at all, which is identical with the wish (see chapter V., D.) that his father would die. As a little boy, during the prolonged absence of his father, the dreamer was guilty of a sexual aggression against another child, and was punished by the threat: "Just you wait until your father comes home!"

If we should seek to trace the relations between the dream-content and the dream-thoughts a little farther, we shall do this best by making the dream itself our point of departure, and asking ourselves: What do certain formal characteristics of the dream-presentation signify in relation to the dream-thoughts? First and foremost among the formal characteristics which are bound to impress us in dreams are the differences in the sensory intensity of the single dream-images, and in the distinctness of various parts of the dream, or of whole dreams as compared with one another. The differences in the intensity of individual dream-images cover the whole gamut, from a sharpness of definition which one is inclined - although without warrant - to rate more highly than that of reality, to a provoking indistinctness which we declare to be characteristic of dreams, because it really is not wholly comparable to any of the degrees of indistinctness which we occasionally perceive in real objects. Moreover, we usually describe the impression which we receive of an indistinct object in a dream as fleeting, while we think of the more distinct dream-images as having been perceptible also for a longer period of time. We must now ask ourselves by what conditions in the dream-material these differences in the distinctness of the individual portions of the dream-content are brought about.

Before proceeding farther, it is necessary to deal with certain expectations which seem to be almost inevitable. Since actual sensations experienced during sleep may constitute part of the dream-material, it will probably be assumed that these sensations, or the dream-elements resulting from them, are emphasized by a special intensity, or conversely, that anything which is particularly vivid in the dream can probably be traced to such real sensations during sleep. My experience, however, has never confirmed this. It is not true that those elements of a dream which are derivatives of real impressions perceived in sleep (nerve stimuli) are distinguished by their special vividness from others which are based on memories. The factor of reality is inoperative in determining the intensity of dream-images.

Further, it might be expected that the sensory intensity (vividness) of single dream-images is in proportion to the psychic intensity of the elements corresponding to them in the dream-thoughts. In the latter, intensity is identical with psychic value; the most intense elements are in fact the most significant, and these constitute the central point of the dream-thoughts. We know, however, that it is precisely these elements which are usually not admitted to the dream-content, owing to the vigilance of the censorship. Still, it might be possible for their most immediate derivatives, which represent them in the dream, to reach a higher degree of intensity without, however, for that reason constituting the central point of the dreamrepresentation.

This assumption also vanishes as soon as we compare the dream and the dream-material. The intensity of the elements in the one has nothing to do with the intensity of the elements in the other; as a matter of fact, a complete transvaluation of all psychic values takes place between the dream-material and the dream. The very element of the dream which is transient and hazy, and screened by more vigorous images, is often discovered to be the one and only direct derivative of the topic that completely dominates the dream-thoughts.

The intensity of the dream-elements proves to be determined in a different manner: that is, by two factors which are mutually independent. It will readily be understood that, those elements by means of which the wish-fulfilment expresses itself are those which are intensely represented. But analysis tells us that from the most vivid elements of the dream the greatest number of trains of thought proceed, and that those which are most vivid are at the same time those which are best determined. No change of meaning is involved if we express this latter empirical proposition in the following formula: The greatest intensity is shown by those elements of the dream for whose formation the most extensive condensation-work was required. We may, therefore, expect that it will be possible to express this condition, as well as the other condition of the wish-fulfilment, in a single formula.

I must utter a warning that the problem which I have just been considering - the causes of the greater or lesser intensity or distinctness of single elements in dreams - is not to be confounded with the other problem - that of variations in the distinctness of whole dreams or sections of dreams.

In the former case the opposite of distinctness is haziness; in the latter, confusion. It is, of course, undeniable that in both scales the two kinds of intensities rise and fall in unison. A portion of the dream which seems clear to us usually contains vivid elements; an obscure dream, on the contrary, is composed of less vivid elements. But the problem offered by the scale of definition, which ranges from the apparently clear to the indistinct or confused, is far more complicated than the problem of fluctuations in vividness of the dream-elements. For reasons which will be given later, the former cannot at this stage be further discussed. In isolated cases one observes, not without surprise, that the impression of distinctness or indistinctness produced by a dream has nothing to do with the dream-structure, but proceeds from the dream-material, as one of its ingredients. Thus, for example, I remember a dream which on waking seemed so particularly well-constructed, flawless and clear that I made up my mind, while I was still in a somnolent state, to admit a new category of dreams - those which had not been subject to the mechanism of condensation and distortion, and which might thus be described as phantasies during sleep. A closer examination, however, proved that this unusual dream suffered from the same structural flaws and breaches as exist in all other dreams; so I abandoned the idea of a category of dreamphantasies.[17] The content of the dream, reduced to its lowest terms, was that I was expounding to a friend a difficult and long-sought theory of bisexuality, and the wish-fulfilling power of the dream was responsible for the fact that this theory (which, by the way, was not communicated in the dream) appeared to be so lucid and flawless. Thus, what I believed to be a judgment as regards the finished dream was a part, and indeed the most essential part, of the dream-content. Here the dream-work reached out, as it were, into my first waking thoughts, and presented to me, in the form of a judgment of the dream, that part of the dream-material which it had failed to represent with precision in the dream. I was once confronted with the exact counterpart of this case by a female patient who at first absolutely declined to relate a dream which was necessary for the analysis "because it was so hazy and confused," and who finally declared, after repeatedly protesting the inaccuracy of her description, that it seemed to her that several persons - herself, her husband, and her father - had occurred in the dream, and that she had not known whether her husband was her father, or who really was her father, or something of that sort. Comparison of this dream with the ideas which occurred to the dreamer in the course of the sitting showed beyond a doubt that it dealt with the rather commonplace story of a maidservant who has to confess that she is expecting a child, and hears doubts

---

[17] I do not know today whether I was justified in doing so.

expressed as to "who the father really is."[18] The obscurity manifested by this dream, therefore, was once more a portion of the dream-exciting material. A fragment of this material was represented in the form of the dream. The form of the dream or of dreaming is employed with astonishing frequency to represent the concealed content.

Glosses on the dream, and seemingly harmless comments on it, often serve in the most subtle manner to conceal - although, of course, they really betray - a part of what is dreamed. As, for example, when the dreamer says: Here the dream was wiped out, and the analysis gives an infantile reminiscence of listening to someone cleaning himself after defecation. Or another example, which deserves to be recorded in detail: A young man has a very distinct dream, reminding him of phantasies of his boyhood which have remained conscious. He found himself in a hotel at a seasonal resort; it was night; he mistook the number of his room, and entered a room in which an elderly lady and her two daughters were undressing to go to bed. He continues: "Then there are some gaps in the dream; something is missing; and at the end there was a man in the room, who wanted to throw me out, and with whom I had to struggle." He tries in vain to recall the content and intention of the boyish phantasy to which the dream obviously alluded. But we finally become aware that the required content had already been given in his remarks concerning the indistinct part of the dream. The gaps are the genital apertures of the women who are going to bed: Here something is missing describes the principal characteristic of the female genitals. In his young days he burned with curiosity to see the female genitals, and was still inclined to adhere to the infantile sexual theory which attributes a male organ to women.

A very similar form was assumed in an analogous reminiscence of another dreamer. He dreamed: I go with Fraulein K into the restaurant of the Volksgarten... then comes a dark place, an

---

[18] Accompanying hysterical symptoms; amenorrhoea and profound depression were the chief troubles of this patient.

interruption... then I find myself in the salon of a brothel, where I see two or three women, one in a chemise and drawers.

Analysis. Fraulein K is the daughter of his former employer; as he himself admits, she was a sister-substitute. He rarely had the opportunity of talking to her, but they once had a conversation in which "one recognized one's sexuality, so to speak, as though one were to say: I am a man and you are a woman." He had been only once to the above-mentioned restaurant, when he was accompanied by the sister of his brother-in-law, a girl to whom he was quite indifferent. On another occasion he accompanied three ladies to the door of the restaurant. The ladies were his sister, his sister-in-law, and the girl already mentioned. He was perfectly indifferent to all three of them, but they all belonged to the sister category. He had visited a brothel but rarely, perhaps two or three times in his life.

The interpretation is based on the dark place, the interruption in the dream, and informs us that on occasion, but in fact only rarely, obsessed by his boyish curiosity, he had inspected the genitals of his sister, a few years his junior. A few days later the misdemeanor indicated in the dream recurred to his conscious memory.

All dreams of the same night belong, in respect of their content, to the same whole; their division into several parts, their grouping and number, are all full of meaning and may be regarded as pieces of information about the latent dream-thoughts. In the interpretation of dreams consisting of several main sections, or of dreams belonging to the same night, we must not overlook the possibility that these different and successive dreams mean the same thing, expressing the same impulses in different material. That one of these homologous dreams which comes first in time is usually the most distorted and most bashful, while the next dream is bolder and more distinct.

Even Pharaoh's dream of the ears and the kine, which Joseph interpreted, was of this kind. It is given by Josephus in greater detail than in the Bible. After relating the first dream, the King said: "After I had seen this vision I awaked out of my sleep, and, being in disorder, and considering with myself what this appearance should be, I fell asleep again, and saw another dream much more wonderful than the foregoing, which still did more affright and disturb me." After listening to the relation of the dream, Joseph said: "This dream, O King, although seen under two forms, signifies one and the same event of things."[19]

Jung, in his Beitrag zur Psychologie des Geruchtes, relates how a veiled erotic dream of a schoolgirl was understood by her friends without interpretation, and continued by them with variations, and he remarks, with reference to one of these narrated dreams, that "the concluding idea of a long series of dream-images had precisely the same content as the first image of the series had endeavoured to represent. The censorship thrust the complex out of the way as long as possible by a constant renewal of symbolic screenings, displacements, transformations into something harmless, etc." Scherner was well acquainted with this peculiarity of dream-representation, and describes it in his Leben des Traumes in terms of a special law in the Appendix to his doctrine of organic stimulation: "But finally, in all symbolic dream-formations emanating from definite nerve stimuli, the phantasy observes the general law that at the beginning of the dream it depicts the stimulating object only by the remotest and freest allusions, but towards the end, when the graphic impulse becomes exhausted, the stimulus itself is nakedly represented by its appropriate organ or its function; whereupon the dream, itself describing its organic motive, achieves its end...."

A pretty confirmation of this law of Scherner's has been furnished by Otto Rank in his essay: Ein Traum, der sich selbst deutet. This dream, related to him by a girl, consisted of two dreams of the same night, separated by an interval of time, the second of which ended with an orgasm. It was possible to interpret this orgastic dream in detail in spite of the few ideas contributed by the dreamer, and the wealth of relations between the two

---

[19] Josephus; Antiquities of the Jews, book II, chap. V, trans. by Wm. Whitson (David McKay, Philadelphia).

dream-contents made it possible to recognize that the first dream expressed in modest language the same thing as the second, so that the latter - the orgastic dream - facilitated a full explanation of the former. From this example, Rank very justifiably argues the significance of orgastic dreams for the theory of dreams in general.

But, in my experience, it is only in rare cases that one is in a position to translate the lucidity or confusion of a dream, respectively, into a certainty or doubt in the dream-material. Later on I shall have to disclose a hitherto unmentioned factor in dream-formation, upon whose operation this qualitative scale in dreams is essentially dependent.

In many dreams in which a certain situation and environment are preserved for some time, there occur interruptions which may be described in the following words: "But then it seemed as though it were, at the same time, another place, and there such and such a thing happened." In these cases, what interrupts the main action of the dream, which after a while may be continued again, reveals itself in the dream-material as a subordinate clause, an interpolated thought. Conditionality in the dream-thoughts is represented by simultaneity in the dream-content (wenn or wann = if or when, while).

We may now ask: What is the meaning of the sensation of inhibited movement which so often occurs in dreams, and is so closely allied to anxiety? One wants to move, and is unable to stir from the spot; or wants to accomplish something, and encounters obstacle after obstacle. The train is about to start, and one cannot reach it; one's hand is raised to avenge an insult, and its strength fails, etc. We have already met with this sensation in exhibition-dreams, but have as yet made no serious attempt to interpret it. It is convenient, but inadequate, to answer that there is motor paralysis in sleep, which manifests itself by means of the sensation alluded to. We may ask: Why is it, then, that we do not dream continually of such inhibited movements? And we may permissibly suspect that this sensation, which may at any time occur during sleep, serves some sort of purpose for representation, and is evoked only when the need of this representation is present in the dream-material.

Inability to do a thing does not always appear in the dream as a sensation; it may appear simply as part of the dream-content. I think one case of this kind is especially fitted to enlighten us as to the meaning of this peculiarity. I shall give an abridged version of a dream in which I seem to be accused of dishonesty. The scene is a mixture made up of a private sanatorium and several other places. A manservant appears, to summon me to an inquiry. I know in the dream that something has been missed, and that the inquiry is taking place because I am suspected of having appropriated the lost article. Analysis shows that inquiry is to be taken in two senses; it includes the meaning of medical examination. Being conscious of my innocence, and my position as consultant in this sanatorium, I calmly follow the manservant. We are received at the door by another manservant, who says, pointing at me, "Have you brought him? Why, he is a respectable man." Thereupon, and unattended, I enter a great hall where there are many machines, which reminds me of an inferno with its hellish instruments of punishment. I see a colleague strapped to an appliance; he has every reason to be interested in my appearance, but he takes no notice of me. I understand that I may now go. Then I cannot find my hat, and cannot go after all.

The wish that the dream fulfils is obviously the wish that my honesty shall be acknowledged, and that I may be permitted to go; there must therefore be all sorts of material in the dream-thoughts which comprise a contradiction of this wish. The fact that I may go is the sign of my absolution; if, then, the dream provides at its close an event which prevents me from going, we may readily conclude that the suppressed material of the contradiction is asserting itself in this feature. The fact that I cannot find my hat therefore means: "You are not after all an honest man."

The inability to do something in the dream is the expression of a contradiction, a No; so that our earlier assertion, to the effect that the dream is not capable of expressing a negation, must be revised accordingly.[20]

In other dreams in which the inability to do something occurs, not merely as a situation, but also as a sensation, the same contradiction is more emphatically expressed by the sensation of inhibited movement, or a will to which a counter-will is opposed. Thus the sensation of inhibited movement represents a conflict of will. We shall see later on that this very motor paralysis during sleep is one of the fundamental conditions of the psychic process which functions during dreaming. Now an impulse which is conveyed to the motor system is none other than the will, and the fact that we are certain that the impulse will be inhibited in sleep makes the whole process extraordinarily well-adapted to the representation of a will towards something and of a No which opposes itself thereto. From my explanation of anxiety, it is easy to understand why the sensation of the inhibited will is so closely allied to anxiety, and why it is so often connected with it in dreams. Anxiety is a libidinal impulse which emanates from the unconscious and is inhibited by the preconscious.[21] Therefore, when a sensation of inhibition in the dream is accompanied by anxiety, the dream must be concerned with a volition which was at one time capable of arousing libido; there must be a sexual impulse.

As for the judgment which is often expressed during a dream: "Of course, it is only a dream," and the psychic force to which it may be ascribed, I shall discuss these questions later on. For the present I will merely say that they are intended to depreciate the importance of what is being dreamed. The interesting problem

---

[20] A reference to an experience of childhood emerges, in the complete analysis, through the following connecting-links: "The Moor has done his duty, the Moor can go." And then follows the waggish question: "How old is the Moor when he has done his duty?" - "A year, then he can go (walk)." (It is said that I came into the world with so much black curly hair that my young mother declared that I was a little Moor.) The fact that I cannot find my hat is an experience of the day which has been exploited in various senses. Our servant, who is a genius at stowing things away, had hidden the hat. A rejection of melancholy thoughts of death is concealed behind the conclusion of the dream: "I have not nearly done my duty yet; I cannot go yet." Birth and death together - as in the dream of Goethe and the paralytic, which was a little earlier in date.

[21] This theory is not in accordance with more recent views.

allied to this, as to what is meant if a certain content in the dream is characterized in the dream itself as having been dreamed - the riddle of a dream within a dream - has been solved in a similar sense by W. Stekel, by the analysis of some convincing examples. Here again the part of the dream dreamed is to be depreciated in value and robbed of its reality; that which the dreamer continues to dream after waking from the dream within a dream is what the dream-wish desires to put in place of the obliterated reality. It may therefore be assumed that the part dreamed contains the representation of the reality, the real memory, while, on the other hand, the continued dream contains the representation of what the dreamer merely wishes. The inclusion of a certain content in a dream within a dream is, therefore, equivalent to the wish that what has been characterized as a dream had never occurred. In other words: when a particular incident is represented by the dream-work in a dream, it signifies the strongest confirmation of the reality of this incident, the most emphatic affirmation of it. The dream-work utilizes the dream itself as a form of repudiation, and thereby confirms the theory that a dream is a wish-fulfilment.

D. Regard for Representability

We have hitherto been concerned with investigating the manner in which our dreams represent the relations between the dream-thoughts, but we have often extended our inquiry to the further question as to what alterations the dream-material itself undergoes for the purposes of dreamformation.

We now know that the dream-material, after being stripped of a great many of its relations, is subjected to compression, while at the same time displacements of the intensity of its elements enforce a psychic transvaluation of this material. The displacements which we have considered were shown to be substitutions of one particular idea for another, in some way related to the original by its associations, and the displacements were made to facilitate the condensation, inasmuch as in this manner, instead of two elements, a common mean between them found its way into the dream. So far, no mention has been made of any other kind of displacement. But we learn from the analyses that displacement of another kind does occur, and that it manifests itself in an exchange of the verbal expression for the thought in question. In both cases we are dealing with a displacement along a chain of associations, but the same process takes place in different psychic spheres, and the result of this displacement in the one case is that one element is replaced by another, while in the other case an element exchanges its verbal shape for another.

This second kind of displacement occurring in dream-formation is not only of great theoretical interest, but also peculiarly well-fitted to explain the appearance of phantastic absurdity in which dreams disguise themselves. Displacement usually occurs in such a way that a colourless and abstract expression of the dream-thought is exchanged for one that is pictorial and concrete. The advantage, and along with it the purpose, of this substitution is obvious. Whatever is pictorial is capable of representation in dreams and can be fitted into a situation in which abstract expression would confront the dream-representation with difficulties not unlike those which would arise if a political leading article had to be represented in an illustrated journal. Not only the possibility of representation, but also the interests of condensation and of the censorship, may be furthered by this exchange. Once the abstractly expressed and unserviceable dream-thought is translated into pictorial language, those contacts and identities between this new expression and the rest of the dream-material which are required by the dream-work, and which it contrives whenever they are not available, are more readily provided, since in every language concrete terms, owing to their evolution, are richer in associations than are abstract terms. It may be imagined that a good part of the intermediate work in dream-formation, which seeks to reduce the separate dreamthoughts to the tersest and most unified expression in the dream, is effected in this manner, by fitting paraphrases of the various thoughts. The one thought whose mode of expression has perhaps been determined by other factors will therewith exert a distributive and selective influence on the expressions available for the others, and it may even do this from the very start, just as it would in the creative activity of a poet. When a poem is to be written in rhymed couplets, the second rhyming line is bound by two conditions: it must express the meaning allotted to it, and its expression must permit of a rhyme with the first line. The best poems are, of course, those in which one does not detect the effort to find a rhyme, and in which both thoughts have as a matter of course, by mutual induction, selected the verbal expression which, with a little subsequent adjustment, will permit of the rhyme.

In some cases the change of expression serves the purposes of dream-condensation more directly, in that it provides an arrangement of words which, being ambiguous, permits of the expression of more than one of the dream-thoughts. The whole range of verbal wit is thus made to serve the purpose of the dream-work. The part played by words in dream-formation ought not to surprise us. A word, as the point of junction of a number of ideas, possesses, as it were, a predestined ambiguity, and the neuroses (obsessions, phobias) take advantage of the opportunities for condensation and disguise afforded by words quite as eagerly as do dreams.[22] That dream-distortion also profits by this displacement of expression may be readily demonstrated. It is indeed confusing if one ambiguous word is substituted for two with single meanings, and the replacement of sober, everyday language by a plastic mode of expression baffles our understanding, especially since a dream never tells us whether the elements presented by it are to be interpreted literally or metaphorically, whether they refer to the dream-material directly, or only by means of interpolated expressions. Generally speaking, in the interpretation of any element of a dream it is doubtful whether it (a) is to be accepted in the negative or the positive sense (contrast relation); (b) is to be interpreted historically (as a memory); (c) is symbolic; or whether (d) its valuation is to be based upon its

---

[22] Compare Wit and its Relation to the Unconscious.

wording. - In spite of this versatility, we may say that the representation effected by the dream-work, which was never even intended to be understood, does not impose upon the translator any greater difficulties than those that the ancient writers of hieroglyphics imposed upon their readers.

I have already given several examples of dream-representations which are held together only by ambiguity of expression (her mouth opens without difficulty, in the dream of Irma's injection; I cannot go yet after all, in the last dream related, etc.) I shall now cite a dream in the analysis of which plastic representation of the abstract thoughts plays a greater part. The difference between such dream-interpretation and the interpretation by means of symbols may nevertheless be clearly defined; in the symbolic interpretation of dreams, the key to the symbolism is selected arbitrarily by the interpreter, while in our own cases of verbal disguise these keys are universally known and are taken from established modes of speech. Provided one hits on the right idea on the right occasion, one may solve dreams of this kind, either completely or in part, independently of any statements made by the dreamer.

A lady friend of mine, dreams: *She is at the opera. It is a Wagnerian performance, which has lasted until 7.45 in the morning. In the stalls and pit there are tables, at which people are eating and drinking. Her cousin and his young wife, who have just returned from their honeymoon, are sitting at one of these tables; beside them is a member of the aristocracy. The young wife is said to have brought him back with her from the honeymoon quite openly, just as she might have brought back a hat. In the middle of the stalls there is a high tower, on the top of which there is a platform surrounded by an iron railing. There, high overhead, stands the conductor, with the features of Hans Richter, continually running round behind the railing, perspiring terribly; and from this position he is conducting the orchestra, which is arranged round the base of the tower. She herself is sitting in a box with a friend of her own sex (known to me). Her* younger sister tries to hand her up, from the stalls, a large lump of coal, alleging that she had not known that it would be so long, and that she must by this time be miserably cold. (As though the boxes ought to have been heated during the long performance.)

Although in other respects the dream gives a good picture of the situation, it is, of course, nonsensical enough: the tower in the middle of the stalls, from which the conductor leads the orchestra, and above all the coal which her sister hands up to her. I purposely asked for no analysis of this dream. With some knowledge of the personal relations of the dreamer, I was able to interpret parts of it independently of her. I knew that she had felt intense sympathy for a musician whose career had been prematurely brought to an end by insanity. I therefore decided to take the tower in the stalls verbally. It then emerged that the man whom she wished to see in the place of Hans Richter towered above all the other members of the orchestra. This tower must be described as a composite formation by means of apposition; by its substructure it represents the greatness of the man, but by the railing at the top, behind which he runs round like a prisoner or an animal in a cage (an allusion to the name of the unfortunate man),[23] it represents his later fate. Lunatic-tower is perhaps the expression in which the two thoughts might have met.

Now that we have discovered the dream's method of representation, we may try, with the same key, to unlock the meaning of the second apparent absurdity, that of the coal which her sister hands up to the dreamer. Coal should mean secret love.

No fire, no coal so hotly glows
As the secret love of which no one knows.

She and her friend remain seated[24] while her younger sister, who still has a prospect of marrying, hands her up the coal because she did not know that it would be so long. What would be so long is not told in the dream. If it were an anecdote, we should

---
[23] Hugo Wolf.
[24] The German *sitzen geblieben* is often applied to women who have not succeeded in getting married. - TR.

say the performance; but in the dream we may consider the sentence as it is, declare it to be ambiguous, and add before she married. The interpretation secret love is then confirmed by the mention of the cousin who is sitting with his wife in the stalls, and by the open love-affair attributed to the latter. The contrasts between secret and open love, between the dreamer's fire and the coldness of the young wife, dominate the dream. Moreover, here once again there is a person in a high position as a middle term between the aristocrat and the musician who is justified in raising high hopes.

In the above analysis we have at last brought to light a third factor, whose part in the transformation of the dream-thoughts into the dream-content is by no means trivial: namely, consideration of the suitability of the dream-thoughts for representation in the particular psychic material of which the dream makes use - that is, for the most part in visual images. Among the various subordinate ideas associated with the essential dream-thoughts, those will be preferred which permit of visual representation, and the dream-work does not hesitate to recast the intractable thoughts into an: other verbal form, even though this is a more unusual form provided it makes representation possible, and thus puts an end to the psychological distress caused by strangulated thinking. This pouring of the thought-content into another mould may at the same time serve the work of condensation, and may establish relations with another thought which otherwise would not have been established. It is even possible that this second thought may itself have previously changed its original expression for the purpose of meeting the first one halfway.

Herbert Silberer[25] has described a good method of directly observing the transformation of thoughts into images which occurs in dreamformation, and has thus made it possible to study in isolation this one factor of the dream-work. If, while in a state of fatigue and somnolence, he imposed upon himself a mental

---

[25] Bleuler-Freud Jahrbuch, i (1909).

effort, it frequently happened that the thought escaped him and in its place there appeared a picture in which he could recognize the substitute for the thought. Not quite appropriately, Silberer described this substitution as auto-symbolic. I shall cite here a few examples from Silberer's work, and on account of certain peculiarities of the phenomena observed I shall refer to the subject later on.

"Example 1. I remember that I have to correct a halting passage in an essay.

"Symbol. I see myself planing a piece of wood.

"Example 5. I endeavour to call to mind the aim of certain metaphysical studies which I am proposing to undertake.

"This aim, I reflect, consists in working one's way through, while seeking for the basis of existence, to ever higher forms of consciousness or levels of being.

"Symbol. I run a long knife under a cake as though to take a slice out of it.

"Interpretation. My movement with the knife signifies working one's way through... The explanation of the basis of the symbolism is as follows:

At table it devolves upon me now and again to cut and distribute a cake, a business which I perform with a long, flexible knife, and which necessitates a certain amount of care. In particular, the neat extraction of the cut slices of cake presents a certain amount of difficulty; the knife must be carefully pushed under the slices in question (the slow working one's way through in order to get to the bottom). But there is yet more symbolism in the picture. The cake of the symbol was really a dobos-cake - that is, a cake in which the knife has to cut through several layers (the levels of consciousness and thought).

"Example 9. I lost the thread in a train of thought. I make an effort to find it again, but I have to recognize that the point of departure has completely escaped me.

"Symbol. Part of a form of type, the last lines of which have fallen out."

In view of the part played by witticisms, puns, quotations, songs, and proverbs in the intellectual life of educated persons, it would be entirely in accordance with our expectations to find disguises of this sort used with extreme frequency in the representation of the dream-thoughts. Only in the case of a few types of material has a generally valid dream-symbolism established itself on the basis of generally known allusions and verbal equivalents. A good part of this symbolism, however, is common to the psychoneuroses, legends, and popular usages as well as to dreams.

In fact, if we look more closely into the matter, we must recognize that in employing this kind of substitution the dream-work is doing nothing at all original. For the achievement of its purpose, which in this case is representation without interference from the censorship, it simply follows the paths which it finds already marked out in unconscious thinking, and gives the preference to those transformations of the repressed material which are permitted to become conscious also in the form of witticisms and allusions, and with which all the phantasies of neurotics are replete.

Here we suddenly begin to understand the dream-interpretations of Scherner, whose essential correctness I have vindicated elsewhere. The preoccupation of the imagination with one's own body is by no means peculiar to or characteristic of the dream alone. My analyses have shown me that it is constantly found in the unconscious thinking of neurotics, and may be traced back to sexual curiosity, whose object, in the adolescent youth or maiden, is the genitals of the opposite sex, or even of the same sex. But, as Scherner and Volkelt very truly insist, the house does not constitute the only group of ideas which is employed for the symbolization of the body, either in dreams or in the unconscious phantasies of neurosis. To be sure, I know patients who have steadily adhered to an architectural symbolism for the body and the genitals (sexual interest, of course, extends far beyond the region of the external genital organs) - patients for whom posts and pillars signify legs (as in the Song of Songs), to whom every door suggests a bodily aperture (hole), and every water-pipe the urinary system, and so on. But the groups of ideas appertaining to plant-life. or to the kitchen, are just as often chosen to conceal sexual images;[26] in respect of the former everyday language, the sediment of imaginative comparisons dating from the remotest times, has abundantly paved the way (the vineyard of the Lord, the seed of Abraham, the garden of the maiden in the Song of Songs). The ugliest as well as the most intimate details of sexual life may be thought or dreamed of in apparently innocent allusions to culinary operations, and the symptoms of hysteria will become absolutely unintelligible if we forget that sexual symbolism may conceal itself behind the most commonplace and inconspicuous matters as its safest hiding-place. That some neurotic children cannot look at blood and raw meat, that they vomit at the sight of eggs and macaroni, and that the dread of snakes, which is natural to mankind, is monstrously exaggerated in neurotics - all this has a definite sexual meaning. Wherever the neurosis employs a disguise of this sort, it treads the paths once trodden by the whole of humanity in the early stages of civilization - paths to whose thinly veiled existence our idiomatic expressions, proverbs, superstitions, and customs testify to this day.

I here insert the promised flower-dream of a female patient, in which I shall print in Roman type everything which is to be sexually interpreted.

This beautiful dream lost all its charm for the dreamer once it had been interpreted.

(a) Preliminary dream: She goes to the two maids in the kitchen and scolds them for taking so long to prepare a little bite of food. She also sees a very large number of heavy kitchen utensils in the kitchen, heaped into piles and turned upside down in order

---

[26] A mass of corroborative material may be found in the three supplementary volumes of Edward Fuchs's Illustrierte Sittengeschichte; privately printed by A. Lange, Munich.

to drain. Later addition: The two maids go to fetch water, and have, as it were, to climb into a river which reaches up to the house or into the courtyard.[27]

(b) Main dream:[28] She is descending from a height[29] over curiously constructed railings, or a fence which is composed of large square trelliswork hurdles with small square apertures.[30] It is really not adapted for climbing; she is constantly afraid that she cannot find a place for her foot, and she is glad that her dress doesn't get caught anywhere, and that she is able to climb it so respectably.[31] As she climbs she is carrying a big branch in her hand,[32] really like a tree, which is thickly studded with red flowers; a spreading branch, with many twigs.[33] With this is connected the idea of cherry-blossoms (Bluten = flowers), but they look like fully opened camellias, which of course do not grow on trees. As she is descending, she first has one, then suddenly two, and then again only one.[34] When she has reached the ground the lower flowers have already begun to fall. Now that she has reached the bottom she sees an "odd man" who is combing - as she would like to put it - just such a tree, that is, with a piece of wood he is scraping thick bunches of hair from it, which hang from it like moss. Other men have chopped off such branches in a garden, and have flung them into the road, where they are lying about, so that a number of people take some of them. But she asks whether this is right, whether she may take one, too.[35] In the garden there stands a young man (he is a foreigner, and known

---

[27] For the interpretation of this preliminary dream, which is to be regarded as casual, see earlier in this chapter, C.

[28] Her career.

[29] Exalted origin, the wish-contrast to the preliminary dream.

[30] A composite formation, which unites two localities, the so-called garret (German: Boden = "floor," "garret") of her father's house, in which she used to play with her brother, the object of her later phantasies, and the farm of a malicious uncle, who used to tease her.

[31] Wish-contrast to an actual memory of her uncle's farm, to the effect that she used to expose herself while she was asleep.

[32] Just as the angel bears a lily-stem in the Annunciation.

[33] For the explanation of this composite formation, see earlier in this chapter, C.; innocence, menstruation, La Dame aux Camelias.

[34] Referring to the plurality of the persons who serve her phantasies.

[35] Whether it is permissible to masturbate. [Sich einem herunterreissen means "to pull off" and colloquially "to masturbate." - TR.]

to her) toward whom she goes in order to ask him how it is possible to transplant such branches in her own garden.[36] He embraces her, whereupon she struggles and asks him what he is thinking of, whether it is permissible to embrace her in such a manner. He says there is nothing wrong in it, that it is permitted.[37] He then declares himself willing to go with her into the other garden, in order to show her how to put them in, and he says something to her which she does not quite understand: "Besides this I need three metres (later she says: square metres) or three fathoms of ground." It seems as though he were asking her for something in return for his willingness, as though he had the intention of indemnifying (reimbursing) himself in her garden, as though he wanted to evade some law or other, to derive some advantage from it without causing her an injury. She does not know whether or not he really shows her anything.

The above dream, which has been given prominence on account of its symbolic elements, may be described as a biographical dream. Such dreams occur frequently in psychoanalysis, but perhaps only rarely outside it.[38]

I have, of course, an abundance of such material, but to reproduce it here would lead us too far into the consideration of neurotic conditions.

Everything points to the same conclusion, namely, that we need not assume that any special symbolizing activity of the psyche is operative in dream-formation; that, on the contrary, the dream makes use of such symbolizations as are to be found ready-made in unconscious thinking, since these, by reason of their case of representation, and for the most part by reason of their being exempt from the censorship, satisfy more effectively the requirements of dream-formation.

E. Representation in Dreams by Symbols: Some Further

---

[36] The branch (Ast) has long been used to represent the male organ, and, moreover, contains a very distinct allusion to the family name of the dreamer.

[37] Refers to the matrimonial precautions, as does that which immediately follows.

[38] An analogous biographical dream is recorded later in this chapter, among the examples of dream symbolism.

Typical Dreams - The analysis of the last biographical dream shows that I recognized the symbolism in dreams from the very outset. But it was only little by little that I arrived at a full appreciation of its extent and significance, as the result of increasing experience, and under the influence of the works of W. Stekel, concerning which I may here fittingly say something.

This author, who has perhaps injured psychoanalysis as much as he has benefited it, produced a large number of novel symbolic translations, to which no credence was given at first, but most of which were later confirmed and had to be accepted. Stekel's services are in no way belittled by the remark that the sceptical reserve with which these symbols were received was not unjustified. For the examples upon which he based his interpretations were often unconvincing, and, moreover, he employed a method which must be rejected as scientifically unreliable. Stekel found his symbolic meanings by way of intuition, by virtue of his individual faculty of immediately understanding the symbols. But such an art cannot be generally assumed; its efficiency is immune from criticism, and its results have therefore no claim to credibility. It is as though one were to base one's diagnosis of infectious diseases on the olfactory impressions received beside the sick-bed, although of course there have been clinicians to whom the sense of smell - atrophied in most people - has been of greater service than to others, and who really have been able to diagnose a case of abdominal typhus by their sense of smell.

The progressive experience of psycho-analysis has enabled us to discover patients who have displayed in a surprising degree this immediate understanding of dream-symbolism. Many of these patients suffered from dementia praecox, so that for a time there was an inclination to suspect that all dreamers with such an understanding of symbols were suffering from that disorder. But this did not prove to be the case; it is simply a question of a personal gift or idiosyncrasy without perceptible pathological significance. When one has familiarized oneself with the extensive employment of symbolism for the representation of sexual material in dreams, one naturally asks oneself whether many of these symbols have not a permanently established meaning, like the signs in shorthand; and one even thinks of attempting to compile a new dream-book on the lines of the cipher method. In this connection it should be noted that symbolism does not appertain especially to dreams, but rather to the unconscious imagination, and particularly to that of the people, and it is to be found in a more developed condition in folklore, myths, legends, idiomatic phrases, proverbs, and the current witticisms of a people than in dreams. We should have, therefore, to go far beyond the province of dream-interpretation in order fully to investigate the meaning of symbolism, and to discuss the numerous problems - for the most part still unsolved - which are associated with the concept of the symbol.[39] We shall here confine ourselves to saying that representation by a symbol comes under the heading of the indirect representations, but that we are warned by all sorts of signs against indiscriminately classing symbolic representation with the other modes of indirect representation before we have clearly conceived its distinguishing characteristics. In a number of cases, the common quality shared by the symbol and the thing which it represents is obvious; in others, it is concealed; in these latter cases the choice of the symbol appears to be enigmatic. And these are the very cases that must be able to elucidate the ultimate meaning of the symbolic relation; they point to the fact that it is of a genetic nature. What is today symbolically connected was probably united, in primitive times, by conceptual and linguistic identity.[40] The symbolic relationship seems to be a residue and reminder of a former identity. It may

---

[39] Cf. the works of Bleuler and his Zurich disciples, Maeder, Abraham, and others, and of the non-medical authors (Kleinpaul and others) to whom they refer. But the most pertinent things that have been said on the subject will be found in the work of O. Rank and H. Sachs, Die Bedeutung der Psychoanalyse fur die Geisteswissenschaft, (1913), chap. i.

[40] This conception would seem to find an extraordinary confirmation in a theory advanced by Hans Sperber ("Uber den Einfluss sexueller momente auf Entstehung und Entwicklung der Sprache," in Imago, i. [1912]). Sperber believes that primitive words denoted sexual things exclusively, and subsequently lost their sexual significance and were applied to other things and activities, which were compared with the sexual.

also be noted that in many cases the symbolic identity extends beyond the linguistic identity, as had already been asserted by Schubert (1814).[41]

Dreams employ this symbolism to give a disguised representation to their latent thoughts. Among the symbols thus employed there are, of course, many which constantly, or all but constantly, mean the same thing. But we must bear in mind the curious plasticity of psychic material. Often enough a symbol in the dream-content may have to be interpreted not symbolically but in accordance with its proper meaning; at other times the dreamer, having to deal with special memory-material, may take the law into his own hands and employ anything whatever as a sexual symbol, though it is not generally so employed. Wherever he has the choice of several symbols for the representation of a dream-content, he will decide in favour of that symbol which is in addition objectively related to his other thought-material; that is to say, he will employ an individual motivation besides the typically valid one.

Although since Scherner's time the more recent investigations of dream-problems have definitely established the existence of dream-symbolism - even Havelock Ellis acknowledges that our dreams are indubitably full of symbols - it must yet be admitted that the existence of symbols in dreams has not only facilitated dream-interpretation, but has also made it more difficult. The technique of interpretation in accordance with the dreamer's free associations more often than otherwise leaves us in the lurch as far as the symbolic elements of the dream-content are concerned. A return to the arbitrariness of dream-interpretation as it was practised in antiquity, and is seemingly revived by Stekel's wild interpretations, is contrary to scientific method. Consequently, those elements in the dream-content which are

---

[41] For example, a ship sailing on the sea may appear in the urinary dreams of Hungarian dreamers, despite the fact that the term of to ship, for to urinate, is foreign to this language (Ferenczi). In the dreams of the French and the other romance peoples room serves as a symbolic representation for woman, although these peoples have nothing analogous to the German Frauenzimmer. Many symbols are as old as language itself, while others are continually being coined (e.g., the aeroplane, the Zeppelin).

to be symbolically regarded compel us to employ a combined technique, which on the one hand is based on the dreamer's associations, while on the other hand the missing portions have to be supplied by the interpreter's understanding of the symbols. Critical circumspection in the solution of the symbols must coincide with careful study of the symbols in especially transparent examples of dreams in order to silence the reproach of arbitrariness in dream-interpretation. The uncertainties which still adhere to our function as dream-interpreters are due partly to our imperfect knowledge (which, however, can be progressively increased) and partly to certain peculiarities of the dream-symbols themselves. These often possess many and varied meanings, so that, as in Chinese script, only the context can furnish the correct meaning. This multiple significance of the symbol is allied to the dream's faculty of admitting over-interpretations, of representing, in the same content, various wish-impulses and thought-formations, often of a widely divergent character.

After these limitations and reservations, I will proceed. The Emperor and the Empress (King and Queen)[42] in most cases really represent the dreamer's parents; the dreamer himself or herself is the prince or princess. But the high authority conceded to the Emperor is also conceded to great men, so that in some dreams, for example, Goethe appears as a father symbol (Hitschmann). - All elongated objects, sticks, tree-trunks, umbrellas (on account of the opening, which might be likened to an erection), all sharp and elongated weapons, knives, daggers, and pikes, represent the male member. A frequent, but not very intelligible symbol for the same is a nail-file (a reference to rubbing and scraping?). - Small boxes, chests, cupboards, and ovens correspond to the female organ; also cavities, ships, and all kinds of vessels. - A room in a dream generally represents a woman; the description of its various entrances and exits is scarcely calculated

---

[42] In the U.S.A. the father is represented in dreams as the President, and even more often as the Governor - a title which is frequently applied to the parent in everyday life. - TR.

to make us doubt this interpretation.[43] The interest as to whether the room is open or locked will be readily understood in this connection. (Cf. Dora's dream in Fragment of an Analysis of Hysteria.) There is no need to be explicit as to the sort of key that will unlock the room; the symbolism of lock and key has been gracefully if broadly employed by Uhland in his song of the Graf Eberstein. - The dream of walking through a suite of rooms signifies a brothel or a harem. But, as H. Sachs has shown by an admirable example, it is also employed to represent marriage (contrast). An interesting relation to the sexual investigations of childhood emerges when the dreamer dreams of two rooms which were previously one, or finds that a familiar room in a house of which he dreams has been divided into two, or the reverse. In childhood the female genitals and anus (the "behind")[44] are conceived of as a single opening according to the infantile cloaca theory, and only later is it discovered that this region of the body contains two separate cavities and openings. Steep inclines, ladders and stairs, and going up or down them, are symbolic representations of the sexual act.[45] Smooth walls over which one climbs, facades of houses, across which one lets oneself down - often with a sense of great anxiety - correspond to erect human bodies, and probably repeat in our dreams childish memories of climbing up parents or nurses. Smooth walls are men; in anxiety dreams one often holds firmly to projections on houses. Tables, whether bare or covered, and boards, are women, perhaps by virtue of contrast, since they have no protruding contours. Wood generally speaking, seems, in accordance with its linguistic

---

[43] "A patient living in a boarding-house dreams that he meets one of the servants, and asks her what her number is; to his surprise she answers: 14. He has, in fact, entered into relations with the girl in question, and has often had her in his bedroom. She feared, as may be imagined, that the landlady suspected her, and had proposed, on the day before the dream, that they should meet in one of the unoccupied rooms. In reality this room had the number 14, while in the dream the woman bore this number. A clearer proof of the identification of woman and room could hardly be imagined," (Ernest Jones, Intern. Zeitschr. f. Psychoanalyse, ii, [1914]). (Cf. Artemidorus, The Symbolism of Dreams [German version by F. S. Krauss, Vienna, 1881, p. 110]: "Thus, for example, the bedroom signifies the wife, supposing one to be in the house.")

[44] Cf. "the cloaca theory" in Three Contributions to the Theory of Sex.

[45] See p. 123-124 above.

relations, to represent feminine matter (Materie). The name of the island Madeira means wood in Portuguese. Since bed and board (mensa et thorus) constitute marriage, in dreams the latter is often substituted for the former, and as far as practicable the sexual representation-complex is transposed to the eating-complex. - Of articles of dress, a woman's hat may very often be interpreted with certainty as the male genitals. In the dreams of men, one often finds the necktie as a symbol for the penis; this is not only because neckties hang down in front of the body, and are characteristic of men, but also because one can select them at pleasure, a freedom which nature prohibits as regards the original of the symbol. Persons who make use of this symbol in dreams are very extravagant in the matter of ties, and possess whole collections of them.[46] All complicated machines and appliances are very probably the genitals - as a rule the male genitals - in the description of which the symbolism of dreams is as indefatigable as human wit. It is quite unmistakable that all weapons and tools are used as symbols for the male organ: e.g., ploughshare, hammer, gun, revolver, dagger, sword, etc.

Again, many of the landscapes seen in dreams, especially those that contain bridges or wooded mountains, may be readily recognized as descriptions of the genitals. Marcinowski collected a series of examples in which the dreamer explained his dream by means of drawings, in order to represent the landscapes and places appearing in it. These drawings clearly showed the distinction between the manifest and the latent meaning of the dream. Whereas, naively regarded, they seemed to represent plans, maps, and so forth, closer investigation showed that they were representations of the human body, of the genitals, etc., and only after conceiving them thus could the dream be understood.[47] Finally, where one finds incomprehensible neologisms one may

---

[46] Cf. in the Zentralblatt fur Psychoanalyse, ii, 675, the drawing of a nineteen-year-old manic patient: a man with a snake as a neck-tie, which is turning towards a girl. Also the story Der Schamhaftige (Anthropophyteia, vi, 334): A woman entered a bathroom, and there came face to face with a man who hardly had time to put on his shirt. He was greatly embarrassed, but at once covered his throat with the front of his shirt, and said: "Please excuse me, I have no necktie."

[47] Cf. Pfister's works on cryptography and picture-puzzles.

suspect combinations of components having a sexual significance. - Children, too, often signify the genitals, since men and women are in the habit of fondly referring to their genital organs as little man, little woman, little thing. The little brother was correctly recognized by Stekel as the penis. To play with or to beat a little child is often the dream's representation of masturbation.

The dream-work represents castration by baldness, hair-cutting, the loss of teeth, and beheading. As an insurance against castration, the dream uses one of the common symbols of the penis in double or multiple form and the appearance in a dream of a lizard - an animal whose tail, if pulled off, is regenerated by a new growth - has the same meaning. Most of those animals which are utilized as genital symbols in mythology and folklore play this part also in dreams: the fish, the snail, the cat, the mouse (on account of the hairiness of the genitals), but above all the snake, which is the most important symbol of the male member. Small animals and vermin are substitutes for little children, e.g., undesired sisters or brothers. To be infected with vermin is often the equivalent for pregnancy. - As a very recent symbol of the male organ I may mention the airship, whose employment is justified by its relation to flying, and also, occasionally, by its form. - Stekel has given a number of other symbols, not yet sufficiently verified, which he has illustrated by examples. The works of this author, and especially his book: Die Sprache des Traumes, contain the richest collection of interpretations of symbols, some of which were ingeniously guessed and were proved to be correct upon investigation, as, for example, in the section on the symbolism of death. The author's lack of critical reflection, and his tendency to generalize at all costs, make his interpretations doubtful or inapplicable, so that in making use of his works caution is urgently advised. I shall therefore restrict myself to mentioning a few examples.

Right and left, according to Stekel, are to be understood in dreams in an ethical sense. "The right-hand path always signifies the way to righteousness, the left-hand path the path to crime. Thus the left may signify homosexuality, incest, and perversion, while the right signifies marriage, relations with a prostitute, etc. The meaning is always determined by the individual moral standpoint of the dreamer".

Relatives in dreams generally stand for the genitals. Here I can confirm this meaning only for the son, the daughter, and the younger sister - that is, wherever little thing could be employed. On the other hand, verified examples allow us to recognize sisters as symbols of the breasts, and brothers as symbols of the larger hemispheres. To be unable to overtake a carriage is interpreted by Stekel as regret at being unable to catch up with a difference in age. The luggage of a traveller is the burden of sin by which one is oppressed (ibid.) But a traveller's luggage often proves to be an unmistakable symbol of one's own genitals. To numbers, which frequently occur in dreams, Stekel has assigned a fixed symbolic meaning, but these interpretations seem neither sufficiently verified nor of universal validity, although in individual cases they can usually be recognized as plausible. We have, at all events, abundant confirmation that the figure three is a symbol of the male genitals. One of Stekel's generalizations refers to the double meaning of the genital symbols. "Where is there a symbol," he asks, "which (if in any way permitted by the imagination) may not be used simultaneously in the masculine and the feminine sense?" To be sure, the clause in parenthesis retracts much of the absolute character of this assertion, for this double meaning is not always permitted by the imagination. Still, I think it is not superfluous to state that in my experience this general statement of Stekel's requires elaboration. Besides those symbols which are just as frequently employed for the male as for the female genitals, there are others which preponderantly, or almost exclusively, designate one of the sexes, and there are yet others which, so far as we know, have only the male or only the female signification. To use long, stiff objects and weapons as symbols of the female genitals, or hollow objects (chests, boxes, etc.) as symbols of the male genitals, is certainly not permitted by the imagination.

It is true that the tendency of dreams, and of the unconscious phantasy, to employ the sexual symbols bisexually, reveals an archaic trait, for in childhood the difference in the genitals is unknown, and the same genitals are attributed to both sexes. One may also be misled as regards the significance of a bisexual symbol if one forgets the fact that in some dreams a general reversal of sexes takes place, so that the male organ is represented by the female, and vice versa. Such dreams express, for example, the wish of a woman to be a man.

The genitals may even be represented in dreams by other parts of the body: the male member by the hand or the foot, the female genital orifice by the mouth, the ear, or even the eye. The secretions of the human body - mucus, tears, urine, semen, etc. - may be used in dreams interchangeably. This statement of Stekel's, correct in the main, has suffered a justifiable critical restriction as the result of certain comments of R. Reitler's (Internat. Zeitschr. fur Psych., i, 1913). The gist of the matter is the replacement of an important secretion, such as the semen, by an indifferent one.

These very incomplete indications may suffice to stimulate others to make a more painstaking collection.[48] I have attempted a much more detailed account of dream-symbolism in my General Introduction to Psycho-Analysis. - I shall now append a few instances of the use of such symbols, which will show how impossible it is to arrive at the interpretation of a dream if one excludes dream-symbolism, but also how in many cases it is imperatively forced upon one. At the same time, I must expressly warn the investigator against overestimating the importance of symbols in the interpretation of dreams, restricting the work of dream-translation to the translation of symbols, and neglecting the technique of utilizing the associations of the dreamer. The two techniques of dream-interpretation must supplement one another; practically, however, as well as theoretically, precedence is retained by the latter process, which assigns the final significance

---

[48] In spite of all the differences between Scherner's conception of dream-symbolism and the one developed here, I must still insist that Scherner should be recognized as the true discoverer of symbolism in dreams, and that the experience of psycho analysis has brought his book (published in 1861) into posthumous repute. -

to the utterances of the dreamer, while the symbol-translation which we undertake play an auxiliary part.

1. The hat as the symbol of a man (of the male genitals):[49]

(A fragment from the dream of a young woman who suffered from agoraphobia as the result of her fear of temptation.) -

I am walking in the street in summer; I am wearing a straw hat of peculiar shape, the middle piece of which is bent upwards, while the side pieces hang downwards (here the description hesitates), and in such a fashion that one hangs lower than the other. I am cheerful and in a confident mood, and as I pass a number of young officers I think to myself: You can't do anything to me.

As she could produce no associations to the hat, I said to her: "The hat is really a male genital organ, with its raised middle piece and the two downward-hanging side pieces." It is perhaps peculiar that her hat should be supposed to be a man, but after all one says: Unter die Haube kommen (to get under the cap) when we mean: to get married. I intentionally refrained from interpreting the details concerning the unequal dependence of the two side pieces, although the determination of just such details must point the way to the interpretation. I went on to say that if, therefore, she had a husband with such splendid genitals she would not have to fear the officers; that is, she would have nothing to wish from them, for it was essentially her temptation - phantasies which prevented her from going about unprotected and unaccompanied. This last explanation of her anxiety I had already been able to give her repeatedly on the basis of other material.

It is quite remarkable how the dreamer behaved after this interpretation. She withdrew her description of the hat and would not admit that she had said that the two side pieces were hanging down. I was, however, too sure of what I had heard to allow myself to be misled, and so I insisted that she did say it. She was quiet for a while, and then found the courage to ask why it was that one of her husband's testicles was lower than the other, and

---

[49] From "Nachtrage sur Traumdeutung" in Zentralblatt fur Psychoanalyse, i, Nos. 5 and 6, (1911).

whether it was the same with all men. With this the peculiar detail of the hat was explained, and the whole interpretation was accepted by her.

The hat symbol was familiar to me long before the patient related this dream. From other but less transparent cases I believed that I might assume the hat could also stand for the female genitals.[50]

2. The little one as the genital organ. Being run over as a symbol of sexual intercourse.

(Another dream of the same agoraphobic patient.)

Her mother sends away her little daughter so that she has to go alone. She then drives with her mother to the railway station, and sees her little one walking right along the track, so that she is bound to be run over. She hears the bones crack. (At this she experiences a feeling of discomfort but no real horror.) She then looks through the carriage window, to see whether the parts cannot be seen behind. Then she reproaches her mother for allowing the little one to go out alone.

Analysis. - It is not an easy matter to give here a complete interpretation of the dream. It forms part of a cycle of dreams, and can be fully understood only in connection with the rest. For it is not easy to obtain the material necessary to demonstrate the symbolism in a sufficiently isolated condition. The patient at first finds that the railway journey is to be interpreted historically as an allusion to a departure from a sanatorium for nervous diseases, with whose director she was, of course, in love. Her mother fetched her away, and before her departure the physician came to the railway station and gave her a bunch of flowers; she felt uncomfortable because her mother witnessed this attention. Here the mother, therefore, appears as the disturber of her tender feelings, a role actually played by this strict woman during her daughter's girlhood. - The next association referred to the sentence:

---

[50] Cf. Kirchgraber for a similar example (Zentralblatt fur Psychoanalyse, iii, [1912], p. 95). Stekel reported a dream in which the hat with an obliquely-standing feather in the middle symbolized the (impotent) man.

She then looks to see whether the parts cannot be seen behind. In the dream-facade one would naturally be compelled to think of the pieces of the little daughter who had been run over and crushed. The association, however, turns in quite a different direction. She recalls that she once saw her father in the bath-room, naked, from behind; she then begins to talk about sex differences, and remarks that in the man the genitals can be seen from behind, but in the woman they cannot. In this connection she now herself offers the interpretation that the little one is the genital organ, and her little one (she has a four-year-old daughter) her own rgan. She reproaches her mother for wanting her to live as though she had no genitals, and recognizes this reproach in the introductory sentence of the dream: the mother sends her little one away, so that she has to go alone. In her phantasy, going alone through the streets means having no man, no sexual relations (coire = to go together), and this she does not like. According to all her statements, she really suffered as a girl through her mother's jealousy, because her father showed a preference for her.

The deeper interpretation of this dream depends upon another dream of the same night, in which the dreamer identifies herself with her brother.

She was a tomboy, and was always being told that she should have been born a boy. This identification with the brother shows with especial clearness that the little one signifies the genital organ. The mother threatened him (her) with castration, which could only be understood as a punishment for playing with the genital parts, and the identification, therefore, shows that she herself had masturbated as a child, though she had retained only a memory of her brother's having done so. An early knowledge of the male genitals, which she lost later, must, according to the assertions of this second dream, have been acquired at this time. Moreover, the second dream points to the infantile sexual theory that girls originate from boys as a result of castration. After I had told her of this childish belief, she at once confirmed it by an anecdote in which the boy asks the girl: "Was it cut off?" to which the girl replies: "No, it's always been like that."

Consequently the sending away of the little one, of the genital organ, in the first dream refers also to the threatened castration. Finally, she blames her mother for not having borne her as a boy.

That being run over symbolizes sexual intercourse would not be evident from this dream if we had not learned it from many other sources.

3. Representation of the genitals by buildings, stairs, and shafts.

(Dream of a young man inhibited by a father complex.)

He is taking a walk with his father in a place which is certainly the Prater, for one can see the Rotunda, in front of which there is a small vestibule to which there is attached a captive balloon; the balloon, however, seems rather limp. His father asks him what this is all for; he is surprised at it, but he explains it to his father. They come into a courtyard in which lies a large sheet of tin. His father wants to pull off a big piece of this, but first looks round to see if anyone is watching. He tells his father that all he needs to do is to speak to the overseer, and then he can take as much as he wants to without any more ado. From this courtyard a flight of stairs leads down into a shaft, the walls of which are softly upholstered, rather like a leather arm-chair. At the end of this shaft there is a long platform, and then a new shaft begins...

Analysis. This dreamer belonged to a type of patient which is not at all promising from a therapeutic point of view; up to a certain point in the analysis such patients offer no resistance whatever, but from that point onwards they prove to be almost inaccessible. This dream he analysed almost independently. "The Rotunda," he said, "is my genitals, the captive balloon in front is my penis, about whose flaccidity I have been worried." We must, however, interpret it in greater detail: the Rotunda is the buttocks, constantly associated by the child with the genitals; the smaller structure in front is the scrotum. In the dream his father asks him what this is all for - that is, he asks him about the purpose and arrangement of the genitals. It is quite evident that this state of affairs should be reversed, and that he ought to be the questioner. As such questioning, on the part of the father never occurred in reality, we must conceive the dream-thought as a wish, or perhaps take it conditionally, as follows. "If I had asked my father for sexual enlightenment..." The continuation of this thought we shall presently find in another place.

The courtyard in which the sheet of tin is spread out is not to be conceived symbolically in the first instance, but originates from his father's place of business. For reasons of discretion I have inserted the tin for another material in which the father deals without, however, changing anything in the verbal expression of the dream. The dreamer had entered his father's business, and had taken a terrible dislike to the somewhat questionable practices upon which its profit mainly depended. Hence the continuation of the above dream-thought ("if I had asked him") would be: "He would have deceived me just as he does his customers." For the pulling off, which serves to represent commercial dishonesty, the dreamer himself gives a second explanation, namely, masturbation. This is not only quite familiar to us (see above), but agrees very well with the fact that the secrecy of masturbation is expressed by its opposite (one can do it quite openly). Thus, it agrees entirely with our expectations that the autoerotic activity should be attributed to the father, just as was the questioning in the first scene of the dream. The shaft he at once interprets as the vagina, by referring to the soft upholstering of the walls. That the action of coition in the vagina is described as a going down instead of in the usual way as a going up agrees with what I have found in other instances.[51]

The details - that at the end of the first shaft there is a long platform, and then a new shaft - he himself explains biographically. He had for some time had sexual intercourse with women, but had given it up on account of inhibitions, and now hopes to be able to begin it again with the aid of treatment. The dream, however, becomes indistinct towards the end, and to the

---

[51] Cf. comment in the Zentralblatt fur Psychoanalyse, i; and see above, note (8) in earlier paragraph.

experienced interpreter it becomes evident that in the second scene of the dream the influence of another subject has already begun to assert itself; which is indicated by his father's business, his dishonest practices, and the vagina represented by the first shaft, so that one may assume a reference to his mother.

4. The male organ symbolized by persons and the female by a landscape.

(Dream of a woman of the lower class, whose husband is a policeman, reported by B. Dattner.)

...Then someone broke into the house and she anxiously called for a policeman. But he went peacefully with two tramps into a church,[52] to which a great many steps led up,[53] behind the church there was a mountain[54] on top of which there was a dense forest.[55] The policeman was provided with a helmet, a gorget, and a cloak.[56] The two vagrants, who went along with the policeman quite peaceably, had sack-like aprons tied round their loins.[57] A road led from the church to the mountain. This road was overgrown on each side with grass and brushwood, which became thicker and thicker as it reached the top of the mountain, where it spread out into quite a forest. -

5. Castration dreams of children.

(a) A boy aged three years and five months, for whom his father's return from military service is clearly inconvenient, wakes one morning in a disturbed and excited state, and constantly repeats the question: Why did Daddy carry his head on a plate? Last night Daddy carried his head on a plate.

(b) A student who is now suffering from a severe obsessional neurosis remembers that in his sixth year he repeatedly had the following dream: He goes to the barber to have his hair cut.

---

[52] Or Chapel = vagina.
[53] Symbol of coitus.
[54] Mons veneris.
[55] Crines pubis.
[56] Demons in cloaks and hoods are, according to the explanation of a specialist, of a phallic character.
[57] The two halves of the scrotum.

Then a large woman with severe features comes up to him and cuts off his head. He recognizes the woman as his mother.

6. A modified staircase dream.

To one of my patients, a sexual abstainer, who was very ill, whose phantasy was fixated upon his mother, and who repeatedly dreamed of climbing stairs while accompanied by his mother, I once remarked that moderate masturbation would probably have been less harmful to him than his enforced abstinence. The influence of this remark provoked the following dream:

His piano teacher reproaches him for neglecting his pianoplaying, and for not practicing the Etudes of Moscheles and Clementi's Gradus ad Parnassum. With reference to this he remarked that the Gradus, too, is a stairway, and that the piano itself is a stairway, as it has a scale.

It may be said that there is no class of ideas which cannot be enlisted in the representation of sexual facts and wishes.

7. The sensation of reality and the representation of repetition.

A man, now thirty-five, relates a clearly remembered dream which he claims to have had when he was four years of age: The notary with whom his father's will was deposited - he had lost his father at the age of three - brought two large Emperor-pears, of which he was given one to eat. The other lay on the window sill of the living-room. He woke with the conviction of the reality of what he had dreamt, and obstinately asked his mother to give him the second pear; it was, he said, still lying on the windowsill. His mother laughed at this.

Analysis. The notary was a jovial old gentleman who, as he seems to remember, really sometimes brought pears with him. The window-sill was as he saw it in the dream. Nothing else occurs to him in this connection, except, perhaps, that his mother has recently told him a dream. She has two birds sitting on her head; she wonders when they will fly away, but they do not fly away, and one of them flies to her mouth and sucks at it.

The dreamer's inability to furnish associations justifies the attempt to interpret it by the substitution of symbols. The two pears - pommes on poires - are the breasts of the mother who nursed him; the window-sill is the projection of the bosom, analogous to the balconies in the dream of houses. His sensation of reality after waking is justified, for his mother had actually suckled him for much longer than the customary term, and her breast was still available. The dream is to be translated: "Mother, give (show) me the breast again at which I once used to drink." The once is represented by the eating of the one pear, the again by the desire for the other. The temporal repetition of an act is habitually represented in dreams by the numerical multiplication of an object It is naturally a very striking phenomenon that symbolism should already play a part in the dream of a child of four, but this is the rule rather than the exception. One may say that the dreamer has command of symbolism from the very first.

The early age at which people make use of symbolic representation, even apart from the dream-life, may be shown by the following uninfluenced memory of a lady who is now twenty-seven: She is in her fourth year. The nursemaid is driving her, with her brother, eleven months younger, and a cousin, who is between the two in age, to the lavatory, so that they can do their little business there before going for their walk. As the oldest, she sits on the seat and the other two on chambers. She asks her (female) cousin: Have you a purse, too? Walter has a little sausage, I have a purse. The cousin answers: Yes, I have a purse, too. The nursemaid listens, laughing, and relates the conversation to the mother, whose reaction is a sharp reprimand.

Here a dream may be inserted whose excellent symbolism permitted of interpretation with little assistance from the dreamer:

8. The question of symbolism in the dreams of normal persons. [58]

An objection frequently raised by the opponents of psycho-analysis - - and recently also by Havelock Ellis[59] - - is that, although dreamsymbolism may perhaps be a product of the neurotic psyche, it has no validity whatever in the case of normal

---

[58] Alfred Robitsek in the Zentralblatt fur Psychoanalyse, ii (1911), p. 340.
[59] The World of Dreams, London (1911), p. 168.

persons. But while psychoanalysis recognizes no essential distinctions, but only quantitative differences, between the psychic life of the normal person and that of the neurotic, the analysis of those dreams in which, in sound and sick persons alike, the repressed complexes display the same activity, reveals the absolute identity of the mechanisms as well as of the symbolism. Indeed, the natural dreams of healthy persons often contain a much simpler, more transparent, and more characteristic symbolism than those of neurotics, which, owing to the greater strictness of the censorship and the more extensive dream-distortion resulting therefrom, are frequently troubled and obscured, and are therefore more difficult to translate. The following dream serves to illustrate this fact. This dream comes from a non-neurotic girl of a rather prudish and reserved type. In the course of conversation I found that she was engaged to be married, but that there were hindrances in the way of the marriage which threatened to postpone it. She related spontaneously the following dream: -

I arrange the centre of a table with flowers for a birthday. On being questioned she states that in the dream she seemed to be at home (she has no home at the time) and experienced a feeling of happiness.

The popular symbolism enables me to translate the dream for myself. It is the expression of her wish to be married: the table, with the flowers in the centre, is symbolic of herself and her genitals. She represents her future fulfilled, inasmuch as she is already occupied with the thoughts of the birth of a child; so the wedding has taken place long ago.

I call her attention to the fact that the centre of a table is an unusual expression, which she admits; but here, of course, I cannot question her more directly. I carefully refrain from suggesting to her the meaning of the symbols, and ask her only for the thoughts which occur to her mind in connection with the individual parts of the dream. In the course of the analysis her reserve gave way to a distinct interest in the interpretation, and a frankness which was made possible by the serious tone of the conversation. To my question as to what kind of flowers they had been, her first answer is: expensive flowers; one has to pay for them; then she adds that they were lilies-of-the-valley, violets, and pinks or carnations. I took the word lily in this dream in its popular sense, as a symbol of chastity; she confirmed this, as purity occurred to her in association with lily. Valley is a common feminine dream-symbol. The chance juxtaposition of the two symbols in the name of the flower is made into a piece of dreamsymbolism, and serves to emphasize the preciousness of her virginity - expensive flowers; one has to pay for them - and expresses the expectation that her husband will know how to appreciate its value. The comment, expensive flowers, etc. has, as will be shown, a different meaning in every one of the three different flower-symbols.

I thought of what seemed to me a venturesome explanation of the hidden meaning of the apparently quite asexual word violets by an unconscious relation to the French viol. But to my surprise the dreamer's association was the English word violate. The accidental phonetic similarity of the two words violet and violate is utilized by the dream to express in the language of flowers the idea of the violence of defloration (another word which makes use of flower-symbolism), and perhaps also to give expression to a masochistic tendency on the part of the girl. An excellent example of the word bridges across which run the paths to the unconscious. One has to pay for them here means life, with which she has to pay for becoming a wife and a mother.

In association with pinks, which she then calls carnations, I think of carnal. But her association is colour, to which she adds that carnations are the flowers which her fiance gives her frequently and in large quantities. At the end of the conversation she suddenly admits, spontaneously, that she has not told me the truth; the word that occurred to her was not colour, but incarnation, the very word I expected. Moreover, even the word colour is not a remote association; it was determined by the meaning of carnation (i.e., flesh-colour) - that is, by the complex. This lack of honesty shows that the resistance here is at its greatest because the symbolism is here most transparent, and the struggle between libido and repression is most intense in connection with this phallic theme. The remark that these flowers were often given her by her fiance is, together with the double meaning of carnation, a still further indication of their phallic significance in the dream. The occasion of the present of flowers during the day is employed to express the thought of a sexual present and a return present. She gives her virginity and expects in return for it a rich love-life. But the words: expensive flowers; one has to pay for them may have a real, financial meaning. The flower-symbolism in the dream thus comprises the virginal female, the male symbol, and the reference to violent defloration. It is to be noted that sexual flower-symbolism, which, of course, is very widespread, symbolizes the human sexual organs by flowers, the sexual organs of plants; indeed, presents of flowers between lovers may have this unconscious significance.

The birthday for which she is making preparations in the dream probably signifies the birth of a child. She identifies herself with the bridegroom, and represents him preparing her for a birth (having coitus with her). It is as though the latent thought were to say: "If I were he, I would not wait, but I would deflower the bride without asking her; I would use violence." Indeed, the word violate points to this. Thus even the sadistic libidinal components find expression.

In a deeper stratum of the dream the sentence I arrange, etc., probably has an auto-erotic, that is, an infantile significance.

She also has a knowledge - possibly only in the dream - of her physical need; she sees herself flat like a table, so that she emphasizes all the more her virginity, the costliness of the centre (another time she calls it a centre-piece of flowers). Even the horizontal element of the table may contribute something to the symbol. The concentration of the dream is worthy of remark: nothing is superfluous, every word is a symbol.

Later on she brings me a supplement to this dream: I decorate the flowers with green crinkled paper. She adds that it was fancy paper of the sort which is used to disguise ordinary flower-pots. She says also: "To hide untidy things, whatever was to be seen which was not pretty to the eye; there is a gap, a little space in the flowers. The paper looks like velvet or moss." With decorate she associates decorum, as I expected. The green colour is very prominent, and with this she associates hope, yet another reference to pregnancy. In this part of the dream the identification with the man is not the dominant feature, but thoughts of shame and frankness express themselves. She makes herself beautiful for him; she admits physical defects, of which she is ashamed and which she wishes to correct. The associations velvet and moss distinctly point to crines pubis.

The dream is an expression of thoughts hardly known to the waking state of the girl; thoughts which deal with the love of the senses and its organs; she is prepared for a birth-day, i.e., she has coitus; the fear of defloration and perhaps the pleasurably toned pain find expression; she admits her physical defects and overcompensates them by means of an over-estimation of the value of her virginity. Her shame excuses the emerging sensuality by the fact that the aim of it all is the child. Even material considerations, which are foreign to the lover, find expression here. The affect of the simple dream - the feeling of bliss - shows that here strong emotional complexes have found satisfaction.

I close with the
9. Dream of a chemist.

(A young man who has been trying to give up his habit of masturbation by substituting intercourse with a woman.)

Preliminary statement: On the day before the dream he had been instructing a student as to Grignard's reaction, in which magnesium is dissolved in absolutely pure ether under the catalytic influence of iodine. Two days earlier there had been an explosion in the course of the same reaction, in which someone had burned his hand.

Dream I. He is going to make phenylmagnesiumbromide; he sees the apparatus with particular distinctness, but he has substituted himself for the magnesium. He is now in a curious, wavering attitude. He keeps on repeating to himself: "This is the right thing, it is working, my feet are beginning to dissolve, and my knees are getting soft." Then he reaches down and feels for his feet, and meanwhile (he does not know how) he takes his legs out of the carboy, and then again he says to himself: "That can't be... Yes, it has been done correctly." Then he partially wakes, and repeats the dream to himself, because he wants to tell it to me. He is positively afraid of the analysis of the dream. He is much excited during this state of semi-sleep, and repeats continually: "Phenyl, phenyl."

II. He is in... with his whole family. He is supposed to be at the Schottentor at half-past eleven in order to keep an appointment with the lady in question, but he does not wake until half-past eleven. He says to himself: "It is too late now; when you get there it will be half-past twelve." The next moment he sees the whole family gathered about the table - his mother and the parlourmaid with the soup tureen with peculiar distinctness.

Then he says to himself: "Well, if we are sitting down to eat already, I certainly can't get away."

Analysis. He feels sure that even the first dream contains a reference to the lady whom he is to meet at the place of rendezvous (the dream was dreamed during the night before the expected meeting). The student whom he was instructing is a particularly unpleasant fellow; the chemist had said to him: "That isn't right, because the magnesium was still unaffected," and the student had answered, as though he were quite unconcerned:

"Nor it is." He himself must be this student; he is as indifferent to his analysis as the student is to his synthesis; the he in the dream, however, who performs the operation, is myself. How unpleasant he must seem to me with his indifference to the result!

Again, he is the material with which the analysis (synthesis) is made. For the question is the success of the treatment. The legs in the dream recall an impression of the previous evening. He met a lady at a dancing class of whom he wished to make a conquest; he pressed her to him so closely that she once cried out. As he ceased to press her legs he felt her firm, responding pressure against his lower thighs as far as just above the knees, the spot mentioned in the dream. In this situation, then, the woman is the magnesium in the retort, which is at last working. He is feminine towards me, as he is virile towards the woman. If he succeeds with the woman, the treatment will also succeed. Feeling himself and becoming aware of his knees refers to masturbation, and corresponds to his fatigue of the previous day... The rendezvous had actually been made for halfpast eleven. His wish to oversleep himself and to keep to his sexual object at home (that is, masturbation) corresponds to his resistance.

He says, in respect to the repetition of the name phenyl, that all these radicals ending in yl have always been pleasing to him; they are very convenient to use: benzyl, acetyl, etc. That, however, explained nothing. But when I proposed the root Schlemihl he laughed heartily, and told me that during the summer he had read a book by Prevost which contained a chapter: "Les exclus de l'amour," and in this there was some mention of Schlemilies; and in reading of these outcasts he said to himself: "That is my case." He would have played the Schlemihl if he had missed the appointment.

It seems that the sexual symbolism of dreams has already been directly confirmed by experiment. In 1912 Dr. K. Schrotter, at the instance of H.

Swoboda, produced dreams in deeply hypnotized persons by suggestions which determined a large part of the dream-content. If the suggestion proposed that the subject should dream of normal or abnormal sexual relations, the dream carried out these orders by replacing sexual material by the symbols with which psycho-analytic dream-interpretation has made us familiar. Thus, following the suggestion that the dreamer should dream of homosexual relations with a lady friend, this friend appeared in the dream carrying a shabby travelling-bag, upon which there was a label with the printed words: "For ladies only." The dreamer was believed never to have heard of dream-symbolization or of dream-interpretation.

Unfortunately, the value of this important investigation was diminished by the fact that Dr. Schrotter shortly afterwards committed suicide. Of his dream-experiments be gave us only a preliminary report in the Zentralblatt fur Psychoanalyse.

Only when we have formed a due estimate of the importance of symbolism in dreams can we continue the study of the typical dreams which was interrupted in an earlier chapter. I feel justified in dividing these dreams roughly into two classes; first, those which always really have the same meaning, and second, those which despite the same or a similar content must nevertheless be given the most varied interpretations. Of the typical dreams belonging to the first class I have already dealt fairly fully with the examination-dream.

On account of their similar affective character, the dreams of missing a train deserve to be ranked with the examination-dreams; moreover, their interpretation justifies this approximation. They are consolation-dreams, directed against another anxiety perceived in dreams - the fear of death.

To depart is one of the most frequent and one of the most readily established of the death-symbols. The dream therefore says consolingly:

"Reassure yourself, you are not going to die (to depart)," just as the examination-dream calms us by saying: "Don't be afraid; this time, too, nothing will happen to you." The difficulty is understanding both kinds of dreams is due to the fact that the anxiety is attached precisely to the expression of consolation.

The meaning of the dreams due to dental stimulus which I have often enough had to analyse in my patients escaped me for a long time because, much to my astonishment, they habitually offered too great a resistance to interpretation. But finally an overwhelming mass of evidence convinced me that in the case of men nothing other than the masturbatory desires of puberty furnish the motive power of these dreams. I shall analyse two such dreams, one of which is also a flying dream. The two dreams were dreamed by the same person - a young man of pronounced homosexuality which, however, has been inhibited in life.

He is witnessing a performance of Fidelio from the stalls the of the operahouse; sitting next to L, whose personality is congenial to him, and whose friendship he would like to have. Suddenly he flies diagonally right across the stalls; he then puts his hand in his mouth and draws out two of his teeth.

He himself describes the flight by saying that it was as though he were thrown into the air. As the opera performed was Fidelio, he recalls the words: -

He who a charming wife acquires.... -

But the acquisition of even the most charming wife is not among the wishes of the dreamer. Two other lines would be more appropriate: -

He who succeeds in the lucky (big) throw

The friend of a friend to be.... -

The dream thus contains the lucky (big) throw which is not, however, a wish-fulfilment only. For it conceals also the painful reflection that in his striving after friendship he has often had the misfortune to be thrown out, and the fear lest this fate may be repeated in the case of the young man by whose side he has enjoyed the performance of Fidelio. This is now followed by a confession, shameful to a man of his refinement, to the effect that once, after such a rejection on the part of a friend, his profound sexual longing caused him to masturbate twice in succession.

The other dream is as follows: Two university professors of his acquaintance are treating him in my place. One of them does something to his penis; he is afraid of an operation. The other thrusts an iron bar against his mouth, so that he loses one or two teeth. He is bound with four silk handkerchiefs.

The sexual significance of this dream can hardly be doubted. The silk handkerchiefs allude to an identification with a homosexual of his acquaintance. The dreamer, who has never achieved coition (nor has he ever actually sought sexual intercourse) with men, conceives the sexual act on the lines of masturbation with which he was familiar during puberty.

I believe that the frequent modifications of the typical dream due to dental stimulus - that, for example, in which another person draws the tooth from the dreamer's mouth - will be made intelligible by the same explanation.[60] It may, however, be difficult to understand how dental stimulus can have come to have this significance. But here I may draw attention to the frequent displacement from below to above which is at the service of sexual repression, and by means of which all kinds of sensations and intentions occurring in hysteria, which ought to be localized in the genitals, may at all events be realized in other, unobjectionable parts of the body. We have a case of such displacement when the genitals are replaced by the face in the symbolism of unconscious thought. This is corroborated by the fact that verbal usage relates the buttocks to the cheeks, and the labia minora to the lips which enclose the orifice of the mouth. The nose is compared to the penis in numerous allusions, and in each case the presence of hair completes the resemblance. Only one feature - the teeth - is beyond all possibility of being compared in this way; but it is just this coincidence of agreement and disagreement which makes the teeth suitable for purposes of representation under the pressure of sexual repression. -

I will not assert that the interpretation of dreams due to dental stimulus as dreams of masturbation (the correctness of which I cannot doubt) has been freed of all obscurity.[61] I carry the explanation as far as I am able, and must leave the rest unsolved. But I must refer to yet another relation indicated by a colloquial

---

[60] The extraction of a tooth by another is usually to be interpreted as castration (cf. haircutting; Stekel). One must distinguish between dreams due to dental stimulus and dreams referring to the dentist, such as have been recorded, for example, by Coriat (Zentralblatt fur Psychoanalyse, iii, 440). -

[61] According to C. G. Jung, dreams due to dental stimulus in the case of women have the significance parturition dreams. E. Jones has given valuable confirmation of this. The common element of this interpretation with that represented above may be found in the fact that in both cases (castration-birth) there is a question of removing a part from the whole body.

expression. In Austria there is in use an indelicate designation for the act of masturbation, namely: "To pull one out," or "to pull one off."[62] I am unable to say whence these colloquialisms originate, or on what symbolisms they are based; but the teeth would very well fit in with the first of the two.

Dreams of pulling teeth, and of teeth falling out, are interpreted in popular belief to mean the death of a connection. Psychoanalysis can admit of such a meaning only at the most as a joking allusion to the sense already indicated.

To the second group of typical dreams belong those in which one is flying or hovering, falling, swimming, etc. What do these dreams signify?

Here we cannot generalize. They mean, as we shall learn, something different in each case; only, the sensory material which they contain always comes from the same source.

We must conclude from the information obtained in psychoanalysis that these dreams also repeat impressions of our childhood - that is, that they refer to the games involving movement which have such an extraordinary attraction for children. Where is the uncle who has never made a child fly by running with it across the room, with outstretched arms, or has never played at falling with it by rocking it on his knee and then suddenly straightening his leg, or by lifting it above his head and suddenly pretending to withdraw his supporting hand? At such moments children shout with joy and insatiably demand a repetition of the performance, especially if a little fright and dizziness are involved in it. In after years they repeat their sensations in dreams, but in dreams they omit the hands that held them, so that now they are free to float or fall. We know that all small children have a fondness for such games as rocking and see-sawing; and when they see gymnastic performances at the circus their recollection of such games is refreshed. In some boys the hysterical attack consists simply in the reproduction of such performances, which they accomplish with great dexterity. Not infrequently sexual sensations are excited

---

[62] Cf. the biographical dream earlier in this chapter. -

by these games of movement, innocent though they are in themselves. To express the matter in a few words: it is these romping games of childhood which are being repeated in dreams of flying, falling, vertigo, and the like, but the pleasurable sensations are now transformed into anxiety. But, as every mother knows, the romping of children often enough ends in quarrelling and tears.

I have therefore good reason for rejecting the explanation that it is the condition of our cutaneous sensations during sleep, the sensation of the movements of the lungs, etc., that evoke dreams of flying and falling. As I see it, these sensations have themselves been reproduced from the memory to which the dream refers - that they are therefore dream-content, and not dream - sources.[63]

This material, consisting of sensations of motion, similar in character, and originating from the same sources, is now used for the representation of the most manifold dream-thoughts. Dreams of flying or hovering, for the most part pleasurably toned, will call for the most widely differing interpretations - interpretations of a quite special nature in the case of some dreamers, and interpretations of a typical nature in that of others. One of my patients was in the habit of dreaming very frequently that she was hovering a little way above the street without touching the ground. She was very short of stature, and she shunned every sort of contamination involved by intercourse with human beings. Her dream of suspension - which raised her feet above the ground and allowed her head to tower into the air - fulfilled both of her wishes. In the case of other dreamers of the same sex, the dream of flying had the significance of the longing: "If only I were a little bird!" Similarly, others become angels at night, because no one has ever called them angels by day. The intimate connection between flying and the idea of a bird makes it comprehensible that the dream of flying, in the case of male dreamers, should usually have a coarsely sensual significance;[64] and we should not be surprised to hear that this or that dreamer is always very proud of his ability to fly. -

---

[63] This passage, dealing with dreams of motion, is repeated on account of the context. Cf. chapter V., D.

Dr. Paul Federn (Vienna) has propounded the fascinating theory that a great many flying dreams are erection dreams, since the remarkable phenomenon of erection, which constantly occupies the human phantasy, cannot fail to be impressive as an apparent suspension of the laws of gravity (cf. the winged phalli of the ancients).

It is a noteworthy fact that a prudent experimenter like Mourly Vold, who is really averse to any kind of interpretation, nevertheless defends the erotic interpretation of the dreams of flying and hovering.[65] He describes the erotic element as "the most important motive factor of the hovering dream," and refers to the strong sense of bodily vibration which accompanies this type of dream, and the frequent connection of such dreams with erections and emissions. -

Dreams of falling are more frequently characterized by anxiety. Their interpretation, when they occur in women, offers no difficulty, because they nearly always accept the symbolic meaning of falling, which is a circumlocution for giving way to an erotic temptation. We have not yet exhausted the infantile sources of the dream of falling; nearly all children have fallen occasionally, and then been picked up and fondled; if they fell out of bed at night, they were picked up by the nurse and taken into her bed.

People who dream often, and with great enjoyment, of swimming, cleaving the waves, etc., have usually been bed-wetters, and they now repeat in the dream a pleasure which they have long since learned to forego. We shall soon learn, from one example or another, to what representations dreams of swimming easily lend themselves.

The interpretation of dreams of fire justifies a prohibition of the nursery, which forbids children to play with fire so that they may not wet the bed at night. These dreams also are based on reminiscences of the enuresis nocturna of childhood. In my

---

[64] A reference to the German slang word vogeln (to copulate) from Vogel (a bird). - TR.
[65] "Uber den Traum," Ges. Schriften, Vol. III.

"Fragment of an Analysis of Hysteria"[66] I have given the complete analysis and synthesis of such a dream of fire in connection with the infantile history of the dreamer, and have shown for the representation of what maturer impulses this infantile material has been utilized.

It would be possible to cite quite a number of other typical dreams, if by such one understands dreams in which there is a frequent recurrence, in the dreams of different persons, of the same manifest dream-content. For example: dreams of passing through narrow alleys, or a whole suite of rooms; dreams of burglars, in respect of whom nervous people take measures of precaution before going to bed; dreams of being chased by wild animals (bulls, horses); or of being threatened with knives, daggers, and lances. The last two themes are characteristic of the manifest dreamcontent of persons suffering from anxiety, etc. A special investigation of this class of material would be well worth while. In lieu of this I shall offer two observations, which do not, however, apply exclusively to typical dreams.

The more one is occupied with the solution of dreams, the readier one becomes to acknowledge that the majority of the dreams of adults deal with sexual material and give expression to erotic wishes. Only those who really analyse dreams, that is, those who penetrate from their manifest content to the latent dream-thoughts, can form an opinion on this subject; but never those who are satisfied with registering merely the manifest content (as, for example, Nacke in his writings on sexual dreams). Let us recognize at once that there is nothing astonishing in this fact, which is entirely consistent with the principles of dream-interpretation. No other instinct has had to undergo so much suppression, from the time of childhood onwards, as the sexual instinct in all its numerous components:[67] from no other instincts are so many and such intense unconscious wishes left over, which now, in the sleeping state, generate dreams. In dream-interpretation this importance of the sexual complexes must never

---

[66] Collected Papers, III.
[67] Cf. Three Contributions to the Theory of Sex.

be forgotten, though one must not, of course, exaggerate it to the exclusion of all other factors. -

Of many dreams it may be ascertained, by careful interpretation, that they may even be understood bisexually, inasmuch as they yield an indisputable over-interpretation, in which they realize homosexual impulses - that is, impulses which are contrary to the normal sexual activity of the dreamer. But that all dreams are to be interpreted bisexually, as Stekel[68] maintains, and Adler,[69] seems to me to be a generalization as insusceptible of proof as it is improbable, and one which, therefore, I should be loth to defend; for I should, above all, be at a loss to know how to dispose of the obvious fact that there are many dreams which satisfy other than erotic needs (taking the word in the widest sense), as, for example, dreams of hunger, thirst, comfort, etc. And other similar assertions, to the effect that "behind every dream one finds a reference to death" (Stekel), or that every dream shows "an advance from the feminine to the masculine line" (Adler), seem to me to go far beyond the admissible in the interpretation of dreams. The assertion that all dreams call for a sexual interpretation, against which there is such an untiring polemic in the literature of the subject, is quite foreign to my Interpretation of Dreams. It will not be found in any of the eight editions of this book, and is in palpable contradiction to the rest of its contents. -

We have stated elsewhere that dreams which are conspicuously innocent commonly embody crude erotic wishes, and this we might confirm by numerous further examples. But many dreams which appear indifferent, in which we should never suspect a tendency in any particular direction, may be traced, according to the analysis, to unmistakably sexual wish-impulses, often of an unsuspected nature. For example, who, before it had been interpreted, would have suspected a sexual wish in the following

---

[68] W. Stekel, Die Sprache des Traumes (1911).
[69] Alf. Adler, "Der Psychische Hermaphroditismus im Leben und in der Neurose," in Fortschritte der Medizin (1910), No. 16, and later papers in the Zentralblatt fur Psychoanalyse, i (1910-11). -

dream? The dreamer relates: Between two stately palaces there stands, a little way back, a small house, whose doors are closed. My wife leads me along the little bit of road leading to the house and pushes the door open, and then I slip quickly and easily into the interior of a courtyard that slopes steeply upwards.

Anyone who has had experience in the translating of dreams will, of course, at once be reminded that penetration into narrow spaces and the opening of locked doors are among the commonest of sexual symbols, and will readily see in this dream a representation of attempted coition from behind (between the two stately buttocks of the female body). The narrow, steep passage is, of course, the vagina; the assistance attributed to the wife of the dreamer requires the interpretation that in reality it is only consideration for the wife which is responsible for abstention from such an attempt. Moreover, inquiry shows that on the previous day a young girl had entered the household of the dreamer; she had pleased him, and had given him the impression that she would not be altogether averse to an approach of this sort. The little house between the two palaces is taken from a reminiscence of the Hradschin in Prague, and once more points to the girl, who is a native of that city.

If, in conversation with my patients, I emphasize the frequency of the Oedipus dream - the dream of having sexual intercourse with one's mother - I elicit the answer: "I cannot remember such a dream." Immediately afterwards, however, there arises the recollection of another, an unrecognizable, indifferent dream, which the patient has dreamed repeatedly, and which on analysis proves to be a dream with this very content - that is, yet another Oedipus dream. I can assure the reader that disguised dreams of sexual intercourse with the dreamer's mother are far more frequent than undisguised dreams to the same effect.[70]

Typical example of a disguised Oedipus dream:

A man dreams: He has a secret affair with a woman whom another man wishes to marry. He is concerned lest the other should discover this relation and abandon the marriage; he therefore behaves very affectionately to the man; he nestles up to him and kisses him. The facts of the dreamer's life touch the dream-content only at one point. He has a secret affair with a married woman, and an equivocal expression of her husband, with whom he is on friendly terms, aroused in him the suspicion that he might have noticed something of this relationship. There is, however, in reality, yet another factor, the mention of which was avoided in the dream, and which alone gives the key to it. The life of the husband is threatened by an organic malady. His wife is prepared for the possibility of his sudden death, and our dreamer consciously harbours the intention of marrying the young widow after her husband's decease. It is through this objective situation that the dreamer finds himself transferred into the constellation of the Oedipus dream; his wish is to be enabled to kill the man, so that he may win the woman for his wife; his dream gives expression to the wish in a hypocritical distortion. Instead of representing her as already married to the other man, it represents the other man only as wishing to marry her, which indeed corresponds with his own secret intention, and the hostile whishes directed against the man are concealed under demonstrations of affection, which are reminiscences of his childish relations to his father.

---

[70] I have published a typical example of such a disguised Oedipus dream in No. 1 of the Zentralblatt für Psychoanalyse (see below): another, with a detailed analysis, was published in No. 4 of the same journal by Otto Rank. For other disguised Oedipus dreams in which the eye appears as a symbol, see Rank (Int. Zeitschr. für Ps. A., i, [1913]). Papers upon eye dreams and eye symbolism by Eder, Ferenczi, and Reitler will be found in the same issue. The blinding in the Oedipus legend and elsewhere is a substitute for castration. The ancients, by the way, were not unfamiliar with the symbolic interpretation of the undisguised Oedipus dream (see O. Rank, Jahrb. ii, p. 534: "Thus, a dream of Julius Caesar's of sexual relations with his mother has been handed down to us, which the oreirocopists interpreted as a favourable omen signifying his taking possession of the earth (Mother Earth). Equally well known is the oracle delivered to the Tarquinii, to the effect that that one of them would become the ruler of Rome who should be the first to kiss his mother (osculum matri tulerit), which Brutus conceived as referring to Mother Earth (terram osculo contigit, scilicet quod ea communis mater omnium mortalium esset, Livy, I, lvi). Cf. here the dream of Hippias in Herodotus vi, 107. These myths and interpretations point to a correct psychological insight. I have found that those persons who consider themselves preferred or favoured by their mothers manifest in life that confidence in themselves, and that unshakable optimism, which often seem heroic, and not infrequently compel actual success.

There are dreams of landscapes and localities in which emphasis is always laid upon the assurance: "I have been here before." but this Deja vu has a special significance in dreams. In this case the locality is the genitals of the mother; of no other place can it be asserted with such certainty that one has been here before. I was once puzzled by the account of a dream given by a patient afflicted with obsessional neurosis. He dreamed that he called at a house where he had been twice before. But this very patient had long ago told me of an episode of his sixth year. At that time he shared his mother's bed, and had abused the occasion by inserting his finger into his mother's genitals while she was asleep.

A large number of dreams, which are frequently full of anxiety, and often have for content the traversing of narrow spaces, or staying long in the water, are based upon phantasies concerning the intra-uterine life, the sojourn in the mother's womb, and the act of birth. I here insert the dream of a young man who, in his phantasy, has even profited by the intra-uterine opportunity of spying upon an act of coition between his parents.

He is in a deep shaft, in which there is a window, as in the Semmering tunnel. Through this he sees at first an empty landscape, and then he composes a picture in it, which is there all at once and fills up the empty space. The picture represents a field which is being deeply tilled by an implement, and the wholesome air, the associated idea of hard work, and the bluish-black clods of earth make a pleasant impression on him. He then goes on and sees a work on education lying open... and is surprised that so much attention is devoted in it to the sexual feelings (of children), which makes him think of me.

Here is a pretty water-dream of a female patient, which was turned to special account in the course of treatment.

At her usual holiday resort on the... Lake, she flings herself into the dark water at a place where the pale moon is reflected in the water. Dreams of this sort are parturition dreams; their interpretation is effected by reversing the fact recorded in the manifest dream-content; thus, instead of flinging oneself into the water, read coming out of the water - that is, being born.[71] The place from which one is born may be recognized if one thinks of the humorous sense of the French la lune. The pale moon thus becomes the white bottom, which the child soon guesses to be the place from which it came. Now what can be the meaning of the patient's wishing to be born at a holiday resort? I asked the dreamer this, and she replied without hesitation: "Hasn't the treatment made me as though I were born again?" Thus the dream becomes an invitation to continue the treatment at this summer resort - that is, to visit her there; perhaps it also contains a very bashful allusion to the wish to become a mother herself.[72] -

Another dream of parturition, with its interpretation, I take from a paper by E. Jones. "She stood at the seashore watching a small boy, who seemed to be hers, wading into the water. This he did till the water covered him and she could only see his head bobbing up and down near the surface. The scene then changed to the crowded to hall of an hotel. Her husband left her, and she 'entered into conversation with' a stranger.

"The second half of the dream was discovered in the analysis to represent flight from her husband, and the entering into intimate relations with a third person, behind whom was plainly indicated Mr. X's brother, mentioned in a former dream. The first part of the dream was a fairly evident birth-phantasy. In dreams, as in mythology, the delivery of a child from the uterine waters is commonly represented, by way of distortion, as the entry of the child into water; among many other instances, the births of Adonis, Osiris, Moses, and Bacchus are well-known illustrations of this.

---

[71] For the mythological meaning of water-birth, see Rank: Der Mythus von der Geburt des Helden (1909).

[72] It was not for a long time that I learned to appreciate the significance of the phantasies and unconscious thoughts relating to life in the womb. They contain the explanation of the curious dread, felt by so many people, of being buried alive, as well as the profoundest unconscious reason for the belief in a life after death, which represents only the projection into the future of this mysterious life before birth. The act of birth, moreover, is the first experience attended by anxiety, and is thus, the source and model of the affect of anxiety. -

The bobbing up and down of the head in the water at once recalled to the patient the sensation of quickening which she had experienced in her only pregnancy. Thinking of the boy going into the water induced a reverie in which she saw herself taking him out of the water, carrying him into the nursery, washing and dressing him, and installing him in her household.

"The second half of the dream, therefore, represents thoughts concerning the elopement, which belonged to the first half of the underlying latent content; the first half of the dream corresponded with the second half of the latent content, the birth phantasy. Besides this inversion in the order, further inversions took place in each half of the dream. In the first half the child entered the water, and then his head bobbed; in the underlying dream-thoughts the quickening occurred first, and then the child left the water (a double inversion). In the second half her husband left her; in the dream-thoughts she left her husband."

Another parturition dream is related by Abraham - the dream of a young woman expecting her first confinement: From one point of the floor of the room a subterranean channel leads directly into the water (path of parturition - amniotic fluid). She lifts up a trap in the floor, and there immediately appears a creature dressed in brownish fur, which almost resembles a seal. This creature changes into the dreamer's younger brother, to whom her relation has always been material in character.

Rank has shown from a number of dreams that parturition-dreams employ the same symbols as micturition-dreams. The erotic stimulus expresses itself in these dreams as in urethral stimulus. The stratification of meaning in these dreams corresponds with a chance in the significance of the symbol since childhood.

We may here turn back to the interrupted theme (see chapter III) of the part played by organic, sleep-disturbing stimuli in dream-formation.

Dreams which have come into existence under these influences not only reveal quite frankly the wish-fulfilling tendency, and the character of convenience-dreams, but they very often display a quite transparent symbolism as well, since waking not infrequently follows a stimulus whose satisfaction in symbolic disguise has already been vainly attempted in the dream. This is true of emission dreams as well as those evoked by the need to urinate or defecate. The peculiar character of emission dreams permits us directly to unmask certain sexual symbols already recognized as typical, but nevertheless violently disputed, and it also convinces us that many an apparently innocent dream-situation is merely the symbolic prelude to a crudely sexual scene. This, however, finds direct representation, as a rule, only in the comparatively infrequent emission dreams, while it often enough turns into an anxiety-dream, which likewise leads to waking.

The symbolism of dreams due to urethral stimulus is especially obvious, and has always been divined. Hippocrates had already advanced the theory that a disturbance of the bladder was indicated if one dreamt of fountains and springs (Havelock Ellis). Scherner, who has studied the manifold symbolism of the urethral stimulus, agrees that "the powerful urethral stimulus always turns into the stimulation of the sexual sphere and its symbolic imagery.... The dream due to urethral stimulus is often at the same time the representative of the sexual dream."

O. Rank, whose conclusions (in his paper on Die Symbolschichtung im Wecktraum) I have here followed, argues very plausibly that a large number of "dreams due to urethral stimulus" are really caused by sexual stimuli, which at first seek to gratify themselves by way of regression to the infantile form of urethral erotism. Those cases are especially instructive in which the urethral stimulus thus produced leads to waking and the emptying of the bladder, whereupon, in spite of this relief, the dream is continued, and expresses its need in undisguisedly erotic images.[73]

---

[73] "The same symbolic representations which in the infantile sense constitute the basis of the vesical dream appear in the recent sense in purely sexual significance: water = urine = semen = amniotic fluid; ship = to pump ship (urinate) = seed-capsule; getting wet = enuresis = coitus = pregnancy; swimming = full bladder = dwelling-place of the unborn; rain = urination = symbol of fertilization: traveling (journeying - alighting) = getting out of bed = having sexual intercourse (honeymoon journey); urinating = sexual ejaculation" (Rank, I, c).

In a quite analogous manner dreams due to intestinal stimulus disclose the pertinent symbolism, and thus confirm the relation, which is also amply verified by ethno-psychology, of gold and feces.[74] "Thus, for example, a woman, at a time when she is under the care of a physician on account of an intestinal disorder, dreams of a digger for hidden treasure who is burying a treasure in the vicinity of a little wooden shed which looks like a rural privy. A second part of the dream has as its content how she wipes the posterior of her child, a little girl, who has soiled herself."

Dreams of rescue are connected with parturition dreams. To rescue, especially to rescue from the water, is, when dreamed by a woman, equivalent to giving birth; this sense is, however, modified when the dreamer is a man.[75]

Robbers, burglars, and ghosts, of which we are afraid before going to bed, and which sometimes even disturb our sleep, originate in one and the same childish reminiscence. They are the nightly visitors who have waked the child in order to set it on the chamber, so that it may not wet the bed, or have lifted the coverlet in order to see clearly how the child is holding its hands while sleeping. I have been able to induce an exact recollection of the nocturnal visitor in the analysis of some of these anxiety dreams. The robbers were always the father; the ghosts more probably correspond to female persons in white night-gowns.

F. Examples - Arithmetic and Speech in Dreams

Before I proceed to assign to its proper place the fourth of the factors which control the formation of dreams, I shall cite a few examples from my collection of dreams, partly for the purpose of illustrating the co-operation of the three factors with which we are already acquainted, and partly for the purpose of adducing

---

[74] Freud, "Character and Anal Erotism," Collected Papers, II; Rank, Die Symbolschictung, etc.; Dattner, Intern. Zeitschr. f. Psych. i (1913); Reik Intern. Zeitschr., iii (1915). -

[75] For such a dream see Pfister, "Ein Fall von psychoanalytischer Seelensorge und Seelenheilung," in Evangelische Freiheit (1909). Concerning the symbol of "rescuing," see my paper, "The Future Prospects of Psycho-Analytic Therapy". Also "Contribution to the Theory of Love, I: A Special Type of Object Choice in Men" in Collected Papers, iv. Also Rank, "Beilege zur Rettungs-phantasie," in the Zentralblatt fur Psychoanalyse i (1910); Reik; "Zur Rettungssymbolic," ibid.

evidence for certain unsupported assertions which have been made, or of bringing out what necessarily follows from them. It has, of course, been difficult in the foregoing account of the dream-work to demonstrate my conclusions by means of examples.

Examples in support of isolated statements are convincing only when considered in the context of an interpretation of a dream as a whole; when they are wrested from their context, they lose their value; on the other hand, a dream-interpretation, even when it is by no means profound, soon becomes so extensive that it obscures the thread of the discussion which it is intended to illustrate. This technical consideration must be my excuse if I now proceed to mix together all sorts of things which have nothing in common except their reference to the text of the foregoing chapter.

We shall first consider a few examples of very peculiar or unusual methods of representation in dreams. A lady dreamed as follows: *A servantgirl is standing on a ladder as though to clean the windows, and has with her a chimpanzee and a gorilla cat (later corrected, angora cat). She throws the animals on to the dreamer; the chimpanzee nestles up to her, and this is very disgusting.* This dream has accomplished its purpose by a very simple means, namely, by taking a mere figure of speech literally, and representing it in accordance with the literal meaning of its words.

Monkey, like the names of animals in general, is an opprobrious epithet, and the situation of the dream means merely to hurl invectives. This same collection will soon furnish us with further examples of the employment of this simple artifice in the dream-work.

Another dream proceeds in a very similar manner: *A woman with a child which has a conspicuously deformed cranium; the dreamer has heard that the child acquired this deformity owing to its position in its mother's womb. The doctor says that the cranium might be given a better shape by means of compression, but that this would injure the brain. She thinks that because it is a boy it won't suffer so much from deformity.* This dream contains a plastic representation of the abstract concept: Childish impressions, with which the dreamer has become familiar in the course of the treatment.

In the following example the dream-work follows rather a different course. The dream contains a recollection of an excursion to the Hilmteich, near Graz: *There is a terrible storm outside; a miserable hotel - the water is dripping from the walls, and the beds are damp.* (The latter part of the content was less directly expressed than I give it.) The dream signifies *superfluous*. The abstract idea occurring in the dream-thoughts is first made equivocal by a certain abuse of language; it has perhaps been replaced by *overflowing*, or by *fluid* and *super-fluid* (-fluous), and has then been brought to representation by an accumulation of like impressions. Water within, water without, water in the beds in the form of dampness - everything fluid and super fluid. That for the purposes of dream-representation the spelling is much less considered than the sound of words ought not to surprise us when we remember that rhyme exercises a similar privilege.

The fact that language has at its disposal a great number of words which were originally used in a pictorial and concrete sense, but are at present used in a colourless and abstract fashion, has, in certain other cases, made it very easy for the dream to represent its thoughts. The dream has only to restore to these words their full significance, or to follow their change of meaning a little way back. For example, a man dreams that his friend, who is struggling to get out of a very tight place, calls upon him for help. The analysis shows that the tight place is a hole, and that the dreamer symbolically uses these very words to his friend: "Be careful, or you'll get yourself into a hole."[76] Another dreamer climbs a mountain from which he obtains an extraordinarily extensive view. He identifies himself with his brother, who is editing a review dealing with the Far East. In a dream in *Der Grune Heinrich*, a spirited horse is plunging about in a field of the finest oats, every grain of which is really "a sweet almond, a

---

[76] English Example. - TR.

raisin and a new penny" wrapped in red silk and tied with a bit of pig's bristle." The poet (or the dreamer) immediately furnishes the meaning of this dream, for the horse felt himself pleasantly tickled, so that he exclaimed: "The oats are pricking me" ("I feel my oats").

In the old Norse sagas (according to Henzen) prolific use is made in dreams of colloquialisms and witty expressions; one scarcely finds a dream without a double meaning or a play upon words.

It would be a special undertaking to collect such methods of representation and to arrange them in accordance with the principles upon which they are based. Some of the representations are almost witty. They give one the impression that one would have never guessed their meaning if the dreamer himself had not succeeded in explaining it.

1. A man dreams that he is asked for a name, which, however, he cannot recall. He himself explains that this means: "I shouldn't dream of it."

2. A female patient relates a dream in which all the persons concerned were singularly large. "That means," she adds, "that it must deal with an episode of my early childhood, for at that time all grown-up people naturally seemed to me immensely large." She herself did not appear in the dream.

The transposition into childhood is expressed differently in other dreams - by the translation of time into space. One sees persons and scenes as though at a great distance, at the end of a long road, or as though one were looking at them through the wrong end of a pair of opera-glasses.

3. A man who in waking life shows an inclination to employ abstract and indefinite expressions, but who otherwise has his wits about him, dreams, in a certain connection, that he reaches a railway station just as a train is coming in. But then the platform moves towards the train, which stands still; an absurd inversion of the real state of affairs. This detail, again, is nothing more than

an indication to the effect that something else in the dream must be inverted. The analysis of the same dream leads to recollections of picture-books in which men were represented standing on their heads and walking on their hands.

4. The same dreamer, on another occasion, relates a short dream which almost recalls the technique of a rebus. His uncle gives him a kiss in an automobile. He immediately adds the interpretation, which would never have occurred to me: it means auto-erotism. In the waking state this might have been said in jest.

5. At a New Year's Eve dinner the host, the patriarch of the family, ushered in the New Year with a speech. One of his sons-in-law, a lawyer, was not inclined to take the old man seriously, especially when in the course of his speech he expressed himself as follows: "When I open the ledger for the Old Year and glance at its pages I see everything on the asset side and nothing, thank the Lord, on the side of liability; all you children have been a great asset, none of you a liability." On hearing this the young lawyer thought of X, his wife's brother, who was a cheat and a liar, and whom he had recently extricated from the entanglements of the law. That night, in a dream. he saw the New Year's celebration once more, and heard the speech, or rather saw it. Instead of speaking, the old man actually opened the ledger, and on the side marked assets he saw his name amongst others, but on the other side, marked liability, there was the name of his brother-in-law, X. However, the word liability was changed into Lie-Ability, which he regarded as X's main characteristic.[77]

6. A dreamer treats another person for a broken bone. The analysis shows that the fracture represents a broken marriage vow, etc.

7. In the dream-content the time of day often represents a certain period of the dreamer's childhood. Thus, for example, 5:15 a.m. means to one dreamer the age of five years and three months; when he was that age, a younger brother was born.

8. Another representation of age in a dream: A woman is walking with two little girls; there is a difference of fifteen months

---

[77] Reported by Brill in his Fundamental Conceptions of Psychoanalysis.

in their ages. The dreamer cannot think of any family of her acquaintance in which this is the case. She herself interprets it to mean that the two children represent her own person, and that the dream reminds her that the two traumatic events of her childhood were separated by this period of time 3 1/2 and 4 3/4 years).

9. It is not astonishing that persons who are undergoing psychoanalytic treatment frequently dream of it, and are compelled to give expression in their dreams to all the thoughts and expectations aroused by it. The image chosen for the treatment is as a rule that of a journey, usually in a motorcar, this being a modern and complicated vehicle; in the reference to the speed of the car the patient's ironical humour is given free play. If the unconscious, as an element of waking thought, is to be represented in the dream, it is replaced, appropriately enough, by subterranean localities, which at other times, when there is no reference to analytic treatment, have represented the female body or the womb. Below in the dream very often refers to the genitals, and its opposite, above, to the face, mouth or breast. By wild beasts the dream-work usually symbolizes passionate impulses; those of the dreamer, and also those of other persons of whom the dreamer is afraid; or thus, by means of a very slight displacement, the persons who experience these passions. From this it is not very far to the totemistic representation of the dreaded father by means of vicious animals, dogs, wild horses, etc. One might say that wild beasts serve to represent the libido, feared by the ego, and combated by repression. Even the neurosis itself, the sick person, is often separated from the dreamer and exhibited in the dream as an independent person.

One may go so far as to say that the dream-work makes use of all the means accessible to it for the visual representation of the dream-thoughts, whether these appear admissible or inadmissible to waking criticism, and thus exposes itself to the doubt as well as the derision of all those who have only hearsay knowledge of dream-interpretation, but have never themselves practised it. Stekel's book, *Die Sprache des Traumes*, is especially rich in such examples, but I avoid citing illustrations from this work as the author's lack of critical judgment and his arbitrary technique would make even the unprejudiced observer feel doubtful.

10. From an essay by V. Tausk ("Kleider und Farben in Dienste der Traumdarstellung," in Interna. Zeitschr. fur Ps. A., ii [1914]):

(a) A dreams that he sees his former governess wearing a dress of black lustre, which fits closely over her buttocks. That means he declares this woman to be lustful.

(b) C in a dream sees a girl on the road to X bathed in a white light and wearing a white blouse.

The dreamer began an affair with a Miss White on this road.

11. In an analysis which I carried out in the French language I had to interpret a dream in which I appeared as an elephant. I naturally had to ask why I was thus represented: "Vous me trompez," answered the dreamer (Trompe = trunk).

The dream-work often succeeds in representing very refractory material, such as proper names, by means of the forced exploitation of very remote relations. In one of my dreams old Brucke has set me a task. I make a preparation, and pick something out of it which looks like crumpled tinfoil. (I shall return to this dream later.) The corresponding association, which is not easy to find, is stanniol, and now I know that I have in mind the name of the author Stannius, which appeared on the title-page of a treatise on the nervous system of fishes, which in my youth I regarded with reverence. The first scientific problem which my teacher set me did actually relate to the nervous system of a fish - the Ammocoetes. Obviously, this name could not be utilized in the picture-puzzle.

Here I must not fail to include a dream with a curious content, which is worth noting also as the dream of a child, and which is readily explained by analysis: A lady tells me: "I can remember that when I was a child I repeatedly dreamed that God wore a conical paper hat on His head. They often used to make me wear such a hat at table, so that I shouldn't be able to look at the plates of the other children and see how much they had received of any particular dish. Since I had heard that God was omniscient, the dream signified that I knew everything in spite of the hat which I was made to wear."

What the dream-work consists in, and its unceremonious handling of its material, the dream-thoughts, may be shown in an instructive manner by the numbers and calculations which occur in dreams. Superstition, by the way, regards numbers as having a special significance in dreams. I shall therefore give a few examples of this kind from my collection.

1. From the dream of a lady, shortly before the end of her treatment:

She wants to pay for something or other; her daughter takes 3 florins 65 kreuzer from her purse; but the mother says: "What are you doing? It costs only 21 kreuzer." This fragment of the dream was intelligible without further explanation owing to my knowledge of the dreamer's circumstances. The lady was a foreigner, who had placed her daughter at school in Vienna, and was able to continue my treatment as long as her daughter remained in the city. In three weeks the daughter's scholastic year would end, and the treatment would then stop. On the day before the dream the principal of the school had asked her whether she could not decide to leave the child at school for another year. She had then obviously reflected that in this case she would be able to continue the treatment for another year. Now, this is what the dream refers to, for a year is equal to 365 days; the three weeks remaining before the end of the scholastic year, and of the treatment, are equivalent to 21 days (though not to so many hours of treatment). The numerals, which in the dream-thoughts refer to periods of time, are given money values in the dream, and simultaneously a deeper meaning finds expression - for time is money. 365 kreuzer, of course, are 3 florins 65 kreuzer. The smallness of the sums which appear in the dream is a self-evident wish-fulfilment; the wish has reduced both the cost of the treatment and the year's school fees.

2. In another dream the numerals are involved in even more complex relations. A young lady, who has been married for some years, learns that an acquaintance of hers, of about the same age, Elise L, has just become engaged. Thereupon she dreams: She is sitting in the theatre with her husband and one side of the stalls is quite empty. Her husband tells her that Elise L and her fiance had also wished to come to the theatre, but that they only could have obtained poor seats; three for 1 florin 50 kreuzer, and of course they could not take those. She thinks they didn't lose much, either.

What is the origin of the 1 florin 50 kreuzer? A really indifferent incident of the previous day. The dreamer's sister-in-law had received 150 florins as a present from her husband, and hastened to get rid of them by buying some jewellery. Let us note that 150 florins is 100 times 1 florin 50 kreuzer. But whence the 3 in connection with the seats in the theatre? There is only one association for this, namely, that the fiance is three months younger than herself. When we have ascertained the significance of the fact that one side of the stalls is empty we have the solution of the dream. This feature is an undisguised allusion to a little incident which had given her husband a good excuse for teasing her. She had decided to go to the theatre that week; she had been careful to obtain tickets a few days beforehand, and had had to pay the advance booking-fee. When they got to the theatre they found that one side of the house was almost empty; so that she certainly need not have been in such a hurry.

I shall now substitute the dream-thoughts for the dream: "It surely was nonsense to marry so early; there was no need for my being in such a hurry. From Elise L's example I see that I should have got a husband just the same - and one a hundred times better - If I had only waited (antithesis to the haste of her sister-in-law), I could have bought three such men for the money (the dowry)!" - Our attention is drawn to the fact that the numerals in this dream have changed their meanings and their relations to a much greater extent than in the one previously considered.

The transforming and distorting activity of the dream has in this case been greater - a fact which we interpret as meaning that these dreamthoughts had to overcome an unusual degree of endopsychic resistance before they attained to representation. And we must not overlook the fact that the dream contains an absurd element, namely, that two persons are expected to take three seats. It will throw some light on the question of the interpretation of absurdity in dreams if I remark that this absurd detail of the dream-content is intended to represent the most strongly emphasized of the dream-thoughts: "It was nonsense to marry so early." The figure 3, which occurs in a quite subordinate relation between the two persons compared (three months' difference in their ages), has thus been adroitly utilized to produce the idea of nonsense required by the dream. The reduction of the actual 150 florins to 1 florin 50 kreuzer corresponds to the dreamer's disparagement of her husband in her suppressed thoughts.

3. Another example displays the arithmetical powers of dreams, which have brought them into such disrepute. A man dreams: He is sitting in the B's house (the B's are a family with which he was formerly acquainted), and he says: "It was nonsense that you didn't give me Amy for my wife."

Thereupon, he asks the girl: "How old are you?" Answer: "I was born in 1882." "Ah, then you are 28 years old."

Since the dream was dreamed in the year 1898, this is obviously bad arithmetic, and the inability of the dreamer to calculate may, if it cannot be otherwise explained, be likened to that of a general paralytic. My patient was one of those men who cannot help thinking about every woman they see. The patient who for some months came next after him in my consulting-room was a young lady; he met this lady after he had constantly asked about her, and he was very anxious to make a good impression on her. This was the lady whose age he estimated at 28. So much for explaining the result of his apparent calculation. But 1882 was the year in which he had married. He had been unable to refrain from entering into conversation with the two other women whom he met at my house - the two by no means youthful maids who alternately opened the door to him - and as he did not find them very responsive, he had told himself that they probably regarded him as elderly and serious.

Bearing in mind these examples, and others of a similar nature (to follow), we may say: The dream-work does not calculate at all, whether correctly or incorrectly; it only strings together, in the form of a sum, numerals which occur in the dream-thoughts, and which may serve as allusions to material which is insusceptible of representation. It thus deals with figures, as material for expressing its intentions, just as it deals with all other concepts, and with names and speeches which are only verbal images.

For the dream-work cannot compose a new speech. No matter how many speeches; and answers, which may in themselves be sensible or absurd, may occur in dreams, analysis shows us that the dream has taken from the dream-thoughts fragments of speeches which have really been delivered or heard, and has dealt with them in the most arbitrary fashion. It has not only torn them from their context and mutilated them, accepting one fragment and rejecting another, but it has often fitted them together in a novel manner, so that the speech which seems coherent in a dream is dissolved by analysis into three or four components. In this new application of the words the dream has often ignored the meaning which they had in the dream-thoughts, and has drawn an entirely new meaning from them.[78] Upon closer inspection, the more distinct and compact ingredients of the dream-speech may be distinguished from others, which serve as connectives, and have probably been supplied, just as we supply omitted letters and syllables in reading. The dream-speech thus has the structure of breccia, in which the larger pieces of various material are held together by a solidified cohesive medium.

---

[78] Analyses of other numerical dreams have been given by Jung, Marcinowski and others. Such dreams often involve very complicated arithmetical operations, which are none the less solved by the dreamer with astonishing confidence. Cf. also Ernest Jones, "Uber unbewusste Zahlenbehandlung," Zentralb. fur Psychoanalyse, 4, ii, [1912].

Neurosis behaves in the same fashion. I know a patient who - involuntarily and unwillingly - hears (hallucinates) songs or fragments of songs without being able to understand their significance for her psychic life. She is certainly not a paranoiac. Analysis shows that by exercising a certain license she gave the text of these songs a false application. "Oh, thou blissful one! Oh, thou happy one!" This is the first line of Christmas carol, but by not continuing it to the word, Christmastide, she turns it into a bridal song, etc. The same mechanism of distortion may operate, without hallucination, merely in association.

Strictly speaking, of course, this description is correct only for those dream-speeches which have something of the sensory character of a speech, and are described as speeches. The others, which have not, as it were, been perceived as heard or spoken (which have no accompanying acoustic or motor emphasis in the dream) are simply thoughts, such as occur in our waking life, and find their way unchanged into many of our dreams.

Our reading, too, seems to provide an abundant and not easily traceable source for the indifferent speech-material of dreams. But anything that is at all conspicuous as a speech in a dream can be referred to actual speeches which have been made or heard by the dreamer.

We have already found examples of the derivation of such dream-speeches in the analyses of dreams which have been cited for other purposes.

Thus, in the innocent market-dream (chapter V., A.) where the speech: *That is no longer to be had* serves to identify me with the butcher, while a fragment of the other speech: *I don't know that, I don't take that,* precisely fulfils the task of rendering the dream innocent. On the previous day, the dreamer, replying to some unreasonable demand on the part of her cook, had waved her aside with the words: *I don't know that, behave yourself properly,* and she afterwards took into the dream the first, indifferent-sounding part of the speech in order to allude to the latter part, which fitted well into the phantasy underlying the dream, but which might also have betrayed it.

Here is one of many examples which all lead to the same conclusion: A large courtyard in which dead bodies are being burned. The dreamer says, "I'm going, I can't stand the sight of it." (Not a distinct speech.) Then he meets two butcher boys and asks, "Well, did it taste good?" And one of them answers, "No, it wasn't good." As though it had been human flesh.

The innocent occasion of this dream is as follows: After taking supper with his wife, the dreamer pays a visit to his worthy but by no means appetizing neighbour. The hospitable old lady is just sitting down to her own supper, and presses him (among men a composite, sexually significant word is used jocosely in the place of this word) to taste it. He declines, saying that he has no appetite. She replies: "Go on with you, you can manage it all right," or something of the kind. The dreamer is thus forced to taste and praise what is offered him. "But that's good!" When he is alone again with his wife, he complains of his neighbour's importunity, and of the quality of the food which he has tasted. "I can't stand the sight of it," a phrase that in the dream, too, does not emerge as an actual speech, is a thought relating to the physical charms of the lady who invites him, which may be translated by the statement that he has no desire to look at her.

The analysis of another dream - which I will cite at this stage for the sake of a very distinct speech, which constitutes its nucleus, but which will be explained only when we come to evaluate the affects in dreams - is more instructive. I dream very vividly: I have gone to Brucke's laboratory at night, and on hearing a gentle knocking at the door, I open it to (the deceased) Professor Fleischl, who enters in the company of several strangers, and after saying a few words sits down at his table. Then follows a second dream: My friend Fl has come to Vienna, unobtrusively, in July; I meet him in the street, in conversation with my (deceased) friend P, and I go with them somewhere, and they sit down facing each other as though at a small table, while I sit facing them at the narrow end of the table. Fl speaks of his sister, and says: "In three-quarters of an hour she was dead," and then something like

"That is the threshold." As P does not understand him, Fl turns to me, and asks me how much I have told P of his affairs. At this, overcome by strange emotions, I try to tell Fl that P (cannot possibly know anything, of course, because he) is not alive. But noticing the mistake myself, I say: "Non vixit." Then I look searchingly at P, and under my gaze he becomes pale and blurred, and his eyes turn a sickly blue - and at last he dissolves. I rejoice greatly at this; I now understand that Ernst Fleischl, too, is only an apparition, a revenant, and I find that it is quite possible that such a person should exist only so long as one wishes him to, and that he can be made to disappear by the wish of another person.

This very pretty dream unites so many of the enigmatical characteristics of the dream-content - the criticism made in the dream itself, inasmuch as I myself notice my mistake in saying Non vixit instead of Non vivit, the unconstrained intercourse with deceased persons, whom the dream itself declares to be dead, the absurdity of my conclusion, and the intense satisfaction which it gives me - that "I would give my life" to expound the complete solution of the problem. But in reality I am incapable of doing what I do in the dream, i.e., of sacrificing such intimate friends to my ambition. And if I attempted to disguise the facts, the true meaning of the dream, with which I am perfectly familiar, would be spoiled. I must therefore be content to select a few of the elements of the dream for interpretation, some here, and some at a later stage.

The scene in which I annihilate P with a glance forms the centre of the dream. His eyes become strange and weirdly blue, and then he dissolves.

This scene is an unmistakable imitation of a scene that was actually experienced. I was a demonstrator at the Physiological Institute; I was on duty in the morning, and Brucke learned that on several occasions I had been unpunctual in my attendance at the students' laboratory. One morning, therefore, he arrived at the hour of opening, and waited for me. What he said to me was brief and to the point; but it was not what he said that mattered. What overwhelmed me was the terrible gaze of his blue eyes, before which I melted away - as P does in the dream, for P has exchanged roles with me, much to my relief. Anyone who remembers the eyes of the great master, which were wonderfully beautiful even in his old age, and has ever seen him angered, will readily imagine the emotions of the young transgressor on that occasion.

But for a long while I was unable to account for the Non vixit with which I pass sentence in the dream. Finally, I remembered that the reason why these two words were so distinct in the dream was not because they were heard or spoken, but because they were seen. Then I knew at once where they came from. On the pedestal of the statue of the Emperor joseph in the Vienna Hofburg are inscribed the following beautiful words:

Saluti patriae vixit
non diu sed totus.[79]

[He lived for the safety of the public, not for a long time, but always.] The motive of the mistake: patriae [fatherland] for publicae, has probably been correctly divined by Wittels.

From this inscription I had taken what fitted one inimical train of thought in my dream-thoughts, and which was intended to mean: "That fellow has nothing to say in the matter, he is not really alive." And I now recalled that the dream was dreamed a few days after the unveiling of the memorial to Fleischl, in the cloisters of the University, upon which occasion I had once more seen the memorial to Brucke, and must have thought with regret (in the unconscious) how my gifted friend P, with all his devotion to science, had by his premature death forfeited his just claim to a memorial in these halls. So I set up this memorial to him in the dream; Josef is my friend P's baptismal name.[80]

---

[79] The inscription in fact reads: Saluti publicae vixit non diu sed totus.
[80] As an example of over-determination: My excuse for coming late was that after working late into the night, in the morning I had to make the long journey from Kaiser-Josef-Strasse to Wahringer Strasse.

According to the rules of dream-interpretation, I should still not be justified in replacing *non vivit*, which I need, by *non vixit*, which is placed at my disposal by the recollection of the Kaiser Josef memorial. Some other element of the dream-thoughts must have contributed to make this possible. Something now calls my attention to the fact that in the dream scene two trains of thought relating to my friend P meet, one hostile, the other affectionate - the former on the surface, the latter covered up - and both are given representation in the same words: *non vixit*. As my friend P has deserved well of science, I erect a memorial to him; as he has been guilty of a malicious wish (expressed at the end of the dream), I annihilate him. I have here constructed a sentence with a special cadence, and in doing so I must have been influenced by some existing model.

But where can I find a similar antithesis, a similar parallel between two opposite reactions to the same person, both of which can claim to be wholly justified, and which nevertheless do not attempt to affect one another? Only in one passage which, however, makes a profound impression upon the reader - Brutus's speech of justification in Shakespeare's *Julius Caesar*: "As Caesar loved me, I weep for him; as he was fortunate, I rejoice at it; as he was valiant, I honour him; but as he was ambitious, I slew him." Have we not here the same verbal structure, and the same antithesis of thought, as in the dream-thoughts? So I am playing Brutus in my dream. If only I could find in my dream-thoughts another collateral connection to confirm this! I think it might be the following: My friend Fl comes to Vienna in July. This detail is not the case in reality. To my knowledge, my friend has never been in Vienna in July. But the month of July is named after Julius Caesar, and might therefore very well furnish the required allusion to the intermediate thought - that I am playing the part of Brutus.[81]

Strangely enough, I once did actually play the part of Brutus. When I was a boy of fourteen, I presented the scene between

---

[81] And also, Caesar = Kaiser.

Brutus and Caesar in Schiller's poem to an audience of children: with the assistance of my nephew, who was a year older than I, and who had come to us from England - and was thus a revenant - for in him I recognized the playmate of my early childhood. Until the end of my third year we had been inseparable; we had loved each other and fought each other and, as I have already hinted, this childish relation has determined all my later feelings in my intercourse with persons of my own age. My nephew John has since then had many incarnations, which have revivified first one and then another aspect of a character that is ineradicably fixed in my unconscious memory. At times he must have treated me very badly, and I must have opposed my tyrant courageously, for in later years I was often told of a short speech in which I defended myself when my father - his grandfather - called me to account: "Why did you hit John?" "I hit him because he hit me." It must be this childish scene which causes non vivit to become non vixit, for in the language of later childhood striking is known as wichsen (German: wichsen = to polish, to wax, i.e., to thrash); and the dream-work does not disdain to take advantage of such associations. My hostility towards my friend P, which has so little foundation in reality - he was greatly my superior, and might therefore have been a new edition of my old playmate - may certainly be traced to my complicated relations with John during our childhood. I shall, as I have said, return to this dream later on.

G. Absurd Dreams - Intellectual Performances in Dreams

I

Hitherto, in our interpretation of dreams, we have come upon the element of absurdity in the dream-content so frequently that we must no longer postpone the investigation of its cause and its meaning. We remember, of course, that the absurdity of dreams has furnished the opponents of dream-interpretation with their chief argument for regarding the dream as merely the meaningless product of an attenuated and fragmentary activity of the psyche.

I will begin with a few examples in which the absurdity of the dream-content is apparent only, disappearing when the dream is more thoroughly examined. These are certain dreams which - accidently [sic], one begins by thinking - are concerned with the dreamer's dead father.

1. Here is the dream of a patient who had lost his father six years before the date of the dream:

His father had been involved in a terrible accident. He was travelling by the night express when the train was derailed, the seats were telescoped, and his head was crushed from side to side. The dreamer sees him lying on his bed; from his left eyebrow a wound runs vertically upwards. The dreamer is surprised that his father should have met with an accident (since he is dead already, as the dreamer adds in relating his dream). His father's eyes are so clear.

According to the prevailing standards of dream-criticism, this dream-content would be explained as follows: At first, while the dreamer is picturing his father's accident, he has forgotten that his father has already been many years in his grave; in the course of the dream this memory awakens, so that he is surprised at his own dream even while he is dreaming it. Analysis, however, tells us that it is quite superfluous to seek for such explanations. The dreamer had commissioned a sculptor to make a bust of his father, and he had inspected the bust two days before the dream. It is this which seems to him to have come to grief (the German word means gone wrong or met with an accident). The sculptor has never seen his father, and has had to work from photographs. On the very day before the dream the son had sent an old family servant to the studio in order to see whether he, too, would pass the some judgment upon the marble bust - namely, that it was too narrow between the temples. And now follows the memory-material which has contributed to the formation of the dream: The dreamer's father had a habit, whenever he was harassed by business cares or domestic difficulties, of pressing his temples between his hands, as though his head was growing too large and be was trying to compress it. When the dreamer was four years old, he was present when a pistol was accidentally discharged, and his father's eyes were blackened (his eyes are so clear). When his father was thoughtful or depressed, he had a deep furrow in his forehead just where the dream shows his wound.

The fact that in the dream this wrinkle is replaced by a wound points to the second occasion for the dream. The dreamer had taken a photograph of his little daughter; the plate had fallen from his hand, and when he picked it up it revealed a crack which ran like a vertical furrow across the child's forehead, extending as far as the eyebrow. He could not help feeling a superstitious foreboding, for on the day before his mother's death the negative of her portrait had been cracked.

Thus, the absurdity of this dream is simply the result of a carelessness of verbal expression, which does not distinguish between the bust or the photograph and the original. We are all accustomed to making remarks like: "Don't you think it's exactly your father?" The appearance of absurdity in this dream might, of course, have been easily avoided. If it were permissible to form an opinion on the strength of a single case, one might be tempted to say that this semblance of absurdity is admitted or even desired.

II

Here is another example of the same kind from my own dreams (I lost my father in the year 1896):

After his death, my father has played a part in the political life of the Magyars, and has united them into a political whole; and here I see, indistinctly, a little picture: a number of men, as though in the Reichstag; a man is standing on one or two chairs; there are others round about him. I remember that on his deathbed he looked so like Garibaldi, and I am glad that this promise has really come true.

Certainly this is absurd enough. It was dreamed at the time when the Hungarians were in a state of anarchy, owing to Parliamentary obstruction, and were passing through the crisis from which Koloman Szell subsequently delivered them. The trivial circumstance that the scenes beheld in dreams consist of such little pictures is not without significance for the elucidation of this element. The customary visual dream-representations of our thoughts present images that impress us as being life-size; my dream-picture, however, is the reproduction of a wood-cut inserted in the text of an illustrated history of Austria, representing Maria Theresa in the Reichstag of Pressburg - the famous scene of Moriamur pro rege nostro.[82]

Like Maria Theresa, my father, in my dream, is surrounded by the multitude; but he is standing on one or two chairs (Stuhlen), and is thus, like a Stuhlrichter (presiding judge). (He has united them; here the intermediary is the phrase: "We shall need no judge.") Those of us who stood about my father's death-bed did actually notice that he looked very like Garibaldi. He had a post-mortem rise of temperature; his cheeks shone redder and redder... involuntarily we continue: "And behind him, in unsubstantial (radiance), lay that which subdues us all - the common fate."

This uplifting of our thoughts prepares us for the fact that we shall have to deal with this common fate. The post-mortem rise in temperature corresponds to the words after his death in the dream-content. The most agonizing of his afflictions had been a complete paralysis of the intestines (obstruction) during the last few weeks of his life. All sorts of disrespectful thoughts associate themselves with this. One of my contemporaries, who lost his father while still at the Gymnasium - upon which occasion I was profoundly moved, and tendered him my friendship - once told me, derisively, of the distress of a relative whose father had died in the street, and had been brought home, when it appeared, upon undressing the corpse, that at the moment of death, or post-mortem, an evacuation of the bowels (Stuhlentleerung) had taken place. The daughter was deeply distressed by this circumstance, because this ugly detail would inevitably spoil her memory of her father. We have now penetrated to the wish that

---

[82] [We die for our king.] I have forgotten in what author I found a reference to a dream which was overrun with unusually small figures, the source of which proved to be one of the engravings of Jacques Callot, which the dreamer had examined during the day. These engravings contain an enormous number of very small figures; a whole series of them deals with the horrors of the Thirty Years War.

is embodied in this dream. To stand after one's death before one's children great and undefiled: who would not wish that? What now has become of the absurdity of this dream? The appearance of absurdity was due only to the fact that a perfectly permissible figure of speech, in which we are accustomed to ignore any absurdity that may exist as between its components, has been faithfully represented in the dream. Here again we can hardly deny that the appearance of absurdity is desired and has been purposely produced.

The frequency with which dead persons appear in our dreams as living and active and associating with us has evoked undue astonishment, and some curious explanations, which afford conspicuous proof of our misunderstanding of dreams. And yet the explanation of these dreams is close at hand. How often it happens that we say to ourselves: "If my father were still alive, what would he say to this?" The dream can express this if in no other way than by his presence in a definite situation. Thus, for instance, a young man whose grandfather has left him a great inheritance dreams that the old man is alive, and calls his grandson to account, reproaching him for his lavish expenditure. What we regard as an objection to the dream on account of our better knowledge that the man is already dead, is in reality the consoling thought that the dead man does not need to learn the truth, or satisfaction over the fact that he can no longer have a say in the matter.

Another form of absurdity found in dreams of deceased relatives does not express scorn and derision; it serves to express the extremest repudiation, the representation of a suppressed thought which one would like to believe the very last thing one would think of. Dreams of this kind appear to be capable of solution only if we remember that a dream makes no distinction between desire and reality. For example, a man who nursed his father during his last illness, and who felt his death very keenly, dreamed some time afterwards the following senseless dream: His father was again living, and conversing with him as usual, but (and this was the remarkable thing) he had nevertheless died, though he did not know it. This dream is intelligible if, after he had nevertheless died, we insert in consequence of the dreamer's wish, and if after but he did not know it, we add that the dreamer had entertained this wish. While nursing him, the son had often wished that his father was dead; that is, he had had the really compassionate thought that it would be a good thing if death would at last put an end to his sufferings. While he was mourning his father's death, even this compassionate wish became an unconscious reproach, as though it had really contributed to shorten the sick man's life. By the awakening of the earliest infantile feelings against his father, it became possible to express this reproach as a dream; and it was precisely because of the extreme antithesis between the dream-instigator and the day - thoughts that this dream had to assume so absurd a form.[83]

As a general thing, the dreams of a deceased person of whom the dreamer has been fond confront the interpreter with difficult problems, the solution of which is not always satisfying. The reason for this may be sought in the especially pronounced ambivalence of feeling which controls the relation of the dreamer to the dead person. In such dreams it is quite usual for the deceased person to be treated at first as living; then it suddenly appears that he is dead; and in the continuation of the dream he is once more living. This has a confusing effect. I at last divined that this alternation of death and life is intended to represent the indifference of the dreamer ("It is all one to me whether he is alive or dead"). This indifference, of course, is not real, but wished; its purpose is to help the dreamer to deny his very intense and often contradictory emotional attitudes, and so it becomes the dream-representation of his ambivalence. For other dreams in which one meets with deceased persons the following rule will often be a guide: If in the dream the dreamer is not reminded that the dead person is dead, he sets himself on a par with the dead; he dreams of his own death. The sudden realization or

---

[83] Cf. "Formulations regarding the Two Principles in Mental Functioning," Collected Papers, IV.

astonishment in the dream ("but he has long been dead!") is a protest against this identification, and rejects the meaning that the dreamer is dead. But I will admit that I feel that dream-interpretation is far from having elicited all the secrets of dreams having this content.

III

In the example which I shall now cite, I can detect the dream-work in the act of purposely manufacturing an absurdity for which there is no occasion whatever in the dream-material. It is taken from the dream which I had as a result of meeting Count Thun just before going away on a holiday. I am driving in a cab, and I tell the driver to drive to a railway station. "Of course, I can't drive with you on the railway track itself," I say, after the driver had reproached me, as though I had worn him out; at the same time, it seems as though I had already made with him a journey that one usually makes by train. Of this confused and senseless story analysis gives the following explanation: During the day I had hired a cab to take me to a remote street in Dornbach. The driver, however, did not know the way, and simply kept on driving, in the manner of such worthy people, until I became aware of the fact and showed him the way, indulging in a few derisive remarks. From this driver a train of thought led to the aristocratic personage whom I was to meet later on. For the present, I will only remark that one thing that strikes us middle-class plebeians about the aristocracy is that they like to put themselves in the driver's seat. Does not Count Thun guide the Austrian car of State? The next sentence in the dream, however, refers to my brother, whom I thus also identify with the cab-driver. I had refused to go to Italy with him this year (Of course, I can't drive with you on the railway track itself), and this refusal was a sort of punishment for his accustomed complaint that I usually wear him out on this tour (this finds its way into the dream unchanged) by rushing him too quickly from place to place, and making him see too many beautiful things in a single day. That evening my brother had accompanied me to the railway station, but shortly before the carriage had reached the Western station of the Metropolitan Railway he had jumped out in order to take the train to Purkersdorf. I suggested to him that he might remain with me a little longer, as he did not travel to Purkersdorf by the Metropolitan but by the Western Railway. This is why, in my dream, I made in the cab a journey which one usually makes by train. In reality, however, it was the other way about: what I told my brother was: "The distance which you travel on the Metropolitan Railway you could travel in my company on the Western Railway." The whole confusion of the dream is therefore due to the fact that in my dream I replace "Metropolitan Railway" by cab, which, to be sure, does good service in bringing the driver and my brother into conjunction. I then elicit from the dream some nonsense which is hardly disentangled by elucidation, and which almost constitutes a contradiction of my earlier speech (of course, I cannot drive with you on the railway track itself). But as I have no excuse whatever for confronting the Metropolitan Railway with the cab, I must intentionally have given the whole enigmatical story this peculiar form in my dream.

But with what intention? We shall now learn what the absurdity in the dream signifies, and the motives which admitted it or created it. In this case the solution of the mystery is as follows: In the dream I need an absurdity, and something incomprehensible, in connection with driving (Fahren = riding, driving) because in the dream-thoughts I have a certain opinion that demands representation. One evening, at the house of the witty and hospitable lady who appears, in another scene of the same dream, as the housekeeper, I heard two riddles which I could not solve: As they were known to the other members of the party, I presented a somewhat ludicrous figure in my unsuccessful attempts to find the solutions. They were two puns turning on the words Nachkommen (to obey orders - offspring) and Vorfahren (to drive - forefathers, ancestry). They ran, I believe, as follows:

The coachman does it
At the master's behests;

Everyone has it;
In the grave it rests.
(Vorfahren)

A confusing detail was that the first halves of the two riddles were identical:

The coachman does it
At the master's behests;
Not everyone has it,
In the cradle it rests.
(Nachkommen)

When I saw Count Thun drive up (vorfahren) in state, and fell into the Figaro-like mood, in which one finds that the sole merit of such aristocratic gentlemen is that they have taken the trouble to be born (to become Nachkommen), these two riddles became intermediary thoughts for the dreamwork.

As aristocrats may readily be replaced by coachmen, and since it was once the custom to call a coachman Herr Schwager (brother-in-law), the work of condensation could involve my brother in the same representation. But the dream-thought at work in the background is as follows: It is nonsense to be proud of one's ancestors (Vorfahren). I would rather be an ancestor (Vorfahr) myself. On account of this opinion, it is nonsense, we have the nonsense in the dream. And now the last riddle in this obscure passage of the dream is solved - namely that I have driven before (vorher gefahren, vorgefaltren) with this driver.

Thus, a dream is made absurd if there occurs in the dream-thoughts, as one of the elements of the contents, the opinion: "That is nonsense"; and, in general, if criticism and derision are the motives of one of the dreamer's unconscious trains of thought. Hence, absurdity is one of the means by which the dream-work represents contradiction; another means is the inversion of material relation between the dream-thoughts and the dreamcontent; another is the employment of the feeling of motor inhibition. But the absurdity of a dream is not to be translated by a simple no; it is intended to reproduce the tendency of the dream-thoughts to express laughter or derision simultaneously with the contradiction. Only with this intention does the dream-work produce anything ridiculous. Here again it transforms a part of the latent content into a manifest form.[84]

> Herr Ludwig ist ein grosser Poet
> Und singt er, so sturzt Apollo
> Vor ihm auf die Knie und bittet und fleht,
> Halt ein, ich werde sonst toll, oh!

As a matter of fact, we have already cited a convincing example of this significance of an absurd dream. The dream (interpreted without analysis) of the Wagnerian performance which lasted until 7.45 a.m., and in which the orchestra is conducted from a tower, etc. (see this chapter, D.), is obviously saying: It is a crazy world and an insane society. He who deserves a thing doesn't get it, and he who doesn't care for it does get it. In this way the dreamer compares her fate with that of her cousin. The fact that dreams of a dead father were the first to furnish us with examples of absurdity in dreams is by no means accidental. The conditions for the creation of absurd dreams are here grouped together in a typical fashion.

The authority proper to the father has at an early age evoked the criticism of the child, and the strict demands which he has made have caused the child, in self-defence, to pay particularly close attention to every weakness of his father's; but the piety with which the father's personality is surrounded in our thoughts, especially after his death, intensifies the censorship which prevents the expression of this criticism from becoming conscious.

IV

Here is another absurd dream of a deceased father:

I receive a communication from the town council of my native city concerning the cost of accommodation in the hospital in the year 1851. This was necessitated by a seizure from which I was

---

[84] Here the dream-work parodies the thought which it qualifies as ridiculous, in that it creates something ridiculous in relation to it. Heine does the same thing when he wishes to deride the bad rhymes of the King of Bavaria. He does it by using even worse rhymes:

suffering. I make fun of the matter for, in the first place, I was not yet born in 1851, and in the second place, my father, to whom the communication might refer, is already dead. I go to him in the adjoining room, where he is lying in bed, and tell him about it. To my surprise he remembers that in the year 1851 he was once drunk and had to be locked up or confined. It was when he was working for the firm of T. "Then you, too, used to drink?" I ask. "You married soon after?" I reckon that I was born in 1856, which seems to me to be immediately afterwards.

In the light of the foregoing exposition, we shall translate the insistence with which this dream exhibits its absurdities as a sure sign of a particularly embittered and passionate polemic in the dream-thoughts. All the greater, then, is our astonishment when we perceive that in this dream the polemic is waged openly, and that my father is denoted as the person who is made a laughing-stock. Such frankness seems to contradict our assumption of a censorship controlling the dream-work. The explanation is that here the father is only an interposed figure, while the quarrel is really with another person, who appears in the dream only in a single allusion. Whereas a dream usually treats of revolt against other persons, behind whom the father is concealed, here it is the other way about: the father serves as the man of straw to represent another, and hence the dream dares to concern itself openly with a person who is usually hallowed, because there is present the certain knowledge that he is not in reality intended. We learn of this condition of affairs by considering the occasion of the dream. It was dreamed after I had heard that an older colleague, whose judgment was considered infallible, had expressed disapproval and astonishment on hearing that one of my patients had already been undergoing psychoanalytic treatment at my hands for five years. The introductory sentences of the dream allude in a transparently disguised manner to the fact that this colleague had for a time taken over the duties which my father could no longer perform (statement of expenses, accommodation in the hospital); and when our friendly relations began to alter for the worse I was thrown into the same emotional conflict as that which arises in the case of a misunderstanding between father and son (by reason of the part played by the father, and his earlier functions). The dream-thoughts now bitterly resent the reproach that I am not making better progress, which extends itself from the treatment of this patient to other things. Does my colleague know anyone who can get on any faster? Does he not know that conditions of this sort are usually incurable and last for life? What are four or five years in comparison to a whole lifetime, especially when life has been made so much easier for the patient during the treatment?

The impression of absurdity in this dream is brought about largely by the fact that sentences from different divisions of the dream-thoughts are strung together without any reconciling transition. Thus, the sentence, I go to him it the adjoining room, etc., leaves the subject from which the preceding sentences are taken, and faithfully reproduces the circumstances under which I told my father that I was engaged to be married. Thus the dream is trying to remind me of the noble disinterestedness which the old man showed at that time, and to contrast this with the conduct of another newly-introduced person. I now perceive that the dream is allowed to make fun of my father because in the dream-thoughts, in the full recognition of his merits, he is held up as an example to others. It is in the nature of every censorship that one is permitted to tell untruths about forbidden things rather than the truth. The next sentence, to the effect that my father remembers that he was once drink, and was locked up in consequence, contains nothing that really relates to my father any more. The person who is screened by him is here a no less important personage than the great Meynert, in whose footsteps I followed with such veneration, and whose attitude towards me, after a short period of favouritism, changed into one of undisguised hostility. The dream recalls to me his own statement that in his youth he had at one time formed the habit of intoxicating himself with chloroform, with the result that he had to enter a sanatorium; and also my second experience with him, shortly before his death. I had an embittered literary controversy with him in reference to masculine hysteria, the existence of which he denied, and when I visited him during his last illness, and asked him how he felt, he described his condition at some length, and concluded with the words: "You know, I have always been one of the prettiest cases of masculine hysteria." Thus, to my satisfaction, and to my astonishment, he admitted what he so long and so stubbornly denied. But the fact that in this scene of my dream I can use my father to screen Meynert is explained not by any discovered analogy between the two persons, but by the fact that it is the brief yet perfectly adequate representation of a conditional sentence in the dream-thoughts which, if fully expanded, would read as follows: "Of course, if I belonged to the second generation, if I were the son of a professor or a privy councillor, I should have progressed more rapidly." In my dream I make my father a professor and a privy councillor. The most obvious and most annoying absurdity of the dream lies in the treatment of the date 1851, which seems to me to be indistinguishable from 1856, as though a difference of five years meant nothing whatever. But it is just this one of the dream-thoughts that requires expression. Four or five years - that is precisely the length of time during which I enjoyed the support of the colleague mentioned at the outset; but it is also the duration of time I kept my fiance waiting before I married her; and by a coincidence that is eagerly exploited by the dream-thoughts, it is also the time I have kept my oldest patient waiting for a complete cure. "What are five years?" ask the dream-thoughts. "That is no time at all to me, that isn't worth consideration. I have time enough ahead of me, and just as what you wouldn't believe came true at last, so I shall accomplish this also." Moreover, the number 51, when considered apart from the number of the century, is determined in yet another manner and in an opposite sense; for which reason it occurs several times over in the dream. It is the age at which man seems particularly exposed to danger; the age at which I have seen colleagues die suddenly, among them one who had been appointed a few days earlier to a professorship for which he had long been waiting.

V

Another absurd dream which plays with figures:

An acquaintance of mine, Herr M, has been attacked in an essay by no less a person than Goethe and, as we all think, with unjustifiable vehemence. Herr M is, of course, crushed by this attack. He complains of it bitterly at a dinner-party; but his veneration for Goethe has not suffered as a result of this personal experience. I try to elucidate the temporal relations a little, as they seem improbable to me. Goethe died in

1832; since his attack upon M must, of course, have taken place earlier, M was at the time quite a young man. It seems plausible to me that he was 18 years old. But I do not know exactly what the date of the present year is, and so the whole calculation lapses into obscurity. The attack, by the way, is contained in Goethe's well-known essay on "Nature."

We shall soon find the means of justifying the nonsense of this dream. Herr M, with whom I became acquainted at a dinner-party, had recently asked me to examine his brother, who showed signs of general paralysis. The conjecture was right; the painful thing about this visit was that the patient gave his brother away by alluding to his youthful pranks, though our conversation gave him no occasion to do so. I had asked the patient to tell me the year of his birth, and had repeatedly got him to make trifling calculations in order to show the weakness of his memory - which tests, by the way, he passed quite well. Now I can see that I behave like a paralytic in the dream (I do not know exactly what the date of the present year is). Other material of the dream is drawn from another recent source. The editor of a medical periodical, a friend of mine, had accepted for his paper a very unfavourable crushing review of the last book of my Berlin friend, Fl, the critic being a very youthful reviewer, who was not very competent to pass judgment. I thought I had a right to interfere, and called the editor to account; he greatly regretted his acceptance of the review, but he would not promise any redress. I thereupon broke off my relations with the periodical, and in my letter of resignation I expressed the hope that our personal relations would not suffer as a result of the incident. The third source of this dream is an account given by a female patient - it was fresh in my memory at the time - of the psychosis of her brother who had fallen into a frenzy crying "Nature, Nature." The physicians in attendance thought that the cry was derived from a reading of Goethe's beautiful essay, and that it pointed to the patient's overwork in the study of natural philosophy. I thought, rather, of the sexual meaning in which even our less cultured people use the word Nature, and the fact that the unfortunate man afterwards mutilated his genitals seems to show that I was not far wrong. Eighteen years was the age of this patient at the time of this access of frenzy.

If I add, further, that the book of my so severely criticized friend ("One asks oneself whether the author or oneself is crazy" had been the opinion of another critic) treats of the temporal conditions of life, and refers the duration of Goethe's life to the multiple of a number significant from the biological point of view, it will readily be admitted that in my dream I am putting myself in my friend's place. (I try to elucidate the temporal relations a little.) But I behave like a paretic, and the dream revels in absurdity. This means that the dream-thoughts say, ironically: "Naturally, he is the fool, the lunatic, and you are the clever people who know better. Perhaps, however, it is the other way about?" Now, the other way about is abundantly represented in my dream, inasmuch as Goethe has attacked the young man, which is absurd, while it is perfectly possible even today for a young fellow to attack the immortal Goethe; and inasmuch as I reckon from the year of Goethe's death, while I made the paretic reckon from the year of his birth.

But I have further promised to show that no dream is inspired by other than egoistical motives. Accordingly, I must account for the fact that in this dream I make my friend's cause my own, and put myself in his place. My critical conviction in waking life would not justify my doing so. Now, the story of the eighteen-year-old patient, and the divergent interpretations of his cry, "Nature," allude to the fact that I have put myself into opposition to the majority of physicians by claiming a sexual aetiology for the psychoneuroses. I may say to myself: "You will meet with the same kind of criticism as your friend; indeed you have already done so to some extent"; so that I may now replace the he in the dream-thoughts by we. "Yes, you are right; we two are the fools." That mea res agitur is clearly shown by the mention of the short, incomparably beautiful essay of Goethe's, for it was a popular lecture on this essay which induced me to study the natural sciences when I left the Gymnasium, and was still undecided as to my future.

VI

I have to show that yet another dream in which my ego does not appear is none the less egoistic. In chapter V., D., I referred to a short dream in which Professor M says: "My son, the myopic..."; and I stated that this was only a preliminary dream, preceding another in which I play a part.

Here is the main dream, previously omitted, which challenges us to explain its absurd and unintelligible word-formation.

On account of something or other that is happening in Rome, it is necessary for the children to flee, and this they do. The scene is then laid before a gate, a double gate in the ancient style (the Porta Romana in Siena, as I realize while I am dreaming). I am sitting on the edge of a well, and I am greatly depressed; I am almost weeping. A woman - a nurse, a nun - brings out the two boys and hands them over to their father, who is not myself. The elder is distinctly my eldest son, but I do not see the face of the other boy. The woman asks the eldest boy for a parting kiss. She is remarkable for a red nose. The boy refuses her the kiss, but says to her, extending her his hand in parting, "Auf Geseres," and to both of us (or to one of us) "Auf Ungeseres." I have the idea that this indicates a preference.

This dream is built upon a tangle of thoughts induced by a play I saw at the theatre, called Das neue Ghetto (The New

Ghetto). The Jewish question, anxiety as to the future of my children, who cannot be given a fatherland, anxiety as to educating them so that they may enjoy the privileges of citizens - all these features may easily be recognized in the accompanying dream-thoughts.

"By the waters of Babylon we sat down and wept." Siena, like Rome, is famous for its beautiful fountains. In the dream I have to find some sort of substitute for Rome (cf. chapter V., B.) from among localities which are known to me. Near the Porta Romana of Siena we saw a large, brightly-lit building, which we learned was the Manicomio, the insane asylum. Shortly before the dream I had heard that a co-religionist had been forced to resign a position, which he had secured with great effort, in a State asylum.

Our interest is aroused by the speech: "Auf Geseres," where one might expect, from the situation continued throughout the dream, "Auf Wiedersehen" (Au revoir), and by its quite meaningless antithesis: "Auf Ungeseres." (Un is a prefix meaning "not.")

According to information received from Hebrew scholars, Geseres is a genuine Hebrew word, derived from the verb goiser, and may best be rendered by "ordained sufferings, fated disaster." From its employment in the Jewish jargon one would take it to mean "wailing and lamentation."

Ungeseres is a coinage of my own, and is the first to attract my attention, but for the present it baffles me. The little observation at the end of the dream - that Ungeseres indicates an advantage over Geseres - opens the way to the associations, and therewith to understanding. This relation holds good in the case of caviar; the unsalted kind is more highly prized than the salted. "Caviar to the general" - "noble passions." Herein lies concealed a jesting allusion to a member of my household, of whom I hope - for she is younger than I - that she will watch over the future of my children; this, too, agrees with the fact that another member of my household, our worthy nurse, is clearly indicated by the nurse (or nun) of the dream. But a connecting-link is wanting between the pair, salted - unsalted and Geseres - Ungeseres. This is to be found in gesauert and ungesauert (leavened and unleavened). In their flight or exodus from Egypt the children of Israel had not time to allow their dough to become leavened, and in commemoration of this event they eat unleavened bread at Passover to this day. Here, too, I can find room for the sudden association which occurred to me in this part of the analysis. I remembered how we, my friend from Berlin and myself, had strolled about the streets of Breslau, a city which was strange to us, during the last days of Easter. A little girl asked me the way to a certain street; I had to tell her that I did not know it; I then remarked to my friend, "I hope that later on in life the child will show more perspicacity in selecting the persons whom she allows to direct her." Shortly afterwards a sign caught my eye: "Dr. Herod, consulting hours..." I said to myself: "I hope this colleague does not happen to be a children's specialist." Meanwhile, my friend had been developing his views on the biological significance of bilateral symmetry, and had begun a sentence with the words: "If we had only one eye in the middle of the forehead, like Cyclops..." This leads us to the speech of the professor in the preliminary dream: "My son, the myopic." And now I have been led to the chief source for Geseres. Many years ago, when this son of Professor M's, who is today an independent thinker, was still sitting on his school-bench, he contracted an affection of the eye which, according to the doctor, gave some cause for anxiety. He expressed the opinion that so long as it was confined to one eye it was of no great significance, but that if it should extend to the other eye it would be serious. The affection subsided in the one eye without leaving any ill effects; shortly afterwards, however, the same symptoms did actually appear in the other eye. The boy's terrified mother immediately summoned the physician to her distant home in the country. But the doctor was now of a different opinion (took the other side). "What sort of 'Geseres' is this you are making?" he asked the mother, impatiently. "If one side got well, the other will, too." And so it turned out. And now as to the connection between this and myself and my family. The school-bench upon which Professor M's son learned his first lessons has become the property of my eldest son; it was given to him by the boy's mother, and it is into his mouth that I put the words of farewell in the dream. One of the wishes that may be connected with this transference may now be readily guessed. This school-bench is intended by its construction to guard the child from becoming shortsighted and one-sided. Hence myopia (and behind it the Cyclops), and the discussion about bilateralism. The fear of one-sidedness has a twofold significance; it might mean not only physical one-sidedness, but intellectual one-sidedness also. Does it not seem as though the scene in the dream, with all its craziness, were contradicting precisely this anxiety? When on the one hand the boy has spoken his words of farewell, on the other hand he calls out the very opposite, as though to establish an equilibrium. He is acting, as it were, in obedience to bilateral symmetry!

Thus, a dream frequently has the profoundest meaning in the places where it seems most absurd. In all ages those who have had something to say and have been unable to say it without danger to themselves have gladly donned the cap and bells. He for whom the forbidden saying was intended was more likely to tolerate it if he was able to laugh at it, and to flatter himself with the comment that what he disliked was obviously absurd. Dreams behave in real life as does the prince in the play who is obliged to pretend to be a madman, and hence we may say of dreams what Hamlet said of himself, substituting an unintelligible jest for the actual truth: "I am but mad north-northwest; when the wind is southerly I know a hawk from a handsaw" (Act II. sc. ii).[85]

Thus, my solution of the problem of absurdity in dreams is that the dream-thoughts are never absurd - at least, not those of

---

[85] This dream furnishes a good example in support of the universally valid doctrine that dreams of the same night, even though they are separated in the memory, spring from the same thought-material. The dream-situation in which I am rescuing my children from the city of Rome, moreover, is distorted by a reference back to an episode of my childhood. The meaning is that I envy certain relatives who years ago had occasion to transplant their children to the soil of another country.

the dreams of sane persons - and that the dream-work produces absurd dreams, and dreams with individually absurd elements, when the dream-thoughts contain criticism, ridicule, and derision, which have to be given expression. My next concern is to show that the dream-work is exhausted by the cooperation of the three factors enumerated - and of a fourth which has still to be mentioned - that it does no more than translate the dreamthoughts, observing the four conditions prescribed, and that the question whether the mind goes to work in dreams with all its intellectual

faculties, or with only part of them, is wrongly stated, and does not meet the actual state of affairs. But since there are plenty of dreams in which judgments are passed, criticisms made, and facts recognized in which astonishment at some individual element of the dream appears, and explanations are attempted, and arguments adduced, I must meet the objections deriving from these occurrences by the citation of selected examples.

My answer is as follows: Everything in dreams which occurs as the apparent functioning of the critical faculty is to be regarded, not as the intellectual performance of the dream-work, but as belonging to the substance of the dream-thoughts, and it has found its way from these, as a completed structure, into the manifest dream-content. I may go even farther than this! I may even say that the judgments which are passed upon the dream as it is remembered after waking, and the feelings which are aroused by the reproduction of the dream, belong largely to the latent dream-content, and must be fitted into place in the interpretation of the dream.

1. One striking example of this has already been given. A female patient does not wish to relate her dream because it was too vague. She saw a person in the dream, and does not know whether it was her husband or her father. Then follows a second dream-fragment, in which there occurs a manure-pail, with which the following reminiscence is associated. As a young housewife she once declared jestingly, in the presence of a young male relative who frequented the house, that her next business would be to procure a new manure-pail. Next morning one was sent to her, but it was filled with lilies

of the valley. This part of the dream served to represent the phrase, "Not grown on my own manure."[86] If we complete the analysis, we find in the dream-thoughts the after-effect of a story heard in youth; namely, that a girl had given birth to a child, and that it was not clear who was the father. The dream-representation here overlaps into the waking thought, and allows one of the elements of the dream-thoughts to be represented by a judgment, formed in the waking state, of the whole dream.

2. A similar case: One of my patients has a dream which strikes him as being an interesting one, for he says to himself, immediately after waking.

"I must tell that to the doctor." The dream is analysed, and shows the most distinct allusion to an affair in which he had become involved during the treatment, and of which he had decided to tell me nothing.[87]

3. Here is a third example from my own experience:

I go to the hospital with P, through a neighbourhood in which there are houses and gardens. Thereupon I have an idea that I have already seen this locality several times in my dreams. I do not know my way very well; P shows me a way which leads round a corner to a restaurant (indoor); here I ask for Frau Doni, and I hear that she is living at the back of the house, in a small room, with three children. I go there, and on the way I meet an undefined person with my two little girls. After I have been with them for a while, I take them with me. A sort of reproach against my wife for having left them there.

On waking I am conscious of a great satisfaction, whose motive seems to be the fact that I shall now learn from the analysis what is meant by I have already dreamed of this.[88] But the analysis of

---

[86] This German expression is equivalent to our saying: "I am not responsible for that," "That's not my funeral," or "That's not due to my own efforts." - TR.

[87] The injunction or resolve already contained in the dream: "I must tell that to the doctor," when it occurs in dreams during psycho-analytic treatment, is constantly accompanied by a great resistance to confessing the dream, and is not infrequently followed by the forgetting of the dream.

[88] A subject which has been extensively discussed in recent volumes If the Revue Philosophique (paramnesia in dreams).

the dream tells me nothing about this; it shows me only that the satisfaction belongs to the latent dream-content, and not to a judgment of the dream. It is satisfaction concerning the fact that I have had children by my marriage. P's path through life and my own ran parallel for a time; now he has outstripped me both socially and financially, but his marriage has remained childless.

Of this the two occasions of the dream give proof on complete analysis. On the previous day I had read in the newspaper the obituary notice of a certain Frau Dona A - y (which I turn into Doni), who had died in childbirth; I was told by my wife that the dead woman had been nursed by the same midwife whom she herself had employed at the birth of our two youngest boys. The name Dona had caught my attention, for I had recently met with it for the first time in an English novel. The other occasion for the dream may be found in the date on which it was dreamed; this was the night before the birthday of my eldest boy, who, it seems, is poetically gifted.

4. The same satisfaction remained with me after waking from the absurd dream that my father, after his death, had played a political role among the Magyars. It is motivated by the persistence of the feeling which accompanied the last sentence of the dream: I remember that on his deathbed he looked so like Garibaldi, and I am glad that it has really come true... (Followed by a forgotten continuation.) I can now supply from the analysis what should fill this gap. It is the mention of my second boy, to whom I have given the baptismal name of an eminent historical personage who attracted me greatly during my boyhood, especially during my stay in England. I had to wait for a year before I could fulfil my intention of using this name if the next child should be a son, and with great satisfaction I greeted him by this name as soon as he was born. It is easy to see how the father's suppressed desire for greatness is, in his thoughts, transferred to his children; one is inclined to believe that this is one of the ways by which the suppression of this desire (which becomes necessary in the course of life) is effected. The little fellow won his right to inclusion in the text of this dream by virtue of the fact that the same accident

– that of soiling his clothes (quite pardonable in either a child or in a dying person) – had occurred to him. Compare with this the allusion Stuhlrichter (presiding judge) and the wish of the dream: to stand before one's children great and undefiled.

5. If I should now have to look for examples of judgments or expressions of opinion which remain in the dream itself, and are not continued in, or transferred to, our waking thoughts, my task would be greatly facilitated were I to take my examples from dreams which have already been cited for other purposes. The dream of Goethe's attack on Herr M appears to contain quite a number of acts of judgment. I try to elucidate the temporal relations a little, as they seem improbable to me. Does not this look like a critical impulse directed against the nonsensical idea that Goethe should have made a literary attack upon a young man of my acquaintance? It seems plausible to me that he was 18 years old. That sounds quite like the result of a calculation, though a silly one; and the I do not know exactly what is the date of the present year would be an example of uncertainty or doubt in dreams.

But I know from analysis that these acts of judgment, which seem to have been performed in the dream for the first time, admit of a different construction, in the light of which they become indispensable for interpreting the dream, while at the same time all absurdity is avoided. With the sentence I try to elucidate the temporal relations a little, I put myself in the place of my friend, who is actually trying to elucidate the temporal relations of life. The sentence then loses its significance as a judgment which objects to the nonsense of the previous sentences. The interposition, Which seems improbable to me, belongs to the following: It seems plausible to me. With almost these identical words I replied to the lady who told me of her brother's illness: "It seems improbable to me" that the cry of "Nature, Nature," was in any way connected with Goethe; it seems much more plausible to me that it has the sexual significance which is known to you. In this case, it is true, a judgment was expressed, but in reality, not in a dream, and on an occasion which is remembered and utilized by the dream-thoughts. The dream-content appropriates this judgment like any other fragment of the dream-thoughts.

The number 18 with which the judgment in the dream is meaninglessly connected still retains a trace of the context from which the real judgment was taken. Lastly, the I do not know exactly what is the date of the present year is intended for no other purpose than that of my identification with the paralytic, in examining whom this particular fact was established.

In the solution of these apparent acts of judgment in dreams, it will be well to keep in mind the above-mentioned rule of interpretation, which tells us that we must disregard the coherence which is established in the dream between its constituent parts as an unessential phenomenon, and that every dream-element must be taken separately and traced back to its source. The dream is a compound, which for the purposes of investigation must be broken up into its elements. On the other hand, we become alive to the fact that there is a psychic force which expresses itself in our dreams and establishes this apparent coherence; that is, the material obtained by the dream-work undergoes a secondary elaboration. Here we have the manifestations of that psychic force which we shall presently take into consideration as the fourth of the factors which co-operate in dream-formation.

6. Let us now look for other examples of acts of judgment in the dreams which have already been cited. In the absurd dream about the communication from the town council, I ask the question, "You married soon after?" I reckon that I was born in 1856, which seems to me to be directly afterwards. This certainly takes the form of an inference. My father married shortly after his attack, in the year 1851. I am the eldest son, born in 1856; so this is correct. We know that this inference has in fact been falsified by the wish-fulfilment, and that the sentence which dominates the dream-thoughts is as follows: Four or five years - that is no time at all - that need not be counted. But every part of this

chain of reasoning may be seen to be otherwise determined from the dream-thoughts, as regards both its content and its form. It is the patient of whose patience my colleague complains who intends to marry immediately the treatment is ended. The manner in which I converse with my father in this dream reminds me of an examination or cross-examination, and thus of a university professor who was in the habit of compiling a complete docket of personal data when entering his pupils' names: You were born when? - 1856. - Patre? - Then the applicant gave the Latin form of the baptismal name of the father and we students assumed that the Hofrat drew inferences from the father's name which the baptismal name of the candidate would not always have justified. Hence, the drawing of inferences in the dream would be merely the repetition of the drawing of inferences which appears as a scrap of material in the dream-thoughts. From this we learn something new. If an inference occurs in the dreamcontent, it assuredly comes from the dream-thoughts; but it may be contained in these as a fragment of remembered material, or it may serve as the logical connective of a series of dream-thoughts. In any case, an inference in the dream represents an inference taken from the dreamthoughts.[89]

It will be well to continue the analysis of this dream at this point. With the inquisition of the professor is associated the recollection of an index (in my time published in Latin) of the university students; and further, the recollection of my own course of study. The five years allowed for the study of medicine were, as usual, too little for me. I worked unconcernedly for some years longer; my acquaintances regarded me as a loafer, and doubted whether I should get through. Then, suddenly, I decided to take my examinations, and I got through in spite of the postponement. A fresh confirmation of the dream-thoughts with which I defiantly meet my critics: "Even though you won't believe it, because I am taking my time, I shall reach the conclusion

---

[89] These results correct at several points my earlier statements concerning the representation of logical relations (chapter VI., C.). These described the general procedure of the dream-work, but overlooked its most delicate and most careful operations.

(German, Schluss = end, conclusion, inference). It has often happened like that." In its introductory portion, this dream contains several sentences which, we can hardly deny, are of the nature of an argument. And this argument is not at all absurd; it might just as well occur in my waking thoughts. In my dream I make fun of the communication from the town council, for in the first place I was not yet born in 1851, and in the second place my father, to whom it might refer, is already dead. Not only is each of these statements perfectly correct in itself, but they are the very arguments that I should employ if I received such a communication. We know from the foregoing analysis that this dream has sprung from the soil of deeply embittered and scornful dream-thoughts; and if we may also assume that the motive of the censorship is a very powerful one, we shall understand that the dream-thought has every occasion to create a flawless refutation of an unreasonable demand, in accordance with the pattern contained in the dream-thoughts. But the analysis shows that in this case the dream-work has not been required to make a free imitation, but that material taken from the dream-thoughts had to be employed for the purpose. It is as though in an algebraic equation there should occur, besides the figures, plus and minus signs, and symbols of powers and of roots, and as though someone, in copying this equation, without understanding it, should copy both the symbols and the figures, and mix them all up together. The two arguments may be traced to the following material: It is painful to me to think that many of the hypotheses upon which I base my psychological solution of the psychoneuroses which will arouse scepticism and ridicule when they first become known. For instance, I shall have to assert that impressions of the second year of life, and even the first, leave an enduring trace upon the emotional life of subsequent neuropaths, and that these impressions - although greatly distorted and exaggerated by the memory - may furnish the earliest and profoundest basis of a hysterical symptom. Patients to whom I explain this at a suitable moment are wont to parody my explanation by offering to search for reminiscences of the period when they were not yet born. My disclosure of the unsuspected part played by the father in the earliest sexual impulses of female patients may well have a similar reception. (Cf. the discussion in chapter V., D). Nevertheless, it is my well-founded conviction that both doctrines are true. In confirmation of this I recall certain examples in which the death of the father occurred when the child was very young, and subsequent incidents, otherwise inexplicable, proved that the child had unconsciously reserved recollections of the person who had so early gone out of its life. I know that both my assertions are based upon inferences whose validity will be attacked. It is the doing of the wish-fulfilment that precisely the material of those inferences, which I fear will be contested, should be utilized by the dream-work for establishing incontestable conclusions. 7. In one dream, which I have hitherto only touched upon, astonishment at the subject emerging is distinctly expressed at the outset. The elder Brucke must have set me some task or other; strangely enough, it relates to the preparation of the lower part of my own body, the pelvis and legs, which I see before me as though in the dissecting-room, but without feeling the absence of part of my body, and without a trace of horror. Louise N is standing beside me, and helps me in the work. The pelvis is eviscerated; now the upper, now the lower aspect is visible, and the two aspects are commingled. Large fleshy red tubercles are visible (which, even in the dream, make me think of haemorrhoids). Also something lying over them had to be carefully picked off; it looked like crumpled tinfoil.[90] Then I was once more in possession of my legs, and I made a journey through the city, but I took a cab (as I was tired). To my astonishment, the cab drove into the front door of a house, which opened and allowed it to pass into a corridor, which was broken off at the end, and eventually led on into the open.[91] Finally I wandered through changing landscapes, with an Alpine guide, who carried my things. He carried me for some distance, out of consideration for my tired legs. The ground was swampy; we

---

[90] Stanniol, allusion to Stannius; the nervous system of fishes; cf chapter VI., F.
[91] The place in the corridor of my apartment-house where the perambulators of the other tenants stand; it is also otherwise hyper-determined several times over.

went along the edge; people were sitting on the ground, like Red Indians or gypsies; among them a girl. Until then I had made my way along on the slippery ground, in constant astonishment that I was so well able to do so after making the preparation. At last we came to a small wooden house with an open window at one end. Here the guide set me down, and laid two planks, which stood in readiness, on the window-sill so as to bridge the chasm which had to be crossed from the window. Now I grew really alarmed about my legs.

Instead of the expected crossing, I saw two grown-up men lying upon wooden benches which were fixed on the walls of the hut, and something like two sleeping children next to them; as though not the planks but the children were intended to make the crossing possible. I awoke with terrified thoughts.

Anyone who his been duly impressed by the extensive nature of dream-condensation will readily imagine what a number of pages the exhaustive analysis of this dream would fill. Fortunately for the context, I shall make this dream only the one example of astonishment in dreams, which makes its appearance in the parenthetical remark, strangely enough. Let us consider the occasion of the dream. It is a visit of this lady, Louise N, who helps me with my work in the dream. She says: "Lend me something to read." I offer her She, by Rider Haggard. A strange book, but full of hidden meaning," I try to explain; "the eternal feminine, the immortality of our emotions -" Here she interrupts me: "I know that book already.

Haven't you something of your own?" "No, my own immortal works are still unwritten." "Well, when are you going to publish your so-called 'latest revelations,' which, you promised us, even we should be able to read?" she asks, rather sarcastically. I now perceive that she is a mouthpiece for someone else, and I am silent. I think of the effort it cost me to make public even my work on dreams, in which I had to surrender so much of my own intimate nature. ("The best that you know you can't tell the boys.") The preparation of my own body which I am ordered to make in my dream is thus the self-analysis involved in the communication of my dreams. The elder Brucke very properly finds a place here; in the first years of my scientific work it so happened that I neglected the publication of a certain discovery until his insistence forced me to publish it. But the further trains of thought, proceeding from my conversation with Louise N, go too deep to become conscious; they are side-tracked by way of the material which has been incidentally awakened in me by the mention of Rider Haggard's She. The comment strangely enough applies to this book, and to another by the same author, The Heart of the World; and numerous elements of the dream are taken from these two fantastic romances. The swampy ground over which the dreamer is carried, the chasm which has to be crossed by means of planks, come from She; the Red Indians, the girl, and the wooden house, from The Heart of the World. In both novels a woman is the leader, and both treat of perilous wanderings; She has to do with an adventurous journey to an undiscovered country, a place almost untrodden by the foot of man. According to a note which I find in my record of the dream, the fatigue in my legs was a real sensation from those days. Probably a weary mood corresponded with this fatigue, and the doubting question: "How much farther will my legs carry me?" In She, the end of the adventure is that the heroine meets her death in the mysterious central fire, instead of winning immortality for herself and for others. Some related anxiety has mistakably arisen in the dream-thoughts. The wooden house is assuredly also a coffin - that is, the grave. But in representing this most unwished-for of all thoughts by means of a wish-fulfilment, the dream-work has achieved its masterpiece. I was once in a grave, but it was an empty Etruscan grave near Orvieto - a narrow chamber with two stone benches on the walls, upon which were lying the skeletons of two adults. The interior of the wooden house in the dream looks exactly like this grave, except that stone has been replaced by wood. The dream seems to say: "If you must already sojourn in your grave, let it be this Etruscan grave," and by means of this interpolation it transforms the most mournful expectation into one that is really to be desired. Unfortunately, as we shall learn, the dream is able to change into its opposite only the idea accompanying an affect, but not always the affect itself. Hence, I awake with thoughts of terror, even after the idea that perhaps my children will achieve what has been denied to their father has forced its way to representation: a fresh allusion to the strange romance in which the identity of a character is preserved through a series of generations covering two thousand years.

8. in the context of another dream there is a similar expression of astonishment at what is experienced in the dream. This, however, is connected with such a striking, far-fetched, and almost intellectual attempt at explanation that if only on this account I should have to subject the whole dream to analysis, even if it did not possess two other interesting features. On the night of the eighteenth of July I was travelling on the Southern Railway, and in my sleep I heard someone call out: "Hollthurn, 10 minutes." I immediately think of Holothuria - of a natural history museum - that here is a place where valiant men have vainly resisted the domination of their overlord. - Yes, the counter-reformation in Austria! - As though it were a place in Styria or the Tyrol. Now I see indistinctly a small museum, in which the relics of the acquisitions of these men are preserved. I should like to leave the train, but I hesitate to do so. There are women with fruit on the platform; they squat on the ground, and in that position invitingly hold up their baskets. - I hesitated, in doubt as to whether we have time, but here we are still stationary. - I am suddenly in another compartment in which the leather and the seats are so narrow that one's spine directly touches the back.[92] I am surprised at this, but I may have changed carriages while asleep. Several people, among them an English brother and sister; a row of books plainly on a shelf on the wall. - I see The Wealth of Nations, and Matter and Motion (by Maxwell), thick books

---

[92] This description is not intelligible even to myself, but I follow the principle of reproducing the dream in those words which occur to me while I am writing it down. The wording itself is a part of the dream-representation.

bound in brown linen. The man asks his sister about a book of Schiller's, whether she has forgotten it. These books seem to belong now to me, now to them. At this point I wish to join in the conversation in order to confirm or support what is being said. I wake sweating all over, because all the windows are shut, The train stops at Marburg.

While writing down the dream, a part of it occurs to me which my memory wished to pass over. I tell the brother and sister (in English), referring to a certain book: "It is from..." but I correct myself: "It is by..." The man remarks to his sister: "He said it correctly."

The dream begins with the name of a station, which seems to have almost waked me. For this name, which was Marburg, I substitute Hollthurn.

The fact that I heard Marburg the first, or perhaps the second time it was called out, is proved by the mention of Schiller in the dream; he was born in Marburg, though not the Styrian Marburg.[93] Now on this occasion, although I was travelling first class, I was doing so under very disagreeable circumstances. The train was overcrowded; in my compartment I had come upon a lady and gentleman who seemed very fine people, and had not the good breeding, or did not think it worth while, to conceal their displeasure at my intrusion. My polite greeting was not returned, and although they were sitting side by side (with their backs to the engine), the woman before my eyes hastened to pre-empt the seat opposite her, and next to the window, with her umbrella; the door was immediately closed, and pointed remarks about the opening of windows were exchanged. Probably I was quickly recognized as a person hungry for fresh air. It was a hot night, and the atmosphere of the compartment, closed on both sides, was almost suffocating. My experience as a traveller leads me to believe that such inconsiderate and overbearing

---

[93] Schiller was not born in one of the Marbergs, but in Marbach, as every German schoolboy knows, and I myself knew. This again is one of those errors (Cf. chapter VI., B) which creep in as substitutes for an intentional falsification in another place and which I have endeavoured to explain in The Psycho-pathology of Everyday Life.

conduct marks people who have paid for their tickets only partly, or not at all. When the conductor came round, and I presented my dearly bought ticket, the lady exclaimed haughtily and almost threateningly: "My husband has a pass." She was an imposing-looking person, with a discontented expression, in age not far removed from the autumn of feminine beauty; the man had no chance to say anything; he sat there motionless. I tried to sleep. In my dream I take a terrible revenge on my disagreeable travelling companions; no one would suspect what insults and humiliations are concealed behind the disjointed fragments of the first half of the dream. After this need has been satisfied, the second wish, to exchange my compartment for another, makes itself felt. The dream changes its scene so often, and without making the slightest objection to such changes, that it would not have seemed at all remarkable had I at once, from my memories, replaced my travelling companions by more agreeable persons. But here was a case where something or other opposes the change of scene, and finds it necessary to explain it. How did I suddenly get into another compartment? I could not positively remember having changed carriages. So there was only one explanation. I must have left the carriage while asleep - an unusual occurrence, examples of which, however, are known to neuropathologists. We know of persons who undertake railway journeys in a crepuscular state, without betraying their abnormal condition by any sign whatever, until at some stage of their journey they come to themselves, and are surprised by the gap in their memory. Thus, while I am still dreaming, I declare my own case to be such a case of automatisme ambulatoire.

Analysis permits of another solution. The attempt at explanation, which so surprises me if I am to attribute it to the dream-work, is not original, but is copied from the neurosis of one of my patients. I have already spoken in another chapter of a highly cultured and kindly man who began, shortly after the death of his parents, to accuse himself of murderous tendencies, and who was distressed by the precautionary measures which he had to take to secure himself against these tendencies. His was a case of severe obsessional ideas with full insight. To begin with, it was painful to him to walk through the streets, as he was obsessed by the necessity of accounting for all the persons he met; he had to know whither they had disappeared; if one of them suddenly eluded his pursuing glance, he was left with a feeling of distress and the idea that he might possibly have made away with the man. Behind this obsessive idea was concealed, among other things, a Cain-phantasy, for "all men are brothers." Owing to the impossibility of accomplishing this task, he gave up going for walks, and spent his life imprisoned within his four walls. But reports of murders which had been committed in the world outside were constantly reaching his room by way of the newspapers, and his conscience tormented him with the doubt that he might be the murderer for whom the police were looking. The certainty that he had not left the house for weeks protected him for a time against these accusations, until one day there dawned upon him the possibility that he might have left his house while in an unconscious state, and might thus have committed murder without knowing anything about it. From that time onwards he locked his front door, and gave the key to his old housekeeper, strictly forbidding her to give it into his hands, even if he demanded it.

This, then, is the origin of the attempted explanation that I may have changed carriages while in an unconscious state; it has been taken into the dream ready-made, from the material of the dream-thoughts, and is evidently intended to identify me with the person of my patient. My memory of this patient was awakened by natural association. My last night journey had been made a few weeks earlier in his company. He was cured, and we were going into the country together to his relatives, who had sent for me; as we had a compartment to ourselves, we left all the windows open throughout the night, and for as long as I remained awake we had a most interesting conversation. I knew that hostile impulses towards his father in childhood, in a sexual connection, had been at the root of his illness. By identifying myself with him, I wanted to make an analogous confession to myself. The second scene of the dream really resolves itself into a wanton phantasy to the effect that my two elderly travelling companions had acted so uncivilly towards me because my arrival on the scene had prevented them from exchanging kisses and embraces during the night, as they had intended. This phantasy, however, goes back to an early incident of my childhood when, probably impelled by sexual curiosity, I had intruded into my parents' bedroom, and was driven thence by my father's emphatic command.

I think it would be superfluous to multiply such examples. They would all confirm what we have learned from those already cited: namely, that an act of judgment in a dream is merely the repetition of an original act of judgment in the dream-thoughts. In most cases it is an unsuitable repetition, fitted into an inappropriate context; occasionally, however, as in our last example, it is so artfully applied that it may almost give one the impression of independent intellectual activity in the dream. At this point we might turn our attention to that psychic activity which, though it does not appear to co-operate constantly in the formation of dreams, yet endeavours to fuse the dream-elements of different origin into a flawless and significant whole. We consider it necessary, however, first of all to consider the expressions of affect which appear in dreams, and to compare these with the affects which analysis discovers in the dream-thoughts.

H. The Affects in Dreams

A shrewd remark of Stricker's called our attention to the fact that the expressions of affects in dreams cannot be disposed of in the contemptuous fashion in which we are wont to shake off the dream-content after we have waked. "If I am afraid of robbers in my dreams, the robbers, to be sure, are imaginary, but the fear of them is real"; and the same thing is true if I rejoice in my dream. According to the testimony of our feelings, an affect experienced in a dream is in no way inferior to one of like intensity experienced in waking life, and the dream presses its claim to be accepted as part of our real psychic experiences, by virtue of its affective rather than its ideational content. In the waking state, we do not put the one before the other, since we do not know how to evaluate an affect psychically except in connection with an ideational content. If an affect and an idea are ill-matched as regards their nature or their intensity, our waking judgment becomes confused. The fact that in dreams the ideational content does not always produce the affective result which in our waking thoughts we should expect as its necessary consequence has always been a cause of astonishment. Strumpell declared that ideas in dreams are stripped of their psychic values. But there is no lack of instances in which the reverse is true; when an intensive manifestation of affect appears in a content which seems to offer no occasion for it. In my dream I may be in a horrible, dangerous, or disgusting situation, and yet I may feel no fear or aversion; on the other hand, I am sometimes terrified by harmless things, and sometimes delighted by childish things.

This enigma disappeared more suddenly and more completely than perhaps any other dream-problem if we pass from the manifest to the latent content. We shall then no longer have to explain it, for it will no longer exist. Analysis tells us that the ideational contents have undergone displacements and substitutions, while the affects have remained unchanged. No wonder, then, that the ideational content which has been altered by dream-distortion no longer fits the affect which has remained intact; and no cause for wonder when analysis has put the correct content into its original place.[94]

In a psychic complex which has been subjected to the influence of the resisting censorship, the affects are the unyielding

---

[94] If I am not greatly mistaken, the first dream which I was able to elicit from my grandson (aged 20 months) points to the fact that the dreamwork had succeeded in transforming its material into a wish-fulfilment, while the affect which belonged to it remained unchanged even in the sleeping state. The night before its father was to return to the front the child cried out, sobbing violently: "Papa, Papa - Baby." That may mean: Let Papa and Baby still be together; while the weeping takes cognizance of the imminent departure. The child was at the time very well able to express the concept of separation. Fort (= away, replaced by a peculiarly accented, long-drawn-out ooooh) had been his first word, and for many months before this first dream he had played at away with all his toys; which went back to his early self-conquest in allowing his mother to go away.

constituent, which alone can guide us to the correct completion. This state of affairs is revealed in the psychoneuroses even more distinctly than in dreams. Here the affect is always in the right, at least as regards its quality; its intensity may, of course, be increased by displacement of the neurotic attention. When the hysterical patient wonders that he should be so afraid of a trifle, or when the sufferer from obsessions is astonished that he should reproach himself so bitterly for a mere nothing, they are both in error, inasmuch as they regard long conceptual content - the trifle, the mere nothing - as the essential thing, and they defend themselves in vain, because they make this conceptual content the starting-point of their thought-work. Psychoanalysis, however, puts them on the right path, inasmuch as it recognizes that, on the contrary, it is the affect that is justified, and looks for the concept which pertains to it, and which has been repressed by a substitution. All that we need assume is that the liberation of affect and the conceptual content do not constitute the indissoluble organic unity as which we are wont to regard them, but that the two parts may be welded together, so that analysis will separate them. Dream-interpretation shows that this is actually the case.

I will first of all give an example in which analysis explains the apparent absence of affect in a conceptual content which ought to compel a liberation of affect.

I

The dreamer sees three lions in a desert, one of which is laughing, but she is not afraid of them. Then, however, she must have fled from them, for she is trying to climb a tree. But she finds that her cousin, the French teacher, is already up in the tree, etc. The analysis yields the following material: The indifferent occasion of the dream was a sentence in the dreamer's English exercise: "The lion's greatest adornment is his mane." Her father used to wear a beard which encircled his face like a Mane. The name of her English teacher is Miss Lyons. An acquaintance of hers sent her the ballads of Loewe (Loewe = lion). These, then, are the three lions; why should she be afraid of them? She has read a story in which a negro who has incited his fellows to revolt is hunted with bloodhounds, and climbs a tree to save himself. Then follow fragmentary recollections in the merriest mood, such as the following directions for catching lions (from Die Fliegende Blatter): "Take a desert and put it through a sieve; the lions will be left behind." Also a very amusing, but not very proper anecdote about an official who is asked why he does not take greater pains to win the favour of his chief, and who replies that he has been trying to creep into favour, but that his immediate superior was already up there. The whole matter becomes intelligible as soon as one learns that on the dream-day the lady had received a visit from her husband's superior. He was very polite to her, and kissed her hand, and she was not at all afraid of him, although he is a big bug (Grosses Tier = big animal) and plays the part of a social lion in the capital of her country. This lion is, therefore, like the lion in A Midsummer Night's Dream, who is unmasked as Snug the joiner; and of such stuff are all the dream-lions of which one is not afraid.

II

As my second example, I will cite the dream of the girl who saw her sister's little son lying as a corpse in his coffin, but who, it may be added, was conscious of no pain or sorrow. Why she was unmoved we know from the analysis. The dream only disguised her wish to see once more the man she loved; the affect had to be attuned to the wish, and not to its disguisement. There was thus no occasion for sorrow.

In a number of dreams the affect does at least remain connected with the conceptual content which has replaced the content really belonging to it.

In others, the dissolution of the complex is carried farther. The affect is entirely separated from the idea belonging to it, and finds itself accommodated elsewhere in the dream, where it fits into the new arrangement of the dream-elements. We have seen that the same thing happens to acts of judgment in dreams. If an important inference occurs in the dream-thoughts, there is one in the dream also; but the inference in the dream may be displaced to entirely different material. Not infrequently this displacement is effected in accordance with the principle of antithesis.

I will illustrate the latter possibility by the following dream, which I have subjected to the most exhaustive analysis.

III

A castle by the sea; afterwards it lies not directly on the coast, but on a narrow canal leading to the sea. A certain Herr P is the governor of the castle. I stand with him in a large salon with three windows, in front of which rise the projections of a wall, like battlements of a fortress. I belong to the garrison, perhaps as a volunteer naval officer. We fear the arrival of enemy warships, for we are in a state of war. Herr P intends to leave the castle; he gives me instructions as to what must be done if what we fear should come to pass. His sick wife and his children are in the threatened castle. As soon as the bombardment begins, the large hall is to be cleared. He breathes heavily, and tries to get away; I detain him, and ask him how I am to send him news in case of need. He says something further, and immediately afterwards he sinks to the floor dead. I have probably taxed him unnecessarily with my questions. After his death, which makes no further impression upon me, I consider whether the widow is to remain in the castle, whether I should give notice of the death to the higher command, whether I should take over the control of the castle as the next in command. I now stand at the window, and scrutinize the ships as they pass by; they are cargo steamers, and they rush by over the dark water; several with more than one funnel, others with bulging decks (these are very like the railway stations in the preliminary dream, which has not been related). Then my brother is standing beside me, and we both look out of the window on to the canal. At the sight of one ship we are alarmed, and call out: "Here comes the warship!" It turns out, however, that they are only the ships which I have already seen, returning. Now comes a small ship, comically truncated, so that it ends amidships; on the deck one sees curious things like cups or little boxes. We call out as with one voice: "That is the breakfast ship."

The rapid motion of the ships, the deep blue of the water, the brown smoke of the funnels - all these together produce an intense and gloomy impression.

The localities in this dream are compiled from several journeys to the Adriatic (Miramare, Duino, Venice, Aquileia). A short but enjoyable Easter trip to Aquileia with my brother, a few weeks before the dream, was still fresh in my memory; also the naval war between America and Spain, and, associated with this my anxiety as to the fate of my relatives in America, play a part in the dream. Manifestations of affect appear at two places in the dream. In one place an affect that would be expected is lacking: it expressly emphasized that the death of the governor makes no impression upon me; at another point, when I see the warships, I am frightened, and experience all the sensations of fright in my sleep. The distribution of affects in this well-constructed dream has been effected in such a way that any obvious contradiction is avoided. For there is no reason why I should be frightened at the governor's death, and it is fitting that, as the commander of the castle, I should be alarmed by the sight of the warship. Now analysis shows that Herr P is nothing but a substitute for my own ego (in the dream I am his substitute). I am the governor who suddenly dies. The dream-thoughts deal with the future of my family after my premature death. No other disagreeable thought is to be found among the dream-thoughts. The alarm which goes with the sight of the warship must be transferred from it to this disagreeable thought. Inversely, the analysis shows that the region of the dream-thoughts from which the warship comes is laden with most cheerful reminiscences. In Venice, a year before the dream, one magically beautiful day, we stood at the windows of our room on the Riva Schiavoni and looked out over the blue lagoon, on which there was more traffic to be seen than usual. Some English ships were expected; they were to be given a festive reception; and suddenly my wife cried, happy as a child: "Here comes the English warship!" In the dream I am frightened by the very same words; once more we see that speeches in dreams have their origin in speeches in real life. I shall presently show that even the element English in this speech has not been lost for the dream-work. Here, then, between the dream-thoughts and the dream-content, I turn joy into fright, and I need only point to the fact that by means of this transformation I give expression to part of the latent dream-content. The example shows, however, that the dreamwork is at liberty to detach the occasion of an affect from its connections in the dream-thoughts, and to insert it at any other place it chooses in the dream-content.

I will take the opportunity which is here, incidentally offered of subjecting to a closer analysis the breakfast ship, whose appearance in the dream so absurdly concludes a situation that has been rationally adhered to. If I look more closely at this dream-object, I am impressed after the event by the fact that it was black. and that by reason of its truncation at its widest beam it achieved, at the truncated end, a considerable resemblance to an object which had aroused our interest in the museums of the Etruscan cities. This object was a rectangular cup of black clay, with two handles, upon which stood things like coffee-cups or tea-cups, very similar to our modern service for the breakfast table. Upon inquiry we learned that this was the toilet set of an Etruscan lady, with little boxes for rouge and powder; and we told one another jestingly that it would not be a bad idea to take a thing like that home to the lady of the house. The dream-object, therefore, signifies a black toilet (toilette = dress), or mourning. and refers directly to a death. The other end of the dream-object reminds us of the boat (German, Nachen, from the Greek root, nechus, as a philological friend informs me), upon which corpses were laid in prehistoric times, and were left to be buried by the sea. This is associated with the return of the ships in the dream.

"Silently on his rescued boat the old man drifts into harbour." It is the return voyage after the shipwreck (German: Schiff-bruch = ship-breaking); the breakfast ship looks as though it were broken off amidships. But whence comes the name breakfast ship? This is where English comes in, which we have left over from the warships. Breakfast, a breaking of the fast. Breaking again belongs to shipwreck (Schiff-bruch), and fasting is associated with the black (mourning).

But the only thing about this breakfast ship which has been newly created by the dream is its name. The thing existed in reality, and recalls to me one of the merriest moments of my last journey. As we distrusted the fare in Aquileia, we took some food with us from Goerz, and bought a bottle of the excellent Istrian wine in Aquileia; and while the little mail-steamer slowly travelled through the canale delle Mee and into the lonely expanse of lagoon in the direction of Grado, we had breakfast on deck in the highest spirits - we were the only passengers - and it tasted to us as few breakfasts have ever tasted. This, then, was the breakfast ship, and it is behind this very recollection of the gayest joie de vivre that the dream hides the saddest thoughts of an unknown and mysterious future.

The detachment of affects from the groups of ideas which have occasioned their liberation is the most striking thing that happens to them in dream-formation, but it is neither the only nor even the most essential change which they undergo on the way from the dream-thoughts to the manifest dream. If the affects in the dream-thoughts are compared with those in the dream, one thing at once becomes clear: Wherever there is an affect in the dream, it is to be found also in the dream-thoughts; the converse, however, is not true. In general, a dream is less rich in affects than the psychic material from which it is elaborated. When I have reconstructed the dream-thoughts, I see that the most intense psychic impulses are constantly striving in them for self-assertion, usually in conflict with others which are sharply opposed to them. Now, if I turn back to the dream.

I often find it colourless and devoid of any very intensive affective tone. Not only the content, but also the affective tone of my thoughts is often reduced by the dream-work to the level of the indifferent. I might say that a suppression of the affects has been accomplished by the dream-work.

Take, for example, the dream of the botanical monograph. It corresponds to a passionate plea for my freedom to act as I am acting, to arrange my life as seems right to me, and to me alone. The dream which results from this sounds indifferent; I have written a monograph; it is lying before me; it is provided with coloured plates, and dried plants are to be found in each copy. It is like the peace of a deserted battlefield; no trace is left of the tumult of battle.

But things may turn out quite differently; vivid expressions of affect may enter into the dream itself; but we will first of all consider the unquestioned fact that so many dreams appear indifferent, whereas it is never possible to go deeply into the dream-thoughts without deep emotion.

The complete theoretical explanation of this suppression of affects during the dream-work cannot be given here; it would require a most careful investigation of the theory of the affects and of the mechanism of repression. Here I can put forward only two suggestions. I am forced - for other reasons - to conceive the liberation of affects as a centrifugal process directed towards the interior of the body, analogous to the processes of motor and secretory innervation. Just as in the sleeping state the emission of motor impulses towards the outer world seems to be suspended, so the centrifugal awakening of affects by unconscious thinking during sleep may be rendered more difficult. The affective impulses which occur during the course of the dream-thoughts may thus in themselves be feeble, so that those that find their way into the dream are no stronger.

According to this line of thought, the suppression of the affects would not be a consequence of the dream-work at all, but a consequence of the state of sleep. This may be so, but it cannot possibly be all the truth. We must remember that all the more complex dreams have revealed themselves as the result of a compromise between conflicting psychic forces. On the one hand, the wish-forming thoughts have to oppose the contradiction of a censorship; on the other hand, as we have often seen, even in unconscious thinking, every train of thought is harnessed to its contradictory counterpart. Since all these trains of thought are capable of arousing affects, we shall, broadly speaking, hardly go astray if we conceive the suppression of affects as the result of the inhibition which the contrasts impose upon one another, and the censorship upon the urges which it has suppressed. The inhibition of affects would accordingly be the second consequence of the dream-censorship, just as dream-distortion was the first consequence.

I will here insert an example of a dream in which the indifferent emotional tone of the dream-content may be explained by the antagonism of the dream-thoughts. I must relate the following short dream, which every reader will read with disgust.

IV

Rising ground, and on it something like an open-air latrine; a very long bench, at the end of which is a wide aperture. The whole of the back edge is thickly covered with little heaps of excrement of all sizes and degrees of freshness. A thicket behind the bench. I urinate upon the bench; a long stream of urine rinses everything clean, the patches of excrement come off easily and fall into the opening. Nevertheless, it seems as though something remained at the end.

Why did I experience no disgust in this dream?

Because, as the analysis shows, the most pleasant and gratifying thoughts have cooperated in the formation of this dream. Upon analysing it, I immediately think of the Augean stables which were cleansed by Hercules. I am this Hercules. The rising ground and the thicket belong to Aussee, where my children are now staying. I have discovered the infantile aetiology of the neuroses, and have thus guarded my own children from falling ill. The bench (omitting the aperture, of course) is the faithful copy of a piece of furniture of which an affectionate female patient has made me a present. This reminds me how my patients honour me. Even the museum of human excrement is susceptible of a gratifying interpretation. However much it disgusts me, it is a souvenir of the beautiful land of Italy, where in the small cities, as everyone knows, the privies are not equipped in any other way. The stream of urine that washes everything clean is an unmistakable allusion to greatness. It is in this manner that Gulliver extinguishes the great fire in Lilliput; to be sure, he thereby incurs the displeasure of the tiniest of queens. In this way, too, Gargantua, the superman of Master Rabelais, takes vengeance upon the Parisians, straddling Notre-Dame and training his stream of urine upon the city. Only yesterday I was turning over the leaves of Garnier's illustrations to Rabelais before I went to bed. And, strangely enough, here is another proof that I am the superman! The platform of Notre-Dame was my favourite nook in Paris; every free afternoon I used to go up into the towers of the cathedral and there clamber about between the monsters and gargoyles. The circumstance that all the excrement vanishes so rapidly before the stream of urine corresponds to the motto: *Afflavit et dissipati sunt*, which I shall some day make the title of a chapter on the therapeutics of hysteria.

And now as to the affective occasion of the dream. It had been a hot summer afternoon; in the evening, I had given my lecture on the connection between hysteria and the perversions, and everything which I had to say displeased me thoroughly, and seemed utterly valueless. I was tired; I took not the least pleasure in my difficult work, and longed to get away from this rummaging in human filth; first to see my children, and then to revisit the beauties of Italy. In this mood I went from the lecture-hall to a cafe to get some little refreshment in the open air, for my appetite had forsaken me. But a member of my audience went with me; he begged for permission to sit with me while I drank my coffee and gulped down my roll, and began to say flattering things to me. He told me how much he had learned from me, that he now saw everything through different eyes, that I had cleansed the Augean stables of error and prejudice, which encumbered the theory of the neuroses - in short, that I was a very great man. My mood was ill-suited to his hymn of praise; I struggled with my disgust, and went home earlier in order to get rid of him; and before I went to sleep I turned over the leaves of Rabelais, and read a short story by C. F. Meyer entitled Die Leiden eines Knaben (The Sorrows of a Boy).

The dream had originated from this material, and Meyer's novel had supplied the recollections of scenes of childhood.[95] The day's mood of annoyance and disgust is continued in the dream, inasmuch as it is permitted to furnish nearly all the material for the dream-content. But during the night the opposite mood of vigorous, even immoderate self-assertion awakened and dissipated the earlier mood. The dream had to assume such a form as would accommodate both the expressions of self-depreciation and exaggerated self-glorification in the same material. This compromise-formation resulted in an ambiguous dream-content, but, owing to the mutual inhibition of the opposites, in an indifferent emotional tone.

According to the theory of wish-fulfilment, this dream would not have been possible had not the opposed, and indeed suppressed, yet pleasureemphasized megalomanic train of thought been added to the thoughts of disgust. For nothing painful is intended to be represented in dreams; the painful elements of our daily thoughts are able to force their way into our dreams only if at the same time they are able to disguise a wishfulfilment.

The dream-work is able to dispose of the affects of the dream-thoughts in yet another way than by admitting them or reducing them to zero. It can transform them into their opposites. We are acquainted with the rule that for the purposes of interpretation every element of the dream may represent its opposite, as well as itself. One can never tell beforehand which is to be posited; only the context can decide this point. A suspicion of this state of affairs has evidently found its way into the popular consciousness; the dream-books, in their interpretations, often proceed according to the principle of contraries. This transformation into the

---

[95] Cf. the dream about Count Thun, last scene.

contrary is made possible by the intimate associative ties which in our thoughts connect the idea of a thing with that of its opposite. Like every other displacement, this serves the purposes of the censorship, but it is often the work of wish-fulfilment, for wish-fulfilment consists in nothing more than the substitution of an unwelcome thing by its opposite. Just as concrete images may be transformed into their contraries in our dreams, so also may the affects of the dream-thoughts, and it is probable that this inversion of affects is usually brought about by the dream-censorship. The suppression and inversion of affects is useful even in social life, as is shown by the familiar analogy of the dream-censorship and, above all, hypocrisy. If I am conversing with a person to whom I must show consideration while I should like to address him as an enemy, it is almost more important that I should conceal the expression of my affect from him than that I should modify the verbal expression of my thoughts. If I address him in courteous terms, but accompany them by looks or gestures of hatred and disdain, the effect which I produce upon him is not very different from what it would have been had I cast my unmitigated contempt into his face. Above all, then, the censorship bids me suppress my affects. and if I am a master of the art of dissimulation I can hypocritically display the opposite affect - smiling where I should like to be angry, and pretending affection where I should like to destroy.

We have already had an excellent example of such an inversion of affect in the service of the dream-censorship. In the dream of my uncle's beard I feel great affection for my friend R, while (and because) the dream-thoughts berate him as a simpleton. From this example of the inversion of affects we derived our first proof of the existence of the censorship. Even here it is not necessary to assume that the dream-work creates a counteraffect of this kind that is altogether new; it usually finds it lying ready in the material of the dream-thoughts, and merely intensifies it with the psychic force of the defence-motives until it is able to predominate in the dream-formation. In the dream of my uncle, the affectionate counteraffect probably has its origin in an infantile source (as the continuation of the dream would suggest), for owing to the peculiar nature of my earliest childhood experiences the relation of uncle and nephew has become the source of all my friendships and hatreds (cf. analysis chapter VI., F.).

An excellent example of such a reversal of affect is found in a dream recorded by Ferenczi.[96] "An elderly gentleman was awakened at night by his wife, who was frightened because he laughed so loudly and uncontrollably in his sleep. The man afterwards related that he had had the following dream: I lay in my bed, a gentleman known to me came in, I wanted to turn on the light, but I could not; I attempted to do so repeatedly, but in vain. Thereupon my wife got out of bed, in order to help me, but she, too, was unable to manage it; being ashamed of her neglige in the presence of the gentleman, she finally gave it up and went back to her bed; all this was so comical that I had to laugh terribly. My wife said: 'What are you laughing at, what are you laughing at?' but I continued to laugh until I woke. The following day the man was extremely depressed, and suffered from headache: 'From too much laughter, which shook me up,' he thought.

"Analytically considered, the dream looks less comical. In the latent dream-thoughts the gentleman known to him who came into the room is the image of death as the 'great unknown,' which was awakened in his mind on the previous day. The old gentleman, who suffers from arteriosclerosis, had good reason to think of death on the day before the dream. The uncontrollable laughter takes the place of weeping and sobbing at the idea that he has to die. It is the light of life that he is no longer able to turn on. This mournful thought may have associated itself with a failure to effect sexual intercourse, which he had attempted shortly before this, and in which the assistance of his wife en neglige was of no avail; he realized that he was already on the decline. The dream-work knew how to transform the sad idea of impotence and death into a comic scene, and the sobbing into laughter."

---

[96] Internat. Zeitschr. f. Psychoanalyse, IV (1916).

There is one class of dreams which has a special claim to be called hypocritical, and which severely tests the theory of wish-fulfilment. My attention was called to them when Frau Dr. M. Hilferding proposed for discussion by the Psychoanalytic Society of Vienna a dream recorded by Rosegger, which is here reprinted:

In Waldheimat, vol. xi, Rosegger writes as follows in his story, Fremd gemacht:

"I usually enjoy healthful sleep, yet I have gone without repose on many a night; in addition to my modest existence as a student and literary man, I have for long years dragged out the shadow of a veritable tailor's life - like a ghost from which I could not become divorced.

"It is not true that I have occupied myself very often or very intensely with thoughts of my past during the day. A stormer of heaven and earth who has escaped from the hide of the Philistine has other things to think about. And as a gay young fellow, I hardly gave a thought to my nocturnal dreams; only later, when I had formed the habit of thinking about everything, or when the Philistine within me began to assert itself a little, did it strike me that - when I dreamed at all - I was always a journeyman tailor, and that in that capacity I had already worked in my master's shop for a long time without any pay. As I sat there beside him, and sewed and pressed, I was perfectly well aware that I no longer belonged there, and that as a burgess of the town I had other things to attend to; but I was always on a holiday, or away in the country, and so I sat beside my master and helped him. I often felt far from comfortable about it, and regretted the waste of time which I might have employed for better and more useful purposes. If anything was not quite correct in measure and cut I had to put up with a scolding from my master. Of wages there was never a question. Often, as I sat with bent back in the dark workshop, I decided to give notice and make myself scarce. Once I actually did so, but the master took no notice of me, and next time I was sitting beside him again and sewing.

"How happy I was when I woke up after such weary hours! And I then resolved that, if this intrusive dream should ever occur again, I would energetically throw it off, and would cry aloud: 'It is only a delusion, I am lying in bed, and I want to sleep'... And the next night I would be sitting in the tailor's shop again.

"So it went on for years, with dismal regularity. Once when the master and I were working at Alpelhofer's, at the house of the peasant with whom I began my apprenticeship, it happened that my master was particularly dissatisfied with my work. 'I should like to know where in the world your thoughts are?' he cried, and looked at me sullenly. I thought the most sensible thing to do would be to get up and explain to the master that I was working with him only as a favour, and then take my leave. But I did not do this. I even submitted when the master engaged an apprentice, and ordered me to make room for him on the bench. I moved into the corner, and kept on sewing. On the same day another journeyman was engaged; a bigoted fellow; he was the Bohemian who had worked for us nineteen years earlier, and then had fallen into the lake on his way home from the public-house. When he tried to sit down there was no room for him. I looked at the master inquiringly, and he said to me: 'You have no talent for tailoring; you may go; you're a stranger henceforth.' My fright on that occasion was so overpowering that I woke.

"The grey of morning glimmered through the clear windows of my familiar home. Objets d'art surrounded me; in the tasteful bookcase stood the eternal Homer, the gigantic Dante, the incomparable Shakespeare, the glorious Goethe - all radiant and immortal. From the adjoining room resounded the clear little voices of the children, who were waking up and prattling to their mother. I felt as though I had rediscovered that idyllically sweet, peaceful, poetical and spiritualized life in which I have so often and so deeply been conscious of contemplative human happiness. And yet I was vexed that I had not given my master notice first, but had been dismissed by him.

"And how remarkable this seems to me: since that night, when my master 'made a stranger' of me, I have enjoyed restful sleep; I no longer dream of my tailoring days, which now lie in the remote past: which in their unpretentious simplicity were really so cheerful, but which, none the less, have cast a long shadow over the later years of my life."

In this series of dreams of a poet who, in his younger years, had been a journeyman tailor, it is hard to recognize the domination of the wishfulfilment.

All the delightful things occurred in his waking life, while the dream seemed to drag along with it the ghost-like shadow of an unhappy existence which had long been forgotten. Dreams of my own of a similar character enable me to give some explanation of such dreams.

As a young doctor, I worked for a long time in the Chemical Institute without being able to accomplish anything in that exacting science, so that in the waking state I never think about this unfruitful and actually somewhat humiliating period of my student days. On the other hand, I have a recurring dream to the effect that I am working in the laboratory, making analyses, and experiments, and so forth; these dreams, like the examination-dreams, are disagreeable, and they are never very distinct. During the analysis of one of these dreams my attention was directed to the word analysis, which gave me the key to an understanding of them. Since then I have become an analyst. I make analyses which are greatly praised - psycho-analyses, of course. Now I understand: when I feel proud of these analyses in my waking life, and feel inclined to boast of my achievements, my dreams hold up to me at night those other, unsuccessful analyses, of which I have no reason to be proud; they are the punitive dreams of the upstart, like those of the journeyman tailor who became a celebrated poet. But how is it possible for a dream to place itself at the service of self-criticism in its conflict with parvenu pride, and to take as its content a rational warning instead of a prohibited wish-fulfilment? I have already hinted that the answer to this question presents many difficulties. We may conclude that the foundation of the dream consisted at first of an arrogant phantasy of ambition; but that in its stead only its suppression and abasement has reached the dream-content. One must remember that there are masochistic tendencies in mental life to which such an inversion might be attributed. I see no objection to regarding such dreams as punishment-dreams, as distinguished from wish-fulfilling dreams. I should not see in this any limitation of the theory of dreams hitherto as presented, but merely a verbal concession to the point of view to which the convergence of contraries seems strange. But a more thorough investigation of individual dreams of this class allows us to recognize yet another element. In an indistinct, subordinate portion of one of my laboratory dreams, I was just at the age which placed me in the most gloomy and most unsuccessful year of my professional career; I still had no position, and no idea how I was going to support myself, when I suddenly found that I had the choice of several women whom I might marry! I was, therefore, young again and, what is more, she was young again - the woman who has shared with me all these difficult years. In this way, one of the wishes which constantly gnaws at the heart of the aging man was revealed as the unconscious dream-instigator. The conflict raging in other psychic strata between vanity and self-criticism had certainly determined the dream-content, but the more deeply-rooted wish for youth had alone made it possible as a dream. One often says to oneself even in the waking state: "To be sure, things are going well with you today, and once you found life very hard; but, after all, life was sweet in those days, when you were still so young."[97]

Another group of dreams, which I have often myself experienced, and which I have recognized to be hypocritical, have as their content a reconciliation with persons with whom one has long ceased to have friendly relations. The analysis constantly discovers an occasion which might well induce me to cast aside the last remnants of consideration for these former friends, and

---

[97] Ever since psycho-analysis has dissected the personality into an ego and a super-ego (Group Psychology and the Analysis of the Ego, p. 664 below), it has been easy to recognize in these punishment-dreams wishfulfilments of the super-ego.

to treat them as strangers or enemies. But the dream chooses to depict the contrary relation.

In considering dreams recorded by a novelist or poet, we may often enough assume that he has excluded from the record those details which he felt to be disturbing and regarded as unessential. His dreams thus set us a problem which could be readily solved if we had an exact reproduction of the dream-content.

O. Rank has called my attention to the fact that in Grimm's fairy-tale of the valiant little tailor, or Seven at One Stroke, there is related a very similar dream of an upstart. The tailor, who has become a hero, and has married the king's daughter, dreams one night while lying beside the princess, his wife, about his trade; having become suspicious, on the following night she places armed guards where they can listen to what is said by the dreamer, and arrest him. But the little tailor is warned, and is able to correct his dream.

The complicated processes of removal, diminution, and inversion by which the affects of the dream-thoughts finally become the affects of the dream may be very well survived in suitable syntheses of completely analysed dreams. I shall here discuss a few examples of affective manifestations in dreams which will, I think, prove this conclusively in some of the cases cited.

V

In the dream about the odd task which the elder Brucke sets me - that of preparing my own pelvis - I am aware in the dream itself of not feeling appropriate horror. Now this is a wish-fulfilment in more senses than one. The preparation signifies the self-analyses which I perform, as it were, by publishing my book on dreams, which I actually found so painful that I postponed the printing of the completed manuscript for more than a year. The wish now arises that I may disregard this feeling of aversion, and for that reason I feel no horror (Grauen, which also means to grow grey) in the dream. I should much like to escape Grauen in the other sense too, for I am already growing quite grey, and the grey in my hair warns me to delay no longer. For we know that at the end of the dream this thought secures representation: "I shall have to leave my children to reach the goal of their difficult journey without my help."

In the two dreams that transfer the expression of satisfaction to the moments immediately after waking, this satisfaction is in the one case motivated by the expectation that I am now going to learn what is meant by I have already dreamed of this, and refers in reality to the birth of my first child, and in the other case it is motivated by the conviction that "that which has been announced by a premonitory sign" is now going to happen, and the satisfaction is that which I felt on the arrival of my second son. Here the same affects that dominated in the dream-thoughts have remained in the dream, but the process is probably not quite so simple as this in any dream. If the two analyses are examined a little more closely it will be seen that this satisfaction, which does not succumb to the censorship, receives reinforcement from a source which must fear the censorship, and whose affect would certainly have aroused opposition if it had not screened itself by a similar and readily admitted affect of satisfaction from the permitted source, and had, so to speak, sneaked in behind it. I am unfortunately unable to show this in the case of the actual dream, but an example from another situation will make my meaning intelligible. I will put the following case: Let there be a person near me whom I hate so strongly that I have a lively impulse to rejoice should anything happen to him. But the moral side of my nature does not give way to this impulse; I do not dare to express this sinister wish, and when something does happen to him which he does not deserve I suppress my satisfaction, and force myself to thoughts and expressions of regret. Everyone will at some time have found himself in such a position. But now let it happen that the hated person, through some transgression of his own, draws upon himself a well-deserved calamity; I shall now be allowed to give free rein to my satisfaction at his being visited by a just punishment, and I shall be expressing an opinion which coincides with that of other impartial persons. But I observe that my satisfaction proves to be more intense than that of others, for it has received reinforcement from another source - from my hatred, which was hitherto prevented by the inner censorship from furnishing the affect, but which, under the altered circumstances, is no longer prevented from doing so. This case generally occurs in social life when antipathetic persons or the adherents of an unpopular minority have been guilty of some offence. Their punishment is then usually commensurate not with their guilt, but with their guilt plus the ill-will against them that has hitherto not been put into effect. Those who punish them doubtless commit an injustice, but they are prevented from becoming aware of it by the satisfaction arising from the release within themselves of a suppression of long standing. In such cases the quality of the affect is justified, but not its degree; and the self-criticism that has been appeased in respect of the first point is only too ready to neglect to scrutinize the second point. Once you have opened the doors, more people enter than it was your original intention to admit.

A striking feature of the neurotic character, namely, that in it causes capable of evoking affect produce results which are qualitatively justified but quantitatively excessive, is to be explained on these lines, in so far as it admits of a psychological explanation at all. But the excess of affect proceeds from unconscious and hitherto suppressed affective sources which are able to establish an associative connection with the actual occasion, and for whose liberation of affect the unprotested and permitted source of affects opens up the desired path. Our attention is thus called to the fact that the relation of mutual inhibition must not be regarded as the only relation obtaining between the suppressed and the suppressing psychic institution. The cases in which the two institutions bring about a pathological result by co-operation and mutual reinforcement deserve just as much attention. These hints regarding the psychic mechanism will contribute to our understanding of the expressions of affects in dreams.

A gratification which makes its appearance in a dream, and which, of course, may readily be found in its proper place in the dream-thoughts, may not always be fully explained by means of this reference. As a rule, it is necessary to search for a second source in the dream-thoughts, upon which the pressure of the censorship rests, and which, under this pressure, would have yielded not gratification but the contrary affect, had it not been enabled by the presence of the first dream-source to free its gratification-affect from repression, and reinforce the gratification springing from the other source. Hence affects which appear in dreams appear to be formed by the confluence of several tributaries, and are overdetermined in respect of the material of the dream-thoughts. Sources of affect which are able to furnish the same affect combine in the dreamwork in order to produce it.[98]

Some insight into these involved relations is gained from the analysis of the admirable dream in which Non vixit constitutes the central point. In this dream expressions of affect of different qualities are concentrated at two points in the manifest content. Hostile and painful impulses (in the dream itself we have the phrase overcome by strange emotions) overlap one another at the point where I destroy my antagonistic friend with a couple of words. At the end of the dream I am greatly pleased, and am quite ready to believe in a possibility which I recognize as absurd when I am awake, namely, that there are revenants who can be swept away by a mere wish. I have not yet mentioned the occasion of this dream. It is an important one, and leads us far down into the meaning of the dream. From my friend in Berlin (whom I have designated as Fl) I had received the news that he was about to undergo an operation, and that relatives of his living in Vienna would inform me as to his condition. The first few messages after the operation were not very reassuring, and caused me great anxiety. I should have liked to go to him myself, but at that time I was afflicted with a painful complaint which made every movement a torment. I now learn from the dream-thoughts that I feared for this dear friend's life. I knew that his only sister, with whom I had never been acquainted, had died young, after a very

---

[98] I have since explained the extraordinary effect of pleasure produced by tendency wit on analogous lines.

brief illness. (In the dream Fl tells me about his sister, and says: "In three-quarters of an hour she was dead.") I must have imagined that his own constitution was not much stronger, and that I should soon be travelling, in spite of my health, in response to far worse news - and that I should arrive too late, for which I should eternally reproach myself.[99] This reproach, that I should arrive too late, has become the central point of the dream, but it has been represented in a scene in which the revered teacher of my student years - Brucke - reproaches me for the same thing with a terrible look from his blue eyes. What brought about this alteration of the scene will soon become apparent: the dream cannot reproduce the scene itself as I experienced it. To be sure, it leaves the blue eyes to the other man, but it gives me the part of the annihilator, an inversion which is obviously the work of the wish-fulfilment. My concern for the life of my friend, my self-reproach for not having gone to him, my shame (he had come to me in Vienna unobtrusively), my desire to consider myself excused on account of my illness - all this builds up an emotional tempest which is distinctly felt in my sleep, and which rages in that region of the dream-thoughts.

But there was another thing in the occasion of the dream which had quite the opposite effect. With the unfavourable news during the first days of the operation I received also an injunction to speak to no one about the whole affair, which hurt my feelings, for it betrayed an unnecessary distrust of my discretion. I knew, of course, that this request did not proceed from my friend, but that it was due to clumsiness or excessive timidity on the part of the messenger; yet the concealed reproach affected me very disagreeably, because it was not altogether unjustified. As we know, only reproaches which have something in them have the power to hurt. Years ago, when I was younger than I am now, I knew two men who were friends, and who honoured me with their friendship; and I quite superfluously told one of them what the

---

[99] It is this fancy from the unconscious dream-thoughts which peremptorily demands non vivit instead of non vixit. "You have come too late, he is no longer alive." The fact that the manifest situation of the dream aims at the non vivit has been mentioned in chapter VI., G.

other had said of him. This incident, of course, had nothing to do with the affairs of my friend Fl, but I have never forgotten the reproaches to which I had to listen on that occasion. One of the two friends between whom I made trouble was Professor Fleischl; the other one I will call by his baptismal name, Josef, a name which was borne also by my friend and antagonist P, who appears in this dream.

In the dream the element unobtrusively points to the reproach that I cannot keep anything to myself, and so does the question of Fl as to how much of his affairs I have told P. But it is the intervention of that old memory which transposes the reproach for arriving too late from the present to the time when I was working in Brucke's laboratory; and by replacing the second person in the annihilation scene of the dream by a Josef, I enable this scene to represent not only the first reproach - that I have arrived too late - but also that other reproach, more strongly affected by the repression, to the effect that I do not keep secrets. The work of condensation and displacement in this dream, as well as the motives for it, are now obvious.

My present trivial annoyance at the injunction not to divulge secrets draws reinforcement from springs that flow far beneath the surface, and so swells to a stream of hostile impulses towards persons who are in reality dear to me. The source which furnishes the reinforcement is to be found in my childhood. I have already said that my warm friendships as well as my enmities with persons of my own age go back to my childish relations to my nephew, who was a year older than I. In these he had the upper hand, and I early learned how to defend myself; we lived together, were inseparable, and loved one another, but at times, as the statements of older persons testify, we used to squabble and accuse one another. In a certain sense, all my friends are incarnations of this first figure; they are all revenants. My nephew himself returned when a young man, and then we were like Caesar and Brutus. An intimate friend and a hated enemy have always been indispensable to my emotional life; I have always been able to create them anew, and not infrequently my childish ideal has been so closely approached that friend and enemy have coincided in the same person; but not simultaneously, of course, nor in constant alternation, as was the case in my early childhood.

How, when such associations exist, a recent occasion of emotion may cast back to the infantile occasion and substitute this as a cause of affect, I shall not consider now. Such an investigation would properly belong to the psychology of unconscious thought, or a psychological explanation of the neuroses. Let us assume, for the purposes of dream-interpretation, that a childish recollection presents itself, or is created by the phantasy with, more or less, the following content: We two children quarrel on account of some object - just what we shall leave undecided, although the memory, or illusion of memory, has a very definite object in view - and each claims that he got there first, and therefore has the first right to it.

We come to blows; Might comes before Right; and, according to the indications of the dream, I must have known that I was in the wrong (noticing the error myself); but this time I am the stronger, and take possession of the battlefield; the defeated combatant hurries to my father, his grandfather, and accuses me, and I defend myself with the words, which I have heard from my father: "I hit him because he hit me." Thus, this recollection, or more probably phantasy, which forces itself upon my attention in the course of the analysis - without further evidence I myself do not know how - becomes a central item of the dream-thoughts, which collects the affective impulses prevailing in the dream-thoughts, as the bowl of a fountain collects the water that flows into it. From this point the dream-thoughts flow along the following channels: "It serves you right that you have had to make way for me; why did you try to push me off? I don't need you; I'll soon find someone else to play with," etc. Then the channels are opened through which these thoughts flow back again into the dream-representation. For such an "ote-toi que je m'y mette,"[100] I once had to reproach my deceased friend Josef.

---

[100] Make room for me.

He was next to me in the line of promotion in Brucke's laboratory, but advancement there was very slow. Neither of the two assistants budged from his place, and youth became impatient. My friend, who knew that his days were numbered, and was bound by no intimate relation to his superior, sometimes gave free expression to his impatience. As this superior was a man seriously ill, the wish to see him removed by promotion was susceptible of an obnoxious secondary interpretation. Several years earlier, to be sure, I myself had cherished, even more intensely, the same wish - to obtain a post which had fallen vacant; wherever there are gradations of rank and promotion the way is opened for the suppression of covetous wishes. Shakespeare's Prince Hal cannot rid himself of the temptation to see how the crown fits, even at the bedside of his sick father. But, as may readily be understood, the dream inflicts this inconsiderate wish not upon me, but upon my friend.[101]

"As he was ambitious, I slew him." As he could not expect that the other man would make way for him, the man himself has been put out of the way. I harbour these thoughts immediately after attending the unveiling of the memorial to the other man at the University. Part of the satisfaction which I feel in the dream may therefore be interpreted: A just punishment; it serves you right.

At the funeral of this friend a young man made the following remark, which seemed rather out of place: "The preacher talked as though the world could no longer exist without this one human being." Here was a stirring of revolt in the heart of a sincere man, whose grief had been disturbed by exaggeration. But with this speech are connected the dream-thoughts: "No one is really irreplaceable; how many men have I already escorted to the grave! But I am still alive; I have survived them all; I claim the field." Such a thought, at the moment when I fear that if I make a journey to see him I shall find my friend no longer among the

---

[101] It will have been obvious that the name Josef plays a great part in my dreams (see the dream about my uncle). It is particularly easy for me to hide my ego in my dreams behind persons of this name, since Joseph was the name of the dream-interpreter in the Bible.

living, permits only of the further development that I am glad once more to have survived someone; that it is not I who have died but he; that I am master of the field, as once I was in the imagined scene of my childhood. This satisfaction, infantile in origin, at the fact that I am master of the field, covers the greater part of the affect which appears in the dream. I am glad that I am the survivor; I express this sentiment with the naive egoism of the husband who says to his wife: "If one of us dies, I shall move to Paris." My expectation takes it as a matter of course that I am not the one to die. It cannot be denied that great self-control is needed to interpret one's dreams and to report them. One has to reveal oneself as the sole villain among all the noble souls with whom one shares the breath of life. Thus, I find it quite comprehensible that revenants should exist only as long as one wants them, and that they can be obliterated by a wish. It was for this reason that my friend Josef was punished. But the revenants are the successive incarnations of the friend of my childhood; I am also gratified at having replaced this person for myself over and over again, and a substitute will doubtless soon be found even for the friend whom I am now on the point of losing. No one is irreplaceable.

But what has the dream-censorship been doing in the meantime? Why does it not raise the most emphatic objection to a train of thoughts characterized by such brutal selfishness, and transform the satisfaction inherent therein into extreme discomfort? I think it is because other unobjectionable trains of thought referring to the same persons result also in satisfaction, and with their affect cover that proceeding from the forbidden infantile sources. In another stratum of thought I said to myself, at the ceremony of unveiling the memorial: "I have lost so many dear friends, some through death, some through the dissolution of friendship; is it not good that substitutes have presented themselves, that I have gained a friend who means more to me than the others could, and whom I shall now always retain, at an age when it is not easy to form new friendships?" The gratification of having found this substitute for my lost friend can be taken over into the dream without interference, but behind it there sneaks in the hostile feeling of malicious gratification from the infantile source. Childish affection undoubtedly helps to reinforce the rational affection of today; but childish hatred also has found its way into the representation.

But besides this, there is in the dream a distinct reference to another train of thoughts which may result in gratification. Some time before this, after long waiting, a little daughter was born to my friend. I knew how he had grieved for the sister whom he had lost at an early age, and I wrote to him that I felt that he would transfer to this child the love he had felt for her, that this little girl would at last make him forget his irreparable loss.

Thus this train also connects up with the intermediary thoughts of the latent dream-content, from which paths radiate in the most contrary directions: "No one is irreplaceable. See, here are only revenants; all those whom one has lost return." And now the bonds of association between the contradictory components of the dream-thoughts are more tightly drawn by the accidental circumstance that my friend's little daughter bears the same name as the girl playmate of my own youth, who was just my own age, and the sister of my oldest friend and antagonist. I heard the name Pauline with satisfaction, and in order to allude to this coincidence I replaced one Josef in the dream by another Josef, and found it impossible to suppress the identical initials in the name Fleischl and Fl. From this point a train of thought runs to the naming of my own children. I insisted that the names should not be chosen according to the fashion of the day, but should be determined by regard for the memory of those dear to us. The children's names make them revenants. And, finally, is not the procreation of children for all men the only way of access to immortality?

I shall add only a few observations as to the affects of dreams considered from another point of view. In the psyche of the sleeper an affective tendency - what we call a mood - may be contained as its dominating element, and may induce a corresponding mood in the dream. This mood may be the result of the experiences and thoughts of the day, or it may be of somatic origin; in either case it will be accompanied by the corresponding trains of thought. That this ideational content of the dream-thoughts should at one time determine the affective tendency primarily, while at another time it is awakened in a secondary manner by the somatically determined emotional disposition, is indifferent for the purposes of dream-formation. This is always subject to the restriction that it can represent only a wish-fulfilment, and that it may lend its psychic energy to the wish alone. The mood actually present will receive the same treatment as the sensation which actually emerges during sleep, which is either neglected or reinterpreted in the sense of a wish-fulfilment. Painful moods during sleep become the motive force of the dream, inasmuch as they awake energetic wishes which the dream has to fulfil. The material in which they inhere is elaborated until it is serviceable for the expression of the wish-fulfilment. The more intense and the more dominating the element of the painful mood in the dream-thoughts, the more surely will the most strongly suppressed wish-impulses take advantage of the opportunity to secure representation; for thanks to the actual existence of discomfort, which otherwise they would have to create, they find that the more difficult part of the work necessary to ensure representation has already been accomplished; and with these observations we touch once more upon the problem of anxiety-dreams, which will prove to be the boundary-case of dream-activity.

I. The Secondary Elaboration

We will at last turn our attention to the fourth of the factors participating in dream-formation. If we continue our investigation of the dream-content on the lines already laid down - that is, by examining the origin in the dream-thoughts of conspicuous occurrences - we come upon elements that can be explained only by making an entirely new assumption. I have in mind cases where one manifests astonishment, anger, or resistance in a dream, and that, too, in respect of part of the dream-content itself. Most of these impulses of criticism in dreams are not directed against the dream-content, but prove to be part of the dream-material, taken over and fittingly applied, as I have already shown by suitable examples. There are, however, criticisms of this sort which are not so derived: their correlatives cannot be found in the dream-material. What, for instance, is meant by the criticism not infrequent in dreams: "After all, it's only a dream"? This is a genuine criticism of the dream, such as I might make if I were awake, Not infrequently it is only the prelude to waking; even oftener it is preceded by a painful feeling, which subsides when the actuality of the dream-state has been affirmed. The thought: "After all, it's only a dream" in the dream itself has the same intention as it has on the stage on the lips of Offenbach's Belle Helene; it seeks to minimize what has just been experienced, and to secure indulgence for what is to follow. It serves to lull to sleep a certain mental agency which at the given moment has every occasion to rouse itself and forbid the continuation of the dream, or the scene. But it is more convenient to go on sleeping and to tolerate the dream, "because, after all, it's only a dream." I imagine that the disparaging criticism: "After all, it's only a dream," appears in the dream at the moment when the censorship, which is never quite asleep, feels that it has been surprised by the already admitted dream. It is too late to suppress the dream, and the agency therefore meets with this remark the anxiety or painful emotion which rises into the dream. It is an expression of the esprit d'escalier on the part of the psychic censorship.

In this example we have incontestable proof that everything which the dream contains does not come from the dream-thoughts, but that a psychic function, which cannot be differentiated from our waking thoughts, may make contributions to the dream-content. The question arises, does this occur only in exceptional cases, or does the psychic agency, which is otherwise active only as the censorship, play a constant part in dreamformation?

One must decide unhesitatingly for the latter view. It is indisputable that the censoring agency, whose influence we have so far recognized only in the restrictions of and omissions in the dream-content, is likewise responsible for interpolations in and amplifications of this content. Often these interpolations are readily recognized; they are introduced with hesitation, prefaced by an "as if"; they have no special vitality of their own, and are constantly inserted at points where they may serve to connect two portions of the dream-content or create a continuity between two sections of the dream. They manifest less ability to adhere in the memory than do the genuine products of the dream-material; if the dream is forgotten, they are forgotten first, and I strongly suspect that our frequent complaint that although we have dreamed so much we have forgotten most of the dream, and have remembered only fragments, is explained by the immediate falling away of just these cementing thoughts. In a complete analysis, these interpolations are often betrayed by the fact that no material is to be found for them in the dream-thoughts. But after careful examination I must describe this case as the less usual one; in most cases the interpolated thoughts can be traced to material in the dream-thoughts which can claim a place in the dream neither by its own merits nor by way of over-determination. Only in the most extreme cases does the psychic function in dreamformation which we are now considering rise to original creation; whenever possible it makes use of anything appropriate that it can find in the dream-material.

What distinguishes this part of the dream-work, and also betrays it, is its tendency. This function proceeds in a manner which the poet maliciously attributes to the philosopher: with its rags and tatters it stops up the breaches in the structure of the dream. The result of its efforts is that the dream loses the appearance of absurdity and incoherence, and approaches the pattern of an intelligible experience. But the effort is not always crowned with complete success. Thus, dreams occur which may, upon superficial examination, seem faultlessly logical and correct; they start from a possible situation, continue it by means of consistent changes, and bring it - although this is rare - to a not unnatural conclusion. These dreams have been subjected to the most searching elaboration by a psychic function similar to our waking thought; they seem to have a meaning, but this meaning is very far removed from the real meaning of the dream. If we analyse them, we are convinced that the secondary elaboration has handled the material with the greatest freedom, and has retained as little as possible of its proper relations. These are the dreams which have, so to speak, already been once interpreted before we subject them to waking interpretation. In other dreams this tendencious elaboration has succeeded only up to a point; up to this point consistency seems to prevail, but then the dream becomes nonsensical or confused; but perhaps before it concludes it may once more rise to a semblance of rationality In yet other dreams the elaboration has failed completely; we find ourselves helpless, confronted with a senseless mass of fragmentary contents.

I do not wish to deny to this fourth dream-forming power, which will soon become familiar to us - it is in reality the only one of the four dreamcreating factors which is familiar to us in other connections - I do not wish to deny to this fourth factor the faculty of creatively making new contributions to our dreams. But its influence is certainly exerted, like that of the other factors, mainly in the preference and selection of psychic material already formed in the dream-thoughts. Now there is a case where it is to a great extent spared the work of building, as it were, a facade to the dream by the fact that such a structure, only waiting to be used, already exists in the material of the dream-thoughts. I am accustomed to describe the element of the dream-thoughts which I have in mind as phantasy; I shall perhaps avoid misunderstanding if I at once point to the daydream as an analogy in waking life.[102] The part played by this element in our psychic life has not yet been fully recognized and revealed by psychiatrists; though M. Benedikt has, it seems to me, made a highly promising beginning. Yet the significance of the day-dream has not escaped the unerring insight of the poets; we are all familiar with the description of the day-dreams of one of his subordinate characters which Alphonse Daudet has given us in his Nabab. The study of the

---

[102] Reve, petit roman = day-dream, story.

psychoneuroses discloses the astonishing fact that these phantasies or day-dreams are the immediate predecessors of symptoms of hysteria - at least, of a great many of them; for hysterical symptoms are dependent not upon actual memories, but upon the phantasies built up on a basis of memories. The frequent occurrence of conscious day-phantasies brings these formations to our ken; but while some of these phantasies are conscious, there is a superabundance of unconscious phantasies, which must perforce remain unconscious on account of their content and their origin in repressed material. A more thorough examination of the character of these dayphantasies shows with what good reason the same name has been given to these formations as to the products of nocturnal thought - dreams. They have essential features in common with nocturnal dreams; indeed, the investigation of day-dreams might really have afforded the shortest and best approach to the understanding of nocturnal dreams.

Like dreams, they are wish-fulfilments; like dreams, they are largely based upon the impressions of childish experiences; like dreams, they obtain a certain indulgence from the censorship in respect of their creations. If we trace their formation, we become aware how the wish-motive which has been operative in their production has taken the material of which they are built, mixed it together, rearranged it, and fitted it together into a new whole. They bear very much the same relation to the childish memories to which they refer as many of the baroque palaces of Rome bear to the ancient ruins, whose hewn stones and columns have furnished the material for the structures built in the modern style.

In the secondary elaboration of the dream-content which we have ascribed to our fourth dream-forming factor, we find once more the very same activity which is allowed to manifest itself, uninhibited by other influences, in the creation of day-dreams. We may say, without further preliminaries, that this fourth factor of ours seeks to construct something like a day-dream from the material which offers itself. But where such a day-dream has already been constructed in the context of the dream-thoughts, this factor of the dream-work will prefer to take possession of it, and contrive that it gets into the dream-content. There are dreams that consist merely of the repetition of a day-phantasy, which has perhaps remained unconscious - as, for instance, the boy's dream that he is riding in a war-chariot with the heroes of the Trojan war. In my Autodidasker dream the second part of the dream at least is the faithful repetition of a day-phantasy - harmless in itself - of my dealings with Professor N. The fact that the exciting phantasy forms only a part of the dream, or that only a part of it finds its way into the dream-content, is due to the complexity of the conditions which the dream must satisfy at its genesis. On the whole, the phantasy is treated like any other component of the latent material; but it is often still recognizable as a whole in the dream. In my dreams there are often parts which are brought into prominence by their producing a different impression from that produced by the other parts. They seem to me to be in a state of flux, to be more coherent and at the same time more transient than other portions of the same dream. I know that these are unconscious phantasies which find their way into the context of the dream, but I have never yet succeeded in registering such a phantasy. For the rest, these phantasies, like all the other component parts of the dream-thoughts, are jumbled together, condensed, superimposed, and so on; but we find all the transitional stages, from the case in which they may constitute the dream-content, or at least the dream-facade, unaltered, to the most contrary case, in which they are represented in the dream-content by only one of their elements, or by a remote allusion to such an element. The fate of the phantasies in the dream-thoughts is obviously determined by the advantages they can offer as against the claims of the censorship and the pressure of condensation.

In my choice of examples for dream-interpretation I have, as far as possible, avoided those dreams in which unconscious phantasies play a considerable part, because the introduction of this psychic element would have necessitated an extensive discussion of the psychology of unconscious thought. But even in this connection I cannot entirely avoid the phantasy, because it often finds its way into the dream complete, and still more often perceptibly glimmers through it. I might mention yet one more dream, which seems to be composed of two distinct and opposed phantasies, overlapping here and there, of which the first is superficial, while the second becomes, as it were, the interpretation of the first.[103] The dream - it is the only one of which I possess no careful notes - is roughly to this effect: The dreamer - a young unmarried man - is sitting in his favourite inn, which is seen correctly; several persons come to fetch him, among them someone who wants to arrest him. He says to his table companions, "I will pay later, I am coming back." But they cry, smiling scornfully: "We know all about that; that's what everybody says." One guest calls after him: "There goes another one." He is then led to a small place where he finds a woman with a child in her arms. One of his escorts says: "This is Herr Muller." A commissioner or some other official is running through a bundle of tickets or papers, repeating Muller, Muller, Muller. At last the commissioner asks him a question, which he answers with a "Yes." He then takes a look at the woman, and notices that she has grown a large beard.

The two component parts are here easily separable. What is superficial is the phantasy of being arrested; this seems to be newly created by the dream-work. But behind it the phantasy of marriage is visible, and this material, on the other hand, has been slightly modified by the dream-work, and the features which may be common to the two phantasies appear with special distinctness, as in Galton's composite photographs. The promise of the young man, who is at present a bachelor, to return to his place at his accustomed table - the scepticism of his drinking companions,

---

[103] I have analysed an excellent example of a dream of this kind, having its origin in the stratification of several phantasies, in the Fragment of an Analysis of a Case of Hysteria (Collected Papers, vol. III). I undervalued the significance of such phantasies for dream-formation as long as I was working principally on my own dreams, which were rarely based upon day-dreams but most frequently upon discussions and mental conflicts. With other persons it is often much easier to prove the complete analogy between the nocturnal dream and the day-dream. In hysterical patients an attack may often be replaced by a dream; it is then obvious that the day-dream phantasy is the first step for both these psychic formations.

made wise by their many experiences - their calling after him: "There goes (marries) another one" - are all features easily susceptible of the other interpretation, as is the affirmative answer given to the official. Running through a bundle of papers and repeating the same name corresponds to a subordinate but easily recognized feature of the marriage ceremony - the reading aloud of the congratulatory telegrams which have arrived at irregular intervals, and which, of course, are all addressed to the same name. In the personal appearance of the bride in this dream the marriage phantasy has even got the better of the arrest phantasy which screens it. The fact that this bride finally wears a beard I can explain from information received - I had no opportunity of making an analysis. The dreamer had, on the previous day, been crossing the street with a friend who was just as hostile to marriage as himself, and had called his friend's attention to a beautiful brunette who was coming towards them. The friend had remarked: "Yes, if only these women wouldn't get beards as they grow older, like their fathers."

Of course, even in this dream there is no lack of elements with which the dream-distortion has done deep work. Thus, the speech, "I will pay later," may have reference to the behaviour feared on the part of the father-in-law in the matter of a dowry. Obviously all sorts of misgivings are preventing the dreamer from surrendering himself with pleasure to the phantasy of marriage. One of these misgivings - at with marriage he might lose his freedom - has embodied itself in the transformation of a scene of arrest.

If we once more return to the thesis that the dream-work prefers to make use of a ready-made phantasy, instead of first creating one from the material of the dream-thoughts, we shall perhaps be able to solve one of the most interesting problems of the dream. I have related the dream of Maury, who is struck on the back of the neck by a small board, and wakes after a long dream - a complete romance of the period of the French Revolution. Since the dream is produced in a coherent form, and completely fits the explanation of the waking stimulus, of whose occurrence the sleeper could have had no forboding, only one assumption seems possible, namely, that the whole richly elaborated dream must have been composed and dreamed in the short interval of time between the falling of the board on cervical vertebrae and the waking induced by the blow.

We should not venture to ascribe such rapidity to the mental operations of the waking state, so that we have to admit that the dream-work has the privilege of a remarkable acceleration of its issue.

To this conclusion, which rapidly became popular, more recent authors (Le Lorrain, Egger, and others) have opposed emphatic objections; some of them doubt the correctness of Maury's record of the dream, some seek to show that the rapidity of our mental operations in waking life is by no means inferior to that which we can, without reservation, ascribe to the mental operations in dreams. The discussion raises fundamental questions, which I do not think are at all near solution. But I must confess that Egger's objections, for example, to Maury's dream of the guillotine, do not impress me as convincing. I would suggest the following explanation of this dream: Is it so very improbable that Maury's dream may have represented a phantasy which had been preserved for years in his memory, in a completed state, and which was awakened - I should like to say, alluded to - at the moment when he became aware of the waking stimulus? The whole difficulty of composing so long a story, with all its details, in the exceedingly short space of time which is here at the dreamer's disposal then disappears; the story was already composed. If the board had struck Maury's neck when he was awake, there would perhaps have been time for the thought: "Why, that's just like being guillotined." But as he is struck by the board while asleep, the dream-work quickly utilizes the incoming stimulus for the construction of a wish-fulfilment, as if it thought (this is to be taken quite figuratively): "Here is a good opportunity to realize the wish-phantasy which I formed at such and such a time while I was reading." It seems to me undeniable that this dream-romance is just such a one as a young man is wont to construct under the influence of exciting impressions. Who has not been fascinated - above all, a Frenchman and a student of the history of civilization - by descriptions of the Reign of Terror, in which the aristocracy, men and women, the flower of the nation, showed that it was possible to die with a light heart, and preserved their ready wit and the refinement of their manners up to the moment of the last fateful summons? How tempting to fancy oneself in the midst of all this, as one of these young men who take leave of their ladies with a kiss of the hand, and fearlessly ascend the scaffold! Or perhaps ambition was the ruling motive of the phantasy - the ambition to put oneself in the place of one of those powerful personalities who, by their sheer force of intellect and their fiery eloquence, ruled the city in which the heart of mankind was then beating so convulsively; who were impelled by their convictions to send thousands of human beings to their death, and were paving the way for the transformation of Europe; who, in the meantime, were not sure of their own heads, and might one day lay them under the knife of the guillotine, perhaps in the role of a Girondist or the hero Danton? The detail preserved in the memory of the dream, accompanied by an enormous crowd, seems to show that Maury's phantasy was an ambitious one of just this character.

But the phantasy prepared so long ago need not be experienced again in sleep; it is enough that it should be, so to speak, "touched off." What I mean is this: If a few notes are struck, and someone says, as in Don Juan: "That is from The Marriage of Figaro by Mozart," memories suddenly surge up within me, none of which I can recall to consciousness a moment later. The phrase serves as a point of irruption from which a complete whole is simultaneously put into a condition of stimulation. It may well be the same in unconscious thinking. Through the waking stimulus the psychic station is excited which gives access to the whole guillotine phantasy. This phantasy, however, is not run through in sleep, but only in the memory of the awakened sleeper. Upon waking, the sleeper remembers in detail the phantasy which was transferred as a whole into the dream. At the same time, he has no means of assuring himself that he is really remembering something which was dreamed. The same explanation - namely, that one is dealing with finished phantasies which have been evoked as wholes by the waking stimulus - may be applied to other dreams which are adapted to the waking stimulus - for example, to Napoleon's dream of a battle before the explosion of a bomb. Among the dreams collected by Justine Tobowolska in her dissertation on the apparent duration of time in dreams,[104] I think the most corroborative is that related by Macario (1857) as having been dreamed by a playwright, Casimir Bonjour. Bonjour intended one evening to witness the first performance of one of his own plays, but he was so tired that he dozed off in his chair behind the scenes just as the curtain was rising. In his sleep he went through all the five acts of his play, and observed all the various signs of emotion which were manifested by the audience during each individual scene. At the close of the performance, to his great satisfaction, he heard his name called out amidst the most lively manifestations of applause. Suddenly he woke. He could hardly believe his eyes or his ears; the performance had not gone beyond the first lines of the first scene; he could not have been asleep for more than two minutes. As for the dream, the running through the five acts of the play and the observing the attitude of the public towards each individual scene need not, we may venture to assert, have been something new, produced while the dreamer was asleep; it may have been a repetition of an already completed work of the phantasy. Tobowolska and other authors have emphasized a common characteristic of dreams that show an accelerated flow of ideas: namely, that they seem to be especially coherent, and not at all like other dreams, and that the dreamer's memory of them is summary rather than detailed. But these are precisely the characteristics which would necessarily be exhibited by ready-made phantasies touched off by the dream-work - a conclusion

---

[104] Justine Tobowolska, Etude sur les illusions de temps dans les reves du sommeil normal (1900).

which is not, of course, drawn by these authors. I do not mean to assert that all dreams due to a waking stimulus admit of this explanation, or that the problem of the accelerated flux of ideas in dreams is entirely disposed of in this manner.

And here we are forced to consider the relation of this secondary elaboration of the dream-content to the other factors of the dream-work. May not the procedure perhaps be as follows? The dream-forming factors, the efforts at condensation, the necessity of evading the censorship, and the regard for representability by the psychic means of the dream first of all create from the dream-material a provisional dream-content, which is subsequently modified until it satisfies as far as possible the exactions of a secondary agency. No, this is hardly probable. We must rather assume that the requirements of this agency constitute from the very first one of the conditions which the dream must satisfy, and that this condition, as well as the conditions of condensation, the opposing censorship, and representability, simultaneously influence, in an inductive and selective manner, the whole mass of material in the dream-thoughts. But of the four conditions necessary for dream-formation, the last recognized is that whose exactions appear to be least binding upon the dream. The following consideration makes it seem very probable that this psychic function, which undertakes the so-called secondary elaboration of the dream-content, is identical with the work of our waking thought: Our waking (preconscious) thought behaves towards any given perceptual material precisely as the function in question behaves towards the dream-content. It is natural to our waking thought to create order in such material, to construct relations, and to subject it to the requirements of an intelligible coherence. Indeed, we go rather too far in this respect; the tricks of conjurers befool us by taking advantage of this intellectual habit of ours. In the effort to combine in an intelligible manner the sensory impressions which present themselves we often commit the most curious mistakes, and even distort the truth of the material before us. The proofs of this fact are so familiar that we need not give them further consideration here. We overlook errors which make nonsense of a printed page because we imagine the proper words. The editor of a widely read French journal is said to have made a bet that he could print the words from in front or from behind in every sentence of a long article without any of his readers noticing it. He won his bet. Years ago I came across a comical example of false association in a newspaper. After the session of the French Chamber in which Dupuy quelled the panic, caused by the explosion of a bomb thrown by an anarchist, with the courageous words, "La seance continue,"[105] the visitors in the gallery were asked to testify as to their impressions of the outrage. Among them were two provincials. One of these said that immediately after the end of a speech he had heard a detonation, but that he had thought that it was the parliamentary custom to fire a shot whenever a speaker had finished. The other, who had apparently already listened to several speakers, had got hold of the same idea, but with this variation, that he supposed the shooting to be a sign of appreciation following a specially successful speech.

Thus, the psychic agency which approaches the dream-content with the demand that it must be intelligible, which subjects it to a first interpretation, and in doing so leads to the complete misunderstanding of it, is none other than our normal thought. In our interpretation the rule will be, in every case, to disregard the apparent coherence of the dream as being of suspicious origin and, whether the elements are confused or clear, to follow the same regressive path to the dream-material.

At the same time, we note those factors upon which the above-mentioned scale of quality in dreams - from confusion to clearness - is essentially independent. Those parts of the dream seem to us clear in which the secondary elaboration has been able to accomplish something; those seem confused where the powers of this performance have failed. Since the confused parts of the dream are often likewise those which are less vividly presented, we may conclude that the secondary dream-work is responsible

---

[105] The meeting will continue.

also for a contribution to the plastic intensity of the individual dream-structures.

If I seek an object of comparison for the definitive formation of the dream, as it manifests itself with the assistance of normal thinking, I can think of none better than those mysterious inscriptions with which Die Fliegende Blatter has so long amused its readers. In a certain sentence which, for the sake of contrast, is in dialect, and whose significance is as scurrilous as possible, the reader is led to expect a Latin inscription. For this purpose the letters of the words are taken out of their syllabic groupings, and are rearranged. Here and there a genuine Latin word results; at other points, on the assumption that letters have been obliterated by weathering, or omitted, we allow ourselves to be deluded about the significance of certain isolated and meaningless letters. If we do not wish to be fooled we must give up looking for an inscription, must take the letters as they stand, and combine them, disregarding their arrangement, into words of our mother tongue.

The secondary elaboration is that factor of the dream-work which has been observed by most of the writers on dreams, and whose importance has been duly appreciated. Havelock Ellis gives an amusing allegorical description of its performances: "As a matter of fact, we might even imagine the sleeping consciousness as saying to itself: 'Here comes our master, Waking Consciousness, who attaches such mighty importance to reason and logic and so forth. Quick! gather things up, put them in order - any order will do - before he enters to take possession.'"[106]

The identity of this mode of operation with that of waking thought is very clearly stated by Delacroix in his Sur la structure logique du reve: "Cette fonction d'interpretation n'est pas particuliere au reve; c'est le meme travail de coordination logique que nous faisons sur nos sensations pendant la veille."[107]

---

[106] The World of Dreams, pp. 10, 11 (London, 1911).
[107] This function of interpretation is not particular to the dream; it is the same work of logical coordination that we use on our sensations when awake.

J. Sully is of the same opinion; and so is Tobowolska: "Sur ces successions incoherentes d'hallucinations, l'esprit s'efforce de faire le meme travail de coordination logique qu'il fait pendant le veille sur les sensations. Il relie entre elles par un lien imaginaire toutes ces images decousues et bouche les ecarts trop grands qui se trouvaient entre elles"[108].

Some authors maintain that this ordering and interpreting activity begins even in the dream and is continued in the waking state. Thus Paulhan: "Cependant j'ai souvent pense qu'il pouvait y avoir une certain deformation, ou plutot reformation du reve dans le souvenir.... La tendance systematisante de l'imagination pourrait fort bien achever apres le reveil ce qu'elle a ebauche pendant le sommeil. De la sorte, la rapidite reelle de la pensee serait augmentee en apparence par les perfectionnements dus a l'imagination eveillee."[109]

Leroy and Tobowolska: "Dans le reve, au contraire, l'interpretation et la coordination se font non seulement a l'aide des donnees du reve, mais encore a l'aide de celles de la veille...."[110]

It was therefore inevitable that this one recognized factor of dream-formation should be over-estimated, so that the whole process of creating the dream was attributed to it. This creative work was supposed to be accomplished at the moment of waking, as was assumed by Goblot, and with deeper conviction by Foucault, who attributed to waking thought the faculty of creating the dream out of the thoughts which emerged in sleep.

---

[108] With these series of incoherent halucinations, the mind must do the same work of logical coordination that it does with the sensations when awake. With a bon of imagination, it reunites all the disconnected images, and fills in the gaps found which are too great.

[109] However, I have often thought that there might be a certain deformation, or rather reformation, of the dream when it is recalled.... The systematizing tendency of the imagination can well finish, after waking, the sketch begun in sleep. In that way, the real speed of thought will be augmented in appearance by improvements due to the wakened imagination.

[110] In the dream, on the contrary, the interpretation and coordination are made not only with the aid of what is given by the dream, but also with what is given by the wakened mind.

In respect to this conception, Leroy and Tobowolska express themselves as follows: "On a cru pouvoir placer le reve au moment du reveil et ils ont attribue a la pensee de la veille la fonction de construire le reve avec les images presentes dans la pensee du sommeil."[111]

To this estimate of the secondary elaboration I will add the one fresh contribution to the dream-work which has been indicated by the sensitive observations of H. Silberer. Silberer has caught the transformation of thoughts into images in flagranti, by forcing himself to accomplish intellectual work while in a state of fatigue and somnolence. The elaborated thought vanished, and in its place there appeared a vision which proved to be a substitute for - usually abstract - thoughts. In these experiments it so happened that the emerging image, which may be regarded as a dream-element, represented something other than the thoughts which were waiting for elaboration: namely, the exhaustion itself, the difficulty or distress involved in this work; that is, the subjective state and the manner of functioning of the person exerting himself rather than the object of his exertions. Silberer called this case, which in him occurred quite often, the functional phenomenon, in contradistinction to the material phenomenon which he expected.

"For example: one afternoon I am lying, extremely sleepy, on my sofa, but I nevertheless force myself to consider a philosophical problem. I endeavour to compare the views of Kant and Schopenhauer concerning time. Owing to my somnolence I do not succeed in holding on to both trains of thought, which would have been necessary for the purposes of comparison. After several vain efforts, I once more exert all my willpower to formulate for myself the Kantian deduction in order to apply it to Schopenhauer's statement of the problem. Thereupon, I directed my attention to the latter, but when I tried to return to Kant, I found that he had again escaped me, and I tried in vain to fetch

---

[111] It was thought that the dream could be placed at the moment of waking, and they attributed to the waking thoughts the function of constructing the dream from the images present in the sleeping thoughts.

him back. And now this fruitless endeavour to rediscover the Kantian documents mislaid somewhere in my head suddenly presented itself, my eyes being closed, as in a dream-image, in the form of a visible, plastic symbol: I demand information of a grumpy secretary, who, bent over a desk, does not allow my urgency to disturb him; half straightening himself, he gives me a look of angry refusal."[112]

Other examples, which relate to the fluctuation between sleep and waking: "Example No. 2. Conditions: Morning, while awaking. While to a certain extent asleep (crepuscular state), thinking over a previous dream, in a way repeating and finishing it, I feel myself drawing nearer to the waking state, yet I wish to remain in the crepuscular state...'Scene: I am stepping with one foot over a stream, but I at once pull it back again and resolve to remain on this side.'[113]

"Example No. 6. Conditions the same as in Example No. 4 (he wishes to remain in bed a little longer without oversleeping). I wish to indulge in a little longer sleep. .."Scene: I am saying good-bye to somebody, and I agree to meet him (or her) again before long."

I will now proceed to summarize this long disquisition on the dream-work. We were confronted by the question whether in dream-formation the psyche exerts all its faculties to their full extent, without inhibition, or only a fraction of them, which are restricted in their action. Our investigations lead us to reject such a statement of the problem as wholly inadequate in the circumstances. But if, in our answer, we are to remain on the ground upon which the question forces us, we must assent to two conceptions which are apparently opposed and mutually exclusive. The psychic activity in dream-formation resolves itself into two achievements: the production of the dream-thoughts and the transformation of these into the dream-content. The dream-thoughts are perfectly accurate, and are formed with all

---
[112] Jahrb., i, p. 514.
[113] Jahrb., iii, p. 625.

the psychic profusion of which we are capable; they belong to the thoughts which have not become conscious, from which our conscious thoughts also result by means of a certain transposition.

There is doubtless much in them that is worth knowing, and also mysterious, but these problems have no particular relation to our dreams, and cannot claim to be treated under the head of dream-problems.[114] On the other hand, we have the process which changes the unconscious thoughts into the dream-content, which is peculiar to the dream-life and characteristic of it. Now, this peculiar dream-work is much farther removed from the pattern of waking thought than has been supposed by even the most decided depreciators of the psychic activity in dreamformation.

It is not so much that it is more negligent, more incorrect, more forgetful, more incomplete than waking thought; it is something altogether different, qualitatively, from waking thought, and cannot therefore be compared with it. It does not think, calculate, or judge at all, but limits itself to the work of transformation. It may be exhaustively described if we do not lose sight of the conditions which its product must satisfy. This product, the dream, has above all to be withdrawn from the censorship, and to this end the dream-work makes use of the displacement of psychic intensities, even to the transvaluation of

---

[114] Formerly I found it extraordinarily difficult to accustom my readers to the distinction between the manifest dream-content and the latent dream-thoughts. Over and over again arguments and objections were adduced from the uninterpreted dream as it was retained in the memory, and the necessity of interpreting the dream was ignored. But now, when the analysts have at least become reconciled to substituting for the manifest dream its meaning as found by interpretation, many of them are guilty of another mistake, to which they adhere just as stubbornly. They look for the essence of the dream in this latent content, and thereby overlook the distinction between latent dream-thoughts and the dream-work. The dream is fundamentally nothing more than a special form of our thinking, which is made possible by the conditions of the sleeping state. It is the dream-work which produces this form, and it alone is the essence of dreaming - the only explanation of its singularity. I say this in order to correct the reader's judgment of the notorious prospective tendency of dreams. That the dream should concern itself with efforts to perform the tasks with which our psychic life is confronted is no more remarkable than that our conscious waking life should so concern itself, and I will only add that this work may be done also in the preconscious, a fact already familiar to us.

all psychic values; thoughts must be exclusively or predominantly reproduced in the material of visual and acoustic memory-traces, and from this requirement there proceeds the regard of the dream-work for representability, which it satisfies by fresh displacements. Greater intensities have (probably) to be produced than are at the disposal of the night dream-thoughts, and this purpose is served by the extensive condensation to which the constituents of the dream-thoughts are subjected. Little attention is paid to the logical relations of the thought-material; they ultimately find a veiled representation in the formal peculiarities of the dream. The affects of the dream-thoughts undergo slighter alterations than their conceptual content. As a rule, they are suppressed; where they are preserved, they are freed from the concepts and combined in accordance with their similarity. Only one part of the dream-work - the revision, variable in amount, which is effected by the partially wakened conscious thought - is at all consistent with the conception which the writers on the subject have endeavoured to extend to the whole performance of dream-formation.

Chapter 7
The Psychology Of The Dream Processes

Among the dreams which have been communicated to me by others, there is one which is at this point especially worthy of our attention. It was told me by a female patient who had heard it related in a lecture on dreams. Its original source is unknown to me. This dream evidently made a deep impression upon the lady, since she went so far as to imitate it, i.e., to repeat the elements of this dream in a dream of her own; in order, by this transference, to express her agreement with a certain point in the dream.

The preliminary conditions of this typical dream were as follows: A father had been watching day and night beside the sick-bed of his child. After the child died, he retired to rest in an adjoining room, but left the door ajar so that he could look from his room into the next, where the child's body lay surrounded by tall candles. An old man, who had been installed as a watcher, sat beside the body, murmuring prayers. After sleeping for a few hours the father dreamed that the child was standing by his bed, clasping his arm and crying reproachfully: "7father, don't you see that I am burning?" The father woke up and noticed a bright light coming from the adjoining room. Rushing in, he found that the old man had fallen asleep, and the sheets and one arm of the beloved body were burnt by a fallen candle.

The meaning of this affecting dream is simple enough, and the explanation given by the lecturer, as my patient reported it, was correct. The bright light shining through the open door on to the sleeper's eyes gave him the impression which he would have received had he been awake: namely, that a fire had been started near the corpse by a falling candle. It is quite possible that he had taken into his sleep his anxiety lest the aged watcher should not be equal to his task.

We can find nothing to change in this interpretation; we can only add that the content of the dream must be overdetermined, and that the speech of the child must have consisted of phrases which it had uttered while still alive, and which were associated with important events for the father.

Perhaps the complaint, "I am burning," was associated with the fever from which the child died, and "7father, don't you see?" to some other affective occurrence unknown to us.

Now, when we have come to recognize that the dream has meaning, and can be fitted into the context of psychic events, it may be surprising that a dream should have occurred in circumstances which called for such an immediate waking. We shall then note that even this dream is not lacking in a wish-fulfilment. The dead child behaves as though alive; he warns his father himself; he comes to his father's bed and clasps his arm, as he probably did in the recollection from which the dream obtained the first part of the child's speech. It was for the sake of this wish-fulfilment that the father slept a moment longer. The dream was given precedence over waking reflection because it was able to show the child still living. If the father had waked first, and had then drawn the conclusion which led him into the adjoining room, he would have shortened the child's life by this one moment.

There can be no doubt about the peculiar features in this brief dream which engage our particular interest. So far, we have endeavoured mainly to ascertain wherein the secret meaning of the dream consists, how it is to be discovered, and what means the dream-work uses to conceal it. In other words, our greatest interest has hitherto been centered on the problems of interpretation. Now, however, we encounter a dream which is easily explained, and the meaning of which is without disguise; we note that nevertheless this dream preserves the essential characteristics which conspicuously differentiate a dream from our waking thoughts, and this difference demands an explanation. It is only when we have disposed of all the problems of interpretation that we feel how incomplete is our psychology of dreams.

But before we turn our attention to this new path of investigation, let us stop and look back, and consider whether we have not overlooked something important on our way hither. For we must understand that the easy and comfortable part of our journey lies behind us. Hitherto, all the paths that we have followed have led, if I mistake not, to light, to explanation, and to full understanding; but from the moment when we seek to penetrate more deeply into the psychic processes in dreaming, all paths lead into darkness. It is quite impossible to explain the dream as a psychic process, for to explain means to trace back to the known, and as yet we have no psychological knowledge to which we can refer such explanatory fundamentals as may be inferred from the psychological investigation of dreams. On the contrary, we shall be compelled to advance a number of new assumptions, which do little more than conjecture the structure of the psychic apparatus and the play of the energies active in it; and we shall have to be careful not to go too far beyond the simplest logical construction, since otherwise its value will be doubtful. And even if we should be unerring in our inferences, and take cognizance of all the logical possibilities, we should still be in danger of arriving at a completely mistaken result, owing to the probable incompleteness of the preliminary statement of our elementary data. We shall not be able to arrive at any conclusions as to the structure and function of the psychic instrument from even the most careful investigation of dreams, or of any other isolated activity; or, at all events, we shall not be able to confirm our conclusions. To do this we shall have to collate such phenomena as the comparative study of a whole series of psychic activities proves to be reliably constant. So that the psychological assumptions which we base on the analysis of the dream-processes will have to mark time, as it were, until they can join up with the results of other investigations which, proceeding from another starting-point, will seek to penetrate to the heart of the same problem.

A. The Forgetting of Dreams

I propose, then, that we shall first of all turn our attention to a subject which brings us to a hitherto disregarded objection, which threatens to undermine the very foundation of our efforts at dream-interpretation. The objection has been made from more than one quarter that the dream which we wish to interpret is really unknown to us, or, to be more precise, that we have no guarantee that we know it as it really occurred. What we recollect of the dream, and what we subject to our methods of interpretation, is, in the first place, mutilated by the unfaithfulness of our memory, which seems quite peculiarly incapable of retaining dreams, and which may have omitted precisely the most significant parts of their content. For when we try to consider our dreams attentively, we often have reason to complain that we have dreamed much than we remember; that unfortunately we know nothing more than this one fragment, and that our recollection of even this fragment seems to us strangely uncertain.

Moreover, everything goes to prove that our memory reproduces the dream not only incompletely but also untruthfully, in a falsifying manner. As, on the one hand, we may doubt whether what we dreamed was really as disconnected as it is in our recollections, so on the other hand we may doubt whether a dream was really as coherent as our account of it; whether in our attempted reproduction we have not filled in the gaps which really existed, or those which are due to forgetfulness, with new and arbitrarily chosen material; whether we have not embellished the dream, rounded it off and corrected it, so that any conclusion as to its real content becomes impossible. Indeed, one writer (Spitta)[1] surmises that all that is orderly and coherent is really first put into the dream during the attempt to recall it. Thus we are in danger of being deprived of the very object whose value we have undertaken to determine.

---

[1] Similar views are expressed by Foucault and Tannery.

In all our dream-interpretations we have hitherto ignored these warnings. On the contrary, indeed, we have found that the smallest, most insignificant, and most uncertain components of the dream-content invited interpretations no less emphatically than those which were distinctly and certainly contained in the dream. In the dream of Irma's injection we read: "I quickly called in Dr. M," and we assumed that even this small addendum would not have got into the dream if it had not been susceptible of a special derivation. In this way we arrived at the history of that unfortunate patient to whose bedside I quickly called my older colleague. In the seemingly absurd dream which treated the difference between fifty-one and fifty-six as a quantity negligible the number fifty-one was mentioned repeatedly. Instead of regarding this as a matter of course, or a detail of indifferent value, we proceeded from this to a second train of thought in the latent dream-content, which led to the number fifty-one, and by following up this clue we arrived at the fears which proposed fifty-one years as the term of life in the sharpest opposition to a dominant train of thought which was boastfully lavish of the years. In the dream Non vixit I found, as an insignificant interpolation, that I had at first overlooked the sentence: As P does not understand him, Fl asks me, etc. The interpretation then coming to a standstill, I went back to these words, and I found through them the way to the infantile phantasy which appeared in the dream-thoughts as an intermediate point of junction. This came about by means of the poet's verses:

Selten habt ihr mich verstanden,
Selten auch verstand ich Euch,
Nur wenn wir im Kot uns fanden
So verstanden wir uns gleich![2]

Every analysis will afford evidence of the fact that the most insignificant features of the dream are indispensable to interpretation, and will show how the completion of the task is delayed if we postpone our examination of them. We have given

---

[2] Seldom have you understood me, Seldom have I understood you, But when we found ourselves in the mire, We at once understood each other!

equal attention, in the interpretation of dreams, to every nuance of verbal expression found in them; indeed, whenever we are confronted by a senseless or insufficient wording, as though we had failed to translate the dream into the proper version, we have respected even these defects of expression. In brief, what other writers have regarded as arbitrary improvisations, concocted hastily to avoid confusion, we have treated like a sacred text. This contradiction calls for explanation.

It would appear, without doing any injustice to the writers in question, that the explanation is in our favour. From the standpoint of our newlyacquired insight into the origin of dreams, all contradictions are completely reconciled. It is true that we distort the dream in our attempt to reproduce it; we once more find therein what we have called the secondary and often misunderstanding elaboration of the dream by the agency of normal thinking. But this distortion is itself no more than a part of the elaboration to which the dream-thoughts are constantly subjected as a result of the dream-censorship. Other writers have here suspected or observed that part of the dream-distortion whose work is manifest; but for us this is of little consequence, as we know that a far more extensive work of distortion, not so easily apprehended, has already taken the dream for its object from among the hidden dream-thoughts. The only mistake of these writers consists in believing the modification effected in the dream by its recollection and verbal expression to be arbitrary, incapable of further solution, and consequently liable to lead us astray in our cognition of the dream. They underestimate the determination of the dream in the psyche. Here there is nothing arbitrary. It can be shown that in all cases a second train of thought immediately takes over the determination of the elements which have been left undetermined by the first. For example, I wish quite arbitrarily to think of a number; but this is not possible; the number that occurs to me is definitely and necessarily determined by thoughts within me which may be quite foreign to my momentary purpose.[3] The modifications which the dream

---
[3] Cf. The Psycho-pathology of Everday Life.

undergoes in its revision by the waking mind are just as little arbitrary. They preserve an associative connection with the content, whose place they take, and serve to show us the way to this content, which may itself be a substitute for yet another content.

In analysing the dreams of patients I impose the following test of this assertion, and never without success. If the first report of a dream seems not very comprehensible, I request the dreamer to repeat it. This he rarely does in the same words. But the passages in which the expression is modified are thereby made known to me as the weak points of the dream's disguise; they are what the embroidered emblem on Siegfried's raiment was to Hagen. These are the points from which the analysis may start. The narrator has been admonished by my announcement that I intend to take special pains to solve the dream, and immediately, obedient to the urge of resistance, he protects the weak points of the dream's disguise, replacing a treacherous expression by a less relevant one. He thus calls my attention to the expressions which he has discarded. From the efforts made to guard against the solution of the dream, I can also draw conclusions about the care with which the raiment of the dream has been woven. The writers whom I have mentioned are, however, less justified when they attribute so much importance to the doubt with which our judgment approaches the relation of the dream. For this doubt is not intellectually warranted; our memory can give no guarantees, but nevertheless we are compelled to credit its statements far more frequently than is objectively justifiable. Doubt concerning the accurate reproduction of the dream, or of individual data of the dream, is only another offshoot of the dream-censorship, that is, of resistance to the emergence of the dream-thoughts into consciousness. This resistance has not yet exhausted itself by the displacements and substitutions which it has effected, so that it still clings, in the form of doubt, to what has been allowed to emerge. We can recognize this doubt all the more readily in that it is careful never to attack the intensive elements of the dream, but only the weak and indistinct ones. But we already know that a transvaluation of all the psychic values has taken place between the dream-thoughts and the dream. The distortion has been made possible only by devaluation; it constantly manifests itself in this way and sometimes contents itself therewith. If doubt is added to the indistinctness of an element of the dream-content, we may, following this indication, recognize in this element a direct offshoot of one of the outlawed dream-thoughts. The state of affairs is like that obtaining after a great revolution in one of the republics of antiquity or the Renaissance. The once powerful, ruling families of the nobility are now banished; all high posts are filled by upstarts; in the city itself only the poorer and most powerless citizens, or the remoter followers of the vanquished party, are tolerated. Even the latter do not enjoy the full rights of citizenship. They are watched with suspicion. In our case, instead of suspicion we have doubt. I must insist, therefore, that in the analysis of a dream one must emancipate oneself from the whole scale of standards of reliability; and if there is the slightest possibility that this or that may have occurred in the dream, it should be treated as an absolute certainty. Until one has decided to reject all respect for appearances in tracing the dream-elements, the analysis will remain at a standstill. Disregard of the element concerned has the psychic effect, in the person analysed, that nothing in connection with the unwished ideas behind this element will occur to him. This effect is really not self-evident; it would be quite reasonable to say, "Whether this or that was contained in the dream I do not know for certain; but the following ideas happen to occur to me." But no one ever does say so; it is precisely the disturbing effect of doubt in the analysis that permits it to be unmasked as an offshoot and instrument of the psychic resistance. Psycho-analysis is justifiably suspicions. One of its rules runs: Whatever disturbs the progress of the work is a resistance. [4]

---

[4] This peremptory statement: "Whatever disturbs the progress of the work is a resistance" might easily be misunderstood. It has, of course, the significance merely of a technical rule, a warning for the analyst. It is not denied that during an analysis events may occur which cannot be ascribed to the intention of the person analysed. The patient's father may die in other ways than by being murdered by the patient, or a war may break out and interrupt the analysis. But despite the obvious exaggeration of the above statement there is still something new and useful in it. Even if the disturbing event is real and independent of the patient, the extent of the disturbing influence does often depend only on him, and the resistance reveals itself unmistakably in the ready and immoderate exploitation of such an opportunity.

The forgetting of dreams, too, remains inexplicible until we seek to explain it by the power of the psychic censorship. The feeling that one has dreamed a great deal during the night and has retained only a little of it may have yet another meaning in a number of cases: it may perhaps mean that the dream-work has continued in a perceptible manner throughout the night, but has left behind it only one brief dream. There is, however, no possible doubt that a dream is progressively forgotten on waking. One often forgets it in spite of a painful effort to recover it. I believe, however, that just as one generally overestimates the extent of this forgetting, so also one overestimates the lacunae in our knowledge of the dream due to the gaps occurring in it. All the dream-content that has been lost by forgetting can often be recovered by analysis; in a number of cases, at all events, it is possible to discover from a single remaining fragment, not the dream, of course - which, after all, is of no importance - but the whole of the dream-thoughts. It requires a greater expenditure of attention and self-suppression in the analysis; that is all; but it shows that the forgetting of the dream is not innocent of hostile intention.[5]

A convincing proof of the tendencious nature of dream-forgetting - of the fact that it serves the resistance - is obtained on analysis by investigating a preliminary stage of forgetting.[6] It often happens that, in the midst of an interpretation, an omitted fragment of the dream suddenly emerges which is described as having been previously forgotten. This part of the dream that has been wrested from forgetfulness is always the most important part. It lies on the shortest path to the solution of the dream, and for that every reason it was most exposed to the resistance. Among the examples of dreams that I have included in the text of this treatise, it once happened that I had subsequently to interpolate a

---

[5] As an example of the significance of doubt and uncertainty in a dream with a simultaneous shrinking of the dream-content to a single element, see my General Introduction to Psycho-Analysis the dream of the sceptical lady patient, the analysis of which was successful, despite a short postponement.

[6] Concerning the intention of forgetting in general, see my The Psycho-pathology of Everyday Life.

fragment of dream-content. The dream is a dream of travel, which revenges itself on two unamiable traveling companions; I have left it almost entirely uninterpreted, as part of its content is obscene. The part omitted reads: "I said, referring to a book of Schiller's: 'It is from...' but corrected myself, as I realized my mistake: 'It is by...' Whereupon the man remarked to his sister, 'Yes, he said it correctly.'"[7]

Self-correction in dreams, which to some writers seems so wonderful, does not really call for consideration. But I will draw from my own memory an instance typical of verbal errors in dreams. I was nineteen years of age when I visited England for the first time, and I spent a day on the shore of the Irish Sea. Naturally enough, I amused myself by picking up the marine animals left on the beach by the tide, and I was just examining a starfish (the dream begins with Hollthurn - Holothurian) when a pretty little girl came up to me and asked me: "Is it a starfish? Is it alive?" I replied, "Yes, he is alive," but then felt ashamed of my mistake, and repeated the sentence correctly. For the grammatical mistake which I then made, the dream substitutes another which is quite common among German people. "Das Buch ist von Schiller" is not to be translated by "the book is from," but by "the book is by." That the dream-work accomplishes this substitution, because the word from, owing to its consonance with the German adjective fromm (pious, devout) makes a remarkable condensation possible, should no longer surprise us after all that we have heard of the intentions of the dream-work and its unscrupulous selection of means. But what relation has this harmless recollection of the seashore to my dream? It explains, by means of a very innocent example, that I have used the word - the word denoting gender, or sex or the sexual (he) - in the wrong place. This is surely one of the keys to the solution of the dream. Those who have heard of the derivation of the booktitle

---

[7] Such corrections in the use of foreign languages are not rare in dreams, but they are usually attributed to foreigners. Maury (p. 143), while he was studying English, once dreamed that he informed someone that he had called on him the day before in the following words: "I called for you yesterday." The other answered correctly: "You mean: I called on you yesterday."

Matter and Motion (Moliere in Le Malade Imaginaire: La Matiere est-elle laudable? - A Motion of the bowels) will readily be able to supply the missing parts.

Moreover, I can prove conclusively, by a demonstratio ad oculos, that the forgetting of the dream is in a large measure the work of the resistance.

A patient tells me that he has dreamed, but that the dream has vanished without leaving a trace, as if nothing had happened. We set to work, however; I come upon a resistance which I explain to the patient; encouraging and urging him, I help him to become reconciled to some disagreeable thought; and I have hardly succeeded in doing so when he exclaims: "Now I can recall what I dreamed!" The same resistance which that day disturbed him in the work of interpretation caused him also to forget the dream. By overcoming this resistance I have brought back the dream to his memory.

In the same way the patient, having reached a certain part of the work, may recall a dream which occurred three, four, or more days ago, and which has hitherto remained in oblivion.[8]

Psycho-analytical experience has furnished us with yet another proof of the fact that the forgetting of dreams depends far more on the resistance than on the mutually alien character of the waking and sleeping states, as some writers have believed it to depend. It often happens to me, as well as to other analysts, and to patients under treatment, that we are waked from sleep by a dream, as we say, and that immediately thereafter, while in full possession of our mental faculties, we begin to interpret the dream. Often in such cases I have not rested until I have achieved a full understanding of the dream, and yet it has happened that after waking I have forgotten the interpretation - work as completely as I have forgotten the dream-content itself, though I have been aware that I have dreamed and that I had interpreted the dream. The dream has far more frequently taken the result of the

---

[8] Ernest Jones describes an analogous case of frequent occurrence; during the analysis of one dream another dream of the same night is often recalled which until then was not merely forgotten, but was not even suspected.

interpretation with it into forgetfulness than the intellectual faculty has succeeded in retaining the dream in the memory.

But between this work of interpretation and the waking thoughts there is not that psychic abyss by which other writers have sought to explain the forgetting of dreams. When Morton Prince objects to my explanation of the forgetting of dreams on the ground that it is only a special case of the amnesia of dissociated psychic states, and that the impossibility of applying my explanation of this special amnesia to other types of amnesia makes it valueless even for its immediate purpose, he reminds the reader that in all his descriptions of such dissociated states he has never attempted to discover the dynamic explanation underlying these phenomena. For had he done so, he would surely have discovered that repression (and the resistance produced thereby) is the cause not of these dissociations merely, but also of the amnesia of their psychic content.

That dreams are as little forgotten as other psychic acts, that even in their power of impressing themselves on the memory they may fairly be compared with the other psychic performances, was proved to me by an experiment which I was able to make while preparing the manuscript of this book. I had preserved in my notes a great many dreams of my own which, for one reason or another, I could not interpret, or, at the time of dreaming them, could interpret only very imperfectly. In order to obtain material to illustrate my assertion, I attempted to interpret some of them a year or two later. In this attempt I was invariably successful; indeed, I may say that the interpretation was effected more easily after all this time than when the dreams were of recent occurrence. As a possible explanation of this fact, I would suggest that I had overcome many of the internal resistances which had disturbed me at the time of dreaming. In such subsequent interpretations I have compared the old yield of dream-thoughts with the present result, which has usually been more abundant, and I have invariably found the old dream-thoughts unaltered among the present ones. However, I soon recovered from my surprise when I reflected that I had long been accustomed to interpret dreams of former years that had occasionally been related to me by my patients as though they had been dreams of the night before; by the same method, and with the same success. In the section on anxiety-dreams I shall include two examples of such delayed dream-interpretations. When I made this experiment for the first time I expected, not unreasonably, that dreams would behave in this connection merely like neurotic symptoms. For when I treat a psychoneurotic for instance, an hysterical patient, by psychoanalysis, I am compelled to find explanations for the first symptoms of the malady, which have long since disappeared, as well as for those still existing symptoms which have brought the patient to me; and I find the former problem easier to solve than the more exigent one of today. In the Studies in Hysteria,[9] published as early as 1895, I was able to give the explanation of a first hysterical attack which the patient, a woman over forty years of age, had experienced in her fifteenth year.[10]

I will now make a few rather unsystematic remarks relating to the interpretations of dreams, which will perhaps serve as a guide to the reader who wishes to test my assertions by the analysis of his own dreams.

He must not expect that it will be a simple and easy matter to interpret his own dreams. Even the observation of endoptic phenomena, and other sensations which are commonly immune from attention, calls for practice, although this group of observations is not opposed by any psychic motive. It is very much more difficult to get hold of the unwished ideas. He who seeks to do so must fulfil the requirements laid down in this treatise, and while following the rules here given, he must endeavour to restrain all criticism, all preconceptions, and all affective or intellectual bias in himself during the work of analysis.

---

[9] Studien uber Hysterie, Case II.
[10] Dreams which have occurred during the first years of childhood, and which have sometimes been retained in the memory for decades with perfect sensorial freshness, are almost always of great importance for the understanding of the development and the neurosis of the dreamer. The analysis of them protects the physician from errors and uncertainties which might confuse him even theoretically.

He must be ever mindful of the precept which Claude Bernard held up to the experimenter in the physiological laboratory: "Travailler comme une bete" - that is, he must be as enduring as an animal, and also as disinterested in the results of his work. He who will follow this advice will no longer find the task a difficult one. The interpretation of a dream cannot always be accomplished in one session; after following up a chain of associations you will often feel that your working capacity is exhausted; the dream will not tell you anything more that day; it is then best to break off, and to resume the work the following day. Another portion of the dream-content then solicits your attention, and you thus obtain access to a fresh stratum of the dream-thoughts. One might call this the fractional interpretation of dreams.

It is most difficult to induce the beginner in dream-interpretation to recognize the fact that his task is not finished when he is in possession of a complete interpretation of the dream which is both ingenious and coherent, and which gives particulars of all the elements of the dream-content.

Besides this, another interpretation, an over-interpretation of the same dream, one which has escaped him, may be possible. It is really not easy to form an idea of the wealth of trains of unconscious thought striving for expression in our minds, or to credit the adroitness displayed by the dreamwork in killing - so to speak - seven flies at one stroke, like the journeyman tailor in the fairy-tale, by means of its ambiguous modes of expression. The reader will constantly be inclined to reproach the author for a superfluous display of ingenuity, but anyone who has had personal experience of dream-interpretation will know better than to do so.

On the other hand, I cannot accept the opinion, first expressed by H. Silberer, that every dream - or even that many dreams, and certain groups of dreams - calls for two different interpretations, between which there is even supposed to be a fixed relation. One of these, which Silberer calls the psycho-analytic interpretation, attributes to the dream any meaning you please, but in the main an infantile sexual one. The other, the more important interpretation, which he calls the anagogic interpretation, reveals the more serious and often profound thoughts which the dream-work has used as its material. Silberer does not prove this assertion by citing a number of dreams which he has analysed in these two directions. I am obliged to object to this opinion on the ground that it is contrary to facts. The majority of dreams require no over-interpretation, and are especially insusceptible of an anagogic interpretation. The influence of a tendency which seeks to veil the fundamental conditions of dream-formation and divert our interest from its instinctual roots is as evident in Silberer's theory as in other theoretical efforts of the last few years. In a number of cases I can confirm Silberer's assertions; but in these the analysis shows me that the dream-work was confronted with the task of transforming a series of highly abstract thoughts, incapable of direct representation, from waking life into a dream. The dream-work attempted to accomplish this task by seizing upon another thought-material which stood in loose and often allegorical relation to the abstract thoughts, and thereby diminished the difficulty of representing them. The abstract interpretation of a dream originating in this manner will be given by the dreamer immediately, but the correct interpretation of the substituted material can be obtained only by means of the familiar technique.

The question whether every dream can be interpreted is to be answered in the negative. One should not forget that in the work of interpretation one is opposed by the psychic forces that are responsible for the distortion of the dream. Whether one can master the inner resistances by one's intellectual interest, one's capacity for self-control, one's psychological knowledge, and one's experience in dream-interpretation depends on the relative strength of the opposing forces. It is always possible to make some progress; one can at all events go far enough to become convinced that a dream has meaning, and generally far enough to gain some idea of its meaning. It very often happens that a second dream enables us to confirm and continue the interpretation assumed for the first. A whole series of dreams, continuing for weeks or months, may have a common basis, and should therefore be interpreted as a continuity. In dreams that follow one another, we often observe that one dream takes as its central point something that is only alluded to in the periphery of the next dream, and conversely, so that even in their interpretations the two supplement each other. That different dreams of the same night are always to be treated, in the work of interpretation, as a whole, I have already shown by examples.

In the best interpreted dreams we often have to leave one passage in obscurity because we observe during the interpretation that we have here a tangle of dream-thoughts which cannot be unravelled, and which furnishes no fresh contribution to the dream-content. This, then, is the keystone of the dream, the point at which it ascends into the unknown. For the dream-thoughts which we encounter during the interpretation commonly have no termination, but run in all directions into the net-like entanglement of our intellectual world. It is from some denser part of this fabric that the dream-wish then arises, like the mushroom from its mycelium.

Let us now return to the facts of dream-forgetting. So far, of course, we have failed to draw any important conclusion from them. When our waking life shows an unmistakable intention to forget the dream which has been formed during the night, either as a whole, immediately after waking, or little by little in the course of the day, and when we recognize as the chief factor in this process of forgetting the psychic resistance against the dream which has already done its best to oppose the dream at night, the question then arises: What actually has made the dreamformation possible against this resistance? Let us consider the most striking case, in which the waking life has thrust the dream aside as though it had never happened. If we take into consideration the play of the psychic forces, we are compelled to assert that the dream would never have come into existence had the resistance prevailed at night as it did by day. We conclude, then, that the resistance loses some part of its force during the night; we know that it has not been discontinued, as we have demonstrated its share in the formation of dreams - namely, the work of distortion. We have therefore to consider the possibility that at night the resistance is merely diminished, and that dream-formation becomes possible because of this slackening of the resistance; and we shall readily understand that as it regains its full power on waking it immediately thrusts aside what it was forced to admit while it was feeble. Descriptive psychology teaches us that the chief determinant of dream-formation is the dormant state of the psyche; and we may now add the following explanation: The state of sleep makes dream-formation possible by reducing the endopsychic censorship.

We are certainly tempted to look upon this as the only possible conclusion to be drawn from the facts of dream-forgetting, and to develop from this conclusion further deductions as to the comparative energy operative in the sleeping and waking states. But we shall stop here for the present. When we have penetrated a little farther into the psychology of dreams we shall find that the origin of dream-formation may be differently conceived. The resistance which tends to prevent the dream-thoughts from becoming conscious may perhaps be evaded without suffering reduction. It is also plausible that both the factors which favour dream-formation, the reduction as well as the evasion of the resistance, may be simultaneously made possible by the sleeping state. But we shall pause here, and resume the subject a little later.

We must now consider another series of objections against our procedure in dream-interpretation. For we proceed by dropping all the directing ideas which at other times control reflection, directing our attention to a single element of the dream, noting the involuntary thoughts that associate themselves with this element. We then take up the next component of the dream-content, and repeat the operation with this; and, regardless of the direction taken by the thoughts, we allow ourselves to be led onwards by them, rambling from one subject to another. At the same time, we harbour the confident hope that we may in the end, and without intervention on our part, come upon the dream-thoughts from which the dream originated. To this the critic may make the following objection:

That we arrive somewhere if we start from a single element of the dream is not remarkable. Something can be associatively connected with every idea. The only thing that is remarkable is that one should succeed in hitting upon the dream-thoughts in this arbitrary and aimless excursion. It is probably a self-deception; the investigator follows the chain of associations from the one element which is taken up until he finds the chain breaking off, whereupon he takes up a second element; it is thus only natural that the originally unconfined associations should now become narrowed down. He has the former chain of associations still in mind, and will therefore in the analysis of the second dream-idea hit all the more readily upon single associations which have something in common with the associations of the first chain. He then imagines that he has found a thought which represents a point of junction between two of the dream-elements. As he allows himself all possible freedom of thought-connection, excepting only the transitions from one idea to another which occur in normal thinking, it is not difficult for him finally to concoct out of a series of intermediary thoughts, something which he calls the dream-thoughts; and without any guarantee, since they are otherwise unknown, he palms these off as the psychic equivalent of the dream. But all this is a purely arbitrary procedure, an ingenious-looking exploitation of chance, and anyone who will go to this useless trouble can in this way work out any desired interpretation for any dream whatever.

If such objections are really advanced against us, we may in defence refer to the impression produced by our dream-interpretations, the surprising connections with other dream-elements which appear while we are following up the individual ideas, and the improbability that anything which so perfectly covers and explains the dream as do our dream-interpretations could be achieved otherwise than by following previously established psychic connections. We might also point to the fact that the procedure in dream-interpretation is identical with the procedure followed in the resolution of hysterical symptoms, where the correctness of the method is attested by the emergence and disappearance of the symptoms - that is, where the interpretation of the text is confirmed by the interpolated illustrations. But we have no reason to avoid this problem - namely, how one can arrive at a pre-existent aim by following an arbitrarily and aimlessly maundering chain of thoughts - since we shall be able not to solve the problem, it is true, but to get rid of it entirely.

For it is demonstrably incorrect to state that we abandon ourselves to an aimless excursion of thought when, as in the interpretation of dreams, we renounce reflection and allow the involuntary ideas to come to the surface. It can be shown that we are able to reject only those directing ideas which are known to us, and that with the cessation of these the unknown - or, as we inexactly say, unconscious - directing ideas immediately exert their influence, and henceforth determine the flow of the involuntary ideas. Thinking without directing ideas cannot be ensured by any influence we ourselves exert on our own psychic life; neither do I know of any state of psychic derangement in which such a mode of thought establishes itself.[11] The psychiatrists have here

---

[11] Only recently has my attention been called to the fact that Ed. von Hartmann took the same view with regard to this psychologically important point: Incidental to the discussion of the role of the unconscious in artistic creation (Philos. d. Unbew., Vol. i, Sect. B., Chap. V) Eduard von Hartmann clearly enunciated the law of association of ideas which is directed by unconscious directing ideas, without however realizing the scope of this law. With him it was a question of demonstrating that "every combination of a sensuous idea when it is not left entirely to chance, but is directed to a definite end, is in need of help from the unconscious," and that the conscious interest in any particular thoughtassociation is a stimulus for the unconscious to discover from among the numberless possible ideas the one which corresponds to the directing idea. "It is the unconscious that selects, and appropriately, in accordance with the aims of the interest: and this holds true for the associations in abstract thinking (as sensible representations and artistic combinations as well as for flashes of wit)." Hence, a limiting of the association of ideas to ideas that evoke and are evoked in the sense of pure association-psychology is untenable. Such a restriction "would be justified only if there were states in human life in which man was free not only from any conscious purpose, but also from the domination or cooperation of any unconscious interest, any passing mood. But such a state hardly ever comes to pass, for even if one leaves one's train of thought seemingly altogether to chance, or if one surrenders oneself entirely to the involuntary dreams of phantasy, yet always other leading interests, dominant feelings and moods prevail at one time rather than another, and these will always exert an influence on the association of ideas.". In semi-conscious dreams there always appear only such ideas as correspond to the (unconscious) momentary main interest. By rendering prominent the feelings and moods over the free thought-series, the methodical procedure of psycho-analysis is thoroughly justified even from the standpoint of Hartmann's Psychology. Du Prel concludes from the fact that a name which we vainly try to recall suddenly occurs to the mind that there is an unconscious but none the less purposeful thinking, whose result then appears in consciousness.

far too prematurely relinquished the idea of the solidity of the psychic structure. I know that an unregulated stream of thoughts, devoid of directing ideas, can occur as little in the realm of hysteria and paranoia as in the formation or solution of dreams.

Perhaps it does not occur at all in the endogenous psychic affections, and, according to the ingenious hypothesis of Lauret, even the deliria observed in confused psychic states have meaning and are incomprehensible to us only because of omissions. I have had the same conviction whenever I have had an opportunity of observing such states. The deliria are the work of a censorship which no longer makes any effort to conceal its sway, which, instead of lending its support to a revision that is no longer obnoxious to it, cancels regardlessly anything to which it objects, thus causing the remnant to appear disconnected. This censorship proceeds like the Russian censorship on the frontier, which allows only those foreign journals which have had certain passages blacked out to fall into the bands of the readers to be protected.

The free play of ideas following any chain of associations may perhaps occur in cases of destructive organic affections of the brain. What, however, is taken to be such in the psychoneuroses may always be explained as the influence of the censorship on a series of thoughts which have been pushed into the foreground by the concealed directing ideas.[12] It has been considered an unmistakable sign of free association unencumbered by directing ideas if the emerging ideas (or images) appear to be connected by means of the so-called superficial associations - that is, by assonance, verbal ambiguity, and temporal coincidence, without inner relationship of meaning; in other words, if they are connected by all those associations which we allow ourselves to exploit in wit and playing upon words. This distinguishing mark holds good with associations which lead us from the elements of the dream-content to the intermediary thoughts, and from these to the dream-thoughts proper; in many analyses of dreams we have

---

[12] Jung has brilliantly corroborated this statement by analyses of dementia praecox. (Cf. The Psychology of Dementia Praecox, translated by A. A. Brill. Monograph Series, [Journal of Nervous and Mental Diseases Publishing Co., New York].)

found surprising examples of this. In these no connection was too loose and no witticism too objectionable to serve as a bridge from one thought to another. But the correct understanding of such surprising tolerance is not far to seek. Whenever one psychic element is connected with another by an obnoxious and superficial association, there exists also a correct and more profound connection between the two, which succumbs to the resistance of the censorship.

The correct explanation for the predominance of the superficial associations is the pressure of the censorship, and not the suppression of the directing ideas. Whenever the censorship renders the normal connective paths impassable, the superficial associations will replace the deeper ones in the representation. It is as though in a mountainous region a general interruption of traffic, for example an inundation, should render the broad highways impassable: traffic would then have to be maintained by steep and inconvenient tracks used at other times only by the hunter.

We can here distinguish two cases which, however, are essentially one. In the first case, the censorship is directed only against the connection of two thoughts which, being detached from one another, escape its opposition. The two thoughts then enter successively into consciousness; their connection remains concealed; but in its place there occurs to us a superficial connection between the two which would not otherwise have occurred to us, and which as a rule connects with another angle of the conceptual complex instead of that from which the suppressed but essential connection proceeds. Or, in the second case, both thoughts, owing to their content, succumb to the censorship; both then appear not in their correct form but in a modified, substituted form; and both substituted thoughts are so selected as to represent, by a superficial association, the essential relation which existed between those that they have replaced. Under the pressure of the censorship, the displacement of a normal and vital association by one superficial and apparently absurd has thus occurred in both cases.

Because we know of these displacements, we unhesitatingly rely upon even the superficial associations which occur in the course of dreaminterpretation.[13]

The psycho-analysis of neurotics makes abundant use of the two principles: that with the abandonment of the conscious directing ideas the control over the flow of ideas is transferred to the concealed directing ideas; and that superficial associations are only a displacement-substitute for suppressed and more profound ones. Indeed, psycho-analysis makes these two principles the foundation-stones of its technique. When I request a patient to dismiss all reflection, and to report to me whatever comes into his mind, I firmly cling to the assumption that he will not be able to drop the directing idea of the treatment, and I feel justified in concluding that what he reports, even though it may seem to be quite ingenuous and arbitrary, has some connection with his morbid state. Another directing idea of which the patient has no suspicion is my own personality. The full appreciation, as well as the detailed proof of both these explanations, belongs to the description of the psycho-analytic technique as a therapeutic method. We have here reached one of the junctions, so to speak, at which we purposely drop the subject of dreaminterpretation.[14]

Of all the objections raised, only one is justified and still remains to be met; namely, that we ought not to ascribe all the associations of the interpretation-work to the nocturnal dream - work. By interpretation in the waking state we are actually opening a path running back from the dream-elements to the dream-thoughts. The dream-work has followed the contrary direction, and it is not at all probable that these paths are equally passable in opposite

---

[13] The same considerations naturally hold good of the case in which superficial associations are exposed in the dream-content, as, for example, in both the dreams reported by Maury. I know from my work with neurotics what kind of reminiscence is prone to represent itself in this manner. It is the consultation of encyclopedias by which most people have satisfied their need of an explanation of the sexual mystery when obsessed by the curiosity of puberty.

[14] The above statements, which when written sounded very improbable, have since been corroborated and applied experimentally by Jung and his pupils in the Diagnostiche Assoziationsstudien.

directions. On the contrary, it appears that during the day, by means of new thought-connections, we sink shafts that strike the intermediary thoughts and the dream-thoughts now in this place, now in that. We can see how the recent thought-material of the day forces its way into the interpretation-series, and how the additional resistance which has appeared since the night probably compels it to make new and further detours. But the number and form of the collaterals which we thus contrive during the day are, psychologically speaking, indifferent, so long as they point the way to the dream-thoughts which we are seeking.

B. Regression

Now that we have defended ourselves against the objections raised, or have at least indicated our weapons of defence, we must no longer delay entering upon the psychological investigations for which we have so long been preparing. Let us summarize the main results of our recent investigations: The dream is a psychic act full of import; its motive power is invariably a wish craving fulfilment; the fact that it is unrecognizable as a wish, and its many peculiarities and absurdities, are due to the influence of the psychic censorship to which it has been subjected during its formation. Besides the necessity of evading the censorship, the following factors have played a part in its formation: first, a need for condensing the psychic material; second, regard for representability in sensory images; and third (though not constantly), regard for a rational and intelligible exterior of the dream-structure. From each of these propositions a path leads onward to psychological postulates and assumptions. Thus, the reciprocal relation of the wish-motives, and the four conditions, as well as the mutual relations of these conditions, must now be investigated; the dream must be inserted in the context of the psychic life.

At the beginning of this section we cited a certain dream in order that it might remind us of the problems that are still unsolved. The interpretation of this dream (of the burning child) presented no difficulties, although in the analytical sense it was not given in full. We asked ourselves why, after all, it was necessary that the father should dream instead of waking, and we recognized the wish to represent the child as living as a motive of the dream. That there was yet another wish operative in the dream we shall be able to show after further discussion. For the present, however, we may say that for the sake of the wish-fulfilment the thought-process of sleep was transformed into a dream.

If the wish-fulfilment is cancelled out, only one characteristic remains which distinguishes the two kinds of psychic events. The dream-thought would have been: "I see a glimmer coming from the room in which the body is lying. Perhaps a candle has fallen over, and the child is burning!"

The dream reproduces the result of this reflection unchanged, but represents it in a situation which exists in the present and is perceptible by the senses like an experience of the waking state. This, however, is the most common and the most striking psychological characteristic of the dream; a thought, usually the one wished for, is objectified in the dream, and represented as a scene, or - as we think - experienced.

But how are we now to explain this characteristic peculiarity of the dream-work, or - to put it more modestly - how are we to bring it into relation with the psychic processes?

On closer examination, it is plainly evident that the manifest form of the dream is marked by two characteristics which are almost independent of each other. One is its representation as a present situation with the omission of perhaps; the other is the translation of the thought into visual images and speech.

The transformation to which the dream-thoughts are subjected because the expectation is put into the present tense is, perhaps, in this particular dream not so very striking. This is probably due to the special and really subsidiary role of the wish-fulfilment in this dream. Let us take another dream, in which the dream-wish does not break away from the continuation of the waking thoughts in sleep; for example, the dream of Irma's injection. Here the dream-thought achieving representation is in the conditional: "If only Otto could be blamed for Irma's illness!" The dream suppresses the conditional, and replaces it by a simple present tense: "Yes, Otto is to blame for Irma's illness." This, then, is the first of the transformations which even the undistorted dream imposes on the dream-thoughts. But we will not linger over this first peculiarity of the dream.

We dispose of it by a reference to the conscious phantasy, the day-dream, which behaves in a similar fashion with its conceptual content. When Daudet's M. Joyeuse wanders unemployed through the streets of Paris while his daughter is led to believe that he has a post and is sitting in his office, he dreams, in the present tense, of circumstances that might help him to obtain a recommendation and employment. The dream, then, employs the present tense in the same manner and with the same right as the day-dream. The present is the tense in which the wish is represented as fulfilled.

The second quality peculiar to the dream alone, as distinguished from the day-dream, is that the conceptual content is not thought, but is transformed into visual images, to which we give credence, and which we believe that we experience. Let us add. however, that not all dreams show this transformation of ideas into visual images. There are dreams which consist solely of thoughts, but we cannot on that account deny that they are substantially dreams. My dream Autodidasker - the day-phantasy about Professor N is of this character; it is almost as free of visual elements as though I had thought its content during the day. Moreover, every long dream contains elements which have not undergone this transformation into the visual, and which are simply thought or known as we are wont to think or know in our waking state. And we must here reflect that this transformation of ideas into visual images does not occur in dreams alone, but also in hallucinations and visions, which may appear spontaneously in health, or as symptoms in the psychoneuroses. In brief, the relation which we are here investigating is by no means anexclusive one; the fact remains, however, that this characteristic of the dream, whenever it occurs, seems to be its most noteworthy characteristic, so that we cannot think of the dream-life without it. To understand it, however, requires a very exhaustive discussion.

Among all the observations relating to the theory of dreams to be found in the literature of the subject, I should like to lay stress upon one as being particularly worthy of mention. The famous G. T. H. Fechner makes the conjecture,[15] in a discussion as to the nature of the dreams, that the dream is staged elsewhere than in the waking ideation. No other assumption enables us to comprehend the special peculiarities of the dreamlife.

The idea which is thus put before us is one of psychic locality. We shall wholly ignore the fact that the psychic apparatus concerned is known to us also as an anatomical preparation, and we shall carefully avoid the temptation to determine the psychic locality in any anatomical sense. We shall remain on psychological ground, and we shall do no more than accept the invitation to think of the instrument which serves the psychic activities much as we think of a compound microscope, a photographic camera, or other apparatus. The psychic locality, then, corresponds to a place within such an apparatus in which one of the preliminary phases of the image comes into existence. As is well known, there are in the microscope and the telescope such ideal localities or planes, in which no tangible portion of the apparatus is located. I think it superfluous to apologize for the imperfections of this and all similar figures. These comparisons are designed only to assist us in our attempt to make intelligible the complication of the psychic performance by dissecting it and referring the individual performances to the individual components of the apparatus. So far as I am aware, no attempt has yet been made to divine the construction of the psychic instrument by means of such dissection. I see no harm in such an attempt; I think that we should give free rein to our conjectures, provided we keep our heads and do not mistake the scaffolding for the building. Since for the first approach to any unknown subject we need the help

---

[15] Psychophysik, Part. II.

only of auxiliary ideas, we shall prefer the crudest and most tangible hypothesis to all others.

Accordingly, we conceive the psychic apparatus as a compound instrument, the component parts of which we shall call instances, or, for the sake of clearness, systems. We shall then anticipate that these systems may perhaps maintain a constant spatial orientation to one another, very much as do the different and successive systems of lenses of a telescope. Strictly speaking, there is no need to assume an actual spatial arrangement of the psychic system. It will be enough for our purpose if a definite sequence is established, so that in certain psychic events the system will be traversed by the excitation in a definite temporal order. This order may be different in the case of other processes; such a possibility is left open.

For the sake of brevity, we shall henceforth speak of the component parts of the apparatus as Psi-systems. The first thing that strikes us is the fact that the apparatus composed of Psi-systems has a direction. All our psychic activities proceed from (inner or outer) stimuli and terminate in innervations. We thus ascribe to the apparatus a sensory and a motor end; at the sensory end we find a system which receives the perceptions, ind at the motor end another which opens the sluices of motility. The psychic process generally runs from the perceptive end to the motor end. The most general scheme of the psychic apparatus has therefore the following appearance.

But this is only in compliance with the requirement, long familiar to us, that the psychic apparatus must be constructed like a reflex apparatus. The reflex act remains the type of every psychic activity as well.

We now have reason to admit a first differentiation at the sensory end. The percepts that come to us leave in our psychic apparatus a trace, which we may call a memory-trace. The function related to this memory-trace we call the memory. If we hold seriously to our resolution to connect the psychic processes into systems, the memory-trace can consist only of lasting changes in the elements of the systems. But, as has already been shown elsewhere, obvious difficulties arise when one and the same system is faithfully to preserve changes in its elements and still to remain fresh and receptive in respect of new occasions of change. In accordance with the principle which is directing our attempt, we shall therefore ascribe these two functions to two different systems. We assume that an initial system of this apparatus receives the stimuli of perception but retains nothing of them - that is, it has no memory; and that behind this there lies a second system, which transforms the momentary excitation of the first into lasting traces.

We know that of the percepts which act upon the P-system, we retain permanently something else as well as the content itself. Our percepts prove also to be connected with one another in the memory, and this is especially so if they originally occurred simultaneously. We call this the fact of association. It is now clear that, if the P-system is entirely lacking in memory, it certainly cannot preserve traces for the associations; the individual P-elements would be intolerably hindered in their functioning if a residue of a former connection should make its influence felt against a new perception. Hence we must rather assume that the memory-system is the basis of association. The fact of association, then, consists in this - that in consequence of a lessening of resistance and a smoothing of the ways from one of the mem-elements, the excitation transmits itself to a second rather than to a third mem-element.

On further investigation we find it necessary to assume not one but many such mem-systems, in which the same excitation transmitted by the P elements undergoes a diversified fixation. The first of these mem-systems will in any case contain the fixation of the association through simultaneity, while in those lying farther away the same material of excitation will be arranged according to other forms of combination; so that relationships of similarity, etc., might perhaps be represented by these later systems. It would, of course, be idle to attempt to express in words the psychic significance of such a system. Its characteristic would lie in the intimacy of its relations to elements of raw material of memory

– that is (if we wish to hint at a more comprehensive theory) in the gradations of the conductive resistance on the way to these elements. An observation of a general nature, which may possibly point to something of importance, may here be interpolated. The P-system, which possesses no capacity for preserving changes, and hence no memory, furnishes to consciousness the complexity and variety of the sensory qualities. Our memories, on the other hand, are unconscious in themselves; those that are most deeply impressed form no exception. They can be made conscious, but there is no doubt that they unfold all their activities in the unconscious state. What we term our character is based, indeed, on the memory – traces of our impressions, and it is precisely those impressions that have affected us most strongly, those of our early youth, which hardly ever become conscious. But when memories become conscious again they show no sensory quality, or a very negligible one in comparison with the perceptions. If, now, it can be confirmed that for consciousness memory and quality are mutually exclusive in the Psi-systems, we have gained a most promising insight into the determinations of the neuron excitations.[16]

What we have so far assumed concerning the composition of the psychic apparatus at the sensible end has been assumed regardless of dreams and of the psychological explanations which we have hitherto derived from them. Dreams, however, will serve as a source of evidence for our knowledge of another part of the apparatus. We have seen that it was impossible to explain dream-formation unless we ventured to assume two psychic instances, one of which subjected the activities of the other to criticism, the result of which was exclusion from consciousness.

We have concluded that the criticizing instance maintains closer relations with the consciousness than the instance criticized. It stands between the latter and the consciousness like a screen. Further, we have found that there is reason to identify the criticizing instance with that which directs our waking life and

---

[16] Since writing this, I have thought that consciousness occurs actually in the locality of the memory-trace.

determines our voluntary conscious activities. If, in accordance with our assumptions, we now replace these instances by systems, the criticizing system will therefore be moved to the motor end. We now enter both systems in our diagram, expressing, by the names given them, their relation to consciousness.

The last of the systems at the motor end we call the preconscious (Pcs.) to denote that the exciting processes in this system can reach consciousness without any further detention, provided certain other conditions are fulfilled, e.g., the attainment of a definite degree of intensity, a certain apportionment of that function which we must call attention, etc. This is at the same time the system which holds the keys of voluntary motility. The system behind it we call the unconscious (Ucs), because it has no access to consciousness except through the preconscious, in the passage through which the excitation-process must submit to certain changes.[17]

In which of these systems, then, do we localize the impetus to dream-formation? For the sake of simplicity, let us say in the system Ucs. We shall find, it is true, in subsequent discussions, that this is not altogether correct; that dream-formation is obliged to make connection with dreamthoughts which belong to the system of the preconscious. But we shall learn elsewhere, when we come to deal with the dream-wish, that the motive-power of the dream is furnished by the Ucs, and on account of this factor we shall assume the unconscious system as the starting-point for dream-formation. This dream-excitation, like all the other thought-structures, will now strive to continue itself in the Pcs, and thence to gain admission to the consciousness.

Experience teaches us that the path leading through the preconscious to consciousness is closed to the dream-thoughts during the day by the resisting censorship. At night they gain admission to consciousness; the question arises: In what way and because of what changes? If this admission were rendered possible

---

[17] The further elaboration of this linear diagram will have to reckon with the assumption that the system following the Pcs represents the one to which we must attribute consciousness (Cs), so that P = Cs.

to the dream-thoughts by the weakening, during the night, of the resistance watching on the boundary between the unconscious and the preconscious, we should then have dreams in the material of our ideas, which would not display the hallucinatory character that interests us at present.

The weakening of the censorship between the two systems, Ucs and Pcs, can explain to us only such dreams as the Autodidasker dream but not dreams like that of the burning child, which - as will be remembered - we stated as a problem at the outset in our present investigations.

What takes place in the hallucinatory dream we can describe in no other way than by saying that the excitation follows a retrogressive course. It communicates itself not to the motor end of the apparatus, but to the sensory end, and finally reaches the system of perception. If we call the direction which the psychic process follows from the unconscious into the waking state progressive, we may then speak of the dream as having a regressive character.[18]

This regression is therefore assuredly one of the most important psychological peculiarities of the dream-process; but we must not forget that it is not characteristic of the dream alone. Intentional recollection and other component processes of our normal thinking likewise necessitate a retrogression in the psychic apparatus from some complex act of ideation to the raw material of the memory-traces which underlie it. But during the waking state this turning backwards does not reach beyond the memory-images; it is incapable of producing the hallucinatory revival of the perceptual images. Why is it otherwise in dreams? When we spoke of the condensation-work of the dream we could not avoid the assumption that by the dream-work the intensities adhering to the ideas are completely transferred from one to another. It is

---

[18] The first indication of the element of regression is already encountered in the writings of Albertus Magnus. According to him the imaginatio constructs the dream out of the tangible objects which it has retained. The process is the converse of that operating in the waking state. Hobbes states (Leviathan, ch. 2): "In sum our dreams are the reverse of our imagination, the motion, when we are awake, beginning at one end, and when we dream at another".

probably this modification of the usual psychic process which makes possible the cathexis[19] of the system of P to its full sensory vividness in the reverse direction to thinking.

I hope that we are not deluding ourselves as regards the importance of this present discussion. We have done nothing more than give a name to an inexplicable phenomenon. We call it regression if the idea in the dream is changed back into the visual image from which it once originated. But even this step requires justification. Why this definition if it does not teach us anything new? Well, I believe that the word regression is of service to us, inasmuch as it connects a fact familiar to us with the scheme of the psychic apparatus endowed with direction. At this point, and for the first time, we shall profit by the fact that we have constructed such a scheme. For with the help of this scheme we shall perceive, without further reflection, another peculiarity of dream-formation. If we look upon the dream as a process of regression within the hypothetical psychic apparatus, we have at once an explanation of the empirically proven fact that all thought-relations of the dream-thoughts are either lost in the dream-work or have difficulty in achieving expression. According to our scheme, these thought-relations are contained not in the first memsystems, but in those lying farther to the front, and in the regression to the perceptual images they must forfeit expression. In regression, the structure of the dream-thoughts breaks up into its raw material.

But what change renders possible this regression which is impossible during the day? Let us here be content with an assumption. There must evidently be changes in the cathexis of the individual systems, causing the latter to become more accessible or inaccessible to the discharge of the excitation; but in any such apparatus the same effect upon the course of the excitation might be produced by more than one kind of change. We naturally think of the sleeping state, and of the many cathectic changes which this evokes at the sensory end of the apparatus. During the

---

[19] From the Greek Kathexo, to occupy, used here in place of the author's term Besetzung, to signify a charge or investment of energy. - TR.

day there is a continuous stream flowing from the Psi-system of the P toward the motility end; this current ceases at night, and can no longer block the flow of the current of excitation in the opposite direction. This would appear to be that seclusion from the outer world which, according to the theory of some writers, is supposed to explain the psychological character of the dream. In the explanation of the regression of the dream we shall, however, have to take into account those other regressions which occur during morbid waking states. In these other forms of regression the explanation just given plainly leaves us in the lurch. Regression occurs in spite of the uninterrupted sensory current in a progressive direction.

The hallucinations of hysteria and paranoia, as well as the visions of mentally normal persons, I would explain as corresponding, in fact, to regressions, i.e., to thoughts transformed into images; and would assert that only such thoughts undergo this transformation as are in intimate connection with suppressed memories, or with memories which have remained unconscious. As an example, I will cite the case of one of my youngest hysterical patients - a boy of twelve, who was prevented from falling asleep by "green faces with red eyes," which terrified him. The source of this manifestation was the suppressed, but once conscious memory of a boy whom he had often seen four years earlier, and who offered a warning example of many bad habits, including masturbation, for which he was now reproaching himself. At that time his mother had noticed that the complexion of this ill-mannered boy was greenish and that he had red (i.e., red-rimmed) eyes. Hence his terrifying vision, which merely determined his recollection of another saying of his mother's, to the effect that such boys become demented, are unable to learn anything at school, and are doomed to an early death. A part of this prediction came true in the case of my little patient; he could not get on at school, and, as appeared from his involuntary associations, he was in terrible dread of the remainder of the prophecy. However, after a brief period of successful treatment his sleep was restored, his anxiety removed, and he finished his scholastic year with an excellent record. Here I may add the interpretation of a vision described to me by an hysterical woman of forty, as having occurred when she was in normal health.

One morning she opened her eyes and saw her brother in the room, although she knew him to be confined in an insane asylum. Her little son was asleep by her side. Lest the child should be frightened on seeing his uncle, and fall into convulsions, she pulled the sheet over his face. This done, the phantom disappeared. This apparition was the revision of one of her childish memories, which, although conscious, was most intimately connected with all the unconscious material in her mind. Her nurserymaid had told her that her mother, who had died young (my patient was then only eighteen months old), had suffered from epileptic or hysterical convulsions, which dated back to a fright caused by her brother (the patient's uncle) who appeared to her disguised as a spectre with a sheet over his head. The vision contains the same elements as the reminiscence, viz., the appearance of the brother, the sheet, the fright, and its effect. These elements, however, are arranged in a fresh context, and are transferred to other persons. The obvious motive of the vision, and the thought which it replaced, was her solicitude lest her little son, who bore a striking resemblance to his uncle, should share the latter's fate.

Both examples here cited are not entirely unrelated to the state of sleep, and may for that reason be unfitted to afford the evidence for the sake of which I have cited them. I will, therefore, refer to my analysis of an hallucinatory paranoic woman patient[20] and to the results of my hitherto unpublished studies on the psychology of the psychoneuroses, in order to emphasize the fact that in these cases of regressive thoughttransformation one must not overlook the influence of a suppressed memory, or one that has remained unconscious, this being usually of an infantile character. This memory draws into the regression, as it were, the thoughts with which it is connected, and which are kept from

---

[20] Selected Papers on Hysteria, "7further Observations on the Defence-Neuro-Psychoses".

expression by the censorship - that is, into that form of representation in which the memory itself is psychically existent. And here I may add, as a result of my studies of hysteria, that if one succeeds in bringing to consciousness infantile scenes (whether they are recollections or phantasies) they appear as hallucinations, and are divested of this character only when they are communicated. It is known also that even in persons whose memories are not otherwise visual, the earliest infantile memories remain vividly visual until late in life.

If, now, we bear in mind the part played in the dream-thoughts by the infantile experiences, or by the phantasies based upon them, and recollect how often fragments of these re-emerge in the dream-content, and how even the dream-wishes often proceed from them, we cannot deny the probability that in dreams, too, the transformation of thoughts into visual images may be the result of the attraction exercised by the visually represented memory, striving for resuscitation, upon the thoughts severed from the consciousness and struggling for expression. Pursuing this conception. we may further describe the dream as the substitute for the infantile scene modified by transference to recent material. The infantile scene cannot enforce its own revival, and must therefore be satisfied to return as a dream.

This reference to the significance of the infantile scenes (or of their phantastic repetitions) as in a certain degree furnishing the pattern for the dream-content renders superfluous the assumption made by Scherner and his pupils concerning inner sources of stimuli. Scherner assumes a state of visual excitation, of internal excitation in the organ of sight, when the dreams manifest a special vividness or an extraordinary abundance of visual elements. We need raise no objection to this assumption; we may perhaps content ourselves with assuming such a state of excitation only for the psychic perceptive system of the organ of vision; we shall, however, insist that this state of excitation is a reanimation by the memory of a former actual visual excitation. I cannot, from my own experience, give a good example showing such an influence of an infantile memory; my own dreams are altogether less rich in perceptual elements than I imagine those of others to be; but in my most beautiful and most vivid dream of late years I can easily trace the hallucinatory distinctness of the dream-contents to the visual qualities of recently received impressions. In chapter VI., H, I mentioned a dream in which the dark blue of the water, the brown of the smoke issuing from the ship's funnels, and the sombre brown and red of the buildings which I saw made a profound and lasting impression upon my mind. This dream, if any, must be attributed to visual excitation, but what was it that had brought my organ of vision into this excitable state? It was a recent impression which had joined itself to a series of former impressions. The colours I beheld were in the first place those of the toy blocks with which my children had erected a magnificent building for my admiration, on the day preceding the dream. There was the sombre red on the large blocks, the blue and brown on the small ones. Joined to these were the colour impressions of my last journey in Italy: the beautiful blue of the Isonzo and the lagoons, the brown hue of the Alps. The beautiful colours seen in the dream were but a repetition of those seen in memory.

Let us summarize what we have learned about this peculiarity of dreams: their power of recasting their idea-content in visual images. We may not have explained this character of the dream-work by referring it to the known laws of psychology, but we have singled it out as pointing to unknown relations, and have given it the name of the regressive character. Wherever such regression has occurred, we have regarded it as an effect of the resistance which opposes the progress of thought on its normal way to consciousness, and of the simultaneous attraction exerted upon it by vivid memories.[21] The regression in dreams is perhaps facilitated by the cessation of the progressive stream flowing from the senseorgans during the day; for which auxiliary factor there

---

[21] In a statement of the theory of repression it should be explained that a thought passes into repression owing to the co-operation of two of the factors which influence it. On the one side (the censorship of Cs) it is pushed, and from the other side (the Ucs) it is pulled, much as one is helped to the top of the Great Pyramid.

must be some compensation, in the other forms of regression, by the strengthening of the other regressive motives. We must also bear in mind that in pathological cases of regression, just as in dreams, the process of energy-transference must be different from that occurring in the regressions of normal psychic life, since it renders possible a full hallucinatory cathexis of the perceptive system. What we have described in the analysis of the dream-work as regard for representability may be referred to the selective attraction of visually remembered scenes touched by the dream-thoughts.

As to the regression, we may further observe that it plays a no less important part in the theory of neurotic symptom-formation than in the theory of dreams. We may therefore distinguish a threefold species of regression: (a) a topical one, in the sense of the scheme of the Psi-systems here exponded; (b) a temporal one, in so far as it is a regression to older psychic formations; and (c) a formal one, when primitive modes of expression and representation take the place of the customary modes. These three forms of regression are, however, basically one, and in the majority of cases they coincide, for that which is older in point of time is at the same time formally primitive and, in the psychic topography, nearer to the perception-end.

We cannot leave the theme of regression in dreams without giving utterance to an impression which has already and repeatedly forced itself upon us, and which will return to us reinforced after a deeper study of the psychoneuroses: namely, that dreaming is on the whole an act of regression to the earliest relationships of the dreamer, a resuscitation of his childhood, of the impulses which were then dominant and the modes of expression which were then available. Behind this childhood of the individual we are then promised an insight into the phylogenetic childhood, into the evolution of the human race, of which the development of the individual is only an abridged repetition influenced by the fortuitous circumstances of life. We begin to suspect that Friedrich Nietzsche was right when he said that in a dream "there persists a primordial part of humanity which we can no longer reach by a direct path," and we are encouraged to expect, from the analysis of dreams, a knowledge of the archaic inheritance of man, a knowledge of psychical things in him that are innate. It would seem that dreams and neuroses have preserved for us more of the psychical antiquities than we suspected; so that psycho-analysis may claim a high rank among those sciences which endeavour to reconstruct the oldest and darkest phases of the beginnings of mankind.

It is quite possible that we shall not find this first part of our psychological evaluation of dreams particularly satisfying. We must, however, console ourselves with the thought that we are, after all, compelled to build out into the dark. If we have not gone altogether astray, we shall surely reach approximately the same place from another starting-point, and then, perhaps, we shall be better able to find our bearings.

C. The Wish-Fulfilment

The dream of the burning child (cited above) affords us a welcome opportunity for appreciating the difficulties confronting the theory of wishfulfilment.

That a dream should be nothing but a wish-fulfilment must undoubtedly seem strange to us all - and not only because of the contradiction offered by the anxiety-dream. Once our first analyses had given us the enlightenment that meaning and psychic value are concealed behind our dreams, we could hardly have expected so unitary a determination of this meaning. According to the correct but summary definition of Aristotle, the dream is a continuation of thinking in sleep. Now if, during the day, our thoughts perform such a diversity of psychic acts - judgments, conclusions, the answering of objections, expectations, intentions, etc. - why should they be forced at night to confine themselves to the production of wishes only? Are there not, on the contrary, many dreams that present an altogether different psychic act in dream-form - for example, anxious care - and is not the father's unusually transparent dream of the burning child such a dream?

From the gleam of light that falls upon his eyes while he is asleep the father draws the apprehensive conclusion that a candle has fallen over and may be burning the body; he transforms this conclusion into a dream by embodying it in an obvious situation enacted in the present tense. What part is played in this dream by the wish-fulfilment? And how can we possibly mistake the predominance of the thought continued from the waking state or evoked by the new sensory impression?

All these considerations are justified, and force us to look more closely into the role of the wish-fulfilment in dreams, and the significance of the waking thoughts continued in sleep.

It is precisely the wish-fulfilment that has already caused us to divide all dreams into two groups. We have found dreams which were plainly wishfulfilments; and others in which the wish-fulfilment was unrecognizable and was often concealed by every available means. In this latter class of dreams we recognized the influence of the dream-censorship. The undisguised wish-dreams were found chiefly in children; short, frank wishdreams seemed (I purposely emphasize this word) to occur also in adults.

We may now ask whence in each case does the wish that is realized in the dream originate? But to what opposition or to what diversity do we relate this whence? I think to the opposition between conscious daily life and an unconscious psychic activity which is able to make itself perceptible only at night. I thus, find a threefold possibility for the origin of a wish. Firstly, it may have been excited during the day, and owing to external circumstances may have remained unsatisfied; there is thus left for the night an acknowledged and unsatisfied wish. Secondly, it may have emerged during the day, only to be rejected; there is thus left for the night an unsatisfied but suppressed wish. Thirdly, it may have no relation to daily life, but may belong to those wishes which awake only at night out of the suppressed material in us. If we turn to our scheme of the psychic apparatus, we can localize a wish of the first order in the system Pcs. We may assume that a wish of the second order has been forced back from the

Pcs system into the Ucs system, where alone, if anywhere, can it maintain itself; as for the wish-impulse of the third order, we believe that it is wholly incapable of leaving the Ucs system. Now, have the wishes arising from these different sources the same value for the dream, the same power to incite a dream?

On surveying the dreams at our disposal with a view to answering this question, we are at once moved to add as a fourth source of the dream-wish the actual wish-impetus which arises during the night (for example, the stimulus of thirst, and sexual desire). It then seems to us probable that the source of the dream-wish does not affect its capacity to incite a dream. I have in mind the dream of the child who continued the voyage that had been interrupted during the day, and the other children's dreams cited in the same chapter; they are explained by an unfulfilled but unsuppressed wish of the daytime. That wishes suppressed during the day assert themselves in dreams is shown by a great many examples. I will mention a very simple dream of this kind. A rather sarcastic lady, whose younger friend has become engaged to be married, is asked in the daytime by her acquaintances whether she knows her friend's fiance, and what she thinks of him. She replies with unqualified praise, imposing silence on her own judgment, although she would have liked to tell the truth, namely, that he is a commonplace fellow - one meets such by the dozen (Dutzendmensch). The following night she dreams that the same question is put to her, and that she replies with the formula: "In case of subsequent orders, it will suffice to mention the reference number." Finally, as the result of numerous analyses, we learn that the wish in all dreams that have been subject to distortion has its origin in the unconscious, and could not become perceptible by day. At first sight, then, it seems that in respect of dream-formation all wishes are of equal value and equal power. I cannot prove here that this is not really the true state of affairs, but I am strongly inclined to assume a stricter determination of the dream-wish. Children's dreams leave us in no doubt that a wish unfulfilled during the day may instigate a dream. But we must not forget that this is, after all, the wish of a child; that it is a wish-impulse of the strength peculiar to childhood. I very much doubt whether a wish unfulfilled in the daytime would suffice to create a dream in an adult. It would rather seem that, as we learn to control our instinctual life by intellection, we more and more renounce as unprofitable the formation or retention of such intense wishes as are natural to childhood. In this, indeed, there may be individual variations; some retain the infantile type of the psychic processes longer than others; just as we find such differences in the gradual decline of the originally vivid visual imagination. In general, however, I am of the opinion that unfulfilled wishes of the day are insufficient to produce a dream in adults. I will readily admit that the wish-impulses originating in consciousness contribute to the instigation of dreams, but they probably do no more. The dream would not occur if the preconscious wish were not reinforced from another source.

That source is the unconscious. I believe that the conscious wish becomes effective in exciting a dream only when it succeeds in arousing a similar unconscious wish which reinforces it. From the indications obtained in the psychoanalysis of the neuroses, I believe that these unconscious wishes are always active and ready to express themselves whenever they find an opportunity of allying themselves with an impulse from consciousness, and transferring their own greater intensity to the lesser intensity of the latter.[22] It must, therefore, seem that the conscious wish alone has been realized in the dream; but a slight peculiarity in the form of the dream will put us on the track of the powerful ally from the unconscious. These ever-active and, as it were, immortal wishes of our unconscious recall the legendary Titans who, from time immemorial, have been buried under the mountains which were once hurled upon them by the victorious gods, and even now

---

[22] They share this character of indestructibility with all other psychic acts that are really unconscious - that is, with psychic acts belonging solely to the system Ucs. These paths are opened once and for all; they never fall into disease; they conduct the excitation process to discharge as often as they are charged again with unconscious excitation. To speak metaphorically, they suffer no other form of annihilation than did the shades of the lower regions in the Odyssey, who awoke to new life the moment they drank blood. The processes depending on the preconscious system are destructible in quite another sense. The psychotherapy of the neuroses is based on this difference.

quiver from time to time at the convulsions of their mighty limbs. These wishes, existing in repression, are themselves of infantile origin, as we learn from the psychological investigation of the neuroses. Let me, therefore, set aside the view previously expressed, that it matters little whence the dream-wish originates, and replace it by another, namely: the wish manifested in the dream must be an infantile wish. In the adult it originates in the Ucs, while in the child, in whom no division and censorship exist as yet between the Pcs and Ucs, or in whom these are only in process of formation, it is an unfulfilled and unrepressed wish from the waking state. I am aware that this conception cannot be generally demonstrated, but I maintain that it can often be demonstrated even where one would not have suspected it, and that it cannot be generally refuted.

In dream-formation, the wish-impulses which are left over from the conscious waking life are, therefore, to be relegated to the background. I cannot admit that they play any part except that attributed to the material of actual sensations during sleep in relation to the dream-content. If I now take into account those other psychic instigations left over from the waking life of the day, which are not wishes, I shall merely be adhering to the course mapped out for me by this line of thought. We may succeed in provisionally disposing of the energetic cathexis of our waking thoughts by deciding to go to sleep. He is a good sleeper who can do this; Napoleon I is reputed to have been a model of this kind. But we do not always succeed in doing it, or in doing it completely. Unsolved problems, harassing cares, overwhelming impressions, continue the activity of our thought even during sleep, maintaining psychic processes in the system which we have termed the preconscious. The thought-impulses continued into sleep may be divided into the following groups:

1. Those which have not been completed during the day, owing to some accidental cause.

2. Those which have been left uncompleted because our mental powers have failed us, i.e., unsolved problems.

3. Those which have been turned back and suppressed during the day. This is reinforced by a powerful fourth group:

4. Those which have been excited in our Ucs during the day by the workings of the Pcs; and finally we may add a fifth, consisting of:

5. The indifferent impressions of the day, which have therefore been left unsettled.

We need not underrate the psychic intensities introduced into sleep by these residues of the day's waking life, especially those emanating from the group of the unsolved issues. It is certain that these excitations continue to strive for expression during the night, and we may assume with equal certainty that the state of sleep renders impossible the usual continuance of the process of excitation in the preconscious and its termination in becoming conscious. In so far as we can become conscious of our mental processes in the ordinary way, even during the night, to that extent we are simply not asleep. I cannot say what change is produced in the Pcs system by the state of sleep,[23] but there is no doubt that the psychological characteristics of sleep are to be sought mainly in the cathectic changes occurring just in this system, which dominates, moreover, the approach to motility, paralysed during sleep. On the other hand, I have found nothing in the psychology of dreams to warrant the assumption that sleep produces any but secondary changes in the conditions of the Ucs system. Hence, for the nocturnal excitations in the Pcs there remains no other path than that taken by the wish-excitations from the Ucs; they must seek reinforcement from the Ucs, and follow the detours of the unconscious excitations. But what is the relation of the preconscious day-residues to the dream? There is no doubt that they penetrate abundantly into the dream; that they utilize the dream-content to obtrude themselves upon consciousness even during the night; indeed, they sometimes even dominate the dream-content, and impel it to continue the work of the day; it

---

[23] I have endeavoured to penetrate farther into the relations of the sleeping state and the conditions of hallucination in my essay, "Metapsychological Supplement to the Theory of Dreams," Collected Papers.

is also certain that the day-residues may just as well have any other character as that of wishes. But it is highly instructive, and for the theory of wish-fulfilment of quite decisive importance, to see what conditions they must comply with in order to be received into the dream.

Let us pick out one of the dreams cited above, e.g., the dream in which my friend Otto seems to show the symptoms of Basedow's disease (chapter V., D). Otto's appearance gave me some concern during the day, and this worry, like everything else relating to him, greatly affected me.

I may assume that this concern followed me into sleep. I was probably bent on finding out what was the matter with him. During the night my concern found expression in the dream which I have recorded. Not only was its content senseless, but it failed to show any wish-fulfilment. But I began to search for the source of this incongruous expression of the solicitude felt during the day, and analysis revealed a connection. I identified my friend Otto with a certain Baron L and myself with a Professor R. There was only one explanation of my being impelled to select just this substitute for the day-thought. I must always have been ready in the Ucs to identify myself with Professor R, as this meant the realization of one of the immortal infantile wishes, viz., the wish to become great. Repulsive ideas respecting my friend, ideas that would certainly have been repudiated in a waking state, took advantage of the opportunity to creep into the dream; but the worry of the day had likewise found some sort of expression by means of a substitute in the dream-content. The day-thought, which was in itself not a wish, but on the contrary a worry, had in some way to find a connection with some infantile wish, now unconscious and suppressed, which then allowed it - duly dressed up - to arise for consciousness. The more domineering the worry the more forced could be the connection to be established; between the content of the wish and that of the worry there need be no connection, nor was there one in our example.

It would perhaps be appropriate, in dealing with this problem, to inquire how a dream behaves when material is offered to it in the dreamthoughts which flatly opposes a wish-fulfilment; such as justified worries, painful reflections and distressing realizations. The many possible results may be classified as follows: (a) The dream-work succeeds in replacing all painful ideas by contrary ideas. and suppressing the painful affect belonging to them. This, then, results in a pure and simple satisfaction-dream, a palpable wish-fulfilment, concerning which there is nothing more to be said. (b) The painful ideas find their way into the manifest dream-content, more or less modified, but nevertheless quite recognizable. This is the case which raises doughts about the wish-theory of dreams, and thus calls for further investigation. Such dreams with a painful content may either be indifferent in feeling, or they may convey the whole painful affect, which the ideas contained in them seem to justify, or they may even lead to the development of anxiety to the point of waking.

Analysis then shows that even these painful dreams are wish-fulfilments. An unconscious and repressed wish, whose fulfilment could only be felt as painful by the dreamer's ego, has seized the opportunity offered by the continued cathexis of painful day-residues, has lent them its support, and has thus made them capable of being dreamed. But whereas in case (a) the unconscious wish coincided with the conscious one, in case (b) the discord between the unconscious and the conscious - the repressed material and the ego - is revealed, and the situation in the fairy-tale, of the three wishes which the fairy offers to the married couple, is realized. The gratification in respect of the fulfilment of the repressed wish may prove to be so great that it balances the painful affects adhering to the day-residues; the dream is then indifferent in its affective tone, although it is on the one hand the fulfilment of a wish, and on the other the fulfilment of a fear. Or it may happen that the sleeper's ego plays an even more extensive part in the dream-formation, that it reacts with violent resentment to the accomplished satisfaction of the repressed wish, and even goes so far as to make an end of the dream by means of anxiety. It is thus not difficult to recognize that dreams of pain and anxiety are, in accordance with our theory, just as much wish-fulfilments as are the straightforward dreams of gratification.

Painful dreams may also be punishment dreams. It must be admitted that the recognition of these dreams adds something that is, in a certain sense, new to the theory of dreams. What is fulfilled by them is once more an unconscious wish - the wish for the punishment of the dreamer for a repressed, prohibited wish - impulse. To this extent, these dreams comply with the requirement here laid down: that the motive-power behind the dream-formation must be furnished by a wish belonging to the unconscious. But a finer psychological dissection allows us to recognize the difference between this and the other wish-dreams. In the dreams of group (b) the unconscious dream-forming wish belonged to the repressed material. In the punishment-dreams it is likewise an unconscious wish, but one which we must attribute not to the repressed material but to the ego.

Punishment-dreams point, therefore, to the possibility of a still more extensive participation of the ego in dream-formation. The mechanism of dream-formation becomes indeed in every way more transparent if in place of the antithesis conscious and unconscious, we put the antithesis: ego and repressed. This, however, cannot be done without taking into account what happens in the psychoneuroses, and for this reason it has not been done in this book. Here I need only remark that the occurrence of punishment-dreams is not generally subject to the presence of painful dayresidues.

They originate, indeed, most readily if the contrary is true, if the thoughts which are day-residues are of a gratifying nature, but express illicit gratifications. Of these thoughts nothing, then, finds its way into the manifest dream except their contrary, just as was the case in the dreams of group (a). Thus it would be the essential characteristic of punishment-dreams that in them it is not the unconscious wish from the repressed material (from the system Ucs) that is responsible for dream-formation but the punitive wish reacting against it, a wish pertaining to the ego, even though it is unconscious (i.e., preconscious).[24] I will elucidate some of the foregoing observations by means of a dream of my own, and above all I will try to show how the dream-work deals with a day-residue involving painful expectation:

Indistinct beginning. I tell my wife I have some news for her, something very special. She becomes frightened, and does not wish to hear it. I assure her that on the contrary it is something which will please her greatly, and I begin to tell her that our son's Officers' Corps has sent a sum of money (5,000 k.?)... something about honourable mention... distribution... at the same time I have gone with her into a sitting room, like a storeroom, in order to fetch something from it. Suddenly I see my son appear; he is not in uniform but rather in a tight-fitting sports suit (like a seal?) with a small cap. He climbs on to a basket which stands to one side near a chest, in order to put something on this chest. I address him; no answer.

It seems to me that his face or forehead is bandaged, he arranges something in his mouth, pushing something into it. Also his hair shows a glint of grey. I reflect: Can he be so exhausted? And has he false teeth? Before I can address him again I awake without anxiety, but with palpitations. My clock points to 2.30 a.m.

To give a full analysis is once more impossible. I shall therefore confine myself to emphasizing some decisive points. Painful expectations of the day had given occasion for this dream; once again there had been no news for over a week from my son, who was fighting at the Front. It is easy to see that in the dream-content the conviction that he has been killed or wounded finds expression. At the beginning of the dream one can observe an energetic effort to replace the painful thoughts by their contrary. I have to impart something very pleasing, something about sending money, honourable mention, and distribution. (The sum of money originates in a gratifying incident of my medical practice; it is therefore trying to lead the dream away altogether

---

[24] Here one may consider the idea of the super-ego which was later recognized by psycho-analysis.

from its theme.) But this effort fails. The boy's mother has a presentiment of something terrible and does not wish to listen. The disguises are too thin; the reference to the material to be suppressed shows through everywhere. If my son is killed, then his comrades will send back his property; I shall have to distribute whatever he has left among his sisters, brothers and other people. Honourable mention is frequently awarded to an officer after he has died the "hero's death." The dream thus strives to give direct expression to what it at first wished to deny, whilst at the same time the wish-fulfilling tendency reveals itself by distortion. (The change of locality in the dream is no doubt to be understood as threshold symbolism, in line with Silberer's view.) We have indeed no idea what lends it the requisite motive-power. But my son does not appear as falling (on the field of battle) but climbing. - He was, in fact, a daring mountaineer. - He is not in uniform, but in a sports suit; that is, the place of the fatality now dreaded has been taken by an accident which happened to him at one time when he was ski-running, when he fell and fractured his thigh. But the nature of his costume, which makes him look like a seal, recalls immediately a younger person, our comical little grandson; the grey hair recalls his father, our son-in-law, who has had a bad time in the War. What does this signify? But let us leave this: the locality, a pantry, the chest, from which he wants to take something (in the dream, to put something on it), are unmistakable allusions to an accident of my own, brought upon myself when I was between two and three years of age. I climbed on a foot-stool in the pantry, in order to get something nice which was on a chest or table. The footstool tumbled over and its edge struck me behind the lower jaw. I might very well have knocked all my teeth out. At this point, an admonition presents itself: it serves you right - like a hostile impulse against the valiant warrior. A profounder analysis enables me to detect the hidden impulse, which would be able to find satisfaction in the dreaded mishap to my son. It is the envy of youth which the elderly man believes that he has thoroughly stifled in actual life. There is no mistaking the fact that it was the very intensity of the painful apprehension lest such a misfortune should really happen that searched out for its alleviation such a repressed wish-fulfilment. I can now clearly define what the unconscious wish means for the dream. I will admit that there is a whole class of dreams in which the incitement originates mainly or even exclusively from the residues of the day; and returning to the dream about my friend Otto, I believe that even my desire to become at last a professor extraordinarius would have allowed me to sleep in peace that night, had not the day's concern for my friend's health continued active. But this worry alone would not have produced a dream; the motive-power needed by the dream had to be contributed by a wish, and it was the business of my concern to find such a wish for itself, as the motive power of the dream. To put it figuratively, it is quite possible that a day-thought plays the part of the entrepreneur in the dream; but the entrepreneur, who, as we say, has the idea, and feels impelled to realize it, can do nothing without capital; he needs a capitalist who will defray the expense, and this capitalist, who contributes the psychic expenditure for the dream, is invariably and indisputably, whatever the nature of the waking thoughts, a wish from the unconscious.

In other cases the capitalist himself is the entrepreneur; this, indeed, seems to be the more usual case. An unconscious wish is excited by the day's work, and this now creates the dream. And the dream-processes provide a parallel for all the other possibilities of the economic relationship here used as an illustration. Thus the entrepreneur may himself contribute a little of the capital, or several entrepreneurs may seek the aid of the same capitalist, or several capitalists may jointly supply the capital required by the entrepreneurs. Thus there are dreams sustained by more than one dream-wish, and many similar variations, which may be readily imagined, and which are of no further interest to us. What is still lacking to our discussion of the dream-wish we shall only be able to complete later on.

The tertium comparationis in the analogies here employed, the quantitative element of which an allotted amount is placed at the free disposal of the dream, admits of a still closer application to the elucidation of the dream-structure. As shown in chapter VI., B., we can recognize in most dreams a centre supplied with a special sensory intensity. This is, as a rule, the direct representation of the wish-fulfilment; for, if we reverse the displacements of the dream-work, we find that the psychic intensity of the elements in the dream-thoughts is replaced by the sensory intensity of the elements in the dream-content. The elements in the neighbourhood of the wish-fulfilment have often nothing to do with its meaning, but prove to be the offshoots of painful thoughts which are opposed to the wish. But owing to their connection with the central element, often artificially established, they secure so large a share of its intensity as to become capable of representation. Thus, the representative energy of the wishfulfilment diffuses itself over a certain sphere of association, within which all elements are raised to representation, including even those that are in themselves without resources. In dreams containing several dynamic wishes we can easily separate and delimit the spheres of the individual wish-fulfilments, and we shall find that the gaps in the dream are often of the nature of boundary-zones.

Although the foregoing remarks have restricted the significance of the day-residues for the dream, they are none the less deserving of some further attention. For they must be a necessary ingredient in dream-formation, inasmuch as experience reveals the surprising fact that every dream shows in its content a connection with a recent waking impression, often of the most indifferent kind. So far we have failed to understand the necessity for this addition to the dream-mixture (chapter V., A.). This necessity becomes apparent only when we bear in mind the part played by the unconscious wish, and seek further information in the psychology of the neuroses. We shall then learn that an unconscious idea, as such, is quite incapable of entering into the preconscious, and that it can exert an influence there only by establishing touch with a harmless idea already belonging to the preconscious, to which it transfers its intensity, and by which it allows itself to be screened. This is the fact of transference, which furnishes the explanation of so many surprising occurrences in the psychic life of neurotics. The transference may leave the idea from the preconscious unaltered, though the latter will thus acquire an unmerited intensity, or it may force upon this some modification derived from the content of the transferred idea. I trust the reader will pardon my fondness for comparisons with daily life, but I feel tempted to say that the situation for the repressed idea is like that of the American dentist in Austria, who may not carry on his practice unless he can get a duly installed doctor of medicine to serve him as a signboard and legal "cover." Further, just as it is not exactly the busiest physicians who form such alliances with dental practitioners, so in the psychic life the choice as regards covers for repressed ideas does not fall upon such preconscious or conscious ideas as have themselves attracted enough of the attention active in the preconscious. The unconscious prefers to entangle with its connections either those impressions and ideas of the preconscious which have remained unnoticed as being indifferent or those which have immediately had attention withdrawn from them again (by rejection). it is a well-known proposition of the theory of associations, confirmed by all experience, that ideas which have formed a very intimate connection in one direction assume a negative type of attitude towards whole groups of new connections. I have even attempted at one time to base a theory of hysterical paralysis on this principle.

If we assume that the same need of transference on the part of the repressed ideas, of which we have become aware through the analysis of the neurosis, makes itself felt in dreams also, we can at once explain two of the problems of the dream: namely, that every dream-analysis reveals an interweaving of a recent impression, and that this recent element is often of the most indifferent character. We may add what we have already learned elsewhere, that the reason why these recent and indifferent elements so frequently find their way into the dream-content as substitutes for the very oldest elements of the dream-thoughts is that they have the least to fear from the resisting censorship. But while this freedom from censorship explains only the preference shown to the trivial elements, the constant presence of recent elements points to the necessity for transference. Both groups of impressions satisfy the demand of the repressed ideas for material still free from associations, the indifferent ones because they have offered no occasion for extensive associations, and the recent ones because they have not had sufficient time to form such associations.

We thus see that the day-residues, among which we may now include the indifferent impressions, not only borrow something from the Ucs when they secure a share in dream-formation - namely, the motive-power at the disposal of the repressed wish - but they also offer to the unconscious something that is indispensable to it, namely, the points of attachment necessary for transference. If we wished to penetrate more deeply into the psychic processes, we should have to throw a clearer light on the play of excitations between the preconscious and the unconscious, and indeed the study of the psychoneuroses would impel us to do so; but dreams, as it happens, give us no help in this respect. Just one further remark as to the day-residues. There is no doubt that it is really these that disturb our sleep, and not our dreams which, on the contrary, strive to guard our sleep. But we shall return to this point later.

So far we have discussed the dream-wish; we have traced it back to the sphere of the Ucs, and have analysed its relation to the day-residues, which, in their turn, may be either wishes, or psychic impulses of any other kind, or simply recent impressions. We have thus found room for the claims that can be made for the dream-forming significance of our waking mental activity in all its multifariousness. It might even prove possible to explain, on the basis of our train of thought, those extreme cases in which the dream, continuing the work of the day, brings to a happy issue an unsolved problem of waking life. We merely lack a suitable example to analyse, in order to uncover the infantile or repressed source of wishes, the tapping of which has so successfully reinforced the efforts of the preconscious activity. But we are not a step nearer to answering the question: Why is it that the unconscious can furnish in sleep nothing more than the motive-power for a wish-fulfilment? The answer to this question must elucidate the psychic nature of the state of wishing: and it will be given with the aid of the notion of the psychic apparatus.

We do not doubt that this apparatus, too, has only arrived at its present perfection by a long process of evolution. Let us attempt to restore it as it existed in an earlier stage of capacity. From postulates to be confirmed in other ways, we know that at first the apparatus strove to keep itself as free from stimulation as possible, and therefore, in its early structure, adopted the arrangement of a reflex apparatus, which enabled it promptly to discharge by the motor paths any sensory excitation reaching it from without. But this simple function was disturbed by the exigencies of life, to which the apparatus owes the impetus toward further development. The exigencies of life first confronted it in the form of the great physical needs. The excitation aroused by the inner need seeks an outlet in motility, which we may describe as internal change or expression of the emotions. The hungry child cries or struggles helplessly. But its situation remains unchanged; for the excitation proceeding from the inner need has not the character of a momentary impact, but of a continuing pressure. A change can occur only if, in some way (in the case of the child by external assistance), there is an experience of satisfaction, which puts an end to the internal excitation. An essential constituent of this experience is the appearance of a certain percept (of food in our example), the memory-image of which is henceforth associated with the memory-trace of the excitation arising from the need. Thanks to the established connection, there results, at the next occurrence of this need, a psychic impulse which seeks to revive the memory-image of the former percept, and to re-evoke the former percept itself; that is, it actually seeks to re-establish the situation of the first satisfaction. Such an impulse is what we call a wish; the reappearance of the perception constitutes the wish-fulfilment, and the full cathexis of the perception, by the excitation springing from the need, constitutes the shortest path to the wish-fulfilment. We may assume a primitive state of the psychic apparatus in which this path is actually followed, i.e., in which the wish ends in hallucination. This first psychic activity therefore aims at an identity of perception: that is, at a repetition of that perception which is connected with the satisfaction of the need.

This primitive mental activity must have been modified by bitter practical experience into a secondary and more appropriate activity. The establishment of identity of perception by the short regressive path within the apparatus does not produce the same result in another respect as follows upon cathexis of the same perception coming from without. The satisfaction does not occur, and the need continues. In order to make the internal cathexis equivalent to the external one, the former would have to be continuously sustained, just as actually happens in the hallucinatory psychoses and in hunger-phantasies, which exhaust their performance in maintaining their hold on the object desired. In order to attain to more appropriate use of the psychic energy, it becomes necessary to suspend the full regression, so that it does not proceed beyond the memory-image, and thence can seek other paths, leading ultimately to the production of the desired identity from the side of the outer world.[25] This inhibition, as well as the subsequent deflection of the excitation, becomes the task of a second system, which controls voluntary motility, i.e., a system whose activity first leads on to the use of motility for purposes remembered in advance. But all this complicated mental activity, which works its way from the memory-image to the production of identity of perception via the outer world, merely represents a roundabout way to wishfulfilment made necessary by experience.[26] Thinking is indeed nothing but a substitute for the hallucinatory wish; and if the dream is called a wish-fulfilment, this becomes something self-evident, since nothing but a wish

---

[25] In other words: the introduction of a test of reality is recognized as necessary.
[26] Le Lorrain justly extols the wish-fulfilments of dreams: "Sans fatigue serieuse, sans etre oblige de recourir a cette lutte opiniatre et longue qui use et corrode les jouissances poursuivies." [Without serious fatigue, without being obliged to have recourse to that long and stubborn struggle which exhausts and wears away pleasures sought.]

can impel our psychic apparatus to activity. The dream, which fulfils its wishes by following the short regressive path, has thereby simply preserved for us a specimen of the primary method of operation of the psychic apparatus, which has been abandoned as inappropriate. What once prevailed in the waking state, when our psychic life was still young and inefficient, seems to have been banished into our nocturnal life; just as we still find in the nursery those discarded primitive weapons of adult humanity, the bow and arrow. Dreaming is a fragment of the superseded psychic life of the child. In the psychoses, those modes of operation of the psychic apparatus which are normally suppressed in the waking state reassert themselves, and thereupon betray their inability to satisfy our demands in the outer world.[27]

The unconscious wish-impulses evidently strive to assert themselves even during the day, and the fact of transference, as well as the psychoses, tells us that they endeavour to force their way through the preconscious system to consciousness and the command of motility. Thus, in the censorship between Ucs and Pcs, which the dream forces us to assume, we must recognize and respect the guardian of our psychic health. But is it not carelessness on the part of this guardian to diminish his vigilance at night, and to allow the suppressed impulses of the Ucs to achieve expression, thus again making possible the process of hallucinatory regression? I think not, for when the critical guardian goes to rest - and we have proof that his slumber is not profound - he takes care to close the gate to motility. No matter what impulses from the usually inhibited Ucs may bustle about the stage, there is no need to interfere with them; they remain harmless, because they are not in a position to set in motion the motor apparatus which alone can operate to produce any change in the outer world. Sleep guarantees the security of the fortress which has to be guarded. The state of affairs is less harmless when a displacement of energies is produced, not by the decline at night in the energy put forth by the critical censorship, but by the pathological enfeeblement of the

---

[27] I have further elaborated this train of thought elsewhere, where I have distinguished the two principles involved as the pleasure-principle and the reality-principle. Formulations regarding the Two Principles in Mental Functioning, in Collected Papers.

latter, or the pathological reinforcement of the unconscious excitations, and this while the preconscious is cathected and the gates of motility are open. The guardian is then overpowered; the unconscious excitations subdue the Pcs, and from the Pcs they dominate our speech and action, or they enforce hallucinatory regressions, thus directing an apparatus not designed for them by virtue of the attraction exerted by perceptions on the distribution of our psychic energy. We call this condition psychosis.

We now find ourselves in the most favourable position for continuing the construction of our psychological scaffolding, which we left after inserting the two systems, Ucs and Pcs. However, we still have reason to give further consideration to the wish as the sole psychic motive-power in the dream. We have accepted the explanation that the reason why the dream is in every case a wish-fulfilment is that it is a function of the system Ucs, which knows no other aim than wish-fulfilment, and which has at its disposal no forces other than the wish-impulses. Now if we want to continue for a single moment longer to maintain our right to develop such far-reaching psychological speculations from the facts of dreaminterpretation, we are in duty bound to show that they insert the dream into a context which can also embrace other psychic structures. If there exists a system of the Ucs - or something sufficiently analogous for the purposes of our discussion - the dream cannot be its sole manifestation; every dream may be a wish-fulfilment, but there must be other forms of abnormal wish-fulfilment as well as dreams. And in fact the theory of all psychoneurotic symptoms culminates in the one proposition that they, too, must be conceived as wish-fulfilments of the unconscious.[28] Our explanation makes the dream only the first member of a series of the greatest importance for the psychiatrist, the understanding of which means the solution of the purely psychological part of the psychiatric problem.[29] But in other members of this group of wish-fulfilments - for example,

---

[28] Expressed more exactly: One portion of the symptom corresponds to the unconscious wish-fulfilment, while the other corresponds to the reaction-formation opposed to it.
[29] Hughlings Jackson has expressed himself as follows: "?find out all about dreams, and you will have found out all about insanity."

in the hysterical symptoms - I know of one essential characteristic which I have so far failed to find in the dream. Thus, from the investigations often alluded to in this treatise, I know that the formation of an hysterical symptom needs a junction of both the currents of our psychic life. The symptom is not merely the expression of a realized unconscious wish; the latter must be joined by another wish from the preconscious, which is fulfilled by the same symptom; so that the symptom is at least doubly determined, once by each of the conflicting systems. Just as in dreams, there is no limit to further over-determination. The determination which does not derive from the Ucs is, as far as I can see, invariably a thoughtstream of reaction against the unconscious wish; for example, a self-punishment. Hence I can say, quite generally, that an hysterical symptom originates only where two contrary wish-fulfilments, having their source in different psychic systems, are able to meet in a single expression.[30]

Examples would help us but little here, as nothing but a complete unveiling of the complications in question can carry conviction. I will therefore content myself with the bare assertion, and will cite one example, not because it proves anything, but simply as an illustration. The hysterical vomiting of a female patient proved, on the one hand, to be the fulfilment of an unconscious phantasy from the years of puberty - namely, the wish that she might be continually pregnant, and have a multitude of children; and this was subsequently supplemented by the wish that she might have them by as many fathers as possible. Against this immoderate wish there arose a powerful defensive reaction. But as by the vomiting the patient might have spoilt her figure and her beauty, so that she would no longer find favour in any man's eyes, the symptom was also in keeping with the punitive trend of thought, and so, being admissible on both sides, it was allowed to become a reality. This is the same way of acceding to a wish-fulfilment as the queen of the Parthians was pleased to

---

[30] Cf. my latest formulation (in Zeitschrift fur Sexual-wissenschaft, Bd. I) of the origin of hysterical symptoms in the treatise on "Hysterical Phantasies and their Relation to Bisexuality". This forms chapter X of Selected Papers on Hysteria.

adopt in the case of the triumvir Crassus. Believing that he had undertaken his campaign out of greed for gold, she caused molten gold to be poured into the throat of the corpse. "Here thou hast what thou hast longed for!"

Of the dream we know as yet only that it expresses a wish-fulfilment of the unconscious; and apparently the dominant preconscious system permits this fulfilment when it has compelled the wish to undergo certain distortions. We are, moreover, not in fact in a position to demonstrate regularly the presence of a train of thought opposed to the dream-wish, which is realized in the dream as well as its antagonist. Only now and then have we found in dream-analyses signs of reaction-products as, for instance, my affection for my friend R in the dream of my uncle (chapter IV.).

But the contribution from the preconscious which is missing here may be found in another place. The dream can provide expression for a wish from the Ucs by means of all sorts of distortions, once the dominant system has withdrawn itself into the wish to sleep, and has realized this wish by producing the changes of cathexis within the psychic apparatus which are within its power; thereupon holding on to the wish in question for the whole duration of sleep.[31]

Now this persistent wish to sleep on the part of the preconscious has a quite general facilitating effect on the formation of dreams. Let us recall the dream of the father who, by the gleam of light from the death-chamber, was led to conclude that his child's body might have caught fire. We have shown that one of the psychic forces decisive in causing the father to draw this conclusion in the dream instead of allowing himself to be awakened by the gleam of light was the wish to prolong the life of the child seen in the dream by one moment. Other wishes originating in the repressed have probably escaped us, for we are unable to analyse this dream. But as a second source of motive-power in this dream we may add the father's desire to sleep, for, like the life of the child, the father's sleep is prolonged for a moment by the dream.

[31] This idea has been borrowed from the theory of sleep of Liebault, who revived hypnotic research in modern times (Du Sommeil provoque, etc., Paris [1889]).

The underlying motive is: "Let the dream go on, or I must wake up." As in this dream, so in all others, the wish to sleep lends its support to the unconscious wish. In chapter III we cited dreams which were manifestly dreams of convenience. But in truth all dreams may claim this designation. The efficacy of the wish to go on sleeping is most easily recognized in the awakening dreams, which so elaborate the external sensory stimulus that it becomes compatible with the continuance of sleep; they weave it into a dream in order to rob it of any claims it might make as a reminder of the outer world. But this wish to go on sleeping must also play its part in permitting all other dreams, which can only act as disturbers of the state of sleep from within. "Don't worry; sleep on; it's only a dream," is in many cases the suggestion of the Pcs to consciousness when the dream gets too bad; and this describes in a quite general way the attitude of our dominant psychic activity towards dreaming, even though the thought remains unuttered. I must draw the conclusion that throughout the whole of our sleep we are just as certain that we are dreaming as we are certain that we are sleeping. It is imperative to disregard the objection that our consciousness is never directed to the latter knowledge, and that it is directed to the former knowledge only on special occasions, when the censorship feels, as it were, taken by surprise. On the contrary, there are persons in whom the retention at night of the knowledge that they are sleeping and dreaming becomes quite manifest, and who are thus apparently endowed with the conscious faculty of guiding their dream-life. Such a dreamer, for example, is dissatisfied with the turn taken by a dream; he breaks it off without waking, and begins it afresh, in order to continue it along different lines, just like a popular author who, upon request, gives a happier ending to his play. Or on another occasion, when the dream places him in a sexually exciting situation, he thinks in his sleep: "I don't want to continue this dream and exhaust myself by an emission; I would rather save it for a real situation."

The Marquis Hervey (Vaschide) declared that he had gained such power over his dreams that he could accelerate their course at will, and turn them in any direction he wished. It seems that in him the wish to sleep had accorded a place to another, a preconscious wish, the wish to observe his dreams and to derive pleasure from them. Sleep is just as compatible with such a wish-resolve as it is with some proviso as a condition of waking up (wet-nurse's sleep), We know, too, that in all persons an interest in dreams greatly increases the number of dreams remembered after waking.

Concerning other observations as to the guidance of dreams, Ferenczi states: "The dream takes the thought that happens to occupy our psychic life at the moment, and elaborates it from all sides. It lets any given dream-picture drop when there is a danger that the wish-fulfilment will miscarry, and attempts a new kind of solution, until it finally succeeds in creating a wish-fulfilment that satisfies in one compromise both instances of the psychic life."

D. Waking Caused by Dreams - The Function of Dreams - The Anxiety Dream Now that we know that throughout the night the preconscious is orientated to the wish to sleep, we can follow the dream-process with proper understanding. But let us first summarize what we already know about this process. We have seen that day-residues are left over from the waking activity of the mind, residues from which it has not been possible to withdraw all cathexis. Either one of the unconscious wishes has been aroused through the waking activity during the day or it so happens that the two coincide; we have already discussed the multifarious possibilities. Either already during the day or only on the establishment of the state of sleep the unconscious wish has made its way to the day-residues, and has effected a transference to them. Thus there arises a wish transferred to recent material; or the suppressed recent wish is revived by a reinforcement from the unconscious. This wish now endeavours to make its way to consciousness along the normal path of the thought processes, through the preconscious, to which indeed it belongs by virtue of one of its constituent elements. It is, however, confronted by the censorship which still subsists, and to whose influence it soon succumbs. It now takes on the distortion for which the way has already been paved by the transference to recent material. So far it is on the way to becoming something resembling an obsession, a delusion, or the like, i.e., a thought reinforced by a transference, and distorted in expression owing to the censorship. But its further progress is now checked by the state of sleep of the preconscious; this system has presumably protected itself against invasion by diminishing its excitations. The dream-process, therefore, takes the regressive course, which is just opened up by the peculiarity of the sleeping state, and in so doing follows the attraction exerted on it by memorygroups, which are, in part only, themselves present as visual cathexis, not as translations into the symbols of the later systems. On its way to regression it acquires representability. The subject of compression will be discussed later. The dream-process has by this time covered the second part of its contorted course. The first part threads its way progressively from the unconscious scenes or phantasies to the preconscious, while the second part struggles back from the boundary of the censorship to the tract of the perceptions. But when the dream-process becomes a perceptioncontent, it has, so to speak, eluded the obstacle set up in the Pcs by the censorship and the sleeping state. It succeeds in drawing attention to itself, and in being remarked by consciousness. For consciousness, which for us means a sense-organ for the apprehension of psychic qualities, can be excited in waking life from two sources: firstly, from the periphery of the whole apparatus, the perceptive system; and secondly, from the excitations of pleasure and pain which emerge as the sole psychic qualities yielded by the transpositions of energy in the interior of the apparatus. All other processes in the Psi-systems, even those in the preconscious, are devoid of all psychic quality, and are therefore not objects of consciousness, inasmuch as they do not provide either pleasure or pain for its perception. We shall have to assume that these releases of pleasure and pain automatically regulate the course of the cathectic processes. But in order to make possible more delicate performances, it subsequently proved necessary to render the flow of ideas more independent of pain-signals. To accomplish this, the Pcs system needed qualities of its own which could attract consciousness, and most probably received them through the connection of the preconscious processes with the memorysystem of speech-symbols, which was not devoid of quality. Through the qualities of this system, consciousness, hitherto only a sense-organ for perceptions, now becomes also a sense-organ for a part of our thought-processes. There are now, as it were, two sensory surfaces, one turned toward perception and the other toward the preconscious thought-processes.

I must assume that the sensory surface of consciousness which is turned to the preconscious is rendered far more unexcitable by sleep than the surface turned toward the P-system. The giving up of interest in the nocturnal thought-process is, of course, an appropriate procedure. Nothing is to happen in thought; the preconscious wants to sleep. But once the dream becomes perception, it is capable of exciting consciousness through the qualities now gained. The sensory excitation performs what is in fact its function; namely, it directs a part of the cathectic energy available in the Pcs to the exciting cause in the form of attention. We must therefore admit that the dream always has a waking effect - that is, it calls into activity part of the quiescent energy of the Pcs. Under the influence of this energy, it now undergoes the process which we have described as secondary elaboration with a view to coherence and comprehensibility. This means that the dream is treated by this energy like any other perception-content; it is subjected to the same anticipatory ideas as far, at least, as the material allows. As far as this third part of the dream-process has any direction, this is once more progressive.

To avoid misunderstanding, it will not be amiss to say a few words as to the temporal characteristics of these dream-processes. In a very interesting discussion, evidently suggested by Maury's puzzling guillotine dream, Goblot tries to demonstrate that a dream takes up no other time than the transition period between sleeping and waking. The process of waking up requires time;

during this time the dream occurs. It is supposed that the final picture of the dream is so vivid that it forces the dreamer to wake; in reality it is so vivid only because when it appears the dreamer is already very near waking. "Un reve, c'est un reveil qui commence."[32]

It has already been pointed out by Dugas that Goblot, in order to generalize his theory, was forced to ignore a great many facts. There are also dreams from which we do not awaken; for example, many dreams in which we dream that we dream. From our knowledge of the dream-work, we can by no means admit that it extends only over the period of waking. On the contrary, we must consider it probable that the first part of the dream-work is already begun during the day, when we are still under the domination of the preconscious. The second phase of the dream-work, viz., the alteration by the censorship, the attraction exercised by unconscious scenes, and the penetration to perception, continues probably all through the night, and accordingly we may always be correct when we report a feeling that we have been dreaming all night, even although we cannot say what we have dreamed. I do not however, think that it is necessary to assume that up to the time of becoming conscious the dreamprocesses really follow the temporal sequence which we have described; viz., that there is first the transferred dream-wish, then the process of distortion due to the censorship, and then the change of direction to regression, etc. We were obliged to construct such a sequence for the sake of description; in reality, however, it is probably rather a question of simultaneously trying this path and that, and of the excitation fluctuating to and fro, until finally, because it has attained the most apposite concentration, one particular grouping remains in the field. Certain personal experiences even incline me to believe that the dream-work often requires more than one day and one night to produce its result, in which case the extraordinary art manifested in the construction of the dream is shorn of its miraculous character. In my opinion, even the regard for the comprehensibility of the

---

[32] A dream is the beginning of wakening.

dream as a perceptual event may exert its influence before the dream attracts consciousness to itself. From this point, however, the process is accelerated, since the dream is henceforth subjected to the same treatment as any other perception. It is like fire works, which require hours for their preparation and then flare up in a moment.

Through the dream-work, the dream-process now either gains sufficient intensity to attract consciousness to itself and to arouse the preconscious (quite independently of the time or profundity of sleep), or its intensity is insufficient, and it must wait in readiness until attion, becoming more alert immediately before waking, meets it half-way. Most dreams seem to operate with relatively slight psychic intensities, for they wait for the process of waking. This, then, explains the fact that as a rule we perceive something dreamed if we are suddenly roused from a deep sleep. Here, as well as in spontaneous waking, our first glance lights upon the perception-content created by the dream-work, while the next falls on that provided by the outer world.

But of greater theoretical interest are those dreams which are capable of waking us in the midst of our sleep. We may bear in mind the purposefulness which can be demonstrated in all other cases, and ask ourselves why the dream, that is, the unconscious wish, is granted the power to disturb our sleep, i.e., the fulfilment of the preconscious wish. The explanation is probably to be found in certain relations of energy which we do not yet understand. If we did so, we should probably find that the freedom given to the dream and the expenditure upon it of a certain detached attention represent a saving of energy as against the alternative case of the unconscious having to be held in check at night just as it is during the day. As experience shows, dreaming, even if it interrupts our sleep several times a night, still remains compatible with sleep. We wake up for a moment, and immediately fall asleep again. It is like driving off a fly in our sleep; we awake ad hoc. When we fall asleep again we have removed the cause of disturbance. The familiar examples of the sleep of wet-nurses, etc., show that the fulfilment of the wish to sleep is quite compatible with the maintenance of a certain amount of attention in a given direction.

But we must here take note of an objection which is based on a greater knowledge of the unconscious processes. We have ourselves described the unconscious wishes as always active, whilst nevertheless asserting that in the daytime they are not strong enough to make themselves perceptible.

But when the state of sleep supervenes, and the unconscious wish has shown its power to form a dream, and with it to awaken the preconscious, why does this power lapse after cognizance has been taken of the dream? Would it not seem more probable that the dream should continually renew itself, like the disturbing fly which, when driven away, takes pleasure in returning again and again? What justification have we for our assertion that the dream removes the disturbance to sleep?

It is quite true that the unconscious wishes are always active. They represent paths which are always practicable, whenever a quantum of excitation makes use of them. It is indeed an outstanding peculiarity of the unconscious processes that they are indestructible. Nothing can be brought to an end in the unconscious; nothing is past or forgotten. This is impressed upon us emphatically in the study of the neuroses, and especially of hysteria. The unconscious path of thought which leads to the discharge through an attack is forthwith passable again when there is a sufficient accumulation of excitation. The mortification suffered thirty years ago operates, after having gained access to the unconscious sources of affect, during all these thirty years as though it were a recent experience. Whenever its memory is touched, it revives, and shows itself to be cathected with excitation which procures a motor discharge for itself in an attack. It is precisely here that psychotherapy must intervene, its task being to ensure that the unconscious processes are settled and forgotten. Indeed, the fading of memories and the weak affect of impressions which are no longer recent, which we are apt to take as self-evident, and to explain as a primary effect of time on our psychic memory-residues, are in reality secondary changes brought about by laborious work. It is the preconscious that accomplishes this work; and the only course which psychotherapy can pursue is to bring the Ucs under the dominion of the Pcs.

There are, therefore, two possible issues for any single unconscious excitation-process. Either it is left to itself, in which case it ultimately breaks through somewhere and secures, on this one occasion, a discharge for its excitation into motility, or it succumbs to the influence of the preconscious, and through this its excitation becomes bound instead of being discharged. It is the latter case that occurs in the dream-process. The cathexis from the Pcs which goes to meet the dream once this has attained to perception, because it has been drawn thither by the excitation of consciousness, binds the unconscious excitation of the dream and renders it harmless as a disturber of sleep. When the dreamer wakes up for a moment, he has really chased away the fly that threatened to disturb his sleep. We may now begin to suspect that it is really more expedient and economical to give way to the unconscious wish, to leave clear its path to regression so that and it may form a dream, and then to bind and dispose of this dream by means of a small outlay of preconscious work, than to hold the unconscious in check throughout the whole period of sleep. It was, indeed, to be expected that the dream, even if originally it was not a purposeful process, would have seized upon some definite function in the play of forces of the psychic life. We now see what this function is. The dream has taken over the task of bringing the excitation of the Ucs, which had been left free, back under the domination of the preconscious; it thus discharges the excitation of the Ucs, acts as a safetyvalve for the latter, and at the same time, by a slight outlay of waking activity, secures the sleep of the preconscious. Thus, like the other psychic formations of its group, the dream offers itself as a compromise, serving both systems simultaneously, by fulfilling the wishes of both, in so far as they are mutually compatible. A glance at Robert's "elimination theory" will show that we must agree with this author on his main point, namely, the determination of the function of dreams, though we differ from him in our general presuppositions and in our estimation of the dreamprocess.[33]

But an obvious reflection must show us that this secondary function of the dream has no claim to recognition within the framework of any dreaminterpretation.

Thinking ahead, making resolutions, sketching out attempted solutions which can then perhaps be realized in waking life - these and many more performances are functions of the unconscious and preconscious activities of the mind which continue as day-residues in the sleeping state, and can then combine with an unconscious wish to form a dream. The function of thinking ahead in the dream is thus rather a function of preconscious waking thought, the result of which may be disclosed to us by the analysis of dreams or other phenomena.

After the dream has so long been fused with its manifest content, one must now guard against confusing it with the latent dream-thoughts.

The above qualification - in so far as the two wishes are mutually compatible - contains a suggestion that there may be cases in which the function of the dream fails. The dream-process is, to begin with, admitted as a wish-fulfilment of the unconscious, but if this attempted wish-fulfilment disturbs the preconscious so profoundly that the latter can no longer maintain its state of rest, the dream has broken the compromise, and has failed to perform the second part of its task. It is then at once broken off, and replaced by complete awakening. But even here it is not

[33] Is this the only function which we can attribute to dreams? I know of no other. A. Maeder, to be sure, has endeavoured to claim for the dream yet other secondary functions. He started from the just observation that many dreams contain attempts to provide solutions of conflicts, which are afterwards actually carried through. They thus behave like preparatory practice for waking activities. He therefore drew a parallel between dreaming and the play of animals and children, which is to be conceived as a training of the inherited instincts, and a preparation for their later serious activity, thus setting up a fonction ludique for the dream. A little while before Maeder, Alfred Adler likewise emphasized the function of thinking ahead in the dream. (An analysis which I published in 1905 contained a dream which may be conceived as a resolution-dream, which was repeated night after night until it was realized.)

really the fault of the dream if, though at other times the guardian, it has now to appear as the disturber of sleep, nor need this prejudice us against its averred purposive character. This is not the only instance in the organism in which a contrivance that is usually to the purpose becomes inappropriate and disturbing so soon as something is altered in the conditions which engender it; the disturbance, then, at all events serves the new purpose of indicating the change, and of bringing into play against it the means of adjustment of the organism. Here, of course, I am thinking of the anxiety-dream, and lest it should seem that I try to evade this witness against the theory of wish-fulfilment whenever I encounter it, I will at least give some indications as to the explanation of the anxiety-dream.

That a psychic process which develops anxiety may still be a wish-fulfilment has long ceased to imply any contradiction for us. We may explain this occurrence by the fact that the wish belongs to one system (the Ucs), whereas the other system (the Pcs) has rejected and suppressed it.[34]

The subjection of the Ucs by the Pcs is not thoroughgoing even in perfect psychic health; the extent of this suppression indicates the degree of our psychic normality. Neurotic symptoms indicate to us that the two systems are in mutual conflict; the symptoms are the result of a compromise in this conflict, and they temporarily put an end to it. On the one hand, they afford the Ucs a way out for the discharge of its excitation - they serve it as a kind of sally-gate - while, on the other hand, they give the Pcs the possibility of dominating the Ucs in some degree. It is instructive to consider, for example, the significance of a hysterical phobia, or of agoraphobia. A neurotic is said to be incapable of crossing the street alone, and this we should rightly call a symptom. Let someone now remove this symptom by constraining him to this action which he deems himself incapable of performing. The result will be an attack of anxiety, just as an attack of anxiety in the street has often been the exciting cause of the establishment

---

[34] General Introduction to Psycho-Analysis.

of an agoraphobia. We thus learn that the symptom has been constituted in order to prevent the anxiety from breaking out. The phobia is thrown up before the anxiety like a frontier fortress.

We cannot enlarge further on this subject unless we examine the role of the affects in these processes, which can only be done here imperfectly. We will therefore affirm the proposition that the principal reason why the suppression of the Ucs becomes necessary is that, if the movement of ideas in the Ucs were allowed to run its course, it would develop an affect which originally had the character of pleasure, but which, since the process of repression, bears the character of pain. The aim, as well as the result, of the suppression is to prevent the development of this pain. The suppression extends to the idea-content of the Ucs, because the liberation of pain might emanate from this idea-content. We here take as our basis a quite definite assumption as to the nature of the development of affect. This is regarded as a motor or secretory function, the key to the innervation of which is to be found in the ideas of the Ucs. Through the domination of the Pcs these ideas are as it were strangled, that is, inhibited from sending out the impulse that would develop the affect. The danger which arises, if cathexis by the Pcs ceases, thus consists in the fact that the unconscious excitations would liberate an affect that - in consequence of the repression that has previously occurred - could only be felt as pain or anxiety.

This danger is released if the dream-process is allowed to have its own way. The conditions for its realization are that repressions shall have occurred, and that the suppressed wish-impulses can become sufficiently strong. They, therefore, fall entirely outside the psychological framework of dream-formation. Were it not for the fact that our theme is connected by just one factor with the theme of the development of anxiety, namely, by the setting free of the Ucs during sleep, I could refrain from the discussion of the anxiety-dream altogether, and thus avoid all the obscurities involved in it.

The theory of the anxiety-dream belongs, as I have already repeatedly stated, to the psychology of the neuroses. I might further add that anxiety in dreams is an anxiety-problem and not a dream-problem. Having once exhibited the point of contact of the psychology of the neuroses with the theme of the dream-process, we have nothing further to do with it. There is only one thing left which I can do. Since I have asserted that neurotic anxiety has its origin in sexual sources, I can subject anxiety-dreams to analysis in order to demonstrate the sexual material in their dreamthoughts.

For good reasons, I refrain from citing any of the examples so abundantly placed at my disposal by neurotic patients, and prefer to give some anxiety-dreams of children.

Personally, I have had no real anxiety-dream for decades, but I do recall one from my seventh or eighth year which I subjected to interpretation some thirty years later. The dream was very vivid, and showed me my beloved mother, with a peculiarly calm, sleeping countenance, carried into the room and laid on the bed by two (or three) persons with birds' beaks. I awoke crying and screaming, and disturbed my parents' sleep. The peculiarly draped, excessively tall figures with beaks I had taken from the illustrations of Philippson's Bible; I believe they represented deities with the heads of sparrowhawks from an Egyptian tomb-relief. The analysis yielded, however, also the recollection of a house-porter's boy, who used to play with us children on a meadow in front of the house; I might add that his name was Philip. It seemed to me then that I first heard from this boy the vulgar word signifying sexual intercourse, which is replaced among educated persons by the Latin word coitus, but which the dream plainly enough indicates by the choice of the birds' heads. I must have guessed the sexual significance of the word from the look of my worldlywise teacher. My mother's expression in the dream was copied from the countenance of my grandfather, whom I had seen a few days before his death snoring in a state of coma. The interpretation of the secondary elaboration in the dream must therefore have been that my mother was dying; the tomb-relief, too, agrees with this. I awoke with this anxiety, and could not calm myself until I had waked my parents. I remember that I suddenly became calm when I saw my mother; it was as though I had needed the assurance: then she was not dead. But this secondary interpretation of the dream had only taken place when the influence of the developed anxiety was already at work. I was not in a state of anxiety because I had dreamt that my mother was dying; I interpreted the dream in this manner in the preconscious elaboration because I was already under the domination of the anxiety. The latter, however, could be traced back, through the repression to a dark, plainly sexual craving, which had found appropriate expression in the visual content of the dream.

A man twenty-seven years of age, who had been seriously ill for a year, had repeatedly dreamed, between the ages of eleven and thirteen, dreams attended with great anxiety, to the effect that a man with a hatchet was running after him; he wanted to run away, but seemed to be paralysed, and could not move from the spot. This may be taken as a good and typical example of a very common anxiety-dream, free from any suspicion of a sexual meaning. In the analysis, the dreamer first thought of a story told him by his uncle (chronologically later than the dream), viz., that he was attacked at night in the street by a suspicious-looking individual; and he concluded from this association that he might have heard of a similar episode at the time of the dream. In association with the hatchet, he recalled that during this period of his life he once hurt his hand with a hatchet while chopping wood. This immediately reminded him of his relations with his younger brother, whom he used to maltreat and knock down. He recalled, in particular, one occasion when he hit his brother's head with his boot and made it bleed, and his mother said: "I'm afraid he will kill him one day." While he seemed to be thus held by the theme of violence, a memory from his ninth year suddenly emerged. His parents had come home late and had gone to bed, whilst he was pretending to be asleep. He soon heard panting, and other sounds that seemed to him mysterious, and he could also guess the position of his parents in bed. His further thoughts showed that he had established an analogy between this relation between his parents and his own relation to his younger brother. He subsumed what was happening between his parents under the notion of "an act of violence and a fight." The fact that he had frequently noticed blood in his mother's bed corroborated this conception.

That the sexual intercourse of adults appears strange and alarming to children who observe it, and arouses anxiety in them, is, I may say, a fact established by everyday experience. I have explained this anxiety on the ground that we have here a sexual excitation which is not mastered by the child's understanding, and which probably also encounters repulsion because their parents are involved, and is therefore transformed into anxiety. At a still earlier period of life the sexual impulse towards the parent of opposite sex does not yet suffer repression, but as we have seen expresses itself freely.

For the night terrors with hallucinations (pavor nocturnus) so frequent in children I should without hesitation offer the same explanation. These, too, can only be due to misunderstood and rejected sexual impulses which, if recorded, would probably show a temporal periodicity, since an intensification of sexual libido may equally be produced by accidentally exciting impressions and by spontaneous periodic processes of development.

I have not the necessary observational material for the full demonstration of this explanation.[35] On the other hand, pediatrists seem to lack the point of view which alone makes intelligible the whole series of phenomena, both from the somatic and from the psychic side. To illustrate by a comical example how closely, if one is made blind by the blinkers of medical mythology, one may pass by the understanding of such cases, I will cite a case which I found in a thesis on pavor nocturnus.

A boy of thirteen, in delicate health, began to be anxious and dreamy; his sleep became uneasy, and once almost every week it was interrupted by an acute attack of anxiety with hallucinations. The memory of these dreams was always very distinct. Thus he

---

[35] This material has since been provided in abundance by the literature of psychoanalysis.

was able to relate that the devil had shouted at him: "Now we have you, now we have you!" and then there was a smell of pitch and brimstone, and the fire burned his skin. From this dream he woke in terror; at first he could not cry out; then his voice came back to him, and he was distinctly heard to say: "No, no, not me; I haven't done anything," or: "Please, don't; I will never do it again!" At other times he said: "Albert has never done that!" Later he avoided undressing, "because the fire attacked him only when he was undressed." In the midst of these evil dreams, which were endangering his health, he was sent into the country, where he recovered in the course of eighteen months. At the age of fifteen he confessed one day: "Je n'osais pas l'avouer, mais j'eprouvais continuellement des picotements et des surexcitations aux parties;[36] a la fin, cela m'enervait tant que plusieurs fois j'ai pense me jeter par la fenetre du dortoir."[37]

It is, of course, not difficult to guess: 1. That the boy had practised masturbation in former years, that he had probably denied it, and was threatened with severe punishment for his bad habit (His confession: Je ne le ferai plus;[38] his denial: Albert n'a jamais fait ca.)[39] 2. That, under the advancing pressure of puberty, the temptation to masturbate was re-awakened through the titillation of the genitals. 3. That now, however, there arose within him a struggle for repression, which suppressed the libido and transformed it into anxiety, and that this anxiety now gathered up the punishments with which he was originally threatened.

Let us, on the other hand, see what conclusions were drawn by the author:

"1. It is clear from this observation that the influence of puberty may produce in a boy of delicate health a condition of extreme weakness, and that this may lead to a very marked cerebral anaemia.[40]

---

[36] The emphasis [on 'parties'] is my own, though the meaning is plain enough without it.
[37] I did not dare admit it, but I continually felt tinglings and overexcitements of the parts; at the end, it wearied me so much that several times I thought to throw myself from the dormitory window.
[38] I will not do it again.
[39] Albert never did that.
[40] The italics ['very marked cerebral anaemia.'] are mine.

"2. This cerebral anaemia produces an alteration of character, demono-maniacal hallucinations, and very violent nocturnal, and perhaps also diurnal, states of anxiety.

"3. The demonomania and the self-reproaches of the boy can be traced to the influences of a religious education which had acted upon him as a child.

"4. All manifestations disappeared as a result of a lengthy sojourn in the country, bodily exercise, and the return of physical strength after the termination of puberty.

"5. Possibly an influence predisposing to the development of the boy's cerebral state may be attributed to heredity and to the father's former syphilis."

Then finally come the concluding remarks: "Nous avons fait entrer cette observation dans le cadre delires apyretiques d'inanition, car c'est a l'ischemie cerebrale que nous rattachons cet etat particulier."[41]

E. The Primary and Secondary Processes. Repression

In attempting to penetrate more profoundly into the psychology of the dream-processes, I have undertaken a difficult task, to which, indeed, my powers of exposition are hardly adequate. To reproduce the simultaneity of so complicated a scheme in terms of a successive description, and at the same time to make each part appear free from all assumptions, goes fairly beyond my powers. I have now to atone for the fact that in my exposition of the psychology of dreams I have been unable to follow the historic development of my own insight. The lines of approach to the comprehension of the dream were laid down for me by previous investigations into the psychology of the neuroses, to which I should not refer here, although I am constantly obliged to do so; whereas I should like to work in the opposite direction, starting from the dream, and then proceeding to establish its junction with the psychology of the neuroses. I am conscious of

---

[41] We put this case in the file of apyretic delirias of inanition, for it is to cerebral anaemia that we attach this particular state.

all the difficulties which this involves for the reader, but I know of no way to avoid them.

Since I am dissatisfied with this state of affairs, I am glad to dwell upon another point of view, which would seem to enhance the value of my efforts. As was shown in the introductory section, I found myself confronted with a theme which had been marked by the sharpest contradictions on the part of those who had written on it. In the course of our treatment of the problems of the dream, room has been found for most of these contradictory views. We have been compelled to take decided exception to two only of the views expressed: namely, that the dream is a meaningless process, and that it is a somatic process. Apart from these, we have been able to find a place for the truth of all the contradictory opinions at one point or another of the complicated tissue of the facts, and we have been able to show that each expressed something genuine and correct. That our dreams continue the impulses and interests of waking life has been generally confirmed by the discovery of the hidden dreamthoughts.

These concern themselves only with things that seem to us important and of great interest. Dreams never occupy themselves with trifles.

But we have accepted also the opposite view, namely, that the dream gathers up the indifferent residues of the day, and cannot seize upon any important interest of the day until it has in some measure withdrawn itself from waking activity. We have found that this holds true of the dreamcontent, which by means of distortion gives the dream-thought an altered expression. We have said that the dream-process, owing to the nature of the mechanism of association, finds it easier to obtain possession of recent or indifferent material, which has not yet been put under an embargo by our waking mental activity; and that, on account of the censorship, it transfers the psychic intensity of the significant but also objectionable material to the indifferent. The hypermnesia of the dream and its ability to dispose of infantile material have become the main foundations of our doctrine; in our theory of dreams we have assigned to a wish of infantile origin the part of the indispensable motive-power of dream-formation. It has not, of course, occurred to us to doubt the experimentally demonstrated significance of external sensory stimuli during sleep; but we have placed this material in the same relation to the dream-wish as the thought-residues left over from our waking activity. We need not dispute the fact that the dream interprets objective sensory stimuli after the manner of an illusion; but we have supplied the motive for this interpretation, which has been left indeterminate by other writers. The interpretation proceeds in such a way that the perceived object is rendered harmless as a source of disturbance of sleep, whilst it is made usable for the wish-fulfilment. Though we do not admit as a special source of dreams the subjective state of excitation of the sensory organs during sleep (which seems to have been demonstrated by Trumbull Ladd), we are, nevertheless, able to explain this state of excitation by the regressive revival of the memories active behind the dream. As to the internal organic sensations, which are wont to be taken as the cardinal point of the explanation of dreams, these, too, find a place in our conception, though indeed a more modest one. These sensations - the sensations of falling, of soaring, or of being inhibited - represent an ever-ready material, which the dream-work can employ to express the dream-thought as often as need arises.

That the dream-process is a rapid and momentary one is, we believe, true as regards the perception by consciousness of the preformed dreamcontent; but we have found that the preceding portions of the dream-process probably follow a slow, fluctuating course. As for the riddle of the superabundant dream-content compressed into the briefest moment of time, we have been able to contribute the explanation that the dream seizes upon ready-made formations of the psychic life. We have found that it is true that dreams are distorted and mutilated by the memory, but that this fact presents no difficulties, as it is only the last manifest portion of a process of distortion which has been going on from the very beginning of the dream-work. In the embittered controversy, which has seemed irreconcilable, whether the psychic life is asleep at night, or can make the same use of all its faculties as during the day, we have been able to conclude that both sides are right, but that neither is entirely so. In the dreamthoughts we found evidence of a highly complicated intellectual activity, operating with almost all the resources of the psychic apparatus; yet it cannot be denied that these dream-thoughts have originated during the day, and it is indispensable to assume that there is a sleeping state of the psychic life. Thus, even the doctrine of partial sleep received its due, but we have found the characteristic feature of the sleeping state not in the disintegration of the psychic system of connections, but in the special attitude adopted by the psychic system which is dominant during the day - the attitude of the wish to sleep. The deflection from the outer world retains its significance for our view, too; though not the only factor at work, it helps to make possible the regressive course of the dream-representation. The abandonment of voluntary guidance of the flow of ideas is incontestable; but psychic life does not thereby become aimless, for we have seen that upon relinquishment of the voluntary directing ideas, involuntary ones take charge. On the other hand, we have not only recognized the loose associative connection of the dream, but have brought a far greater area within the scope of this kind of connection than could have been suspected; we have, however, found it merely an enforced substitute for another, a correct and significant type of association. To be sure, we too have called the dream absurd, but examples have shown us how wise the dream is when it simulates absurdity. As regards the functions that have been attributed to the dream, we are able to accept them all.

That the dream relieves the mind, like a safety-valve, and that, as Robert has put it, all kinds of harmful material are rendered harmless by representation in the dream, not only coincides exactly with our own theory of the twofold wish-fulfilment in the dream, but in its very wording becomes more intelligible for us than it is for Robert himself. The free indulgence of the psyche in the play of its faculties is reproduced in our theory as the non-interference of the preconscious activity with the dream. The return of the embryonal standpoint of psychic life in the dream, and Havelock Ellis's remark that the dream is "an archaic world of vast emotions and imperfect thoughts," appear to us as happy anticipations of our own exposition, which asserts that primitive modes of operations that are suppressed during the day play a part in the formation of dreams. We can fully identify ourselves with Sully's statement, that "our dreams bring back again our earlier and successively developed personalities, our old ways of regarding things, with impulses and modes of reaction which ruled us long ago"; and for us, as for Delage, the suppressed material becomes the mainspring of the dream.

We have fully accepted the role that Scherner ascribes to the dream-phantasy, and his own interpretations, but we have been obliged to transpose them, as it were, to another part of the problem. It is not the dream that creates the phantasy, but the activity of unconscious phantasy that plays the leading part in the formation of the dream-thoughts. We remain indebted to Scherner for directing us to the source of the dream-thoughts, but almost everything that he ascribes to the dream-work is attributable to the activity of the unconscious during the day, which instigates dreams no less than neurotic symptoms. The dream-work we had to separate from this activity as something quite different and far more closely controlled.

Finally, we have by no means renounced the relation of the dream to psychic disturbances, but have given it, on new ground, a more solid foundation.

Held together by the new features in our theory as by a superior unity, we find the most varied and most contradictory conclusions of other writers fitting into our structure; many of them are given a different turn, but only a few of them are wholly rejected. But our own structure is still unfinished. For apart from the many obscure questions in which we have involved ourselves by our advance into the dark regions of psychology, we are now, it would seem, embarrassed by a new contradiction. On the one hand, we have made it appear that the dream-thoughts proceed from perfectly normal psychic activities, but on the other hand we have found among the dream-thoughts a number of entirely abnormal mental processes, which extend also to the dream-content, and which we reproduce in the interpretation of the dream. All that we have termed the dreamwork seems to depart so completely from the psychic processes which we recognize as correct and appropriate that the severest judgments expressed by the writers mentioned as to the low level of psychic achievement of dreams must appear well founded.

Here, perhaps, only further investigations can provide an explanation and set us on the right path. Let me pick out for renewed attention one of the constellations which lead to dream-formation.

We have learned that the dream serves as a substitute for a number of thoughts derived from our daily life, and which fit together with perfect logic. We cannot, therefore, doubt that these thoughts have their own origin in our normal mental life. All the qualities which we value in our thought-processes, and which mark them out as complicated performances of a high order, we shall find repeated in the dream-thoughts. There is, however, no need to assume that this mental work is performed during sleep; such an assumption would badly confuse the conception of the psychic state of sleep to which we have hitherto adhered. On the contrary, these thoughts may very well have their origin in the daytime, and, unremarked by our consciousness, may have gone on from their first stimulus until, at the onset of sleep, they have reached completion. If we are to conclude anything from this state of affairs, it can only be that it proves that the most complex mental operations are possible without the cooperation of consciousness - a truth which we have had to learn anyhow from every psycho-analysis of a patient suffering from hysteria or obsessions. These dream-thoughts are certainly not in themselves incapable of consciousness; if we have not become conscious of them during the day, this may have been due to various reasons. The act of becoming conscious depends upon a definite psychic function - attention - being brought to bear. This seems to be available only in a determinate quantity, which may have been diverted from the train of thought in question by other aims. Another way in which such trains of thought may be withheld from consciousness is the following: From our conscious reflection we know that, when applying our attention, we follow a particular course. But if that course leads us to an idea which cannot withstand criticism, we break off and allow the cathexis of attention to drop. Now, it would seem that the train of thought thus started and abandoned may continue to develop without our attention returning to it, unless at some point it attains a specially high intensity which compels attention. An initial conscious rejection by our judgment, on the ground of incorrectness or uselessness for the immediate purpose of the act of thought, may, therefore, be the cause of a thought-process going on unnoticed by consciousness until the onset of sleep.

Let us now recapitulate: We call such a train of thought a preconscious train, and we believe it to be perfectly correct, and that it may equally well be a merely neglected train or one that has been interrupted and suppressed. Let us also state in plain terms how we visualize the movement of our thought. We believe that a certain quantity of excitation, which we call cathectic energy, is displaced from a purposive idea along the association paths selected by this directing idea. A neglected train of thought has received no such cathexis, and the cathexis has been withdrawn from one that was suppressed or rejected; both have thus been left to their own excitations. The train of thought cathected by some aim becomes able under certain conditions to attract the attention of consciousness, and by the mediation of consciousness it then receives hyper-cathexis. We shall be obliged presently to elucidate our assumptions as to the nature and function of consciousness.

A train of thought thus incited in the Pcs may either disappear spontaneously, or it may continue. The former eventuality we conceive as follows: it diffuses its energy through all the association paths emanating from it, and throws the entire chain of thoughts into a state of excitation, which continues for a while, and then subsides, through the excitation which had called for discharge being transformed into dormant cathexis. If this first eventuality occurs, the process has no further significance for dream-formation. But other directing ideas are lurking in our preconscious, which have their source in our unconscious and ever-active wishes. These may gain control of the excitation in the circle of thoughts thus left to itself, establish a connection between it and the unconscious wish, and transfer to it the energy inherent in the unconscious wish. Henceforth the neglected or suppressed train of thought is in a position to maintain itself, although this reinforcement gives it no claim to access to consciousness. We may say, then, that the hitherto preconscious train of thought has been drawn into the unconscious.

Other constellations leading to dream-formation might be as follows: The preconscious train of thought might have been connected from the beginning with the unconscious wish, and for that reason might have met with rejection by the dominating aim - cathexis. Or an unconscious wish might become active for other (possibly somatic) reasons, and of its own accord seek a transference to the psychic residues not cathected by the Pcs. All three cases have the same result: there is established in the preconscious a train of thought which, having been abandoned by the preconscious cathexis, has acquired cathexis from the unconscious wish.

From this point onward the train of thought is subjected to a series of transformations which we no longer recognize as normal psychic processes, and which give a result that we find strange, a psychopathological formation. Let us now emphasize and bring together these transformations:

1. The intensities of the individual ideas become capable of discharge in their entirety, and pass from one idea to another, so that individual ideas are formed which are endowed with great intensity. Through the repeated occurrence of this process, the

intensity of an entire train of thought may ultimately be concentrated in a single conceptual unit. This is the fact of compression or condensation with which we become acquainted when investigating the dream-work. It is condensation that is mainly responsible for the strange impression produced by dreams, for we know of nothing analogous to it in the normal psychic life that is accessible to consciousness. We get here, too, ideas which are of great psychic significance as nodal points or as end-results of whole chains of thought, but this value is not expressed by any character actually manifest for our internal perception; what is represented in it is not in any way made more intensive. In the process of condensation the whole set of psychic connections becomes transformed into the intensity of the idea-content. The situation is the same as when, in the case of a book, I italicize or print in heavy type any word to which I attach outstanding value for the understanding of the text. In speech, I should pronounce the same word loudly, and deliberately, and with emphasis. The first simile points immediately to one of the examples which were given of the dream-work (trimethylamine in the dream of Irma's injection). Historians of art call our attention to the fact that the most ancient sculptures known to history follow a similar principle, in expressing the rank of the persons represented by the size of the statues. The king is made two or three times as tall as his retinue or his vanquished enemies. But a work of art of the Roman period makes use of more subtle means to accomplish the same end. The figure of the Emperor is placed in the centre, erect and in his full height, and special care is bestowed on the modelling of this figure; his enemies are seen cowering at his feet; but he is no longer made to seem a giant among dwarfs. At the same time, in the bowing of the subordinate to his superior, even in our own day, we have an echo of this ancient principle of representation.

The direction followed by the condensations of the dream is prescribed on the one hand by the true preconscious relations of the dream-thoughts, and, on the other hand, by the attraction of the visual memories in the unconscious. The success of the condensation-work produces those intensities which are required for penetration to the perception-system.

2. By the free transference of intensities, and in the service of the condensation, intermediary ideas - compromises, as it were - are formed (cf. the numerous examples). This, also, is something unheard of in the normal movement of our ideas, where what is of most importance is the selection and the retention of the right conceptual material. On the other hand, composite and compromise formations occur with extraordinary frequency when we are trying to find verbal expression for preconscious thoughts; these are considered slips of the tongue.

3. The ideas which transfer their intensities to one another are very loosely connected, and are joined together by such forms of association as are disdained by our serious thinking, and left to be exploited solely by wit. In particular, assonances and punning associations are treated as equal in value to any other associations.

4. Contradictory thoughts do not try to eliminate one another, but continue side by side, and often combine to form condensation-products, as though no contradiction existed; or they form compromises for which we should never forgive our thought, but which we frequently sanction in our action.

These are some of the most conspicuous abnormal processes to which the dream-thoughts which have previously been rationally formed are subjected in the course of the dream-work. As the main feature of these processes, we may see that the greatest importance is attached to rendering the cathecting energy mobile and capable of discharge; the content and the intrinsic significance of the psychic elements to which these cathexes adhere become matters of secondary importance. One might perhaps assume that condensation and compromise-formation are effected only in the service of regression, when the occasion arises for changing thoughts into images. But the analysis - and still more plainly the synthesis - of such dreams as show no regression towards images, e.g., the dream Autodidasker: Conversation with

Professor N, reveals the same processes of displacement and condensation as do the rest.

We cannot, therefore, avoid the conclusion that two kinds of essentially different psychic processes participate in dream-formation; one forms perfectly correct and fitting dream-thoughts, equivalent to the results of normal thinking, while the other deals with these thoughts in a most astonishing and, as it seems, incorrect way. The latter process we have already set apart in chapter VI as the dream-work proper. What can we say now as to the derivation of this psychic process?

It would be impossible to answer this question here if we had not penetrated a considerable way into the psychology of the neuroses, and especially of hysteria. From this, however, we learn that the same "incorrect" psychic processes - as well as others not enumerated - control the production of hysterical symptoms. In hysteria, too, we find at first a series of perfectly correct and fitting thoughts, equivalent to our conscious ones, of whose existence in this form we can, however, learn nothing, i.e., which we can only subsequently reconstruct. If they have forced their way anywhere to perception, we discover from the analysis of the symptom formed that these normal thoughts have been subjected to abnormal treatment, and that by means of condensation and compromise-formation, through superficial associations which cover up contradictions, and eventually along the path of regression, they have been conveyed into the symptom. In view of the complete identity between the peculiarities of the dream-work and those of the psychic activity which issues in psychoneurotic symptoms, we shall feel justified in transferring to the dream the conclusions urged upon us by hysteria.

From the theory of hysteria we borrow the proposition that such an abnormal psychic elaboration of a normal train of thought takes place only when the latter has been used for the transference of an unconscious wish which dares from the infantile life and is in a state of repression. Complying with this proposition, we have built up the theory of the dream on the assumption that the actuating dream-wish invariably originates in the unconscious; which, as we have ourselves admitted, cannot be universally demonstrated, even though it cannot be refuted. But in order to enable us to say just what repression is, after employing this term so freely, we shall be obliged to make a further addition to our psychological scaffolding.

We had elaborated the fiction of a primitive psychic apparatus, the work of which is regulated by the effort to avoid accumulation of excitation, and as far as possible to maintain itself free from excitation. For this reason it was constructed after the plan of a reflex apparatus; motility, in the first place as the path to changes within the body, was the channel of discharge at its disposal. We then discussed the psychic results of experiences of gratification, and were able at this point to introduce a second assumption, namely, that the accumulation of excitation - by processes that do not concern us here - is felt as pain, and sets the apparatus in operation in order to bring about again a state of gratification, in which the diminution of excitation is perceived as pleasure. Such a current in the apparatus, issuing from pain and striving for pleasure, we call a wish. We have said that nothing but a wish is capable of setting the apparatus in motion and that the course of any excitation in the apparatus is regulated automatically by the perception of pleasure and pain. The first occurrence of wishing may well have taken the form of a hallucinatory cathexis of the memory of gratification. But this hallucination, unless it could be maintained to the point of exhaustion, proved incapable of bringing about a cessation of the need, and consequently of securing the pleasure connected with gratification.

Thus, there was required a second activity - in our terminology the activity of a second system - which would not allow the memory-cathexis to force its way to perception and thence to bind the psychic forces, but would lead the excitation emanating from the need-stimulus by a detour, which by means of voluntary motility would ultimately so change the outer world as to permit the real perception of the gratifying object. Thus far we have already elaborated the scheme of the psychic apparatus; these two systems are the germ of what we set up in the fully developed apparatus as the Ucs and Pcs.

To change the outer world appropriately by means of motility requires the accumulation of a large total of experiences in the memory-systems, as well as a manifold consolidation of the relations which are evoked in this memory-material by various directing ideas. We will now proceed further with our assumptions. The activity of the second system, groping in many directions, tentatively sending forth cathexes and retracting them, needs on the one hand full command over all memory-material, but on the other hand it would be a superfluous expenditure of energy were it to send along the individual thought-paths large quantities of cathexis, which would then flow away to no purpose and thus diminish the quantity needed for changing the outer world. Out of a regard for purposiveness, therefore, I postulate that the second system succeeds in maintaining the greater part of the energic cathexes in a state of rest, and in using only a small portion for its operations of displacement. The mechanics of these processes is entirely unknown to me; anyone who seriously wishes to follow up these ideas must address himself to the physical analogies, and find some way of getting a picture of the sequence of motions which ensues on the excitation of the neurones. Here I do no more than hold fast to the idea that the activity of the first Psi-system aims at the free outflow of the quantities of excitation, and that the second system, by means of the cathexes emanating from it, effects an inhibition of this outflow, a transformation into dormant cathexis, probably with a rise of potential. I therefore assume that the course taken by any excitation under the control of the second system is bound to quite different mechanical conditions from those which obtain under the control of the first system. After the second system has completed its work of experimental thought, it removes the inhibition and damming up of the excitations and allows them to flow off into motility.

An interesting train of thought now presents itself if we consider the relations of this inhibition of discharge by the second system to the process of regulation by the pain-principle. Let us now seek out the counterpart of the primary experience of gratification, namely, the objective experience of fear. Let a perception-stimulus act on the primitive apparatus and be the source of a pain-excitation. There will then ensue uncoordinated motor manifestations, which will go on until one of these withdraws the apparatus from perception, and at the same time from the pain. On the reappearance of the percept this manifestation will immediately be repeated (perhaps as a movement of flight), until the percept has again disappeared. But in this case no tendency will remain to recathect the perception of the source of pain by hallucination or otherwise. On the contrary, there will be a tendency in the primary apparatus to turn away again from this painful memory-image immediately if it is in any way awakened, since the overflow of its excitation into perception would, of course, evoke (or more precisely, begin to evoke) pain. This turning away from a recollection, which is merely a repetition of the former flight from perception, is also facilitated by the fact that, unlike the perception, the recollection has not enough quality to arouse consciousness, and thereby to attract fresh cathexis. This effortless and regular turning away of the psychic process from the memory of anything that had once been painful gives us the prototype and the first example of psychic repression. We all know how much of this turning away from the painful, the tactics of the ostrich, may still be shown as present even in the normal psychic life of adults.

In obedience to the pain-principle, therefore, the first Psi-system is quite incapable of introducing anything unpleasant into the thought-nexus. The system cannot do anything but wish. If this were to remain so, the activity of thought of the second system, which needs to have at its disposal all the memories stored up by experience, would be obstructed. But two paths are now open: either the work of the second system frees itself completely from the pain-principle, and continues its course, paying no heed to the pain attached to given memories, or it contrives to cathect the memory of the pain in such a manner as to preclude the liberation of pain. We can reject the first possibility, as the pain-principle also proves to act as a regulator of the cycle of excitation in the second system; we are therefore thrown back upon the second possibility, namely, that this system cathects a memory in such a manner as to inhibit any outflow of excitation from it, and hence, also, the outflow, comparable to a motorinnervation, needed for the development of pain. And thus, setting out from two different starting-points, i.e., from regard for the pain-principle, and from the principle of the least expenditure of innervation, we are led to the hypothesis that cathexis through the second system is at the same time an inhibition of the discharge of excitation. Let us, however, keep a close hold on the fact - for this is the key to the theory of repression - that the second system can only cathect an idea when it is in a position to inhibit any pain emanating from this idea. Anything that withdrew itself from this inhibition would also remain inaccessible for the second system, i.e., would immediately be given up by virtue of the pain-principle.

The inhibition of pain, however, need not be complete; it must be permitted to begin, since this indicates to the second system the nature of the memory, and possibly its lack of fitness for the purpose sought by the process of thought.

The psychic process which is alone tolerated by the first system I shall now call the primary process; and that which results under the inhibiting action of the second system I shall call the secondary process. I can also show at another point for what purpose the second system is obliged to correct the primary process. The primary process strives for discharge of the excitation in order to establish with the quantity of excitation thus collected an identity of perception; the secondary process has abandoned this intention, and has adopted instead the aim of an identity of thought.

All thinking is merely a detour from the memory of gratification (taken as a purposive idea) to the identical cathexis of the same memory, which is to be reached once more by the path of motor experiences. Thought must concern itself with the connecting-paths between ideas without allowing itself to be misled by their intensities. But it is obvious that condensations of ideas and intermediate or compromise-formations are obstacles to the attainment of the identity which is aimed at; by substituting one idea for another they swerve away from the path which would have led onward from the first idea. Such procedures are, therefore, carefully avoided in our secondary thinking. It will readily be seen, moreover, that the pain-principle, although at other times it provides the thought-process with its most important clues, may also put difficulties in its way in the pursuit of identity of thought. Hence, the tendency of the thinking process must always be to free itself more and more from exclusive regulation by the pain-principle, and to restrict the development of affect through the work of thought to the very minimum which remains effective as a signal. This refinement in functioning is to be achieved by a fresh hyper-cathexis, effected with the help of consciousness. But we are aware that this refinement is seldom successful, even in normal psychic life, and that our thinking always remains liable to falsification by the intervention of the pain-principle.

This, however, is not the breach in the functional efficiency of our psychic apparatus which makes it possible for thoughts representing the result of the secondary thought-work to fall into the power of the primary psychic process; by which formula we may now describe the operations resulting in dreams and the symptoms of hysteria. This inadequacy results from the converging of two factors in our development, one of which pertains solely to the psychic apparatus, and has exercised a determining influence on the relation of the two systems, while the other operates fluctuatingly, and introduces motive forces of organic origin into the psychic life. Both originate in the infantile life, and are a precipitate of the alteration which our psychic and somatic organism has undergone since our infantile years.

When I termed one of the psychic processes in the psychic apparatus the primary process, I did so not only in consideration of its status and function, but was also able to take account of the temporal relationship actually involved. So far as we know, a psychic apparatus possessing only the primary process does not exist, and is to that extent a theoretical fiction but this at least is a fact: that the primary processes are present in the apparatus from the beginning, while the secondary processes only take shape gradually during the course of life, inhibiting and overlaying the primary, whilst gaining complete control over them perhaps only in the prime of life. Owing to this belated arrival of the secondary processes, the essence of our being, consisting of unconscious wish-impulses, remains something which cannot be grasped or inhibited by the preconscious; and its part is once and for all restricted to indicating the most appropriate paths for the wish-impulses originating in the unconscious. These unconscious wishes represent for all subsequent psychic strivings a compulsion to which they Must submit themselves, although they may perhaps endeavour to divert them and to guide them to superior aims. In consequence of this retardation, an extensive region of the memorymaterial remains in fact inaccessible to preconscious cathexis.

Now among these wish-impulses originating in the infantile life. indestructible and incapable of inhibition, there are some the fulfilments of which have come to be in contradiction with the purposive ideas of our secondary thinking. The fulfilment of these wishes would no longer produce an affect of pleasure, but one of pain; and it is just this conversion of affect that constitutes the essence of what we call repression. In what manner and by what motive forces such a conversion can take place constitutes the problem of repression, which we need here only to touch upon in passing. It will suffice to note the fact that such a conversion of affect occurs in the course of development (one need only think of the emergence of disgust, originally absent in infantile life), and that it is connected with the activity of the secondary system. The memories from which the unconscious wish evokes a liberation of affect have never been accessible to the Pcs, and for that reason this liberation cannot be inhibited. It is precisely on account of this generation of affect that these ideas are not now accessible even by way of the preconscious thoughts to which they have transferred the energy of the wishes connected with them. On the contrary, the pain-principle comes into play, and causes the Pcs to turn away from these transference-thoughts. These latter are left to themselves, are repressed, and thus, the existence of a store of infantile memories, withdrawn from the beginning from the Pcs, becomes the preliminary condition of repression.

In the most favourable case, the generation of pain terminates so soon as the cathexis is withdrawn from the transference-thoughts in the Pcs, and this result shows that the intervention of the pain-principle is appropriate. It is otherwise, however, if the repressed unconscious wish receives an organic reinforcement which it can put at the service of its transference-thoughts, and by which it can enable them to attempt to break through with their excitation, even if the cathexis of the Pcs has been taken away from them. A defensive struggle then ensues, inasmuch as the Pcs reinforces the opposite to the repressed thoughts (counter-cathexis), and the eventual outcome is that the transference-thoughts (the carriers of the unconscious wish) break through in some form of compromise through symptom-formation. But from the moment that the repressed thoughts are powerfully cathected by the unconscious wish-impulse, but forsaken by the preconscious cathexis, they succumb to the primary psychic process, and aim only at motor discharge; or, if the way is clear, at hallucinatory revival of the desired identity of perception. We have already found, empirically, that the incorrect processes described are enacted only with thoughts which are in a state of repression. We are now in a position to grasp yet another part of the total scheme of the facts. These incorrect Processes are the primary processes of the psychic apparatus; they occur wherever ideas abandoned by the preconscious cathexis are left to themselves and can become filled with the uninhibited energy which flows from the unconscious and strives for discharge. There are further facts which go to show that the processes described as incorrect are not really falsifications of our normal procedure, or defective thinking. but the modes of operation of the psychic apparatus when freed from inhibition.

Thus we see that the process of the conveyance of the preconscious excitation to motility occurs in accordance with the same procedure, and that in the linkage of preconscious ideas with words we may easily find manifested the same displacements and confusions (which we ascribe to inattention). Finally, a proof of the increased work made necessary by the inhibition of these primary modes of procedure might be found in the fact that we achieve a comical effect, a surplus to be discharged through laughter, if we allow these modes of thought to come to consciousness.

The theory of the psychoneuroses asserts with absolute certainty that it can only be sexual wish-impulses from the infantile life, which have undergone repression (affect-conversion) during the developmental period of childhood, which are capable of renewal at later periods of development (whether as a result of our sexual constitution, which has, of course, grown out of an original bisexuality, or in consequence of unfavourable influences in our sexual life); and which therefore supply the motive-power for all psychoneurotic symptom-formation. It is only by the introduction of these sexual forces that the gaps still demonstrable in the theory of repression can be filled. Here, I will leave it undecided whether the postulate of the sexual and infantile holds good for the theory of dreams as well; I am not completing the latter, because in assuming that the dream-wish invariably originates in the unconscious I have already gone a step beyond the demonstrable.[42] Nor will I inquire further into the nature of the difference between the play of psychic forces in dream-formation and in the formation of hysterical symptoms, since

---

[42] Here, as elsewhere, there are gaps in the treatment of the subject, which I have deliberately left, because to fill them up would, on the one hand, require excessive labour, and, on the other hand, I should have to depend on material which is foreign to the dream. Thus, for example, I have avoided stating whether I give the word suppressed a different meaning from that of the word repressed. No doubt, however, it will have become clear that the latter emphasizes more than the former the relation to the unconscious. I have not gone into the problem, which obviously arises, of why

there is missing here the needed fuller knowledge of one of the two things to be compared. But there is another point which I regard as important, and I will confess at once that it was only on account of this point that I entered upon all the discussions concerning the two psychic systems, their modes of operation, and the fact of repression. It does not greatly matter whether I have conceived the psychological relations at issue with approximate correctness, or, as is easily possible in such a difficult matter, wrongly and imperfectly. However our views may change about the interpretation of the psychic censorship or the correct and the abnormal elaboration of the dream-content. it remains certain that such processes are active in dream-formation, and that in their essentials they reveal the closest analogy with the processes observed in the formation of hysterical symptoms. Now the dream is not a pathological phenomenon; it does not presuppose any disturbance of our psychic equilibrium; and it does not leave behind it any weakening of our efficiency or capacities. The objection that no conclusions can be drawn about the dreams of healthy persons from my own dreams and from those of my neurotic patients may be rejected without comment. If, then, from the nature of the given phenomena we infer the nature of their motive forces, we find that the psychic mechanism utilized by the neuroses is not newly-created by a morbid disturbance that lays hold of the psychic life, but lies in readiness

---

the dream-thoughts undergo distortion by the censorship even when they abandon the progressive path to consciousness, and choose the path of regression. And so with other similar omissions. I have, above all, sought to give some idea of the problems to which the further dissection of the dream-work leads, and to indicate the other themes with which these are connected. It was, however, not always easy to decide just where the pursuit should be discontinued. That I have not treated exhaustively the part which the psycho-sexual life plays in the dream, and have avoided the interpretation of dreams of an obviously sexual content, is due to a special reason - which may not perhaps be that which the reader would expect. It is absolutely alien to my views and my neuropathological doctrines to regard the sexual life as a pudendum with which neither the physician nor the scientific investigator should concern himself. To me, the moral indignation which prompted the translator of Artemidorus of Daldis to keep from the reader's knowledge the chapter on sexual dreams contained in the Symbolism of Dreams is merely ludicrous. For my own part, what decided my procedure was solely the knowledge that in the explanation of sexual dreams I should be bound to get deeply involved in the still unexplained problems of perversion and bisexuality; it was for this reason that I reserved this material for treatment elsewhere.

in the normal structure of our psychic apparatus. The two psychic systems, the frontier-censorship between them, the inhibition and overlaying of the one activity by the other, the relations of both to consciousness - or whatever may take place of these concepts on a juster interpretation of the actual relations - all these belong to the normal structure of our psychic instrument, and the dream shows us one of the paths which lead to a knowledge of this structure. If we wish to be content with a minimum of perfectly assured additions to our knowledge, we shall say that the dream affords proof that the suppressed material continues to exist even in the normal person and remains capable of psychic activity. Dreams are one of the manifestations of this suppressed material; theoretically, this is true in all cases; and in tangible experience, it has been found true in at least a great number of cases, which happen to display most plainly the more striking features of the dream-life. The suppressed psychic material, which in the waking state has been prevented from expression and cut off from internal perception by the mutual neutralization of contradictory attitudes, finds ways and means, under the sway of compromise-formations, of obtruding itself on consciousness during the night. Flectere si nequeo superos, Acheronta movebo.[43] At any rate, the interpretation of dreams is the via regia to a knowledge of the unconscious element in our psychic life.

By the analysis of dreams we obtain some insight into the composition of this most marvellous and most mysterious of instruments; it is true that this only takes us a little way, but it gives us a start which enables us, setting out from the angle of other (properly pathological) formations, to penetrate further in our disjoining of the instrument. For disease - at all events that which is rightly called functional - does not necessarily presuppose the destruction of this apparatus, or the establishment of new cleavages in its interior: it can be explained dynamically by the strengthening and weakening of the components of the play of forces, so many of the activities of which are covered up in normal

---

[43] If I cannot influence the gods, I will stir up Acheron.

functioning. It might be shown elsewhere how the fact that the apparatus is a combination of two instances also permits of a refinement of its normal functioning which would have been impossible to a single system.[44]

F. The Unconscious and Consciousness. Reality.

If we look more closely, we may observe that the psychological considerations examined in the foregoing chapter require us to assume, not the existence of two systems near the motor end of the psychic apparatus, but two kinds of processes or courses taken by excitation. But this does not disturb us; for we must always be ready to drop our auxiliary ideas, when we think we are in a position to replace them by something which comes closer to the unknown reality. Let us now try to correct certain views which may have taken a misconceived form as long as we regarded the two systems, in the crudest and most obvious sense, as two localities within the psychic apparatus - views which have left a precipitate in the terms repression and penetration. Thus, when we say that an unconscious thought strives for translation into the preconscious in order subsequently to penetrate through to consciousness, we do not mean that a second idea has to be formed, in a new locality, like a paraphrase, as it were, whilst the original persists by its side; and similarly, when we speak of penetration into consciousness, we wish carefully to detach from this notion any idea of a change of locality. When we say that a preconscious idea is repressed and subsequently absorbed by the unconscious, we might be tempted by these images, borrowed from the idea of a struggle for a particular territory, to assume that an arrangement is really broken up in the one psychic locality and replaced by a new one in the other locality. For these comparisons we will substitute a description which would seem

---

[44] The dream is not the only phenomenon that permits us to base our psycho-pathology on psychology. In a short unfinished series of articles in the Monatsschrift fur Psychiatrie und Neurologie ("uber den psychischen Mechanismus der Vergesslichkeit," 1898, and "uber Deckerinnerungen," 1899) I attempted to interpret a number of psychic manifestations from everyday life in support of the same conception. (These and other articles on "7forgetting," "Lapses of Speech," etc., have now been published in the Psycho-pathology of Everyday Life.)

to correspond more closely to the real state of affairs; we will say that an energic cathexis is shifted to or withdrawn from a certain arrangement, so that the psychic formation falls under the domination of a given instance or is withdrawn from it. Here again we replace a topographical mode of representation by a dynamic one; it is not the psychic formation that appears to us as the mobile element, but its innervation.[45]

Nevertheless, I think it expedient and justifiable to continue to use the illustrative idea of the two systems. We shall avoid any abuse of this mode of representation if we remember that ideas, thoughts, and psychic formations in general must not in any case be localized in organic elements of the nervous system but, so to speak, between them, where resistances and association-tracks form the correlate corresponding to them. Everything that can become an object of internal perception is virtual, like the image in the telescope produced by the crossing of light-rays. But we are justified in thinking of the systems - which have nothing psychic in themselves, and which never become accessible to our psychic perception - as something similar to the lenses of the telescope, which project the image. If we continue this comparison, we might say that the censorship between the two systems corresponds to the refraction of rays on passing into a new medium.

Thus far, we have developed our psychology on our own responsibility; it is now time to turn and look at the doctrines prevailing in modern psychology, and to examine the relation of these to our theories. The problem of the unconscious in psychology is, according to the forcible statement of Lipps,[46] less a psychological problem than the problem of psychology. As long as psychology disposed of this problem by the verbal explanation that the psychic is the conscious, and that unconscious psychic occurrences are an obvious contradiction, there was no possibility of a physician's observations of abnormal mental states

---
[45] This conception underwent elaboration and modification when it was recognized that the essential character of a preconscious idea was its connection with the residues of verbal ideas.
[46] Der Begriff des Unbewussten in der Psychologie. Lecture delivered at the Third International Psychological Congress at Munich, 1897.

being turned to any psychological account. The physician and the philosopher can meet only when both acknowledge that unconscious psychic processes is the appropriate and justified expression for all established fact. The physician cannot but reject, with a shrug of his shoulders, the assertion that consciousness is the indispensable quality of the psychic; if his respect for the utterances of the philosophers is still great enough, he may perhaps assume that he and they do not deal with the same thing and do not pursue the same science. For a single intelligent observation of the psychic life of a neurotic, a single analysis of a dream, must force upon him the unshakable conviction that the most complicated and the most accurate operations of thought, to which the name of psychic occurrences can surely not be refused, may take place without arousing consciousness.[47] The physician, it is true, does not learn of these unconscious processes until they have produced an effect on consciousness which admits of communication or observation. But this effect on consciousness may show a psychic character which differs completely from the unconscious process, so that internal perception cannot possibly recognize in the first a substitute for the second. The physician must reserve himself the right to penetrate, by a Process of deduction, from the effect on consciousness to the unconscious psychic process; he learns in this way that the effect on consciousness is only a remote psychic product of the unconscious process, and that the latter has not become conscious as such, and has, moreover, existed and operated without in any way betraying itself to consciousness.

Du Prel says: "The problem: what is the psyche, manifestly requires a preliminary examination as to whether consciousness and psyche are identical. But it is just this preliminary question which is answered in the negative by the dream, which shows that the concept of the psyche extends beyond that of consciousness, much as the gravitational force of a star extends beyond its sphere of luminosity".

---

[47] I am happy to be able to point to an author who has drawn from the study of dreams the same conclusion as regards the relation between consciousness and the unconscious.

"It is a truth which cannot be sufficiently emphasized that the concepts of consciousness and of the psyche are not co-extensive".

A return from the over-estimation of the property of consciousness is the indispensable preliminary to any genuine insight into the course of psychic events. As Lipps has said, the unconscious must be accepted as the general basis of the psychic life. The unconscious is the larger circle which includes the smaller circle of the conscious; everything conscious has a preliminary unconscious stage, whereas the unconscious can stop at this stage, and yet claim to be considered a full psychic function. The unconscious is the true psychic reality; in its inner nature it is just as much unknown to us as the reality of the external world, and it is just as imperfectly communicated to us by the data of consciousness as is the external world by the reports of our sense-organs.

We get rid of a series of dream-problems which have claimed much attention from earlier writers on the subject when the old antithesis between conscious life and dream-life is discarded, and the unconscious psychic assigned to its proper place. Thus, many of the achievements which are a matter for wonder in a dream are now no longer to be attributed to dreaming, but to unconscious thinking, which is active also during the day. If the dream seems to make play with a symbolical representation of the body, as Scherner has said, we know that this is the work of certain unconscious phantasies, which are probably under the sway of sexual impulses and find expression not only in dreams, but also in hysterical phobias and other symptoms. If the dream continues and completes mental work begun during the day, and even brings valuable new ideas to light, we have only to strip off the dream-disguise from this, as the contribution of the dream-work, and a mark of the assistance of dark powers in the depths of the psyche (cf. the devil in Tartini's sonata-dream). The intellectual achievement as such belongs to the same psychic forces as are responsible for all such achievements during the day. We are probably much too inclined to over-estimate the conscious character even of intellectual and artistic production. From the reports of certain writers who have been highly productive, such as Goethe and Helmholtz, we learn, rather, that the most essential and original part of their creations came to them in the form of inspirations, and offered itself to their awareness in an almost completed state. In other cases, where there is a concerted effort of all the psychic forces, there is nothing strange in the fact that conscious activity, too, lends its aid. But it is the much-abused privilege of conscious activity to hide from us all other activities wherever it participates.

It hardly seems worth while to take up the historical significance of dreams as a separate theme. Where, for instance, a leader has been impelled by a dream to engage in a bold undertaking, the success of which has had the effect of changing history, a new problem arises only so long as the dream is regarded as a mysterious power and contrasted with other more familiar psychic forces. The problem disappears as soon as we regard the dream as a form of expression for impulses to which a resistance was attached during the day, whilst at night they were able to draw reinforcement from deep-lying sources of excitation.[48] But the great respect with which the ancient peoples regarded dreams is based on a just piece of psychological divination. It is a homage paid to the unsubdued and indestructible element in the human soul, to the demonic power which furnishes the dream-wish, and which we have found again in our unconscious.

It is not without purpose that I use the expression in our unconscious, for what we so call does not coincide with the unconscious of the philosophers, nor with the unconscious of Lipps. As they use the term, it merely means the opposite of the conscious. That there exist not only conscious but also unconscious psychic processes is the opinion at issue, which is so hotly contested and so energetically defended. Lipps enunciates the more comprehensive doctrine that everything psychic exists as unconscious, but that some of it may exist also as conscious.

---

[48] Cf. (chapter II.), the dream (Sa-Turos) of Alexander the Great at the siege of Tyre.

But it is not to prove this doctrine that we have adduced the phenomena of dreams and hysterical symptom-formation; the observation of normal life alone suffices to establish its correctness beyond a doubt. The novel fact that we have learned from the analysis of psycho-pathological formations, and indeed from the first member of the group, from dreams, is that the unconscious - and hence all that is psychic - occurs as a function of two separate systems, and that as such it occurs even in normal psychic life. There are consequently two kinds of unconscious, which have not as yet been distinguished by psychologists. Both are unconscious in the psychological sense; but in our sense the first, which we call Ucs, is likewise incapable of consciousness; whereas the second we call Pcs because its excitations, after the observance of certain rules, are capable of reaching consciousness; perhaps not before they have again undergone censorship, but nevertheless regardless of the Ucs system. The fact that in order to attain consciousness the excitations must pass through an unalterable series, a succession of instances, as is betrayed by the changes produced in them by the censorship, has enabled us to describe them by analogy in spatial terms. We described the relations of the two systems to each other and to consciousness by saying that the system Pcs is like a screen between the system Ucs and consciousness. The system Pcs not only bars access to consciousness, but also controls the access to voluntary motility, and has control of the emission of a mobile cathectic energy, a portion of which is familiar to us as attention.[49]

We must also steer clear of the distinction between the super-conscious and the subconscious, which has found such favour in the more recent literature on the psychoneuroses, for just such a distinction seems to emphasize the equivalence of what is psychic and what is conscious.

What role is now left, in our representation of things, to the phenomenon of consciousness, once so all-powerful and over-shadowing all else?

---

[49] Cf. here my remarks in the Proceedings of the Society for Psychical Research, vol. xxvi, in which the descriptive, dynamic and systematic meanings of the ambiguous word Unconscious are distinguished from one another.

None other than that of a sense-organ for the perception of psychic qualities. According to the fundamental idea of our schematic attempt we can regard conscious perception only as the function proper to a special system for which the abbreviated designation Cs commends itself. This system we conceive to be similar in its mechanical characteristics to the perception-system P, and hence excitable by qualities, and incapable of retaining the trace of changes: i.e., devoid of memory. The psychic apparatus which, with the sense-organ of the P-systems, is turned to the outer world, is itself the outer world for the sense-organ of Cs, whose teleological justification depends on this relationship. We are here once more confronted with the principle of the succession of instances which seems to dominate the structure of the apparatus. The material of excitation flows to the sense-organ Cs from two sides: first from the P-system, whose excitation, qualitatively conditioned, probably undergoes a new elaboration until it attains conscious perception; and, secondly, from the interior of the apparatus itself, whose quantitative processes are perceived as a qualitative series of pleasures and pains once they have reached consciousness after undergoing certain changes.

The philosophers, who became aware that accurate and highly complicated thought-structures are possible even without the co-operation of consciousness, thus found it difficult to ascribe any function to consciousness; it appeared to them a superfluous mirroring of the completed psychic process. The analogy of our Cs system with the perception-systems relieves us of this embarrassment. We see that perception through our sense-organs results in directing an attention-cathexis to the paths along which the incoming sensory excitation diffuses itself; the qualitative excitation of the P-system serves the mobile quantity in the psychic apparatus as a regulator of its discharge. We may claim the same function for the overlying sense-organ of the Cs system. By perceiving new qualities, it furnishes a new contribution for the guidance and suitable distribution of the mobile cathexis-quantities. By means of perceptions of pleasure and pain, it influences the course of the cathexes within the psychic apparatus, which otherwise operates unconsciously and by the displacement of quantities. It is probable that the pain-principle first of all regulates the displacements of cathexis automatically, but it is quite possible that consciousness contributes a second and more subtle regulation of these qualities, which may even oppose the first, and perfect the functional capacity of the apparatus, by placing it in a position contrary to its original design, subjecting even that which induces pain to cathexis and to elaboration. We learn from neuro-psychology that an important part in the functional activity of the apparatus is ascribed to these regulations by the qualitative excitations of the sense-organs. The automatic rule of the primary pain-principle, together with the limitation of functional capacity bound up with it, is broken by the sensory regulations, which are themselves again automatisms. We find that repression, which, though originally expedient, nevertheless finally brings about a harmful lack of inhibition and of psychic control, overtakes memories much more easily than it does perceptions, because in the former there is no additional cathexis from the excitation of the psychic sense-organs. Whilst an idea which is to be warded off may fail to become conscious because it has succumbed to repression, it may on other occasions come to be repressed simply because it has been withdrawn from conscious perception on other grounds. These are clues which we make use of in therapy in order to undo accomplished repressions.

The value of the hyper-cathexis which is produced by the regulating influence of the Cs sense-organs on the mobile quantity is demonstrated in a teleological context by nothing more clearly than by the creation of a new series of qualities, and consequently a new regulation, which constitutes the prerogative of man over animals. For the mental processes are in themselves unqualitative except for the excitations of pleasure and pain which accompany them: which, as we know, must be kept within limits as possible disturbers of thought. In order to endow them with quality, they are associated in man with verbal memories, the qualitative residues of which suffice to draw upon them the attention of consciousness, which in turn endows thought with a new mobile cathexis.

It is only on a dissection of hysterical mental processes that the manifold nature of the problems of consciousness becomes apparent. One then receives the impression that the transition from the preconscious to the conscious cathexis is associated with a censorship similar to that between Ucs and Pcs. This censorship, too, begins to act only when a certain quantitative limit is reached, so that thought-formations which are not very intense escape it. All possible cases of detention from consciousness and of penetration into consciousness under certain restrictions are included within the range of psychoneurotic phenomena; all point to the intimate and twofold connection between the censorship and consciousness. I shall conclude these psychological considerations with the record of two such occurrences.

On the occasion of a consultation a few years ago, the patient was an intelligent-looking girl with a simple, unaffected manner. She was strangely attired; for whereas a woman's dress is usually carefully thought out to the last pleat, one of her stockings was hanging down and two of the buttons of her blouse were undone. She complained of pains in one of her legs, and exposed her calf without being asked to do so. Her chief complaint, however, was as follows: She had a feeling in her body as though something were sticking into it which moved to and fro and shook her through and through. This sometimes seemed to make her whole body stiff. On hearing this, my colleague in consultation looked at me: the trouble was quite obvious to him. To both of us it seemed peculiar that this suggested nothing to the patient's mother, though she herself must repeatedly have been in the situation described by her child. As for the girl, she had no idea of the import of her words, or she would never have allowed them to pass her lips. Here the censorship had been hoodwinked so successfully that under the mask of an innocent complaint a phantasy was admitted to consciousness which otherwise would have remained in the preconscious.

Another example: I began the psycho-analytic treatment of a boy fourteen who was suffering from tic convulsif, hysterical vomiting, headache, etc., by assuring him that after closing his eyes he would see pictures or that ideas would occur to him, which he was to communicate to me. He replied by describing pictures. The last impression he had received before coming to me was revived visually in his memory. He had been playing a game of checkers with his uncle, and now he saw the checkerboard before him. He commented on various positions that were favourable or unfavourable, on moves that were not safe to make. He then saw a dagger lying on the checker-board - an object belonging to his father, but which his phantasy laid on the checkerboard. Then a sickle was lying on the board; a scythe was added; and finally, he saw the image of an old peasant mowing the grass in front of his father's house far away. A few days later I discovered the meaning of this series of pictures. Disagreeable family circumstances had made the boy excited and nervous. Here was a case of a harsh, irascible father, who had lived unhappily with the boy's mother, and whose educational methods consisted of threats; he had divorced his gentle and delicate wife, and remarried; one day he brought home a young woman as the boy's new mother. The illness of the fourteen-year-old boy developed a few days later. It was the suppressed rage against his father that had combined these images into intelligible allusions. The material was furnished by a mythological reminiscence. The sickle was that with which Zeus castrated his father; the scythe and the image of the peasant represented Kronos, the violent old man who devours his children, and upon whom Zeus wreaks his vengeance in so unfilial a manner. The father's marriage gave the boy an opportunity of returning the reproaches and threats which the child had once heard his father utter because he played with his genitals (the draught-board; the prohibited moves; the dagger with which one could kill). We have here long-impressed memories and their unconscious derivatives which, under the guise of meaningless pictures, have slipped into consciousness by the devious paths opened to them.

If I were asked what is the theoretical value of the study of dreams, I should reply that it lies in the additions to psychological knowledge and the beginnings of an understanding of the neuroses which we thereby obtain. Who can foresee the importance a thorough knowledge of the structure and functions of the psychic apparatus may attain, when even our present state of knowledge permits of successful therapeutic intervention in the curable forms of psychoneuroses? But, it may be asked, what of the practical value of this study in regard to a knowledge of the psyche and discovery of the hidden peculiarities of individual character? Have not the unconscious impulses revealed by dreams the value of real forces in the psychic life? Is the ethical significance of the suppressed wishes to be lightly disregarded, since, just as they now create dreams, they may some day create other things?

I do not feel justified in answering these questions. I have not followed up this aspect of the problem of dreams. In any case, however, I believe that the Roman Emperor was in the wrong in ordering one of his subjects to be executed because the latter had dreamt that he had killed the Emperor. He should first of all have endeavoured to discover the significance of the man's dreams; most probably it was not what it seemed to be.

And even if a dream of a different content had actually had this treasonable meaning, it would still have been well to recall the words of Plato - that the virtuous man contents himself with dreaming of that which the wicked man does in actual life. I am therefore of the opinion that dreams should be acquitted of evil. Whether any reality is to be attributed to the unconscious wishes, I cannot say. Reality must, of course, be denied to all transitory and intermediate thoughts. If we had before us the unconscious wishes, brought to their final and truest expression, we should still do well to remember that psychic reality is a special form of existence which must not be confounded with material reality. It seems, therefore, unnecessary that people should refuse to accept the responsibility for the immorality of their dreams. With an appreciation of the mode of functioning of the psychic apparatus, and an insight into the relations between conscious and unconscious, all that is ethically offensive in our dream-life and the life of phantasy for the most part disappears.

"What a dream has told us of our relations to the present (reality) we will then seek also in our consciousness and we must not be surprised if we discover that the monster we saw under the magnifying-glass of the analysis is a tiny little infusorian" (H. Sachs).

For all practical purposes in judging human character, a man's actions and conscious expressions of thought are in most cases sufficient. Actions, above all, deserve to be placed in the front rank; for many impulses which penetrate into consciousness are neutralized by real forces in the psychic life before they find issue in action; indeed, the reason why they frequently do not encounter any psychic obstacle on their path is because the unconscious is certain of their meeting with resistances later. In any case, it is highly instructive to learn something of the intensively tilled soil from which our virtues proudly emerge. For the complexity of human character, dynamically moved in all directions, very rarely accommodates itself to the arbitrament of a simple alternative, as our antiquated moral philosophy would have it.

And what of the value of dreams in regard to our knowledge of the future? That, of course, is quite out of the question. One would like to substitute the words: in regard to our knowledge of the past. For in every sense a dream has its origin in the past. The ancient belief that dreams reveal the future is not indeed entirely devoid of the truth. By representing a wish as fulfilled the dream certainly leads us into the future; but this future, which the dreamer accepts as his present, has been shaped in the likeness of the past by the indestructible wish.